ILLUSTRATED
THEATRE PRODUCTION
GUIDE

ILLUSTRATED THEATRE PRODUCTION GUIDE
SECOND EDITION

JOHN HOLLOWAY

ELSEVIER

AMSTERDAM • BOSTON • HEIDELBERG • LONDON
NEW YORK • OXFORD • PARIS • SAN DIEGO
SAN FRANCISCO • SINGAPORE • SYDNEY • TOKYO

Focal Press is an imprint of Elsevier

Focal Press

Focal Press is an imprint of Elsevier
30 Corporate Drive, Suite 400, Burlington, MA 01803, USA
The Boulevard, Langford Lane, Kidlington, Oxford, OX5 1GB, UK

Notices
Knowledge and best practice in this field are constantly changing. As new research and experience broaden our understanding, changes in research methods, professional practices, or medical treatment may become necessary.

Practitioners and researchers must always rely on their own experience and knowledge in evaluating and using any information, methods, compounds, or experiments described herein. In using such information or methods they should be mindful of their own safety and the safety of others, including parties for whom they have a professional responsibility.

To the fullest extent of the law, neither the Publisher nor the authors, contributors, or editors, assume any liability for any injury and/or damage to persons or property as a matter of products liability, negligence or otherwise, or from any use or operation of any methods, products, instructions, or ideas contained in the material herein.

Library of Congress Cataloging-in-Publication Data
Holloway, John, 1954-
    Illustrated theatre production guide / John Holloway.—2nd ed.
        p.   cm.
    Includes bibliographical references and index.
    ISBN 978-0-240-81204-5 (pbk. : alk. paper)   1. Stage management.   2. Theaters—Stage-setting and scenery.   I. Title.
    PN2085.H64 2010
    792.02'32—dc22

                                                                    2009046558

British Library Cataloguing-in-Publication Data
A catalogue record for this book is available from the British Library.

ISBN: 978-0-240-81204-5

For information on all Focal Press publications
visit our website at www.elsevierdirect.com

11 12 13 5 4 3

Printed in the United States of America

CONTENTS

COMPANION WEB SITE
http://booksite.focalpress.com/companion/Holloway/
Passcode: **theatre045**

WEB SITE MATERIALS:
Doors and Windows Bonus Chapter
How-To Videos
How Do You Make ... do-it yourself projects
Terms for Theatre Production Reference Guide
Key Term lists
Green Tips
Production Charts and other extras

PREFACE

Working in the theatre is fun. Or at least it should be! Theatre people are bright, hard-working, and committed to an artistic pursuit. If they were not, they would never survive the long hours and hard work that a theatre career demands. It is not a job for wimps!

I wrote those words for the preface to the first addition of this book in 2002, and they still ring true today. I first began working on shows in high school, back in the early 1970s, and have had a great time doing it ever since. I love going to the theatre on opening night and seeing how my work, and the work of others, affects the audience. I'm really happy to have started in the business when I did, because it has given me a chance to see the art and craft of theatre production grow from something more like a sideline into an actual occupation.

I've expanded this second edition quite a bit from the original, so that is now about half again as long, with somewhere around 1,200 illustrations, so I hope that the name is apt! Most of those illustrations are drawings, so that your eye is immediately drawn to the most important feature. But this latest edition includes quite a few more photographs where that seemed like a good idea. And of course the all-important screenshots. How could one discuss a computer program without them?

Don't forget to check out these new features:

- Important terms to remember shown in italics
- Terms listed by chapter on line
- Glossary of Terms for Theatre Production online
- How-To videos online
- Green Tips for Theatre

The new edition contains quite a few more historical references than the first one did. I view theatre work an effort in the humanities, and think that it is important for college students to understand the context of certain inventions, so there are many times when the historical period of a process or event is mentioned. I'm hoping that you will find them as interesting as I do. My next book will be a historical perspective of the technology of the early years of stage lighting, and I suppose you can see that work blossoming in this one.

I'm very pleased to have greatly expanded the section on electricity and stage lighting, as well as the totally new chapters on sound, stage management, and the use of computers in the theatre. I think they go a long way in fulfilling the promise of a book about all phases of theatrical production, not just the building of scenery.

I WOULD LIKE TO THANK ...

I would like to thank quite a few people for their help in creating this book. First of all, the readers who spent their valuable time reading some perhaps not-quite-so-polished earlier versions of the book and gave me their ideas about how to improve things. Dennis Dorn from the University of Wisconsin, Robert Amsden of Ripon College, Amy Schneider of Florida State, Rita K. Carver, and Charlie Hukill from McMurray University. Thanks to my engineer friend, Rhonda Shay. Closer to home, I'm indebted to these members of my IATSE local #346: Michael Lavin, Lynda Matusek, and John Ferguson.

Thanks to Rebecca Amsler for taking so many photographs, and then patiently resending me the files after I lost them for the third time.

A great debt is owed to Ann and Tom Barry for teaching me so much about the touring business. I was really green starting out, and they put up with me anyway. Special thanks to Ann for not firing me after that incident at the theatre in Minneapolis. Thanks to Nanette Golia, Nick Rouse, and Mark Krauss for teaching me how to behave on the road.

Most of all, I would like to thank my good friend from Eastern Michigan University, Jeromy Hopgood, who was instrumental in breaking me out of my PC mindset and getting me to understand the finer qualities of Macintosh programs. Actually, Jeromy was a great help with all of the new chapters, and I'm looking forward to his even greater involvement in subsequent editions of the book.

If you would like to contact me about this book, my email address is john.holloway@uky.edu. I put that address in the first edition of the book, and have been delighted to receive emails from places like the Netherlands and Hong Kong. Here's a big shout-out to our friends in New Zealand and Australia!

This poem is from the November 3, 1894, edition of the *New York Clipper*, a great old sports and entertainment newspaper of that time. I still like the way it lauds the creations of stage workers, although wages have gone up somewhat from "five bones" a week since then. IATSE, the International Alliance of Theatrical Stage Employees, was founded four years later in 1898, so perhaps that helped to boost salaries.

THE STAGE CARPENTER.

WRITTEN FOR THE NEW YORK CLIPPER.
BY MONROE H. ROSENFELD.

He wanders up, he wanders down,
 A phantom on the scene;
He talks to none, he does his work
 With countenance serene;
Although his purse is never fat,
 'Tis like his figure—lean.

What is there he cannot construct?
 An elephant to him
Is but a simple plight, or eke
 A dragon fierce and grim,
And golden goblets all begemmed,
 That never will grow dim.

He builds a ship, a paradise,
 Where angels music speak—
Bright angels with a salary
 Of just five bones a week;
And yet, in spite of genius,
 His actions are so meek.

Tanks are his special workmanship,
 And buzz saws meet his line;
And cottages and other things—
 At these he's very fine;
And he can make a thunder cloud,
 And moons that move and shine.

But who applauds his mystic art?
 The bass drum wouldn't nod
At him, while on his daily rounds
 The carpenter doth plod;
The manager? He knows him not—
 A stranger in the fold.

I wonder if he ever thinks
 Who cleverly will make
A little box for him, some day,
 That will not be a fake,
When Life's last scene on him shall close
 And Heaven's joy awake!

INTRODUCTION

PHILOSOPHY OF THEATRE PRODUCTION

Theatre production is very complex field of study. There's a huge amount of factual information about very different topics such as pipe sizes, paint solvents, and wire gauges, but the traditions of the theatre and the philosophy of how artists in theatre work together are also important. Theatre is all about creative problem solving in a group setting. My hope is that if you learn some basic methods of problem solving that have worked well for others in the past, that you can use those ideas to help solve problems you encounter in the future. But technique is also important, so the goal of learning about process is balanced here with the presentation of some very specific skills used in working with wood, metal, plastics, and less physical things like electricity, computer programs, and personalities.

One of the things you will learn early on about theatre and the entertainment business in general is that shows are "Here today, gone later today." That can be sad if you are working a great show with good friends and hate to see that time come to an end. But just remember that there is always another show down the road. Accommodating a rapidly changing environment means that your work needs to be easily installed and removed. Theatre lighting uses lots of temporary wiring with unusual connectors patching them together. It's really different from distribution systems you see elsewhere. Scenery is different also. Traditional methods of working in the theatre are different from working in other building trades, because theatre has special needs. Some of the basic principles of scenery building are:

- Scenery is built in units.
- Scenery should be portable.
- Scenery should be lightweight.
- Scenery should be easy to take apart and reassemble.

THEATRE LOADING DOCK DOORS

SCENERY MUST GENERALLY BE MOVED FROM
PLACE TO PLACE, SO BUILD IT IN UNITS
SMALL ENOUGH TO FIT THROUGH THE LOADING DOOR

Scenery Building

Building scenery is different from most other types of general construction, in that scenery quite often needs to do more than just sit there and look pretty. At times, the action of the play dictates that units must fly in and out, roll off stage, disappear, reappear, or sink into the floor. Building scenery effectively requires an understanding of things like theatre rigging systems, casters for rolling units around the stage, and the physical nature of the proscenium stage and peculiar things like trapdoors.

Whenever possible, building and painting scenery *in a shop* is a much better practice than building it in place *on the stage*. It sounds trite, but this actually does match the real-world practice better than you might think. Of course, shops in large cities must be able to move their product to a theatre or a TV studio. But even regional theatres must generally be able to transport what they build. In order for a resident theatre to remain solvent, it must have shows running all the time. The next production must be built while the present one is still in performance. Resident theatres most likely have only a week, or perhaps two, between shows to get the next one loaded in, through tech rehearsals, and open to the public. These are intense periods with lots of things to do and you cannot afford to wait until you are in the theatre to start building the scenery.

It's important to realize that there are many different levels of theatre production, and that what works for one does not always work for another. The nature of scenery built in New York for a touring show and the type of scenery built for a university show are often quite different. Broadway shows have really big budgets that a university or regional theatre can never match. The tour versions of these shows sometimes use the original set, but more often a special version is made that is more "tour-friendly." Television is vastly different from any sort of theatre work. As a result, there are lots of different ways to approach most production problems. I have tried to take the best of different worlds and bring them together in a style of production that can work for most theatres. You may not need to worry about moving your show from town to town, but certainly it must at least travel from the shop to the stage. Learning to build scenery in units, or parts that can be transported and easily assembled, is very important if you have aspirations toward professional theatre.

Lighting in a theatre is also different from what one would expect in most architectural environments. Fixtures must be relocated from one show to the next so that they are properly placed for effects. The equipment itself is very specialized to accommodate rapid relocation. Theatres frequently use portable power distribution networks and very complex control systems. The chapters on lighting and electricity begin with a survey of electrical theory, and progress to more specific information about the current state of theatre lighting equipment and practices.

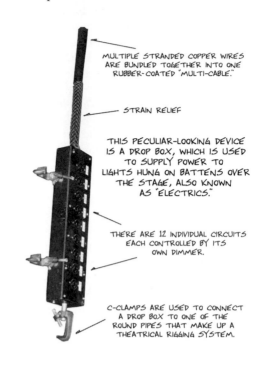

MULTIPLE STRANDED COPPER WIRES ARE BUNDLED TOGETHER INTO ONE RUBBER-COATED "MULTI-CABLE."

STRAIN RELIEF

THIS PECULIAR-LOOKING DEVICE IS A DROP BOX, WHICH IS USED TO SUPPLY POWER TO LIGHTS HUNG ON BATTENS OVER THE STAGE, ALSO KNOWN AS "ELECTRICS."

THERE ARE 12 INDIVIDUAL CIRCUITS EACH CONTROLLED BY ITS OWN DIMMER.

C-CLAMPS ARE USED TO CONNECT A DROP BOX TO ONE OF THE ROUND PIPES THAT MAKE UP A THEATRICAL RIGGING SYSTEM.

Different Work Environments

In talking to the editors at Focal Press about this book, I became more aware of how my background in different types of entertainment venues has influenced the way I build scenery, and my basic philosophy of how to approach the craft. My MFA is in scenery design, but most of my work experience has been as a technical director. I have been teaching college for 30 years, but am also a long-standing member of Local 346 of IATSE (the International Alliance of Theatrical Stage Employees). As a union stagehand, I have had the opportunity to travel with national touring companies of Broadway shows, and have set up hundreds of tour shows and rock concerts. The touring experience impressed me with the need to make sure that scenery is portable, and with how that aspect of the craft leads to many clever inventions that are always fun to figure out. Being a teacher at a university has exposed me to many creative people, and the enjoyment of being in on the development of artistic endeavors that most stagehands are never exposed to. My earliest work experiences were in regional theatres. I have also built scenery for television shows, commercials, and news programs.

It is interesting how different the two worlds of the union stagehand and the college theatre student are, and how little they sometimes seem to know about each other. In large cities, stagehands are mostly engaged in setting up shows and running them. The apprentice exam in my local is mostly about electrics, the fly system, and followspot operation. These are things that stagehands are most frequently asked to do. Being a stagehand is often a family tradition. It is a craft that is learned by being an apprentice and then moving on to journeyman. Except for very specific union shops, most stagehand work occurs in theatres or convention centers. Most IATSE stagehands know a great deal about load-ins, load-outs, and running shows, but probably not so much about building scenery.

A GROUP OF IA STAGEHANDS
WAITING BY THE STAGE DOOR

In a college theatre environment, students are immersed in all phases of theatrical activity, from acting and directing to design and production. A student may hang lights for one show, act in another, and build costumes for a third. College theatres generally build all their own scenery, and constructing scenery in the shop is an important activity requiring a huge amount of effort. College is a place for young people to see what careers are available, learn something about them, and then decide which one is most appealing to them personally.

COLLEGE STUDENTS
IN A SCENE SHOP

In a union situation, very specific departments are set up to ensure that proper organization is achieved.

They are carpentry, electrics, sound (a.k.a. audio), wardrobe, props, and hair. Each department is peopled with experts in those fields. You almost never hear anyone use the words "lighting" or "costumes" in reference to the people who work in those departments. They are electricians and dressers. Workers in one field may not necessarily know that much about what happens in another department, unless it has a direct bearing on their own, but they are absolute masters of their particular craft.

There are many differences in terminology. In a union situation a *strike* requires you *not* to work. At a university, it is a very intense work period when a show is broken down. Union workers call that a *load-out*. A commercial show that is in *production* is going through the same process that schools call a *tech*. In general, production is a catchall term that means just about anything to do with a play that isn't related to acting, singing, or dancing.

WORK PROCESS

Regardless of the type of theatre you work in, the actual process of mounting a show is more or less the same. Designers work with the director to invent a way of presenting the author's work to the audience. Shops go to work and build the scenery, lighting effects, and props that the designers have created. The show is set up in a theatre, and the cueing process begins. Whether you call it tech or production, cue setting requires many hours of starting, stopping, and waiting around for things to begin again.

Commercial theatre (which has investors and must show a profit) is usually developed along the lines of the *long run* concept of production, in which a show is put up with the intention that it will run until it stops making money and then close. That could mean at the end of 10 years, or it could mean the end of Act I—that sort of thing is difficult to forecast. The scenery for such a show will most likely be trashed after the show closes. That scenery is built with only one specific use in mind. Universities and most resident or regional theatre companies are often organized around the concept of *stock theatre*. These theatre companies produce many plays that are scheduled with the idea of having a "season" every year. They tend to save scenery, props, costumes, and so on in order to reuse them for another production, or perhaps the same show will be run again if it was popular enough. Some theatres save and reuse lots of things. Some theatres save very little. Things like platforms, escape stairs, curtains, and so forth are so generic that it just makes sense to reuse them in order to keep costs down. This book often discusses the pros and cons of what should constitute stock items.

Actually, recycling scenery is mostly dependent on design factors. You can't reuse something that isn't asked for. Sometimes designers will specifically ask for something from a previous show. That works well with Victorian doors that all look pretty much the same, especially if they were last used 5 years ago. Alas, there are relatively few shows that cry out for a sign advertising *Mrs. Lovett's Meat Pies* or *River City Pool Hall*. Even so, it is possible to dispose of such items in something other than a regular landfill, thus having a less negative impact on the environment.

ORGANIZATION OF THE CHAPTERS

The first part of the book covers theatres and their equipment. It outlines how to use rigging equipment, and the spaces you find in different sorts of theatres. It is important to have a strong understanding of how shows run in a theatre in order to understand how to build scenery. Scenery must be built in a way that accommodates stage equipment, and the sort of rigging used in theatres dictates how the scenery must be rigged to fly in and out. The construction phase of lighting work occurs mostly in the theatre. Rather than actually building things, most of the electrician's work involves hanging and focusing lights. There are many ancillary projects like setting up dimmers and running cables. The inside-the-theatre chapters are presented first because of a desire to help you to understand how the theatre itself influences the construction of the scenery.

The second group of chapters has to do with materials and tools. In this new edition, I've included some information about stage managing, creating sound cues on the computer, and computer-aided drawing, or CAD. Computers are immensely important in the modern theatre, and no theatre practitioner can afford to be computer-illiterate these days. I can only assume that they will be even more important in the future than they are now.

The final chapters are concerned with how you actually make things. As far as building scenery is concerned, you may find that the same sorts of structures tend to repeat themselves over and over. In reality, most joinery, whether wood or steel, follows some pretty straightforward concepts that should be apparent by the time you finish with the book. Most construction is based on flat structures that are grouped together to form more three-dimensional objects. If you learn the ideas behind one type of construction based on the way parts overlap one another, you can use the same ideas for lots of other projects.

A number of projects are described at the end of the book. You can build them directly from the plans you find there, but it would be better to change them in some way to better reflect something you actually need for a show, so that they have an even more practical quality to them. It is very important to be able to take basic information and extrapolate it to work in different situations. That is the goal of inference learning: not just to memorize facts and figures, but to comprehend the reasoning behind a process or method. That allows you to take information and use it in new and creative ways.

You may notice that from time to time there are small encouragements to be neat with your work. That comes under the heading of craftsmanship. Taking pride in your work is very important, especially if you want to go on to be a professional. The farther you go in theatre, the more important it becomes. Many regional theatres are very well known for the excellent work they produce, and shows built for the Broadway market are impeccably well turned out. In my younger years, I worked for a carpenter who said, "The audience sees the front, but I have to look at the back. My view should be just as good as theirs." Finely crafted work should be its own reward.

CHAPTER 1

THEATRE TYPES

An understanding of the development of the physical nature of modern theatres requires an understanding of the past and its effect on the design of theatre buildings. Throughout history, the design of theatrical structures has been heavily influenced by the engineering and construction methods that were known to a particular culture. Styles of producing plays (and other types of entertainment) have also been a factor. The type of venue needed for a play is entirely different from one that can be used for a chariot race or in modern times a rock concert. The Greeks did not arbitrarily select the amphitheater as a type of structure because they liked being outdoors. They used the construction methods available in their time period to create the most useful and efficient space possible to be used in producing the type of entertainment that was popular in their culture. Large indoor structures were simply not possible until more modern engineering methods were developed.

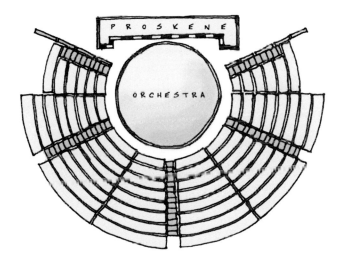

SYMMETRICAL GREEK THEATRE

GREEK AMPHITHEATRES

The earliest Greek-style theatres took advantage of existing hillsides to form a sloping audience area that curved around a circular performance area. Pre–Industrial Revolution technology did not provide their culture with heavy earth-moving equipment to form the slopes from scratch, and often large amphitheaters were somewhat asymmetrical as a result of following the existing terrain.

doi: 10.1016/C2009-0-23409-X

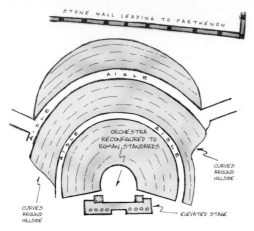

STONE WALL LEADING TO PARTHENON

ORCHESTRA
RECONFIGURED TO
ROMAN STANDARDS

AISLE

CURVES
AROUND
HILLSIDE

CURVES
AROUND
HILLSIDE

ELEVATED STAGE

SHAPE MODIFIED TO FIT EXISTING HILLSIDE

THE ROMANS CONVERTED THE ORCHESTRA
AT THE THEATRE OF DIONYSUS TO MEET THEIR SPECIFICATIONS

Modern outdoor theatres are generically known as amphitheatres, especially if they resemble the original Greek model. Modified versions are very popular for outdoor historical dramas that run only in the summertime.

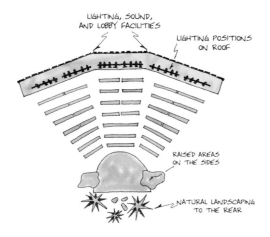

LIGHTING, SOUND,
AND LOBBY FACILITIES

LIGHTING POSITIONS
ON ROOF

RAISED AREAS
ON THE SIDES

NATURAL LANDSCAPING
TO THE REAR

THEATRES FOR OUTDOOR DRAMAS
OFTEN BORROW HEAVILY FROM
CLASSICAL MODELS

Greek theatres are an excellent early example of the science of *sightlines* as used in designing a performance space. The study of sightlines is a notion whereby the ability of the audience to see the performance area can be enhanced by the proper arrangement of the seating area. This term can also be used to indicate which portions of a stage space are visible to the audience. Obviously, another person sitting directly in front of you will

impede your ability to properly view the stage. By *raking* the seating rows up and away from the front of the stage, sightlines are vastly improved.

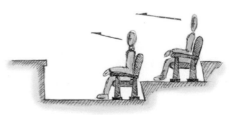

RAKED SEATING IMPROVES SIGHTLINES

In a Greek-style amphitheater, with a round performance area or *orchestra*, it was necessary to curve the seating rows around the shape of the orchestra in order to ensure that audience members would be as close as possible to the action of the drama. This created the traditional fan shape that is often associated with Greek amphitheatres. Classical architects were very interested in graceful geometrical shapes and symmetry.

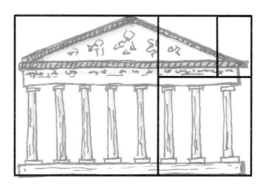

THE PARTHENON WAS CONSTRUCTED
WITH PROPORTIONS CHOSEN FROM THE GOLDEN MEAN

THE WIDTH OF A RECTANGLE SHOULD BE 1.6 TIMES ITS HEIGHT.

PLACING A SQUARE IN A RECTANGLE THUS PROPORTIONED
CREATES ANOTHER RECTANGLE OF THE SAME PROPORTIONS.

Having the audience and performers in close proximity to one another is an important factor in the relationship between actor and audience. Most Greek theatres were actually quite large in relation to a modern, indoor theatre. To counterbalance that loss of intimacy, a *chorus* of performers was used, all making the same movements and reciting the same lines, which had more impact on the audience than a single actor would. When the Greek choral form of entertainment began to give way to individual actors speaking lines of dialogue, a raised platform area was provided to give them prominence, or focus. This area was called the *skene* by the Greeks, and is the root of our word *proscenium*.

ACTOR ON SKENE GAINS HEIGHT ADVANTAGE OVER ACTOR STANDING IN ORCHESTRA

THIS ACTOR GAINS FOCUS EVEN THOUGH HE IS FARTHER AWAY

ROMAN ADVANCES

Many historians have noted that although the Greek culture tended to create ideas, their Roman counterparts concentrated on developing them into something more practical. As a simplification, it has been said that the Greeks asked "why" and the Romans asked "how." The Roman society spawned excellent civil engineers. They used their talents to create many civic improvements like roads, aqueducts, and public buildings. Most of these achievements involved the use of *arches*. An arch is formed when the downward force of gravity acting on the stones of a curved open structure is counterbalanced by its own curved shape, with the force being redirected outward. In a structure created by several arches place side by side, the outward pressure from one arch is counterbalanced by one or more adjacent structures. Egyptian pyramids were solid structures that required a vast amount of stone to construct. A Greek building such as the Parthenon depends on the strength of stone beams to span between columns and to carry the weight of the roof, but stone is not well suited to that purpose, because it lacks tensile strength. Arches, when made into domes and barrel-vault roofs, can be used to create open interiors, and don't require nearly as much stone material.

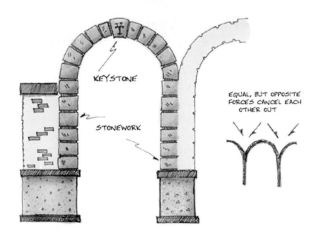

KEYSTONE

STONEWORK

EQUAL, BUT OPPOSITE FORCES CANCEL EACH OTHER OUT

HOW ARCHES WORK

This concept allowed the Romans to use a series of arches to build the *Colosseum*, a freestanding oval structure best suited to the games, races, and physical contests that were the most popular types of entertainment in that period. The Colosseum was an architectural marvel of its day, not only because of its size, but also because of its clever high-tech features like stage elevators and trap doors that allowed performers to enter the space unexpectedly. These same devices are often used in modern arena rock concerts, and for the same reason, because they present an unexpected event to the audience.

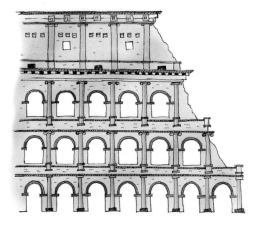

THE COLOSSEUM IN ROME IS CONSTRUCTED FROM MANY SMALL ARCHES

THAT APPROACH USES FEWER MATERIALS AND CREATES A MORE OPEN SPACE THAN IF THE WALLS WERE SOLID

Roman theatres for plays were constructed in much the same manner as the Greek ones were, with the major differences being that the elevated stage area was greatly enlarged and elaborated upon, and the circular choral area was cut in half to form a semicircle. Individual actors had become more important in the drama. As with the Colosseum, the Romans were able to build freestanding banks of tiered seats for their theatres rather than depending entirely upon the geography of hillsides. These theatres generally were somewhat smaller in scope than their Greek counterparts, perhaps due to more urban settings, but it would seem also because the plays themselves had a more modern structure requiring greater intimacy between performer and audience. The archetypical Roman theatre seems to have had a lot in common with a more modern type, the thrust theatre (defined later in this chapter).

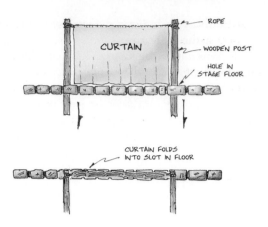

DISAPPEARING ROMAN CURTAIN

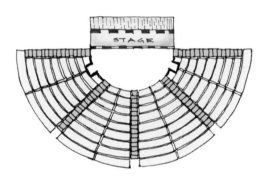

TYPICAL ROMAN THEATRE

The Romans were also innovative in the introduction of a front curtain that could be used to mask the stage from the view of the audience. As these early theatres were open-air, daytime-use structures, there was no way to hang a curtain from above as in a modern theatre. In at least one instance, the Romans used instead a series of poles coming out of the stage floor to hold up the drape. When these poles were lowered, the stage and its occupants were revealed. This seems at best a cumbersome arrangement, but lacking the technology to construct large, open spans inside a building, it was the best method available at the time. It is mentioned here as a contrast to the ease with which curtains may be hung in a modern proscenium theatre using a counterweight system. The ability to construct the type of structure needed to house today's modern rigging systems did not appear until much more recent times.

PROSCENIUM THEATRES

The next period to greatly influence the progress of theatrical design was the Italian Renaissance. The development of theories pertaining to illusionist painting and perspective rendering created the need for much more advanced production methods. The type of scenery utilized during the Renaissance period was often based on the methods used in *one-point perspective* drawing, in which a single vanishing point is located somewhere near the bottom center of the viewing plane.

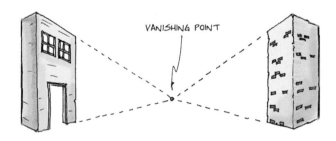

FORCED PERSPECTIVE DRAWING

Objects in the foreground are shown in a larger scale than those objects in the distance. This technique creates an illusion of depth and three-dimensionality. The effect was further realized by using a series of viewing planes spaced at intervals, moving away from the audience. Objects farther upstage were rendered in a smaller size. For a city scene, this would require a number of building images painted on flat panels, with each successive building being rendered in a scale somewhat smaller than the one preceding it. This style of design is known generically as *wing and drop* scenery. The "wings" were the panels off to the side of the stage, and the "drop" was a painted cloth dropping down in the rear from the ceiling of the stage. All of the action of the play had to occur in front of the first plane in order to ensure that the carefully created illusion of depth was not shattered. Naturally, an actor who ventured too near the rear of the stage would appear grotesquely large in proportion to the scale of the scenery. This latter technique can be seen in modern-day amusement parks and movie special effects.

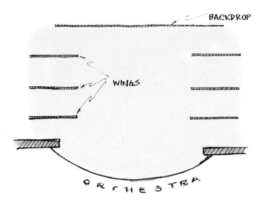

WING AND DROP SCENERY

Because the *vanishing point* in this *forced perspective* style of design must be elevated from the stage floor in order for the lines to appear realistic, the stage floor behind the acting area was raked upward, away from the audience, to achieve the desired effect. This was of course the origination of the terms *upstage* and *downstage*. In later periods, when permanent theatres were larger and grander, the immense size of the settings negated somewhat the requirement that actors remain at a distance from the painted scenery. Hence an actor who traveled toward the back wall would literally be walking upstage, and on the return trip would be treading downstage.

The concepts embraced by wing and drop scenery are still very much alive in the twenty-first century. Historians are fortunate to have several written records of how theatre was staged during the Renaissance period. Books by Sebastiano Serlio and Nicola Sabbattini have survived to the present day and each has a wealth of descriptions and illustrations. The staging of Greek and Roman dramas is not nearly as well known, and most of the information about it is deduced from the surviving scripts. The writings of Serlio and Sabbattini are firsthand accounts of theatre in the sixteenth and seventeenth centuries, and have detailed information about wing and drop staging methods. Scenery designed for proscenium theatres today has many parallels to this earlier style of design, based primarily upon wings, drops, and forced perspective painting.

The question arises of how to easily change the appearance of the stage setting while a show is in progress. In a small theatre, this could be done in a manner similar to sliding closet doors. One set of panels could be pulled offstage, revealing another set behind them—hence the term *stage set*. Some much larger sixteenth-century theatres used the *chariot and pole* system of shifting scenery. This consisted of a series of slots cut into the stage floor running left to right, and a number of symmetrically arranged poles that rose up through them. These upright poles were mounted on carts in a basement. Moving the carts, or chariots, back and forth moved the poles, and thus the scenery. This was of course in an age before the creation of modern rigging from overhead.

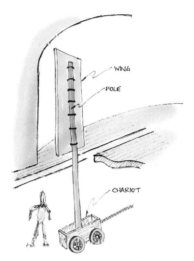

CHARIOT AND POLE SYSTEM

The Renaissance period saw the development of the proscenium theatre as we know it today. The farthermost downstage set of flats or wings became a permanent architectural feature of the building. When supplemented by an overhead masking piece, this feature became recognizable as the proscenium arch so common in our own era. The proscenium not only serves as a frame for the setting, but also separates the audience from the stage, allowing for the use of intricate mechanical devices that are completely hidden from patrons in the auditorium.

By the late nineteenth century, it became possible to construct an overhead tower used for rigging, or *fly house* of the sort in use today. The advent of realism and *box sets* in the early twentieth century eventually did away with the practice of raking the stage for forced perspective settings.

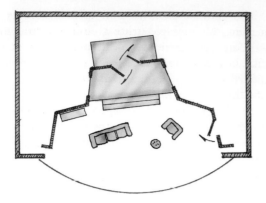

EARLY TYPE OF BOX SET

THE ADVENT OF REALISM IN DRAMA
MOVED DESIGN AWAY FROM
FORCED PERSPECTIVE SCENERY AND
TOWARD THE MORE "REALISTIC" BOX SET

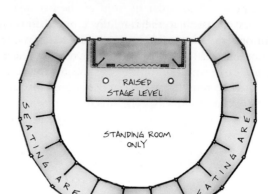

GLOBE THEATRE

THE GLOBE WAS AN EARLY EXAMPLE
OF TODAY'S THRUST THEATRES

The proscenium house is the most common type of theatre used in North America. Its advantages are most obvious when spectacle is an important element of the production, because it has such a large collection of mechanical equipment used for stage effects. Professional touring companies of commercial Broadway shows are restricted to proscenium theatres because of their large audience capacity and also because of the similarity of stage equipment available in all proscenium houses. Although the lobbies and auditoriums of various road houses throughout the country are vastly different in style and size, equipment available upstage of the plaster line is more or less standard. An in-depth discussion of the proscenium theatre can be found in Chapter 2.

MODERN DEVELOPMENTS

Thrust theatres began a surge in popularity in the 1960s and 1970s in an effort to break through to a more actor-friendly type of space. Generally, in a thrust theatre, the audience seating wraps around three-fourths of the stage area, giving the stage the appearance of "thrusting out" into the spectators. This in effect makes the front of the stage longer, making it possible to fit a larger number of seats into a small number of rows. A smaller number of rows going away from the stage results in more audience members being closer to the stage.

It is interesting to note that this type of theatre was also popular in Elizabethan times, and the reasons for its success now and then are largely the same. Thrust theatres are best suited to the production of intimate dramas. Plays that depend on the accurate understanding of words and/or the transmission of small emotional moments are well served by the close proximity of audience and actor found in thrust theatres.

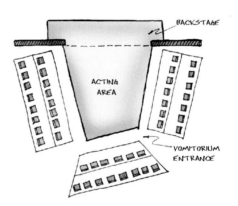

THRUST THEATRE

The thrust theatre is not without its drawbacks, however, as the layout of the stage leads to some rather difficult sightline problems. In a proscenium house, the audience view of the stage is more or less constant throughout the theatre. Although some seats on the extreme sides have a somewhat skewed view of the action, the stage retains a kind of movie-screen quality. In a thrust theatre, the audience view from the far left is completely the opposite of that from the far right. Patrons seated at the downstage edge of the stage see the action from straight ahead. This may lead to some serious staging issues, and require a bit of technique to overcome.

Most thrust theatres have either a modified proscenium opening, or some type of architectural staging at the upstage end of the playing area. Designers must be careful not to place too much emphasis on scenic units in that location, because they may not be entirely visible to a portion of the audience. Likewise, care must be taken not to use visual elements downstage that might block the view of persons sitting in that area. Anything such as a wall, or a refrigerator, or even a large wingback chair is certain to annoy anyone who cannot see past it to the action of the play.

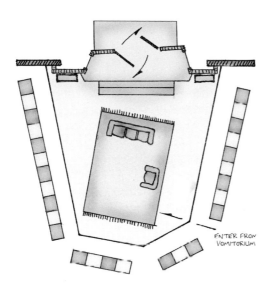

THE SAME BOX SET AS BEFORE, BUT RECONFIGURED FOR A THRUST THEATRE

Seats in a thrust theatre are generally quite steeply raked to help alleviate this issue, and as a result, the appearance of the stage floor assumes a much greater focus than in a proscenium theatre, in which the audience view of the floor is extremely oblique. Low platforms and other intricate floor treatments are popular choices in a thrust theatre. Low-mass scenic elements like lamp posts, bentwood chairs, and small props are also often used in downstage areas. Lighting becomes an extremely crucial element to change the stage picture in the absence of solid physical items.

Thrust theatres are extremely popular with local theatre groups located throughout the country. Many such theatres are founded by actors, so it makes sense that they would choose this type of venue, because it is complementary to acting. Thrusts are also popular with various Shakespearean companies. The original Guthrie Theatre in Minneapolis and the Stratford Shakespeare stage in Ontario, Canada, are prime examples.

Most thrust theatres have an exposed ceiling or grid that allows for multiple lighting positions throughout the theatre. In a traditional proscenium house, care is often taken to attempt to hide the mechanics of lighting, but the more modern thrust type tends to lean in the direction of the adage "form follows function" and lighting equipment is exposed to the audience. This allows for much wider latitude concerning fixture placement, and thus leads to superior lighting design possibilities.

Arena, or theatre in the round, is another popular modern form. As the name suggests, the audience seating wraps entirely around the stage, eliminating the upstage opening found in thrust theatres. Other than the loss of the upstage facade, the sightline rules are primarily the same for arena theatres as they are for thrust theatres.

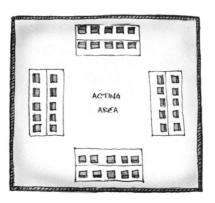

THEATRE IN THE ROUND

At this point, you might be wondering how actors will be able to enter the acting space, as there is apparently no backstage area to enter from. A *vomitorium* entrance can be used to solve this dilemma. A vomitorium is a passageway under the audience seating from the backstage space to the stage itself. They are also popular in thrust theatres, where they provide a more direct route to the downstage area. "Voms" are also used to provide entrance to audience seating in stadiums, sports arenas, and very large proscenium houses.

Another form of theatre space is the *black box* or *flexible* seating theatre. Either of these names is actually quite descriptive. This type of theatre is generally housed in a large, black, rectilinear room. Audience seating chairs may be moved around and set up in whatever configuration is desired. *Risers* are often used to facilitate better sightlines. Some theatres actually have bleacher seats that can be moved around the space.

The black box style of theatre is especially popular with off-off-Broadway types of theatre groups because of its low cost, extreme intimacy, and ability to conform to more experimental genres of performance. The seating may be set up to resemble virtually any style of theatre: proscenium, thrust, and in the round, as well as more offbeat arrangements such as *stadium* (in which the performance area is flanked on two sides by seating, as in a football stadium). Or it may be truly flexible, allowing the performance area to flow in and around the seating (or standing) area. Audience members in this latter concept may move from place to place during the performance, becoming a part of the action, and blurring the dividing line into performance art. Scenic elements become less important in black box theatres, although lighting, props, and sound retain a great deal of influence.

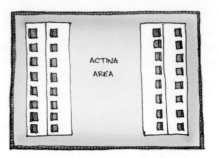

STADIUM SEATING

CHAPTER 2

PROPERTIES OF THE PROSCENIUM THEATRE

This chapter goes into greater detail about the spaces and devices that are generally found in a proscenium theatre. The proscenium theatre is given special prominence in this book because it is the most common sort, because it typifies what you are likely to find in a commercial venue, and because it is the easiest to use in mounting large spectacles. If you are producing a ballet, opera, or Broadway musical, this is the theatre for you.

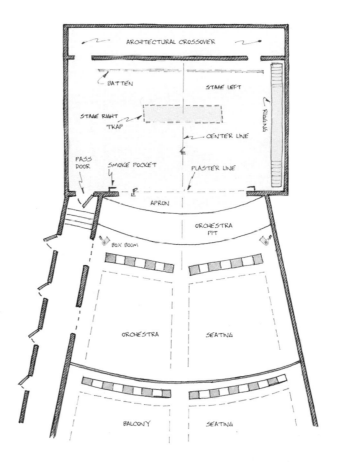

PLAN VIEW OF A PROSCENIUM THEATRE

doi: 10.1016/C2009-0-23409-X

THE AUDITORIUM

Looking at the theatre from overhead in a *plan view*, the central part of the proscenium theatre is the stage itself. Downstage is down toward the audience, and upstage is up toward the back wall. Stage left is to your left if you are facing the audience, and stage right is to your right. Audience left and right are just the opposite. The proscenium frames the stage for the audience, just like the frame on a painting. The area to the side of the stage, past the edge of the proscenium opening, is called a *wing*. Some theatres have very little wing space, and some have a great deal.

Wings are quite important for as a storage space for moving scenery that must be carried or rolled offstage. The *rail*, which constitutes the rigging equipment used to fly scenery over the stage, can be on either side, and as a result it is common for that wing to have less space than the other. In a newer theatre, the architects may have created a hallway directly behind the stage that is used to travel from one side of the stage to the other, and this passageway is known as a *crossover*. An alternative style of crossover runs under the stage and is accessed by a set of stairs on either side. You are more likely to find that style in an older building, especially one in an urban setting. Quite frequently, the staging of a particular show requires that actors exit from one side of the

stage and immediately reappear on the other, and there may not be time for a quick run through the basement. A temporary crossover is often created by hanging drapes across the upstage part of the stage. A space is left between the drapes and the back wall, allowing actors and stagehands easy passage from one side to the other.

You may find a door on the back of the proscenium wall, down left or right, which leads to the *front-of-house* areas (described in more detail shortly). This passage is often referred to as the "passage" or *pass door*.

An imaginary line that runs across the stage from one side to the other directly upstage of the proscenium opening is known as the *plaster line* and is used as a point of reference for locating scenery on the stage. The stage area downstage of the plaster line is referred to as the *apron*. Downstage center on the apron is a most popular spot for actors, but not very useful for scenery, as there is no practical way to move anything to that location. Static pieces that wind up there cannot be hidden by the *main drape*, which is usually located just upstage of the proscenium opening. Off the front edge of the stage, and sometimes partially underneath, is the *orchestra pit*. Superior planning by the architect will have provided an entrance door to the pit from an area under the stage. Unfortunately, many times the pit entrance may be from the house level instead.

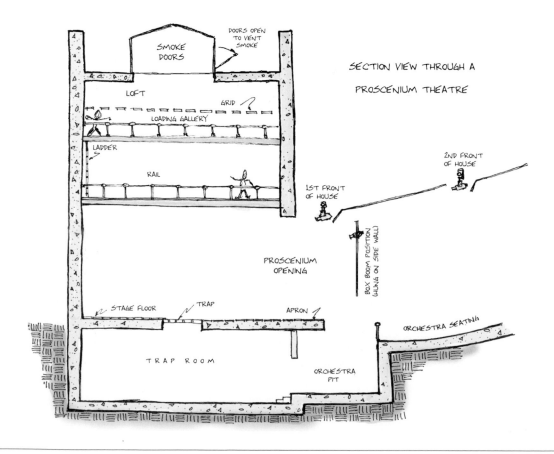

Seats on the lower level of the auditorium are known as *orchestra seats*. You will recall that the round area of a Greek theatre that was often used for singing and dancing by the chorus was also called the orchestra. In many theatres, additional seating is provided through the use of *balconies*. If there are multiple balconies, the lowest one may be called the *mezzanine*. Balconies are stacked up on top of a portion of the orchestra seats in order to reduce the average distance from any one seat to the front of the stage.

PLAN VIEW OF LIGHTING POSITIONS

LIGHTING AND SOUND

Many modern theatres have rooms for lighting and sound in the rear of the auditorium and are often called the *booth*. A position for *followspots*, which are sometimes called front lights, is essential. It is interesting to note that many sound booths are enclosed in glass to provide a sound barrier from the auditorium. That is sometimes okay for sound playback, but it is an awful place to hear the mix of a show that requires sound reinforcement through the use of microphones. Mixers are usually set up in an area cleared of seats in the rear of the auditorium. Some newer theatres have a permanent *house mix position*, which is by far the best option.

Overhead lighting pipes located in the auditorium of a theatre are known as front-of-house or *FOH positions*. These positions may be laid out in many various ways, depending mostly on the uses of the theatre and the architectural features found in it. FOH pipes may be concealed in soffits, rigged on trusses lowered by chain motors, or may exist simply as exposed pipes reachable only by a ladder. Front-of-house positions are numbered in relation to their proximity to the stage. The pipe that is closest to the stage is the first FOH. The next closest will be the second, and so forth. In some theatres, one or more of the FOH positions may be called a *beam position*.

Another popular place for lights in the house of a theatre is the *box boom position*. A boom is any vertical pipe used to hang lights. Box booms are located in the place where theatre box seats were traditionally placed, on the side of the auditorium and close to the front of the stage. This is an excellent lighting angle for side lights across the front of the stage and is a favorite with lighting designers.

There are as many different arrangements of FOH positions as there are theatres that house them. Touring companies that travel with a lighting package usually designate two front-of-house locations: box boom and *balcony rail*. Once in a particular theatre, the design is modified somewhat to accommodate the existing road house positions. Sometimes there is an actual balcony rail, which is a pipe that has been secured to the front edge of the first balcony. Or there may be a more traditional FOH placement, such as a catwalk or a pipe hanging from the ceiling.

Pipes used to hang lights over the stage are called *electrics*. Electrics are also numbered from the front of the stage, and hence the numbers run backward from those used for the FOH positions. The most downstage electric is the first electric, and the next upstage is the second. You could also consider that all lighting positions are numbered with the plaster line as a beginning point.

Some theatres have permanent lighting electrics, which is to say that the same battens are always used for that purpose. Consequently these pipes have a permanently attached *plugging strip* running along the batten to provide power to the lighting instruments. They are generally found in theatres that have their own lighting equipment. Some houses that are strictly for rental purposes may not have any sort of lighting circuits, but rather depend upon the touring company to bring everything in themselves. Many Broadway theatres are of this type.

Other theatres may use a system of *drop boxes* that are moved from one batten to another in order to make any pipe available into an electric. Drop boxes consist of a large diameter multicable containing a number of conductors that feed a junction box with several connectors in it. Many lighting cables may be plugged into one box. Drop boxes may be lowered from above and clamped to any batten being used as an electric. This second type of powering system is much more flexible than the dedicated electric type but also requires more effort to set up and use.

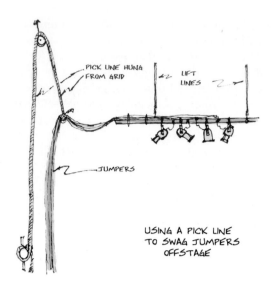

USING A PICK LINE TO SWAG JUMPERS OFFSTAGE

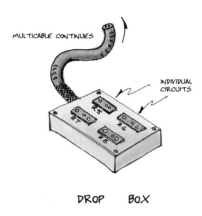

DROP BOX

Quite often you may find that the third or fourth *lineset* upstage of the plaster line is dedicated strictly for use as an electric even if movable drop boxes are used for all the other electrics. This position is the traditional location of the first electric, which is required for virtually all lighting designs. Often this batten is rigged with some kind of *motorized winch* system. The first electric always has a lot of lights on it, and they can be very heavy. A winch system helps avoid the necessity of loading and unloading what can become a large number of stage weights needed to counterbalance the heavy load. Electrics are typically the heaviest pipes in any show, and the first electric is often the weightiest of them all.

Tours of Broadway shows carry their own lighting packages of dimmers, cables, lights, and control equipment. Electrics are formed by running multicable from the lights, off whichever side of the electric the dimmers are located, and down to the floor. It is necessary to swag the cables offstage and out of the way of the fly system, actors, scenery, and other such stuff. This can be accomplished by using a cable pickup line, or *cable pick*. The cable pick is tied to the cable with a clove hitch, and the bundle is raised into the air. Then the pick line is tied off at some convenient spot off-stage. Some theatres have a specific area known as a jump that is used for this purpose, or pick lines can be hung from the pin rail, if the rail is an elevated one and on the proper side of the stage.

THE STAGE

Many theatres have holes in the stage floor equipped with removable covers. These passages are known as *traps*. Traps are useful for productions that require that actors or props disappear into the floor. If a theatre does not possess a trapped floor, and the effect is required, decking will need to be installed to raise the floor level of the setting in order to "invent" the required space. This can obviously become a problematic process. In years past, it was common for chariot and pole–type theatres to have a large number of traps, because the space was already set up along similar lines. Traditions die hard; many modern facilities are thus constructed with large basements under the stage. This area is often used as a dressing room, green room, and/or passageway to the orchestra pit. In some theatres, the only way to load costume racks into the basement is by way of a trap in the floor. Perhaps the traditional availability of traps has caused playwrights to continue writing them into their work, such as in the more recent play *The Foreigner*.

The major architectural element of any proscenium theatre is the *fly house*, or tower. Theatre buildings are quite often easy to spot on a college campus because they are large, square, unattractive buildings with no windows. Older urban theatres were quite often built with a row of in-house offices over the lobby, and were covered on at least one side by another structure. Many of the original Broadway theatres have an entrance on the street that leads backward to the theatre, which is actually at a 90-degree angle to the entrance, so they take up very little street frontage. They are not as easy to spot.

THE FLY TOWER ON THIS 19TH CENTURY THEATRE
WAS EXPANDED UPWARD WITH A METAL-CLAD ADDITION

On the interior, a fly tower is a large open space, very tall, with a *loft* space above. The floor of the loft is a series of beams with spaces in between and is known as a *grid*. The loft space is used for the installation of rigging equipment. That equipment is covered in detail in Chapter 3. In some theatres the rigging is *underhung* from beams in the ceiling in order to save on cost, but this can lead to some serious problems with reaching the equipment when servicing is required.

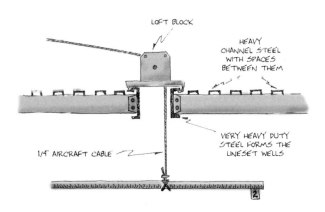

ARRANGEMENT OF STANDARD-STYLE
RIGGING IN THE LOFT OF A PROSCENIUM THEATRE

A good rule of thumb for determining the most desirable height for this type of structure is to triple the height of the proscenium opening, or at least 65 feet. Actual heights vary widely and may easily range from 45 to 110 feet. Newer theatres tend to be taller, but sometimes multiple-use facilities in schools may not have an actual tower and rigging system, using curtains fastened to the ceiling of the stage instead. It isn't possible to fly scenery up out of sight in that type of venue.

Very stringent *fire code* restrictions are placed on theatres because of the large crowds involved, and also due to the many catastrophic accidents that occurred in the days before electric lighting came into vogue. The use of open-flame candles and later gaslights spawned some spectacular and deadly fires. Electric lights are no guarantee against disaster, and theatres today are still required to have fire prevention, detection, and extinguishing devices. Code requirements vary from city to city and state to state, but theatres are generally required to be equipped with smoke detectors, heat detectors, automatic alarms, sprinkler systems, and emergency lighting systems. Local *fire marshals* are the sole arbiters of how to interpret the fire code for any particular theatre. Many municipalities require that scenery be *flame-proofed* and prohibit the use of open flames onstage. Large draperies and wooden scenery can provide ample fuel for voracious fires.

The term *flame-proofing* has a specific meaning. Technically, the definition is that the treated material will not support flames, but will merely smolder and go out if ignited. Often the test is performed by holding a match against the material until it burns itself out. *Fireproof* is a misleading term, as it indicates an inability to burn at all, and virtually anything will burn if heated to a high enough temperature. Flame-proofing is intended to prevent a large, self-sustaining blaze from becoming established. Once that has happened, only a well-trained fire company will be able to extinguish the flames.

On a Wednesday afternoon, December 30, 1903, the Iroquois Theatre in Chicago was showing a matinee of the play *Mr. Bluebeard* when a fire broke out, possibly caused by a calcium spotlight igniting a muslin drop. Stagehands immediately attempted to put the small fire out with their hands, but it grew too fast for them and was soon out of control. Other stagehands attempted to lower the asbestos fire curtain, but it became fouled, possibly from a strong draft from outside or perhaps on a border light framing the proscenium opening. Hundreds died in the auditorium because the exits were inadequate, and a loss of power turned off all the newly installed incandescent lights. Had the painted drop been flame-proofed, the entire tragedy might have been avoided.

Many theatres have a *sprinkler system* that sprays water outward over a specific area, much like a lawn sprinkler does. Never do anything to block the spray heads, because they won't work properly if you do. The sprinkler system supply pipes often run on or around the rigging grid, and you should be especially careful not to disturb them when working in that area. Never tie off a rope to a sprinkler pipe—it isn't meant to hold any weight and you may break it as a result. A huge amount of nasty water will spray out if you do.

WHEN THE HEAT FROM A FIRE TRIPS THE CONTROL MECHANISM, A FIRE SUPPRESSION SPRINKLER SPRAYS WATER IN ALL DIRECTIONS

Most people who die in fires are not necessarily burned, but rather succumb to *smoke inhalation*. This is especially true when modern petrochemical materials such as those used for carpeting and seat padding are considered. For this reason, theatres are generally required to have equipment designed specifically to remove smoke from the building and to separate the audience from any smoke and/or fire that may emanate from the stage. The most easily visible of these is the *fire curtain*.

Fire curtains are traditionally made of *asbestos*, a fibrous mineral that can be stranded and woven into a fabric. Being a mineral (or rock), it is highly resistant to fire. However, virtually everyone is aware now that asbestos can be a very dangerous substance, especially when it becomes frayed and gets into the air. Even so, it is still in use in many theatres, because it does such a great job of preventing fires from spreading. Sealers are applied to lessen the possibility that flaking of the material into the air will occur. When the small airborne fibers get into a person's lungs, damage is done to the tissues. Curtains of this type should be used with care and be left alone as much as possible. There are some substitute materials for fire curtains, but they are not permitted in all jurisdictions. One of them is a very large steel door that slides down into place when a fire is detected. Other theatres are equipped with a deluge system that dumps an incredible amount of water. (Just imagine that going off by accident!) Whatever method is used, the purpose of the system is to seal off the auditorium from the stage house.

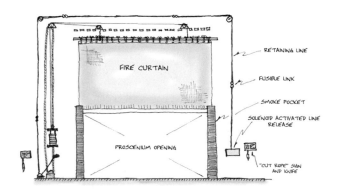

Fire curtains are hung directly upstage of the proscenium wall and are rigged to fall automatically in case of an emergency. There are a variety of ways to rig an asbestos fire curtain, but the most popular uses a self-governing counterweight system. Ropes and pulleys connect the curtain to a balancing counterweight that weighs slightly less than the curtain itself. When a restraining line is released, the fire curtain will drop into place by virtue of its own weight. The curtain can be released in one of several ways, all of which depend on the use of a lightweight rope that is stretched from one side of the proscenium opening to the other. This line restrains the fire curtain from falling. When slack appears in the line, a special knot tied to the counterweight operating line releases the weight, and the curtain falls.

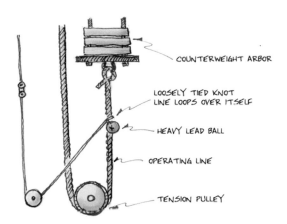

THIS TYPE OF MECHANISM IS OFTEN USED TO RIG A FIRE CURTAIN FOR QUICK RELEASE

There are several ways of severing the line. Many theatres have a knife fastened to the back of the proscenium. (An oft-sighted article: "In case of fire, cut rope.") This seems like the method least likely to work, because the knives are rarely sharp enough to cut through the line with enough speed to match the urgency of the situation.

Another method of releasing the line is through the use of *fusible links*. These links are two small pieces of metal (originally chain links) that have been soldered together with a material that will melt at a temperature of 160 degrees. The high temperature of a fire will cause the link to pull apart, severing the line and dropping

the fire curtain. Fusible links are very frequently used in industrial buildings where roll-up fire doors must lower automatically in a fire.

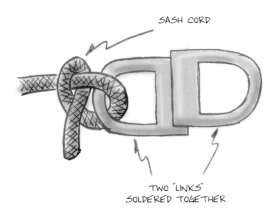

FUSIBLE LINKS ARE CONSTRUCTED SO THAT THE TWO HALVES WILL PULL APART IN THE HEAT OF A FIRE

A final method of operating the fire curtain is through the use of electronic fire detection devices such as heat detectors, smoke detectors, and sprinkler water pressure detectors. These electronic devices can be used to trigger a solenoid that releases the line from its extreme end. Some combination of these various methods is almost certain to bring the curtain in as planned, but if all other methods fail, a good hard yank on the restraining line will break apart one of the fusible links and release the system. Fire curtains are sealed at the edges by heavy steel flanges that wrap around the curtain and help to prevent smoke from entering the auditorium. These flanges are called *smoke pockets*.

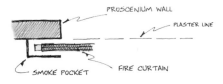

PLAN VIEW OF CURTAIN AND SMOKE POCKET

It is important to keep the fire curtain and all other safety equipment in good working order. Any problems should be taken care of as soon as they arise. If you have tied off the fire-curtain counterweights to circumvent a problem with the system, the curtain will not work in the event of an emergency.

A fire curtain does a great job of protecting the audience from fire and smoke, but it will also seal everyone on the stage in a smoke-filled box. To avoid this, exhaust fans are located on the roof of the fly tower to draw smoke from a fire upward. In older buildings, *smoke doors* are used in place of the fans. Smoke doors are a passive system based on the same principle as a chimney. A shed-type structure that is entirely surrounded by doors is constructed on the roof. The doors are hinged at the bottom so that they will open down and out by force of gravity alone. The same type of fusible links that are used to rig a fire curtain hold them in place. In the heat of a fire, the links melt, fall apart, and release the doors, which then flop open on their own.

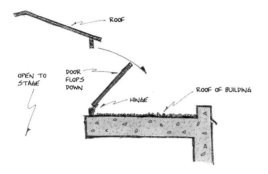

SMOKE DOOR OPERATION

Most fire marshals will agree that the best thing for you to do in a serious fire is to get yourself and others out of the theatre as quickly as possible.

 GREEN IDEAS TIP BOX

Safety is important in a theatre, which can be a dangerous place to work—what with all the stuff hanging overhead and the vast number of electrical devices—but also because of more subtle things like falling into an orchestra pit. Falling into the pit is more likely to happen than you would think, and is especially likely if you consider the danger of walking into a dark theater space where it is very difficult to tell where the apron ends and the pit begins. For this reason, most theatres like to leave a light on at all times, even when the space is not in use. Theatre work lights are often very high-wattage bulbs, because of the size of the space they must light and the same switch often turns on several of them. High-wattage bulbs consume a lot of electricity. Consider instead using a theatre *ghost light* to illuminate the front of the stage when the theatre is not in use. A ghost light is a single bulb (you can make it a compact fluorescent if you like) on a rolling stand that can be moved down to the apron of the stage and plugged in to illuminate the front of it. When someone enters the space in the dark, the ghost light will help him or her to see the line between stage and pit. Ghost lights are a theatre tradition and are also said to keep the ghosts away when the theatre is dark.

CHAPTER 3

RIGGING

Rigging is an entertainment business term with a variety of meanings. A definition of the widest possible latitude might say that rigging means to put something into a workable state. A shirt may be rigged with Velcro when a quick change happens too fast for buttons. Flats may be rigged with stiffeners when they are too floppy to stand on their own. Rigging for a rock show in an arena has its own specific meaning, which is using wire rope and shackles to hang chain motors. In the first part of this chapter, the term *rigging* will cover the equipment used in hanging scenery and lighting over the stage. Ropes, pulleys, arbors, and pipes are all a part of this equipment. The end of the chapter is a survey of how to rig chain motors in a theatre.

CHAIN MOTORS HAVE BEEN USED EXTENSIVELY IN ARENA RIGGING FOR DECADES. THEY HAVE BECOME INCREASINGLY IMPORTANT IN THEATRES IN RECENT YEARS.

TRADITIONAL RIGGING SYSTEMS

There are two main types of theatre rigging systems. The first and oldest type is known as the *hemp* system, and a second, newer type is known as a *counterweight system*. The word *system* is used to denote that there are many parts to each type and that these parts work together in concert to form a method of flying scenery. Some theatre buildings use various types of electric and/or hydraulic winches to fly scenery. Wire rope cable is wound/unwound from a drum, something like a winch that you might find on the front of an off-road vehicle.

doi: 10.1016/C2009-0-23409-X

MOTOR

CABLE DRUM

GEAR CASE

THIS CABLE WINCH IS RATED AT 3000 POUNDS

A CABLE WINCH DOESN'T NEED COUNTERWEIGHTS LIKE OTHER THEATRE SYSTEMS, BUT ALSO DOESN'T HAVE THE DELICATE TOUCH OF A HUMAN FLYMAN.

Thrust and arena theatres often use winches because their placement is more flexible. The winches can be picked up and moved to new locations if necessary. They are more adaptable to fit the different needs of a thrust theatre. Proscenium stages are rectangular, and the rigging is arranged so that all the pipes are parallel with the proscenium. Thrust theatres are irregularly shaped, and a rigging system made of winches that can be arranged in different ways is more useful. The problem with winches in general is that the precise control of automated equipment can be difficult to achieve. These machines have no ability to "feel" when something is going wrong. A good flyman can slip a batten past a crowd of others in a graceful way that a machine cannot possibly mimic. The flyman gets feedback from eyes, touch, and ears that a machine does not. This is an example of how the art of theatre sometimes wins out over the science of technology.

Chain motors have become very popular in recent years as scenery has become heavier and more complex. Most of the time motors are used for items that are dead hung, that is, ones not moving during the normal course of a performance. Chain motors are quite noisy when they operate. That is not so much a problem in the concert business, in which performances are very loud, but they are problematic in a quiet theatre.

Hemp system

The hemp system was developed in the mid-nineteenth century by stagehands who were recruited from the ranks of the merchant marine. As sailors, these stagehands were familiar with methods of using *hemp rope* to hoist heavy objects. As a result, many stagehand terms are derived from nautical sources. This will no doubt become obvious during this discussion of hemp rigging. On a sailing ship, the ropes and pulleys used to manipulate the sails are

known collectively as "the rigging" of the ship. More about ropes and knots can be found in Chapter 4.

When studying the hemp system, it is helpful to imagine a practical rigging problem. For the purposes of the following example, imagine that a curtain needs to be hung across the stage, parallel with the plaster line, and that at some point in the evening's entertainment this curtain will need to be flown up out of sight.

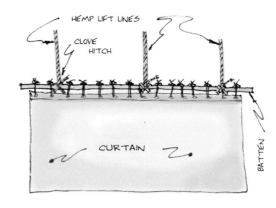

HEMP LIFT LINES

CLOVE HITCH

CURTAIN

BATTEN

BATTEN SUSPENDED WITH HEMP LIFT LINES

If the curtain is laid out on the stage floor or *deck*, it becomes immediately apparent that the first thing required for this rigging job is a horizontal *pipe* or *batten* to which the drapes may be tied. Also we will need some method of hoisting this batten up into the air and leaving it suspended. This can be accomplished by attaching hemp lines to the batten and pulling the lines upward toward the grid. At one time, battens were made from wood, but modern battens are made of steel pipe. When working on the stage, the terms *batten* and *pipe* are interchangeable.

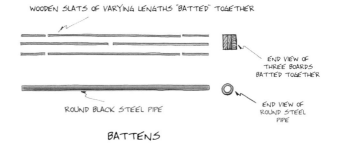

WOODEN SLATS OF VARYING LENGTHS "BATTED" TOGETHER

END VIEW OF THREE BOARDS BATTED TOGETHER

ROUND BLACK STEEL PIPE

END VIEW OF ROUND STEEL PIPE

BATTENS

BACK IN THE DAY, BATTENS WERE MADE BY CONNECTING PIECES OF WOOD TOGETHER, BUT NOW STEEL PIPE IS USED. AT THAT TIME, STEEL PIPE WAS NOT AVAILABLE, AND INDIVIDUAL WOODEN SLATS WERE NOT LONG ENOUGH.

Notice that in the curtain-hanging example, three stagehands are needed to haul the piece up into position, and tie it off at its designated *trim*. The word *trim* is used to indicate proper positioning of a flown piece. *Setting a trim* means to adjust a piece to its proper location and then mark that spot so that it can easily be found again. These stagehands have little choice but to tie off their lines and have them remain in one place.

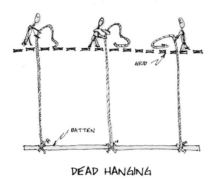

DEAD HANGING

A curtain that has been tied off in one position like this and just hangs there is said to be *dead hung*. In general practice, dead hanging is a last-resort situation, because it is a difficult and time-consuming procedure. It is hard to get all the lines tied off so the pipe is level and at the right height. At the beginning of our rigging example, we said that this drape would need to move on cue, so dead hanging would not be an appropriate solution to this rigging problem.

Other difficulties need to be addressed as well. First, it would be more efficient to use only one stagehand to run the curtain up and down rather than three. This would save on labor and also make sure that all lines are synchronized to move at the same time and speed. Second, it would be wise to find a method of balancing some of the weight of our load. A large curtain may weigh several hundred pounds—far too much for one flyman to handle without assistance. These concerns can be addressed by employing a system of pulleys and weights.

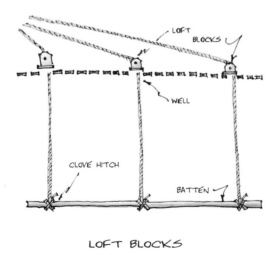

LOFT BLOCKS

Actually, the word *pulley* is somewhat of a misnomer as it has been used here. Generally, a device with a *sheave* (the rotating part of a pulley) used to change the direction of rope travel is referred to as a pulley if it is free to swivel or travel and as a *block* if it is bolted to one spot and stationary. A device that has been bolted to the wood or steel of the grid where it is not allowed to move in any direction is therefore a block. Those particular blocks are known as *loft blocks*, because they are in the loft area of the flyhouse. Loft blocks change the direction of rope travel from vertical to horizontal, that is to say, from an upward motion (leading from batten to grid) to a cross-stage inclination (from the loft block to the side of the stage). When they reach the side of the stage, the three hemp lines are together in one group and are able to be handled by one person.

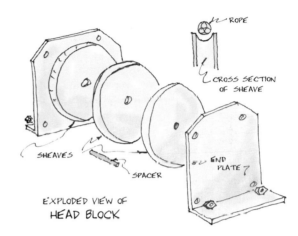

EXPLODED VIEW OF
HEAD BLOCK

It would be much easier to work with the three lines if they were hanging down on the side of the stage rather than remaining horizontal. Pulling down on a rope is more ergonomically efficient, because gravity helps you do it. The change in direction is accomplished using the *head block*. Again, this pulley is referred to as a block because it remains stationary. In our example, the head block has three sheaves, because there are three lines used to lift the batten. The block is constructed so that the three sheaves are side by side in the same housing but turn freely and independently.

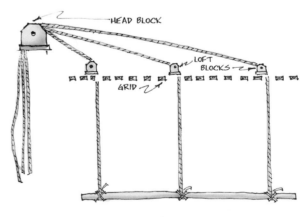

HEMP SYSTEM RIGGING

Our hemp lines are now hanging downward in the direction of the *pin rail*. Better leverage is gained because it is physically much easier to pull down on a rope than it is to pull sideways. It is important to note at this point that when the ropes are pulled down, the batten will move upward. Conversely, when tension is released, gravity will cause the batten to move in a downward direction.

Our example has not yet addressed the problem of counteracting the weight on the batten, but this can be achieved by adding weight to the downward-hanging lift lines. In a hemp house, *sandbags* are used for this purpose. The easiest and most effective means of attaching sandbags to ropes is to use a *clew* that has been fastened to the lift lines themselves. An older method was to use a special rope and knot known as a *sunday*, but a clew is much easier to attach. A clew is little more than a clamp with individual channels in it for the various ropes.

SANDBAGS, CLEWS, AND ROPES IN A
HEMP SYSTEM

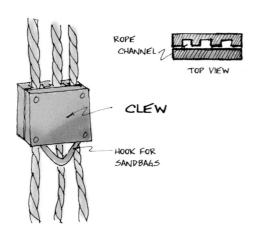

A clew makes it possible to make small adjustments in the lengths of the different lift lines, and thus to adjust the trim of the batten so that it will hang level and parallel to the stage floor. If a proper trim is not reached, the pipe may be bowed or slanted, and the curtain will not hang straight. A hook at the bottom of the clew is used to attach sandbags. Remember that the weight of the bags should be slightly less than the weight of the load on the batten. This condition is referred to as *batten-heavy*. If the lineset is batten-heavy, its own weight will cause it to fly in (down) when the ropes are loosened. If the weight of the sandbags and the weight on the pipe are perfectly balanced, it will be necessary to push up on the rope to get the batten to fly in, which is a method reserved exclusively for magicians.

The final step in operating a hemp system is to secure the group of lines to the pin rail when the batten is not in use. The rail itself is a horizontal pipe, which runs up- and downstage. There are holes drilled through the rail from top to bottom that are used in conjunction with *belaying pins*. In nautical terms, "belay" means to stop, or hold fast. The hemp lift lines are wrapped in a figure-eight around the cleat and into a special knot that will come completely untied whenever the belaying pin is removed from the rail. This method of tying off makes it easier to deal with several ropes at once and to move a lineset in a hurry, and is the same as when *tying off to a cleat* on a ship.

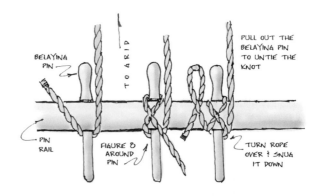

TYING OFF TO A BELAYING PIN

There are a number of shortcomings associated with the hemp system of rigging. The largest of these is the difficulty of attaching sandbags to the line-sets. This is at best a cumbersome task, and when the weight to be added is over 200 or 300 pounds, the sheer size of the bags is a test of anyone's strength and endurance. The largest bags used for electrics at the Lyric Theatre in Baltimore weigh 1,500 pounds! Also, since there are many such linesets arranged side by side, it becomes quite a trial to maneuver the bags past one another as several linesets are being simultaneously worked. On occasion, it is physically impossible, such as when several heavy loads are in close proximity to one another. In addition, there is the problem of the hemp lines stretching. Hemp rope tends to stretch when there is a load placed on it, and also when there is a change in humidity. Several different types of synthetic lines are available that are not affected by humidity, but they too have their own stretching/contracting quirks. Some become shorter and fatter over time—just the opposite of hemp.

The various ropes that make up a lineset are of differing lengths, because the opposite side of the stage is farther away. As the proportional amount of stretch is a function of the length of the rope, the far side of the batten will tend to droop as that line stretches excessively, and the problem will need to be adjusted using the clew. This can be a time consuming chore, and it requires a great deal of skill to be done properly. It is also difficult to deal with tying off the individual hemp lines at the rail, and to keep the massive amount of line that ends up on the floor neat. Several years of apprenticeship is required to develop the necessary skills. As you will see, the invention of the counterweight system was a giant step forward.

Even so, it is good to understand how this early system of rigging worked, because stage-hands are often called upon to rig lines for temporary lifting jobs, and understanding the basic principles of hemp-style rigging will make such tasks much easier.

Counterweight system

The *counterweight system* of rigging works on the same basic principles as the hemp system, but with a number of important refinements. *Aircraft cable*, a very high-strength stranded steel cable, is used in the place of hemp for the lift lines. This product was originally developed for use in linking the control surfaces of early airplanes, hence the odd name.

Most installations are equipped with a $\frac{1}{4}''$ size cable generally rated at around 7,000 pounds *breaking strength*. This far exceeds the breaking strength of any reasonably sized hemp rope. Another advantage of aircraft cable is that the stretching factor is negligible, and

steel is not affected in the least by changes in humidity. However, the very stiff cable is not at all suitable for tying off to a pin rail. It is important to realize that breaking strength is just that: the point at which the cable will break. Most riggers use a safety factor of four, meaning that the load placed on a rigging component should be only one-quarter of the breaking strength. Some components are marked with their breaking strength; others are marked with a working load limit.

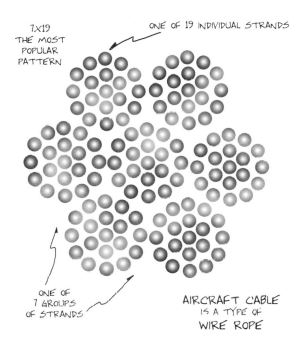

7X19
THE MOST POPULAR PATTERN

ONE OF 19 INDIVIDUAL STRANDS

ONE OF 7 GROUPS OF STRANDS

AIRCRAFT CABLE IS A TYPE OF WIRE ROPE

INDIVIDUAL STAINLESS, OR GALVANIZED STEEL WIRES ARE TWISTED TOGETHER TO FORM A ROPE, JUST LIKE HEMP IS. AIRCRAFT CABLE IS AN ESPECIALLY STRONG AND DURABLE TYPE.

Instead of tying off to a pin rail, the counterweight system uses an arbor that holds steel or lead weights rather than sandbags. The metal used in manufacturing counterweights is dense; these weights thus take up much less space than bags do. Aircraft cable lift lines are attached to the batten, then run upward through the loft blocks, across the grid to the head block, and down to the top of the arbor. A large diagram of that is at the end of the chapter.

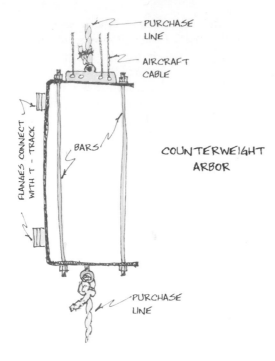

PURCHASE LINE

AIRCRAFT CABLE

FLANGES CONNECT WITH T - TRACK

BARS

COUNTERWEIGHT ARBOR

PURCHASE LINE

CABLE CONNECTED TO A BATTEN
WITH A CLOVE HITCH

Counterweights are added to the arbor to exactly balance out the weight of the batten and its load. The cable may be fastened to the pipe with a clove hitch and *wire rope clamp*, or it may have a *trim chain* that can be used to adjust the exact length of the cable.

CABLE CONNECTED TO A BATTEN
WITH A TRIM CHAIN

It is not necessary to leave the lineset batten-heavy, because there is a positive way to haul the arbor both up and down. This motion is accomplished by the use of a large diameter hemp line known as the *purchase* or *operating line*. A ¾″ line is standard, because the large size is easy to grip. Although I used the term "hemp" for the operating line, most modern systems use one of several types of synthetic materials. Although hemp is still in use many places, it may eventually become a thing of the past, because synthetic fiber ropes are greatly superior.

COUNTERWEIGHT RAIL

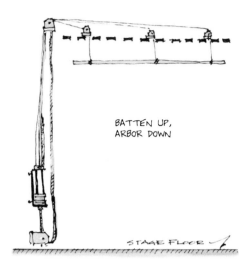

BATTEN UP,
ARBOR DOWN

STAGE FLOOR

The purchase line is attached to the top of the arbor and passes over the head block, down to a *tension pulley*, and back up to the bottom of the arbor, where it is again secured. Pulling down on the rope causes the arbor to move upward. As the arbor travels up, the batten travels down. Hence pulling down on the purchase line will cause the batten to also go down, and, in reverse, pulling up will move the batten upward.

As the purchase line is composed of either hemp or a synthetic such as nylon, it will tend to change length over a period of time. A bottom-tension pulley (remember that pulleys move) serves to keep the line taut at all times. It is set into special guides known as *T-tracks* that allow it to move downward by force of gravity, but cause it to jam rather than slide back up. The rear side of the arbor is guided by the same T-tracks that prevent the arbor from swaying from side to side as it travels up and down. Older systems use a cable-guiding device that is not nearly as effective, especially in a tall house.

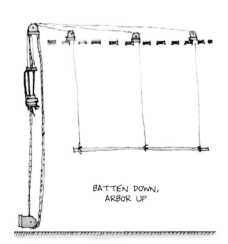

BATTEN DOWN,
ARBOR UP

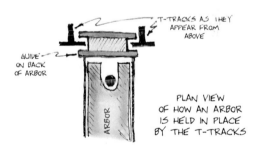

T-TRACKS AS THEY
APPEAR FROM
ABOVE

GUIDE
ON BACK
OF ARBOR

ARBOR

PLAN VIEW
OF HOW AN ARBOR
IS HELD IN PLACE
BY THE T-TRACKS

In some theatres, a lack of wing space means that the floor space under the rail must remain unobstructed, so that scenery and actors may pass back and forth. This is made possible with a 2-to-1 or *double-purchase* counterweight system. In this case, the rail is located approximately halfway between the deck and the grid. With that ratio, if the same type of cable system were used as in the standard counterweight system just discussed, battens would move only halfway up and down. In a double-purchase system, cable length is increased by passing the aircraft cable lift lines around a pulley on top of the arbor, and then tying them off at the grid.

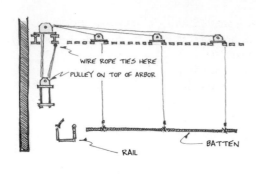

WIRE ROPE TIES HERE

PULLEY ON TOP OF ARBOR

RAIL

BATTEN

A 2 TO 1 OR "DOUBLE PURCHASE" SYSTEM ALLOWS SCENERY TO MOVE OFF STAGE UNDER THE RAIL

is bolted at a 90-degree angle across all of the T-tracks. When an arbor is snug against the top barrier, it is physically unable to move any higher. If the arbor cannot move any higher, the batten cannot sink any lower; at least until the weight limit of the various component parts is reached. This limit should be several thousand pounds at least, depending upon the quality and construction of the system, but in any case, more than the largest amount of weight the arbor can hold.

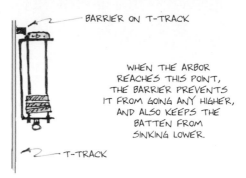

BARRIER ON T-TRACK

WHEN THE ARBOR REACHES THIS POINT, THE BARRIER PREVENTS IT FROM GOING ANY HIGHER, AND ALSO KEEPS THE BATTEN FROM SINKING LOWER.

T-TRACK

What this means is that for every foot the arbor rises, 2 feet of lift line will pass over the head block, and as a consequence, the batten will drop 2 feet. You can clearly see how the names "2-to-1" and "double-purchase" originated. One drawback of this system is that it also requires twice the amount of weight to be loaded into the arbor. If your scenery weighs 150 pounds, then 300 pounds must be loaded onto the arbor. When hanging a heavy load, these arbors tend to fill up in a hurry. Theatres with a double-purchase system may find it best to use heavier lead weights rather than the standard steel ones.

When the batten is flown all the way in and the arbor is all the way out, snug against its barrier, it is safe to load any practical amount of scenery or lighting equipment onto the batten without fear of anything falling to the floor. Of course, this statement presupposes that you securely fasten that load to the batten and that your rigging system is in proper working order.

At this point it seems prudent to offer a word of caution. Flying scenery is dangerous. It involves lifting heavy objects over the heads of actors and stagehands. Accidents can and will result in serious injury. You should be very familiar with any type of rigging system you use and should never exceed the limits of your knowledge. If you are unsure of what you are about to do, stop and seek advice from someone with more experience.

A word of warning! Be sure to completely lower the batten all the way in before adding a load to the pipe. If you stop a few inches short, and a large amount of weight is put on the pipe, it will suddenly slip down until the arbor reaches its full out position at the T-track barrier. This can be very dangerous for the stagehands who are loading the pipe!

Before discussing the operating procedures of a counterweight rigging system, it is wise to review the relationship between battens and arbors. Remember that when a batten has been flown all the way in (down) as far as it will go, its arbor will be all the way up. Actually, the arbor will stop when it reaches its *barrier* at the top of the T-track. When the batten is flown out, the arbor will be stopped by a similar barrier at the bottom of its travel, preventing it from colliding with the tension pulley. This barrier is usually a piece of angle iron with a rubber or wooden cushion bolted to it. This assembly

Let us suppose for a moment that the load on the batten is 400 pounds. With no weights in the arbor of a single-purchase system you would need to pull down on the purchase line with a force of 400 pounds in order to haul the batten into the air. Clearly, it would be terribly unsafe to do this, if it were even possible. You would need to weigh at least 401 pounds yourself, or as a group. Then the batten would have a potential to fall, with the inertia gained from the distance involved and its 400 pounds of mass. That would be illogical, however, because the whole point of using a counterweight system is to allow the weights in the arbor to balance a load placed on the batten.

Counterweights are generally stored on the *loading gallery*. The loading gallery is positioned near the grid, where it is possible to reach the arbors when they are at their highest point of travel. *Counterweights*, which are often referred to as *bricks* because of their shape, are stacked in the arbor in an amount that matches the load on the batten, in our case 400 pounds. Bricks most commonly have rounded indentations at either end that are intended to fit around the upright bars found on an arbor. Bricks are tilted at an angle for placement into the arbor and then laid flat. These weights will not fall out of the arbor when they have been properly placed between the bars.

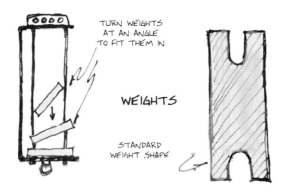

Most arbors have one or more flat pieces of metal connecting the two upright bars. These *spreader plates* slide up and down on the rods, and are intended to prevent the bars from warping out of shape from the weight of the bricks. Spreader plates should be distributed more or less evenly throughout the stack of weights in the arbor.

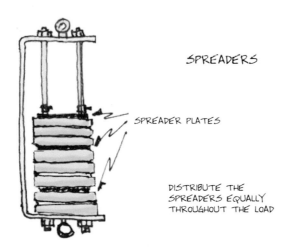

Counterweights are manufactured in a variety of different poundages, but the 20- and/or 25-pound weights seem to be the most popular. Theatres often have a small number of half-sized bricks so that a more exact balance can be reached than is possible with the standard types. Sometimes lead is used in place of steel in manufacturing the weights, with the advantage being that the same size lead brick weighs approximately twice as much. This can be very useful in theatres that have unusually short arbors that cannot hold very many weights, and especially in a double-purchase system.

Remember to load the batten first and the arbor second. This prevents creating a situation where a heavily weighted arbor can fall. If the arbor were to be loaded first, the only thing holding it up would be the rope lock on the rail. That is a completely unsafe procedure, as the rope lock can be expected to hold back only a few dozen pounds at best, and not nearly the 400 that were mentioned earlier. Remember that the batten is always loaded first because it has nowhere else to go. It has no potential for movement.

Conversely, when removing objects from a batten, the arbor should always be unloaded first to avoid the same unsafe situation from occurring in reverse. If the batten were to be unloaded before its corresponding arbor, the system would be very far out of balance, creating a dangerous situation. Again, the weight of the arbor would be held in check from falling only by the pressure of the rope lock on the purchase line. Under normal circumstances, linesets should be safe to load and unload even with the rope lock loosened.

STEPS FOR SAFELY LOADING AND UNLOADING STAGE WEIGHTS

When loading:

- Fly the pipe all the way in.
- Place the load on the pipe, taking care to properly secure it.
- Load the proper amount of stage weights into the arbor.
- Fly the lineset out to its proper trim.

When unloading:

- Fly the pipe in to its extreme bottom position.
- Unload the arbor.
- Remove the load from the batten.

ADVANCED TECHNIQUES

There are a number of added complexities to operating a stage counterweight rigging system. One of them is that the weight of the pipe itself must be balanced out by one or two weights in the arbor that need never be removed. This is often referred to as *pipe weight*. It is helpful to strap these weights down, or to paint them a safety color, or otherwise mark them in some way so that they are not accidentally removed. It is customary that when the *loaders*, as they are called, are finished unloading an arbor they yell down "pipe weight" so that the flyman on the rail below knows that it is safe to unload the pipe and can announce this to the stagehands on the deck.

Unless you are touring and have hung the same show a number of times, it is often difficult to know exactly how much weight should be loaded on a batten. There is a danger of greatly overloading the arbor so that it is vastly heavier than the pipe, thus creating a safety hazard. When an exact weight total is not known, it is best to load the arbor with the purchase line unlocked, slowly and until repeated testing shows that a proper balance has been achieved. If the same scenery or lights are to be hung again at some future date, make a note of the precise weight involved so that this time-consuming procedure can be eliminated. When you are unsure of the weight, load the arbor the safe way. It is very important not to greatly overload the arbor.

Unfortunately, scenery or drapes hung on a pipe may be too large to hang without at least some portion of the load resting on the floor. This will obviously affect your ability to judge the weight of the load by the process just described. In this event, it will be necessary to determine the weight by some other means (such as an educated guess) to within a hundred pounds or so of the actual amount. After the load has been secured to the batten, a *bull line* is used to safely get the piece into the air.

A bull line is a stout length of rope that is comfortably large enough to bear the weight of the load you are hanging. The larger the diameter of the line, the easier it will be for the stagehands to grip. The rope should be lengthy enough so that it reaches the floor even after it's been doubled over the batten, and the pipe has been flown out far enough for the entire weight of the load to be resting on it. Do not tie it to the batten, but do tie both of the ends together so that the line will not accidentally slip off the pipe. If you tie the bull line to the batten you will be subsequently unable to remove it without a ladder or a Genie lift.

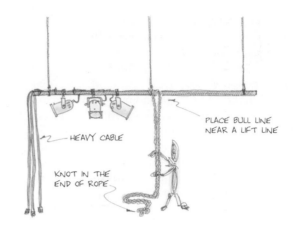

USING A BULL LINE

Stagehands take the place of the eventual load by keeping tension on the bull line as the batten is flown out. Make absolutely certain that the bull line rope is able to handle the strain and that the load is not too much for the stagehands to easily handle. If the load is not more than 100 pounds or so out of weight, you shouldn't have too much trouble. After you've manhandled it all the way out, the arbor will have come in far enough to be fine-tuned from the rail. It is very important that a knowledgeable flyman be on hand when using a bull line.

On occasion, and especially with a double-purchase system, a need arises to hang a piece that is heavier than the amount of counterweight that can be fitted into one arbor. When this happens, it is possible to use a second lineset as a helper. This is known as *marrying* the two pipes. It is a good idea to keep a number of short chains and shackles on hand that may be used for this procedure. Make sure that the hardware in question has a capacity rating high enough to hold the weight involved. How can you know this? Suitable hardware has a rating. Shackles are the best connectors because they generally have a known *working load limit* or *WLL* stamped on their sides. Snap hooks and quick links generally do not. You do not need to use a safety factor when the WLL is known; it is OK to use the entire limit.

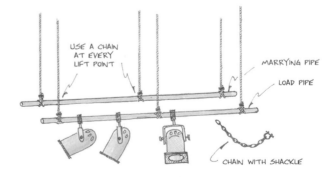

MARRYING PIPES TOGETHER

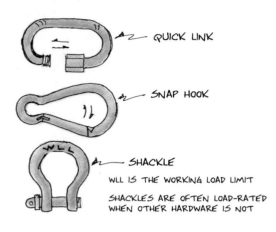

QUICK LINK

SNAP HOOK

SHACKLE

WLL IS THE WORKING LOAD LIMIT

SHACKLES ARE OFTEN LOAD-RATED WHEN OTHER HARDWARE IS NOT

HANGING HARDWARE

this situation occurs, special steps can be taken to ensure that the lineset does not become a "runaway," meaning that the arbor is falling and out of control.

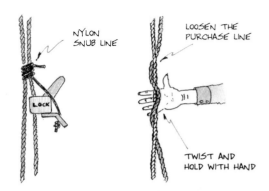

NYLON SNUB LINE

LOCK

LOOSEN THE PURCHASE LINE

TWIST AND HOLD WITH HAND

THREE WAYS TO SAFETY A LINESET

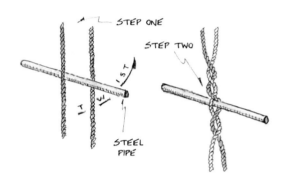

STEP ONE

STEP TWO

1ST

2ND

STEEL PIPE

Use one marrying chain for each of the lift lines in your particular system. Fly in a pipe that is either just upstage or downstage from the one that is being loaded and wrap the chains around the two pipes so that they are tightly bound together. It is best to put the chains next to the lift lines. This will ensure that they are evenly spread out along the length of the pipe.

As a matter of physics, it really doesn't matter how the weight is distributed between the two arbors with regard to their effect on the load. As a practical consequence though, it is easier to load and unload the arbors if a majority of the weight is in the primary arbor. This also places less of a load on the marrying hardware. If the piece must *work,* or move during the show, both linesets must be unlocked and moved together. It takes more physical strength to overcome the inertia of a heavy weight, but it is still possible for one person to fly the piece, because when one purchase line is pulled, the other will automatically follow as a slave.

The aircraft cable making up the lift lines has a certain weight itself. This weight can really add up in a large system. If the arbor and batten are visualized as opposite ends of a set of balance scales, the passage of the aircraft cable from one side of the scales to the other can be seen to make a measurable difference in the balance of the system. Therefore, when the batten is very far in, the lineset will seem a bit batten-heavy, and when it is all the way out, it may seem quite arbor-heavy. This is a natural occurrence and there is not much that can be done about it. In extremely tall and wide houses, a heavy cable running the opposite direction through the head block is sometimes used to account for the difference in the in/out weights.

There are times (such as those calling for a bull line) when loading and unloading weights will require that the system be very arbor-heavy for a short while. When

One method is to tie the front and back parts of the purchase line together with a timber hitch or other suitable choking knot. The friction between the two ropes lashed together will keep them from slipping. It is imperative that the two ropes be very tightly bound.

Another method is to take a short length of pipe and twist the front and back portions of the purchase line together several times until there is enough friction created to prevent the line from slipping. If you wish to leave the lineset unattended for a moment, it is possible to jam one end of the pipe between two of the T-track rails so that it will stay put. (Just make sure that it does.)

The last method is to create slack in the purchase line by pushing down on the front of the tension pulley. Not all systems work this way. If yours does, the pulley will become unjammed and jump up several inches, creating slack in the line. You can then twist the front and rear portions of the purchase line around one another and hold them together tightly with a gloved hand. This last method has the added advantage of allowing the flyman to slowly let the two lines slide through his or her hands while flying the piece out. For loads that are not too greatly out of balance, this technique can take the place of a bull line, but be careful, as it takes a great deal of experience to know the difference. Do not exceed your limitations, and, as they say, better safe than sorry.

Running the Show

Running a show from the rail involves the marking of trims (the limits a purchase line should move), the clear labeling of all linesets in use, making up a cue sheet, and establishing a means of communication from the stage manager. Flymen should exercise a great deal of caution when flying scenery. The inertia of a heavily laden batten can cause severe damage to scenery or props on the deck, as well as to humans. If it is not possible to see the stage while running a cue, it is best to have someone else watch for you. During work calls, a flyman should always announce a batten moving in or out. The most common way is to call "Pipe number so and so, coming in. Heads up!" Remember to speak loudly, from the diaphragm.

Although the term fly*man* is used here in an effort to respect tradition, the rail is by no means an exclusively male domain. There are many fine women flymen, and the term is not intended to exclude them. One of them is listed in the acknowledgments section of this book's preface.

Trims may be marked in one of two basic ways, either with colored tape wrapped around the purchase line or with small pieces of yarn or ribbon that are worked between the strands of the same line. The ribbon is easier to see, and less likely to become dislodged from the purchase line, but it is somewhat more difficult to install and unkind to the rope. The yarn method will not work at all with a newer braided line such as Stage Set X. Whichever method is used, the basic concept is to take the batten to its desired trim, and mark the purchase line where it lines up with a stationary point on the rail. In this way, the pieces to be flown in can be stopped at a precise, predetermined point without hesitation.

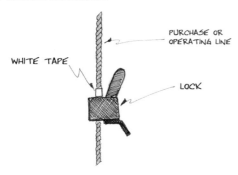

MARKING THE IN TRIM

The best practice is to mark the *in trim* with white tape so that the mark is even with the top of the rope lock when the low trim is reached. If the purchase line is white, use a dark color. As the scenery is flying in, the front part of the purchase line will be moving down. When you see the trim mark come into view, cover the mark with your hand and gently stop the momentum of the lineset as the mark reaches the top of the rope lock. It is important not to run past the mark, as the scenery may hit the deck with some force and make an unpleasant noise.

Running a soft piece past its trim and piling it up on the deck is known as *overhauling*. The error is particularly heinous if it extends to a point where the batten pipe shows to the audience. Should that occur, expect a stern reprimand from the stage manager. With a bit of experience, you should be able to touch in the piece to the deck without making a sound. Slow way down as the trim mark approaches the lock, let it just touch the floor, and then give a small tug on the line to settle the piece against the floor snugly. If you are flying in a hard piece, snugging it against the deck will keep it from drifting back and forth during the scene. You should be able to tell a definite difference in the feel of the purchase line when the piece reaches the deck. With some of the weight on the floor, the arbor will seem heavier.

After the scenery has had its moment in the footlights, it must be flown up or out of view of the audience. It is best *not* to mark the out trim so that it matches up with the top of the rope lock, because you may confuse it with the in trim. Also, because the front section of the purchase line is moving upward when the piece flies out, a mark in that position would be coming from the wrong direction to be easily seen. The tape would be invisible until it suddenly popped up past the lock and had already passed its stopping point. It is far better to mark the high trims on the rear part of the rope. It will be passing downward as the scenery flies up. In this way, you can see the mark approach and more easily stop at the proper trim. With this method, both trim marks will be coming down toward you. Usually there is some horizontal framing member that is a part of the T-track system that can be used as a visual reference for the stopping point. If not, one can easily be established using marker or paint to create a line across the tracks themselves. *Out* trims are most often marked with red tape, but the color does not really matter as long as you are consistent with it. Avoid using the same color tape for both your ins and outs, because that will create confusion.

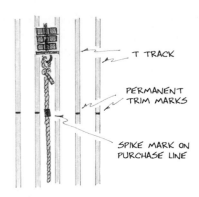

MARKING THE OUT TRIM

On occasion, you may need to mark an intermediate trim. That is a point for scenery to stop somewhere between the high/out and low/in trims. You should mark this trim at the rope lock as you would the low trim, but find some means of differentiating the two, such as by color or by size of the trim mark.

All linesets should be clearly marked by name. Often there is a card holder or marker board on which to write. I personally prefer to use white gaff tape and a black Sharpie marker. The tape is less likely to fall off at some crucial moment. Marking in the clearest possible manner can prevent some fairly embarrassing, though perhaps memorable, moments in the theatre. Clearly marking everything backstage that must be found in the dark is always a good idea. In some theatres, working pieces (linesets that will move during the show) are marked with red tape above the name card so that they are easier for the flymen to spot. Some rails will go so far as to lash together the front and rear purchase lines of all the nonworking linesets so that they will not be grabbed by mistake.

Fly rail *cue sheets* should be made in a large enough format that several people can look at them at the same time. It is not at all unusual for three or four lines to move at the same time, meaning that the same number of flymen will need to review their cues, or *pulls*, all at once. Most often, each flyman is given a number to use as a reference when reading the cue sheet. Sometimes there is a change in personnel, and rather than changing the cue sheet, someone can tell the new person his or her number.

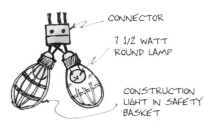

USE THE CLOTHESPIN TO MARK WHICH CUE IS NEXT

The sheet should list the number of the rail cue, the numbers of the flymen involved, the name of the piece each will be pulling, its speed and direction, and the color of *cue light* on which the pull is to occur. Cue lights are double sets of small colored bulbs controlled by the stage manager. You may wish to use a red clothespin or some other small clamp to mark your place on the cue sheet. After a cue is taken, the pin is moved down to the next reference. When the cue light comes on, and the hands gather to check their next pull, the red pin marks the appropriate spot.

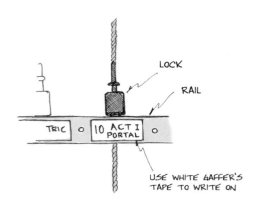

MARKING THE NAME OF A LINESET

The *cue light* coming on is a warning to get ready for the cue. When the light goes out, the cue should be taken immediately. This method allows any number of flymen to see the command at one time, and synchronizes their moves. Trying to run a headset to each person would involve far too many pesky wires and would unnecessarily burden the stage manager with too many verbal commands. Two bulbs are used on each circuit to guard against the inevitable burnout. When there are a series of cues going in a close time period, it is best to use a different color of light for each section of the cue in order to reduce confusion. Switches at the stage manager's desk are used to control the cue lights, which are often used on the deck as well as the fly floor.

Running a fly cue involves knowing which lineset you are to use, the direction of travel (in or out), the speed, and the color of cue light. If a line is to be pulled down so that the scenery is to fly into the view of the audience, you should unlock the lineset when the cue light comes on and stand ready. Watch the light carefully until it goes out. On that command, pull down on the rope until the trim mark is seen. Cover the mark with your hand, slow down the line as the trim mark approaches the lock, and stop it gently in the right spot. Remove your hand, and after checking to see that you are indeed correct, replace the lock and ring.

Sometimes, when the exact positioning of a piece is critical and/or the flymen have proven themselves to be unreliable, a *knuckle buster* may be used. This is essentially a small clamp that may be attached to the purchase line at the low trim mark. It is too large to fit through the lock and is a certain means of assuring that the line cannot travel through the lock any farther than is intended. Even limited experience with a knuckle buster will well acquaint a novice flyman with the origins of its colorful name. They are really a last resort and should be avoided in most situations.

KNUCKLE BUSTER

Flying a piece out to its high trim is essentially the same as flying one in, but there are several important differences. Some pieces of scenery are quite heavy, and as a result, the amount of inertia that must be overcome in order to begin moving the lineset can be rather large and difficult to handle. Bear in mind that it is much easier to pull down on a rope than to pull up. Notice that when a lineset is going out, the front portion of the purchase line (the one nearest you) is also going out, but the back line is going down. Hence, by grabbing the rear line and pulling down, the piece will actually fly up. Pull on the back line, at least until the pipe is up to speed. As the trim mark comes down into view, you can stop by using downward force on the front line at the appropriate point.

Another difference encountered in flying out lies in the position of the scenery just before the cue is taken. By definition, if a piece is to be flown out, then it must be in view of the audience. Often when a lock is pulled open, the lines will tend to creep a bit, and this might be seen by the audience—or even worse, by the stage manager. To avoid that, grasp both the front and back lines together before the lock is undone, and hold them together until the cue is taken. This will prevent the scenery from moving visibly.

Many small nuances make a really experienced flyman an expert in the field, and I've listed just the basic methods in this chapter. Other methods are just as good, but I have found the practices outlined here to be the most easily understood and universally practiced. Perhaps the best advice is to simply watch carefully at all times and pay attention to what is happening around you. There will be many occasions when lines will foul, wrong lines will be pulled, or pieces will move in the wrong direction. If you are watchful, these mistakes can be caught when they are still relatively minor and corrected.

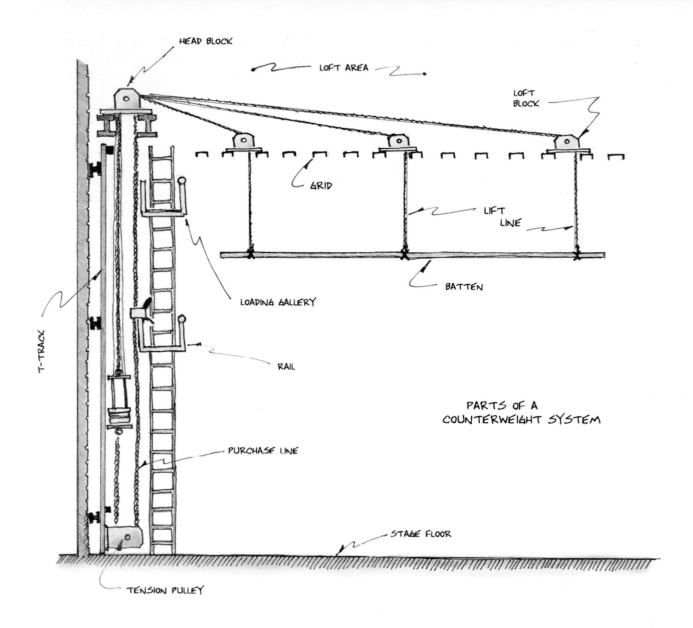

HEAD BLOCK

LOFT AREA

LOFT BLOCK

GRID

LIFT LINE

BATTEN

LOADING GALLERY

T-TRACK

RAIL

PARTS OF A COUNTERWEIGHT SYSTEM

PURCHASE LINE

STAGE FLOOR

TENSION PULLEY

RIGGING WITH CHAIN MOTORS

This type of rigging is sometimes called *arena rigging*, because it was developed to set up lights and sound in multipurpose indoor arenas that are often used for things like ice shows and rock concerts. Wire rope similar to the aircraft cable in theatre rigging is used to suspend industrial-type *chain hoists* from the roof trusses. The chain hoists are then used to lift aluminum trusses, which have scenery and/or lights attached to them. The terms *chain hoist* and *chain motor* are interchangeable.

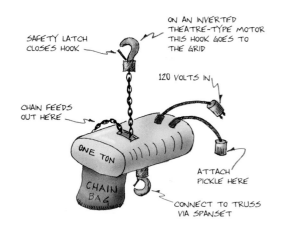

SAFETY LATCH CLOSES HOOK

ON AN INVERTED THEATRE-TYPE MOTOR THIS HOOK GOES TO THE GRID

120 VOLTS IN

CHAIN FEEDS OUT HERE

ONE TON

CHAIN BAG

ATTACH PICKLE HERE

CONNECT TO TRUSS VIA SPANSET

PARTS OF A CM CHAIN MOTOR/HOIST

CM Lodestar motors are by far the most common, although there are a couple of other types. The initials CM stand for Columbus McKinnon, the company that makes them. Lodestar is their premier model. Insurance companies feel better about lifting heavy loads over thousands of people in an audience if you use the best equipment available. An *inverted* type of hoist is made for use in the entertainment field. Normally, in a factory setting, hoists are attached to the ceiling. The chain hangs down, and a hook at the end of it is used to lift heavy loads like a crane. In an arena, lifting the motor itself to the high ceiling is problematic, so the hoists are reconfigured to operate upside-down, with the hook in the air and the motor on the floor. When the hoist does its lifting, it lifts itself along with the load, which slightly de-rates the manufacturer's load limit designation. But in general, these motors are designed to lift the full amount they are rated for, with a safety factor already considered.

The hoist has a sprocket inside of it that the chain runs through, and as the motor turns the sprocket the chain also moves. A very heavy-duty clutch inside the housing keeps the sprocket from slipping when the motor is turned off. The speed is not adjustable, but different motors are designed to run the chain at 16, 32, and 64 feet per minute. Sixteen feet per minute is standard; faster speeds are usually for some type of effect. Chain motors are rated by how much weight they can lift. The *one-ton* size is by far the most common, but *two-ton* and *half-ton* sizes are also available. Half-ton motors are physically smaller and also use a smaller-gauge chain, but the two-tons are the same exact size as the one-tons. The difference is made up by using a different sort of hook with a pulley in it. The chain is fed through the hook so that a 2-to-1 mechanical advantage is achieved. Columbus McKinnon makes many other types of hoists, but they aren't commonly used in the entertainment industry.

No matter what the type, the chain runs through the motor and is fed back out. As the motor lifts a load, the chain is gathered into a *chain bag* attached to the side. There are several different types, and some are better at preventing the chain from falling out of the bag on its own or *running*. That happens when enough chain misfeeds and begins to pull all the rest of the chain out of the bag. The chains are heavy, and can cause serious damage when they run and hit some other part of the rigging.

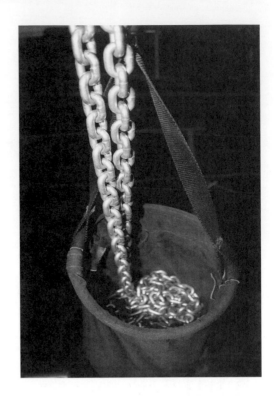

THE CHAIN COMES OUT OF THE MOTOR AND INTO THE BAG. CONNECT THE FREE END OF THE CHAIN TO THE MOTOR TO HELP PREVENT IT FROM RUNNING.

Chains generally come in 60- or 80-foot lengths, meaning that the distance from the hook to the motor is about that long. Rigging the hook with wire rope from the ceiling increases the distance, so even if the ceiling of an arena is 85 feet tall, an 80-foot chain will probably still be long enough. Theatres are generally not that tall, and chain length is not usually an issue. Before rigging, stagehands must run the chain all the way out of the motor so that the hook to motor distance is at its maximum length. That is called *running the chain out*. The motors have a limiting device inside them that will prevent the chain from coming all the way out of the motor at the free end or from hitting the hook at the hook end. The motor will stop on its own when the *limit* is reached. It is considered good practice to run the motor back a *bump* after reaching its limit so as to protect the inner workings of the motor during transport. To bump a motor means to turn it on and off rapidly. Additionally, the term is used to describe moving just a bit. You may be asked to "go up a bump" when setting the trim of a piece of truss.

THE FEMALE CONNECTOR GOES OUT TO THE PICKLE

THE MALE PLUG ON ANY DEVICE IS THE INPUT POWER.

IF POWER WERE FED TO THE MALE CONNECTOR IT WOULD BE A CONSTANT SOURCE OF ELECTRICAL SHOCK

Two-, one-, and half-ton entertainment motors generally work from a 120VAC 60 Hz power supply, which is the common North American line voltage. Two connectors are located on the motor. One is for the input power, and the other is a lower-voltage control circuit. In order to operate the motor, you must connect it to a suitable power source and then use a control mechanism to switch it on and off. The most common type of controller is called a *pickle*, and has a rocker switch on it with three positions. A spring inside automatically selects the center or off position unless the operator intentionally presses another setting. As a safety precaution, when the operator lets go of the button, the switch automatically shuts off the motor. The two other switch positions are up and down. Movement up and down is achieved by having the motor run forward or backward so that the chain feeds either in or out. More complex switching mechanisms may run numerous motors all at the same time. Three position toggle switches on a central panel are used to select up/off/down for the various motors in the system, and a GO button engages them all at once. Like the pickle, the GO button is spring loaded so that releasing it turns everything off automatically. This arrangement is sometimes known as a *dead-man switch*.

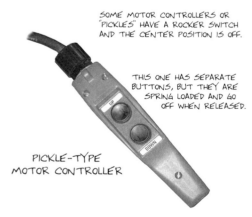

SOME MOTOR CONTROLLERS OR "PICKLES" HAVE A ROCKER SWITCH AND THE CENTER POSITION IS OFF.

THIS ONE HAS SEPARATE BUTTONS, BUT THEY ARE SPRING LOADED AND GO OFF WHEN RELEASED.

PICKLE-TYPE MOTOR CONTROLLER

IT IS IMPORTANT FOR THE SWITCH TO DISENGAGE THE POWER IF THE OPERATOR BECOMES DISTRACTED.

Most of the time, in an arena, motors are used to hoist a system of trusses into the air. Scenery and lights are connected to the truss. That is a means of reducing the number of motors required. An aluminum *box truss* is the preferred type. A box truss is four-sided, and a *delta truss* is three-sided. Box trusses are more heavy-duty and easier to connect together at angles, so they are the most commonly used. Motors in a theatre are most often used to hang lighting trusses, lighting towers, and speaker clusters. These units are designed with motor hoisting in mind. But motors may also be used to hoist scenic units in place, and care should be taken to find a safe hookup location on the piece. Motors can be an excellent way to lift heavy scenery that must be assembled on top of some other unit, and can be thought of as a sort of impromptu crane.

THIS ALUMINUM BOX TRUSS IS 12" SQUARE AND 10 FEET LONG. THE HARDWARE ON THE ENDPLATE CONNECTS WITH ANOTHER SECTION

BOX TRUSS

Trusses are joined to the motors using *slings*, which are often called by the trade name *Spanset*. Spansets are made from a very strong synthetic material, and are formed into a loop, so that there is no discernible end. They come in many different sizes and load capacities. Typically, the Spanset is *choked* to the bottom horizontal member of the box truss, and then again around the top member. Choking means that one Spanset is used on each side of the truss, so that the ends of two loops are left at the top. These two loops are fitted into a shackle, and then into the hook that is on the motor itself. A video of how to do that is available on the Web site. Just to be clear, the other hook is the one at the end of the chain, which would actually be up in the air at this time. Frequently, the motor would already be connected to the overhead support structure, and would be floating in the air by the time the trusses are connected.

FIRST CHOKE SPANSET ON THE BOTTOM
OF THE TRUSS

CLIP SPANSETS FROM BOTH SIDES INTO MOTOR HOOK

When the motor is activated, and the hoist pulls the truss upward, the Spansets pick the truss up from the bottom, a setup that is less likely to pull it apart under load. Rigging from the top of the truss is not allowed by the manufacturer, and the equipment is not rated for it.

Excess chain should be fed into the chain bag from the free end first, so that the part nearest the motor out-feed goes in last. This will help keep the chain from becoming fouled when it feeds back out of the bag, and perhaps avoid its running out entirely. The free end of the chain is generally semipermanently connected to the motor, but if not, you should at least tie it to the bag.

In an arena, steel cables are used to connect the motor's chain to the roof's support structure. In a theatre, the chains are often simply rigged to the grid itself using a pipe. This is especially true if the grid is the standard type constructed from heavy steel channels with spaces between them, forming a slotted floor.

THEN CHOKE SPANSET ON THE TOP
OF THE TRUSS

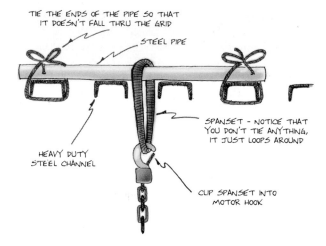

TIE THE ENDS OF THE PIPE SO THAT
IT DOESN'T FALL THRU THE GRID

STEEL PIPE

SPANSET - NOTICE THAT
YOU DON'T TIE ANYTHING,
IT JUST LOOPS AROUND

HEAVY DUTY
STEEL CHANNEL

CLIP SPANSET INTO
MOTOR HOOK

THIS METHOD ONLY WORKS WITH
A HEAVY DUTY STEEL GRID

If the chain is long enough to reach the grid all on its own, clip a Spanset through the hook on the chain and pull it up through a space in the grid at the desired location using a bowline. Slide a piece of *schedule 40, 1.5" ID* or larger pipe through the Spanset and set the rig down across the grid channels with the pipe at a 90-degree angle to them. The channels should be no more than 4" apart, so the pipe is spanning a very small distance. Use some small line to tie off the ends of the pipe to the channel steel so that it does not accidentally turn sideways and fall through the slot. That is really just a safety against its being kicked while rigging, because under load the pipe will be pressed very firmly against the grid. The tie line has no real load on it. The pipe should be about 36" in length, which is long enough so that you have room to tie it down, but not so long as to be unduly cumbersome on the grid. This method will work only in a theatre with an old-style, heavy-duty steel-channel grid. It would be very dangerous to try this on an expanded metal or cable style of grid, so don't do that! If you are not sure, then rig your load from the loft block wells instead.

USING ROPES TO RAISE THE RIGGING

The next chapter of this book discusses ropes and knot tying, and has a thorough description of how to tie the most important rigging knot, the *bowline*. A bowline is used to create a fixed loop in the end of the rope, and is very useful for raising and lowering the steel cables used to hang chain motors. Tie the bowline so that the line of the loop goes through the Spanset, or through the shackle of the rig, depending on the type of rig you are using. The bowline knot will be easy to untie after the rig is secure. A large-diameter, woven exterior nylon fiber rope is best for this work, because it is very supple and bends well, thus making the knots easier to tie. A larger rope is easier to grip, which is important when pulling up the heavy chain by hand.

USE A THICK, 3/4" LINE
FOR RIGGING.

THE THICKER THE ROPE,
THE EASIER IT IS TO
GRIP AND PULL UP.

TIE A BOWLINE THRU
THE SPANSET AND
USE THAT TO
PULL THE RIG
UP TO THE GRID

If you do not have a standard grid with channel steel, you may be able to hang from the loft blocks *wells* that support the loft blocks. Wells are formed with much larger steel than the rest of the grid. Because they run up- and downstage, you can pick a spot that has the right up/down location. The wells must support the weight of the batten loads, plus the weight of the bricks in the arbor, so they are usually very strong. If the span of the opening is more than 10″, you may want to use a larger piece of pipe, perhaps 2″ or 3″ in diameter, but otherwise the method of hanging the motor from the well is pretty much the same as hanging from the grid.

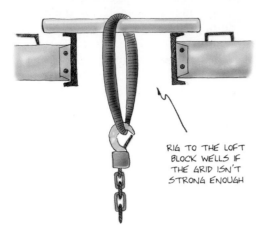

RIG TO THE LOFT BLOCK WELLS IF THE GRID ISN'T STRONG ENOUGH

When rigging from the steel-channel grid, correct placement is easy, because the channels fall every few inches left to right and the open slot runs up- and downstage, so the rig can go most anywhere. If you must rig from the wells, you can still locate the rig at any point up- and downstage (as long as you go between two loft blocks) but placement left and right can be a problem. If the well is not in the proper location left to right, you can use a *bridle* to adjust the rigging.

Bridles require the use of wire rope. In stagehand lingo, this wire rope is simply called *steel*. The most common diameter for the wire rope is 3/8″, because its load rating matches the load capacity of a one-ton motor. The end of the steel is made into a loop by passing it around a *thimble*. The resulting *eye* is used together with a *shackle*, in connecting pieces together. Steel comes in standard lengths of 2, 5, 10, 20, and 30 feet. They can be shackled together to form different sizes.

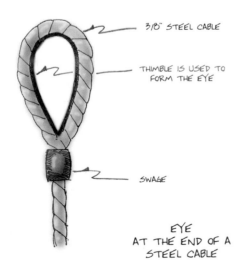

3/8″ STEEL CABLE

THIMBLE IS USED TO FORM THE EYE

SWAGE

EYE
AT THE END OF A
STEEL CABLE

Shackles are used to connect the different parts of the rig together. When 3/8″ steel cable is used, a 5/8″ shackle is considered standard. Larger or smaller shackles might not properly fit through the eye of the steel. A shackle has three distinct parts: the *pin*, the *bell*, and the *hubs*. When connecting two pieces of steel, the eye of one rests on the bell, and the pin is inserted through the eye of the other. Never use a shackle when the load rests only on the two sides, because that tends to deform the bell and places stress on the pin threads.

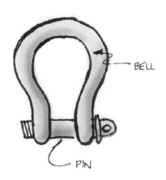

BELL

PIN

PARTS OF A SHACKLE

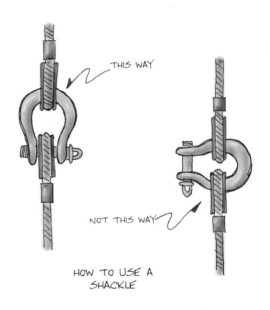

THIS WAY

NOT THIS WAY

HOW TO USE A
SHACKLE

Shackles can also connect three points in a Y shape by using the bell for two of them and the pin for the third. This type of configuration is used when forming the apex of a bridle.

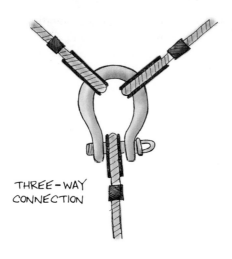

THREE-WAY CONNECTION

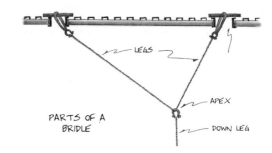

PARTS OF A BRIDLE

LEGS

APEX

DOWN LEG

Deck chain can be used to create a smaller length by using a specific number of the 4" links, in the same way that trim chains are used in standard theatrical rigging. Chains of this sort come from modern cargo ships, and are very heavy.

DECK CHAIN

A simple rig that hangs straight down is call a *dead hang*, but when two pieces of steel are used in conjunction with the motor chain to form a Y shape, the result is known as a *bridle*. The parts of a bridle include the two *legs*, which are the two uppermost sections, and the *downleg*, which forms the upright, lower part of the Y. The downleg could be simply the motor chain, or it could be another piece of steel that connects to the chain. The intersection of the three parts of the Y is called the *apex*. A shackle forms the center of the apex and connects all the parts together.

An even bridle from two wells will make the rig hang dead center between the two points; this is formed by using the same length of steel on each leg. Uneven bridles are formed by using different lengths of steel rope on the two sides. If one of the legs is made up of a standard-length piece of steel, you can design a length for the other that will make the rig fall in the exact spot you wish to hang your load. A bit of geometry is involved—specifically, congruent triangles and the *Pythagorean Theorem* ($a^2 + b^2 = c^2$).

A practical example

Imagine that the wells in the theater are 15 feet apart. You would like to hang the rig so that it is 5 feet from one and 10 feet from the other. A diagram looks like this:

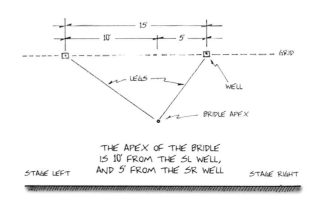

15'

10'   5'

GRID

LEGS

WELL

BRIDLE APEX

THE APEX OF THE BRIDLE IS 10' FROM THE SL WELL, AND 5' FROM THE SR WELL

STAGE LEFT   STAGE RIGHT

Arbitrarily select a reasonable length for one of the legs. Bear in mind that a bridle that hangs down more is easier to hang and puts less stress on the equipment. But a bridle that hangs down too far may place the apex so low that the motor will not be able to fly out far enough. For our example, let's pick a 15-foot bridle leg. Now our diagram looks like this:

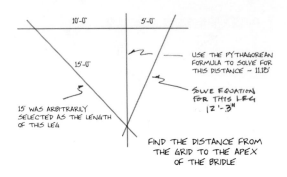

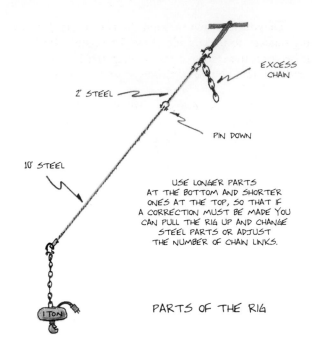

EXCESS CHAIN

2' STEEL

PIN DOWN

10' STEEL

USE LONGER PARTS AT THE BOTTOM AND SHORTER ONES AT THE TOP, SO THAT IF A CORRECTION MUST BE MADE YOU CAN PULL THE RIG UP AND CHANGE STEEL PARTS OR ADJUST THE NUMBER OF CHAIN LINKS.

1 TON

PARTS OF THE RIG

You know the dimensions of two sides of one right triangle, because the apex hangs 10 feet over from the well, and the angular hypotenuse distance is 15 feet. Solve the equation $a^2 + 10^2 = 15^2$ to determine the distance from the grid, down to the apex. The answer is ~11.18 feet. So now our diagram looks like this:

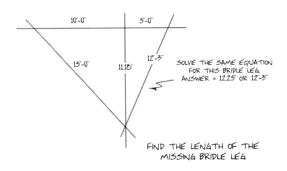

In reality, there are a few more variables, such as the length of the Spanset used and the number of shackles used to connect the rigs. Because so many shackles are used to connect the previous example, the chain link could probably be left out. The standard tolerance for this type of rigging is usually 1 foot, and so close is close enough.

You may need to attach the two legs of the bridle to something other than a pipe on the grid. If you want to hook the bridle up to a steel beam instead, use a *basket* to make the connection. A basket is a loop made from a 5-foot (or 10-foot if necessary) piece of steel. You should make the loop using two shackles so that one holds both the thimble of the 5-foot steel, and the other is used to make the connection.

Now the base and altitude of the second, congruent right triangle are known and the same formula can be used to determine the missing bridle leg length: $11.18^2 + 5^2 = c^2$. The answer is 12.25 feet, or 12' 3". Taking into consideration the standard parts available, this length can be made up from adding 10' + 2' + one 4" link from a deck chain. Shackles are used to connect the parts together.

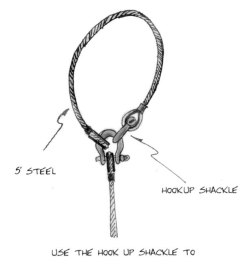

5' STEEL

HOOKUP SHACKLE

USE THE HOOK UP SHACKLE TO ATTACH THE BRIDLE

PARTS OF A BASKET

Tie your bowline through the bell of the connecting shackle, to the outside of the 5-foot steel. If you tie it between the steel and the hookup shackle, there is a tendency for the two of them to pinch in on the rope, making it difficult to remove.

Pull the basket up to the beam it will hang from, and wrap the 5-foot steel around the beam. Remove the pin from the shackle and use it to connect the free end of the steel.

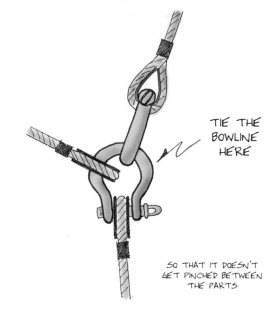

TIE THE
BOWLINE
HERE

SO THAT IT DOESN'T
GET PINCHED BETWEEN
THE PARTS

CHAPTER 4

ROPES AND KNOT TYING

It is not surprising that rope handling skills are very important to stagehand work, considering that sailors were the originators of our craft. Knowledge about rope selection; coiling skills; and quick, accurate knot tying should be learned early in your training. Poorly executed knots can lead to serious injury for anyone unfortunate enough to be underneath a falling piece of scenery or lighting equipment. Rope lines should be selected with an understanding of the capabilities of the line as they relate to what you want to use them for. Knots should be tied with the same understanding. There are literally hundreds of different kinds of knots. It is best to begin with a few of the most common, so that they can be appropriately mastered. Videos of tying some of these knots, and others, are available on the Web site for this book.

THIS TWO-COLOR NYLON ROPE HAS A BRAIDED EXTERIOR WOVEN OVER LINEAR INTERIOR STRANDS. THE END HAS BEEN MELTED TO KEEP IT FROM FRAYING.

TRADITIONAL HEMP ROPE IS MADE BY TWISTING FIBERS TOGETHER. THE END OF THIS LINE HAS BEEN INTENTIONALLY FRAYED TO EXPOSE THE INDIVIDUAL YARNS.

TWO METHODS OF ROPE CONSTRUCTION

ROPES

A good knot should be easy to tie, hold well, be easy to untie, and not place undue stress on the line. Some types of knots, especially if misused, may dangerously reduce the load limit of

doi: 10.1016/C2009-0-23409-X

a rope. When overstressed, ropes almost always break at the point where a knot has been tied or some other kink has disturbed the straight passage of the line. Ropes are said to be *de-rated* when knots, bends, or kinks have made them more likely to break.

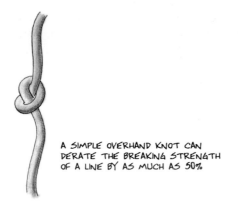

A SIMPLE OVERHAND KNOT CAN DERATE THE BREAKING STRENGTH OF A LINE BY AS MUCH AS 50%

Two basic types of cordage are used in the theatre: those made of stranded fibers that are *twisted* together, and those that are *woven* or *braided* together. Twisted ropes are made from fibers that are spun into loose strands known as *yarns*, which are then twisted together to form the line. The size and weight rating of the rope depends upon the number and size of the yarns, as well as the material used in making the rope. Yarns are usually twisted together in a right-handed orientation (clockwise as you look toward the end), making it easiest to coil ropes in a clockwise direction. Twisting is the oldest form of rope making, and has existed for thousands of years. It requires only a moderate amount of technology to manufacture twisted ropes. Rope fibers of this type may consist of *sisal*, *Manila hemp*, or synthetics like *polypropylene* or *polyester*.

Manila, a variety of the hemp plant, is the best choice for a hemp line used to carry weight over the stage. The grade-one type is easily spotted by the blue fiber that runs through it. Polypropylene and/or polyester ropes have become much more common in recent years. These synthetics start as very long strands and are more easily manufactured into rope. They are somewhat stronger and rot-resistant in most situations that do no include a large amount of ultraviolet (UV) radiation from sunlight. Hemp is rapidly falling out of favor for rigging applications, but there is still a lot of it around.

Braided lines are formed by weaving together many very small yarns to form a cover, or sheath, that fits over an interior group of strands. Because they are not twisted together, these ropes are easier to work with and less likely to become kinked. Cotton was historically used for this type of rope, which requires some fairly complex machinery to create. Hemp fibers come from the stalks of that plant, which are pulverized into individual strands. The fibers are very long and are easy to twist

together, which is why they have been used to make rope for centuries. Although the fibers are long, they are also very stiff, so rope made from them is stiff as well. It is much easier to tie knots with a more flexible line, which is why cotton sash cord became popular in the theatre. It is harder to twist the short cotton fibers into yarns, so rather than make traditional rope from it, the braided exterior concept was developed. Nylon rigging ropes are also made in this way, and so is cotton tie line. Tie line is really just very small-diameter sash cord.

Sash cord gets its name from its original intended use as a line meant to connect the counterbalancing weights used in old-style windows. The sash is the part of a window that moves up and down when it opens and closes. The same properties that make sash cord bend well around a small-diameter window pulley also make it an excellent choice for tying knots. It is very supple and is often used where great strength in a line is not required but 1/8″ tie line is not strong enough.

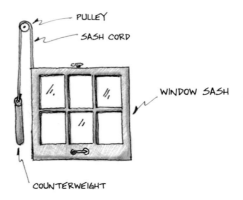

PULLEY — SASH CORD — WINDOW SASH — COUNTERWEIGHT

Number 4 black *tie line* is the most popular choice for securing cable to an electric or for the ties on top of a curtain. Jute tie line was used in the past, but it is so loosely put together that it does not last very long and has fallen into disfavor. It is not at all suitable for use on drapes or other goods that must be frequently tied and untied. The #4 designation comes from an older way of determining the size of a braided line with a gauge number, much like with electrical wires. White is also available, but black is more easily hidden.

BRAIDED TIE LINE COMES ON A 3,000 FOOT SPOOL

Sash cord has become increasingly hard to find in recent years, as the windows it was designed to rig have been mostly replaced by more energy-efficient ones. It is still available from some theatrical suppliers. Newer versions of this same basic type of line, but made from synthetic materials, are readily available from local hardware stores. They come in various sizes, but 3/8″ is frequently the most useful, and can be used to rig a traveler track. Twisted lines don't work at all well on a traveler, because the twist tends to kink up at the pulleys.

More information about ropes, aircraft cable, and chains can be found in Chapter 14.

KNOTS

You should learn some basic terms used in tying knots in order to better understand the descriptions in this chapter. The free end of a line is called the *tail*. It is the part that you actually manipulate to tie the knot. The *standing part* is the long length of a rope that may be formed into a coil, or be tied to the grid, or laid out in some other fashion. It is important to visualize which is which, especially if you are using a short length of cord to learn how to tie the knots in this chapter.

Most knots begin with a *loop* of some sort, which is a rounded turn of the line. To *double-over* means to bend the line over itself so that it runs back, thus creating an artificial tail in the middle of the line.

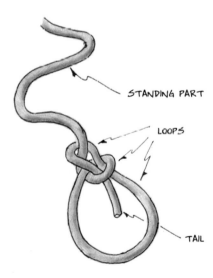

The bow knot

You probably already know how to tie your shoe. But if you start off with an easy knot, it will build confidence for the harder ones ahead. The same actions are used to tie all knots, so working with the bow first will give you an understanding of the terminology. The *bow* is actu-

ally the most-often-used knot in theatre, because it is used to hang drops and curtains. Drapes are traditionally manufactured with a tie every 12 inches, so a 40-foot-long border has 41 knots to tie. Multiply this number by however many curtains are in a show, and the importance of the bow knot becomes clear. The bow contains the same basic building blocks that are used in all knots. It is essentially a square knot in which the two tails are doubled over before making the final half hitch. Pulling on the very end of the tails slides the two loops back through the knot and the bow is untied. If you can visualize that process, it will make it much easier for you to understand more complex knots.

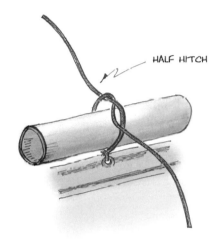

The bow knot requires two tails, or ends. The first part of the knot involves tying a half hitch, which is simply wrapping the two tails around one another, and tightening. The friction of the two lines rubbing against one another tends to make them stay tightly together. But a half hitch will not stay tied on its own; the friction is not great enough.

Double over the two tails so that they are about half of their original length. Now tie a second half hitch using the doubled-over tails. This completes the knot. It is easy to tie, and it is very easy to untie, by pulling on one of the tails. The bow is an excellent example of how a good knot is *easy to tie, and easy to untie*. When you are untying curtains from a batten, pull one tail all the way straight up, and then down to the side; this action will loosen the entire knot in one easy motion.

The choke

This very simple knot is quite useful for attaching a piece of tie line to a pipe or lighting cable so that it grips with holding force and will not slide down. The *choke* is one member of a family of knots that uses a double wrap around a pipe for extra gripping power. It is also the most common manner of attaching a sling, as discussed in Chapter 3. Slings or Spansets are endless nylon bands often used in rigging.

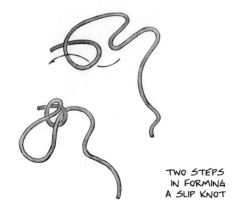

TWO STEPS IN FORMING A SLIP KNOT

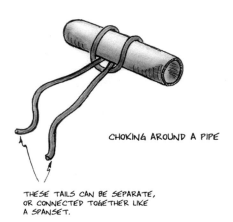

CHOKING AROUND A PIPE

THESE TAILS CAN BE SEPARATE, OR CONNECTED TOGETHER LIKE A SPANSET.

As an example, a choke works well if you want to tie up some lighting cable onto a boom so that it is up off the deck. Apply the choke so that it is about chest-high off the floor. Then coil the cable and secure it with a bow knot.

The greater the force exerted on the choke, the tighter its grip becomes, preventing it from sliding down the pipe and lowering the coil to the deck. This method also works for tying cable (or any other reasonable object) to a truss, handrail, rope, or other tubular item.

The slip knot

The *slip knot* can be used to make a loop in the end of a line that will tighten when force is exerted. It has many useful applications for attaching tie line when speed is essential. The slip knot is also used in tying another knot, the trucker's hitch. Knitters may recognize it as the same knot that is used to start yarn onto a knitting needle.

Make a small loop in the tail near its end. Double the standing part and draw it through the loop. (Remember that the standing part is the long end.) Hold the doubled-over loop and pull on the tail to secure the knot. If the knot has been properly tied, pulling on the standing part makes the loop smaller, while pulling on the loop itself makes it larger. If you tug on the loop and the tail pulls through and the knot is lost, you have tied the knot backward and it will not work properly. An easy way to avoid this problem is to make sure that your first loop is formed very close to the end of the tail. Then there will not be enough of the tail sticking out to make the mistake of pulling it rather than the standing part through the loop.

The clove hitch

The *clove hitch* is used to fasten a line around a pipe, handrail, or other rounded object. It's an important theatrical knot that every stagehand should know and be able to tie without thinking. Like the choke, this knot grips more tightly when force is applied. Unlike the choke, the clove is meant for use with a long line, and especially one that is under load while the knot is tied. One example of that is dead-hanging a drape or a piece of scenery. In that situation, weight is on the line as you haul it up into the air, and a clove hitch is easy to tie under these circumstances, because you can take a wrap around the pipe to safety the line while you tie the knot. The clove hitch would also be a good knot to tie on the hanging pipe.

The clove hitch is a very simple knot to tie. Drape the line over the pipe, and wrap it around the right side of itself. Bring the line around the pipe and wrap it to the left side. Slip it under the first wrap that you took. That's all there is to the clove hitch. However, the clove will hold better if you take an extra half hitch around the standing part to ensure that the line will not accidentally untie itself under stress, especially when the load is repeatedly shifted.

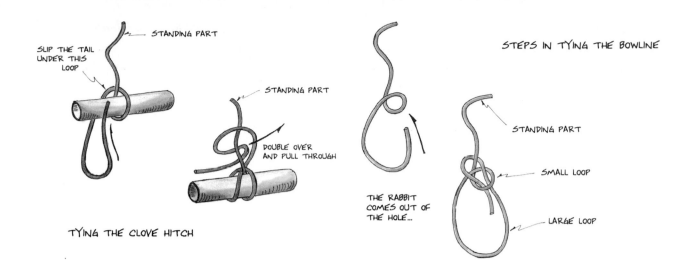

SLIP THE TAIL UNDER THIS LOOP

STANDING PART

STANDING PART

DOUBLE OVER AND PULL THROUGH

TYING THE CLOVE HITCH

THE RABBIT COMES OUT OF THE HOLE...

STANDING PART

SMALL LOOP

LARGE LOOP

Quite often, there is a great deal of excess rope on the floor after hauling something into the air for a dead hang. When this happens, the clove hitch can be tied in the center of the rope by doubling over a few feet of the line and using this doubled-over part as though it were the end. That avoids pulling a huge amount of excess line through the knot. Doubling over to create an end in the middle of a line is a common practice with many different kinds of knots, and is similar to what happens when tying a bow.

The bowline

This knot is pronounced "bowlyn" and not "bow line." If you mispronounce it, you run the risk of becoming an object of ridicule by your fellow stagehands and/or climbing enthusiasts. The *bowline* is used to create a fixed loop in the end of a rope. It is another of the quintessential stagehand knots that everyone must know. It is the basic knot used by rock-and-roll riggers to hang chain motors. The bowline's popularity stems from the fact that it is easy to tie, it is very safe, and it is also easy to untie, which are all essential elements of a good knot. It will be much easier to tie the bowline if you keep these two ideas in mind: make the first loop small, and make the second loop (the one you want to keep) much larger.

The following method of tying a bowline is probably the easiest, although there are others. These instructions are intended for a right-handed person. If you are left-handed, it is probably best to try the right-handed method first, and then adapt it to your own style later. Basically, the left-handed approach is a mirror image of the right and will work just as well.

Hold the line across your left palm so that the long, standing part is lying away from you and the tail is several feet long. The length of the rope making up the tail dictates the size of the loop in the finished knot. For some rigging jobs, the size of the loop is critical. If you need a 2-foot loop in the bowline, start with a bit more than 4 feet of tail.

Coil the rope counterclockwise so that one small loop is in your hand. Pass the tail through the loop from back to front, around the back of the standing part, and then through the small loop, so that the line passes back along itself. Tighten the knot by pulling on the tail in opposition to the standing part.

A story is often told to make it easier to remember the steps in tying the bowline. "There is a hole in the ground (the small loop). A rabbit (the tail) comes up out of the hole and runs behind a tree (the standing part). The rabbit circles the tree and runs back down into the hole." This is a silly story—I didn't make it up!—but it is the traditional method of teaching the bowline. Feel free to embellish it, and adapt it to any animals and/or objects you feel are appropriate.

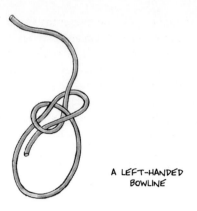

A LEFT-HANDED
BOWLINE

The left-handed approach is really just a mirror image of the instructions that were just given for a regular bowline. Notice that in either version, the tail should wind up to the inside of the large loop rather than to the outside. If you are a left-handed person, you are already aware that lefties are generally shafted by tool manufacturers, so enjoy something technical that works just as well left-handed as it does right-handed.

The square knot

The *square knot* is another very basic knot used in a variety of different situations, such as tying two lines together, tying a bundle, or in combination with other knots.

THE SQUARE KNOT

Tying the square knot requires two tails. Holding one tail in either hand, lay the right tail over the left and twist it around to make a half hitch. Then take the left tail and pass it over the right, making another half hitch. Right over left, left over right, as the saying goes. Tighten this up and you will have a square knot. Right over left twice, or left over right twice will make a granny knot that is harder to untie and is prone to slipping. A true square knot appears as two loops choked over one another and is easily recognizable.

A GRANNY KNOT

The trucker's hitch or snub and loop

The most complicated knot of this chapter has been saved for last. The *trucker's hitch* is a popular knot to use when you need to put a great deal of tension on a line. It is often used to tie down loads for trucking, hence its name. Of course in a modern trailer used for touring, straps and load bars are the preferred method, but there are still plenty of other uses for the trucker's hitch. This knot is excellent for stretching a cyclorama, holding scenery tight to a wall, or making small changes in the trim of a dead-hung piece. I have included two methods of tying the trucker's hitch, using either one piece of rope or two, depending on the situation at hand.

It is easier to learn the two-rope method first. A practical illustration may make it easier to understand how the trucker's hitch is used. Visualize a cyclorama that needs to be stretched to remove its wrinkles. First, clamps must be fastened to the edges of the cyc so that lines can be tied between the clamps and the offstage wall of the theatre. By applying tension to the lines, you can stretch the wrinkles out of the fabric.

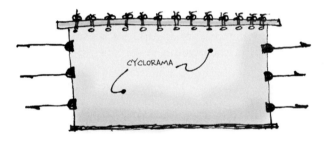

CYCLORAMA

STRETCHING CLAMPS AND LINES
ON A CYCLORAMA

Attach a piece of tie line to the clamp with a bowline. At a convenient distance from the clamp, tie another bowline in the other end of the line. That second bowline creates an eye for the line to pass through. Tie a second piece of tie line to a structure to the side of the stage. Bring the two lines together and pass the tail of the second line through the loop of the first. If you then pull this tail back in the direction of the wall, tension will be placed on the line, and the friction of the tie line doubling back through the loop will keep it from slipping as long as tension is kept on the tail you are holding.

USING TWO LINES FOR A TRUCKER'S HITCH

Finish the knot by tying off to the loop. Hold the doubled-back line with two fingers where it is kinked through the bowline loop. The friction of the two lines and the pressure from just your two fingers should be plenty to keep the line from slipping. If you try to hold it with more than that, your hand will be in the way of tying the rest of the knot. Double over a small portion of the tail and wrap it through just as you would if tying a bow. It will take some practice to get this to work without losing tension on the line. That is the part that most people struggle with, but after a few practice attempts you should get the hang of it.

Untie the knot by pulling on the tail. The doubled-over section will pull through just as it does when untying a bow knot. On the other hand, if you pull the doubled-over tail all the way through when you tie the knot, you won't be able to get it to come loose so easily.

To tie the one-line trucker's hitch, fasten the line at one end with a suitable knot and then tie a slip knot in the middle of the line an easy distance away from the second tie-off point. The slip knot should be tied so that the loop size is dependent on the tail rather than the standing part. If you do this backward, the loop will shrink to nothing when tension is applied, and it will be obvious that something is wrong. The line should be able to pass easily around the second tie-off point without jamming, or the one-line method won't work. To finish the knot, pass the line around the second tie-off point and run it back through the loop, making it fast in the same manner as used in method one.

ONE-LINE METHOD OF TYING
THE TRUCKER'S HITCH

It is possible to make the first small loop by doubling over the line and making a half hitch rather than using a slip knot, but it is very hard to remove this alternative knot later on down the road. If your plan is

to keep the line in place permanently, you might prefer half-hitch loop to a slip-knot one.

Using the trucker's hitch to tension the line provides a two-to-one mechanical advantage and will allow you to pull the line really tight. That is, for every pound of force on the tail, the standing part will be 2 pounds tighter. But it also doubles the load on the line and increases the possibility that it will break.

ROPE COILING AND STORAGE

Coiling a rope for storage can be more complex than amateurs would think. It is fairly easy to roll a rope up into some sort of clump, but not so easy to play it back out in a straight line without a lot of tangles. One thing for sure, you will *never* see a professional stagehand wind a rope up around her elbow, because that means she has no control over how twisted it becomes. This is especially problematic when using a twisted rope like hemp.

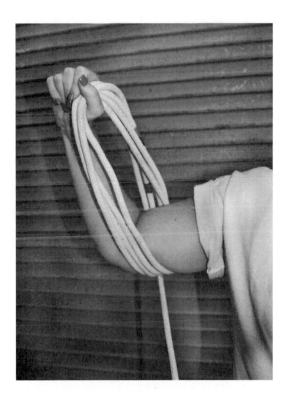

DON'T COIL THIS WAY

Here is the issue: when a rope is coiled into a circle, it must spin one time for each turn in the coil. If you wind the rope around your elbow, you won't be able to put the proper twist into it, and the rope will come out with some of the loops making a figure-eight shape, while others are a circle. The figure-eight shape comes from a turn of the rope that did not get twisted. The arm method also produces a very small coil that will most likely be hard to play back out.

DO THIS INSTEAD

Instead of using the distance between thumb and elbow to set the size of the turns in the coil, let it be a natural function of the length of your arm as it moves in an arc back and forth. Hold the tail of the rope in your right hand and swing your left out to grasp the standing part of the rope a comfortable distance away. As you bring that part of the rope over to the right hand, twist it once with your fingers so that it makes a flat coil. Repeat the procedure, but remember to twist each time you bring the rope back to your right hand to make a new turn of the coil. Sometimes you will find that the rope is actually twisted too many times, so that you must turn the opposite way. Let the feel of the rope tell you which way it needs to twist in order to coil properly. You should finish up with a coil about 2 feet in diameter, which is appropriate for a line that is about half-inch thick, the most common kind.

If the line is really thick, or hugely long, you might try coiling it onto the floor instead of into your hand, but use the same twisting technique. If the line is all kinky from being improperly coiled by someone else, it may take some stretching and massaging to get it back into shape. It may need to spin an incredible amount. Make sure that the far end of the rope is free to spin, because each twist that you make will need to work its way along the standing part and out of the free end.

THIS ROPE IS TOO BIG AND HEAVY TO HOLD, SO COIL IT ON THE FLOOR INSTEAD.

CHAPTER 5

SOFT GOODS

Every stagehand should have a good working knowledge of stage draperies. Curtains are used for just about any show that you can think of, because without them the audience would see all of the magic happening backstage. The term *soft goods* is often used to indicate scenery made from fabric, as opposed to wood or steel. Different types of curtains are intended for use in specific situations. This chapter is a discussion of those different types, as well as construction methods, and the working practices used to hang stage curtains and other fabric scenery. The terms *curtains* and *drapes* are interchangeable.

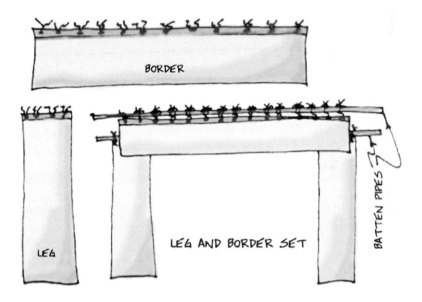

DRAPES AND DROPS

Drapes and *drops* are different things. Drapes are usually made from some kind of opulent fabric like *velour*. They tend to have a generic quality and can be used in many different ways, whereas drops are painted or printed backgrounds designed for a specific purpose. Drops are usually rendered on scenic *muslin* and are essentially large paintings. They are flat, with no folds or pleats. Drops may cover the entire stage picture, or they may be cut in order to cover only the outside edges, as in a portal. They may have some other unusual shape, and/or have textural materials stuck to them. But they are always painted representations of something. You can find a lot more information about painting drops in the book *Scenic Art for the Theatre*, by Susan Crabtree and Peter Beudert (Focal, 1998).

Drapes, on the other hand, are generally unpainted and are most often used as masking. Drapes are often constructed of a heavier fabric, like velour, that has a thick sound- and light-absorbing pile. *Duvetyn* is a less-expensive substitute. Duvetyn has a nappy, textural surface but no actual pile. This nappy surface helps to trap light, making the drapes nonreflective and less obtrusive. Black is the most popular color for all stage drapes, because that color absorbs the most light. Drapes that belong to a certain theatre are often called the house *rags*.

MASKING

Masking is a term used to identify curtains that block the audience view of the backstage area. Curtains that mask the overhead space of a stage are called *borders*. Borders are really wide but not very tall. Ideally, they should be the same width as the battens that they are hung on, so that they run all the way from one side of the stage to the other. *Legs* mask the offstage space or wings. Legs are tall, but usually not very wide. They should be at least several feet taller than the proscenium opening, but not so tall that the bottoms do not clear sightlines when they are flown all the way out. In a theatre with a very short fly tower, that ideal situation might not be met and some sort of happy medium should be reached.

A standard method exists for using legs and borders to mask the stage. It is customary to hang one border in front of a set of two legs in order to create a frame for the stage picture. These *leg and border sets* are used from downstage to upstage in repetition. The legs should be wide enough, and the leg and border sets close enough together so that the audience cannot see around them into the wings. Sometimes this is not possible if there is very little offstage space, and/or if the auditorium is especially wide. Leg and border sets create the *sightlines* for the stage, defining where the audience can and cannot see. It is important for the border to be on a separate lineset from the legs so that they are independently adjustable. Be sure to hang the border downstage of the two legs so that it will cover the pipe they are on.

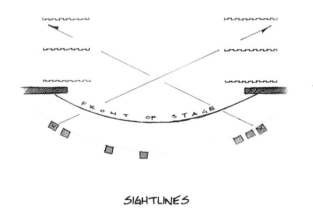

SIGHTLINES

The spaces between the border and leg sets are often referred to as *in one, in two, in three*, etc. This terminology refers to the spaces between the legs and is often used to indicate the place where an actor or a piece of scenery should enter. Example: "Enter through the stage left in one with the chair and place it on the red spike marks downstage." Leg and border sets are a direct descendent of the wing and drop scenery used in early proscenium theatres. Setting up the stage that way was so efficient that it is still done today.

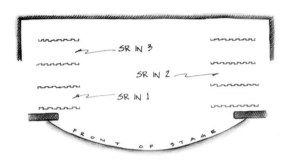

THE "IN BETWEENS"

Another specific piece of masking consists of a large black drape that covers the entire width of the stage, either at the rear of the stage, or about halfway back, or both. This curtain is used as a dark background that covers the back wall and forms a crossover, or as a covering device for shifting scenery upstage while a scene is being played downstage. This type of curtain is commonly known as a *blackout*. It is most often constructed as two solid panels that are hung side by side. You can also put together a blackout from multiple sets of legs that are overlapped to create the same effect. Be sure to overlap the edges by at least 1 foot (also equal to one tie) to prevent a split from showing. Blackouts are often hung on a traveler track, so that when opened that way, they form the two legs in a leg and border set.

SPECIALTY CURTAINS

Some theatres are equipped with a batten that curves around the entire stage area rather than merely from side to side. This type of batten is known as a *cyclorama* or *cyc pipe*. The two arms of the cyc run up/down stage at the off stage ends of a regular pipe. If the cyc is meant to be lighted in order to create a sky effect, it is known as a *sky cyc*.

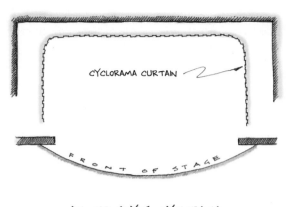

AN OLD-STYLE CYCLORAMA

is lit behind the screen becomes visible. Theatrical scrim curtains work in exactly the same manner.

HOW A SCRIM WORKS

As you could well imagine, it is almost impossible to arrange for entrances and exits if the sides of the stage have been closed off by using a wrap-around cyc. To avoid that problem, a sky cyc can also be used on an ordinary straight batten. It is still called a "cyc" even though it goes only from side to side. This method is so prevalent that most stage workers will assume this is what you mean when a cyc is mentioned. Cycloramas are used extensively in television studios, where they are almost always the wraparound version. In TV, different colors of fabric are used for special effects. This difference in terminology can be confusing to a person who has crossed over from TV to stage or vice versa.

Sharkstooth scrim is one of a family of net-type fabrics that are used in the theatre. The name "sharkstooth" is derived from an open weave structure made up of tiny triangular shapes, which, if you squint and cock your head to the side, may resemble a tooth—or at least someone a hundred years ago thought so. It seems like most scrims these days have a rectangular weave instead. Scrims are used in a variety of ways. They can be painted in much the same manner as muslin, or can be used as a toner for cycs or other drops. Sometimes scrim may be used as a low-tech (but quite effective) method of materializing a person or object, such as the ghost of Hamlet's father.

Scrims have a common operating principle, however they are used. Variations in light intensity are used to create variations in the opacity of the scrim fabric. An analogy can be found in observing the way window screens reflect light. You may have noticed that a window screen restricts your ability to see into a house from the outside when there is bright sunshine lighting it, yet at night, when the only light source is inside the room, a person outside can quite easily see through the screen to the room inside. When light strikes the surface of the screen, the screen itself reflects this light and appears as a solid object. At night when no light reflects off the screen it tends to disappear, and anything that

This principle is put to good use in a process known as a *bleed-through*. A bleed-through is used to change from one scene to another by means of a lighting effect. A painted backdrop scrim is lit from the front so that the painting on it is visible, as well as the actors who are standing in front of it. The bleed-through effect is created by fading light down on the front of the scrim while simultaneously fading light up on the scene behind it. One picture fades out as the other fades in, much the same way that movie editing fades from one scene to another. As the lighting change is completed, the scrim is flown out for an unobscured view. The dreamy quality of bleeding from one scene to another is quite stunning.

Black scrims are often used in front of a sky cyc to create darker, more vivid colors. As an added bonus, the scrim leaves a black background when the cyc lights fade all the way down. This is much like a bleed-through in reverse. More information about scrims and other theatrical fabrics can be found in Chapter 14.

Grand drape or *main* refers to the curtain that is hung in front of the stage to separate it from the auditorium. It is often a decorative, very plush curtain, as it may be all the audience has to look at while waiting for the show to begin. A matching decorative *valance* is often used to finish off the top of the main rag. Grand drapes are almost always sewn with a large amount of *fullness* to give them a more opulent appearance. Fullness is the technique of gathering the fabric at the top to form folds or pleats in the curtain. The greater the amount of pleating, the richer and heavier the curtain appears to be. An amount of fullness is usually given as a percentage. As an example, 100 percent fullness requires a velour panel 80 feet wide to produce a drape 40 feet wide. After a backing is added, the curtain will be quite heavy.

On occasion, scenic designers opt to paint a special drop that is used in place of a front curtain. It is almost always related stylistically to the design of the production, and may indeed include a logo or the name of the play being presented. This practice is principally used for musicals. A drop of this sort is generally referred to as a *show drop*.

A grand drape may be rigged to operate with a *traveler* when there is no room for it to fly in and out. Travelers open the curtain by making it roll across the stage on a track, usually parting in the center. There are several other ways of coping with a lack of overhead space, which is an unfortunately common occurrence in small venues. Small auditoriums and some older movie theatres may be rigged with one of several types of systems that require only limited overhead space.

One of these systems is the *Austrian* curtain. This type of drape has a series of small nylon lift lines evenly spaced across the back of the curtain. Each lift line feeds through a number of small rings that are sewn to the back of the Austrian. As the lift lines are pulled upward, the drape gathers itself up from the bottom, creating small swags as it rises. An Austrian curtain is sewn with many small horizontal pleats to enhance the effect. The fabric is usually some sort of thin satin material, because that fabric bunches up better. This curtain is popular with older movie theatres from the mid-twentieth century.

Another method of dealing with a low overhead is to use an *oleo* curtain, which was quite popular in the days of vaudeville. An oleo is actually a painted drop

like a show curtain. A large round tube is attached to the bottom. Ropes at either side of the tube are used to pull it up and roll it at the same time.

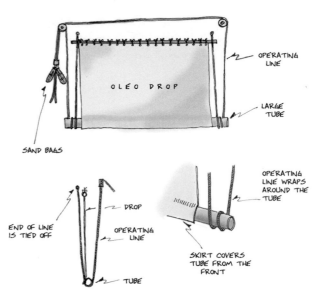

The drop rolls up on the tube as it rotates. A full-stage oleo requires a very large-diameter bottom tube, for two reasons: first, because of the distance the tube must span without sagging, and second, because the large diameter of the tube makes it possible for the drop to roll easily even if it is relatively stiff from being repainted several times. A large oleo is difficult and expensive to construct, although this type of curtain may easily be shop-built in smaller versions and put to good use for window treatments and other smaller openings.

TRAVELER TRACKS

Travelers are the most popular type of low overhead curtain-moving device. Stage travelers are similar to ones that you might see in a house, but they are much larger and able to hold more weight. A traveler consists of a metal *channel* and the rollers that fit into it. The curtain is tied to chains that extend downward from the rollers. A pull rope is used to drag the rollers, and thus the curtain, from side to side. Travelers can be rigged to part in the middle or to extend all the way from one side of the stage to the other.

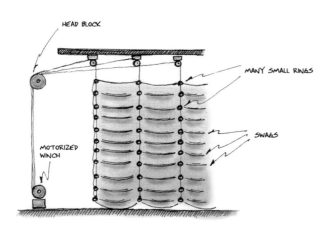

AUSTRIAN CURTAIN

Rigging a traveler is one of those jobs that looks very complicated, because travelers have a large number of moving parts, but in reality the process is fairly straightforward and quite logical once you get the hang of it. The shape of the metal channel that the rollers or *carriers* fit into is such that the wheels of the carriers fit into grooves in the bottom that act as guides, allowing the wheels to roll freely back and forth. Each carrier has a rounded opening just below the wheels for the operating line to fit through. Below this opening is a chain used to attach the curtain to the carrier.

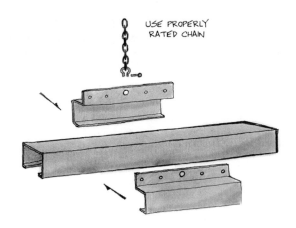

USE PROPERLY RATED CHAIN

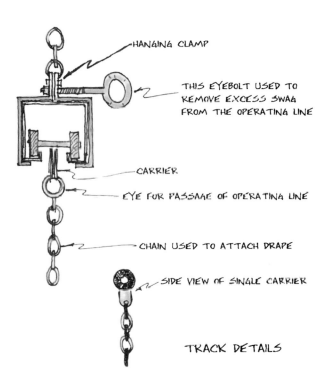

HANGING CLAMP

THIS EYEBOLT USED TO REMOVE EXCESS SWAG FROM THE OPERATING LINE

CARRIER

EYE FOR PASSAGE OF OPERATING LINE

CHAIN USED TO ATTACH DRAPE

SIDE VIEW OF SINGLE CARRIER

TRACK DETAILS

THE HANGING CLAMP FITS AROUND THE OUTSIDE OF THE TRACK SO THE BOTTOM CHANNEL STAYS OPEN

The direction you would like the curtain to move dictates how the traveler should be configured. If the curtain is intended to go all the way from side to side across the entire width of the stage, then you need only one continuous channel.

The onstage leading edge of the curtain is attached to a *master carrier* that has four wheels rather than two and is substantially larger than the single carrier. The master carrier has a clamp on the side so that the operating line can be securely connected to it. The next illustration shows how to rig the line to make the curtain travel all the way across the stage from one side to another.

The traveler channel is hung on a batten using a series of *hanging clamps*. They come in two parts and bolt together around the outside of the channel, and then chain is used to secure the entire rig to a batten. Chain is used, because altering the links of the chain is an excellent way of adjusting the trim so that the traveler can be made level to the stage floor, even if the batten is not. Trim chains are discussed several times in this book, because they are so often used. Make sure that the chain you use is large enough to hold at least four times the weight that will be placed on it, and remember to include the weight of the draperies that will be hung on the traveler. The clamps come in two pieces so that they can be bolted on around the sides only. It is very important not to obstruct the bottom of the traveler track, because that would prevent the carriers from rolling back and forth.

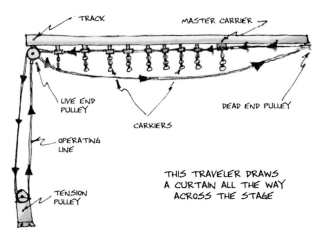

TRACK

MASTER CARRIER

LIVE END PULLEY

DEAD END PULLEY

CARRIERS

OPERATING LINE

TENSION PULLEY

THIS TRAVELER DRAWS A CURTAIN ALL THE WAY ACROSS THE STAGE

Clamp the operating line to the side of the master carrier, and pass it through the center of each of the single carriers. There should be as many single carriers as there are grommets on the drape, except for the first and last ones. The first grommet on the drop is attached to the master carrier. The last grommet gets fastened to the offstage end of the channel.

The *live end pulley* has two sheaves on it: one to change the direction of the rope when it goes down to the floor and another to do the same when it passes back up to the track.

The operating line connects with a *tension pulley* when it gets to the stage floor. As the name implies, this pulley helps to keep the line taut and prevents it from becoming twisted and tangled. If the traveler track stays in one position, it may be possible to permanently attach the tension pulley to the deck. If it is occasionally necessary to fly the traveler out, then it is best to use a temporary method of securing the pulley, and several different types are produced by different manufacturers. A commonly used shop-built method is to secure the pulley to a small section of plywood that can be weighted with counterweights when the traveler is in its down position.

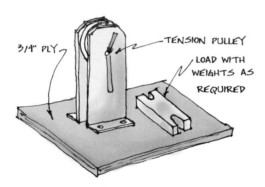

SHOP-BUILT TENSION PULLEY BASE

When the operating line passes back over the second sheave in the live end pulley, it shoots straight down to the *dead-end pulley* at the opposite end of the track, not touching any of the carriers. Here the line reverses direction back to the master carrier, where it is held fast by the clamp. If the track is very wide, it may be necessary to provide some support to the operating line as it crosses the stage from the live-end pulley to the dead-end pulley. Unless the line is exceptionally taut, it will tend to sag in the middle and may become visible to the audience. An *eyebolt* attached to the side of one of the hanging clamps can be used to avoid that.

When hanging the traveler curtain, make sure one side is attached to the master carrier. All but one of the remaining grommets should be secured to successive single carriers, and then the last grommet tied to an end stop at the offstage edge of the track. The *end stop* is used to keep the carriers from running off the end of the track, and it is a handy place to secure the offstage edge of the curtain.

If you would like the traveler to part in the center and move toward both sides, it must be rigged a bit

differently, but the basic concept remains the same. Hang the track in two sections connected by a *lap splice* so that they overlap one another by a foot or more. The fabric curtain must be in two sections in order to split. The two halves of the traveler operate exactly the same way as the side-to-side type, but one half is the "slave" of the other.

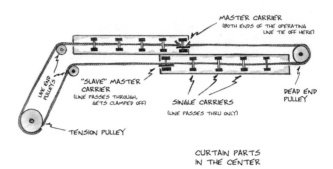

CURTAIN PARTS
IN THE CENTER

Attach the operating line to the master carrier on the tension pulley side of the stage. Feed it through the single carriers, and then pass it through one sheave of the live-end pulley. The line should go down to the floor, through the tension pulley, and then back up through the live-end pulley. So far, this process is exactly the same as before, but now the method differs. The line passes through the clamp on the second master carrier—the one that is in the channel of the track that services the opposite side of the stage. The line passes through the clamp on this second master carrier without being cut.

The operating line continues through the opposite side single carriers and around the dead-end pulley. Then it passes back to the first master carrier and is clamped off there. To operate properly, the placement of the slave carrier must be calibrated with its master. Take the slack out of the operating line and pull on it until the first master carrier is in its full onstage position. Slide the slave carrier along the track to its full onstage position and tighten the clamp to secure it in place. The two master carriers now move symmetrically, but opposite of one another. Hang drapes on either side to complete the rigging job. Follow the same rules as before to connect the on- and offstage edges of the two curtains.

Sometimes cueing requires that a traveler open less than all the way. That can be done with a great deal of accuracy by marking a trim on the operating line. Open the traveler the desired amount. Use tape to mark both sides of the rope with *spike marks* that are right together at a comfortable height for the operator to see. The exact distance from the floor does not affect how the spike marks work. When the stagehand opens the traveler, he or she should stop pulling on the rope when the two spike marks line up with one another. Use different colors of tape to spike multiple positions.

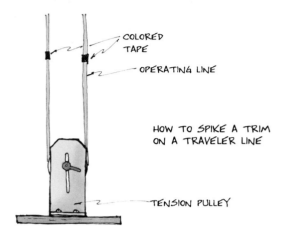

COLORED TAPE

OPERATING LINE

HOW TO SPIKE A TRIM ON A TRAVELER LINE

TENSION PULLEY

Sometimes the sightlines can be improved by hanging *tab curtains* on the sides of the stage so that the audience cannot see into the wings. This is especially common in theatres where the architecture of the building itself creates problematic sightlines. Many touring shows use side tabs because the quality of sightlines in the various theatres they visit cannot be predicted or assured. The name *tab* is used for several different types of curtains, but in this case it refers to a short traveler that runs up- and downstage between two leg and border sets. Tabs are most commonly used across the in-one position, because this is the place where sightlines are usually at their worst. It is possible to rig this type of traveler so that it is self-closing, and hence cannot be accidentally left open to offend the modesty of actors quick-changing in the wings.

A self-closing tab curtain of this type is hung with the traveler track at an angle so that gravity causes the curtain to close on its own. The track itself need be no more than 6 to 8 feet long, because the distance between the first set of legs and the second is only about that far.

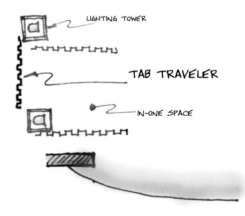

LIGHTING TOWER

TAB TRAVELER

IN-ONE SPACE

The track should hang at about a 5-degree angle, but that is somewhat dependent on the type of curtain, its height and weight, how well the carriers roll, and so on, and some experimentation will be required. You will most likely have to dead-hang the track from the grid or some other structure, because it runs up- and downstage rather than across the stage like a regular batten.

Touring shows often use towers for side lighting, because the lights can travel inside the truss, and also because towers keep the lights from being hit and becoming unfocused during the show. Towers are an excellent place to hang the side tabs, especially if the use of tabs is taken into consideration when the placement of the towers is planned. Tie pulleys to the tower tops before they are raised to make it easy to hoist the track into position with ropes. Pulleys also make it easy to adjust the trim of the track's angle to give the proper amount of closing force.

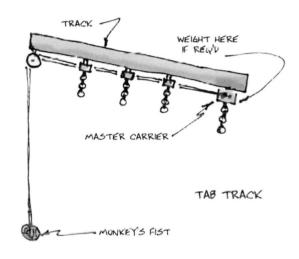

TRACK

WEIGHT HERE IF REQ'D

MASTER CARRIER

TAB TRACK

MONKEY'S FIST

The tab can be rigged so that it opens either from down to up or from up to down. There may be some reason peculiar to the production you are working on to make the tab operate one way or the other, but mechanically it makes no difference. Pulling on the rope causes the tab to open, and gravity closes it for you when the rope is released. If the curtain does not close well, try a slightly greater angle to the traveler track. This will cause the curtain to hang somewhat askew, but considering its position and use, that is not generally a concern. If the curtain is very light, fasten a small weight of some sort to the top of the curtain where it attaches to the master carrier. The added mass should help the rig to overcome the friction of the carrier wheels inside the traveler track.

HANGING THE GOODS

Hanging drops and curtains on a batten involves tying hundreds of bow knots. Like any task in the theatre (or elsewhere, I would imagine), there are a few tricks that make the job a bit easier. After you have determined which lineset to use, you will need to know where to locate the curtain on the batten. If you are hanging legs, the designer's ground plan can be consulted to find the distance of the onstage side of the leg from the *centerline* of the stage. In most theatres, the center of the battens is marked with red tape. If not, there is generally some architectural feature that will give you a clue. Measure along the batten from the center to the appropriate point and mark the pipe. Always measure distances from the center of the batten, never from the end. Plans are notoriously inaccurate about the length of battens. If you are moving from theatre to theatre, there is no way to draw a plan that is accurate for all of them, but the center of the stage is always an easily defined starting point. The intersection of the centerline and the *plaster line* is often considered to be something like the origin of a graph when it comes to laying out points on the stage.

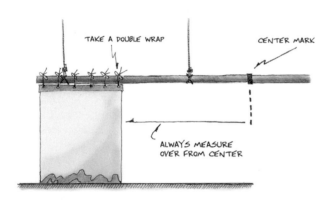

line marked on the webbing and/or have a different colored tie that marks the center.

When a folded drop comes out of a hamper and is laid out on the stage, it may not be obvious which way to turn it before unfolding. Quite often there is a lot of confusion, with ten stagehands arguing about which way the thing should go, but I have found that this strategy always works: lay it out on the floor facing up and with the webbing pointing upstage. The goods will always be in the proper position to face toward the audience.

Begin tying the drop by double-wrapping the center tie, which can often be found by searching for the lone white tie, or for CL (centerline) marked on the webbing with a Sharpie. If the drop is heavy, it is often best to skip along and tie every fifth or sixth tie, stretching the goods each time. Then come back and fill in the open spots. This technique prevents having to pick up the full weight of the drop with every tie. If there is a group working, be sure to reach over the pipe each time or your arm will be in the way of the others. It is important to stretch the drop as you tie it on the batten so that it doesn't get wrinkles in it.

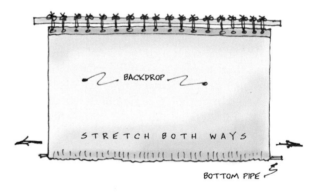

REMOVING WRINKLES WITH A
BOTTOM PIPE

Tie on the leg beginning at the point you measured, and then work your way toward the offstage end of the pipe. It is helpful to begin the first tie with a double wrap around the pipe and then the regular bow knot so that the tie line is choked onto the pipe. This keeps the onstage edge from creeping offstage along the batten as you stretch the goods out tight. Double only the first tie, not all of them. The extra tie doesn't make anything work better and can be a real time-waster during a load out. Often, the leg will be too wide for the batten and will need to be tied back by folding it to the rear and continuing to tie it to the pipe. The other choice is to accordion-pleat the goods at the end of the batten. This approach can sometimes be a better choice when a bottom pipe is involved.

Most drops are hung with the center of the drop aligned with the center of the batten, so there is no need to measure anything. The drop should have a center-

Curtains sewn with fullness often have a chain sewn into the hem, which adds a bit of weight to the bottom and encourages the goods to hang straight. A better solution when possible is to use a *bottom pipe*, but of course it won't fit on a drape with fullness. A bottom pipe works well on any drop or curtain that is sewn flat. When a pipe is used, the weight in the bottom is greater and tends to do a better job of straightening out any horizontal wrinkles. Also, the goods can be stretched along the length of the pipe, thus removing a great many of the vertical wrinkles along the bottom. Drops must be sewn with a *pipe pocket* installed in order to use a bottom pipe. The pipe itself is usually 3/8″ black steel water pipe, cut into lengths about 10 feet long that are connected together with threaded couplings.

Bottom pipe should be installed after the drop has been flown out, with the bottom of the drop about waist-high off the floor. The pipe itself is usually in sections that are screwed or taped together. One stagehand holds the pocket open while two others slide in the length of pipe and then attach the second section to the first. Repeat until the pocket is full, but don't leave too much bare pipe sticking out the end as a hazard. It is often helpful for one or more stagehands to hold up the end of the pipe as it works its way through the pocket and across the stage. Sometimes lightly bouncing the pipe will help it pass. Special care should be exercised when the pocket is old and torn, which unfortunately is a common occurrence. When the pipe is in place, the bottom of the goods can be stretched by gently but firmly pulling on the extreme sides.

ACCOMMODATING DROPS THAT ARE TOO LARGE FOR THE THEATRE

If you are touring, or if you have occasion to rent painted backdrops, you may well have a problem fitting drops into a theatre that is too small for them. If the drop is too wide or the stage is too narrow, then the drops can be folded back on the batten as described earlier. If the drop is too tall, and cannot be flown out far enough to clear the sightlines, then some other remedy is required. There are two possible solutions: tripping the bottom and rolling the top.

Tripping involves using a second batten to fly out the bottom of the drop. On rare occasions, a drop will be sewn with a special pipe pocket halfway down that is intended from the get-go to be used for tripping. This is done when the design of the show calls for a drop that is extraordinarily tall and unlikely to fit anywhere. More commonly, a second method is employed when it suddenly becomes apparent that the drop just won't fit.

A batten directly upstage of the drop is used to pick up the bottom pipe. The easiest way to attach the second batten is to connect a number of small lines that run from the bottom pipe of the drop to the upstage pipe. These *tail-down* lines are required because the tripping batten cannot fly in all the way to the deck to meet the bottom pipe when that bottom pipe is on the floor. A variety of different small line types are workable, but make sure that whatever you use will indeed bear the weight of the drop and bottom pipe safely. Use a number of lines, one every 6 to 8 feet, and not just one on either end. This means, of course, that you will need to poke several holes in the pipe pocket in order to pass the line around the bottom pipe. (This is just one of the reasons that the pocket gets so torn up.) Make sure that all of the tail-downs are the same length so that the pipe will be picked up evenly.

The tripping method works by flying out the tripping pipe just a few feet ahead of the regular pipe. This will pick up the bottom and make the out height of the bottom almost twice as high as it was when you began. Obviously, the two flymen must work well together in a coordinated effort. The linesets will be out of weight most of the time, so this technique will work only if the drop is relatively light.

A second method of shortening a drop is by *rolling*. Rolling the top of the goods reduces the height of the drop but also temporarily takes away part of it. If the top cannot be seen anyway, then this is no great loss. Sometimes there is no extra batten to make tripping possible, and rolling is the only solution. Whether tripping or rolling is appropriate must be decided on a case-by-case basis.

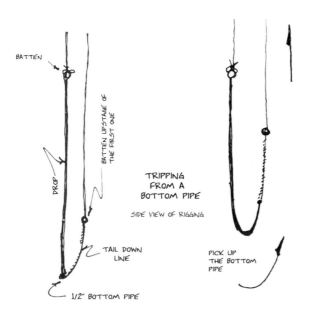

TRIPPING
FROM A
BOTTOM PIPE

SIDE VIEW OF RIGGING

BATTEN

BATTEN UPSTAGE OF THE FIRST ONE

DROP

TAIL DOWN LINE

PICK UP THE BOTTOM PIPE

1/2" BOTTOM PIPE

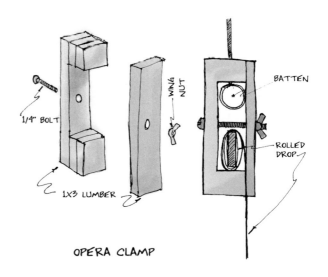

OPERA CLAMP

1/4" BOLT

1X3 LUMBER

WING NUT

BATTEN

ROLLED DROP

Rolling occurs before the drop is hung and requires some special equipment that must be secured beforehand. You will need some *1x4 lumber* and a number of *opera clamps*, as described in the accompanying diagram.

After the supplies are gathered, lay the drop out on the floor face-up and as straight and square as possible. Perhaps the top can be lined up with a long, straight joint on the stage floor. Take several very straight 1×4s and lay them out even with the top of the goods. These boards should go all the way from side to side. Gather a number of stagehands to hold the boards and to rotate them, rolling the fabric onto the boards. It is important to roll together, and to keep everything nice and neat.

Continue to roll until the desired height is reached. Pick up the rolled top and secure it to the batten with the opera clamps. Attach the clamps by rotating the flat part, and make use of the U-shaped part by hanging one end on the pipe and using the other to hold onto the rolled part of the drop. Rotate the flat part to seal in the pipe and drop, and then tighten the wing nut to secure it. If the drop does not hang straight, try again and be more precise. It may be possible to straighten the drop by adjusting the batten trim chains, if there are any.

STORING DROPS AND CURTAINS

Folding curtains and drops is one of the oldest stagehand skills. You can just imagine how early stagehands may have equated drop folding with sail folding.

A few basic concepts govern the folding of any type of hanging goods. One of these is to remember to leave the webbing and ties in an accessible position. This makes it possible to see whatever markings are written on the webbing and also makes it easier to see how to lay the goods out for retying to a batten. Proper folding will also reduce the amount of wrinkling that occurs, and generally keep the goods in better condition. It is not really possible to clean or iron most drops and curtains. Because they are quite expensive, great care is taken to ensure that they are well kept.

Begin any type of folding with the goods laying flat on the floor with the "pretty" side up. It is customary that the back side be touching the floor to save the front from damage. Put a stagehand at each of the four corners to pull the goods out and stretch them. Try to get the goods as flat and smooth as possible. Flopping the corners up and down while pulling makes the job easier, because a small amount of air underneath allows the fabric to float around with less drag.

The stagehands on the bottom two corners should lift up, pull against one another to keep tension on the drop, and then quickly move up to the top two corners. The two stagehands at the top of the drop grab the corners and match them with their own. Again, a bit of air captured in the curtain makes it easier to *float* the

bottom to the top. Too much will cause you to over-shoot. The same two stagehands who carried the bottom to the top the first time return to the middle of the drop, which has now become the bottom by virtue of the folding. Straighten everything out, let the air escape from the inside, and repeat the procedure as many times as necessary until a 2- or 3-foot-wide strip has been created.

Bring both ends to the center. Leave a space about 1 foot wide so that there will be enough slack for the final fold. Repeat bringing the ends to the middle until a 2- or 3-foot bundle is left on either side. Fold one side over the other, and folding is completed.

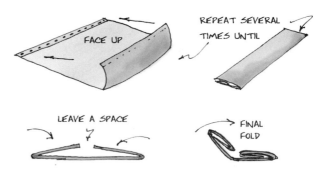

FOLDING A DROP

A word of advice here: a large number of stagehands are on hand at most load-outs, and the natural inclination is for everyone to want to help. That doesn't usually work out well when drop folding, unless the material is really heavy and doesn't want to float. It is best to find something else for the other hands to do to keep them busy and out of the way. If you are folding a light-colored drop, or perhaps a cyclorama, it is a good idea to have the stagehands wash their hands before doing so—especially if it happens at the end of a long and dirty load-out.

Soft goods are traditionally stored in large laundry *hampers*. If you have carefully folded an expensive drop, it just makes sense that you should exercise the same amount of care when easing it into the hamper. Lift it by the four corners and gently place it down into the container. On occasion, you may encounter a piece that is so large and heavy that it is impractical to consider lifting it up and into the hamper. When this happens it is best to roll the drop into it. Once the bottom of the drop has been folded to the top and the sides are to the middle one time, begin rolling the drop from one end to the other. Place a hamper on its side at the far end and simply roll the goods into the hamper like a huge snowball. Because this is a technique for very large pieces, the one curtain will most likely fill it completely.

SOFT GOODS HAMPER

Legs and other goods that are taller than they are wide are folded side to side first. Repeat this until a workable size is reached. Finish the folding by bringing the bottom to the top, rather than both ends to the middle like a full stage drop. This will leave the webbing exposed. The bottom part tends to curl up a bit with every fold, so you will need to straighten it out each time. Repeat the process until a happy size is reached.

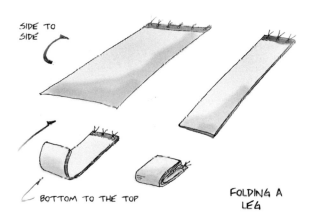

SIDE TO SIDE

BOTTOM TO THE TOP

FOLDING A LEG

Curtains sewn with fullness are a real bear to fold. In all honesty, there is no really good method, and you must do the best you can. Sometimes legs are simply lowered into a hamper when the lineset is brought in, and there is no attempt at all made to fold them. If the drapes are velour, and will be taken back out relatively soon, then this is a fine solution. Velour tends to unwrinkle when it is rehung, but I wouldn't try this with a finely woven fabric with no pile or nap. The problem in folding goods with fullness is of course that the webbing is so much smaller than the body of the curtain, and when stretched out the curtain makes a fan shape. Do your best using the same process as described earlier, but stop and straighten everything at each step as you go along. This would be a good time to invite everyone back to help.

Scrims and other very lightweight drops are sometimes *west-coasted*. In this procedure, many stagehands

are positioned under the drop as it is flown into the deck, the bottom pipe having been removed earlier. The stagehands should position themselves with hands extended so that the scrim furls up on their arms and creates a bundle rather than hitting the floor. Untie about every fifth tie from the batten and retie it around the bundled scrim so that a kind of tube is created with the goods. Untie the remaining ties from the batten and feed the bundle into its hamper.

CONSTRUCTION TECHNIQUES

The construction of stage draperies is quite a difficult chore, and unless you are very experienced at sewing, it is a practice best left to professionals who have a shop devoted to that work. It is not easy to get curtains to hang straight, especially large ones. Undoubtedly there is a vast body of technique that takes substantial practice to acquire. On the other hand, sewing drops is not nearly such a problem. The fabric is much lighter, it comes in wider widths, and methods of laying out the drop, sizing, and preparing for painting give you a bit of latitude in sewing it to a precise size. This margin for error is not found in sewing drapes that must hang straight from the outset.

A good fabric choice for drop construction is 120"-wide, heavyweight, non-flame-proofed muslin. *Muslin* is chosen because the 100-percent cotton type has a good "tooth" for painting, and it sizes well. Heavy-weight muslin is strong enough to hold up over a period of time, but is not as expensive and difficult to work with as canvas is. You can purchase already treated muslin, but it is generally less expensive to buy untreated fabric and flame-proof it yourself with an aftermarket product. This is especially true if you have lots of wooden pieces to treat as well and can spray everything down at once.

Many smaller theatres have a proscenium opening height of around 20 feet. Even if the opening is taller than that, a valance is often used to close down the space a bit. Borders used over the stage trim at around the same height. Drops need to be a few feet taller than the bottom of the borders in order to mask well.

To make this description of drop constructing more understandable, imagine a stage that trims at 18 feet. A height of 20 feet is deemed sufficient for the drop you have to sew. (Of course, in reality the designer dictates the size of the goods, but this gives you an idea of how the process works.) If 120" (10-foot) wide muslin is used, you can create a 20-foot-tall drop out of only two horizontal pieces of fabric. Muslin comes in a variety of widths, so pick one or more that work well for the drop you actually need.

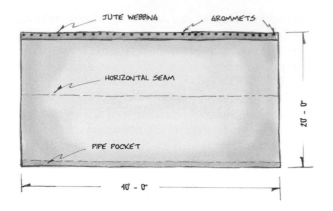

PARTS OF A MUSLIN DROP

A large open space to lay out the pieces is helpful when sewing drops. A dance studio during off hours works really well. The scene shop is not generally a good choice, as it is usually dirty with sawdust and old spattered paint.

Not much equipment is required: a sewing machine that can make a straight stitch through fairly heavy fabric, a large tape measure (like a construction tape, not a sewing tape), some scissors, thread, pins, and grommeting equipment. If you are good with a sewing machine, you may not need the pins. An industrial-type sewing machine works really well. Remember that you need only a straight stitch, so an older, heavier-duty machine is often the best.

Scenic muslin is usually sold by the bolt, roll, or bale. The pieces are 50 to 60 yards long, uncut, from the factory. If you buy less than a full bolt, the price is substantially higher. Because muslin is a mainstay of any scene shop, it makes sense to buy it in quantity. Jute *webbing* is $3\frac{1}{2}''$ wide, comes on a roll that is 72 yards long, and is quite cheap. A new type of webbing is made from polypropylene, and although only 3″ wide, it is really stronger and superior in all respects. The standard size of *grommet* to use is the #2. It is easy to ruin grommets, especially when you are new to the process of installation, so it is best to buy plenty of extras. You will need a #2 grommet hole cutter and setter for the purpose. Plain old #4 tie line is used for the ties.

Unless you are working on some really odd shape of cut drop, the seams in a drop should run horizontally. The drop will hang better that way, with the weight of the pipe pulling on the seams. The webbing is sewn to the top of the drop, and becomes a stable and sturdy strip for the grommets to go. Make a pipe pocket for the bottom out of separate pieces of muslin, and sew onto the drop.

The pipe pocket at the bottom of the drop will add several inches to the finished height. A couple of inches will be taken away by seams, so the finished product

will most likely be an inch or two larger than the ideal. The 120″ measurement for the width of the muslin is somewhat nominal anyway, and the actual size is often an inch or so smaller. Unless there are very unusual circumstances, drop sizes are not that critical. The fabric tends to stretch out and draw up over time. Of course, it would probably *not* be okay if the drop is a foot short.

Lay out the bundle of muslin on the floor and measure off a couple of inches more than 40 feet in length. Use scissors to cut through the thick *selvage edge*, and then rip the muslin straight across the warp. Ripping actually makes a much straighter cut than the scissors can, because the rip follows one thread straight across the fabric. It is also much faster than trying to establish a right angle to use as a guide. Do this a second time for the second piece, and set the muslin off to the side for a few minutes.

It is easiest to begin construction by making the pipe pocket. If the drop will receive heavy use, it is best to beef it up by making it in two layers, the inside being a heavier canvas, and the outside the same muslin as is used for the body of the drop. If the drop will be used for only one in-house show, then you may feel that a simple pocket made from one layer of heavyweight muslin will do. It is important that the outside of the pipe pocket be made of the same material as the rest of the drop to avoid a difference in texture.

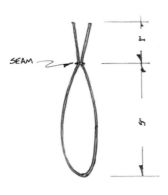

PIPE POCKET

Rip some 12″-wide strips of cloth from scrap, and sew enough of them together end to end to form a strip that is at least as long as the width of the drop, in our case, 40 feet. Fold the strip in half lengthwise and sew it together, creating a tube 6″ wide. Make sure that any seams previously made by sewing together the smaller strips go to the inside where they will not be seen. If you are using an inner sleeve of canvas, the joining seams of that strip should go to the outside, so that the interior of the sleeve is not obstructed. This allows the pipe to slide through easily. Sometimes a very slick and tough nylon fabric is used for the inner sleeve. At any rate, you should wind up with a tube more than 40 feet long, with no seam allowances showing except for the one at the top.

Do not turn the tube inside-out; the top seam will wind up on the back of the drop and will not show. Sew the completed pocket to the bottom piece of muslin. Make sure that your seam allowance is large enough to include the entire selvage, which on scenic muslin is sometimes quite large. Usually about a 1" allowance is enough.

The second stage is to secure the jute webbing to the top section of the muslin. Lay out the muslin on the floor so that it is flat and one edge is in a reasonably straight line. Turn down the straight edge of the muslin an inch, so that the raw edge won't show in the finished product. There is no need to iron it; just crease it with your hand, as you would a piece of thick paper. Muslin typically has a stiff quality from all of the sizing that is in it.

Cut a section of webbing that is about 40'-6" long. Turn under 3 inches at one end and mash it down so that a crease is formed. Pin the webbing to the muslin so that the turned-under section of the jute is down and the edge of the webbing is flush with the edge of the muslin. I find it helpful to use a pin at least every foot or so to make it easier to get the drop through the sewing machine. Fold over and pin down the last 3 inches of the webbing just like you did the first 3 inches. Extra material folded over at the ends creates a greater thickness and more strength in the corner areas, which get the most intense use. The webbing in the illustration is the older, jute type, which has a colored stripe on the back. The newer type does not, and is usually solid black.

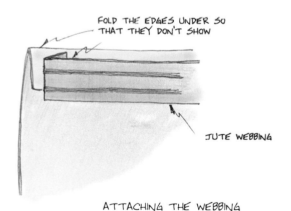

FOLD THE EDGES UNDER SO THAT THEY DON'T SHOW

JUTE WEBBING

ATTACHING THE WEBBING

Sew down the webbing with a straight stitch ¼" from each edge, and also down the middle. A setting of eight or ten stitches per inch is good. An industrial machine is by far the best to use, because of the thickness of the webbing and the extreme length of the seams.

You now have completed top and bottom sections that must be connected together. Make sure that the middle seam, webbing, and pipe pocket seam all fall on what will become the upstage side of the drop. Joining the big parts was saved until the very last, because that way, you have to deal with the weight of the whole drop only once.

When the drop is stretched out and stapled to the floor for painting, the edges should be arranged so that a true rectangle is achieved. Snap lines on the floor to delineate a 20'-0" by 40'-0" area. You may need to make a slight adjustment in size to accommodate the true dimensions of the finished drop.

Rather than letting the sewn material define the shape of the drop, the edges of the muslin should be brought in line with the layout marks on the paint floor. The muslin will shrink, lose its wrinkles, and conform to the shape and size defined by the staples on its perimeter, and it is not necessary to do any stretching. A proper layout is of paramount importance in order to avoid a misshapen product. The drop can be a few inches too wide or too short without much notice being taken, but if it hangs crookedly, everyone will see that.

Grommeting can be done either before or after painting, as time permits. Lay the drop out face-up, and use a tape measure to find the center. Put marks at 1-foot intervals all across the top in either direction. Make sure that the center mark is dead center, because that will make it easier to properly tie the drop onto the batten when it gets to the theatre. Use a specially cut piece of scrap wood to mark a place at each foot interval that is 1" from the top of the drop.

Use a grommet hole cutter to punch holes on the marks in the webbing. It is best to place the drop on top of a block of wood and/or some thick scrap leather when punching the holes to prevent damage to your floor and tool. The leather seems to help keep the punch from dulling so quickly. Arbitrarily move the corner holes in a comfortable distance from the edge so that they are on the sturdiest part of the fabric.

Follow the instructions that come with your grommet setter to attach the #2 brass grommets. Basically, this involves threading the male side through the hole, placing it on the base, slipping the female side over the male, and then using the setter to curl the male side flange down so that it secures the female side. The instructions will most likely say something about not trying to do the job with one hard blow, but rather with many small taps. That is good advice.

GROMMETING SUPPLIES AND TOOLS

GROMMET PRESS

Grommeting is one of those processes that sounds really easy but takes considerable practice to master well. Expect to ruin a few grommets in learning how. A much better alternative to the hammer is a grommet setting tool, which resembles a huge nutcracker. Pressure on the handle smoothly and easily turns down the edge of the male grommet.

Cut some tie line to a length of 30″ and then tie one to each grommet using a square knot. It is traditional to use a contrasting color of tie to mark the center of the drop. Use a Sharpie to mark a small centerline on the front of the drop to be used as a registration mark when painting.

CHAPTER 6

ELECTRICITY

In 1879, Thomas Edison created the first practical incandescent lightbulb with a carbonized filament. Not long after, the tungsten filament still used in today's lightbulbs was developed. Since that time, incandescent electric lamps have been the standard lighting method in theatres. This chapter is intended to help you understand some of the basic principles of electricity: where it comes from and how to predict its behavior.

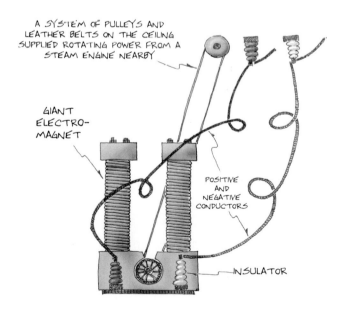

A SYSTEM OF PULLEYS AND
LEATHER BELTS ON THE CEILING
SUPPLIED ROTATING POWER FROM A
STEAM ENGINE NEARBY

GIANT
ELECTRO-
MAGNET

POSITIVE
AND
NEGATIVE
CONDUCTORS

INSULATOR

EARLY "DYNAMOS" LIKE THIS ONE WERE USED
TO SUPPLY DIRECT CURRENT POWER TO THEATRES IN
NEW YORK. DC POWER GENERATION WAS THE
STANDARD FOR BROADWAY THEATRES UNTIL THE 1970S.

doi: 10.1016/C2009-0-23409-X

ELECTRICAL THEORY, UNITS OF MEASUREMENT, AND DEFINITIONS OF TERMS

In 1911, a theory of atomic structure was developed that described an atom as having a central positive nucleus surrounded by orbiting negative *electrons*.

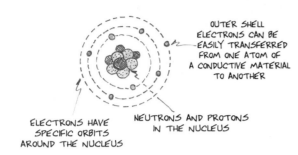

OUTER SHELL ELECTRONS CAN BE EASILY TRANSFERRED FROM ONE ATOM OF A CONDUCTIVE MATERIAL TO ANOTHER

ELECTRONS HAVE SPECIFIC ORBITS AROUND THE NUCLEUS

NEUTRONS AND PROTONS IN THE NUCLEUS

A further development of this idea gave the electrons specific orbits around the nucleus in "shells," and can be used to explain how certain elements combine with one another to make compounds. Although newer atomic theories have been developed since then, this original one is an excellent model for electrical theory discussions, and can be used to explain how electrons work in producing electricity.

Electricity is formed when electrons are moved from one atom to another. This can happen in a number of different ways: statically, like lightning; chemically, like a battery; or by a generator, using induction.

LIGHTNING

ATOMS MOVING PAST EACH OTHER IN CLOUDS FORM A NEGATIVE CHARGE WHICH JUMPS TO THE POSITIVELY CHARGED EARTH. LIGHTNING HAS A HUGE VOLTAGE PRESSURE, MUCH LARGER THAN ANYTHING MAN-MADE. IT NEEDS A LARGE AMOUNT OF PRESSURE TO JUMP SO FAR ACROSS AN OPEN GAP WITH NO CONDUCTOR.

BATTERY

CHEMICALS IN A BATTERY REACT WITH ONE ANOTHER CAUSING ELECTRONS TO GATHER AT THE NEGATIVE TERMINAL –, BY DRAWING THEM FROM THE POSITIVE TERMINAL, +. WHEN THE TWO TERMINALS ARE CONNECTED BY A CONDUCTIVE MATERIAL, THE ELECTRONS MIGRATE FROM – TO +.

INDUCTION

HOT

NEUTRAL

A COIL OF WIRE SPUN IN THE PRESENCE OF A MAGNETIC FIELD CREATES A VOLTAGE PRESSURE, BUT RATHER THAN FLOWING IN ONE DIRECTION LIKE LIGHTNING OR A BATTERY, THE ELECTRONS EBB AND FLOW ON A SCHEDULE DETERMINED BY THE SPEED OF THE GENERATOR.

Lightning strikes the earth when large numbers of electrons gather on the bottom of rain clouds and are attracted to atoms in the earth that are missing electrons. When the pressure becomes great enough, the electrons make a giant spark as they dramatically jump through just thin air. Most of the time, though, when electricity is used for practical purposes, electrons move through a substance called a *conductor*. That material conducts or moves electrons from one place to another.

All metals conduct electricity, some better than others, and they are often used to form conductors. Although copper is the metal of choice for most wiring, high-voltage power lines are generally made from aluminum, because it costs less and is not as heavy.

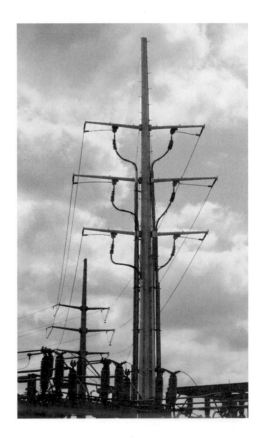

Some elements and/or compounds are extremely poor conductors. They are called *insulators*, and are critical to the practical use of electricity. If every element conducted electrons, there would be no way to contain or control electricity. Rubber, plastics, glass, ceramics, and air are frequently used insulators.

CERAMIC INSULATORS ARE USED FOR
HIGH-VOLTAGE LINES. THE HIGHER THE VOLTAGE,
THE LARGER THE INSULATOR.

The name given to the force that makes electrons move is EMF or *electromotive force*. The amount of the force applied is measured in *volts*.

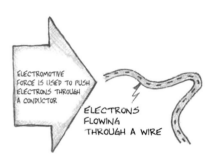

ELECTROMOTIVE FORCE
(EMF)
IS MEASURED IN VOLTS

E is the symbol used for mathematical computations using volts (from EMF), and v is the symbol used to express an amount of voltage. Example:

E = 12v

Where does the force to move electrons come from? The static electricity exhibited by a lightning bolt is a very visible example of the force of an EMF, but lightning is not useful in a practical sense; indeed, it is something to be avoided. The *battery* is a much more stable and controllable source of electromotive force. The type shown in the illustration is often called a *wet cell* storage battery and is the kind used in a car. (At least, a gas-powered car!) Two dissimilar metals are suspended in an electrolytic solution like sulfuric acid. Technically speaking, a battery is actually a number of *cells* linked together to form one larger power source. Each plate in a storage battery is a cell. A number of cells make up a battery of them.

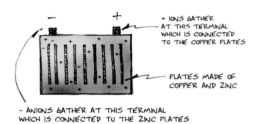

"WET CELL" BATTERIES ARE OFTEN FOUND
IN CARS OR BOATS (OR STAGE LIFTS)

When placed in series with one another, a group of cells produces a higher voltage, because their voltages are added together to get a total. The D-cell batteries pictured here work in the same manner as the wet cell battery, but the electrolytic solution has been made into a highly viscous gel so that it stays put even when the battery is turned upside down.

BATTERY CELLS IN SERIES

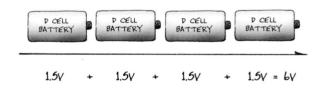

1.5V   +   1.5V   +   1.5V   +   1.5V = 6V

4 D-CELL BATTERIES IN SERIES
ADD UP TO 6 VOLTS OF TOTAL PRESSURE

A chemical reaction occurs between the two metals in the battery, using the fluid they are suspended in as a catalyst. The fluid provides ions that move electrons between the metallic plates. In the case of a wet cell car battery, lead and copper are frequently used, but other types of batteries use other metals. Rechargeable tool batteries use nickel and cadmium suspended in a gel. Acids create a high number of ions and are often used as the catalyst, so take care in working with them. Wet cells are often used as a power source for stage lifts, and if you turn that sort of battery upside down, there is almost sure to be at least some leakage.

Batteries produce a type of current known as *DC* or *direct current*. They create an electromotive force that pushes electrons away from the negative terminal, which is a gathering point for all of the negatively charged ions. In a DC current, the electrons flow in only one direction, from the negative terminal to the positive one.

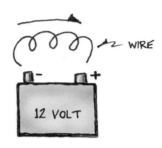

ELECTRONS FLOW FROM
NEGATIVE TO POSITIVE

This graph shows the voltage pressure, E, from a 12-volt car battery over a period of 5 minutes. The x axis represents time, and the y axis the pressure of the voltage as supplied by the battery. The origin, or intersection of the two axes, is the zero starting time. The graph is a straight and horizontal line, because the pressure of the voltage does not change during the 5-minute interval. Battery graphs do go down over time as the battery wears out, but this wouldn't normally happen in so short a time as 5 minutes.

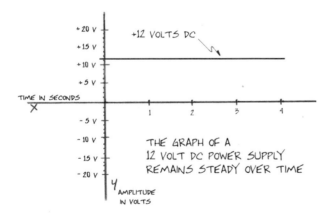

Quadrants II and III are not generally used in electronics graphs, because they fall before time begins at

the origin. Quadrant I is used to indicate a positive voltage pressure, and Quadrant IV a negative voltage pressure. DC currents are generally depicted as positive, because the voltage pressure is always pushing the electrons forward.

The electrons in direct current flow in only one direction, but *alternating current* or AC is different. AC is generally produced by a generator, using the principle of induction, and that process will be covered in detail later on. "Alternating" is a good word to describe this type of current, because it alternates between flowing forward, a positive voltage pressure, and backward, a negative voltage pressure. The graph of an AC voltage looks like the following figure.

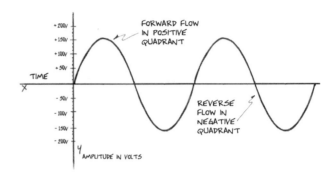

AC CURRENT OVER TWO TIME INTERVALS

The electrons flow forward during the first time interval, and backward during the second time interval. The forward flow is positive, and the backward flow is negative. AC is often said to be pushing and pulling the electrons. The curious shape of this curve is known as a *sine wave*, and is a function of how the electrons are induced to flow in the generator.

The flow of electrons or *current* is often compared to water. A river has a certain amount of water flowing in it, a very large but finite number of H_2O molecules. The number of water molecules represents the current, while the pressure of the moving water represents the voltage. Current is measured in *amperes*, or *amps*.

I is the symbol used for mathematical computations using amps, and A is the symbol used to express an amount of current. Example:

I = 20 A

Technically, 1 ampere is defined as 6×10^{18} electrons moving past a given point in one second. That number is better known as a *coulomb*. This is generally not very useful information in and of itself, but it does demonstrate how a measurement in amperes denotes an actual amount or number of electrons. The mathematical relationship between volts and amps is very important.

IMPORTANT: Remember that amps refers to an amount or number of electrons flowing, whereas volts are used to measure the pressure of the flow.

amperes = an amount of current
volts = the pressure used to push them

Electrical *circuits* are created when current flows through wires and other devices that form a completed pathway. *Schematic* drawings are used to show the electrical connections between various electronic components. Lines represent conductors. Other components are represented by graphic symbols.

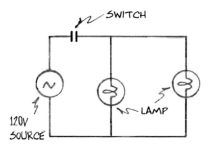

SCHEMATIC FOR A CIRCUIT
WITH A SWITCH AND TWO
LIGHTBULBS

In this circuit, closing the switch causes the bulbs to glow. The brightness of the bulb is a function of the voltage pressure applied to the filament. Increasing the pressure of the voltage makes a bulb brighter. Notice that these bulbs are not connected one after the other, in series, like the cells of a battery. Instead, they are connected across two parallel lines. It is an example of a *parallel circuit*. In a parallel circuit, each resistance (in our case, each lightbulb) has its own path back to the power source.

Resistance is defined as the opposition to current flow. Resistance comes from a number of sources—

devices like lightbulbs or toasters, but also the wires used to connect them. Even good conductors resist the flow of electrons to some degree, and a longer conductor creates more resistance than a shorter one. At the opposite end of the spectrum, insulators conduct electrons so poorly that they are generally regarded as not conducting at all, so in a practical sense they have infinite resistance.

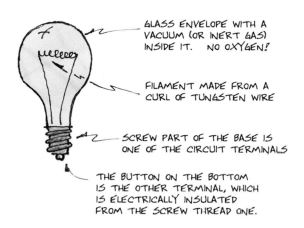

PARTS OF A LIGHTBULB

The tiny tungsten *filament* in the lightbulb resists the flow of electricity, and in the process of doing that, changes some of the electrical energy into heat energy. If the voltage pressure is high enough and the wire gets hot enough, it will incandesce, or glow. In a similar way, the nichrome wire inside a toaster oven turns a bright red when heated to its maximum. Nichrome wire is specially designed to resist oxidizing in the atmosphere, but a lightbulb is different. An inert gas in the glass envelope keeps the tungsten filament from burning up through oxidation. The curl in the filament creates a longer filament, and produces more light in a smaller bulb.

The amount of resistance to electron flow in the wire filament is measured in *ohms* using the uppercase omega, Ω, as a symbol.

R is the symbol used for mathematical computations using resistance, and Ω is the symbol used to express an amount of resistance. Example:

$$R = 150 \ \Omega$$

One additional unit of measurement is watts, which is used to quantify an amount of *power*. Power describes how much work is being done. Lightbulbs do work when they produce light. Toasters do work when they get hot, as well as when they make toast. Other power measurements are things like horsepower, decibels, and BTUs.

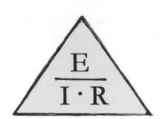

P is the symbol used for mathematical computations using power, and W is the symbol used to express an amount of power. Example:

P = 100 W

SYMBOLS TO REMEMBER

- E = EMF, measured in volts (v)
- I = Current, measured in amps (A)
- R = Resistance, measured in ohms (Ω)

OHM'S LAWS AND THEIR EFFECT ON CIRCUITS

Georg Ohm was a German physicist and electrical experimenter in the 1800s. He discovered a series of formulas that define the mathematical relationship between amperage, voltage, resistance, and watts. His work and primary research led to an understanding of the basic laws of how electricity behaves, and the formulas that connect these four units of measurement are named in his honor, as well the unit of measurement for resistance itself, the ohm (Ω).

The first of Ohm's laws states this mathematical formula:

Voltage is equal to resistance multiplied by the current flow, or **E = IR.**

As with any algebraic formula, it is possible to rearrange the terms in order to solve the equation for a specific unit of measurement. Two algebraic equivalents of the formula would be:

I = E/R
R = E/I

A very handy *magic triangle*, shown in the following figure, makes it easy to remember the different permutations of this formula.

Cover the value to be determined with your finger, and the relationship of the other two is revealed in its proper algebraic form. Example: you need to know the amount of current flowing in a circuit with 100 Ω of resistance and 120 volts of pressure. Cover I, the symbol for current, and the remaining two symbols, E and R, appear in their correct relationship: E/R. The answer would be 120/100 or 1.2 amps. Whenever you solve any equation using Ohm's law, be sure to write the unit of measurement after your answer so that your answer is defined by that unit of measurement. Otherwise, it is just a meaningless number.

A second formula includes the measurement for power. Ohm's power formula states that power is equal to the current flow multiplied by the voltage pressure, or:

P = IE

For obvious reasons it is often called the "pie" formula, and a similar magic triangle can be used for it. Stage electricians generally find the pie formula to be the most useful one, because it helps determine how many lights can be powered from a known amount of current.

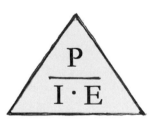

RESISTANCE IN SERIES

One of Ohm's laws states that when resistances are arranged in *series* one after the other, the total amount of resistance in the circuit is equal to the sum of the various resistances. Furthermore, the voltage applied to the circuit is shared between the different resistances in proportion to their size. Current remains constant, as the same number of electrons flows through every point along the path. This concept has some very important implications where dimmers are concerned, especially the early kinds.

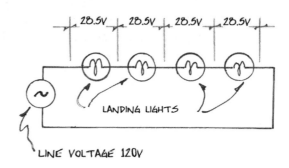

LINE VOLTAGE 120V

28.5V × 4 = 114V
WHICH IS ACTUALLY CLOSE ENOUGH

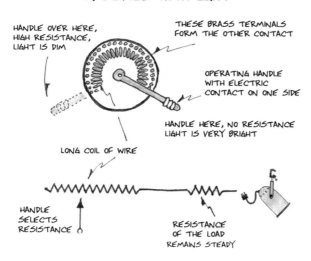

OLD STYLE RESISTANCE DIMMER
IN SERIES WITH LIGHT

HANDLE OVER HERE, HIGH RESISTANCE, LIGHT IS DIM

THESE BRASS TERMINALS FORM THE OTHER CONTACT

OPERATING HANDLE WITH ELECTRIC CONTACT ON ONE SIDE

HANDLE HERE, NO RESISTANCE LIGHT IS VERY BRIGHT

LONG COIL OF WIRE

HANDLE SELECTS RESISTANCE

RESISTANCE OF THE LOAD REMAINS STEADY

BECAUSE THE RESISTANCE OF THE DIMMER AND LIGHT ARE IN SERIES WITH ONE ANOTHER, ADDING RESISTANCE AT THE DIMMER DECREASES VOLTAGE AT THE LIGHT.

Aircraft landing lights (ACL) are sometimes used for special effects lighting on stage, because they put out a tightly focused shaft of light. These lamps were designed to help airplanes land at night, and are mounted on the aircraft like a headlight. Planes use a voltage of 28.5 v, rather than the earthbound 120 v. If ACLs were simply plugged into a standard USA wall voltage of 120 v, the filaments would burn out immediately, because the voltage pressure would be far too much for them to handle. A special power supply could be constructed, but there is an easier way to solve the over-voltage problem and get the lamps to work from a regular wall outlet.

Ohm's law can be used to demonstrate a way to divide up the regular line voltage by using a series circuit created by placing four of the lamps in a row. However, it should be noted that if one of the lamps burns out, all of them will go dark, because the conductive pathway will be disconnected, or *open*. A circuit that has been disconnected in this way is called an *open circuit* and is an indicator that the circuit is not working. The total voltage, 120 v, is shared equally between the lamps so that each one receives ¼ of the total, or about 30 v. The voltage pressure does not have to be exact, and this amount will work fine.

Another example of resistance in series is one that can occur at any time in a scene shop. If you use several power cords plugged together to reach a motorized power tool, you might find that the motor has trouble running properly. It might not even start at all. That is because the resistance of the electric motor on the tool is in series with the resistance present in the power cord itself, and a *voltage divider* has been created. That means that the voltage has been divided between two parts of a circuit—in our case, between the long power cords and the power tool.

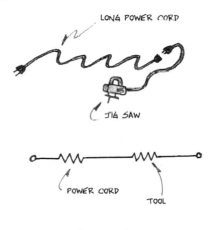

LONG POWER CORD

JIG SAW

POWER CORD

TOOL

POWER CORD AND TOOL
AS VOLTAGE DIVIDER

All wires have a certain resistance to the flow of electrons. A thick-diameter conductor has less resistance per foot than a thin one. Also, a shorter cable has less resistance than a longer one of the same diameter, because there are fewer feet of it creating resistance. A long power cord, especially a small-gauge one, could have quite a bit of resistance in it. The resistance in the cord will split the voltage between the tool and itself. AC electric motors are designed to operate at the full line voltage, and using them with a lower voltage will eventually burn out the windings. You can avoid trouble with the tool motor by using a larger gauge cable that is as short as possible. You should never operate electric motors with a stage dimmer, because they work by lowering voltages, which would of course be destructive.

Early Series Circuits

The first public lighting systems were begun in the 1860s, before the invention of a practical incandescent lamp. These outdoor street lights were often of the *Jablokov* type, an arc lamp made by placing two carbon rods next to each other, with an insulator between them. Contact was made by shorting out the tips of the rods, and an electrical arc began. Electrical arcing is extremely bright and produces a very strong light. The insulation between the rods burned down at the same rate as the rods themselves, and the lamp would stay lit as long as the rods lasted.

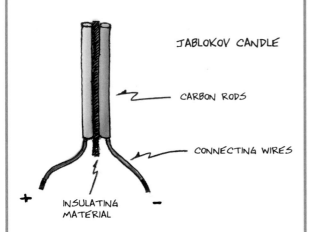

JABLOKOV CANDLE

— CARBON RODS

— CONNECTING WIRES

+   INSULATING   —
     MATERIAL

THE INSULATING MATERIAL SEPARATED THE TWO CARBON RODS, BUT AN ARC JUMPED ACROSS THE ENDS, CREATING A LIGHT SOURCE. THIS CONCEPT WAS AN EARLY VERSION OF WHAT BECAME CARBON ARC FOLLOWSPOTS. THE INSULATOR BURNED UP WITH THE RODS, WHICH NEEDED FREQUENT REPLACEMENT.

At the time, the complexities of Ohm's laws were not universally understood. Arc lamps generally require a DC current. DC currents are difficult to regulate when long wires are used, because the voltage pressure can't be controlled by a transformer, like with AC current. Lamps farther away from the power source tended to get a lower voltage, because of a voltage divider set up with the resistance in the lamp itself in series with the wiring. As a result, some lamps burned faster than others, or did not want to start at all. The late 1800s saw a "war of the currents" over whether DC or AC would be the standardized choice. AC won out, but not without a struggle.

Parallel Circuits

We've been looking at series circuits, in which devices are connected together one after another along a conductor, but these are actually quite rare. In the power cord/motor example, the series circuit is accidental; the compressor motor is actually connected to the building power in parallel. Parallel circuits are the norm in stage lighting systems, as they are elsewhere. They allow a number of different devices to be connected to the circuit, all of them using different amounts of power/watts, but all at the same voltage pressure. In addition, loads can be removed from the system without causing it to go open circuit. Most electrical devices in the United States, Mexico, South America, and Canada are constructed to operate on 120 v, the standard line voltage from a wall receptacle. The following figure shows several schematics showing the same parallel circuit, but with the wires placed differently. A list of the voltages used throughout the world can be found on the website.

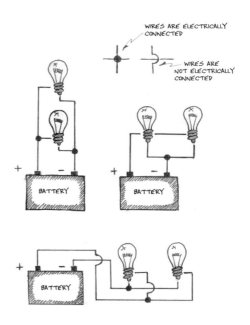

WIRES ARE ELECTRICALLY CONNECTED

WIRES ARE NOT ELECTRICALLY CONNECTED

BATTERY

BATTERY

BATTERY

VARIATIONS ON PARALLEL CIRCUITS

In this example, each lamp has its own discrete path to the voltage source, and if one of the pathways is opened, the others will still operate. In a parallel circuit, the voltage pressure in each part of the circuit remains constant, but the current varies in proportion to how many loads are fed by the conductor that feeds that part of the circuit. This is the opposite of the way in which a series circuit operates.

Although the wiring running between the lights is arranged differently, all of the lamps in this drawing have the same electrical connection to the same voltage. No matter how convoluted the wiring in a lighting system may appear to be, all of the circuits involved are still in parallel, and all of the outlets have the same 120 v service.

Ohm's law for parallel circuits is most often used to determine what the total *current draw* will be for an entire network. Remember that the measurement for current is taken in amperes, which is an indication of how many electrons (how much of them) are moving through the wires. Theatre lighting systems are protected by either fuses or circuit breakers that will disconnect the flow of electricity if too much demand for current is placed on that system. The purpose is to protect the component parts from damage from overloading.

If too many electrons pass through the wiring inside the wall of a house, or through a jumper feeding a stage light, the copper wire will overheat like the tungsten filament inside a lightbulb. The filament is housed inside a glass bulb, and the entire lamp is constructed to cope with such overheating. Wiring is not intended to withstand that sort of extreme use, and a fire will result if too great a load is place on it.

The amount of current draw can be determined by the mathematical relationship between the total power consumed by a circuit in ratio to its voltage pressure. The greater the wattage of lamps in a circuit, the greater the current flow will be.

The pie formula is used to determine current draw when the voltage pressure and wattage are known.

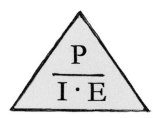

Suppose that the following schematic is given, and that the problem is to find the total current draw:

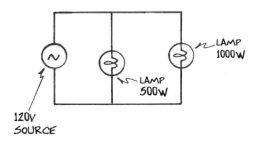

LAMP 1000W

LAMP 500W

120V SOURCE

We are seeking the value of the current flow I, and covering that symbol on the magic triangle gives the formula:

$$I = P/E$$

First the total power consumed by the circuit must be determined.

$$P_{TOTAL} = P_1 + P_2 + P_3 \ldots$$

$$P_{TOTAL} = 500 \text{ W} + 1000 \text{ W}$$

$$P_{TOTAL} = 1500 \text{ W}$$

And if we solve for I:

$$I = P/E$$

$$I = 1500 \text{ W}/120 \text{ v}$$

$$I = 12.5 \text{ A}$$

If we were checking to see whether these two lamps would be safe for the 20 A circuit breaker in a D20 dimmer, the answer would be yes.

DIMMER RATINGS

The most common "size" of modern stage dimmers is the 20 amp, which matches well with equipment used in many other applications. Stage lamp "sizes" are generally given in watts, just like household variety. The permissible wattage on a 20 A circuit can be determined via Ohm's law to be:

P = 20 amps × 120 volts or 2400 watts

It is often easiest to remember the 2400 W rating, and just add up the wattages of the individual lamps to see whether they are more or less than that amount. If your dimmers have a lower current rating, use the same formula to determine the total wattage permissible on them.

500 WATT LIGHTS

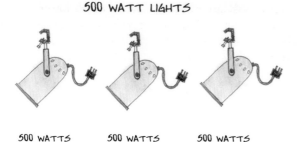

500 WATTS   500 WATTS   500 WATTS

ADD THE WATTAGES TOGETHER TO GET A TOTAL AMOUNT

$$\begin{array}{r} 500 \\ + \ 500 \\ + \ 500 \\ \hline \end{array}$$

TOTAL 1500   WHICH IS LESS THAN 2400.

1000 WATT LIGHTS

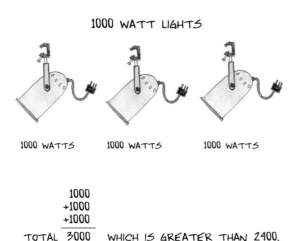

1000 WATTS   1000 WATTS   1000 WATTS

$$\begin{array}{r} 1000 \\ + 1000 \\ + 1000 \\ \hline \end{array}$$

TOTAL 3000   WHICH IS GREATER THAN 2400.

AC CURRENT FROM POWER GENERATION

Remember that there are two basic types of electric current: direct (DC) and alternating (AC). These two types are defined by the way each one causes electrons to move through a conductor. In DC, electrons move in one direction only, from a source of surplus electrons known as the negative terminal (–) toward a collection point known as the positive terminal (+). A *terminal* is an ending point for a circuit. You can find the plus and minus signs on any battery next to its terminals.

THE TERMINALS OF MOST BATTERIES ARE MARKED WITH PLUS AND MINUS SIGNS THAT STAND FOR POSITIVE AND NEGATIVE

9 VOLT BATTERIES ARE COMMONLY USED IN VOLT- OHM METERS AND IN HOME SMOKE DETECTORS

But batteries are not very useful for lighting work, because the power requirements of the lights are too high. It is possible to convert AC current to DC current, but since incandescent lamps will work equally well with AC or DC, there is no reason to do that. Direct current is not often used for lighting purposes, except for very special arc-type lamps that require DC to operate. These are found mostly on followspots or large movie lights, most notably xenon or HMI lamps.

Any type of ordinary filament bulb will operate with either direct or alternating current with no problem, but electric motors are wired for one or the other. The speed of DC motors can be adjusted by varying the voltage supplied to them, much like varying the voltage will cause a light to vary in brightness. Reversing the polarity of the current will make the motor run backward. DC motors are used for equipment like gobo rotators, because their speed and direction are so easily controlled. Alternating current motors will burn out if you try reducing their voltage. AC motor speed can be controlled by altering the frequency of the sine wave, but that is a much different process. Rotators must be connected to a special DC power supply in order to work.

GOBO ROTATOR

THE WIRES ON THE MOTOR ARE MARKED PLUS AND MINUS, WHICH IS AN INDICATOR OF A DC CIRCUIT

IF THE VOLTAGE PRESSURE INCREASES THE MOTOR WILL RUN FASTER. IF THE POLARITY IS REVERSED THE MOTOR WILL RUN BACKWARD.

Alternating current was long ago adopted as the standard method of producing electrical current. It is easier to transmit long distances and requires smaller and less expensive wires. It is the type of current supplied to most homes and businesses. AC differs from DC in that its electrons move through the conducting wire in two opposite directions following a regularly scheduled pattern. There is a constant ebb and flow from the source of power, with electrons first being forced down the wire and then being allowed to lapse back toward the source. The speed at which this change of direction occurs is given in cycles or *hertz* (Hz). Sixty cycles per second is standard in most of the western hemisphere and in Europe. A 50 Hz 230 v system is used in Australia and New Zealand.

AC current is produced in a generator by the interaction of coils of wire and a strong magnetic field. The reaction of the electrons contained in a wire to the effects of an outside magnetic force is called *induction*. When a coil of wire moves through a magnetic field, the magnet forces a current to flow through the wire. The magnetic field thus "induces" a current to flow in the wire, but only as long as either the wire or the magnetic field is in motion. The relationship between magnetism and EMF is crucial to the operation of many common electrical devices. In fact, the entire system of power circuits everywhere in the world is dependent on the principles of the magnetic induction of current flow.

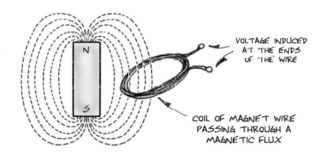

COIL OF MAGNET WIRE
PASSING THROUGH A
MAGNETIC FLUX

VOLTAGE INDUCED
AT THE ENDS
OF THE WIRE

The force of the current, or voltage, induced in the wire by the magnetic force is largely dependent on these factors:

1. The strength of the magnetic force.
2. The proximity of the wire and the magnetic force.
3. The angle of movement through the lines of magnetic force.

The first two factors regarding the strength of an induced voltage are fairly intuitive. It makes sense that the effect would be more pronounced with a stronger

magnet, and also by being closer to it. But the angularity factor is less obvious. More voltage is induced when the wire is passing *across* the lines of magnetic force rather than when the wire is passing *along* the lines of magnetic force.

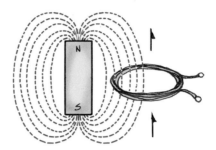

MOVING **ALONG** THE LINES OF FORCE
INDUCES **LITTLE**, IF ANY, CURRENT

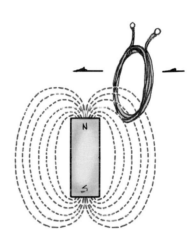

MOVING **THROUGH** THE LINES OF FORCE
INDUCES MUCH **MORE** CURRENT

This important factor explains the unique way alternating current is produced in a generator, where an extremely useful fluctuation in the current is created. If either the wire or the magnetic field is spun in a circular fashion, then the direction of travel through the magnetic field changes from across to along as it completes the circle. As a result, the pressure of the voltage induced will rise and fall in a predictable manner.

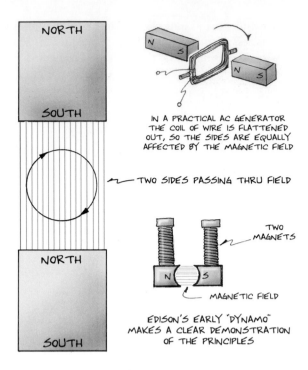

IN A PRACTICAL AC GENERATOR
THE COIL OF WIRE IS FLATTENED
OUT, SO THE SIDES ARE EQUALLY
AFFECTED BY THE MAGNETIC FIELD

TWO SIDES PASSING THRU FIELD

TWO
MAGNETS

MAGNETIC FIELD

EDISON'S EARLY "DYNAMO"
MAKES A CLEAR DEMONSTRATION
OF THE PRINCIPLES

AS THE COIL OF WIRE MAKES A CIRCULAR PATH THRU
THE MAGNETIC FIELD, THE ANGLE OF ITS INTERSECTION
WITH THE LINES OF MAGNETIC FORCE IS CONSTANTLY
CHANGING. THAT ANGLE, AT ANY ONE MOMENT,
DETERMINES THE FORCE OF THE EMF/VOLTAGE.

ANGLE DETERMINES STRENGTH OF EMF

AC is formed in a generator by using magnetic
force and electrical induction to create a voltage in a
coil of wire. Generators can be powered by wind,
falling water, steam from coal/gas/nuclear reactor, or
any other mechanical means that will rotate the coils
of wire.

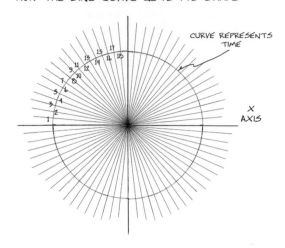

CURVE REPRESENTS
TIME

X
AXIS

THE CIRCUMFERENCE OF THE CIRCLE REPRESENTS ONE CYCLE
OF ALTERNATING CURRENT, AND THE RAYS DIVIDE THE TIME
INTO SECTIONS. EACH SECTION REPRESENTS ONE TIME
DIVISION ON THE GRAPH BELOW. MEASURE FROM THE X AXIS
UP TO THE INTERSECTION OF ONE OF THE RAYS AND THE CIRCLE.
PLOTTING EACH ONE OF THE INTERSECTIONS ON THE GRAPH WILL
PRODUCE A SINE CURVE, BECAUSE THE RATIO OF THIS PROCESS
IS THE SAME AS WHEN A WIRE TRAVELS IN A CIRCLE
THROUGH A MAGNETIC FIELD.

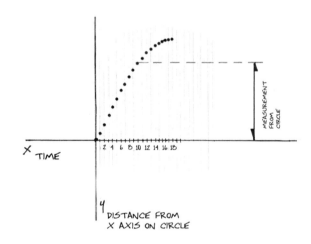

MEASUREMENT FROM CIRCLE

X TIME

DISTANCE FROM
X AXIS ON CIRCLE

CONNECTING THE DOTS WILL FORM A SINE CURVE

As the generator rotor spins, the coil of wire passes
through different parts of the magnetic field, and the
voltage pressure pushing the electrons changes constantly as a result of its angular motion through the
field. Once the coil has rotated 180 degrees, the voltage
is pulled in the opposite direction. The polarity of the
magnetic force is then the mirror image of what it was
in the beginning. The net effect is to push electrons
through the wire during the positive portion of the
rotation, and to pull electrons in the opposite direction
during the second half of the rotation.

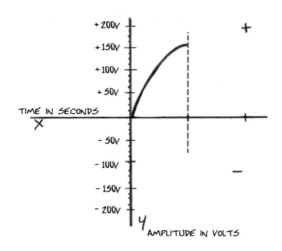

THE POSITIVE PRESSURE OF THE VOLTAGE
INCREASES DURING THE FIRST 1/4 TURN
OF THE COIL OF WIRE IN THE MAGNETIC FIELD.

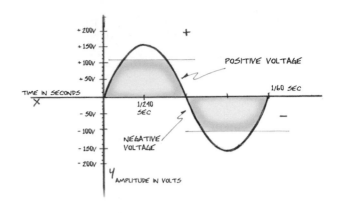

ONE CYCLE OF ALTERNATING CURRENT

THE USEFUL VOLTAGE APPLIED TO THE LOAD IS
THE AVERAGE VOLTAGE. THE RMS AVERAGE VOLTAGE
IS INDICATED BY THE SHADED-IN AREA. THE ACTUAL
PEAK VOLTAGE IS MUCH HIGHER.

ELECTRONS TRAVEL IN ONE DIRECTION WHEN THE CURVE
IS IN THE POSITIVE QUADRANT, BUT REVERSE AND FLOW
THE OPPOSITE DIRECTION WHEN IT IS IN THE NEGATIVE ONE.

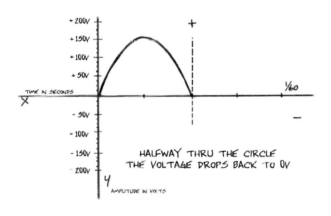

HALFWAY THRU THE CIRCLE
THE VOLTAGE DROPS BACK TO 0V

A graph is typically used to display the manner in which AC produces a voltage. The x axis represents time in seconds; the y axis represents the strength of the EMF, given in volts. The graph shows one complete 360-degree circle through the magnetic field. The shape of this graph is a special type of curve known as a *sine wave*.

A sine curve is a specific shape. You may have noticed that it appears to slope upward most rapidly near the x axis, and that its rate of change slows dramatically near the top of the curve.

Notice that the peak voltage of the graph is around 151 volts, in either the positive or negative quadrants. Even so, the voltage represented on most of the graph is much lower than the nominal 120 volts that AC is stated to have. Because the voltage pressure is constantly changing over time, a special method is used to describe that pressure. AC voltages are expressed as an *RMS* average. RMS stands for *root mean square*, which is a mathematical method of determining the mean distance of a point on the graph of a sine curve from the x axis. For standard line voltage, that mean, or average, is 120 VAC. The sine wave graph is important to stage electricians, because it is the only way to graphically demonstrate how modern stage dimmers work. You will see it again in the discussion of dimmers. This type of graph is also used to show how 240 v single-phase or three-phase power works.

Rather than having a positive and a negative terminal like a direct current battery, AC is said to have a *hot* and a *neutral*. The "hot" is the wire used to push electrons through the circuit. The word *hot* is indicative of the fact that this conductor is energized. The neutral is the wire that provides a resting place for electrons to go when they are not being used. Even though the neutral does not carry any usable electrons, it must be in place for the circuit to be closed and to operate. When wiring electrical devices, it is important to make sure that the hot and neutral wires are attached to the proper terminals, or they may not be safe.

The hot wire is connected to the generator on the side where electrons are being pushed because of the inductive force. The neutral wire is used to complete the electrical circuit, but in many ways mimics the action of a capacitor.

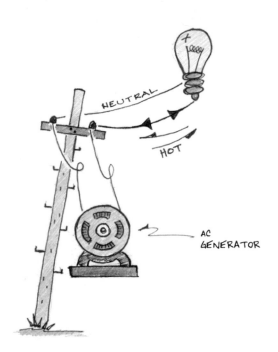

ALTERNATING CURRENT

AC HAS A HOT AND A NEUTRAL RATHER THAN A PLUS AND MINUS LIKE IN DIRECT CURRENT

In electronics, *capacitors* are used to store electrons. Electrons can be "bunched up" inside a capacitor in proportion to the voltage pressure in a circuit and released later on when the pressure drops. The neutral conductor acts in a similar manner, allowing electrons a place to rest temporarily. When the voltage pressure of the sine wave increases, as it does in the positive quadrant of the sine wave, electrons are fed into the neutral. When the voltage pressure drops below zero, electrons begin to move out of the neutral and back into the hot conductor.

Touching a hot conductor will allow at least some electrons to flow into your body, a hand perhaps. It may be that the resistances of the various pathways are such that you will receive only a tingling sensation. However, if you are "grounded out" by a puddle of water or some other method of conduction, you might receive a deadly shock as the current passes through your heart to get to the ions in the puddle of water.

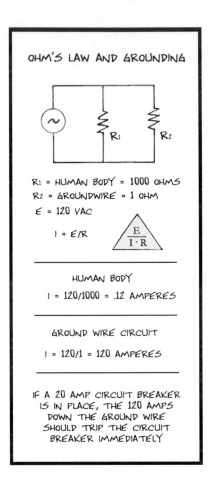

OHM'S LAW AND GROUNDING

R1 = HUMAN BODY = 1000 OHMS
R2 = GROUNDWIRE = 1 OHM
E = 120 VAC

I = E/R $\frac{E}{I \cdot R}$

HUMAN BODY

I = 120/1000 = .12 AMPERES

GROUND WIRE CIRCUIT

I = 120/1 = 120 AMPERES

IF A 20 AMP CIRCUIT BREAKER IS IN PLACE, THE 120 AMPS DOWN THE GROUND WIRE SHOULD TRIP THE CIRCUIT BREAKER IMMEDIATELY

Grounding does not guarantee safety. Normally, a ground wire is used to make AC current safer by providing an alternate path or circuit for electrons to take that has less resistance than the pathway through a person's body. Because the body acts as a resistor in parallel with a short circuit, and the ground wire has only the very small resistance of the wire itself, it will naturally draw off most of the current. If no ground wire is present, the full amount of the current will pass through your body, which can be deadly.

TRANSFORMERS, AC TRANSMISSION, AND THE POWER LOSS FORMULA

Power on overhead lines runs at a very high voltage, because that is the most efficient method of transmission. High-voltage electricity loses less power to resistance over long-distance wires. Power loss in a circuit is determined by the formula $P_{LOSS} = P^2R/E^2$. Because the value of E is squared in the denominator, the higher the voltage is, the smaller the total power loss will be for a given amount of current and resistance. The current running through transmission lines is actually quite tiny. The current can be small because a large voltage and a small current will still create a reasonable amount of power, as demonstrated by the P = IE formula.

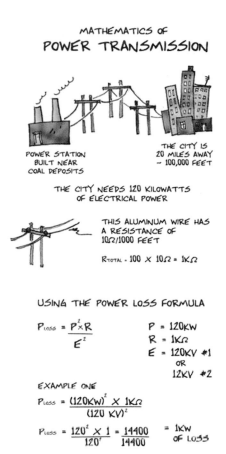

MATHEMATICS OF
POWER TRANSMISSION

POWER STATION BUILT NEAR COAL DEPOSITS

THE CITY IS 20 MILES AWAY ~ 100,000 FEET

THE CITY NEEDS 120 KILOWATTS OF ELECTRICAL POWER

THIS ALUMINUM WIRE HAS A RESISTANCE OF $10\Omega/1000$ FEET

$R_{TOTAL} = 100 \times 10\Omega = 1K\Omega$

USING THE POWER LOSS FORMULA

$$P_{LOSS} = \frac{P^2 \times R}{E^2}$$

P = 120KW
R = 1KΩ
E = 120KV #1
OR
12KV #2

EXAMPLE ONE

$$P_{LOSS} = \frac{(120KW)^2 \times 1K\Omega}{(120 KV)^2}$$

$$P_{LOSS} = \frac{120^2 \times 1}{120^2} = \frac{14400}{14400} \quad = 1KW \text{ OF LOSS}$$

EXAMPLE TWO

$$P_{LOSS} = \frac{(120KW)^2 \times 1K\Omega}{(12 KV)^2}$$

$$P_{LOSS} = \frac{120^2 \times 1}{12^2} = \frac{14400}{144} \quad = 100KW \text{ OF LOSS}$$

TRANSFORMERS

A transformer is used to transform, reduce, or step down, the high voltage to a more user-friendly 120 v. *Transformers* are aptly named, because their function is to "transform" or change the voltage in a circuit. A basic transformer consists of two coils of enamel-coated magnet wire that are wrapped around an armature made of laminated steel plates. The coil of wire that is in series with the incoming voltage is known as the *primary*. The coil of wire that is in series with the outgoing, altered voltage is known as the *secondary*. Both of these coils of wire are wrapped around the same *iron core*. The iron core is used to focus the magnetic force created by the primary.

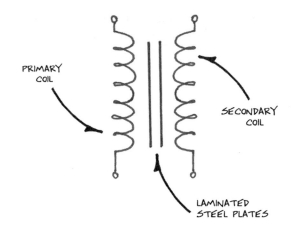

PRIMARY COIL

SECONDARY COIL

LAMINATED STEEL PLATES

SCHEMATIC SYMBOL
OF A TRANSFORMER

In order to understand how a transformer works, you must study it in conjunction with the AC current that feeds it. The rise and fall of an alternating current in relation to its sine wave is central to the workings of a transformer. As the incoming current, in series with the primary coil, gains voltage strength in the first part of its cycle, a building magnetic field is formed around the iron core of the transformer. As the AC cycle continues, the magnetic field reaches its peak, and then collapses to zero as the voltage reaches the x axis on our graph. It then reforms with its magnetic poles *in the opposite direction* as the AC cycle reverses its current flow. That process is repeated over and over—60 times per second. This creates a constantly moving magnetic field, but it is due to electrical forces, not the physical forces found in a rotating generator.

In a transformer, the graph of the voltage in the secondary is the exact opposite of the primary. If the function of the transformer is to lower the voltage of the circuit, a graph of both the primary and secondary voltages might look like the following figure.

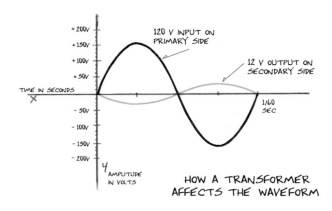

120 V INPUT ON PRIMARY SIDE

12 V OUTPUT ON SECONDARY SIDE

TIME IN SECONDS

1/60 SEC

AMPLITUDE IN VOLTS

HOW A TRANSFORMER
AFFECTS THE WAVEFORM

Transformers do not work with DC current; in fact, they are used to block it from some audio circuits. Even though DC develops a magnetic field in the primary coil as its voltage builds, once it has established that field, it becomes static, and remains in a steady state. Because the field is static and not moving, it will not continue to induce a current in the secondary coil.

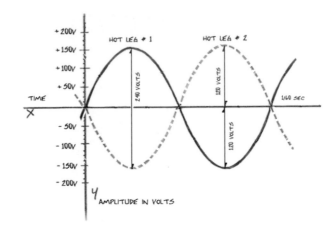

THIS TRANSFORMER IN A RESIDENTIAL AREA STEPS DOWN VOLTAGE TO SEVERAL HOUSES.

THE CENTER TAPPED TRANSFORMER CREATES VOLTAGES THAT ARE EQUAL TO EACH OTHER, BUT OPPOSITE. THE RMS VOLTAGE FROM EITHER ONE TO THE X AXIS IS 120 VAC, BUT FROM THE TOP OF ONE TO THE BOTTOM OF THE OTHER IS 240 VAC. IN THIS DRAWING, THE X AXIS REPRESENTS THE POSITION OF THE NEUTRAL.

In Edison's day, using DC current, it was necessary to have a power generating station every few blocks, because the resistance of the distribution wires themselves, in series with the intended load in a home or business, would seriously degrade the voltage available to the end user. Even though Edison's power company used extremely large conductors for their DC grid, the distances they could effectively span were quite short by modern standards. Today, power transmission lines can be hundreds of miles long, because they use AC power in conjunction with transformers rather than DC.

Different types of transformers are used for specific jobs, sometimes to create a lower voltage, and sometimes to create a higher one. Fluorescent lighting requires a very high voltage, so those fixtures have a special step-up transformer in them. Center-tapped transformers are a special type used to create two voltages of equal but opposite polarity. They are used to create the ubiquitous 120/240-volt service found in homes and elsewhere. The secondary winding of the transformer has a tap in the middle, which means that there are three wires coming from that side. The center one is the ground, or neutral potential. The other two have the same voltage, but the graphs of the sine curves are opposite to one another. The voltage potential from one of the hots to the neutral is 120 volts. From one of the hots to the other hot is 240 volts, peak to peak. So this type of transformer can supply either 120 volts of pressure or 240 volts of pressure.

COPPER WIRE RESISTANCE TABLE

AWG	Feet/Ω	Ω/100ft	Ampacity*
10	490.2 ft	.204Ω	30A
12	308.7 ft	.324Ω	20A
14	193.8 ft	.516Ω	15A
16	122.3 ft	.818Ω	10A
18	76.8 ft	1.30Ω	5A
20	48.1 ft	2.08Ω	3A
22	30.3 ft	3.30Ω	2A
24	19.1 ft	5.24Ω	1A

A LARGER AWG NUMBER MEANS A SMALLER WIRE, JUST THE OPPOSITE OF WHAT YOU MIGHT THINK. LARGER WIRES CARRY MORE CURRENT, AND HAVE LESS RESISTANCE TO CURRENT FLOW. MOST BUILDINGS HAVE AWG #12 AS A STANDARD SIZE FOR LIGHTING CIRCUITS, BUT SOME WIRES ARE MUCH LARGER.

CHAPTER 7

POWER DISTRIBUTION

Power circuits are used to supply AC current to devices throughout a theatre. Often the words *line voltage* or *main* are used to describe the supply of 120 VAC power. This chapter is concerned with the methods used to distribute line voltage from an external source into a theatre and within the theatre itself.

Some of the information in this chapter would apply to electrical work in any field, but the entertainment business uses very specialized equipment that differs substantially from what may be used in other industries. A lot of theatre practice is meant to be temporary, given the changeable nature of the business. Power distribution systems may be set up for one show, and changed for another. Portable cables are used to bring power and data to equipment, rather than using traditional hard-wired methods. Because entertainment depends on rapidly changing from one show to another, special devices are used to connect parts of the system together quickly, and to strike them just as quickly at the end of the show.

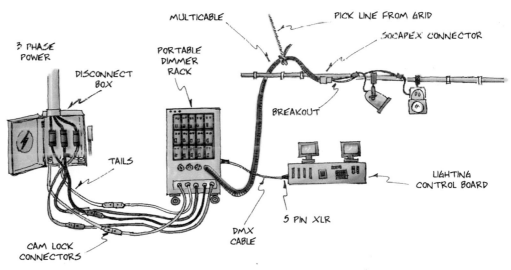

PARTS OF A PORTABLE SYSTEM

A TOURING RIG MAKES A GOOD EXAMPLE, BECAUSE IT IS EASIER TO SEE HOW THE PARTS FIT TOGETHER WHEN THEY AREN'T BURIED INSIDE A WALL

ELECTRICAL SERVICE

Most homes, and some theatre installations, use a *240v service*. The three conductors that make up the system consist of a bare aluminum neutral and two insulated hot legs. The twisted pair of black insulated wires is usually twined around the neutral.

doi: 10.1016/C2009-0-23409-X

A pole transformer steps down a higher voltage to 120 VAC using a center-tapped secondary to create the two hots. The sine curves of the two hot legs are inversely proportional to one another, and as a result, voltage measurements taken show that 120-volt potential exists between either of the two hot legs and the neutral, but this potential is 240 volts between the two hots. This is just like the description in the previous chapter.

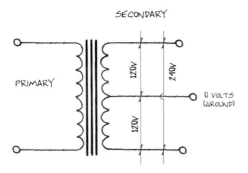

SECONDARY

PRIMARY

120v

240v

120v

0 VOLTS
(GROUND)

A TRANSFORMER FOR 240 VOLT SERVICE
STEPS DOWN VOLTAGE LIKE THIS.

THERE ARE TWO 120 VOLT LEGS AND
ONE NEUTRAL. A CENTER-TAPPED
TRANSFORMER CREATES A +120 VOLT
LEG, AND A -120 VOLT LEG BECAUSE
THE TWO SINE CURVES ARE EXACTLY
OPPOSITE OF ONE ANOTHER. MEASURING
THE VOLTAGE ACROSS EITHER HOT LEG
AND THE NEUTRAL GIVES 120 VOLTS.
MEASURING THE VOLTAGE ACROSS THE
TWO HOTS GIVES 240 VOLTS.

One neutral is used for both hots. It might seem as though the neutral would be carrying twice the current load as either of the two hot wires, and thus should be physically larger in size than either of them in order to carry the load. But, because the two voltages are opposite one another, the electrons in the current from one are gone when the others arrive.

A system using 240v service must split up the current between the dimmers so that half of them are connected to the first hot leg, and the others are connected to the second one. The neutral completes the circuit for both of them. No dimmers should be connected to both hots, as this would supply too much pressure and burn them out in short order.

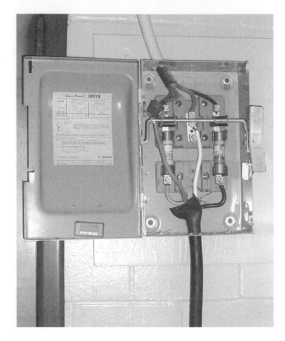

A DISCONNECT BOX FOR
220/240 POWER

THE FUSES CONNECT THE TWO HOTS, THE NEUTRAL
IS IN THE CENTER, AND THE GROUND RUNS UP TOP

THREE-PHASE POWER

In a power station generator, the movement of a coil of wire in a circle inside a magnetic field produces an alternating current that fluctuates from positive to negative in a regular pattern called the *sine wave*. A power station generator is a very large device, and operates more efficiently if more than one current is produced at the same time. *Three-phase power* (3φ) is the most common type of polyphase circuit. The phi symbol, φ, is used to denote phase. Remember that a standard 120v sine wave looks like the following figure.

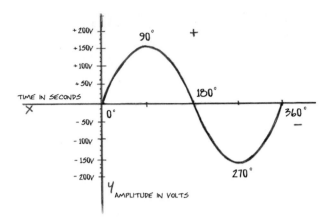

STANDARD 120 VOLT SINE WAVE GRAPH

THE DEGREE MARKINGS REPRESENT THE POSITION
OF THE WIRE COIL IN THE GENERATOR.

As the coil of wire in the generator makes its 360-degree circular journey through the generator's magnetic field, the voltage induced rises to a peak after the first 90 degrees, drops back to zero after 180 degrees, reaches a peak reverse flow at 270 degrees, and then returns to zero at the 360-degree mark. What would happen if there were more than one single coil of wire in the generator? If three *electrically insulated* coils are used instead of one, three separate and distinct currents are formed. If the coils of wire are equally spaced inside the generator, then the sine waves of the three currents will be identical in shape but happen at different times or in different *phases*. The generator will produce three times the electrical power, but use the same amount of mechanical energy to do it. The resulting three-phase current is represented graphically in the following figure.

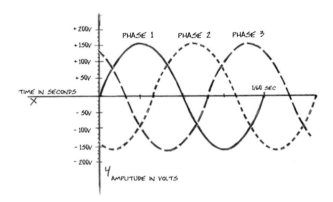

VOLTAGE FLUCTUATION IN THREE-PHASE POWER

It is important to realize that the three phases are actually present on three different conductors that are electrically insulated from one another, and that this graph represents only how the phases relate to one another.

After the three-phase power is generated, it must be distributed on different conductors in order to maintain the separate phase arrangement. On a pole, the conductors might be arranged like the following figure.

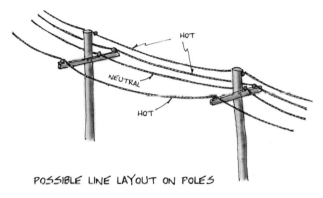

POSSIBLE LINE LAYOUT ON POLES

Notice that there are three hot legs, but only one neutral. Because the current of the phases is running at different times and each places a demand on the neutral in a different way, it is not necessary to have separate neutral conductors for each of the hot legs.

Larger lighting systems are virtually universal in their use of 3ϕ power rather than 240 single phase. Remember that with 240 power, half of the dimmers are connected to one of the 120-volt legs, and the other half is connected to the other hot leg. In 3ϕ power, one-third of the dimmers are connected to each of the three hot legs. There are two configurations of 3ϕ power: *wye* and *delta*. The delta configuration is used primarily in factories and is not often seen in theatres, where the wye configuration is standard. Wye gets its name from the Y shape formed by the three secondary coils that form the output of the transformer. These coils are contained within a transformer that is part of the building structure, probably in a vault in an inaccessible place. They will never be directly used by a stage electrician, but it is helpful to understand how they supply power to the dimming system.

THREE-PHASE POWER, Y CONNECTION

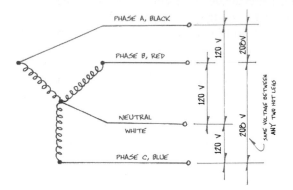

THIS TRANSFORMER IS SET UP IN THE "Y" CONFIGURATION. NOTICE THAT ONE END OF EACH OF THE SECONDARY COILS IS JOINED TOGETHER. EACH OF THE FREE ENDS BECOMES ONE OF THE HOT CONDUCTORS OR "LEGS". THE VOLTAGE POTENTIAL OF ANY HOT LEG AND THE NEUTRAL IS 120 VAC. THE VOLTAGE POTENTIAL BETWEEN ANY TWO OF THE HOT LEGS IS 208 VAC BECAUSE OF THE WAY THE TWO SINE WAVES MERGE TOGETHER. SOME EQUIPMENT IS INTENDED TO OPERATE ON 208 VOLTAGE, BUT MOST OF THE TIME SEPARATE CONNECTIONS ARE MADE TO EACH HOT LEG TO MAKE THREE SEPARATE 120 VOLT SERVICES.

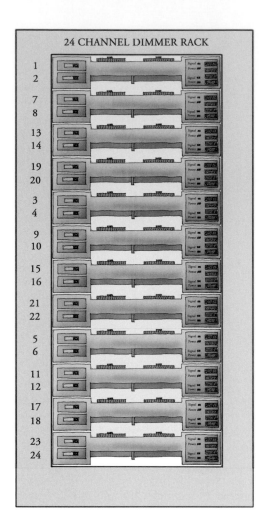

THE NUMBERING SYSTEM SEEMS PECULIAR

For a wye connection, the voltage pressure between any two of the hot legs is 208 volts, and the voltage between any one of the three hot legs and the neutral is 120 volts. In the rack, dimmers are arranged so that one-third are connected to the *phase A* hot leg, one-third to *phase B*, and one-third to *phase C*. As a result, each dimmer has an input of 120 volts. All phases use the same neutral connection, which works out okay, because the different phases are using the neutral at different times. If the loading on each phase A, B, and C is the same, the neutral will not have a voltage potential on it, but if the phases have unequal loads, a dangerous imbalance may exist, and it is possible for the neutral to produce an electrical shock.

You may notice that the dimmers in an ETC Sensor rack seem to have a very odd numbering system, and that the numbers skip around something like the following figure.

There is a reason for the number skipping. When dimmers are inserted into a rack, connectors on the back meet up with a *bus bar*, which is the end of the phase connection. The bus bar is one solid piece, and one-third of the dimmers in the rack must mate with each of the bus bars. The dimmers are in groups of two, so the numbers 1, 2, 7, 8, 13, 14, 19, 20 fall together in order on the phase A bus bar; 3, 4, 9, 10, 15, 16, 20, 21 on the phase B; and 5, 6, 11, 12, 17, 18, 23, 24 on the phase C. *(Note: Sensor racks actually have more dimmers in them, but this number makes it easier to demonstrate.)*

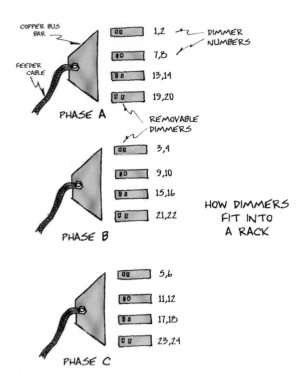

PHASE A

1,2 — DIMMER NUMBERS

7,8

13,14

19,20

REMOVABLE DIMMERS

COPPER BUS BAR

FEEDER CABLE

PHASE B

3,4

9,10

15,16

21,22

HOW DIMMERS FIT INTO A RACK

PHASE C

5,6

11,12

17,18

23,24

THE ODD NUMBERING SYSTEM IS INTENDED TO KEEP ALL PHASES AT THE SAME LOAD LEVEL

determined by the number of fuses in the panel. 240v service has two fuses inside, one for each of the hot legs. Three-phase power has three fuses. Voltages in either case should be 120v from any hot to the neutral, 120v from any hot to the ground wire, and 0v from the ground to the neutral. If the panel contains 240v single-phase the potential from one hot to another should be 240v and for three-phase 208v.

System design engineers prefer to spread the load of all the dimmers evenly between the three phases of the power supply so that the load on the neutral is balanced. If the dimmer numbers of all circuits on the first lighting position are 1 through 24, and all of the lights hung on it are on at the same time, the load should be evenly shared between the three phases. Although it is impossible to predict in advance how a lighting designer may choose to divide up which lights are on at any particular moment, lighting systems engineers feel that this is their best attempt at doing so.

CABLES AND CONNECTORS

In a large, permanent theatre installation, the *feeder cable* to the dimmer racks is most likely in a conduit that runs directly into the dimmer racks and does not need to be changed from show to show. Portable equipment, on the other hand, must be supplied with power by means of a *disconnect box*. This setup is by its very nature temporary, and is the type used by touring shows that travel with their own dimming equipment. The disconnect panel could be either a smaller 240v single-phase type, or it could be three-phase, as in a professional theatre. The type of disconnect you have can be

DISCONNECT FOR 3-PHASE POWER

NOTE THE 3 HOT LEGS WITH FUSES WHITE TAPE ON NEUTRAL BUSS AT LEFT GROUND CONNECTION AT THE BOTTOM

Typically, a disconnect box has a handle on the right-hand side that must be pulled down before the box will open. The handle disengages the power to the connections inside making them safer to handle. Large *cartridge fuses* denote the current carrying capacity of the system. There should be a fuse for each hot leg, but none for the neutral. The total amperage available from the panel is the total of the amounts stamped on the fuses. If 200-amp fuses are in use, the total available current would be 600 amps, which is enough for thirty 20-amp dimmers working at full capacity. At the bottom of the box, directly under each of the fuses, is a *terminal lug,* one for each of the hots. When a disconnect is used for a permanent installation, the dimmers are hardwired to the box, which then may be used more or less as a giant off-on switch for repair purposes.

CAM LOCKS ARE USED FOR SINGLE CONDUCTOR CABLES

IF THE PICTURE WERE IN COLOR YOU COULD SEE HOW THE TAPE IS USED FOR COLOR CODING.

THIS TYPE OF CARTRIDGE FUSE IS FREQUENTLY USED IN A LARGE CAPACITY DISCONNECT PANEL

Tails are used to make the connection with the disconnect box. These are short sections of cable that have a female connector on one end and bare wire on the other. The bare wire is wrenched down to one of the lugs in the disconnect box. It feeds out through an appropriate opening and is given a *strain relief,* which might be a conduit clamp, or simply tying all the conductors up with line, so that pulling on the extensions will not place a mechanical strain on the terminal lug. It is common practice when working with #0000 feeder cable to make the ground connection first, then the neutral, and then the three hots. If there is some misadventure, this procedure will ensure that the ground is in place before any current can reach the equipment.

On a touring setup, the disconnect box is used to supply power to portable dimmer racks. Very special wiring is used for this purpose, most often *#0000 (four-ought)* entertainment cable with a heavy *SO* rubber sheathing on the outside that provides insulation. Each conductor is run separately, and each has its own connector for just the one wire. *Cam lock* connectors are used to connect various sections of the wire. Cam locks come in male and female versions, just like other connectors, with the female being the source of current and the male pointing toward the power. Obviously, if the male connector with its exposed brass fitting were energized, the risk of electrical shock would be huge. Sometimes the neutral wire is run backward, as the theoretical chance of electrical shock is small, and reversing the connectors makes it impossible to accidentally misconnect the neutral and one of the hots.

TWO PIN AND GROUND MALE PIN CONNECTOR

The most common theatrical connector for regular 20-amp power circuits is the *pin connector*, but a second type, the *twist lock*, is also popular. The pin connector has been around for many decades and is extremely durable. The quarter-inch-diameter brass pins are almost impossible to break off. As a safety feature, the ground pin in the center is slightly longer than the other pins, so that the ground connection makes up first. The neutral is located closest to the ground, and the hot is on the far side. Early versions were not grounded, and had no center pin.

20 AMP JUMPER WITH PIN CONNECTORS, COLOR CODING TAPE, AND TIE LINE FOR STORAGE PURPOSES.

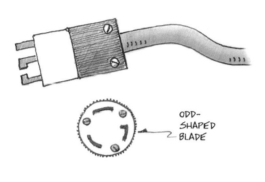

ODD-SHAPED BLADE

TWO PIN AND GROUND TWIST LOCK MALE

Twist locks have the obvious advantage of a positive method of making sure that the connection stays together. When a stagehand twists them together, the two halves lock and won't accidentally become disconnected. On the other hand, pin connectors can come apart when someone accidentally pulls on the cable, unless they are tied or taped together. But twist-lock connectors are not as sturdy as the pin connector, the blades tend to bend easily, and it is sometimes difficult to line them up with the proper holes without looking closely. There are many brands and types of twist locks, for different ampacities. Pin connectors come only in 20-amp (the most common) and 60-amp (very rare) versions.

When a lighting fixture in a theatre is hung too far away from a circuit box for its own pigtail to reach the receptacle, a *jumper* is used to bridge the gap. They are like extension cords for lighting. Most theatres have ready made jumpers in specific lengths on hand at all times. If a theatre has lots of circuits in all the right places, it may not need many jumpers. If the circuits are in inconvenient places, it may need many jumpers.

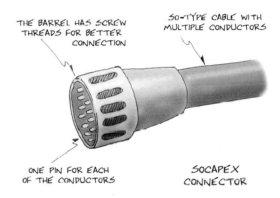

THE BARREL HAS SCREW THREADS FOR BETTER CONNECTION

SO-TYPE CABLE WITH MULTIPLE CONDUCTORS

ONE PIN FOR EACH OF THE CONDUCTORS

SOCAPEX CONNECTOR

Socapex makes a multiconnector with 19 pins for *multicables* that have that many conductors. They are often used when a large number of wires must be run, such as in a touring rig. A six-circuit multicable is much easier to manipulate than six separate runs of 12/3 SO jumpers. A 19-pin Socapex connector can be used to make up a multi that services six lighting circuits, each having a separate hot/neutral/ground, with one pin left spare. A *breakout* is used at the end of the cable to separate it into individual circuits. Frequently, the dimmer system has female Socapex connections on the back so that no breakout is required there.

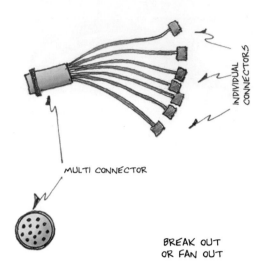

INDIVIDUAL CONNECTORS

MULTI CONNECTOR

BREAK OUT
OR FAN OUT

CATEGOREY FIVE
OR "CAT 5" CABLES
ARE OFTEN USED FOR
ETHERNET CONNECTIONS

Modern lighting systems also use *XLR connectors* for control functions between the board and dimmer racks, moving fixture lights and other peripheral equipment that requires a digital signal to operate. These cables are not expected to carry large amounts of current, and as a result they are physically much smaller. Three-pin XLRs of the sort very commonly used for microphones are also used for moving fixture lights.

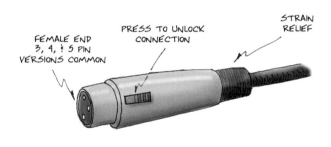

FEMALE END
3, 4, ¦ 5 PIN
VERSIONS COMMON

PRESS TO UNLOCK
CONNECTION

STRAIN
RELIEF

3 PIN XLR CONNECTOR

Four-pin XLRs are often used for color changers/scrollers. Two of the pins transmit data, and the other two carry the DC voltage used to run the motors. The five-pin version is meant for DMX transmission from the light board. DMX 512A is the computer program protocol used in the entertainment industry. It is sometimes very frustrating to have three different, but very similar connector types, but they are actually used for different purposes, so this helps to keep the wrong cable from being selected. *Category 5 computer cables* are also used, if the system has an *Ethernet* hub.

ELECTRICAL WIRES

The size of a wire used to conduct electricity is determined by its *AWG* (*American Wire Gauge*) number. For the most part, the larger the gauge number, the smaller the wire is. So #20 wire is actually much smaller than #10 wire—just the opposite of what might seem intuitive. The largest wire used in the entertainment industry is #0000 (four ought) feeder cable, which is larger in diameter than #00. The conducting wire in #0000 cable is about as big in diameter as a roll of pennies, so you can imagine how heavy it is.

Wire can be made *solid* or *stranded*. Stranded electrical cable is much easier to bend, so it only makes sense that portable cables such as those used in theatres should be of the stranded variety. Solid copper wire is used in permanent installations where the cable never needs to be moved about. Solid wire mistakenly used in a situation requiring mobility will soon develop metal fatigue and become dangerous.

Larger-gauge wires with more copper in them are able to carry more current than small ones, but the voltage capability depends on the insulation surrounding the conductor. Rubber insulation is preferred for theatre cabling, and the code for that is a variant of type S, usually *SO* or *SJ*. SJ insulation is somewhat lighter and thinner than SO. It is rated at 300 volts; the SO is rated at 600 volts. Notice that the copper wire is rated in amps and the insulation is rated in volts. Remember that insulation is designed to contain the voltage pressure, and to keep the wire from shorting out. The copper wire is designed to carry the actual electrons. Although SO insulation is rated at 600 volts, the power running through the wires is only 120v, so the extra protection is really just a safety factor.

APPROXIMATE AMPACITIES OF GAUGES	
#0000	225 amps
#00	175 amps
#4	80 amps
#8	46 amps
#12	20 amps
#16	13 amps
#20	7.5 amps
#30	0.5 amps

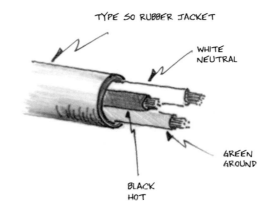

12/3 SO CABLE FOR JUMPERS

The exact ampacity of any conductor is affected by a large number of factors like the metal alloy used, the size and number of the strands, the frequency of the sine wave, temperature, and all sorts of other peculiar details. Most portable lighting cables are made from #12 wire, because it can easily handle a 20-amp load, which is the most common dimmer rating. This cable may be referred to as "12/3 SO," which indicates that it is 12-gauge, three conductors (hot/neutral/ground), with type SO rubber insulation on the outside. Type SO has been the standard for many years, but recently SJ has become very popular as well. SJ is much lighter in weight, and thus more easily carried, but its smaller diameter can be problematic when making a connection to the strain relief of a pin connector designed for the larger-diameter SO.

The various conductors inside a jumper are each sheathed in insulation of their own to keep them separated from one another. Although the outside insulation is black, a standard color coding is used to tell the individual conductors apart on the inside. This color code is not just for theatres, but is used in all different types of electrical work.

TROUBLESHOOTING

Troubleshooting is the name given to a methodology for fault finding. In electrical work, troubleshooting most often occurs when something either doesn't work at all or doesn't work properly. It requires the use of logic to deduct and infer from a given set of facts what could be the cause of a certain fault. Efficient troubleshooting requires an understanding of Ohm's law, series and parallel circuits, induction, and so forth. In short, it requires all of the things you have been reading about so far.

Fault finding requires a logical process of investigation. It is generally best to check the components most likely to have failed first, and/or things that are easiest to check. Checking to see whether the fixture is properly plugged in and whether it has a bulb in it is very easily accomplished, so it intuitively makes sense to try that first. An amazing number of electrical faults are just that simple.

When a theatre light is moved from one place to another, it is necessary to unplug it first. It is human nature to tug on the cord at least a little bit when doing that. Connectors like a stage pin connector or twist-lock often have wires come loose, so look there for an open circuit. Burned-out lamps and connectors with wires loose are the most common causes of a fixture not lighting up when its circuit is hot.

Sometimes, the problem inside a fixture cannot be easily detected with the naked eye. You can use a VOM, or volt-ohm meter, to check all of the components in an entire fixture at one time, without taking anything apart. The fixture must be *de-energized*, or disconnected from the source of power. Use the meter to read resistance, measured in ohms.

Imagine that a group of lights have been hung side by side on the first electric. You bring up all the lights with the lightboard to see whether they all work. One does not, but why? Unplug a light next to the defective one, and plug it into the circuit of the nonworking light. If your test light works, then logic dictates that the problem must be in the original light itself and not in the power coming from the system. If the second lamp does not light, you should intuit that there is no power at the circuit outlet.

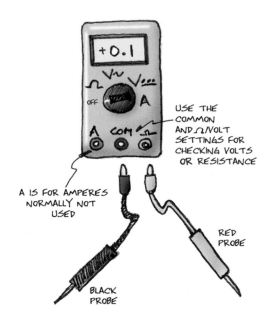

USE THE COMMON AND Ω/VOLT SETTINGS FOR CHECKING VOLTS OR RESISTANCE

A IS FOR AMPERES NORMALLY NOT USED

RED PROBE

BLACK PROBE

TO CHECK RESISTANCE, SUCH AS WHEN TESTING FOR CONTINUITY THROUGH A FIXTURE OR CABLE, SET THE DIAL ON THE METER TO OHMS - Ω. WHEN CHECKING THE VOLTAGE AVAILABLE IN A CIRCUIT SET THE DIAL TO ~V. THAT SETTING IS CORRECT FOR ALTERNATING CURRENT. NOTICE HOW THE TILDE IS SIMILAR TO A SINE WAVE. SOME METERS AUTOMATICALLY SET THEMSELVES TO THE CORRECT RANGE, BUT OTHERS MAY REQUIRE YOU TO MAKE A SELECTION.

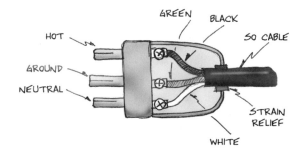

GREEN
BLACK
HOT
SO CABLE
GROUND
NEUTRAL
STRAIN RELIEF
WHITE

THE APPROPRIATE MECHANICS INSIDE A 20 AMP PIN CONNECTOR

MAKE SURE THAT ALL THE TERMINALS ARE TIGHTLY SCREWED DOWN AND THAT THE STRAIN RELIEF HAS A GOOD GRIP ON THE SO INSULATION

Set your meter to read Ωs. Connect the lead from one probe (it doesn't matter which) to the hot pin on the connector and then touch the other probe to the neutral. If the connector is old, and has a lot of corrosion on it, you may need to press the sharp point of the probe into the metal just a bit to get a proper reading. If you get a reading of some low number of ohms, such as less than 20 Ω, then the fixture should be able to light up normally. If you get a reading of infinitely large resistance, then the circuit is open, and most likely a wire is loose or the lamp is blown. Install a new lamp to check which one is at fault.

If you get a very low reading of less than 1 Ω, then there is probably a short circuit in the connector. You can tell that because the meter is reading only the resistance of the pins, and not the resistance through the wire and the lamp filament. Finally, measure the resistance from the ground pin to the metal housing of the fixture itself. A low ohmic reading indicates that the ground wire is working properly, and that it is connected to the metal exterior of the light. An infinitely high reading indicates that the ground wire has become disconnected somewhere.

It is possible for the copper wire inside to break if it is bent back and forth enough times. Stranded wire is meant to take more of that abuse than a solid wire (which should not be used for portable conductors), but even so, it will break after a while. This most often happens right where it bends the most, near the connector or the fixture housing. A fixture that comes on when you jiggle the wire often has a broken conductor.

Your meter can also be used to check a power outlet itself. Set your VOM to AC voltage, which on most meters is marked with a ~ representing the sine wave. Next, you need to set the range of values. Some meters are "auto-ranging," meaning that they will automatically determine the range appropriate to what you are measuring. If not, then you must set the range on the meter itself in accordance with what value you logically expect to find. AC power circuits for stage lighting are always 120 VAC, plus or minus a few volts, when the dimmer is at full. The ranges on most meters are set an order of magnitude apart: 2, 20, 200, and 2k. The 200-volt range is the lowest one larger than 120 volts.

If the power is working properly, you should get a reading of 120 volts between the hot and the neutral conductors. You should also get a reading of 120 volts between the hot and the ground. You should get a reading of 0 volts between the ground and the neutral. It may seem dangerous to connect the meter to 120v service, and you may be worried that it will short out (see the box for explanation), but it will not, as long as you don't accidentally touch anything else with the metal part of the probe. The meter has a very large internal resistance when checking voltage, so the actual current flow inside it is very, very small.

SHORTING OUT VERSUS A BAD CONNECTION

Shorts and *loose connections* are two radically different things. If a fixture "shorts," the hot wire has come loose inside it, and has come into contact with either the neutral or the ground. The entire exterior of a theatre fixture with a metal housing is connected to the ground wire. If the hot should come loose from the socket on the inside of it and it should brush up against the housing, a short circuit will occur when a maximum amount of current rushes through the wires. Often sparks can be seen as the voltage arcs at the point of contact. The circuit breaker will trip, because the very low resistance of the newly created and "shortened" circuit allows too much current to flow all at once. Shorts are common occurrences in connectors where the hot, neutral, and ground wires are very close to one another. The problematic area often has a scorched, blackened look, and is easily recognized.

Loose connections are actually more common than shorts, and most shorts start out as loose connections. When a wire is loose in a connector, an open circuit is formed. Because the circuit is no longer complete, no current can flow, and the light will not come on. The loose wire can be either a hot or a neutral, as both are necessary in order for the circuit to be closed. In either case, the circuit breaker will not have tripped, even though the light remains dark.

A break in the ground wire often goes unnoticed, because lamps work just as well without one. It is a good idea to check fixtures with a meter from time to time to ensure that the grounds are functioning.

In stage work, jumpers are often used to bridge the gap between a circuit box and the light. Because a jumper has a connector on each end, and connectors are frequent failure points, you should consider them in your troubleshooting process. You can use a meter to check them without taking apart the connectors, or just try plugging a light directly into the circuit box to see whether it works without the jumper being series.

The process of checking outlets with a meter is somewhat time-consuming. You can make the job go much faster by investing in a tool that automatically checks an energized circuit. A simple, shop-built checker can be made from a male pin connector, a standard rubber screw base socket, and a 7.5-watt bulb. This unit is small enough to go in your back pocket, and can quickly tell you if a circuit is live or not.

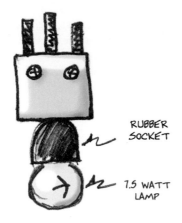

RUBBER SOCKET

7.5 WATT LAMP

A SHOP-BUILT LIGHT LIKE THIS IS SMALL ENOUGH TO CARRY WITH YOU

CIRCUIT TESTER

The *GamChek* is a tool made by Great American that can tell not only whether the circuit is live, but also whether the ground is okay, and whether the hot and neutral are properly wired. Your shop-built tester can't tell you about those things.

Theatre lights have another layer of complexity that our troubleshooting example didn't cover, in that they are fed by a dimmer system, which is controlled by a light board and/or computer. The light may not come on even if all of the electrical connections we've looked into so far are in perfect working condition. If you check the circuit output with either of the two devices mentioned previously and the circuit is not energized, you should turn your attention to the dimmer itself and/or functions of the light board that may need to be corrected. But that is really a control issue, and not an electrical one. Detailed information about the operation of modern dimming equipment is located in Chapter 8, but here are a few of the most common problems:

- Assuming a dimmer per circuit system, is there in fact a dimmer in the slot?
- On ETC systems and many others, if the dimmer is receiving a DMX signal from the board telling it to turn itself on, an LED will light up on the dimmer. If the LED is not lit, no signal is being received.
- If no lights are on anywhere in the system, there may be a global problem with the wiring transmitting the DMX signal and you might need to troubleshoot it, but it is highly unlikely that a cabling issue would affect just one dimmer. You should check to make sure that the proper channel is up on the board, and that the blackout function is not engaged.
- Check whether the dimmer has been properly patched with the channel you are using. If the patch is still set at 1 to 1, then the dimmers should match the channels.
- Very rarely, a problem may develop with a panel-mount connector on a drop box or in a floor pocket.

In general, mechanical issues develop at points of stress, and stress occurs wherever people use the equipment the most.

CHAPTER 8

DIMMERS AND LIGHTING CONTROL

Modern lighting control methods are governed by complex computer systems that make it possible to operate hundreds of lights at one time. They also make it possible to use the many digital lights and accessories developed over the past several decades. Although each manufacturer has its own particular method of handling technical issues, the core technology that makes all of them work is basically the same. Each manufacturer publishes an operator's manual that comes with their equipment. The manual is the best source of information about any specific type of system. Virtually every company makes these manuals available for download online, which is an excellent way to get information about new products.

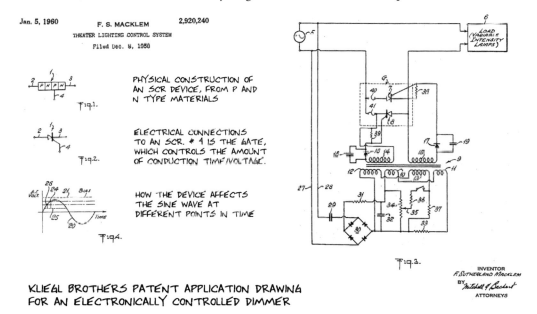

KLIEGL BROTHERS PATENT APPLICATION DRAWING FOR AN ELECTRONICALLY CONTROLLED DIMMER

HISTORICAL PERSPECTIVE

In today's modern world, it is hard to imagine a time before electric lights, but historically speaking, they are a relatively new concept. Gas made from coal was used to light theatres through most of the nineteenth century. The system of controlling the flow of the gas, and hence the brightness of the stage and the distribution of light across it, was quite complex. Gas lights were manipulated by valves, which could make the flames higher or lower, creating artistic effects. When electric lights were first invented, the only means of adjusting them was to switch them on and off. Of course, theatre artists would like to have more subtle control over the look of the stage than simply being able to turn them off and on, so electrical dimmers

doi: 10.1016/C2009-0-23409-X

were invented in order to fade lights in and out and to provide lowered settings for scenes that required them.

Early dimmers worked on the principle of resistance, and created a voltage divider in series with the lightbulbs such that as the dimmer increased its resistance, it got a larger share of the available voltage. When voltage was reduced to the lamps, the light from them faded down. The dimmer's resistance was variable, so lights could fade up and down smoothly. Resistance dimmers of this sort work equally well with either AC or DC current. Most Broadway theatres used DC current well into the twentieth century, because of Edison's influence in New York. But the rest of the country was almost exclusively AC-powered. Resistance dimmers remained popular in New York City until the 1970s.

Other types of dimmers were invented that worked on different principles, but modern electronic dimmers gained widespread acceptance in the 1960s. Electronic dimmers have the distinct advantage that a control system, such as a modern computer board, can be used to operate all of the dimmers at one time. Prior to the invention of electronic dimmers, running lights for a show required numerous electricians, all struggling with switches and dimmer handles.

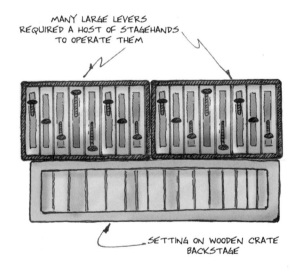

MANY LARGE LEVERS REQUIRED A HOST OF STAGEHANDS TO OPERATE THEM

SETTING ON WOODEN CRATE BACKSTAGE

RESISTANCE DIMMERS OR "PIANO BOARDS" WERE STILL COMMON ON BROADWAY UP UNTIL THE 1970S

Thyristors are a family of semiconductor switching devices that can be used to turn AC electric circuits on and off in relation to a specific point in their sine wave cycle. One of the earliest versions of this device used in theatre lighting was the *silicon-controlled rectifier* or *SCR*, which is still quite common in many power control circuits. More modern dimmers use different components, but the general electronics of how they alter the voltage in an AC circuit remain essentially the same.

Modern electronic dimmers vary the voltage pressure to a lamp by switching the current on and off very rapidly. In the case of an SCR, a control voltage applied to the input gate of the SCR tells it when to conduct. When the line voltage of the circuit drops to zero as it crosses the x axis of the sine wave graph, the SCR shuts off and stops conducting. It must be told by the control circuit to begin conducting again, and remains off until that signal is received. As a result, the control circuit can vary the precise moment that conduction resumes. Remember that the effective voltage of a sine wave is expressed by its root mean square, or RMS.

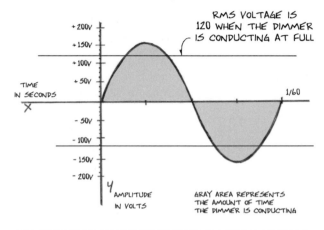

RMS VOLTAGE IS 120 WHEN THE DIMMER IS CONDUCTING AT FULL

TIME IN SECONDS

AMPLITUDE IN VOLTS

GRAY AREA REPRESENTS THE AMOUNT OF TIME THE DIMMER IS CONDUCTING

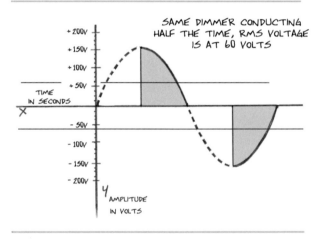

SAME DIMMER CONDUCTING HALF THE TIME, RMS VOLTAGE IS AT 60 VOLTS

TIME IN SECONDS

AMPLITUDE IN VOLTS

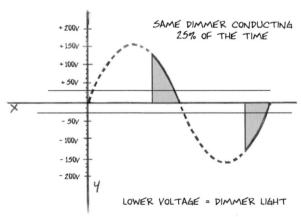

SAME DIMMER CONDUCTING 25% OF THE TIME

LOWER VOLTAGE = DIMMER LIGHT

The graph shows how much time the wave spends conducting, and what effect this has on the RMS voltage. If the control circuit tells the SCR to begin conducting late in the cycle, a smaller voltage is produced. If conduction begins sooner, a larger voltage is produced. SCRs conduct in one direction only, somewhat like a diode, so in order to make use of the entire sine wave, two inversely mounted SCRs are generally used.

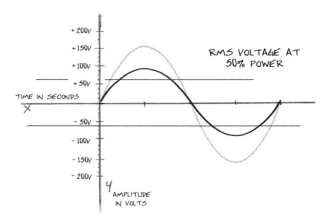

RMS VOLTAGE AT 50% POWER

SINE WAVE DIMMERS WORK DIFFERENTLY, IN THAT THEY ALTER THE AMPLITUDE OF THE WAVEFORM, RATHER THAN CHOPPING IT UP. THE RESULT IS THE SAME, A LOWER VOLTAGE TO THE LIGHT

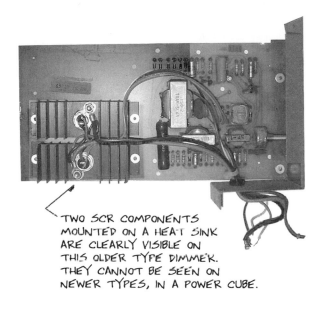

TWO SCR COMPONENTS MOUNTED ON A HEAT SINK ARE CLEARLY VISIBLE ON THIS OLDER TYPE DIMMER. THEY CANNOT BE SEEN ON NEWER TYPES, IN A POWER CUBE.

The newest development in dimmers is the *Sine Wave* type from ETC. Sine Wave dimmers work by lowering the amplitude of the sine curve itself, and thus lowering the RMS apparent voltage. The advantage of the new type lies in its lessening of an effect known as *60-cycle hum*. The filament in most lamps has a curved shape, which mimics the coils of wire used to create a magnetic field through induction. When a current passes through the coil, a magnetic field is established, and when the electrons in the AC current reverse their flow, that magnetic field also reverses. The change in polarity of the magnetic field causes the filament wire to move slightly. When an AC current has a period of 60 cycles per second, the filament moves back and forth at that frequency. Sometimes that movement is audible, especially when the filament is large, as they are in high-wattage lamps, especially those greater than 2 kW. When many lamps are in use, as in a theatre, the noise can be quite loud. When a standard dimmer alters the sine wave to dim lights, the waveform becomes a very rough shape, which increases the hum, especially at reduced voltages. Sine Wave dimmers don't do that, because they don't "chop up" the waveform like a traditional thyristor dimmer does. Altering the amplitude actually reduces the hum effect at lower settings.

Standard ETC Sensor dimmers use two large copper chokes to lessen the 60-cycle hum by smoothing out the waveform. The chokes are the round-shaped inductors in the middle of the dimmer, which occupy most of the space on the inside. There is one choke for each of the two dimmers in the unit. The circuit breakers are on the left, and the power cube is on the right. All of the electronic parts are in the power cube, so if the dimmer fails for some reason, you can repair it easily by replacing the power cube.

ETC SENSOR DIMMER

THERE ARE TWO SENSOR DIMMERS IN EACH MODULE, AND THUS TWO CIRCUIT BREAKERS BOTTOM LEFT AND TWO INDUCTION COILS, OR CHOKES, WHICH ARE IN THE CENTER. A CHOKE IS USED TO SMOOTH OUT THE SINE WAVEFORM.

MOST OF THE ELECTRONICS ARE HELD IN THE "POWER CUBE" TO THE REAR LEFT OF THE MODULE. TYPICALLY, ANY FAILURE OF THE DIMMER CAN BE REPAIRED BY CHANGING OUT THE POWER CUBE

CONTROL EQUIPMENT

The earliest control boards that could take advantage of electronic dimmers came about in the late 1950s, before computers were commonly available. They worked on the principle of presetting groups of dimmer values, which were used by designers to set up a *look* on stage. A look is a specific set of light values created by dimmers that produces an overall effect on stage that the designer wants to see. Quite frequently, designers work by setting up a specific look for a scene, and then varying it to support the action of the play as time passes. If the action of the play returns to the same location several times, the same look, or a variation of it, may be reused each time the action returns.

This method of working developed from the use of *presets*, which could be made up in advance of the cue happening. A group of *sliders* were preset in advance of the cue. One of the earliest examples of this was the *two-scene preset board*, which was very popular in the 1960s and is now making a comeback in small venues. The board was constructed with two sets of sliders, also know as *potentiometers*. These were often called *banks*, and were labeled X/Y or A/B. Each bank had one potentiometer for every dimmer in the system, perhaps 1 through 64. The sliders in a bank were set to specific levels to arrive at a look on stage. The operator could set up the next preset while the first was still in use.

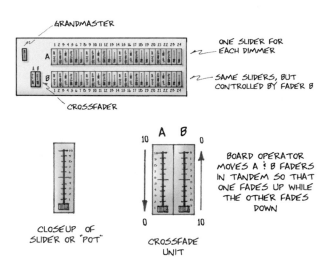

TWO-SCENE PRESET BOARD

THE SYNTAX OF A SYSTEM MEANS THE BASIC GRAMMAR OF HOW IT WORKS. EVEN THE MOST MODERN THEATRE CONTOL CONSOLES OWE MUCH OF THEIR METHOD OF WORKING TO THESE EARLY BOARDS. THAT INCLUDES IDEAS LIKE:

* DESIGNING LIGHTS AROUND THE "LOOKS" CONCEPT

* LINEAR PROGRESSION FROM ONE LOOK TO ANOTHER VIA A "CUE LIST"

* CROSS-FADING FROM ONE LOOK TO ANOTHER

Crossfaders were used to make a smooth change from one preset to the next. A pair of inversely proportional sliders made up the crossfade unit. One read 10 (full) when all the way up, and the other 10 when all

the way down. The operator moved both of these in tandem, causing one scene to fade up while the other faded down.

VERY "RETRO" LOOKING NOW, THIS KLIEGL PERFORMER BOARD WAS STATE OF THE ART IN 1980. THE MONITOR SCREEN WAS BUILT INTO THE HOUSING. THE KEYPAD FUNCTIONS HAD CLOSE TIES TO THE TWO-SCENE PRESET BOARDS THAT PREDATED IT.

Computer boards such as the *Kliegl Performer* constituted a huge change in the lighting design and technology fields, but it is easy to see how they were directly related to earlier types. A careful study of the Performer's keyboard shows its close affiliation with earlier preset board types. Most notably, there is an A/B fader that has A full at the top and B full at the bottom. This was so that the operator could manually fade from one cue to another as was done on a preset board. As an alternative, the operator could use the X or Y fader, which would make the cue happen at the press of the button. This illustrates an important difference between a computer board and any earlier type: the ability for the machine itself to complete a cue over a period of time, with no help from the operator. The fast/slow buttons were used to speed up a lengthy cue to save time when reviewing cues while programming the show.

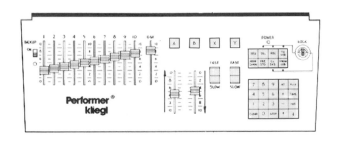

THE KLIEGL BROTHERS PERFORMER KEYPAD WITH A CROSS-FADE UNIT VERY SIMILAR TO WHAT WAS ON PRESET BOARDS OF THE PERIOD

An interesting feature of this board was the inclusion of a backup feature at the left-hand side of the keyboard. The on/off switch can be seen at the far left. *DIP switches* mounted directly on the computer's mother board were used as a matrix to assign one or more channels to each of the sliders. This same type of *dual, in line package* switch is still used today to address some types of digital equipment. By carefully assigning channels into useful groups, and then manipulating them manually, the operator could run a show even if the computer crashed.

Modern control systems don't generally have a backup mode, perhaps because they are more reliable, but more likely because people have become much more trusting of computer systems in general and lighting systems in particular.

Early computer boards stored information digitally, but they still used a 0–10vDC signal to operate the dimmers. It would not be possible to use most of today's accessory equipment with an analog signal, so digital signals are used instead. In the 1980s, various manufacturers agreed to adopt a common system of digital rules that would work with all stage equipment.

DMX 512

The modern *protocol*, or system of rules governing the way that the computer and dimmers communicate with one another, is known as *DMX 512-A*. DMX 512 stands for "Digital Multiplexing 512," which is the method used by lighting equipment manufacturers to send information from a lighting controller to a lighting device. *Multiplexing* is a generic computer term that means to send several different signals over the same line at the same time by varying a factor such as time, space, or frequency. The DMX 512 protocol was first agreed upon in the 1980s as the standard computer "language" for the entertainment industry. It has been revised on occasion, and the newest version is known as DMX 512-A by ANSI, the American National Standards Institute. The full software code instructions can be downloaded from their Web site so that manufacturers can make sure that their equipment is in compliance with the standard. Before DMX became the accepted method, each manufacturer developed its own proprietary code, used only by its company, and as a result a lighting console from one company would not work with dimmers from another one. The adoption of DMX 512 as a standard by all manufacturers meant that incompatibility would no longer be an issue.

Computers communicate with one another via a series of high and low voltages that may also be described

as the numbers 1/0 or true/false. Electronically, these high and low pulses have the graphed appearance of a *square wave*, which is significantly different from the sine wave generated by an alternating current source. In the DMX standard, the ideal high voltage is +5v and the ideal low voltage is –5v. If the wiring involved in connecting the system is very long, has defects in it, or is not the right type, problems with the signal can occur. Resistance may form a voltage divider and cause a drop in voltage on the line, or if the data cable runs too close to an inductive source like a coiled stack of feeder cable, the shape of the square wave could be distorted. The DMX 512-A standard requires that devices be able to receive information when the difference in high/low voltages is as small as 200 mv, or one-fifth of a volt, so in most practical work there shouldn't often be a problem with the voltage drop.

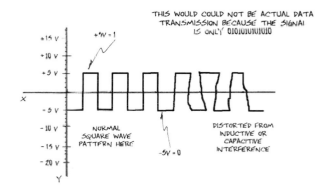

DIGITAL INFORMATION IS SENT VIA SQUARE WAVE

The "512" part of the name comes from the number of separate lines of information that are transmitted at one time by a light board, and corresponds to the number of *channels* available. Each channel has 256 possible values. Computer code numbers are generally some value of 2^n, because they use only two characters (1 and 0) to communicate. 256 is 2^8, and 512 is 2^9.

The light board repeatedly sends out a string of information which tells a dimmer how much voltage to emit, or a moving fixture light what position to take. Each string of information is made up of a long series of high/low voltages that represents each of the 256 values for each of the 512 channels, plus a special start code at the beginning, and a stop code at the end. The start and stop codes are used to synchronize transmission by the light board and its reception by a device. Most electricians won't need to know the intricacies of the code itself, but understanding that there is one makes it easier to understand how the system as a whole operates.

When the DMX 512 standard was set up in the 1980s, it was seen only as a way to control dimmers and not all of the digital equipment in use today. It seemed unlikely at the time that any installation would have more than 512 dimmers, which even now would be a very large number of them. But the DMX signal is now used for much more than just dimmers. As time passed and the issue of digital control of accessory equipment was revealed, it became obvious that 512 channels would no longer be enough, especially when using moving lights. They typically require 16 to 24 channels for each fixture, so the numbers add up rapidly. The DMX standard was set at 512 channels and it was not possible to add more to it without making all previous equipment obsolete. Instead, manufacturers began to use more than one set of DMX in a single light board.

One group of DMX became known as a *universe*, because it is its own complete world, unconnected to any other. It is common for a lighting console to contain two or three universes, and at least one automated board has six universes for working with moving fixture lights. A recently manufactured light board may have multiple *5-pin XLR* outputs, one for each universe. They will be numbered 1-512, 513-1024, and so forth.

Another very interesting and important development used in digital control equipment from the very beginning was the use of *channels* in setting up data recording. *Dimmers* are real, physical devices that control the intensity of lighting fixtures. A channel, on the other hand, is a pathway for information to flow down, and is similar in concept to a television channel. TV channel 22 has one program on it, and channel 37 has another. Information from a cable or satellite provider flows into the television and a program appears on the screen. Information from the lighting computer flows down a control cable to one or more dimmers, and they in turn cause one or more lights to change brightness.

Channels only exist in the digital realm and are really just a means of assigning information to different devices. A channel does not necessarily have to be connected to a dimmer. Accessories like a color scrollers, gobo rotators, and even fog machines can have assigned channel numbers. It is possible to connect more than one dimmer to one channel, but it is not possible to assign more than one channel

number to the same dimmer—which would not be productive, in any case.

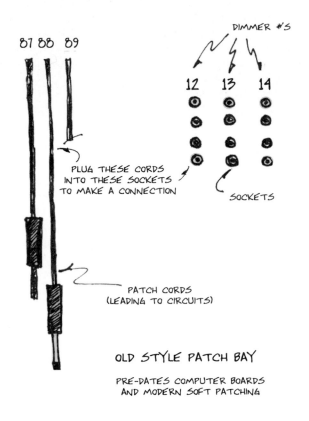

OLD STYLE PATCH BAY

PRE-DATES COMPUTER BOARDS
AND MODERN SOFT PATCHING

Channels and dimmers can be connected with one another by what was once known as *soft-patching,* and now simply *patching*. Although a modern dimmer-per-circuit system has a dimmer for every outlet, early systems generally had a smaller number of dimmers and a larger number of circuits (outlets). A patch panel was used to connect one or more circuits to a dimmer. If the lights in circuits 12, 20, and 58 were designed to always be on at the same value and at the same time, they could all be patched into the same dimmer for convenience and to save on using a limited number of dimmers.

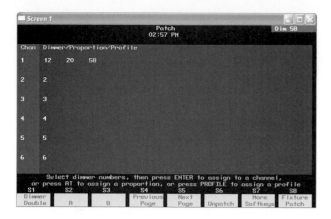

YOU CAN USE THE PATCH SCREEN TO ASSIGN DIMMERS TO CHANNELS ON AN ETC BOARD. HERE DIMMERS 12, 20, & 58 HAVE BEEN PATCHED INTO CHANNEL 1, AND ALL THREE WILL BE ACTIVATED WHEN USING THAT CHANNEL. IN REALITY THOUGH, THERE IS LITTLE REASON TO PATCH MULTIPLE DIMMERS INTO ONE CHANNEL ON A COMPUTER LIGHTING SYSTEM. THE PROGRAM CAN HANDLE AN UNLIMITED NUMBER OF CHANNELS IN ONE CUE.

That approach made sense in a time when dimmers were controlled by hand, and operating too many would be physically difficult. In the present day, all of the dimmers in a system are manipulated by one electrician, literally at the press of a button, so a large number of dimmers has become an asset rather than a liability.

A patch panel was a real, physical entity, but soft-patching occurs only in the computer's memory. After the appropriate menu is selected, dimmers or other accessories are matched with channel numbers. This can be a distinct advantage for a designer or technician, because consecutive channel numbers can be chosen for lights that will commonly be used together, regardless of what circuit/dimmer they may be plugged into. This makes the numbers much easier to remember, and to enter on the keypad. Each target device, like a dimmer, rotator, or strobe unit, has a discrete number location known as its *address*. Dimmers are usually the lowest number addresses, so for a 192-dimmer system, they would be addresses 001 through 192. Addressing devices is covered in more detail later on under the heading "Working with Digital Equipment."

HOOKUP SHEET

Channel	Dimmer	Use	Type	Color	Location
1	2	Down Left Platform	36 deg	Rx 08	3FOH1
2	22	Down Left Platform	36 deg	Rx 60	3FOH12
3	4	Center Platform	36 deg	Rx 08	3FOH2
4	24	Center Platform	36 deg	Rx 60	3FOH13
5	8	Down Right Platform	36 deg	Rx 08	3FOH3
6	26	Down Right Platform	36 deg	Rx 60	3FOH14
7	56	Upstage Platform	36 deg	Rx 08	1FOH7
8	63	Upstage Platform	36 deg	Rx 60	1FOH13
9	5	Front Color Wash	1kFres	SCRLR	3FOH6
10	15	Front Color Wash	1kFres	SCRLR	3FOH12
11	23	Front Color Wash	1kFres	SCRLR	3FOH20
12	98	Back Special	26 deg	NC	2ELEC3
13	97	Scrim Pattern Left	50 deg	Rx 55	1ELEC2
14	107	Scrim Pattern Right	50 deg	Rx 55	1ELEC4
15	96	Down Pattern Wash	50 deg	Rx 16	1ELEC1
16	99	Down Pattern Wash	50 deg	Rx 16	1ELEC3
17	93	Down Pattern Wash	50 deg	Rx 16	1ELEC5
18	102	Down Pattern Wash	50 deg	Rx 16	1ELEC6
19	111	Down Pattern Wash	50 deg	Rx 16	1ELEC7
20	167	Center Side Special Low	26 deg	NC	3ELEC1
21	168	Center Side Special High	26 deg	NC	3ELEC2
22	169	Window Pattern	19 deg	Rx 34	3ELEC3
23	21	Spare	36 deg	NC	3FOH4
24	172	Spare	26 deg	NC	3ELEC4

A HOOKUP SHEET IS USED TO DESCRIBE HOW CHANNELS AND DIMMERS ARE CONNECTED TOGETHER OR "HOOKED UP." CHANNELS ARE LISTED IN CONSECUTIVE ORDER, BECAUSE THEY ARE USED TO PROGRAM THE BOARD. DIMMER NUMBERS ARE RANDOM, AN INDICATION OF HOW THEY ARE SCATTERED ABOUT THE THEATRE. THE HOOKUP ALSO GIVES DETAILS ABOUT HOW AN INSTRUMENT IS USED, TYPE OF FIXTURE, COLOR, AND ITS LOCATION IN THE THEATRE. 3FOH4 = THIRD FRONT OF HOUSE POSITION, FOURTH LIGHT FROM STAGE LEFT.

Entering the patch is guided by use of the *hookup* sheet, a spreadsheet-like document that lists all of the channels in use, and the dimmers that are connected to them. If digital lights and accessories are used, their addresses should also be on the hookup sheet. Patching is accomplished by pressing the patch function key on the control console (also known as a board or desk), which brings up a screen listing the various channels and the dimmers patched into them.

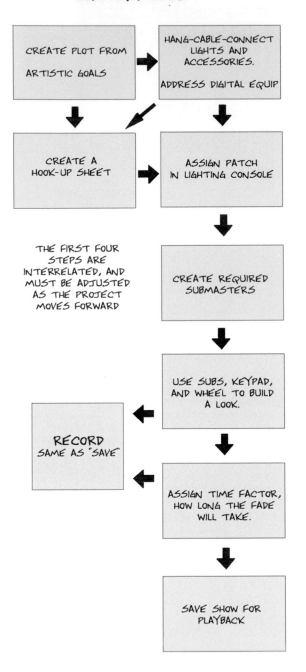

FLOW CHART FOR PROGRAMMING LIGHTING CUES

CREATE PLOT FROM ARTISTIC GOALS

HANG-CABLE-CONNECT LIGHTS AND ACCESSORIES.

ADDRESS DIGITAL EQUIP

CREATE A HOOK-UP SHEET

ASSIGN PATCH IN LIGHTING CONSOLE

THE FIRST FOUR STEPS ARE INTERRELATED, AND MUST BE ADJUSTED AS THE PROJECT MOVES FORWARD

CREATE REQUIRED SUBMASTERS

USE SUBS, KEYPAD, AND WHEEL TO BUILD A LOOK.

RECORD SAME AS "SAVE"

ASSIGN TIME FACTOR, HOW LONG THE FADE WILL TAKE.

SAVE SHOW FOR PLAYBACK

similar throughout. These boards, or *desks*, were originally developed to program cues for static fixtures, meaning regular theatre lights that are not "movers." The programming stream or work organization is different from a moving light desk. Theatre boards are meant to run a single list of cues for a show, from beginning to end. It is assumed that the show will be very tightly scripted, and be exactly the same from night to night. The Expression family of boards was designed to control dimmers. A moving light desk on the other hand is meant to work in a more fluid environment, and has many additional features, such as an effects engine, that can be used to create the many quickly changing effects that moving lights are famous for. The basic theatre-style concepts of recording cues for playback for a show haven't changed all that much from the Kliegl Performer days. Although the Expression was designed to operate static lights, it can also be used to control small numbers of movers.

Many manufacturers offer PC-based versions of the software that is used in their desks, and some programs can be configured to actually run a show with an appropriate output device. The amount of computing power required to run lights is actually quite small. Light boards can be visualized as hardware interfaces that allow you to access the features of the program more easily. It is certainly possible to program lighting cues with a mouse and a keyboard, but the console makes it more ergodynamically convenient.

PARTS OF THE EXPRESSION CONSOLE

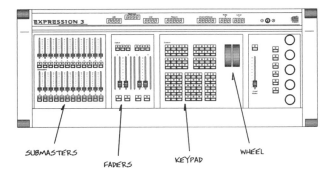

SUBMASTERS   FADERS   KEYPAD   WHEEL

PROGRAMMING THE BOARD

This book uses equipment manufactured by Electronic Theatre Controls or *ETC* in its descriptions, because that company is the most popular at the moment. ETC manufactures the Insight, Express, and Expression boards, and although these different models have different features, navigating the core design philosophy is

Looks are created by *capturing* channels using the keypad and defining values for them using the function keys just to the right of it. Channels can be manipulated singly or in groups to light the stage by entering the channel number and assigning a value between 00 and full. Although the DMX signal has 256 steps, the board divides them into percentages from 0 to 100. The display only has a two-digit capability, so 100 percent shows up as FL rather than 100. Quite often, you may not know the exact level you would like to set for a channel when you begin working with it. The *wheel* can be used to adjust levels in a fluid way. The Expression family of control boards has a moveable wheel to the right of the keypad that allows the user to ramp selected channels up or down by rotating it. Express has a trackpad that works in a similar fashion.

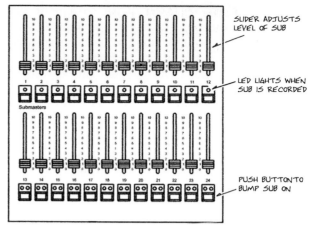

SLIDER ADJUSTS
LEVEL OF SUB

LED LIGHTS WHEN
SUB IS RECORDED

PUSH BUTTON TO
BUMP SUB ON

SUBMASTER SECTION OF AN ETC EXPRESSION

A LIGHT BOARD DOESN'T HAVE THE SAME MEMORY FUNCTIONS COMMONLY FOUND ON A PC OR A MAC. THERE IS NO MOUSE, AND IT DOES NOT ALLOW FOR NAVIGATION BETWEEN FILES. SUBMASTERS ARE A GOOD WAY TO STORE FILES SO THAT THEY CAN BE RECALLED LATER.

THE LED LIGHTS UP WHEN A SERIES OF CHANNELS HAS BEEN RECORDED INTO THE SUBMASTER. THE BUTTON "BUMPS" THE SUB ON FULL. THE SLIDER CAN BE USED TO ADJUST THE LEVEL OF THAT PARTICULAR SUB

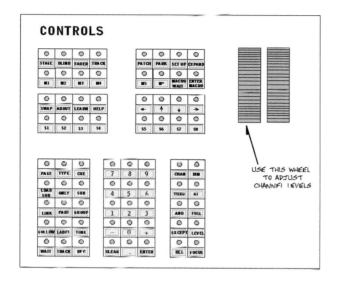

USE THIS WHEEL
TO ADJUST
CHANNEL LEVELS

Channel selection through the numeric keypad is made easier by the function keys found just to the right of it. The *and* key allows several numbers to be added together and manipulated all at the same time, for example, 4 *and* 5 *and* 7 *and* 8, which can then all be set at the same level. The "—" or *through* key allows for a sequential series of numbers, for example, 4 *through* 8, to all be selected at once and set at a specific level. The *at* key is used to preface entering a level command, such as channel 8 *at* 40 percent. If a channel is to be set at 100 percent, the *at* key may be omitted, and the *full* key used instead.

Submasters are frequently used to speed up the cuing process. An Expression console is not a PC, and cannot store files in folders, but submasters are a workaround way of doing that. They function by grouping together sets of channel numbers and values so that they all work as one unit. If one look is to be reused a number of times, it can be recorded as a submaster, so that it is easily recalled. Sometimes systems of light are put into a sub so that they can be brought up as a group on the way to creating a look. For example, red cyc lights in one sub, green and blue in others. Submasters are also a very convenient way to manipulate moving lights, or for setting the values of a number of color scrollers all at one time.

The next step in programming a show on a lighting console is to record each look or other type of change as a *cue number*. On an ETC product, the *record* and *enter* buttons are used to do this, along with the numerical keypad. Generally speaking, the cues are numbered sequentially, one after the other, so that they will be in order for playback. A problem arises when adding cues later on. Additional cues are frequently added during dress rehearsals, so *inserting* cues is necessary and can be done by using the dot "." key. That creates a cue sequence such as 24, 24.1, 24.2, 25, 26.

Each cue number must have a period of *time* associated with it, even if that time is zero. The fade time is recorded as a certain number of seconds using the time key from the left of the numerical keypad. There are actually two timing sequences in a cue, the *fade down* time and the *fade up* time. The computer asks for them separately, but remembers the fade down time when asking about the fade up time. If a straight crossfade is required, entering a time in seconds and pressing the enter button twice will make the up and down times the same. But these two sequences can be manipulated separately if you choose to do so. The need for separate up/down times is rare, but on occasion you may wish to have a light establish itself before others fade down. In that event, it is necessary for one fader to lead and the other to lag, so separate time amounts need to be entered when prompted by the screen. The default time setting is 5 seconds when the board comes from the factory, and if you do not set a time yourself, your cue will automatically be 5 seconds long. You can change the default time using the setup button menu.

Running a show from the *fader controls* is a matter of selecting the required cue and (on command from the stage manager) pushing the GO button. There are actually two separate GO buttons on an ETC Expression board, which means that it is possible to run two completely separate cues at the same time. If a background cue is needed, perhaps a cyc change taking several minutes, that cue can run in one fader while the general show cues are run in the other. Or an effects cue can be run in the background on one of the faders. Care must be taken, though, to clear out the secondary fader at the end of its use, or that cue will continue to run.

There are several other buttons around the faders on an Expression board, which in addition to the faders themselves can be used to modify how a cue is being run and/or how the list of cues is managed.

> GO runs the cue.
> HOLD stops the progress of the cue.
> BACK goes back to the previous cue.
> CLEAR takes down all channels brought up by the cue.
> SLIDER can be used to speed up the cue.

FADER SECTION OF AN ETC BOARD*

THERE ARE ACTUALLY ONLY TWO FADERS, A/B AND C/D
THE SLIDERS MUST BE IN THE UP POSITION
FOR THE GO BUTTON TO WORK. IF THE SLIDER IS DOWN,
THE CUE WILL RUN BUT THE CHANNELS WILL STAY AT ZERO
UNTIL YOU PUSH THE SLIDER UP

*EXPRESSION SPECIFICALLY, OTHERS ARE SIMILAR

After the first cue is brought up, the remaining cues line up in a list on the monitor screen. A > sign is displayed next to the cue in use. Pushing the GO button again will automatically segue to the next cue on the list, without having to enter that cue number. Care must be taken to remove unwanted cues from the list, or they may be brought up by mistake.

There are two sliders in each fader, because of the separate up and down fade functions. This is similar to an old preset board, except that here the sliders are not inversely proportional.

ETC and other manufacturers program their dimmers to maintain the last command. This means that if the DMX signal to the dimmers is lost, the dimmer will stay at the place it was last told to go. If the board is turned off with a cue still up, the lights will stay on. The CLEAR button can be used to turn off those dimmers when the show is finished, or if one cue must be taken down before programming another one.

There are many other board functions, some of which are only accessible by using the *softkeys*, S1 through S8 on the keypad. One of the softkeys is generally a "more softkeys" access, which leads to another series of options. Softkey functions are not necessarily the same for all modes of operation.

At the top left of the keypad is a row of keys that read stage, blind, patch, and set up. These functions are used to switch between modes of work, and each one changes the main monitor view. *Stage* brings up a window showing the channels, and the values for them. Stage mode is normally used when building and running cues. *Blind* is similar to stage, but allows cues to be manipulated while a show is going on, without changing what is happening with the lights on stage. *Patch* is used to make changes in the show patch, and opens a window showing how dimmers and channels are connected. *Set up* mode opens a window that allows system changes similar to what one would find under "control panel" on a PC.

After cues are set, it is important to *save show* in order to preserve the cues for the future. Saving is done by inserting a *3.5-inch floppy disk*, accessing the setup menu, navigating to disk functions, and then selecting *write all to disk*. It is important that the disk be formatted as IBM-compatible. Disk formatting can be done by the board, but that will erase any data on the disk, so make sure that nothing you will need later is on it before formatting. It is important to make two copies of the disk, because the floppy disk storage method is far from infallible. If you finish programming, and turn the board off, your cues should remain in memory and return when the board is powered back up. If the board is to be used within a reasonably short time, you may consider just turning off the monitors instead.

If you are running the same cues from the day before, you do not normally need to reload them into the desk. It is recommended that you not reload unless necessary, because of possible problems with the floppy disk drive. To load cues into the console from a floppy disk, press the set up button, and choose *read all from disk*. It is important to realize that the commands write all to disk and read all to disk control more than just the cues that have been written and stored in the console's memory. These commands also include the patch and submaster settings, as well as any other information you have entered regarding dimmer profiles, personalities, and so on. The command *read show from disk* will read only the cues and not the other information.

If an ETC console is connected to an *Emphasis* server, saving is done on the server instead. In this case, *server* means the accompanying PC. If Emphasis is in use, go to File > Save Show > enter the name of your show, and *save*. Your cue file will be saved on the *shows drive*, normally drive D. It is a good idea to save the cues on a secondary device, and as the server has USB ports, a travel drive is the best option. Follow the process

of Save As > Travel Drive > Enter Show Name > Save. Saving on the travel drive will ensure that your cues survive even if the PC server crashes for some reason. It is often helpful to use the *save as* command to save different versions of the same show. That makes it possible to revert to earlier versions of the cuing process.

Although most of the methods and commands used on ETC equipment are the same from one model to the next, it is interesting to note one important difference between the Expression and Express consoles: the Express has a slider on the console for each of the channels used as dimmers. As a result, the sliders can be used to set levels for the various dimmers rather than going through the regular keypad commands. This is an excellent time-saving measure, but is meant for systems with relatively few dimmers, as it would not be practical to have a console with hundreds of sliders on it. The Express console design makes it easier to work on the fly when it is not possible to program cues for a show because of time constraints. If panel tape is used to mark the purpose of each slider, the board operator can follow along as best she can. This method of working should not be considered ideal, but often occurs.

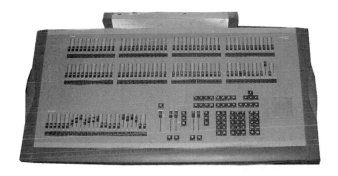

EXPRESS CONSOLE

THE EXPRESS CONSOLE HAS A SLIDER FOR EACH CHANNEL, NOT UNLIKE AN OLDER TWO-SCENE PRESET BOARD

WORKING WITH DIGITAL EQUIPMENT

Over the past two decades, moving lights have gone from being novelty items for rock shows to standard theatre equipment. In the early 1980s, the technology was brand new, and moving fixture lights were the exclusive domain of the *Vari-Light Corporation*. This company didn't sell their fixtures, but rather rented them to rock-and-roll tours and kept their technology a closely guarded secret. The High End Systems *Intellabeam* came on the market as an alternative. Intellabeams used the same core digital technology, but the mechanical systems were very different. Although this particular fixture has been discontinued, High End still sells a very similar product, the *Cyberlight*.

HIGH END SYSTEMS
CYBERLIGHT

In a *moving fixture/yoke* light, a motorized *yoke* allows the optical section to pan and tilt so that the light beam shines in different directions. A Cyberlight is a *moving mirror* light. As its name implies, a mirror in front of the light beam is used to point it in different directions, and the body of the fixture itself does not move. Moving mirror lights respond much more quickly than moving fixture lights, and there is less pressure to keep the light physically small, as only the mirror moves. But mirror fixtures have become unpopular in recent years, perhaps because audiences enjoy seeing lights dance about at a concert, and they have actually become a part of the show.

The digital age has made other sorts of equipment easier to control. *Color scrollers* are motorized strings of gel color on a scroll, which can be rotated across the front of a lighting instrument so that the position of the string determines the color of the filter in the light. Different versions of that technology have been around for quite some time and allow for many different colors on stage from fewer fixtures. One huge disadvantage, though, lies in not being able to smoothly move from one color to the next unless they are right together on the gel string. Often times, scrollers must be reset during a blackout of some sort. A new piece of equipment, the *SeaChanger*, uses dichroic filter technology and can crossfade more easily from one color to the next.

Gobo rotators are tiny motorized units that spin the gobo in its slot. In early versions, they were controlled entirely by an analog 0–10-volt signal from a separate controller. Now, a digital signal is sent to a control unit, and the motors are powered from there. A standard theatre-type console can be used to program all digital devices used in a show, within the limitation of how many channels are available.

SCROLLER

THIS UNIT IS TYPICAL OF MECHANICAL COLOR CHANGERS. THE OPENING IS CLEAR IN THE PICTURE, WHICH IS USUALLY ONE OF THE CHOICES MADE IN GEL STRING COLORS.

STUDIO SPOT

ENTIRE HEAD MOVES ON A ROTATING YOKE

Each accessory device (moving light, color scroller, strobe light, and so on) has an *address*, which is the controller's target when sending out information. This address is changeable, and can be reset by the user. When loading in the show, electricians set the address of each device at a specific number between 001 and 512, depending on what the hookup requires. A multi-channel device set at a certain address will automatically take up whatever following channel numbers are required to assign a different channel for each attribute. Thus, a 16-channel moving light addressed at channel 301 will also use all the following channels up through

316. This illustrates how quickly 512 channels can be taken up in lighting a show. If more than 512 are required, a second set or universe can be added.

The dimmers in a system generally use the lowest numbers in universe 1, and are semi-permanently addressed as devices 001 through 096, 192, 288, or however many dimmers are in use. As a result, any accessory device must have an address higher than that. If moving light addresses are in the zone used by the dimmers, changing dimmer values will inadvertently affect the fixture. When no more addresses are available in the first universe, the second must be used. The address numbering system starts over again in the second universe. The next address after "universe 1, #512," is "universe 2, #001." A single universe cannot recognize a number higher than 512.

Restarting the address number after 512 works perfectly well for individual universes that do not interact with one another, but the control board must communicate with every universe, and a different numbering system must be used so that each address in each universe has a unique channel number for cuing purposes. Channels for the first universe are numbers 001 through 512, the second are 513 through 1024, the third 1025 through 1536, and so forth. The hardware outputs on the board should reflect those numbers, but it is important to remember that they are not used in addressing the device. That isn't possible anyway, because accessories have only a three-digit address capability. On the board, an address of "universe 3, #276" would be controlled by channel 1301.

To configure a light or other device to the third universe, a cable must be run from that port to the first fixture in the line. Most DMX-operated devices have both an input and output for the DMX signal so that up to 32 of them can be run from one board output by *daisy-chaining* them together. The output cable runs from the console to the input of the first light. From that point a *jumper* runs the signal from the output of the first light to the input of the second light. This continues until all of the fixtures are connected. A DMX-controlled device will react only when its particular section of the data stream (its address) tells it to do so. Information for other devices can run through it without difficulty. The end device in the chain should have a *terminator* on it to end the signal. A terminator is an XLR connector with special electronic components that eliminate signal corruption.

If an Emphasis system is in use, *nodes* are used to distribute the DMX signal rather than the outputs on the back of the console. The *Node Configuration Editor* is used to assign the node output to a particular universe of addresses. The node itself gets its information from the server via Ethernet connection.

THIS NODE HAS AN ETHERNET INPUT PORT ON THE SIDE, AND TWO 5-PIN XLR OUTPUTS FOR DMX ON THE FRONT

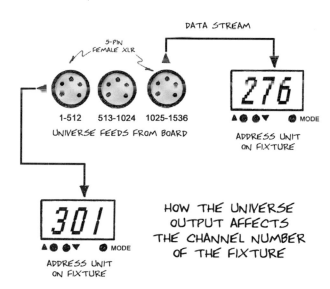

HOW THE UNIVERSE OUTPUT AFFECTS THE CHANNEL NUMBER OF THE FIXTURE

THE CHANNEL NUMBER OF THE FIXTURE AT LEFT WILL BE #301 ON THE BOARD, BECAUSE IT IS IN THE FIRST UNIVERSE. BECAUSE THE FIXTURE ON THE RIGHT IS IN THE THIRD UNIVERSE, ITS CHANNEL NUMBER WILL BE 1025 + 276, OR #1301.

Moving lights contain *attributes*, which is a name used to describe the different controllable properties of the light. Moving fixtures may have anywhere from 12 to 24 such attributes and require the same number of channels, which is why a moving light requires a large number of channels to operate. If a light has 20 different attributes, it will require 20 channels of the DMX signal. Each channel controls one specific attribute, which in turn controls what the light looks like on stage. Setting a value for the channel affects the appearance of the light beam by changing color, shape, intensity, beam angle, or by seeing the light move through space. Setting cues for moving lights requires that levels be entered for the different channels/attributes so that the desired look is achieved.

For most fixtures, channels 1 and 2 control the pan attribute, which is the movement back and forth. Channels 3 and 4 control tilting up and down. The first channel is a *coarse* setting, and the second is a *fine* setting. A reason for the duality lies in the original intent of the DMX protocol as a method of controlling dimmers rather than moving fixtures. Remember that a DMX signal has an output of 512 channels of information. Each channel can be set to only one of 256 different values. If the yoke of a moving fixture pans 360 degrees, each of the 256 *steps* would be slightly more than one degree of rotation. If the fixture is very far away from its intended target, 1 degree of movement could quite a jump, and more precision might be needed.

CYBERLIGHT ATTRIBUTES

CHANNEL	ASSIGNMENT
1	Pan Coarse
2	Pan Fine
3	Tilt Coarse
4	Tilt Fine
5	Color Wheel
6	Cyan (red)
7	Magenta (green)
8	Yellow (blue)
9	Static Litho (pattern)
10	Rotating Litho
11	Rotate
12	Zoom
13	Focus
14	Iris
15	Effects Wheel
16	Frost
17	Shutter
18	Dimmer
19	Motor Speed
20	Control

CHAPTER 9

PHOTOMETRICS AND HANGING THE LIGHTS

Technically, *photometrics* means "those things pertaining to the measuring of light." In common usage, though, photometrics is used to describe how lighting instruments, or fixtures, are defined with regard to their sizes, light output, and uses. In his groundbreaking 1936 work, *A Method for Lighting the Stage* (New York: Theatre Arts Books), Stanley McCandless coined the phrase *lighting instrument*, which he used in referring to lights used for the stage. Perhaps he was attempting to use a scientific name to enhance the image of something that— up to that point—had not been given much thought as an art form. Lights today are still very often called *instruments*, but the term *fixture* is also popular, as it fits in well with the terminology used in commercial lighting practice. In most situations, the words *instrument*, *fixture*, and *light* are used interchangeably.

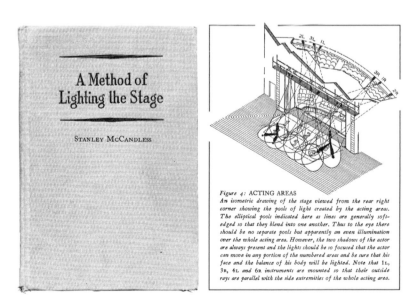

Figure 4: ACTING AREAS
An isometric drawing of the stage viewed from the rear right corner showing the pools of light created by the acting areas. The elliptical pools indicated here as lines are generally soft-edged so that they blend into one another. Thus to the eye there should be no separate pools but apparently an even illumination over the whole acting area. However, the two shadows of the actor are always present and the lights should be so focused that the actor can move in any portion of the numbered areas and be sure that his face and the balance of his body will be lighted. Note that 1L, 3R, 4L and 6R instruments are mounted so that their outside rays are parallel with the side extremities of the whole acting area.

THIS BOOK BY STANLEY McCANDLESS WAS THE BEGINNING OF THE ACADEMIC STUDY OF ENTERTAINMENT LIGHTING

LIGHTING FIXTURE COMPONENTS

The earliest electrified theatre-specific fixtures were basically just lightbulbs with a shiny surface behind them to reflect more of the light in one direction. Not long after, lenses were added, to help focus the light beam down to a more specific shaft of light rather than a simple wash going in all directions. Lenses completed the triad of mechanical parts that make up the core of photometrics as used in a modern lighting instrument: the light source, or *lamp*; the *reflector*; and the *lens*. Most modern fixtures contain all three of these elements, though some of them place two or more within the lamp itself. In any sort of electrical lighting fixture, the lamp is used to create light, the reflector helps to gather the part of that light that emanates in the wrong direction, and the lens helps to either focus or diffuse the beam into a useful shape.

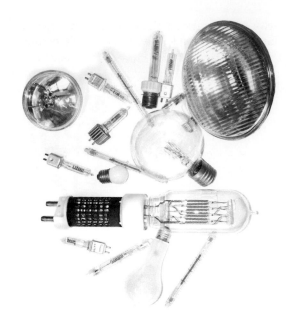

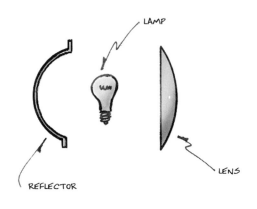

THREE BASIC COMPONENTS
OF A LIGHTING INSTRUMENT

Lamps

It seems appropriate to start this discussion with the lamp, as that is where light begins.

Most lamps generate light by resisting the flow of electricity through the *filament* of the bulb. The tiny wire filament becomes so hot that it incandesces, which means that it has so much heat energy that some of it is dissipated in the form of light energy. To keep the filament from oxidizing, or burning up in the atmosphere, a glass bulb was first used to create a vacuum around the wire filament. Modern versions have an inert gas like argon inside, which creates pressure to keep the filament from *off-gassing* and to make it last longer.

A longer filament generally produces more light energy; the wire is often curled inside the glass bulb so that it can be made longer without using up too much space. Making a bulb smaller in relation to its output is very important for theatre lights, because they are much brighter than ordinary commercial fixtures. A large lamp requires a large fixture, which is problematic when trying to hang many instruments in a small space. One of the problems facing engineers a half-century ago was that the high-wattage lamps used in theatre lights got too hot for the glass bulbs of the period, and they tended to deform from overheating if the filament was too close. To accommodate the heat that was produced, the glass envelope surrounding a 1000-watt lamp had to be several inches in diameter, which was just too big for a practical fixture.

About that time, *quartz glass* was developed to create a lamp that could be very tiny in size, but put out a very large amount of light, and it is that type of glass that is used extensively today for modern lamps. Quartz glass (which is made from a finely ground powder of that mineral) can absorb a tremendous amount of heat without being destroyed. It is important not to touch a quartz lamp with your bare hand when installing one in an instrument, because dirt and oil on your fingers will adhere to the glass. The oil turns black when heated, and that part of the glass will get hotter than the rest. It will melt in short order as a result. Care should be taken to unplug fixtures before changing lamps. If the power to the light has not been switched off, the instantaneous heating of the lamp will seriously burn your hand.

The arrangement of the filament in the lamp is very important to its ability to work well in concert with the reflector and the lens. In a theoretical sense, the source of the light should be from one single point for the reflector to work at its highest efficiency. Of course, this is not entirely possible, given the coiled nature of a practical filament, but even so, manufacturers must take great care to design the filament so that it is extremely compact and comes as close as possible to the theoretical model. The desire for a compact light source has made arc lamps more attractive in moving lights because the arc gap is extremely small, and thus the light comes closer to the theoretical model. Even so, arc lamps are generally not used in static fixtures, because of a dimming issue.

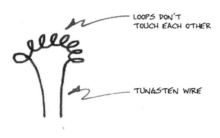

COILING THE FILAMENT
ALLOWS IT TO FIT INTO
A MORE COMPACT SHAPE

The *base* is the part of the lamp used to make connection with the *socket*, which is part of the fixture itself. Everyone is acquainted with the screw base, because this is the type most commonly used in everyday life. Other types include the *two-pin*, the *RSC or double-ended*, and the *mogul bipost*. The *HPL* is a two-pin lamp that is fitted with an aluminum heat sink to dissipate the extreme amount of heat that is generated by this quartz lamp inside a small fixture. Earlier versions of similar lamps were prone to failure in the base or socket because of the heat factor. Even though the glass part of the lamp copes well with high temperatures, the metallic base does not.

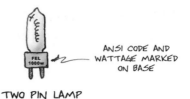

TWO PIN LAMP

DOUBLE-ENDED OR
RECESSED SINGLE CONTACT

HIGH WATTAGE
MOGUL BIPOST

HPL FAMILY

COMMON LAMP TYPES

The letters "HPL" are an example of listing lamps by their *ANSI* (American National Standards Institute) code. ANSI creates standards for many different industries in the United States. They insure that devices are compatible with one another—for example, that any standard-screw-base lightbulb will fit into any standard-screw-base socket. They provide a three-letter ANSI code for every new lamp manufactured. The code is stamped on the shipping container, and should also be visible on the base of the lamp itself. Lamps of the same basic type, but different wattages, have different codes.

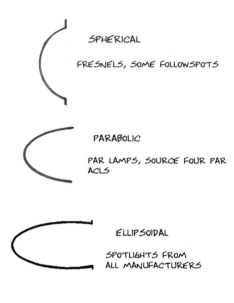

TYPES OF REFLECTORS

The study of how light interacts with the natural world is known as optics. *Geometrical optics* is the study of the *reflection* and *refraction* of light when it interacts with lenses and mirrors. Although light is often described as either waves with specific *wavelengths*, or as particles called *photons*, for the purposes of a study of geometrical optics, it is helpful to visualize light in terms of *rays*. A light ray is assumed to travel in a straight line unless acted upon by a device like a lens or reflector.

Reflectors

A reflector is used to bounce back light rays that are going toward the rear of the fixture. More than that, it is designed to do this in a way that is optically efficient with the rest of the instrument, creating a specific type of light beam. The most commonly used shapes for a reflector are *parabolic*, *ellipsoidal*, and *spherical*. The type of reflector used defines how the light rays travel after they leave the fixture itself.

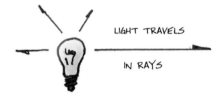

GEOMETRICAL OPTICS

LIGHT RAYS MOVE OUTWARD IN A STRAIGHT LINE UNTIL ACTED ON BY A REFLECTOR OR REFRACTOR

Reflectors are in fact mirrors that have a curved shape, and the properties of that curve affect the manner in which the light rays are reflected. On a flat-plane, reflector, light rays bounce off the surface so that the *angle of incidence* is equal to the angle of *reflection*. The angle of incidence is the angle at which the light ray strikes the mirror's surface.

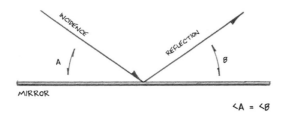

LIGHT RAY IS REFLECTED AT THE
SAME ANGLE IT STRIKES THE MIRROR

If the mirror is held at an angle and the light source remains in the same place, the angles of incidence/reflection will still be equal, but the size of the angle will be altered, and the light will be reflected to a different place.

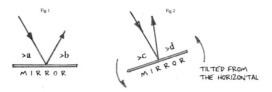

IN FIG 1, ANGLE A AND ANGLE B
ARE EQUAL TO ONE ANOTHER,
BECAUSE THE ANGLE OF INCIDENCE
IS EQUAL TO THE ANGLE OF
REFLECTION. THE SAME STATEMENT
IS TRUE FOR ANGLES C AND D IN FIG 2.

THE ANGLE OF THE LIGHT RAY
STRIKING THE FIRST MIRROR IS
THE SAME ANGLE (TO THE HORIZONTAL)
AS THE SECOND ONE, YET THE FINAL
DIRECTION OF THE TWO REFLECTED RAYS
IS DIFFERENT, BECAUSE THE SECOND
MIRROR HAS BEEN TILTED FROM THE
HORIZONTAL.

The axiom that "the angle of incidence equals the angle of reflection" also holds true for curved surfaces, but the curve determines what the angle will be for each particular point on the curve. Sometimes it is helpful to think of a curve as a series of infinitely small flat surfaces connected together. Viewed in that context, a curved mirror becomes a series of reflectors, each with its own angle of incidence/reflection.

A CURVED SURFACE CAN BE
VISUALIZED AS A SERIES OF
FLAT SURFACES ARRANGED
TOGETHER.

It is important to remember that reflectors are three-dimensional forms, but it is generally easier to visualize them using two-dimensional shapes. Hence, a spherical 3D form becomes a 2D arc when depicted on a flat piece of paper like the page you are reading right now.

Many early fixtures used a spherical reflector derived from lights originally designed for lighthouses. On paper, they are approximated with an arc of a circle. It is the nature of a mirror curved with this shape that rays from a source in the center will be reflected toward the center. This method is not perfect, however, and in the process, light rays on the extreme edges of the reflector are deflected in a more random pattern. Light that falls outside the desired pattern is said to be *ambient*. Imperfections in the reflection of light from a spherical reflector create a good deal of ambient light mixed in with the intended light beam.

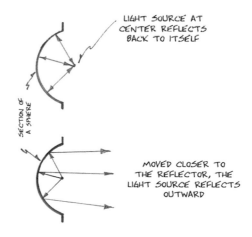

LIGHT SOURCE AT
CENTER REFLECTS
BACK TO ITSELF

SECTION OF
A SPHERE

MOVED CLOSER TO
THE REFLECTOR, THE
LIGHT SOURCE REFLECTS
OUTWARD

SPHERICAL REFLECTOR

The *parabola* is a very interesting shape that occurs in nature in many different ways. When a string is draped between two points and allowed to hang downward in a curve, the shape it forms is a parabola. The arc of a baseball through the air is also a parabola. Parabolas are a frequent object of mathematical study, because they occur in the natural world yet have a scientifically predictable shape.

When a parabola is used as a reflector, the light source at its natural focal point is reflected outward with all rays pointing in one direction. That aspect has obvious advantages when constructing a light fixture to project organized beams of light. In this theoretical construct, the light source is viewed as a single point. In a practical lighting instrument, the filament is not a single point, but rather a coil of tungsten wire with dimensional qualities. If the filament is arranged laterally across the reflector, the light from an instrument of this type will have a beam that is somewhat oval in shape.

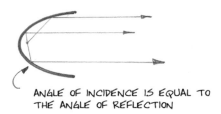

ANGLE OF INCIDENCE IS EQUAL TO THE ANGLE OF REFLECTION

PARABOLIC REFLECTOR

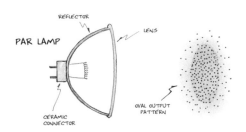

PAR LAMP

REFLECTOR

LENS

CERAMIC CONNECTOR

OVAL OUTPUT PATTERN

THE ACTUAL OUTPUT OF A PARABOLIC REFLECTOR IS GENERALLY AN OVAL SHAPE, PARTLY DUE TO THE SHAPE OF THE FILAMENT, AND PARTLY BECAUSE THEY WERE DEVELOPED TO BE CAR HEADLIGHTS.

A third type of commonly used reflector draws its shape from the *ellipse*. In plane geometry, an ellipse is formed by using two *focal points*, F_1 and F_2. The curved surface of the ellipse is defined by adding (distance) $d_1 + d_2$, where any two values of d_1 and d_2 should equal any other two values for d_1 and d_2. This sum should be the same for any point on the curve.

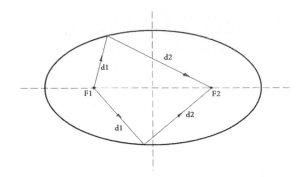

MATHEMATICAL PROPERTIES OF AN ELLIPSE

D1 + D2 SHOULD HAVE THE SAME VALUE NO MATTER WHICH DIRECTION THE RAYS EMANATE FROM ONE OF THE FOCAL POINTS. A RAY FROM ONE FOCAL POINT WILL ALWAYS REFLECT TO THE SECOND FOCAL POINT

A string can also be used to demonstrate this. Fix the ends of the string to the two focal points and stretch it taut in any direction. Use a pencil to draw a line all the way around. The resulting curve will be an ellipse. *Varying the distance between the focal points produces ellipses of different proportions.* If the focal points are moved close to one another, an approximate circle will be formed. If the focal points are so far apart that the string is almost tight between them, a long thin curve will be formed.

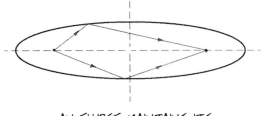

AN ELLIPSE MAINTAINS ITS MATHEMATICAL PROPERTIES EVEN WHEN ELONGATED

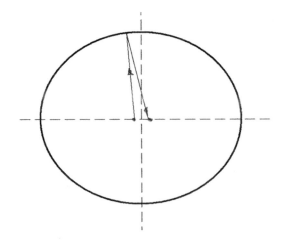

MOVING THE FOCI TOGETHER WILL EVENTUALLY PRODUCE A CIRCLE

The string method of forming an ellipse makes it easier to visualize how light rays are affected by an elliptical reflector, because the curved surface is such that a ray emanating from one focal point will be reflected toward the second one, in the same way that the string was running. The string approximates the angles of incidence and the angles of reflection. In a theoretical construct, all of the light from a lamp in the position of F_1 that hits the reflector will be bounced off and converge again on F_2. Of course in a practical lighting instrument, the reflector cannot be an enclosed unit, because there would be no way for the light to get out and reach the stage. Only part of the ellipse is used, and because of that, some light from the lamp will not be properly reflected and will become ambient light. Even so, the elliptical reflector is very efficient when compared to other types.

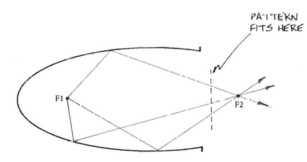

LIGHT RAYS CONVERGE AND DIVERGE, SO ANY TEMPLATE INSERTED BETWEEN THE TWO FOCAL POINTS WILL BE PROJECTED UPSIDE DOWN AND BACKWARD

One interesting aspect of a fixture with an elliptical reflector is that the light rays actually cross over each other as they pass through the second focal point. If this type of fixture is used to project an image by using a metal *pattern* placed between the two focal points, the image will be upside down and reversed. Projecting patterns is a very useful quality of an ellipsoidal instrument.

The exact shape of the ellipse is an important factor in determining the width of the beam of light projected by an ellipsoidal. A narrower ellipse will produce a narrower beam, and a fuller ellipse a wider beam. Different beam angles are important to lighting designers so that they can efficiently shape the light that will be projected onto the stage. Early fixtures used differently shaped reflectors, but the manufacturing process was very expensive, so the modern trend is to construct one type of reflector and create different beam angle spreads with lenses instead.

Lenses

Glass lenses were first invented at the end of the thirteenth century, and use the principle of *refraction* to change the angle at which light rays travel. In the case of a magnifying glass, light rays are gathered by the lens as they pass toward the human eye. In the case of a lighting instrument, light rays are affected as they pass out of the fixture, but the optical principles involved are the same.

Dutch mathematician Willebrord Snell determined that light rays passing through a denser medium were slowed, and that this process bent or refracted the rays so that they moved in a different direction. Most everyone is familiar with the "broken straw" example, in which a straw in a transparent glass appears to bend where it enters the water. The straw is not really bent or broken, but rather only appears to be, because light passing through the water and glass is slowed, and according to Snell, that process refracts the light into a new direction.

A STRAW IN WATER APPEARS TO BE "BROKEN" WHEN THE LIGHT IS REFRACTED

You might actually observe several different effects on the straw, because light is not only bent by the water, but is also affected by the transparent glass container. The density of the material makes a difference in how much refraction takes place. A denser material creates more refraction than a less dense material, so the glass has more of an effect than the water. The angle at which the light ray intersects with the refractive medium is also important. A light ray that strikes the refractor at a steeper angle is bent more than one striking at a shallower angle. If the intersection is at a 90-degree angle, there is no refraction.

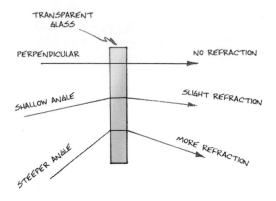

AMOUNT OF REFRACTION IS AFFECTED BY:

DENSITY OF MATERIAL
ANGLE OF INCIDENCE
THICKNESS OF MATERIAL

Augustin Fresnel was a nineteenth-century French scientist working with the properties of light; he developed a specific type of lens often used in lighthouses, and also in theatrical lights. One of the problems of the day was that the very thick lenses used in lighthouse lights tended to crack. This was because impurities made the glass less than 100 percent clear, so part of the light was converted to heat energy. This would cause the lens to heat up when the light was turned on, and the heat caused the glass to expand. When turned off, the glass would contract, and this movement often meant that the somewhat brittle glass would crack, ruining the lens. Fresnel solved this problem by creating a stepped lens that maintained its convex shape on the curved side, but did so in steps, so that the resulting lens was much thinner.

Useful lenses for the theatre are generally of a type known as *Plano-convex*, meaning that they are flat on one side and curved on the other. The curvature of the lens affects the amount of bending that occurs, and by carefully calibrating the curve, it is possible to focus light rays from an instrument into a cohesive unit. The thickness of the lens is directly proportional to the amount of bending that lens will create, because a thicker lens has a more pronounced curve. In a typical ellipsoidal instrument, two Plano-convex lenses are used as a pair to reduce the thickness that would be required if only one were used.

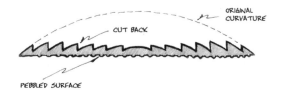

FRESNEL LENS

Although this works perfectly well in theory, the formation of the glass is not completely exact, and a certain amount of ambient light is created. Fresnel lenses are used theatrically in the *Fresnel lighting instrument*, which creates a soft pool of light where precision is not required, unlike an ellipsoidal instrument. Fresnel lenses often have a slightly pebbled surface on the flat, plano side in order to diffuse the pool of light they create. This helps to hide light and dark spots resulting from the imprecision of the stepped lens.

Diffusion is the main objective of some lenses, especially those used on fixtures with a parabolic reflector, such as PAR lamps, or the ETC Source Four PAR. In either of those two types, the lens serves to spread the beam outward a specific amount. The lenses have a similar appearance, and can be identified by the texture of the surface.

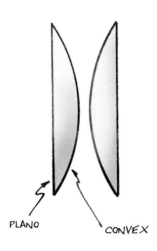

PLANO   CONVEX

TWO THINNER LENSES
CAN HAVE THE SAME
EFFECT AS ONE
THICKER LENS

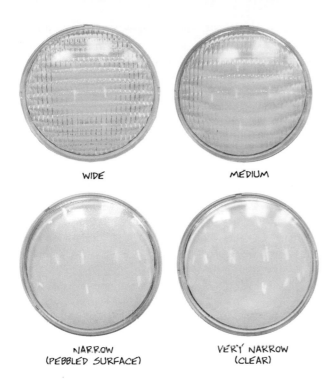

WIDE   MEDIUM

NARROW
(PEBBLED SURFACE)

VERY NARROW
(CLEAR)

SOURCE FOUR PAR LENSES

FRESNEL LIGHT

ETC brand ellipsoidals use lenses to create different *beam angles*. A beam angle is the divergence of the light as it leaves the fixture, measured in degrees. If each light has the same output in lumens or candlepower, the brightness of a light on a reflective surface should be determined by what percentage of the output of the entire fixture falls on that reflective surface. If the reflective surface is far away from the fixture, a narrower, tighter beam of light will preserve more of its luminosity than a wider one will. Thus the apparent light from the narrow angle fixture will be brighter.

FIXTURE PROPERTIES

The Fresnel is perhaps the oldest kind of lighting instrument and has been around longer than any type still in common use. Because Monsieur Fresnel was French, his name has a pronunciation that is odd for most English-speaking persons. The word is pronounced FRUH-nell, rather than frez-null.

Fresnels use a spherical reflector to bounce light vaguely back in the direction of the lens. Both the lamp and the reflector are fastened to a sled that can be moved back and forth, toward or away from the lens. The closer the sled is to the lens, the more spread out the beam pattern will be. This position is referred to as *flood*. When the sled is moved away from the lens, the beam output is sharpened into a position known as *spot*. There are an infinite number of stops between the two extremes.

Regardless of the number of degrees of beam spread, the light output of a Fresnel is always somewhat diffuse, with a bright or hot spot in the center, and a gradual lessening of intensity toward the edge of the beam. A common accessory used in limiting the beam spread of a Fresnel is a set of *barn doors*. This is a set of hinged metal flaps on a mounting plate that can be fitted into the gel frame at the front of the light. They are especially popular in a television studio. By adjusting the angle of the flaps, it is possible to mask the leakage of unwanted ambient light that tends to angle obliquely outward from the imperfect Fresnel lens. A *top hat* is a rounded masking device based on the same principle.

BARN DOORS   TOP HAT

It is interesting to note that ETC does not currently offer a Fresnel lighting instrument in its family of theatre lights. PAR lamps and the Source Four PAR have lessened the popularity of Fresnels in theatres.

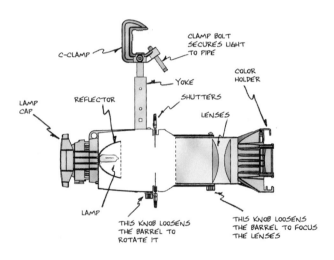

C-CLAMP

CLAMP BOLT SECURES LIGHT TO PIPE

COLOR HOLDER

YOKE

REFLECTOR

LAMP CAP

SHUTTERS

LENSES

LAMP

THIS KNOB LOOSENS THE BARREL TO ROTATE IT

THIS KNOB LOOSENS THE BARREL TO FOCUS THE LENSES

PARTS OF A SOURCE FOUR ELLIPSOIDAL (LEKO)

Sometimes ellipsoidals are called *Lekos*, because they were developed by two people named Lee and Cook at Century lighting, and that company used Leko as a trade name, but they've since gone out of business. Ellipsoidals are the workhorse units of the theatre and are the most commonly used fixtures in stage lighting. Their main advantage lies in the type of optics used and consequently their ability to shape the light beam they produce. An ellipsoidal can be used in more subtle ways than other kinds of lights, because it can be more finely controlled. They are used extensively in theatre, because theatre lighting is a more subtle art form than TV or concert lighting. TV lighting tends to center around

high-wattage Fresnels, and concerts (at which the PAR once was king) now use moving fixture lights almost exclusively. The qualities of high intensity, a coherent beam, and adjustable focus account for the most useful feature of an ellipsoidal: its ability to shape the light beam.

The optics of an ellipsoidal reflector were covered in the earlier section, where you learned that the light beam can be shaped when it is in the space between the two focal points created by the elliptical reflector. The area of an ellipsoidal where shaping of the beam occurs is known as the *gate*. The shaping operation occurs before the light rays have merged and crossed over themselves at the second focal point. Consequently, any image projected by a Leko will appear as reversed when the beam reaches the stage.

Several different approaches may be taken to masking the beam. The most common is to use *shutters*, four thin pieces of metal that slide in and out of the gate and are a permanent part of the instrument. Shutters can make the beam of light into a semicircle, or a square, or, by angling the shutters, a triangle. Shutters are quite useful in shaping the light to fit a specific object such as a window or a door. ETC-brand Source Four instruments have a rotating barrel so that the entire shutter assembly can be turned a few degrees to a more advantageous angle. Lights are hung at all different attitudes, and without this feature, it is sometimes difficult to angle a shutter enough to get the desired shape.

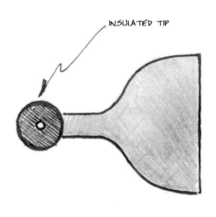

INSULATED TIP

SHUTTER

The left shutter affects the right side of the beam, the bottom the top of the beam, and so forth. It is not possible to precisely shape the output with barn doors, top hats, or any other equipment fitted into the gel frame holder; those devices only work on Fresnels or a wide-angle PAR lamp.

An *iris* can be used to reduce the size of the light beam to a small, round spot. Irises are most often used in followspots, but they are also made in a size that will fit into a standard gobo slot.

A VINTAGE ALTMAN FIXTURE

THE TYPE OF LIGHT, 6×9
IS CLEARLY MARKED ON THE YOKE

THIS TYPE OF LABELING DOESN'T
WORK ON ETC SOURCE FOURS
BECAUSE THE LENS TUBES CAN
BE SWAPPED, AND THE LABEL
WOULD BE WRONG AFTER THAT

TURNING THE OUTER RING
WILL MAKE THE CENTER
OPENING LARGER OR SMALLER

IRIS

There are several ways to describe the size and use of ellipsoidals. An early method was to use the distance between the focal points in a light. The farther apart the two focal points, the narrower the angle. Focal lengths for traditional lights varied from 6 inches to 22 inches. Many of these lights are still in use. The beam spread of a 6×6 is much wider than the beam output of a 6×22, and as a result, the pool of light emitted by the 6×6 (at the same distance) will cover more area on the stage than the 22 will.

The newer system uses degree angles to describe the *beam angle* spread. The new system came about partly because of a change in manufacturing philosophy. ETC and other manufacturers began to design their fixtures so that they all use the same housing and reflector. Different lens arrangements are used to produce different beam angle spreads. These range from a very narrow angle of 5 degrees to an extremely wide angle of 90 degrees. It is possible to purchase extra lenses so that one body can produce different angles by switching *lens tubes*. The most commonly used degree angles are 36 degrees and 26 degrees, which correspond to 6×9s and 6×12s in the older numbering system.

Source Four fixtures have specific beam angle spreads and are generally called by that number of degrees. ETC produces:

90 degrees
70 degrees
50 degrees
36 degrees
26 degrees
10 degrees
5 degrees

COLOR CODING TAPE

EVEN THOUGH THE FACTORY STICKER
HAS FALLEN OFF, THIS LENS TUBE
IS STILL RECOGNIZABLE AS A 36°
BECAUSE OF THE COLORED TAPE ON
THE BARREL

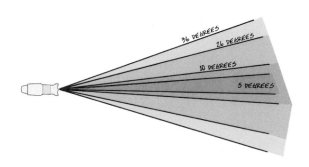

36 DEGREES
26 DEGREES
10 DEGREES
5 DEGREES

RELATIVE BEAM SPREADS FOR ETC LIGHTS

Most of the lenses are interchangeable from one fixture body to the next. The 5- and 10-degree lenses are much larger than the others, which all have the same general appearance. A *beam angle chart* is online at http://booksite.focalpress.com/companion/Holloway/. It shows the approximate size of the beam at different distances.

Other manufacturers have their own methods of describing the beam angle spread, and may manufacture different types.

When fixtures were separated according to their reflector size, there was little need to transfer the lens tube from one fixture to another—they were all the same. It was common practice to *color-code* the light as to its focal length, and the marking was often placed on the yoke of the instrument, frequently written on the metal surface with a paint marker.

Today, most ETC ellipsoidals use the same standard body, but different lenses. The specification of the light cannot be marked on the yoke, but rather must be on the lens tube itself. ETC puts stickers on the tube at the factory, stating 19 degrees, 26 degrees, 36 degrees, and so forth, but these stickers often fall off, and are difficult to read from a distance. It is much easier to tell the lights apart if the lens tube is color-coded in such a way that the code can be read from the ground when the fixture is hanging in the air.

Traditional *PAR cans* are essentially round car headlights that have been manufactured to operate at 120 volts, rather than at the standard automobile voltage of 12v. The fixtures themselves are very simple, lightweight, and inexpensive, because all of the optics are built into the lamp itself. As a consequence, PAR lamps tend to be somewhat more expensive than other types. The parabolic reflector creates a naturally tight beam of light, and the on-board glass lens is used to diffuse it.

PAR cans were the standard rock-and-roll lights for many years, because they are so lightweight and durable, and because rock shows do not require a great deal of precision in focusing. The beam that comes from a "can" is similar to that generated by a Fresnel, except that it is oval in shape and the instrument does not allow for changing from spot to flood. Instead, a variety of lamps may be used. They range in angle from wide to medium to narrow to very narrow.

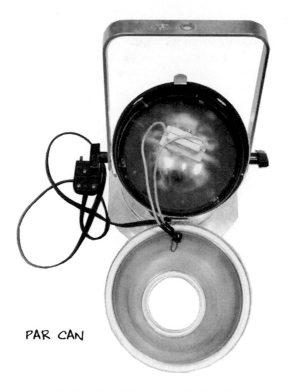

PAR CAN

NOTICE THE CERAMIC ON BACK OF LAMP

THE CERAMIC CONNECTS POWER
TO THE LAMP, AND CAN BE USED TO ROTATE
THE OVAL "HOT DOG" WHEN
FOCUSING THE LIGHT

SOURCE FOUR PAR

NOTICE THAT THE LENS ROTATES
TO ALTER THE DIRECTION OF THE "HOT DOG"

It is possible to rotate the lamp within its housing in order to change the orientation of the oval beam shape from vertical through horizontal, in accordance with how the light can best cover its intended area. PARs come in two main sizes, the 64 and the 56, with a few much smaller sizes. PAR 64s are far and away the most common. "Birdies" are tiny PAR 16 lights which can be mounted on scenery to provide light in odd spaces. The peculiar sizes refer to the diameter of the lamp given in eighths of an inch (PAR 64 = 8″ and PAR 16 = 2″).

The *Source Four PAR* is physically very different from a PAR can, but emits a very similar light. It has a standard reflector and lamp, and the lens is changed to alter the beam angle of the light. A ring known as the *bottle* is rotated to change the direction of the oval, and that oval is much less pronounced than in a regular PAR. These fixtures are more expensive than a standard PAR can, but they have the advantage of using the much cheaper HPL lamp used in many other lights.

Cyc lights, also known as *border lights* or *strip lights*, are used to produce a wide swath of light on stage. As the name implies, these fixtures are manufactured in strips, in which a number of lamps are ganged together in a parallel circuit. Mini Strips have a large number of very small lamps. They are 12v lamps connected in series of 10, and if one filament blows, all the lights go out. The fixture itself is very small—it will fit into places that others will not.

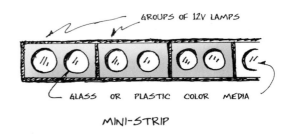

GROUPS OF 12V LAMPS

GLASS OR PLASTIC COLOR MEDIA

MINI-STRIP

Plugging several strip-light units together end to end, it is possible to create a swath of light across the entire stage, and/or as they are most commonly used, across a sky *cyclorama*. Strip lights are evenly spaced lights that provide a wash of color. By using different colors in each circuit, colors on the cyc can be mixed together. If red, green, and blue are used (the primary colors for lighting) an infinite color range may theoretically be achieved. A common practice for cyc lighting is to use a set of strip lights on a batten above, and a set of lights on the floor. A scenic ground row is often used to mask the bottom strips. Confusingly, the bottom strips themselves are also referred to as a *ground row*, and this term can be used to describe either the lights or the scenery.

Strip light circuits are easy to overload, because of the large number of individual lamps that are used. Care should be taken to determine the individual lamp wattage and multiply it by the total number of lamps in use. Compare this wattage rating with the dimmer capacity, or use the P = IE formula to convert to amps. It is possible to buy dimmers of a higher wattage rating, but cables become an issue when the 20-amp rating for standard jumpers is exceeded.

THE FAR CYC IS TYPICAL OF MOST MODERN "STRIP" LIGHTS. IT DOES NOT HAVE A GROUPING OF CIRCUITS, BUT RATHER EACH CELL HAS ITS OWN PIGTAIL.

Lights must be stored when they are not in use. Of course, storage can be handled in a multitude of different ways, but one of the most popular is to use lamp racks. The advantage of using rack storage is that the lights can be rolled around to a specific location where they are being hung. It is a good idea to mark the racks

so that all the electricians know which fixtures go where. Color coding is very popular.

THIS LAMP RACK IS ON WHEELS SO THAT IT CAN BE EASILY ROLLED INTO POSITION

COLOR MEDIA

Colored sheets of plastic are routinely used to create colored light for the stage. They can be called by several different names: *gel, filters, color media*, or simply "color." Modern intelligent lighting often uses *dichroic* filters to change the color of light. Dichroic filters use the principle of prismatic action to change light color, by which white light is split and divided into specific colors through refraction. Dichroic filters are technically very different from a standard plastic gel, which is much more commonly used. The *SeaChanger* is a color-changing device that fits on the front of a standard fixture, and uses dichroic filters to alter the color of the light's output. A different type of device, the color scroller, can be used to automatically shift from one standard gel color to another. Scrollers use the standard plastic media, but it is cut into specific sizes and the different colors are connected together to form a *gel string*, which is then shifted back and forth in front of the light in order to change the fixture's color output.

Gels got that name because they were originally (until the mid-1970s) manufactured from the same sort of gelatin material used to create Jell-O. Gelatin is an organic animal substance used in many different products. It was used to create the original stage lighting gels, because it is easy to insert dye into the material. A method of dyeing clear plastic sheets was not invented until later. Gelatin-based gels would dissolve in water, and that was the basis of a joke where a new stagehand would be asked to "wash the dirty ones."

Most modern color media is created from a mix of polyester and/or polycarbonate plastics. Some manufacturers are able to insert the dye in the base material; others apply it to the surface. The theory is that when color is an integral part of the plastic, it is less likely to bleach out over time and exposure to bright light. The original gelatin gels tended to lose their color saturation rather rapidly, and needed frequent replacement. Modern gels last much longer, and typically need replacement only in a long-running venue.

Gel color typically comes in either a roll form, which is more popular in television and film, or in 20×24-inch sheets. Film electricians or gaffers tend to use rolls of color so that they can cut a large piece and attach it with clothespins to the barn doors of a lighting fixture. The nature of film is that a "setup" for a certain shot will last for only a few minutes before moving on to the next one, so the use of theatre-style frames is not time-efficient. If one were to use the film method in a theatre where shows last from weeks to months to years, pinned-on gels would tend to work themselves loose and are not practical. The 20×24 sheets are more suited to cropping on a paper cutter that can be used to trim them to the appropriate sizes. The most common sizes are:

Source Four Leko: $6\frac{1}{4} \times 6\frac{1}{4}''$
Source Four Par: $7\frac{1}{4} \times 7\frac{1}{4}''$
Pre-ETC Lekos: $7\frac{1}{4} \times 7\frac{1}{4}''$
6" Fresnel: $7\frac{1}{4} \times 7\frac{1}{4}''$
8" Fresnel: $10 \times 10''$
PAR 64: $10 \times 10''$

Quite frequently, these sizes are marked out on a paper cutter so that it is easy to tell at a glance where to cut.

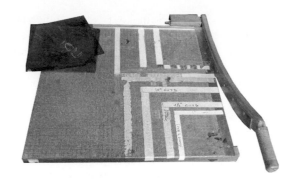

USE TAPE TO MARK OFF COMMONLY NEEDED GEL SIZES

Gels are often called *filters*, because of the nature of how they work in changing the color of light. Light from a theatre instrument at full intensity is white, subject to certain limitations imposed by the Kelvin scale of color temperature. White light is a combination of all different wavelengths of visible light, from just past infrared to just short of ultraviolet. A red painted surface appears as red because the paint reflects only the wavelengths of light that the human eye perceives as the color red. All other wavelengths are absorbed by the object and converted to heat energy. This is why dark objects, which reflect very little light, become much hotter when exposed to direct sunlight on a sunny afternoon than white objects do.

THE RED PAINT OF THE SPORTS CAR REFLECTS ONLY THE RED WAVELENGTHS OF THE WHITE LIGHT

White paint theoretically reflects all wavelengths of light and absorbs none of them. If a red gel is used to illuminate a white object, the object will appear as red—not because the gel is making the object that color, but because the red gel has filtered out the other wavelengths of light, so they are not present to be reflected. Filters subtract undesirable wavelengths as light leaves the instrument, and so not all wavelengths are present in the beam of light emitted from the fixture. The gel removes or "filters" the unwanted wavelengths from the mix before the light from an instrument has a chance to reach the stage.

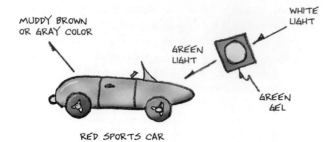

MUDDY BROWN
OR GRAY COLOR

WHITE
LIGHT

GREEN
LIGHT

GREEN
GEL

RED SPORTS CAR

THE GREEN GEL FILTERS OUT MOST OF THE
RED WAVELENGTHS OF LIGHT, SO THERE ARE
NONE TO REFLECT OFF THE SURFACE OF THE CAR.

BECAUSE THE FILTER MECHANISM IS IMPERFECT,
THE GEL IS NOT COMPLETELY SATURATED,
AND THE PAINT IS NOT PURE RED,
SOME REFLECTION TAKES PLACE ANYWAY.

An interesting theoretical process ensues. If a fixture is filtered with a primary green gel so that its output is restricted to *only* green wavelengths and the light from it strikes a red object which reflects *only* red wavelengths, there should be no reflection at all, and the red object should be invisible. What a boon that would be for magicians everywhere. In reality, this does not happen, because the filter is not perfectly constructed and transmits some light other than that which is intended. The red paint is not perfect, either, but rather a mixture of colors where red predominates. Thus the object will not be invisible, but rather a muddy shade of grayish brown. There is a long-standing prohibition against using any sort of green gel on light that may hit an actor's face, because green is the opposite, or *complementary color* of a healthy, sanguine face. The musical *Wicked* is a good example of how rules are meant to be broken.

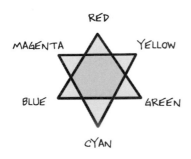

RED

MAGENTA

YELLOW

BLUE

GREEN

CYAN

COMPLEMENTARY COLORS
IN LIGHT

THIS CHART SEEMS VERY ODD TO A PAINTER,
WHO IS ACCUSTOMED TO PIGMENT PRIMARIES
OF YELLOW, RED, AND BLUE, AND SECONDARIES OF
ORANGE, VIOLET, AND GREEN. COLOR THEORY USED
IN LIGHTING IS CLOSER TO A TRUE, MATHEMATICAL
UNDERSTANDING OF THE SUBJECT, WHICH WORKS
WELL WITH ELECTRONIC EQUIPMENT. CYAN IS A LIGHT
BLUE COLOR, SLIGHTLY TINGED WITH GREEN.

The primary colors of light are red, green, and blue, which is different from pigments where the primaries are red, yellow, and blue. The debate about why the difference exists has not been completed. The mixing of red, green, and blue should produce a white light. The mixing of any two of them will produce a secondary color, just as with pigments. Often, there is a need to produce white light from a mixture of two different colors. White is desired so that the true color of the scenery/costumes can show through, but the use of two different colors to achieve the white light means that interesting shadows are cast that help in making the stage picture seem more three-dimensional. If two lights are used, one having a primary color, and the other the opposite secondary color, then a white light will result on any surface receiving an equal amount of each color.

The *CIE color chart* is used to reference how colors react with one another (see Web site). Pick a color on the chart and imagine a line from it through the middle of the white area to a color on the other side. The color at the end of the line will be the complementary, or opposite, color of the first one. Using those two colors together should produce a white light. The artistic goal of producing a white light on the stage in this fashion was more important to Stanley McCandless than for modern lighting designers, but knowing the method reinforces your knowledge of how subtractive mixing works. Color choice is an extremely subjective area.

The effect of gels is governed by factors other than just the chroma, or hue of the color. *Saturation* refers to the amount of color present. Saturated gels have a darker appearance, and they have more dye in the plastic, so that more of the white light is stopped. Most color media is not designed to stop all of the white light going through them, but rather boost the amount of the chosen color wavelength by reducing all the others. A very dark color such as Rx59, Indigo, is highly saturated with dye and transmits only 2 percent of the available light. The very next color in the Roscolux swatch book is No Color Blue, Rx60. It is not very saturated, and transmits 62 percent of the available light. As a result, the Rx60 also transmits a large amount of white light wavelengths along with the blue ones.

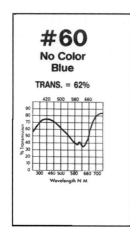
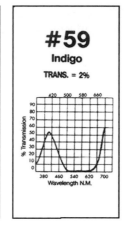

TWO DIFFERENT GRAPHS
OF COLOR TRANSMISSION
IN ROSCOLUX COLORS

The "big three" lighting gel manufacturers are ROSCO, the Great American Market or *GAM*, and the European company *Lee Filters*. ROSCO has a series of colors for the European market that all begin with the letter E, but are not commonly available in the United States. Sheets of gel from any company have an adhesive tag on them with the color number. Pieces of gel cut for individual lights are usually marked with a grease pencil so that they are identifiable from each other.

MARKING THE COLOR WITH A GREASE PENCIL

YOU CAN GET ONE FROM A SUPPLY HOUSE.
THEY ARE OFTEN FREE WITH A GEL ORDER

The letters Rx, G, and L are used to denote the company, and the number of the gel follows. For example: Rx60, L202, and G820 are all very close to the same shade of light blue, which is a very commonly used color, and it is difficult to tell them apart. But each company has colors that are more specific to their line, and most designers have favorite colors that they like to use. At one time, ROSCO had a second line of gels known as *Roscolene*, which are no longer popular, because they tend to fade more over time. RL and Rx were used to differentiate between the two.

Gel manufacturers regularly hand out samples of their products in the form of filter *swatch books*, which contain small pieces of the color media in a flip-out deck like the ones that paint manufacturers offer. Each color is backed by a piece of paper that gives the name and number of the color, its transmission percentage, and a graph showing its transmittance curve. The graph shows the relationship between the wavelength of the light in nanometers, and the percentage of transmittance. In reality, a theater practitioner has little reason to be concerned about the precise wavelengths of light being used, but the graph is a good indicator of how tightly compacted and narrow the filter is when transmitting light.

There are some non-color-related reasons to use gels. *Neutral density* is a type of filter that reduces the amount of light transmitted without changing its apparent color. It is used to reduce the light output of one fixture in relation to another. The graphs of neutral density colors are not a peak like most others, but rather tend to flow across the spectrum in a wavy line. *Frost* and *diffusion* gels are used to scatter light from a fixture that may be too close to spread out normally in accordance with the mechanics of the fixture. Some diffuse the light in all directions; others work in a more linear fashion. The primary colors of red, green, and blue often have frost versions, so that they will scatter and blend together better on a cyclorama. Another type of filter has color, but is not used for artistic reason. *Color-correction* filters are used to change the Kelvin temperature of an incandescent lamp to 56 K for film or television purposes.

Patterns, Gobos, Templates, and Other Ellipsoidal Projection Materials

There are a number of different ways to project an image onto the stage using a pattern or slide fitted into the gate area of an ellipsoidal instrument. The most common is to use metal *templates*, also known as *patterns* or *gobos*. There are several hundred stock types to choose from, or, for a fee, supply companies will create a custom metal template from your user-supplied artwork. It is also possible to have color images transferred to glass plates, but this technology is newer and more expensive. ROSCO offers plastic slides under the name Image Pro.

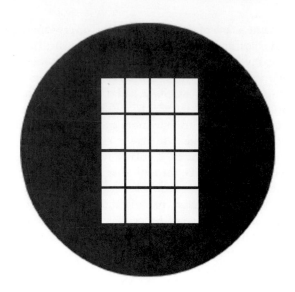

STANDARD GOBOS ARE ETCHED
INTO STAINLESS STEEL SHEETS
THAT CAN WITHSTAND THE INTENSE
HEAT INSIDE A LIGHTING INSTRUMENT

The standard type of pattern is created by etching an image onto a thin sheet of stainless steel. Stainless is preferred, because it holds its shape better under high heat. If a pattern is removed from a light while it is on, the metal can often be seen to glow cherry-red from the heat. Some patterns are made from other alloys when the pattern is too intricate for the normal method.

Patterns are manufactured in several different sizes for use in different sorts of lights. Size A is intended to fit most modern ellipsoidal fixtures, and has the largest image area. The larger image area is generally more efficient. This size pattern fits the standard-size holder used for Source Four and Shakespeare ellipsoidals. Some size A patterns have a round outside shape, and some are rectangular.

One of the problematic aspects of all patterns is that they are fitted inside an instrument where temperatures can reach several hundred degrees Fahrenheit. ROSCO's Image Pro circumvents that issue by cooling the plastic medium with a fan, but even so, the images fade after a short while. Color glass breakups are available, as well as deformed glass that adds no color, but rather creates a texturally interesting, swirling sort of light on the stage.

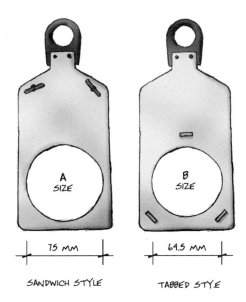

A SIZE   B SIZE

75 MM   64.5 MM

SANDWICH STYLE   TABBED STYE

TWO DIFFERENT TYPES OF GOBO HOLDERS.

THE ONE ON THE LEFT OPENS UP AND IS
DESIGNED FOR RECTANGULAR PATTERNS,
WHILE THE ONE ON THE RIGHT IS DESIGNED
FOR ROUND PATTERNS

Size B is meant for gobo rotators, and has a round outer shape made specifically for that purpose. Although the B size is intended for use in a rotator, it will also work without one, but a special holder with a smaller opening is generally necessary, because the outside diameter of the pattern is almost the same size as the image area of an A size pattern, and they tend to fall out of the holder. It is generally not possible to tape a gobo in the holder, because the tape will burn at the high temperature found inside the ellipsoidal, but aluminum duct tape works okay in a pinch. This type of tape is made from aluminum foil and an adhesive backing and is not the usual kind of duct tape.

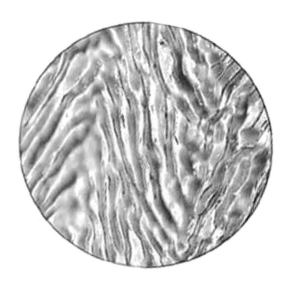

THIS DEFORMED GLASS GOBO FROM ROSCO
CREATES SWIRLING PATTERNS OF LIGHT
WHEN USED IN A ROTATOR

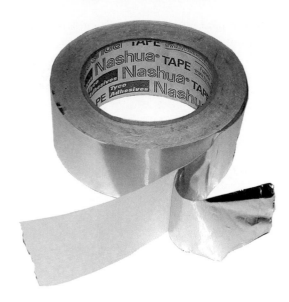

Gobos are often used in groups to provide a textural wash across the stage. In that context, they tend to be repeating irregular shapes that have no definite orientation. Others are used to project a specific image such as a logo or the outline of a building. Remember that patterns fit into the *gate* of an ellipsoidal, in a place where the light rays from the lamp and reflector have yet to converge and cross over themselves. So the image of the pattern will be projected upside down and backward from the way that it has been placed in the fixture. When the pattern has a discernible top and bottom, care must be taken to insert it into the holder in the proper orientation. Left and right can be altered at the fixture by turning the holder over, but because the holder has a handle on it, right side up can be accomplished only when loading the pattern.

THIS TYPE OF DUCT TAPE IS MADE FROM ALUMINUM FOIL, AND HAS A STICKY SIDE THAT IS REVEALED WHEN YOU PULL THE TAPE AWAY FROM ITS PAPER BACKING. THE FOIL DOESN'T BURN UP IN THE LIGHT, BUT SOMETIMES THE GLUE LETS GO.

Size M is used in Source Four Juniors, and is much smaller than the other types. The holder for M gobos is very different looking from the normal kind. Moving lights use patterns also, but each manufacturer tends to use a different size, so there are no standards.

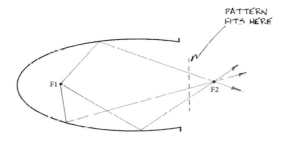

PATTERN FITS HERE

LIGHT RAYS IN AN ELLIPSOIDAL INSTRUMENT CONVERGE AT FOCAL POINT TWO

STANDARD SIZE A FOR REGULAR SOURCE FOUR LIGHTS

FRAME FOR A SIZE M PATTERN FITS A SOURCE FOUR JUNIOR

Gobo rotators are used to spin a pattern, so that the resulting projection is animated. One end of the rotator unit fits inside the light, while the motor is on the outside. Rotators require some sort of external controller, which is connected to the unit via a cable. Speed and direction can be manipulated. Some rotators spin two different patterns at the same time, and can achieve more complicated effects.

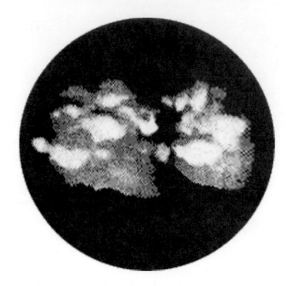

MESH GOBOS ARE FORMED BY MANY SMALL PINHOLES, SO BRIDGES ARE NOT NEEDED. THIS RESULTS IN A MUCH MORE DETAILED IMAGE.

ROSCO invented the Image Pro so that slides can be projected by a standard ellipsoidal fixture. An image is printed onto a special plastic sheet with an inkjet computer printer. The plastic is mounted in a holder. The holder is fitted into the Image Pro unit, which is in turn inserted into the gobo slot on the fixture. The unit itself has a fan built into it, which serves to cool the slide. These images are quite bright, but have a stated lifespan of only 15 hours when the light is at full power. After that, the ink forming the image tends to bleach out.

THIS ROTATOR HAS A FOUR-PIN XLR PLUG THAT PROVIDES BOTH DATA AND POWER TO THE UNIT

Most gobos are made by etching a pattern onto a metal sheet. In doing so, the area occupied by the image is eaten away, and left open. If the design is intricate, a system of islands and bridges are used to create a stencil-like form. Islands are the cut-away part; bridges hold interior parts of the design in place. If a custom-designed pattern is required, the artwork must have sufficient bridges to create a stable design when the metal has been etched away. Another approach is to use many small dots through the metal to create a *mesh* appearance. This method works especially well for amorphous shapes like clouds on a cyclorama. Throwing the fixture slightly out of focus will create an ultrarealistic image.

THE IMAGEPRO UNIT PROVIDES A COOLING BREEZE TO KEEP THE SLIDES FROM MELTING IN THE INTENSE HEAT OF THE LIGHTING INSTRUMENT

Hanging and Focusing the Lights

The plot

Hanging the lights is done to specifications laid down by a designer, who should provide a *light plot*. Most of the time, this is a scale representation of the theatre and its lighting positions, showing the lighting equipment types in their proper locations. Occasionally, plots are more like a schematic drawing, and are not to scale. Computer-aided-design (CAD) plots are often used. *CAD* programs came into their own early on in lighting design, because they are really good at keeping track of all the numbers used for dimmers, channels, circuits, gel colors, and the like. It is also much easier to add and delete lights on the computer and then print out a new plot than it is to do any sort of hand-drafting. However, it should be noted that there were many very artistically satisfying lighting designs created in advance of CAD technology. The computer makes the paperwork a lot easier to put together, but doesn't make anything more artistic. The art part must come from an actual human being.

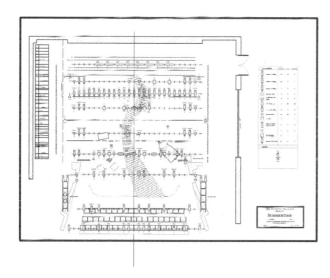

THIS PLOT WAS DRAFTED USING VECTORWORKS AND IS VERY TYPICAL OF THE TYPE OFTEN SEEN

numbers, and instrument numbers. This is just like the legend used on a road map to indicate types of roads, hospitals, airports, and so on. Front-of-house positions should be labeled, as well as the battens being used as electrics. Electrics should have an indication of their *trim height*.

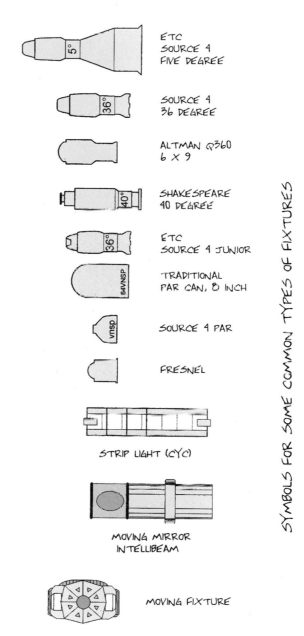

The aesthetic quality of individual light plots tends to vary greatly, but there is a general consensus about the information that should be on the plot. It should include a *legend*, which is a guide to the meanings of various symbols for different types of lights. Part of this is the *key*, an instrument symbol that details the numbering system for gel color, channel numbers, dimmer

Some plots have marks on the battens at 18-inch centers. This is the most common spacing alternative for hanging instruments, unless the lights will be focused directly to the side, where 24-inch centers are more realistic. Maintaining an even spacing ensures adequate room to properly focus the lights. Using corresponding marks on the battens can make a light hang go really fast, because the electricians can simply count over from center to find the proper place for a fixture.

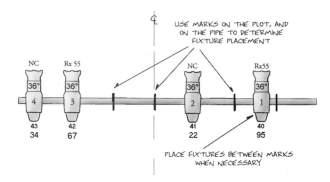

USE REGISTRATION MARKS TO AVOID MEASURING

If no marks are shown, it is necessary to *scale off* the placement of lights using a scale rule. Half-inch scale is standard for theatrical drawings of all types, but quarter-inch is also quite common. Generally speaking, placement is close enough if you can get the measurements correct to within a few inches. An ordinary tape measure works well if the plot is in half-inch scale. For that scale, a half-inch on the drawing is equal to 1 foot on the pipe. Experienced designers tend to use a standard spacing, rather than making each space a different size. This speeds up the hang and leaves more time for focusing.

Preparations

Hanging lights can be done very quickly, if you organize the event before starting. Proper management is the key to success.

Research the plot and its attendant paperwork to find which gel colors will be required, as well as how many and which sizes. Cut the gels and load them into the proper frames. Resident and university theatres often have a filing cabinet filled with previously used gels stored in folders. They are usually sorted according to the color number each is assigned by the manufacturer. The colors have names too, but most everyone uses the numbers to specify the desired colors.

It is helpful to mark the color numbers with a grease pencil. If the marks are placed nearer the center than the edge of the gel, they can be easily read in the dark. Some purists will disagree, but the output of light and the quality of the color will not be noticeably affected, and readable labeling will make finding the proper color during focusing in semi-darkness much easier.

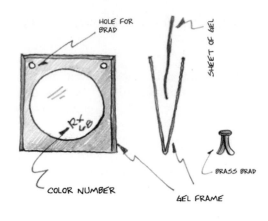

GEL FRAME HOLDER

Holes are provided in the corners of the gel frames so that brass *office brads* may be used to secure the gel. Some people use tape instead, but over a period of time the intense heat generated by the light will cause the tape either to fall off, or to become permanently bonded to the frame, depending on the type of tape used. The manufacturers clearly intend for brads to be used.

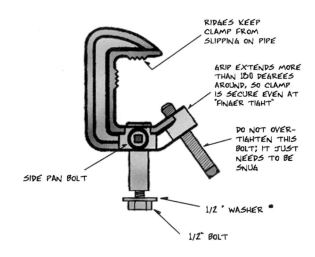

STANDARD IRON C-CLAMP

Virtually all theatres use some form of *C-clamp* to attach lights to a pipe such as a boom or an electric. This C-clamp is a specialized type that is able to grasp a round pipe easily. At the bottom of the C-clamp is a half-inch bolt that connects the clamp to the *yoke*. It also allows the light to move from side to side, or pan. Most of the time the yoke is a piece of flat steel that is bent into a U-shape. It curves around the sides of the body of the light and is attached on either side with bolts or handles.

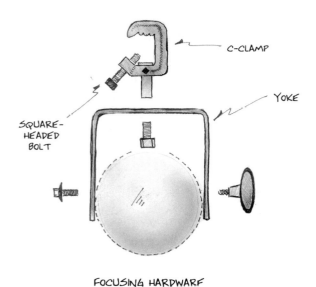

FOCUSING HARDWARE

They allow the light to move up and down, or tilt. When hanging lights on aluminum box truss, a small section of PVC pipe can be used to prevent damage to the soft aluminum pipe making up the truss.

The *half-burger* is an interesting offshoot of the Cheeseborough clamp used to connect pipes together. (The original type is often called a "cheeseburger.") They are often used in hanging moving fixture lights. This type of clamp requires no wrench, because the large wing nut can be merely finger tight.

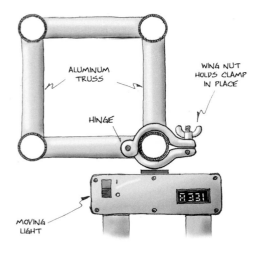

HALF-BURGER

SAFE TO USE ON ALUMINUM TRUSS

If a light is secured to a tower, ladder, box boom, or some other position made of square tubing, the yoke is usually bolted straight to that frame with no clamp. Half-inch bolts are an excellent fit. A washer placed between the yoke and the metal tubing of the tower makes it much easier to pan the light back and forth when focusing.

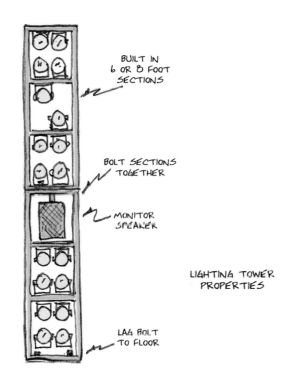

LIGHTING TOWER PROPERTIES

Some tour lights are bolted on to 6- or 8 foot sections of unistrut so that they are hung as a group in order to speed up hanging. The *unistrut* is fitted with two clamps, one at either end. This method works well for a tour show in which the same plot is hung at every stop, but wouldn't make much sense for a one-time setup.

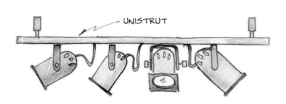

PAR CANS HUNG ON UNISTRUT

On the front of a light is a slot where *gel frames* may be fitted. On the back is a power cord, or *pigtail*, that is used to plug the light into a circuit. Most lights have either handles or bolts (or both) on the side, which are used to secure the light from tilting up and down. Although many lights have a retaining clip that will prevent the gel frame from falling out of the fixture, it is still best to hang the light right side up for easier insertion.

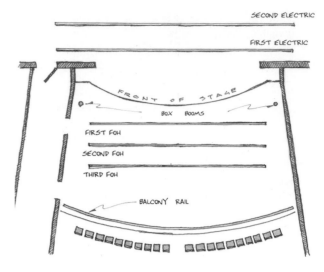

PLAN VIEW OF LIGHTING POSITIONS

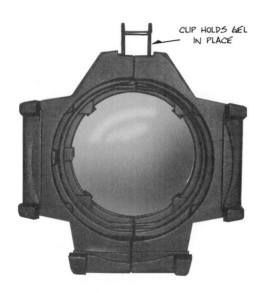

CLIP HOLDS GEL IN PLACE

THE CLIP SHOULD BE ON THE TOP IF THE LIGHT IS RIGHT SIDE UP

Hanging the lights

In a theatre, lights are hung in specific areas, some over the stage itself and some out in the auditorium. Hanging positions in the audience seating area are called *front-of-house* positions or FOH. It is common practice to number the FOH positions starting from the *plaster line*, an imaginary line across the front of the stage just behind the proscenium. The closest position to the plaster line is the first front of house or 1FOH, the second is the 2FOH, and so forth.

Theatres frequently have a lighting position on either side of the proscenium in an area where nineteenth-century theatres had their box seats. For this reason, they are known as *box boom* positions. A *boom* is any vertical pipe used as a hanging position. The stage left boom is called box boom left (BBL) and the stage right is the box boom right (BBR). The exact configuration of box boom positions tend to vary widely from one theatre to another, but most have some sort of hanging position in that area.

An onstage pipe used for hanging lights is called an *electric*. These are normally regular system pipes used for hanging curtains and scenery. Some theatres have dedicated electrics, meaning that certain pipes have been chosen to always be the electrics, and as a consequence they have a plugging strip that connects the lights with dimmers. Electrics are numbered from the plaster line just like FOH positions, but as they are on the opposite side of the line the numbers run the opposite direction, and the most downstage pipe is the first electric. The first electric is a very popular place to hang lights, and is almost always used in any show. It is often made a dedicated electric and has a plugging strip, even if no other pipe is of the dedicated type.

Other positions frequently found on stage are *torm booms*, vertical pipes attached to the back of the proscenium opening, free-standing booms sometimes called *trees*, lighting *towers*, and *ladders*. Booms often have heavy steel bases to help them stay upright, and towers are enclosures of steel tubing that totally encase the lights.

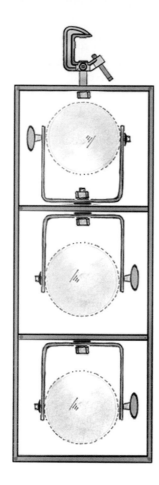

LIGHT LADDER.

MEANT TO BE HUNG
UNDER A BATTEN

centerline of the pipe and work toward the two sides, because it is very likely that the designer may not have known the exact length of the pipe when the drawing was done. The center of the batten is a well-defined location, and the hang will be more accurate this way.

When measuring distances on the plot, it is best to do all of them at one time. Take all the measurements from the center of the pipe to the fixture, and not from one fixture to the next. This will lessen the chance of inaccuracy compiling itself. After getting the measurements from the plot, use a piece of chalk to mark them on the pipe all at one time. Measuring and marking is a job for only one or two hands, but once the chalk marks are in place, a larger crew can jump in to hang the lights *finger-tight* on the pipe. Finger-tight means that the bolt is snugged without using a wrench, which makes it easy to change the placement if necessary. After all the lights are hung, it is a good idea to double-check placement with the plot, and make any changes before it becomes more difficult to do so. C-clamps are constructed so that they will not come off unless the bolt is very, very loose. Finger-tightening will prevent the lights from falling during the short time that you are hanging and double-checking.

Ladders are metal structures that hang down off the end of an electric, and increase the number of fixtures that can be used there for side lighting. Another backstage placement method is the *floor mount*, which can be scattered wherever the design specifies. *Set mount* fixtures are attached directly to scenery when that is the best method of placing them in a desired position.

Hanging on an electric

After you've flown in the first electric, select all the needed equipment from storage and place the lights in their approximate positions on the floor beneath the batten. If both the plan and the batten are marked with 18″ centers, it is an easy matter to count the number of marks and determine the exact placement of an instrument. If you do not have this luxury, it will be necessary to measure the placement of each light as scaled off the drawing. In any case, you should always begin from the

ALWAYS MEASURE FROM THE CENTER OF THE PIPE

Tighten the bolts with a 6- or 8-inch C-wrench only enough so that they do not vibrate loose. Overtightening with a wrench that is too large will damage both the clamp and the batten. Having one person go along and tighten all of the bolts in order, at one time, is an efficient way of ensuring that none of them is left loose accidentally. If you are not sure, it is always best to go through and double-check.

JUST MAKE IT SNUG, DON'T OVERTIGHTEN

If your theatre is equipped with *plugging strips* that are permanently attached to dedicated electric battens, the process of cabling is very easy. Plug the lights into the nearest circuit and record the number on the plot. Recording circuit numbers is essential so that a patching hookup sheet can be generated later on. A soft-patch in the dimmer board is used when the theatre has a dimmer-per-circuit system. If there is a patch panel to connect dimmers and circuits, the patch must be made there. In either case, you will need to know which dimmer or circuit is being used for which light.

Rotate the lights so that they are pointed vaguely in the direction shown on the plot. Most lights have a "this side up" issue that becomes obvious when you look at the gel frame holder. Check to see that all the handles and bolts used in focusing are snug, but not overly tight. Make sure that all shutters are pulled out on all of the Lekos. Shutters are often completely closed when the fixture is in storage, so that they don't become damaged. When left in that position, they won't allow any light to escape and will turn a 575-watt ellipsoidal into a 575-watt heater. The shutters will soon warp out of shape to a point where they will need to be replaced.

Safety cables should be attached so that they go around the yoke of the light and also around the batten. This will keep the light from falling should someone have forgotten to tighten the C-clamp.

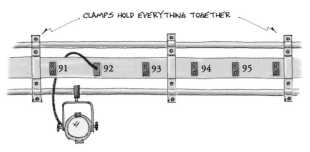

CLAMPS HOLD EVERYTHING TOGETHER

PLUGGING STRIP ON A DOUBLE BATTEN

The only concern with dedicated electrics is the fact that it limits the number and placement of possible hanging positions. *Drop boxes* are much more difficult to work with, but they provide a higher degree of flexibility. A drop box typically consists of a long piece of *multicable* (a large cable with many conductors) that ends with a box containing a number of panel-mounted female connectors.

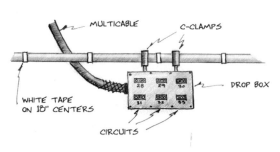

MULTICABLE   C-CLAMPS

WHITE TAPE ON 18" CENTERS

DROP BOX

CIRCUITS

DROP BOX ON A BATTEN

The multicable extends downward from the grid, allowing the drop box to be moved around the stage. When lowering a drop box, it is important to lower the cable in from the grid directly over the batten so that the cable does not foul any of the surrounding pipes. Drop boxes are sometimes hung off to the side of the rigging system and are maneuvered with a *pick line*. As another alternative, individual jumpers can be run off the end of the pipe and from there to a circuit box.

into one dimmer and will show that on the plot. In this case, it will not be necessary to provide an entirely different circuit for each one of these fixtures. The designer indicates ganged-together lights by drawing a line on the plot from one light to another, which is the normal way of indicating two-fering (two for one). A special *two-fer* cable having one male plug connected with two female plugs is used for this purpose.

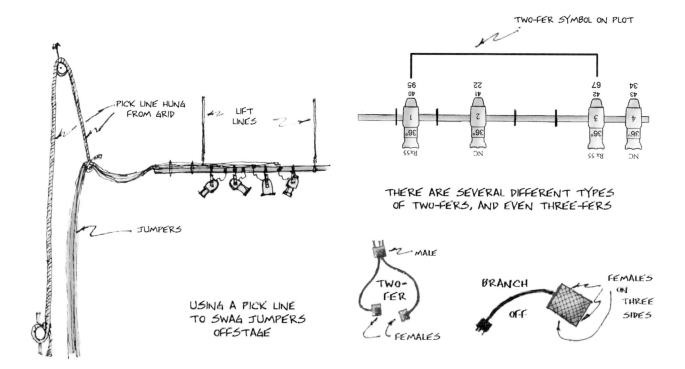

THERE ARE SEVERAL DIFFERENT TYPES OF TWO-FERS, AND EVEN THREE-FERS

When cables hang down off the end of a pipe, it is important to leave enough *swag* in them so that the batten can be flown in and out. Because the hanging process occurs when the electric is all the way down, there will automatically be enough cable for it to reach this point. It is much easier to do repair work from the ground than off a ladder or *Genie* lift.

A good method of attaching drop boxes to an electric is to use a C-clamp that has been bolted through the metal housing of the box. If this is not possible, be sure to use a stout line and a secure knot, because the box and cable are often surprisingly heavy.

You can determine the number of circuits needed, and hence the number of necessary drop boxes, by counting the number of lights on the batten as described by the light plot. Sometimes the designer will know in advance that two or more lights will be ganged together

Although it is the designer's responsibility to have determined in advance the proper power requirements dictated by connecting lamps together in this fashion, it is a good practice to double-check how much power will be required by the total number of lamps linked together by two-fering. This is especially true if two-fering becomes three-fering, or perhaps four-fering. Use the P = IE formula to check if enough power is available. Add the wattages together, and divide by the voltage to get a result. 2400 watts of lighting power translates to a 20-amp circuit, the most common rating.

Extension cords used to connect the pigtail of a lighting instrument with a drop box circuit are referred to as *jumpers*, because they "jump" power from one location to another. Jumpers consist of a single circuit with a male plug at one end and a female at the other.

floor and plug it into a circuit/dimmer. Record this number next to the light as it appears on the plot. Repeat this procedure until all of the lights have been plugged.

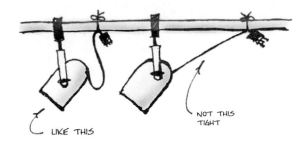

LIKE THIS

NOT THIS TIGHT

LEAVE SOME SLACK FOR FOCUSING

It should be noted that male plugs are never *energized*, meaning that no electricity is supplied *from* them, but rather only *to* them. Female plugs are generally designed so that the conducting material is recessed back into the insulating material of the plug housing, and thus hands are shielded from the electricity. Only female connectors are a source of power.

Jumpers of varying lengths are needed to cover the distance from the fixture pigtails to circuit boxes. It is helpful to color-code the different jumper lengths with vinyl electrical tape so that you can easily tell them apart. Then it is possible to know at a glance which jumper is the proper length for the job. All cables should be fastened to the batten with tie line. Do not use tape or wrap the cable itself around the batten repeatedly. These two methods are quite difficult to remove after the show is over, and the entertainment business is all about quickly changing from one show to another.

Jumpers usually have a piece of tie line attached to keep them together when coiled and not in use. If you tie this piece of line a few inches from the female end, using a clove hitch and a half hitch so that it is permanently attached, it can also serve as the first tie used to secure the jumper to the batten. There are also some great little Velcro strips made for this purpose. Tie the female end near the C-clamp of the light that you intend to cable. Tie it close enough so that there is enough slack in the pigtail for the instrument to pivot easily during focusing. Run the jumper along the

This is a good time to test the system to make sure that all of the elements are in proper working condition (lights, jumpers, and drop box circuits). Run each dimmer to full one at a time to see whether the lights come on as they should. It is important to test your hang while it is still on the ground and relatively easy to troubleshoot, and it is much easier to trade out or repair any faulty equipment before the cable has been tied to the batten. Make sure all of the shutters are pulled out and that safety cables are in place. Some designers like for the color to be put in now before the focus, and some like to do it after.

If the show has not been patched yet, and "set patch at 1-1" has been selected from the setup menu, the circuit/dimmer numbers and the channel numbers will be the same. You can bring up the appropriate channel numbers by reading the circuit/dimmer numbers off the drop box or plugging strip and punching them into the computer.

A *remote focus unit* or RFU is often used to control the dimmers during the light hanging and focusing. The buttons on the front panel match those on the regular console, and can be used to bring the channels up and down. The RFU is generally more convenient than running back and forth from the stage to the tech table.

YOU CAN RUN MOST
BOARD FUNCTIONS
WITH THIS REMOTE.
A WIRELESS VERSION
IS ALSO AVAILABLE.

RFU OR REMOTE FOCUS UNIT

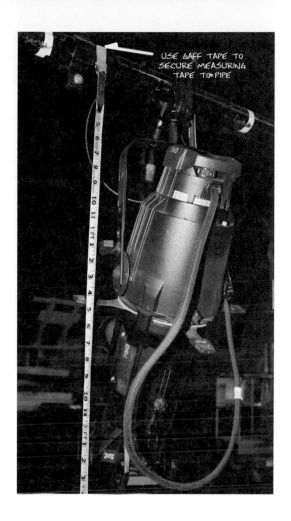

USE GAFF TAPE TO
SECURE MEASURING
TAPE TO PIPE

USE A TAPE MEASURE TO SET THE
TRIM OF THE PIPE OVER THE STAGE

Once troubleshooting is over, and all the lamps are working, the cables should be tied to the batten. Start at the end farthest from the drop boxes and use tie line to secure the cable. Put on a tie every 4 feet or so, and pick up the additional jumpers as you go along, tying them all at once using a bow knot. Thirty inches is a good length for tie lines, because it will usually allow the line to be double-wrapped around the cable. The two turns around the pipe makes it easier to get a tight bundle. If #4 *black tie line* is used, the ties can be recycled several times. When you reach the end where the drop box is, squish the excess cable against the batten and tie it on as neatly as possible. A bit of tidiness now will pay off when you focus, and will also help keep other flown pieces from snagging on the electric. Try to keep the rubber insulation of the jumpers away from the instrument housings, which get very hot during the show. The pigtail wires are usually okay, as they are manufactured from a heat-resistant material.

When the electric is ready to be flown out to its trim, use a small piece of *gaffer's tape* to secure the end of a 50-foot tape measure to the pipe before it goes up. Use the tape measure to determine when the batten has reached the proper trim height. Reel off the tape so that you can hold the exact length on the floor with your foot. When the slack is out of the tape, you are at trim. Once the trim is set the tape measure can be yanked down. (Don't use too much gaff tape!)

Front-of-house positions are so varied that it is impractical to discuss how they may be hung or circuited, but the basic principles just covered should still apply.

TECHNIQUES USED IN FOCUSING THE LIGHTS

Focusing lights is like dancing a tango. You need to observe what your partner is doing, and be ready to respond. The lighting designer leads, and if the electrician follows well, the job can be done very quickly. On tour where the designer is not available, focusing is usually done with the stage manager instead.

FOCUSING FROM A GENIE, WITH TWO HANDS AT THE BASE.

electrician has the hot spot in the proper location without looking too much.

Whatever method is used, the designer gives directions on moving the light. Up-and-down movement is called *tilting*. Side-to-side motion is known as *pan*. The designer might say pan left, and tilt up a bit. This usually means your left, but not always. Some designers just point: up, down, left, right, especially if there is a lot of noise. A clinched fist means "Stop, you've got it." If you are exceptionally in tune with your focusing partner, you will most likely be able to hit them just right without so much talking, and they will just say "Lock it" when you've got it right. *Locking* means to tighten the bolts that hold the light in place.

If the light is an ellipsoidal, *shutter cuts* will be necessary. You may need to sharpen or loosen the focus of the light first by moving the barrel back and forth, just like focusing a projector. A knob on the barrel can be loosened, which allows it and the lenses to move back and forth to adjust the sharpness. It is important to get the barrel set first before going on to the shutters, because adjusting the lens tube changes the size of the light beam, and thus the placement of the shutter cuts.

Use a 6- or 8-inch C-wrench to focus lights. Some people use a safety line on the wrench to prevent it from falling. The lights get hot in a hurry, so you might consider a pair of gloves, but they will definitely get in your way. If you are quick, the lights will not heat up fast enough to make the gloves necessary, and experienced electricians usually avoid them, or use a fingerless type. Either a lift or a ladder is required to focus lights that are up in the air, which means almost all of those on an electric. It is best to have one person on the board or RFU to bring up the proper channels, two moving the lift, and one who actually focuses.

It is common for a designer to begin at one end of an electric and work his or her way down to the other end rather than to hop around from place to place. This prevents having to reposition the lift frequently, which wastes a lot of time. Most experienced designers understand this, and even though it makes their work more difficult, they accommodate the process in order to save time.

Often, the designer asks for a channel number to be brought up, goes to the light's focus point, and just stands there waiting. The general idea is to focus the center or hot spot of the light on the chest or back of the designer, and then lock off the bolts that hold the light in place. Some designers direct the focus by staring at the filament to see when it is brightest. Some stand with their backs to you and watch where their shadow falls within the light. If a relationship of mutual respect is developed, the designer may simply trust that the

THIS KNOB LOOSENS THE BARREL SO THAT YOU CAN SLIDE IT BACK AND FORTH

Push in on the top shutter to mask the bottom of the light beam. Push in on the left shutter to change the right side. Very often, the shutters are hard to move, and you will find that it is easier if you jiggle the handle back and forth a bit to get it started. Try not to change the direction the lamp is pointing, or you will have to start over. Shutters do not just travel straight in and straight out. It is quite possible to tilt them to a severe angle, but not always as far as the designer would like. The barrel on some fixtures can rotate when necessary, but don't immediately start doing that for every light, because it will take too much time; try angling the shutters first and rotate the barrel as a last resort.

If the designer is uncertain which light is casting which shadow, she may ask you to *flag* the light. This means to pass your hand or foot or some other convenient body part in front of the light. This will cause the beam to flash on and off, making it easy to spot its effect on the stage.

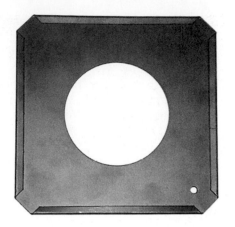

USE A DONUT LIKE THIS IN THE GEL FRAME HOLDER OF AN ELLIPSOIDAL TO SHARPEN THE OUTLINE OF A PATTERN.

If you are focusing a PAR can, it might be necessary to change the direction of the lamp in order to adjust the direction of the oval, or *hot dog*. The ceramic socket in the back of the light can be used for this purpose. There is a limit to how far it will turn in one direction, so it may be necessary to try both ways. Source Four PAR fixtures use a ring around the outside to "spin the bottle" of the reflector.

FLAG THE LIGHT TO SEE ITS AFFECT

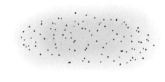

ROTATE THE CERAMIC IN AN OLD-SCHOOL PAR, OR SPIN THE BOTTLE ON A SOURCE FOUR PAR. EITHER WAY THE EFFECT IS TO CHANGE THE ORIENTATION OF THE OVAL PATTERN.

HOW TO CHANGE THE OVAL PATTERN OF A PAR

Patterns or gobos require a special technique, and should be inserted before starting to focus the light. Running the barrel for a sharp focus can make a huge difference in the appearance of the pattern effect. On occasion, a *donut* is used to sharpen the focus even more. A donut of this sort is a black metal sheet that fits into the gel holder slot. It has a hole in the center, and cuts down on ambient light. A donut often has a dramatic effect on contrast.

If you are focusing a Fresnel, you may need to change from *spot* to *flood*. Some fixtures have a crank on the back or side, but most have a knob on the bottom. Loosen it and move it in the right direction. Flood forward, spot back.

When the light has been set, put the gel frame in and move to the next light. If you are on a lift, you can most likely reach several lights before moving. When you are ready to go, tell the guys on the deck. If you say, "Moving stage left," they will know exactly what to do. If you say, "OK" or "Go," or make some other nebulous statement, they may not. Remember that moving *onstage* means toward the center, and moving *offstage* means toward the wing of the side you are closest to.

LIFT AND LADDER SAFETY

Be sure to employ any and all of the safety devices that come with the lift you are using. Follow the instructions given in the instruction booklet. If you do this, there is very little chance of the lift being knocked over. The same cannot be said if you choose to ignore the safety rules. Never set up a lift or a ladder on a raked stage for any reason. A good practice is to always have two stagehands move the lift, and to stand by while work is being done. Use a safety harness when it is required.

OUTRIGGERS HELP TO STABILIZE THE LIFT - BE SURE TO USE THEM

If there is ever a holdup of some sort, be sure to announce what it is and that you are working on the problem so that people on the ground have some idea of what is happening. As a result, they will be less frustrated and impatient.

Bumpers are used on electrics whenever there is a working piece on the next batten that might get fouled

in an instrument or knock one out of focus. A bumper is a section of flat iron bar that has been bent into a circle about 18 or 20 inches in diameter. A C-clamp is used to fasten the bumper to an electric at a convenient location along the pipe. Often three or four are needed for each electric.

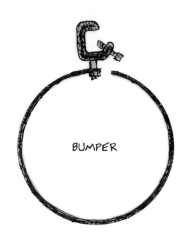

BUMPER

A *side arm* is used to attach lighting equipment that will not fit on the pipe in the normal way. It is really just a long extension of the yoke and C-clamp. The yoke of the fixture bolts to a sliding T so that the length can be adjusted.

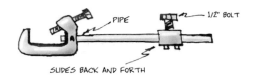

SIDE ARM

Side arms have been adapted for many other purposes. One of these is to prevent a batten from rolling. Lights are usually hung with the yoke pointing straight down, but sometimes there is a reason to *yoke them out* to the side, or even to hang them standing up on the top of the pipe. Sometimes this is to get a better angle with the light, and sometimes it is just a matter of getting more units into less space. At any rate, hanging lights to the side makes the pipe want to roll, and if you let this happen it will change the focus of the lights. To keep the pipe from rolling, fasten a side arm to the batten near one of the lift lines and then attach the pipe part to the aircraft cable with some tie line.

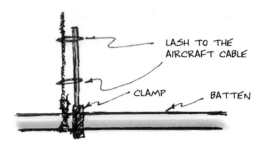

USE A SIDE ARM TO KEEP A BATTEN FIXED

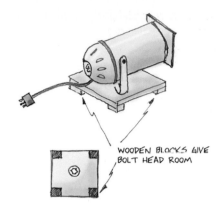

MAKE A SMALL BASE
FOR "ROVER" LIGHTS

A shop-built base is excellent for *floor-mount* lights. A square section of 3/4″ plywood can be used to form the base, and the yoke of the light is bolted to the center of the wood. Feet on the bottom of the ply will keep the assembly from rocking on the bolt. These floor mounts can be easily moved about, or screwed to the deck to prevent being knocked out of focus.

CHAPTER 10

OPERATING A FOLLOWSPOT

Followspots are used in many productions. In some areas of the country, they are known as *front lights*, or perhaps simply as *spotlights* or *spots*. As the name implies, a followspot is a lighting instrument used to follow the action of a play. They are the original moving fixture lights. The basic idea of a followspot is for the operator to *open up* on an actor and then stay with him or her until the scene is over, no matter where he or she may move on the stage. This ensures that the audience's attention will remain focused on that particular actor. A spot may also be used as a special to highlight an inanimate object, or it may be used as effects lighting. Spots can range in size from tiny club instruments of about 1000 watts to the giant behemoths used in sports arenas. IATSE stagehands and others are often called upon to run a spot for concerts, ice shows, wrestling bouts, and other entertainments, as well as for theatre shows. Information about those techniques is included here in order to better understand the full range of followspot operation.

THIS FOLLOWSPOT IS TYPICAL OF THE "MEGA SPOTS" USED IN LARGE SPORTS ARENAS. THE BALLAST RESTING ON THE STAND AT THE BOTTOM IS USED TO CREATE THE LARGE DC CURRENT NEEDED TO OPERATE THE XENON LAMP.

HISTORICAL PERSPECTIVE

Traditionally, a followspot in the theatre was used to create a hard-edged circle of light that said, "Look at me, I'm singing now." This approach is unmistakably presentational, and still works well for 1950s musicals and other shows of that nature. In recent years, that style has often given way to a more subtle method that uses *diffusion* gel in the spot. It creates a softer beam of light that can be used to simply highlight an actor and give him or her focus, without the unnatural look of the hard-edged circle. Spots aren't just for musicals anymore.

In earlier times, followspots used a DC arc between two carbon rods to create an incredibly bright, white beam of light. A large *rectifier* unit was used to supply the necessary DC

doi: 10.1016/C2009-0-23409-X

current. A pair of copper-clad *carbon rods* was clamped into two terminals in front of a parabolic reflector that had a hole in the center for the rods to pass through. A motor and gear system was used to slowly move the two rods together as they were consumed by the heat of the arcing electricity. It was necessary to maintain a precise gap between the two rods in order to ensure maximum light output. The gap itself had to be positioned in just the right place with respect to the reflector in order to work efficiently. New rods had to be inserted and adjusted or *trimmed* several times during a single performance. Keeping the spot running was a difficult process that required almost constant attention and a very experienced operator, who would also need to follow an actor and change colors.

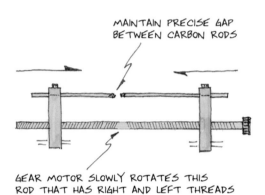

MAINTAIN PRECISE GAP BETWEEN CARBON RODS

GEAR MOTOR SLOWLY ROTATES THIS ROD THAT HAS RIGHT AND LEFT THREADS

ARC MUST BE PROPERLY POSITIONED IN THE REFLECTOR

Carbon-arc lights had one other really problematic aspect: the burning rods gave off toxic fumes, which in more recent years required some sort of exhaust system to be OSHA-compliant.[1] Modern spots use a sealed-beam *arc lamp* like the *Xenon* or *HMI* and don't have the same problem. These lamps still require a rectifier unit to provide the necessary DC current, but the arc

terminals in the lamp itself aren't consumed by the arcing process (at least not during any one performance). This means that the lamp can be permanently clamped in position at the exact focal point vis-à-vis the reflector, and will always be in focus. This greatly simplifies running the spot. Xenon lamps are very expensive up front, but reduced maintenance costs and not having to buy carbon rods more than offset the expense.

A few theatres and/or arenas may still use carbon arcs, but most of them have disappeared. Other venues may have lights that were converted from carbon rods to a sealed beam. However, you can still find an example of carbon-arc technology in the large outdoor spotlights used to attract patrons to gala openings. The brilliant light beams playing across a nighttime sky are visible for miles. These fixtures require an extremely bright light source that a carbon arc can easily produce, and because they are operated outdoors, the fumes are less of an issue. They have been around at least since World War II, when they were used to search for enemy planes in the sky. They have an incredibly long *throw*, or long-distance capability.

Xenon lamps work in much the same way as carbon arcs, but the electrodes used to create the arc are sealed in a glass enclosure so that no oxygen can get in. The electrodes are made from a special alloy that, in conjunction with the gas inside the tube, helps to replace burned parts of the electrode so that they last longer. Even so, they eventually burn out, and this type of lamp is very expensive, sometimes more than the cost of the fixture itself. The lamps get very hot and the gas inside is under pressure, and thus there is a tendency for the lamp to explode, especially if it is removed from the fixture without cooling down, so extreme caution must be used when changing one.

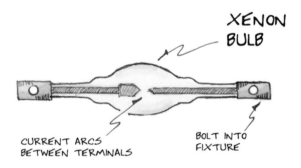

XENON BULB

CURRENT ARCS BETWEEN TERMINALS

BOLT INTO FIXTURE

XENON IS A RARE GAS THAT CAN CONDUCT ELECTRICITY, AND EMITS LIGHT WHEN EXCITED BY ELECTRONS.

THE GAS IS UNDER PRESSURE, AND THE LAMPS REQUIRE SPECIAL HANDLING.

---

[1] Occupational Safety and Health Administration.

Followspots are typically used from a position in the rear of the theatre and require a lamp that is much brighter than that used in a standard fixture, but there are smaller spots that can be fitted with ordinary quartz lamps like the FEL or CYX. It would be possible to run these particular lamps off a dimmer, but arc-type lamps are not dimmable. If the voltage pressure supplied to them decreases below a certain point, the arc won't be able to jump across the gap and will simply sputter out. Instead of dimming, most followspots use a mechanical device to vary the light intensity. Other mechanical devices can change the size/shape of the beam and the color of the light.

Followspots usually have a floor base that supports them from below, rather than hanging from a pipe like other lights. They are generally too heavy to hang and also require room for the operator, and to swing about themselves. One exception to this is the *truss spot*. Truss spots are used extensively in the concert business, where they are literally a spotlight that is mounted on top of a section of truss, which is flown out over the stage or audience. An operator sits on top of the truss to run the show. One artistic advantage is that the angle of the light from high above is much more dramatic than the typical flat beam from a spot in the rear of the house. At a concert, haze in the air reveals a shaft of light extending from the truss to the stage. Most of the reason for using truss spots in a concert can be found in the effect created by these moving colored beams.

For a play, a high angle spot is often used when a subtle halo of diffuse light is required to highlight an actor, but it can also be used in a variety of other ways. In a theatre situation, close spots like this are often mounted at a front-of-house lighting position, or from a tower especially installed for the purpose. It is not unusual for a tower of this sort to be located offstage near an "in one" entrance. Sometimes an ordinary fixture like a PAR or Leko is fitted with special hardware, and is used in place of a dedicated spot fixture because of the tight quarters. The bus and truck tours of *Cats* used two old beam projector lights as followspots, and they were suspended from a truss used as the first electric. A series of gel frames were tied to the operator's platform and were individually inserted into the holder to change the color of the light. A section of hollow pipe on the side of the light was used as a sight. Later tours of *Cats* used an actual truss followspot, but the quality of the lighting effects was not noticeably different between the two. This same type of spot position was used more recently for the tour of *Wicked*. *Spot towers*, larger versions of a regular lighting tower, can be used from behind the proscenium opening as a lighting position. That gives the operator an elevated platform that is made stable by lag bolting to the floor.

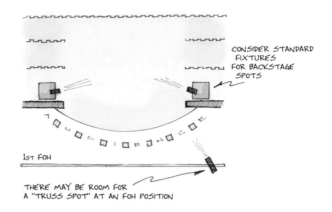

CONSIDER STANDARD FIXTURES FOR BACKSTAGE SPOTS

1ST FOH

THERE MAY BE ROOM FOR A "TRUSS SPOT" AT AN FOH POSITION

OPERATOR CONTROLS

Different followspot models have different mechanical parts, but almost all have the same basic ones. These include the dowser, iris, chopper, and boomerang.

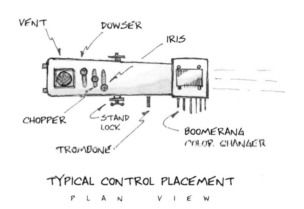

VENT
DOWSER
IRIS
CHOPPER
STAND LOCK
TROMBONE
BOOMERANG COLOR CHANGER

TYPICAL CONTROL PLACEMENT
P L A N   V I E W

A *dowser* is used both to vary the intensity of the light output, and to black out the spot so that no light gets to the stage. The dowser is a metal disc that can be rotated into the light beam. This occurs very close to the lamp, and optically in a manner so that the apparent change is a dimming effect rather than seeing an eclipse-like change to the light beam. On some really large spots, the dowser knob controls an apparatus that resembles a barn door of the type used on a Fresnel light. The two halves of the dowser plate are pulled in from either side for a more effective mechanical shuttering effect.

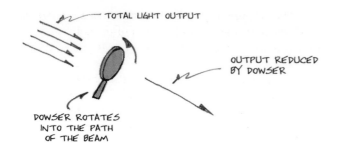

TOTAL LIGHT OUTPUT

OUTPUT REDUCED BY DOWSER

DOWSER ROTATES INTO THE PATH OF THE BEAM

THE SOLID METAL DOWSER BLOCKS PART OF THE LIGHT OUTPUT. SOME DOWSERS ARE CONSTRUCTED DIFFERENTLY, IN THE MANNER OF BARN DOORS, OR VENETIAN BLINDS.

On most lights, the dowser control is on the top of the light itself and is a steel rod with a large plastic ball on the end. Different manufacturers arrange the controls differently, but most of the time, the dowser is the control nearest the back end of the light.

You can make small adjustments in the amount of the light beam that is blacked out, but it is difficult to stop at precise points. Some operators make a mark on the housing in order to stop the lever at a predetermined place, but most of the time, a certain value must be intuited by the *spot op*. Running a followspot is somewhat more artistic than just punching a button at the lighting console.

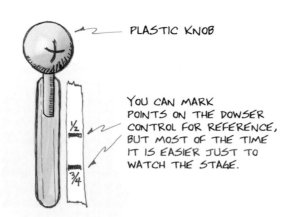

PLASTIC KNOB

YOU CAN MARK POINTS ON THE DOWSER CONTROL FOR REFERENCE, BUT MOST OF THE TIME IT IS EASIER JUST TO WATCH THE STAGE.

½

¾

Dowsers absorb a lot of heat, especially if they are not opened up for a long period of time during the

show. Even so, it is generally not a good idea to turn the spot on and off, as this can actually be harder on the equipment than just leaving it running. Plus, you may have a difficult and noisy time getting it to start back up. Larger types such as the Strong Super Trouper and Gladiator have big power supply units that "clunk" loudly when turned on and off. Virtually all spots have some sort of fan that cools both the power supply and the light itself. This fan should be allowed to run for a while after the spot is turned off, in order to avoid overheating the lamp.

The *iris* is another control found on virtually all followspots. An iris is a system of thin, curved metal plates in a movable housing. The plates overlap one another, and when an outer retaining ring is rotated, the thin plates form a larger or smaller circle. They really act a lot like the kind of ordinary shutters found in a Leko, except that the shape they form is round rather than square. The same kind of mechanism can be found in older film cameras.

Changing the size of the opening varies the size of the pool of light that reaches the stage. If the spotlight is located far from the stage, you will need to iris in for the distance; being closer will mean a larger opening. The design of the show, and individual cues, may require a larger and/or smaller size as well. The iris control knob is often the closest one to the front of the light.

TURNING THE OUTER RING WILL MAKE THE CENTER OPENING LARGER OR SMALLER

IRIS

It is sometimes possible to completely black out the light by closing the iris in all the way. Do not do this. The iris is a delicate device and is very close to the light source, which is extremely hot. If you block all of the output with the iris, the thin metal plates will heat up very rapidly. They will warp out of shape and be ruined.

Some spots have an additional device known as a *trombone* that can also be used to vary the size of the spot. The trombone is a handle on the side of the light that can be pulled back and forth along the length of the spot (hence its name; in action it is like a slide trombone). The trombone works by changing the relationship between the light source and the lens mechanism. Some operators use a combination of iris and trombone in their work. Most of the time in theatres the distance of the talent from the spot position remains fairly constant, and the trombone is not necessary. The trombone is more often used for arena acts like an ice show in which the skaters may move from 300 feet away to only 100 feet away in a matter of seconds.

The iris can be used to create a variety of spot sizes that are selected because of artistic reasons. The largest is generally the *full-body* size, which is large enough to include the entire body of the actor. Sometime you may need to go larger than this to include two characters standing right next to one another. *Three-quarter* means from the knees up and including the head. It is very rare for a designer to ask for a shot that does *not* include the actor's head and face. You should always strive to keep the head in the light, no matter what. The next smaller shot is the *waist*, and then finally the *head-shot*. Sometimes there are special instructions like "head and shoulders, but try and stay off the white guitar as much as possible," which are fairly descriptive in their own right.

The *chopper*, which is also known as a *stripper*, is used to cut off the top and bottom of the light beam so that it is more like a horizontal strip. If you then iris out to a very large size, there will be a strip of light perhaps as wide as the stage. This sometimes happens when a designer wants to have lots of lateral coverage for something like a curtain call. In reality, this effect is rarely used, because it is not very attractive.

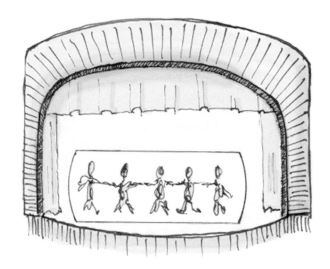

EFFECT OF A CHOPPER
ON A CURTAIN CALL LIGHT

Virtually all followspots have some sort of color changer. This device is often called by the slang term *boomerang*. Normally, six different colors are possible. The gel is loaded into round *frames* that are designed specially for that particular light. The two halves of the frame are fastened to one another with small brass brads like the office kind used to hold papers together, and are also used on other types of gel frames. It is important to do a really neat job of inserting the color media into the spot frames, because they must slide smoothly beside one another while in the light. If either the brads or the gel stick out to the side, the frames will have a tendency to get hung up on each other during the show.

In the light itself, there are six flanges for the frames to slide onto. The flange that is nearest the rear of the light is for frame one. Six goes toward the front end of the light. This is the standard numbering method and it is important to maintain proper orientation so that the correct color will be brought up during the cueing process. The original choice was a somewhat arbitrary selection, but has become the standard method and should be followed exclusively.

FULL BODY   THREE-QUARTER

—KNEE

WAIST   HEAD

COMMON SPOT SIZES

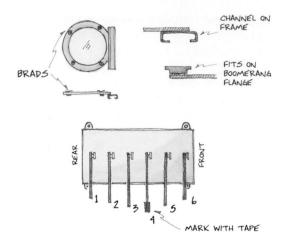

COLOR CHANGER OR "BOOMERANG"

setting up a show and of calling cues, which make it possible for an experienced operator to understand the cues with a minimum of explanation.

The spot-ops are usually given numbers in a clockwise rotation. In an arena, this means starting upstage left and moving around to upstage right. In a theatre show, the house right spot is usually number one and the house left is number two. In any case, the cue caller will tell you your number, and it is important to remember what it is. Traditionally, most theatre shows are designed for two spots, but it is not unusual to have three or even four if the budget will allow it. The numbering system is used to simplify cue calling, and in case of a change in personnel.

There are six levers on the outside of the housing that can be used to bring a particular frame up into the path of the light beam. When a color is up, it filters out all but the precise wavelengths relating to that color. The desired light color passes through, but the remainder of the light waves are stopped and converted into heat energy. Over a period of time, the gel will burn out because of that. There is also a lot of heat from the lamp itself. Gels with heavily saturated colors will last longer if they are placed in the number five and six positions away from the heat. Most lights have a button you can use to cancel out a gel frame and make it drop back out of the light beam. Alternatively, if you pull a different frame lever all the way down, the first color will be automatically canceled and jump back out of the way, hence the name *boomerang*.

A *color correction gel* is often used when video is involved, so that the color temperature of the light from the followspot will match the 56K temperature that is best for TV cameras. The correction is put into the spot so the talent looks good on camera, regardless of what the rest of the stage looks like. It might be used all the way throughout a show, rather than switching colors for artistic reasons. The term *no color* is used to indicate that no gel is to be used on a particular cue.

RUNNING THE SHOW

Running a followspot requires a lot of concentration. Professional stagehands are expected to come in and run a show cold, without ever having seen any the action of the piece. Generally, there is a *lighting director* to call the cues for a musical act, ice show, or circus, while in a theatre show, the cues are called by a stage manager, or possibly by a spot operator who travels with the show and is familiar with it. There are standard methods of

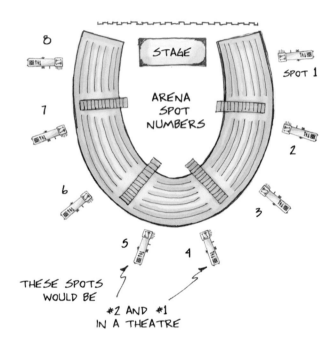

Sometimes the cue caller will assign each spot a *home position*, which is kind of like a default setting in a computer. A call to go to your home position is a way for the cue caller to reset the spots in a familiar, predetermined pattern. This happens more often in concert lighting where home positions are things like the lead singer or the stage right guitar player. In theatre shows, the same spots tend to pick up the same characters in the play so that it is easy for them to remember who to hit.

A typical spot cue might go something like this: "Stand by for spot one to pick up the woman in the red dress up left in a frame one, and spot two on the man in the black suit down right in a frame five. Spo standby and . . . go." If you are spot one, you should push down on the first lever on the boomerang to load frame one. Spot two should do the same with frame five. On the go, both spot ops should run their dowser levers to bring the light up on the target specified by the cue caller. From that point on, it is just a matter of staying with the target until the next cue is called.

Quite often, there are instructions about the timing of fades, intensity of the light, size of the spot, and so on. Very often, cue callers make a blanket statement that fades should be on a one or two count unless there are instructions to the contrary. They might ask for a very long fade like a five count for a very emotional moment, or for the spot to go out all at once on a bump if there is a general blackout. Good spot operators develop an ability to "get in tune" with the tempo of the show, and adjust their actions intuitively.

Most of the time in a theatre show, a spot will stay with the same gel color for an entire cue, but on occasion it is necessary to go from one frame to another with the light still on. Many cue callers express this by saying "*roll* to frame # so and so" or sometimes "*crossfade*." This could be on a bump, but often they want a smooth transition from one color to another. You can do this by slowly engaging the second frame to the point where it cancels the first one. That first frame will want to drop out quickly, but if you catch the lever with your finger you can gently lower the outgoing gel from the light beam in an artistic manner. Running a theatre show is generally a somewhat more subtle enterprise than a concert or circus.

It can sometimes be difficult to locate the next frame lever if you are concentrating on watching the stage and moving the spot to follow an actor. It is helpful to remember that there are six levers, and that quite often number three or four is longer so that you can find it by touch alone. Some operators put tape on number four, for the same reason. It is easy to find numbers six or five by counting backward from the far end.

Most of the time, operators are asked to stay on one person until the light fades out, and then to fade back up on another subject. On occasion, the design calls for the light to move directly from one target to the next. The cue caller may express this by saying, "*slide* over to so and so," or perhaps "*drag* your light." In this instance, you simply move discretely from one place to the other. This often happens when two actors are close together and the idea is to trade one for the other. If you can time it so that this happens as they pass one another, the audience may never notice it, especially if diffusion gel is in use.

A diffusion filter causes the light to change from a sharp-edged beam to a soft-edged beam, rather like the difference between an ellipsoidal and a Fresnel. There are different values of diffusion so that the edge of the beam can be anywhere from a little bit fuzzy to practically unfindable.

It is much more difficult to run a light with a diffuse edge, especially if the stage is bright and the difference in value is hard to see. It is generally easier to keep track of things by choosing to watch the pool of light that has an actor in it, rather than on the actor in a pool of light—a subtle, but very real distinction. If things get really bad, you may have to move your light around a bit to see if you are still on target. If it is that hard for you to see, then probably no one else will notice that you have done it, especially if you manage to avoid running the light off of the actor's face. As a general rule, you should avoid jerking the light around unnecessarily. Stay still, even if you are slightly off-target, wait for the actor to move some, and then readjust.

TRADITIONAL HARD-EDGE SPOT

SPOT WITH DIFFUSION MEDIA

USE YOUR THUMB AND FINGERS TO ARTISTICALLY CHANGE FROM ONE FRAME TO ANOTHER

It is often difficult to have your spot lined up on the actor when the light comes up. It is very distracting to have a light appear near center stage and then uncertainly wander around until it finds the woman in the red dress upstage left. You can avoid this by using some kind of targeting device. This can be as expensive as a high-powered *telescopic rifle sight*, or as low-tech as a bent piece of wire. There are a number of proprietary devices that are made specifically for this purpose and new ones are developed from time to time. You should try different things and find one that works well for you personally. Using a sight of some sort is a really important step that can enhance the artistic qualities of your spotting work.

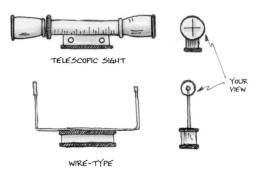

TELESCOPIC SIGHT

YOUR VIEW

WIRE-TYPE

USE A SIGHT TO IMPROVE YOUR AIM

The sight is a personal tool, and you will need to move it from one spot to another each time you work. It is common practice to attach the sight, of whatever type, to a powerful magnet so that it can be easily mounted on the steel housing of the spotlight. Then it is just a matter of adjusting the sight so that it is accurately centered on the light beam coming out of the spot. For best results, make your adjustments at maximum distance, with the iris as small as practical.

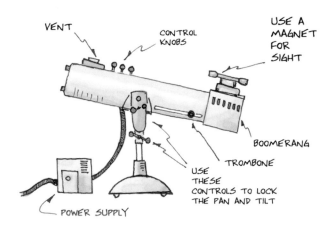

VENT

CONTROL KNOBS

USE A MAGNET FOR SIGHT

BOOMERANG

TROMBONE

USE THESE CONTROLS TO LOCK THE PAN AND TILT

POWER SUPPLY

There are some rather quirky spot instructions that come up on a fairly regular basis, commonly enough so that they have actual names. One of these is the *ballyhoo*. This occurs when the spots criss-cross the audience area in a figure-eight pattern, or perhaps a swirl. This is generally done to excite the crowd, as though the lights are searching for someone. It is even more effective if you change speeds occasionally, as though you are slowly searching, speed over to another possible target, and then slowly search again. Another technique is to *pan* back and forth over a group that is too large for one or more spots to cover effectively. This works well for a line of actors at curtain call, or perhaps even a line of elephants on the back track near ring two.

PAN BACK AND FORTH

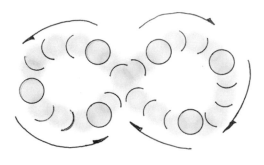

BALLYHOO THRU THE AUDIENCE

CHAPTER 11

SOUND

Sound is a very important element in stage work. It is one of the youngest, as well, and much of the high-tech sound equipment in use today was invented in only the past few years. It is difficult to write about something so changeable in a book such as this one without becoming out of date practically overnight. But the basic ideas about the physics of sound and the concepts of sound reinforcement and playback have been around for many years.

There are three elemental ways to use sound in a play: live sounds, including those made by actors; playback of previously recorded elements; and sound reinforcement through amplification.

THIS MIXING CONSOLE IS SET UP IN A ROAD HOUSE THAT CATERS TO TOURING PRODUCTIONS OF BROADWAY SHOWS

METHODS OF PRODUCING SOUND

Some sounds are better performed live. Gunshots (unless there are lots of them), telephone rings, and doorbells are all good examples of when live sounds are more appropriate. It is difficult to get a realistically loud and sharp gunshot through a sound system. The sound from a telephone is very directional, so having it emanate from the phone itself is more realistic. If the actual telephone is rigged to ring, you can also rig it so that it stops ringing when the actor picks it up. Other sounds like door chimes are so easily set up that it only makes sense for them to be done live. Sometimes the timing of a cue is better when an actor does it, such as the example of chimes, rather than when a stage manager calls the cue to a board operator.

Playback means that sounds are recorded and stored on a machine and then played back during the performance. Playback includes things like preshow music and sound effects. Rain, thunder, cars driving by, and crickets are all good examples of sounds that may be played back. Playback was once done with analog devices like records or tape recordings, but is now exclusively digital.

doi: 10.1016/C2009-0-23409-X

Sound reinforcement is used when the voices of the actors are not strong enough to provide sufficient volume. It is obviously impossible for actors in a rock musical to make themselves heard over the band without help, but reinforcement is also useful in a straight play when the timbre of an actor's voice needs to be softer than that used when "projecting" to the rear of the theatre. Microphones are also often used to amp up the musical instruments in an accompanying orchestra. Sound reinforcement requires a complex system of microphones, mixer, signal processing, amplification, and speakers.

Sound as Waves

Sound is created when pressure waves move through the air. Pressure waves are created by vibrating objects that in turn vibrate the air around them at a certain frequency. Frequency is the number of times per second the vibration happens. The vibrating air can be viewed as waves that travel outward from the source, in much the same way that waves radiate outward from a stone thrown in water. Water doesn't compress, so the waves cause it to rise up from the surface, which makes it easy to see them. Because air is compressible, sound waves take the form of alternating areas of compression and rarefaction, and their movement is invisible.

axis from the positive to the negative zone and back. The positive quadrant represents an area of compression and the negative quadrant an area of rarefaction. The distance of the line from the x axis is representative of the volume of the sound.

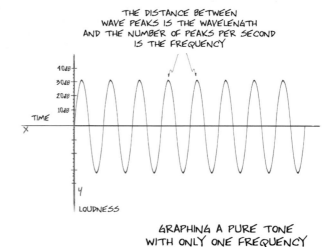

GRAPHING A PURE TONE
WITH ONLY ONE FREQUENCY

In a sound editing program, the graph of a sound is a time/loudness representation instead. Virtually all real-world sounds are a composite of many different tones, all at their own phases and amplitudes, and a realistic graph of that would be so complex as to be meaningless to the viewer. Sound editing programs offer a generalized representation of how loud a sound is, so that editing points, or markers, can be established.

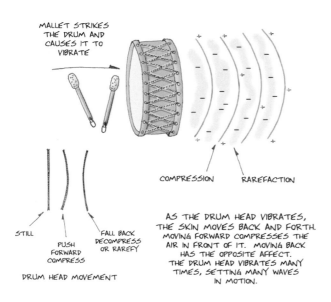

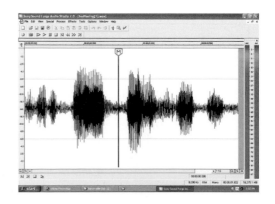

THIS GRAPH SHOWS THE
RELATIVE LOUDNESS OF THE SOUNDS

Sounds are often displayed using a graph, in which the x axis represents time, and the y axis represents the amplitude or loudness of the sound. The frequency can be inferred from how often the wave crosses over the x

In a theoretical model, the waves move through air in all directions in the form of a sphere. As the waves travel farther from the source, their power is reduced according to the law of squares, which is derived from finding the surface area of a sphere.

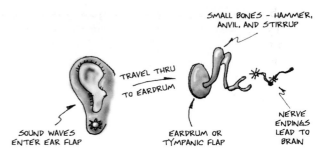

SMALL BONES - HAMMER, ANVIL, AND STIRRUP

TRAVEL THRU TO EARDRUM

SOUND WAVES ENTER EAR FLAP

EARDRUM OR TYMPANIC FLAP

NERVE ENDINGS LEAD TO BRAIN

THE HUMAN EAR IS A TYPE OF TRANSDUCER BECAUSE IT CHANGES SOUND WAVE ENERGY INTO SMALL ELECTRICAL IMPULSES THAT ARE INTERPRETED AS SOUND BY THE NERVE ENDINGS

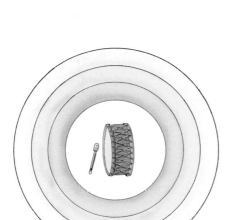

THE ENERGY OF THE DRUMBEAT FADES AS IT TRAVELS OUTWARD IN ALL DIRECTIONS

Sound waves are created when a vibrating source compresses and rarefies the air around it, and the same thing happens in reverse when those atmospheric waves strike a solid object—that object begins to vibrate as well. Some materials are more affected by sound waves than others are. A thin, semirigid material vibrates more readily than a thicker one. The plastic "skin" on the head of a drum is an excellent vibrator, being thin and expansive. In the human ear, the eardrum is a flat layer of skin that reacts in the same way. Small bones in the ear transfer the vibrations to nerves that interpret them as sounds.

SOUND FREQUENCIES

The frequency of a sound is relative to its pitch and is measured in *Hertz* (Hz), as you might expect from studying other wave fields. Frequency means exactly what it seems to: how frequently the oscillations occur. High-pitched sounds have a higher frequency, and low-pitched sounds are a lower frequency. The human ear can detect only a limited range of frequencies, although sounds higher and lower than that exist. Dogs can hear higher and lower frequencies than humans, and in general have much more acute senses than we do. As a person ages, the "skin" on the eardrum tends to thicken and is not as good a sound receiver as it once was. Higher frequencies are more heavily affected than lower ones. Thus older people have less acute hearing, especially in the higher frequency ranges. The eardrum is a very sensitive instrument and should be protected. Sounds that are too loud—especially high-pitched ones—will damage the drum permanently.

Audible sound occurs approximately between 20 Hz and 20,000 Hz, but the amounts are not exact, because some people hear better than others. As a frame of reference, the lowest A note on a piano is 27 Hz, and the highest C is 4186 Hz. Any note an octave above another is twice the frequency of the first one, in a logarithmic scale. Middle A is 440 Hz, and is considered a standard from which other pitches are measured. The concept of an octave is important when considering an equalizer, which is a system of filters that allows the user to boost some frequencies and reduce others.

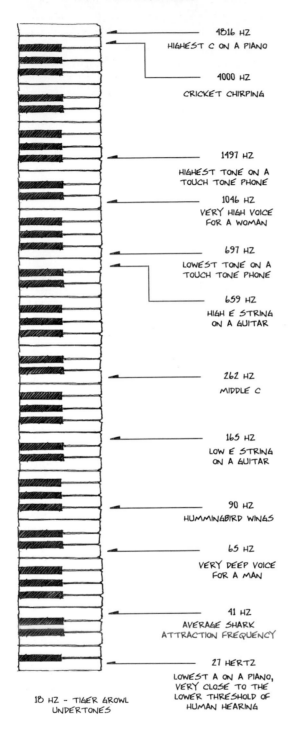

HUMAN HEARING TOPS OUT AROUND 20,000 HERTZ.
THE EAR CANNOT PROCESS VIBRATIONS FASTER
THAN THAT.

25 KHZ + ... BAT SONAR CLICKS

4816 HZ
HIGHEST C ON A PIANO

4000 HZ
CRICKET CHIRPING

1497 HZ
HIGHEST TONE ON A
TOUCH TONE PHONE

1046 HZ
VERY HIGH VOICE
FOR A WOMAN

697 HZ
LOWEST TONE ON A
TOUCH TONE PHONE

659 HZ
HIGH E STRING
ON A GUITAR

262 HZ
MIDDLE C

165 HZ
LOW E STRING
ON A GUITAR

90 HZ
HUMMINGBIRD WINGS

65 HZ
VERY DEEP VOICE
FOR A MAN

41 HZ
AVERAGE SHARK
ATTRACTION FREQUENCY

27 HERTZ
LOWEST A ON A PIANO,
VERY CLOSE TO THE
LOWER THRESHOLD OF
HUMAN HEARING

18 HZ - TIGER GROWL
UNDERTONES

HUMAN HEARING BOTTOMS OUT AROUND 20 HERTZ.
BELOW THAT LEVEL VIBRATIONS ARE PERCIEVED
AS MOVEMENT RATHER THAN SOUND.

How Loudness Is Measured

The standard unit of measurement for sound is the *decibel*. In the SI (Système International d'Unités) system of prefixes for units of measurement, the prefix "deci-" means one-tenth. Thus a decibel or *dB* is one-tenth of a *bel*, a power measurement for sound that is named for telephone inventor Alexander Bell. The scale is logarithmic, so that two bels is twice as loud as one, and five is twice as loud as four. This causes the sounds to become louder very rapidly, so the smaller decibel unit of measurement is used to give the scale more sensitivity. A chart is often used to demonstrate the relative values of dB numbers, so that a frame of reference can be established.

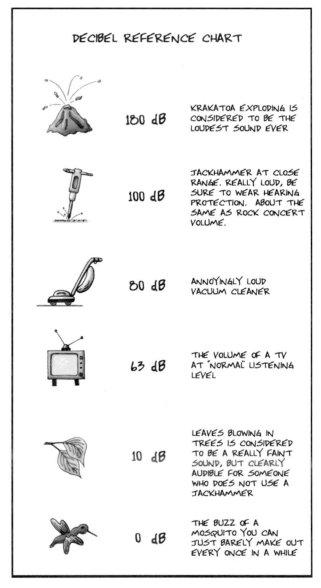

DECIBEL REFERENCE CHART

180 dB — KRAKATOA EXPLODING IS CONSIDERED TO BE THE LOUDEST SOUND EVER

100 dB — JACKHAMMER AT CLOSE RANGE. REALLY LOUD, BE SURE TO WEAR HEARING PROTECTION. ABOUT THE SAME AS ROCK CONCERT VOLUME.

80 dB — ANNOYINGLY LOUD VACUUM CLEANER

63 dB — THE VOLUME OF A TV AT "NORMAL" LISTENING LEVEL

10 dB — LEAVES BLOWING IN TREES IS CONSIDERED TO BE A REALLY FAINT SOUND, BUT CLEARLY AUDIBLE FOR SOMEONE WHO DOES NOT USE A JACKHAMMER

0 dB — THE BUZZ OF A MOSQUITO YOU CAN JUST BARELY MAKE OUT EVERY ONCE IN A WHILE

A *VU meter* is closely related to decibels, but is generally used to reference the force of an audio signal in sound equipment rather than sound waves in the air.

VU stands for volume units. The output of a device is considered to be optimum when the needle is at 0. A volume in the plus range means that the equipment has reached a point where some distortion will occur. The higher the output into the plus range, the higher that amount of distortion will be. Many modern pieces of sound equipment have an LED readout instead of an analog meter, in which a series of green LEDs represent VU measurements up to 0, and red LEDs represent the passage into positive numbers. Sound editing programs have virtual LED bars that reference the same thing.

STANDARD SORT OF VU METER FOUND
ON A MIXING CONSOLE

TINNITUS

Tinnitus is a condition whereby a person's ears tend to have a persistent ringing sensation. Short-term tinnitus is a common result of exposure to loud sounds, especially high-pitched sounds. The problem is proportional to the duration of exposure, and a long exposure is more problematic than a short one. A loud arena concert may reach a noise level of 100 dB or more, and if the show is 2 hours long, an (at least), short-term ringing in the ears is almost sure to occur. (Remember that 100 dB is twice as loud as 90 dB.) Tinnitus is symptomatic of hearing loss, and by the time you notice that your ears are ringing, it is already too late to do anything about it. In recent years, musical artists have come to rely upon wireless *in the ear* monitors rather than using monitor speakers pointed directly at them. The older style needed to be very loud in order to overcome the ambient sounds of the concert, but the in-ear type can be much softer. This protects the ears of the performers, but doesn't help the audience.

PARTS OF A SOUND REINFORCEMENT SYSTEM

Sound reinforcement is used to amplify the voices of actors on the stage, most notably for a musical, but also for some straight plays in large venues. The process is somewhat complex, as the acoustical sounds of the various actors must be transformed into electrical impulses, transmitted to a central location, processed, amplified, and transmitted to a set of speakers that in turn transform the electronic sound back into acoustical sound.

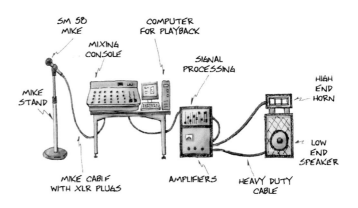

HOW EQUIPMENT IS CONNECTED

MICROPHONE DESIGN

The first duty of the system, picking up aural sounds and converting them to electrical impulses, is the job of the *microphone*. Any device that changes energy from one form to another is called a *transducer*, and microphones change the energy of sound waves traveling through the air into electrical impulses. (*Trans* meaning across, and *ducere* meaning to lead, a microphone leads the energy across to another state.) A *dynamic microphone* uses a coil of wire suspended in a magnetic field to make the transformation. As mentioned in the chapters on electrical theory, a coil of wire moving in a magnetic field produces a voltage. Sounds enter the microphone and vibrate a diaphragm that in turn vibrates the coil of wire. The electrical pulses formed are proportional to the vibrations picked up out of the air. This arrangement requires significant energy to move the coil of wire, because it is somewhat heavy. Dynamic microphones operate best in the middle frequency ranges, where the human voice lies, and are often used for vocal purposes.

Condenser microphones work on a different principle—that of the capacitor. As mentioned in Chapter 6, capacitors have two metal plates separated by an insulating material that can be used to hold an electrical charge. The closeness of the two plates has an effect on the size of the charge. In a condenser microphone ("condenser" is an older word for "capacitor"—they mean the same thing), one of the metal plates is free to move about in relation to the sound waves that enter the mike. The other is fixed, and as the distance between them varies an electrical signal is created. The very small voltage is proportional to the sound waves, but is generally too small to reach the mixing console without some sort of amplification. The *preamp*, as it is called, in a condenser microphone amplifies the signal so that it is stronger, but requires a supply of energy in order to do that.

That power supply is known as *phantom power*, usually 48v DC. Phantom power is supplied via the mixing console. Most boards offer the option of turning it on or off, so it must be turned on when a condenser mic is in use. Most dynamic microphones are not affected by the phantom power supply, and thus it may remain switched on most of the time with little affect to the system.

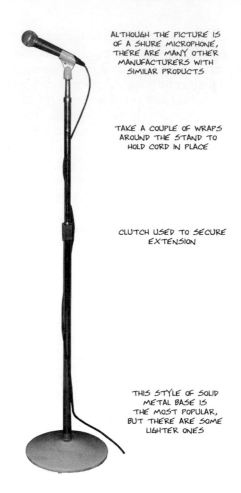

ALTHOUGH THE PICTURE IS OF A SHURE MICROPHONE, THERE ARE MANY OTHER MANUFACTURERS WITH SIMILAR PRODUCTS

TAKE A COUPLE OF WRAPS AROUND THE STAND TO HOLD CORD IN PLACE

CLUTCH USED TO SECURE EXTENSION

THIS STYLE OF SOLID METAL BASE IS THE MOST POPULAR, BUT THERE ARE SOME LIGHTER ONES

MICS USED ON STAGE

The Shure model SM58 is the most easily recognized type of microphone, and has been around for years. They are available in the standard corded version, but also as a wireless type that transmits a signal to a receiver so that the performer can move about anywhere on stage. The SM58 is a dynamic mic, and is designed to pick up sounds close to it, such as when the performer is holding it in his or her hand or is positioned behind a mic stand.

An actor with a handheld microphone makes a very presentational statement, which might be okay for some theatrical productions when the characters are meant to be in the act of performing, but most of the time a less distracting approach is used. One method is to place a type of microphone on the front of the stage that can pick up sounds from a larger area than would be possible with a personal mic like the SM58. *PCC* (phase-coherent-cardioid) microphones are sometimes used on the front of the stage to capture generalized sound from many different actors. They are often meant to pick up the voices of a chorus of singers, when it would be difficult to mike each individual member of the group.

The microphone receivers are generally of the *diversity* type, meaning that they have two antennas installed at different angles, so that if one is unable to pick up the signal the other one takes over. The receivers are usually rack-mounted so that many of them can be fitted into a small space. That is especially important when each actor is wired up individually and 20 to 30 are in use at one time. The radio waves operate in the UHF band, and can be set to an open frequency by the user.

PCC MICROPHONES LIE FLAT ON THE STAGE FLOOR AND TEND TO PICK UP MORE GENERALIZED SOUNDS THAN OTHER TYPES.

Group mikes like the PCC are useful for capturing the overall ambient sound from the stage, but used alone at high gain, they tend to amplify unwanted sounds like footsteps and fabric rustling. In most modern theatre productions, wireless microphone systems are used to boost the voices of individual actors. They use a type of microphone known as a *lavaliere* or lav, which is tiny in comparison to the others and may be hidden on the body of the performer. This type is used by newscasters as well, but broadcast lavs are quite large and worn like a tie pin. They are immediately noticeable when watching a news program. The theatrical type is much smaller and is most often worn behind the ear, or perhaps on the forehead after passing under a wig. The mike is connected to a transmitter via a very small wire. The transmitters are tiny also, and if worn in a pouch connected directly to the actor's body, the performer can change costumes without disturbing the mike. There are many different approaches to "wiring up" a performer.

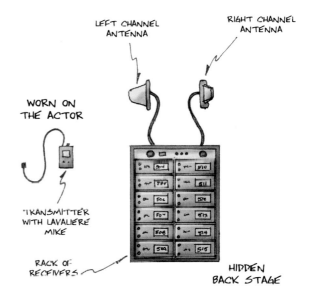

LEFT CHANNEL ANTENNA

RIGHT CHANNEL ANTENNA

WORN ON THE ACTOR

TRANSMITTER WITH LAVALIERE MIKE

RACK OF RECEIVERS

HIDDEN BACK STAGE

WIRELESS BODY MIKE SYSTEMS CONSIST OF LAVALIERE MIKE TRANSMITTERS AND DIVERSITY RECEIVERS. MOST OF THEM UTILIZE THE SAME BROADCAST FREQUENCIES AS UHF TELEVISION STATIONS - 470 MHZ THROUGH 698 MHZ. JUST RECENTLY THE 698 - 806 MEGAHERTZ BAND WAS ALSO AVAILABLE, BUT THE FCC AUCTIONED OFF THOSE FREQUENCIES AFTER THE SHIFT TO DIGITAL MEANT THEY WERE NO LONGER REQUIRED FOR THAT ORIGINAL PURPOSE. MOST SYSTEMS ALLOW THE USER TO SELECT APPROPRIATE UNUSED FREQUENCIES IN THEIR AREA.

MIXING CONSOLE

A sound *mixing console* takes all of the inputs from different microphones, as well as playback devices, and blends them together into the mono or stereo output that is heard by the audience. *Mono* means that all speakers have the same sound, whereas *stereo* indicates that there are two slightly different versions of the same sound coming from different sides of the stage. Stereo imparts a sense of directionality to the sound, so that some specific effects sound like they are coming from one side of the stage or the other. You might choose to pan a sound effect such as a car driving by from one side to the other to enhance the idea that the car is actually moving somewhere. Much more complex multichannel systems are available, but stereo is a standard type of output.

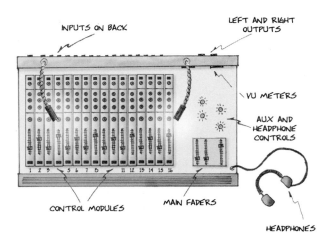

LAYOUT OF A COMMONLY USED MIXING CONSOLE

DESPITE THE SEEMINGLY HUGE NUMBER OF KNOBS AND BUTTONS, THE CONTROL MODULES ARE MOSTLY ALL THE SAME, SO MIXING A SHOW IS NOT AS DAUNTING A PROCESS AS YOU MIGHT THINK.

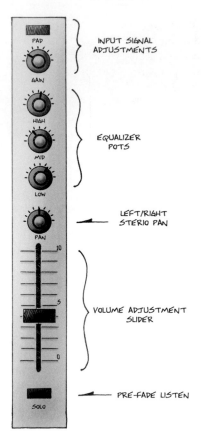

INPUT MODULE

Each input to the mixer board has its own discrete and individual module. The number of *input modules* tends to come in multiples of 16, so that 16, 32, and 48 channel boards are common. Input modules are somewhat different from model to model, but some features are universal. Each of the input modules on a board is identical in most respects, so that although the mixer may have hundreds of knobs and sliders, many of those controls have identical functions, and the setup is not as complex as it may first appear. The signal passing through a module is often called a *channel*.

At the top of each module are a *pad* button and a *gain* knob, which are meant to be used together in preparing the module to receive a signal that is more powerful or less powerful. Microphones emit a very low-power *mic level signal*; playback devices such as a CD player emit a much stronger signal. The latter are often referred to as *line-level inputs*. The pad button should be in the up position for a microphone, and down for a line-level input. The gain knob is used to make finer adjustments to the input power. It is important to adjust the input gain so that the signal is strong enough to be useful, but not so strong as to be out of line with others.

The word *gain* is generally used to indicate an amount of amplification. It is important to make a distinction here: the overall amplification of the signal is adjusted by moving the module slider. The gain knob at the top of the module is really meant only to adjust the input signal, and not to adjust the output of the channel during the show. Use the input gain knob to create a level at which the module slider works effectively in the middle of its travel. If the gain is too high, the input sound will be instantly loud the moment you move its slider upward. If the gain is too low, the sound will be faint even when the slider is all the way up.

Most input modules have at least three *equalizer* knobs, but many have more than that. They are used to *EQ* the sound coming into that one single input. *High-end* or high-frequency tones can be enhanced or reduced. The same is true of *low-end* sounds. The human voice tends to be in the lower mid-range of audible frequencies. Adjusting the EQ can create a richer-than-normal sound.

The *pan* knob is used to adjust how much sound should be coming from the left or right speaker in a stereo system. When wired correctly, turning the knob to the left sends more sound to house left, while turning it to the right sends more sound to the house right speaker. House left and right are the opposite of stage left and right. The board is set up so that it makes intuitive sense to the operator, who is facing the stage.

The *solo* or *PFL* (pre-fade listen) button allows the operator to preview the volume of a channel before bringing it up with the slider. Press the button to hear that channel over your headphones, or to check its strength with the VU meter. These actions do not affect the sound being heard by the audience.

The *slider* below the knobs is used to adjust the volume of the microphone patched into that particular input module. Each channel is controlled separately so that the sound reaching the audience is a balanced mix of all the available sounds. On some boards, some of the channels are designed for microphones and others are meant to be used with playback equipment. They may be slightly different, especially the type of input connector, but the volume of a playback sound is controlled by a slider just like a microphone.

Most boards have one or more *auxiliary sends* that can be used to connect individual channels to a signal processing unit, or perhaps to a performer's monitor that is separate from the main speakers. Typically, *AUX* out buttons are located on the input module, and knobs to the right of the board are used to vary the gain of the output. Pushing in the AUX button on a module connects that channel to the selected AUX output, but *does not* disconnect it from the main output.

Sliders to the far right of the console are used to adjust the overall master left and right stereo volume.

Again, the left should be the house left and the right should be house right.

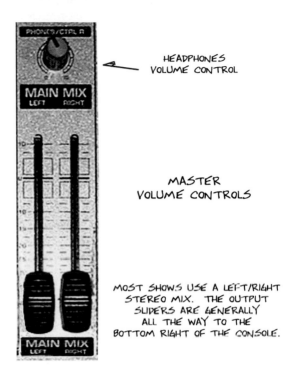

HEADPHONES VOLUME CONTROL

MASTER VOLUME CONTROLS

MOST SHOWS USE A LEFT/RIGHT STEREO MIX. THE OUTPUT SLIDERS ARE GENERALLY ALL THE WAY TO THE BOTTOM RIGHT OF THE CONSOLE.

SIGNAL PROCESSING

After the signal leaves the mixer, it often passes through an *equalizer* used to sweeten the sound and to reduce the effects of feedback. Feedback occurs when a specific frequency of sound feeds itself back into the microphone. A *feedback loop* occurs when the tone reproduces itself louder and louder until it becomes a squeal that drowns out everything else. Often, feedback can be reduced by positioning the microphones away from the speakers. But another cause of feedback has to do with the length of sound waves, and how they interact with a specific room.

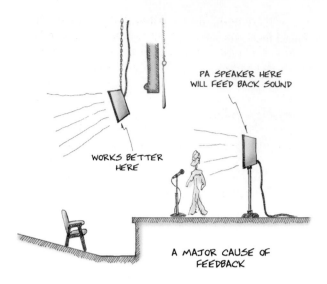

PA SPEAKER HERE
WILL FEED BACK SOUND

WORKS BETTER
HERE

A MAJOR CAUSE OF
FEEDBACK

PLACE THE SPEAKERS WHERE THEY DON'T
SEND SOUND DIRECTLY TO THE MICROPHONES

Each theatre is different in size and shape, so the exact frequency involved is different for each room, but some wavelengths are just the right size to bounce back stronger than others, like an echo. A *third-octave EQ* has filters similar to those found on the input module, but there are many more of them, three per octave of frequency variation. If the EQ is adjusted so that the room's natural feedback frequency is adjusted downward, it will not be as loudly reproduced, and the threat of feedback is lessened. A third-octave EQ is an analog device, but in recent years, it has become possible to attenuate feedback automatically using digital technology. Computer programs can detect that a feedback loop is building and reduce it automatically.

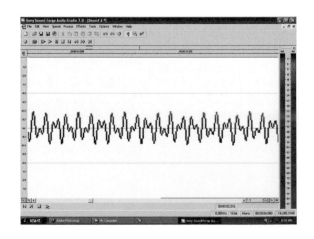

DIGITAL SAMPLE OF THE LOWEST TONE PRODUCED BY
A TOUCH TONE PHONE, 697 Hz. THE TONE WAS
SAMPLED AT A VERY LOW RATE OF 8,000 Hz, SO THE
SQUARE WAVE APPROXIMATION IS CLEARLY EVIDENT.

ANALOG VERSUS DIGITAL SIGNALS

It is important to make a distinction between an analog signal and a digital one. Microphones are analog devices, and the electrical signal they produce is proportional to the sound waves in the air, and can be graphed like a sine wave. Digital signals are a long string of plus and minus voltages that make up a simulation of an analog signal. Analog equipment cannot process a digital signal and digital equipment cannot process an analog signal, unless some sort of conversion is made between the two types. Technically, all digital signals are in the form of a square wave, just like the DMX signal discussed in the chapter on lighting control. Quite often converters are used to change back and forth from analog to digital. A computer's sound card does that when it changes the digital signal from an MP3 file into an analog signal that comes out your speakers. Speakers are inherently analog, as are all devices that deal with audible sound.

In order to become a digital signal, sounds must be sampled. *Sampling* is a process that tests the signal at certain intervals to see what its properties are. The *sample rate* is the time interval involved. A higher sample rate is generally better, because this will ensure that the "samples" of sound are taken often enough to create an accurate digital picture. This is especially true at higher frequencies. The sample rate must be several times the analog rate in order to be effective. Early programs weren't able to sample very rapidly, but the modern types use a fairly standard 44-kHz rate. That allows the computer to sample a 20-kHz audio signal twice for every alternation of the analog signal. Of course, a 20-kHz sound is a very high-pitched squeak, and pleasing tones are for the most part a much slower frequency, and are thus more accurately sampled.

AMPLIFICATION

Sounds are amplified after leaving the mixer. Amplifiers are designed to be low-*noise*, meaning that they tend not to reproduce and amplify buzzing sounds that are present in their own electronics. It is not unusual for the 60-Hz AC line voltage to interfere with sound signals. Each amp has a DC power supply inside it that is used to run the electrical components, and great care is taken by manufacturers to shield the system from inductive magnetic fields. You should avoid connecting them to a power source that also feeds dimmers, because the switching nature of a modern dimmer causes multiple small voltage spikes in the system, which has a negative effect on the amplifier. The power of an amplifier is rated in watts rather than volts or amps, which makes sense, because the watt is a unit used to measure power and volts and amps are not.

THE AUDIO SIGNAL FOLLOWS THIS BASIC PATH

It is important that amplifiers are connected to the signal path after it emerges from the mixer/processors, not before. Amplifiers by their very nature greatly increase the strength of the signal, and if they were used in advance of the mixing console, they would seriously overload its circuits. Most amps can be used either mono or stereo, depending on how they are configured. They have a selection switch on them. If an amp is used to power both the left and right speakers in a system, stereo should be selected and the left and right inputs patched in accordingly. It is very common to use multiple amps for different speakers—one for each speaker or each group of speakers. In that case, configure the amp to mono so that maximum power reaches the speakers.

LOUDSPEAKERS

The amplified signal travels down wires to the *loudspeakers*, which are used to transform the analog electrical signal back into sound waves consisting of compacted and rarefied air that can be heard by the human ear. If all has gone well, the sounds are not unnecessarily distorted, other than as intended by the signal processing equipment. There are several types of loudspeakers, but the most universal is the cone type.

Cone speakers have a paper cone in them that is moved back and forth by a system of magnets and coils of wire. The process is not unlike that used by a microphone to convert, or *transduce*, aural sound into electrical impulses. In this case, the magnetic impulses move a much heavier paper cone much larger distances, which is why the amplifier was necessary. The back-and-forth motion of the cone pushes the air in front of it forward to compress it, and when it moves backward, an opposite area of rarefaction is created. Thus an audible sound wave is created. This process is quite visible in larger speakers. The larger cone moves back and forth a proportionally large distance.

Lower-pitched sounds have a longer wavelength, and are best reproduced by a larger cone. *Woofers* and *subs* are used to reproduce low-end tones. Loudness is relative, and proportional to the amplitude of the signal sent to the speaker. If the amplified signal is too large for the physical properties of the speaker, the cone will be forced to move farther than it is able to, and the paper will be damaged. This is known as a "blown" speaker. Distorted sounds are especially detrimental to speakers.

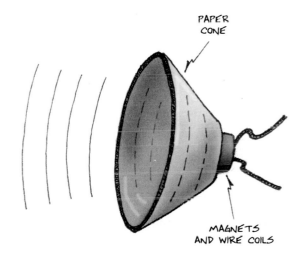

PAPER CONE

MAGNETS AND WIRE COILS

THE CONE OF A SPEAKER IS MADE OF PAPER AND IS QUITE FRAGILE. THE THIN, DELICATE NATURE OF THE CONE MAKES IT MAGNIFY THE VIBRATIONS OF THE MAGNETS AND WIRE FOUND IN THE BACK OF THE PAPER CONE. LOUDER SOUNDS MOVE THE CONE MORE THAN SOFT ONES. IF THE CONE MOVES TOO FAR OR TOO FAST IT WILL BE DAMAGED.

Higher frequencies are often reproduced by *horn* and *driver* loudspeakers. A system of magnets and wires similar to that found in a cone speaker is used to vibrate a diaphragm, but instead of using a paper cone, a plastic horn is used as a resonator. The horn is aptly named, having a small throat and a much larger outer opening.

The plastic horn greatly increases the volume of sound from the diaphragm.

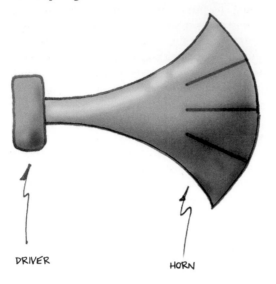

DRIVER   HORN

HORN AND DRIVER

THE DRIVER HAS THE MAGNET AND WIRE THAT
MAKES THE ACTUAL SOUND, BUT THE
HORN PART IS ESSENTIAL AS A RESONATOR

CABLES AND CONNECTORS

Three-pin *XLR connectors* are universally used to connect microphones to sound equipment. Most sound consoles have an input strip along the back, and each mic-compatible module has an XLR input. Most mic cables have a shield in them, so that the wires inside are protected from interference from other electrical sources. Wires from lighting, like a 20-amp jumper, create an inductive field around them that can interfere with the very small voltages present in a microphone cable. You should avoid running mic cables and lighting cables in the same space, especially if the lighting cable has been neatly coiled, because a coil of wire creates a much larger inductive field.

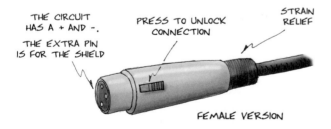

THE CIRCUIT   PRESS TO UNLOCK   STRAIN
HAS A + AND -.   CONNECTION   RELIEF

THE EXTRA PIN
IS FOR THE SHIELD

FEMALE VERSION

XLR MICROPHONE CABLE

Some speakers are connected using a quarter-inch jack, which appears to be one single conductor, but actually has a ring and a tip component. This sort of cable has two conductors in it, one being connected to the ring and one to the tip of the *1/4" jack*. This type of connector is also used for things like a guitar cable, but be careful, because the current output of a guitar is much less than that of a speaker. Speaker cables are much heavier duty.

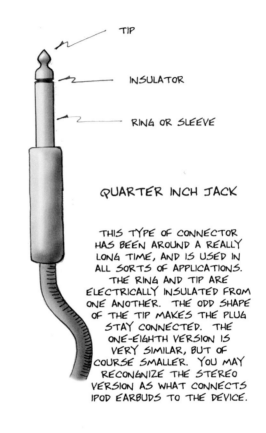

TIP

INSULATOR

RING OR SLEEVE

QUARTER INCH JACK

THIS TYPE OF CONNECTOR
HAS BEEN AROUND A REALLY
LONG TIME, AND IS USED IN
ALL SORTS OF APPLICATIONS.
THE RING AND TIP ARE
ELECTRICALLY INSULATED FROM
ONE ANOTHER. THE ODD SHAPE
OF THE TIP MAKES THE PLUG
STAY CONNECTED. THE
ONE-EIGHTH VERSION IS
VERY SIMILAR, BUT OF
COURSE SMALLER. YOU MAY
RECONGNIZE THE STEREO
VERSION AS WHAT CONNECTS
IPOD EARBUDS TO THE DEVICE.

Other speakers, especially more modern ones, may use a *Speakon* connector, which has the advantage of making a more secure connection to the speaker cabinet. Small tabs on the sides must be manipulated to pull it loose. This type of connector is for speakers only, so there is no confusion with other types of cables.

SPEAKON CONNECTORS ONLY FIT ON
AMPS AND SPEAKERS, SO THEY
AREN'T EASILY CONFUSED WITH
SOMETHING LIKE A 1/4" GUITAR CABLE

A playback device like a CD player often uses *RCA connectors* as outputs. They are used on many televisions and DVD players as well, and will seem very familiar. Most mixing consoles don't have RCA connectors on the back, so you will need an RCA-to-1/4" adaptor to connect a CD player to a sound board.

TIP

RING

RCA CONNECTORS
ARE OFTEN USED TO PATCH DIFFERENT SORTS
OF CONSUMER ELECTRONICS. AUDIO OUTPUTS ARE
USUALLY RED AND WHITE, AND VIDEO YELLOW.

PLAYBACK EQUIPMENT

Playback indicates that sounds have been recorded earlier and are played back during the performance rather than being produced live. Many different types of equipment have been used over the years, beginning with a record player, and progressing to audiotape, MiniDiscs, CDs, and now to sounds stored as files on a computer. It is difficult to imagine what the next thing will be, but it seems like the playing of digital files of one sort or another is here to stay.

There are several different possibilities of how to play back digital files besides using a CD player. It is possible to run sounds from something like Windows Media Player or QuickTime by attaching the headphone output to the mixing console, but the problem is one of reliability and organization. (The headphone output signal is analog, having come from the sound card.) Neither Media Player nor QuickTime is set up to properly organize the files.

Theatre-specific audio programs such as *QLab* and *SXF* have important features that make them useful for playing back digital files. For one thing, the files can be organized into a cue list that automatically updates to the next cue in line once the previous cue has been run. Sound playback programs are mentioned in the next chapter, "Computer Programs for the Theatre."

CHAPTER 12

COMPUTER PROGRAMS FOR THE THEATRE

Computers are an essential part of modern life, and it is hard to imagine a time before they existed. In a short 20 years or so, they have drastically changed the way the world works, especially in a technical field like theatre production. Of course computers don't make anyone more artistic, but they do make just about everyone more efficient. From spreadsheets for the box office to playwriting, it's hard to do theatre today without computers.

I have picked out four programs that are really essential to theatre production, and have written a short description of why they are important, plus a few tips on getting started. If you are like me, the best way to get started with a new program is just to play around with it and determine how to navigate through its features. After you've gotten your feet wet, you can find a guide to help you learn more about the nuances of the programs.

EARLY ON, COMPUTERS FILLED ENTIRE ROOMS LIKE THIS ONE AT A MILITARY COMPLEX. THE LARGE CABINETS ON THE SIDES HELD TAPE STORAGE DEVICES. UNTIL THE 1980S, ONLY LARGE CORPORATIONS, UNIVERSITIES, AND THE MILITARY COULD AFFORD COMPUTERS.

YOU CAN SEE AN EARLY CRT MONITOR IN THE CENTER NEAR THE BACK.

doi: 10.1016/C2009-0-23409-X

ADOBE PHOTOSHOP

Adobe Photoshop is a huge program that has been around for many years, and will no doubt be around for many more. It is used by people in lots of different fields, and has undergone constant revision by the makers. There have been at least a dozen different versions to date. Adobe also produces Photoshop Elements, which is much less expensive than the original and has most of the same features. The less-expensive Elements version is aimed at personal users and is a good way to learn the program on a budget. Photoshop is so widely used that most schools have it in their computer labs, so it is not hard to find a copy to work with. Photoshop works great on either Macs or PCs—it really doesn't make that much difference anymore.

Adobe has excellent online tutorials that you can easily find with a search engine like Google. They have a huge selection of topics that cover most of the program functions you are likely to need. Adobe's tutorials cover all of their products, not just Photoshop.

If you prefer printed material, you might check out the book *Photoshop Essential Skills* by Mark Galer and Philip Andrews (Focal Press, 2008). It was written with the beginner in mind, and is project-based, in much the same way that this book is.

Photoshop is a great tool for designers, especially when used in conjunction with a scanner or a graphic tablet. Almost all of the illustrations in this book were hand-drawn, scanned into Photoshop, and then improved using the tools found in the program. You can use it to create slides for ROSCO's Image Pro gobo projector, labels for props like cans and bottles, pictures for set decoration, stained-glass windows, model parts, and many other things. Lots of designers are using it to produce model parts, painter's elevations, and renderings.

Every modern computer program has a *workspace*, which is what you see on the screen when you open the program. Photoshop opens to a window that has very familiar drop-down menus across the top. The File menu has New, Open, Save, and Save As options, just as you would expect to see, very much the same as a word processing program. But there is one other option, *Import*, which allows you to bring in media from a scanner. That function is great for copying and later manipulating drawings or printed images.

IMAGE contains the function *Image size*, which can be used to change the resolution of an image by breaking it down into a larger number of pixels. This is sort of like what you see on TV when the police want to see the license plate number of a suspect vehicle. Of course, that is only television, and the real thing doesn't work that well, but you can make some images clearer by enhancing the resolution to a higher number of pixels per inch. Each dot on the monitor screen is 1 pixel. A resolution of 72 pixels/inch (ppi) is standard on the Internet, but some images are up to 300 ppi. The file size shoots up dramatically when you raise the resolution, so be careful not to make a giant file that is cumbersome to work with. On the other hand, a resolution that is too small results in pixlation, which means that individual dots are visible on the screen.

Pixel   tion

PIXILATION MAKES AN IMAGE LOOK LIKE IT IS MADE FROM SQUARE-CORNERED DOTS.

Canvas size relates to the area you have to work with, just like an artist's canvas or a piece of paper to draw on. You can change the size to make it bigger, but this will not affect the image on the screen. A larger white space will appear around the image. You can determine via the menu whether the extra space will be all around, or on one specific side.

HISTORY

DROP-DOWN MENUS

PHOTOSHOP WORKSPACE

TOOLS

LAYERS

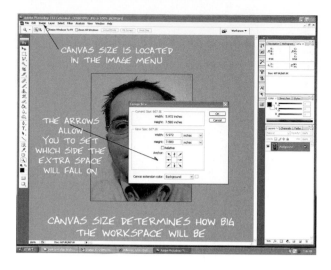

CANVAS SIZE IS LOCATED IN THE IMAGE MENU

THE ARROWS ALLOW YOU TO SET WHICH SIDE THE EXTRA SPACE WILL FALL ON

CANVAS SIZE DETERMINES HOW BIG THE WORKSPACE WILL BE

different icons, including important selection tools like the marquees, lassoes, and the magic wand. Use these tools to select a specific area of an image. They work in different ways, so play around with them to learn which is best for a particular situation. If you have selected an area of the image with one of these tools, a dotted line flashes around it. The selected area is the only part of the image that can be manipulated when the dotted line is visible.

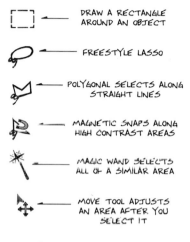

DRAW A RECTANGLE AROUND AN OBJECT

FREESTYLE LASSO

POLYGONAL SELECTS ALONG STRAIGHT LINES

MAGNETIC SNAPS ALONG HIGH CONTRAST AREAS

MAGIC WAND SELECTS ALL OF A SIMILAR AREA

MOVE TOOL ADJUSTS AN AREA AFTER YOU SELECT IT

TRY OUT THE DIFFERENT SELECTION TOOLS

The *Filter menu* allows you to apply effects over the top of your image, so that it looks like a chalk drawing, or a watercolor, or a stained glass window, or many other things. When you click on an effect from the drop-down menu, it gives you a window with options and a preview screen of what the image will look like when the effect is applied.

The *Window menu* allows you to select what tools and information will be displayed on the workspace. If you have too many windows open at the same time, they will crowd out your image, so be judicious about which ones you display. A second monitor is really great for Photoshop, because you can store the open windows on that screen. Or you can use a wide-screen monitor. Most of your work is done with a mouse, so leave the most critical windows on the main monitor, where they are easily reached.

The *brush tool* is used to paint or draw on some part of the screen. You can alter the size of the brush, as well as how sharply defined the edges are, by right-clicking or from a menu at the top of the workspace. Try searching the Internet for free Photoshop brushes for specific textures like stone or water. They can be downloaded and added to your collection. You can also select the color of the "paint" by clicking on the color picker near the bottom of the tool window.

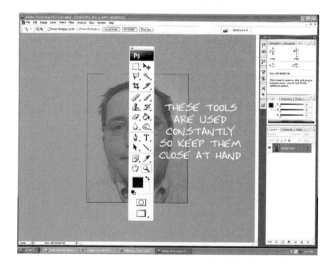

THESE TOOLS ARE USED CONSTANTLY SO KEEP THEM CLOSE AT HAND

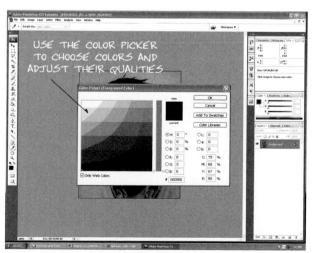

USE THE COLOR PICKER TO CHOOSE COLORS AND ADJUST THEIR QUALITIES

The *Tools window* should definitely be close at hand, because it is used constantly. It contains many

The brush tool can also be a *pencil* tool or a *healing brush* tool. The healing brush is great for "airbrushing" out lines, and other things you would like to cover up.

The *eraser tool* is used to wipe away areas on the image. You must select a brush size to do that, in much the same way that the brush tool sizes are selected. Alternatively, you can use one of the selection tools like the marquee or lasso to select an area and then delete it. The *opacity* of any brush can be selected from a menu above the workspace. Set a low opacity to use brushes to create a translucent wash of color with the brush tool or to fade out something with the eraser tool.

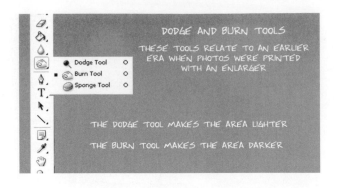

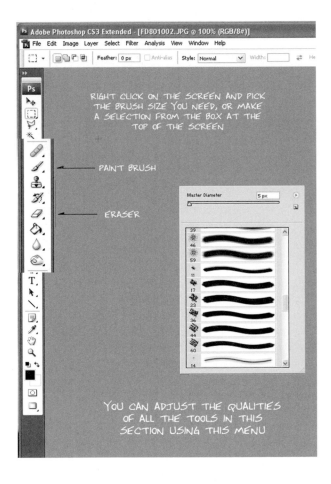

The *dodge* and *burn tools* are very interesting, and are direct descendents of the methods used in printing photographs by hand with an old-school enlarger. Photoshop was invented as a digital way to manipulate photographs, and was meant for photographers. Select the dodge tool and a suitable brush size to highlight specific areas of an image so that they are more visible. The burn tool does just the opposite. Set the opacity of the dodge tool to a medium level and use it to create shadows on an image. The dodge tool won't change any of the colors involved; it just darkens the image, and creates very realistic shadows.

If you would like to make a straight line with any brush tool, click once where the line should start, hold down the Shift key, and click where you want the line to end. Photoshop has a lot of *hot key* shortcuts, which you will learn over time. Most hot keys are centered on the use of the Control Key; often abbreviated Ctrl. Ctrl-S is a very common usage, meaning Save. Frequently the first letter of the intended command is used, such as S for Save or P for Print. The Control Key is PC specific. Macs users should hold down the Apple key instead, as the Control Key on a Mac has a different function. Other than that, hot key use on Macs and PCs is pretty much the same.

Two other windows are very important and somewhat unfamiliar to the new user: *layers* and *history*. Most programs will allow you to undo a number of steps (hot key shortcut: Ctrl-Z) and go back to a point before your mistake. A program like Vectorworks allows a virtually unlimited number of undos, but Photoshop only goes back one step. That is because it uses the history window to record what steps you have taken in producing your image. Navigate to a specific point in the history and click on the listing to revert back to that point in time. Photoshop tells you what each of the steps was, so you don't have to guess.

The layers window shows all of the different layers of images that are present in your work. Dividing an image into layers allows you to work on one part of the image at a time, without changing others. Select the proper layer from the Layers menu in order to work with it. If you do not, you will often get a message like "no pixels selected," which is telling you that you selected a portion of the image other than where that layer is. A new layer is created whenever you use the text tool from the Tools palette. A new layer is also created whenever you copy and paste. Use the arrow tool to move a selected layer around. You can select the entire layer using Ctrl-A.

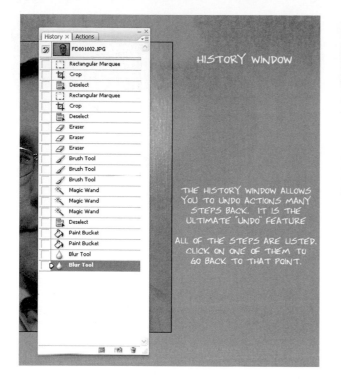

HISTORY WINDOW

THE HISTORY WINDOW ALLOWS YOU TO UNDO ACTIONS MANY STEPS BACK. IT IS THE ULTIMATE "UNDO" FEATURE

ALL OF THE STEPS ARE LISTED. CLICK ON ONE OF THEM TO GO BACK TO THAT POINT.

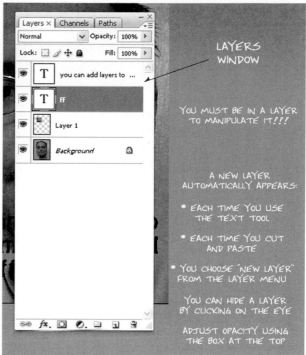

LAYERS WINDOW

YOU MUST BE IN A LAYER TO MANIPULATE IT???

A NEW LAYER AUTOMATICALLY APPEARS:

* EACH TIME YOU USE THE TEXT TOOL

* EACH TIME YOU CUT AND PASTE

* YOU CHOOSE "NEW LAYER" FROM THE LAYER MENU

YOU CAN HIDE A LAYER BY CLICKING ON THE EYE

ADJUST OPACITY USING THE BOX AT THE TOP

You can save your work from the file menu, or by using Ctrl-S. Photoshop does not auto-save, so you should save often to avoid losing work if the computer crashes. You might wish to save different versions using Save as. Files are saved in the Photoshop document format (or *PSD*) by default, but you can select virtually any sort of picture file from the drop-down menu.

Saving as a PSD file preserves the layers in your file, but other file types don't do that.

If you would like to export an image to an older version of Vectorworks, you must save it as a *pict* file extension. Drawing over a drawing is one cool way to use Vectorworks in an artistic manner, and is discussed later on.

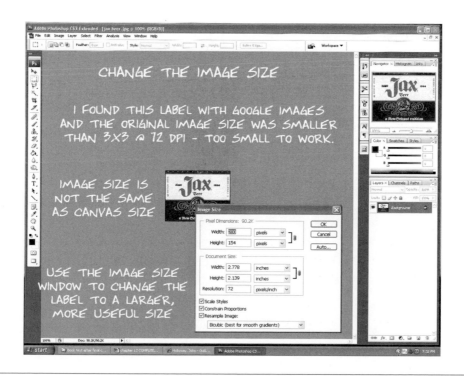

CHANGE THE IMAGE SIZE

I FOUND THIS LABEL WITH GOOGLE IMAGES AND THE ORIGINAL IMAGE SIZE WAS SMALLER THAN 3X3 @ 72 DPI - TOO SMALL TO WORK.

IMAGE SIZE IS NOT THE SAME AS CANVAS SIZE

USE THE IMAGE SIZE WINDOW TO CHANGE THE LABEL TO A LARGER, MORE USEFUL SIZE

A practical example: labels for bottles

You are doing a production of *Cat on a Hot Tin Roof*, and one of the characters must drink a bottle of Jax beer, which was very popular in New Orleans in the 1950s. The bottle is a rather generic brown glass longneck, which is easy to find, but an authentic-looking label is another matter. Search the Internet and find an example of the proper label (isn't everything on there now? eBay is especially helpful) and save the image to your computer. Open it in Photoshop. Check to see what the image size is. Measure the bottle to see what size it should be, and change the image size to fit the bottle. The resolution is probably already 72 pixels per inch, and can remain that way, but if the file size from the Internet was really small, you might try increasing the number of pixels to sharpen the image. Most professional printing happens around 300 dpi.

When you print the image (Ctrl-P), Photoshop will automatically center the image in the middle of the paper. You may need to rotate the canvas so that it is the proper orientation to print: Image > Rotate Canvas.

Making an Image Pro slide

Image Pro is the ROSCO slide projector that fits into the gobo slot of an ellipsoidal lighting instrument. You don't have to make the slide yourself (although that is possible), because ROSCO makes them for you if you email them the image. But you do need to generate the image you would like to use. How can you make a slide of a ghostly head for *Titus Andronicus*?

Take a picture of the actor wearing ghoulish makeup, with dark eyes blood dripping from the mouth,

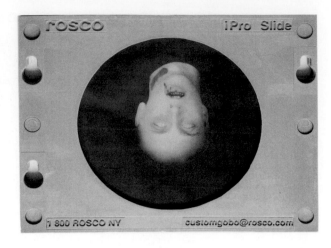

and so forth. Take the photo in front of a black curtain so that the background is as dark as possible. Download the picture onto your computer and open the file in Photoshop. The file will most likely be a JPEG, but will automatically convert to a PSD the moment you add a second layer. Select the part of the head you want, using one of the lasso tools. From the Select menu at the top of the screen, choose Inverse to switch your selection from the head to the background. Use the paint bucket tool from the Tools window to convert the background to pure black, which means that it will not project when the slide comes up on stage. Only the head will show. Choose Inverse again to switch back to a selection of just the head.

From the Image menu at the top of the screen, choose Adjustments > Hue/Saturation. Use that feature to give the head an unearthly greenish cast.

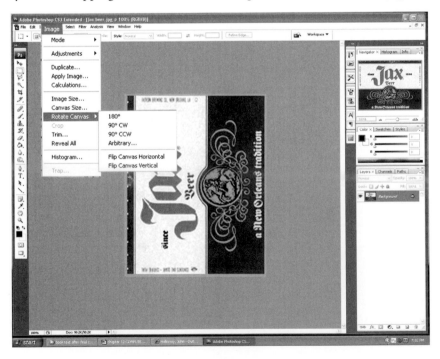

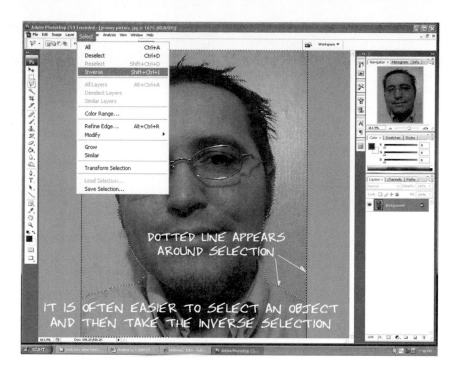

DOTTED LINE APPEARS AROUND SELECTION

IT IS OFTEN EASIER TO SELECT AN OBJECT AND THEN TAKE THE INVERSE SELECTION

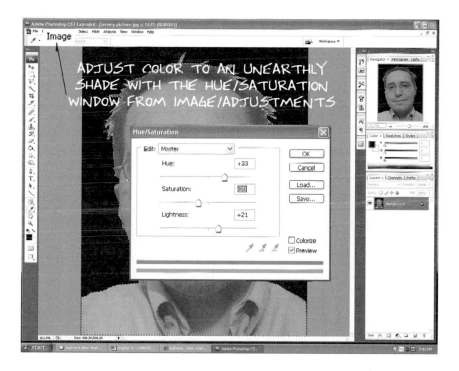

ADJUST COLOR TO AN UNEARTHLY SHADE WITH THE HUE/SATURATION WINDOW FROM IMAGE/ADJUSTMENTS

With the head part still selected, use Ctrl-C to copy the appropriately discolored and disembodied head. Use Ctrl-V to paste it back in the exact same place. Notice that there are now two layers listed in the layers window: one that says background and the other listed as Layer 1. You can't really see that on the screen, because one layer is directly over the other. Layer 1 is the layer you just pasted on the image.

Click on the arrow selection tool, and use the *arrow keys* on the keyboard to *nudge* Layer 1 over a tiny bit. At the top of the Layers window is the opacity option, which you can set at a low number. Adjust the opacity and layer placement so that the picture becomes blurry and more ghostly.

If you are satisfied with the look of your image, you can email it to ROSCO to be printed. Image Pro works best with a high-contrast image, which should be already be the case, because of the black background and ghostly pale face. If not, you can heighten the contrast by selecting Image > Adjustments > Contrast/Brightness. PSD files are larger than other types, because of the way Photoshop stores all the layer information, so it is best to Save As an alternate file type such as a JPEG before emailing.

These two projects pointed out a number of features Photoshop has for manipulating images, but there are many, many more that will not fit into this chapter. Have fun exploring Photoshop's capabilities in creating many more theatre tricks.

SOUND FORGE WORKSPACE

SOUND EDITING PROGRAMS

There is really only one Photoshop, but there are several different sound editing programs that are very similar to one another because they use the same intuitive approach. Sony *Sound Forge Audio Studio* is an inexpensive version of their larger program. Adobe has a similar product called *Soundbooth*. Apple computers are shipped with the program *GarageBand*, which can be upgraded to *Logic*. *Audacity* is an open source software for recording and editing sound. All of them use a graphical, visual approach to displaying the sound file, so that you can look at it to see what the sound is doing at various points in its progress. Sounds occur over time and are fluid in nature, so the visual approach is a good way to look at them in a static form.

The graph shows how the volume of the sound rises and falls over time, which allows the user to look and see where audible events take place. This particular Sound Forge graph has three distinct parts, each of them separated by silence. It is a bell clanging at a railroad crossing, and was extracted from a CD of *sound effects*. We will use this and another sound to build our own effect using tools found in the program. These directions tend to be somewhat Sound Forge–specific, but the basic concepts are true for any application.

Suppose that you would like a cue in which the crossing bell rings twice, a train passes by on the tracks from one side of the stage to the other while the bell continues to sound, after which the bell rings twice more and stops. Let's begin by creating a bell sound that continues for 30 clangs—more than we will likely need. Sound Forge allows you to copy and paste in the same way as many other programs. Use the cursor to select the entire sound by clicking and dragging.

After making your selection, right click and choose copy, or do the same from the Edit menu. Click on the end of the graph to place the cursor there, and paste the copied data. The file now has six bell clangs. Repeat

GARAGE BAND WORKSPACE

EXTRACT AUDIO FROM CD USING SOUND FORGE

- Insert the disk in the appropriate drive, most likely the D or E drive on a PC. (A CD will play in a DVD drive.)
- Select File > Extract Audio from CD.
- After the window opens, choose the appropriate drive that contains the compact disk.
- The window will generate a list of all the sounds on the disk. Click once on any item to *preview* that sound. Double-click to extract the audio, which will show up as a file on the screen.

---

the procedure several times until 30 clangs are lined up in the window. Make sure they are all the same distance apart so that they come at regular intervals. The horizontal axis of this graph represents time, as it usually does on most graphs. When 30 clangs are lined up in the window, their shapes will be compressed into a smaller space, because the graph has been tightened in order to show them all at once.

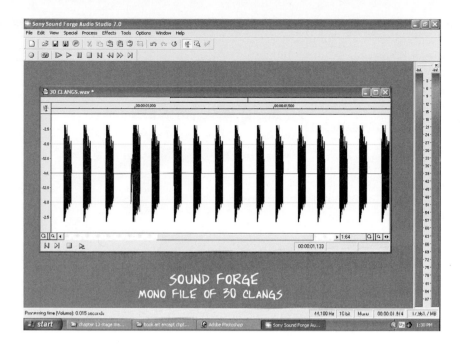

SOUND FORGE
MONO FILE OF 30 CLANGS

Use Extract Audio from the CD to open another file with the sound of a train passing by. Again, the sound is in *mono,* meaning that there is only one track. We would like the sound to *pan* from left to right showing that the train crossed our view in that direction, so we need a *stereo* version of the sound.

CREATE A STEREO TRACK FROM A MONO SOURCE

- Double-click on the window to select the entire file.
- Right-click and choose Copy.
- Open a new file from the File menu, and choose to make it stereo in the dialog box.
- Paste the copied material into the center of the window so that its graph appears in both of them.

The train sound is now in stereo, and can be made to pan from left to right. Select both tracks by double-clicking and they will appear highlighted. From the Process menu, select Pan, and then Left to Right. The waveform will be converted to reflect the change. Notice that the left and right channels are inversely propor-

tional to one another. If you play the sound to preview it, you can hear the sound travel left to right from one speaker to the other.

The clanging sound of the alarm bell should have an equal volume on both the left and right tracks so that it seems to be in the middle of the stage. To make that happen, mix the train and bell sounds together into one cue with the train panning and the bell coming out of both speakers equally.

Begin by making a stereo version of the clang sound that is exactly the same on both the left and right tracks. Then copy both tracks of the train file. Open the clanging bell file by clicking on it; the sounds you copied are still on the clipboard and can be pasted to the bell file. The train sound should start after two clangs, so place the cursor in the space between the second and third clangs. Be sure to engage both the left and right tracks by clicking on the middle of the window between them.

A special technique is used to mix sounds together. If you simply choose Paste, the data you have copied will be inserted at that point in the timeline between other sounds, rather than being mixed with the bell sound. To mix the sounds together instead, choose Edit > Paste Special > Mix. The Sound Forge program gives you the option of adjusting the volumes of the two sounds. If you are unsure, make them the same, preview the sound, and make changes as necessary.

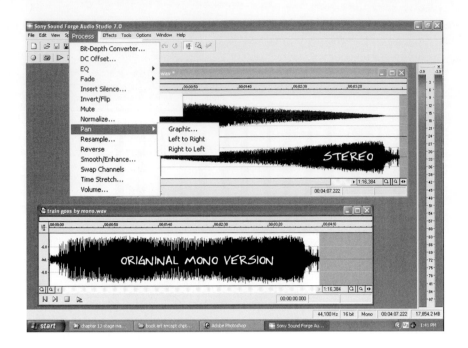

CREATE A STEREO VERSION OF THE TRAIN AND MAKE IT PAN

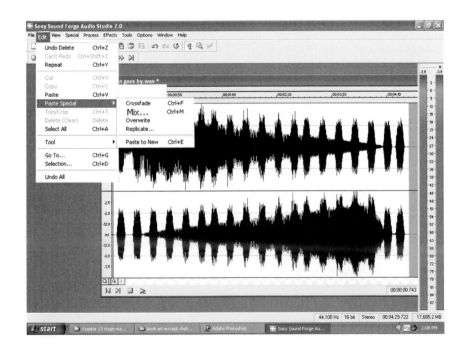

There are some extra clangs at the end of the effect. Trim them by using the cursor to select the unneeded ones and by using the delete button on your keyboard.

The process of building the train cue has given some insight into how to use the cursor to select parts of a sound, how to cut and paste them, how to move from mono to stereo tracks, and how to mix sounds together. Sound Forge is a relatively inexpensive program, but is somewhat limited, because it has only two tracks. But it is also very simple to work with. Some editing programs can work with a huge number of tracks. Choose a program that suits your needs.

The Save As feature allows you to save your files in a number of different formats. One of them is MP3, which is very popular for personal music players. Another is the WAV file, which is often used to make CDs. Pre-6.0 versions of the SFX program used for sound playback will accept only the WAV file format. Most modern equipment can handle either WAV or MP3.

Sound Playback Programs: SFX and QLAB

After you've built your sound cues, a playback program is used to play them over the sound system during the performance, where they become an important element of the show. Theatre shows are tightly scripted, which means that the same things happen in the same order for every performance. As a result, a good playback program must solve the following problems:

1. Keep the cues in an ordered list, from the first one to the last one.
2. Allow the operator to play them back in a dependable fashion, using some type of Go command.
3. Allow the sound designer to designate which speakers the sound cues will output to, and hence where the sounds will come from.
4. Allow the designer to set volume levels for the individual cues.

Generally speaking, fade-ins and fade-outs are either built into the cue itself or are managed on a mixing console.

QLab is a program that works only on Macintosh computers. *SFX* is a PC program that originally worked only on PC computers, although SFX 6.0 was engineered to work on either platform. Version 6.0 is a substantial upgrade from earlier versions.

The biggest advantage of using a computer over individual CDs for playing back sound effects during a show is the *cue list*. It can be arranged so that the sound you need first is cue 1, the next one is cue 2, the next 3, and so forth. The program automatically loads the next cue as soon as the first one begins to run, so that the operator can play all the cues in order by giving a single Go command with a mouse. This eliminates the difficulty of loading disks into a machine and booting them up. Unless you set the default differently, a long-playing cue will continue to run, even after the succeeding cue has been called up. This allows two cues to run simultaneously.

One of the most difficult aspects of setting up SFX on a computer is organizing the outputs so that the signal is routed to the proper speakers. Version 6 has a new *output matrix* that allows the user to exercise a large degree of control over what goes where, but you will

Import sound cues into either QLab or SFX by dragging them with the mouse. This works best if you save all the cues in one folder when you are building them. Adding a word description in the name makes it easier to remember which is which. It is important that

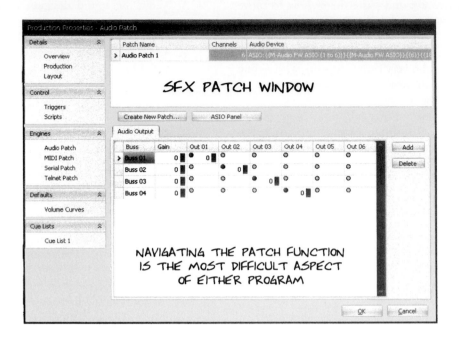

need to spend quite a bit of time with the downloadable manual to determine how to configure it for your particular computer's hardware. QLab is much more intuitive, configured by means of a more user-friendly graphical output matrix.

SFX 6.0 uses the title *Production* to describe a series of cues meant to be used as the sounds for a particular show. When you open the program on your computer, a window will ask what you want to do. One of the options is "create a new production" and, after naming your show, takes you to another window that allows you to configure the patch. There are some very specific hardware issues relating to a specific type of driver software that must be resolved before the program will work on your computer. You can download information about doing so from the SFX Web site.

QLab uses the sound card that comes with the Apple computer, and doesn't require any specialized hardware. For QLab, stereo left and right outputs can be taken directly from the computer's headphone jack, but special interface hardware must be used if more outputs are required. The interface can be connected to a USB port, and receives the digital signals from the computer, translating them into an analog signal that can be fed into a mixing console, or perhaps directly to your system amplifiers.

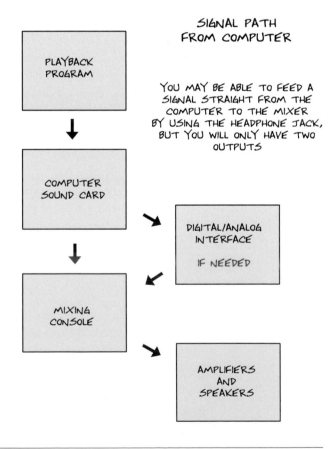

DRAG THE FILES OVER INTO YOUR CUE LIST

CLICK ON THE CUE, AND USE THIS TOOL
TO SET THE OUTPUT VOLUME LEVEL.

THIS PROCESS IS SOMEWHAT
CUMBERSOME ON EITHER PROGRAM.

all of your cues be in sequential order when running the show. If you open the folder with the cues in it to the side of the workspace, you can select cues and drag them over one at a time and in order. If the same cue is used several times, create a new file for each instance. That will keep the process linear for the operator.

The sound cues are not stored directly in the show file, but rather the playback program uses a link to them when the Go command is given. Consequently, it is important to leave a copy of the file on the computer itself, and not just on a removable travel drive. That is important to remember if you've built your cues on another machine and are using a flash memory drive to transfer them to the sound playback computer. A large X appears on the screen when the cue/file link has been broken.

After the cue list has been established in the playback program, you can click on the sounds one at a time to bring up a dialog box allowing you to set certain parameters such as sound level and patch designations. Setting loudness levels on either QLab or SFX is a problematic aspect of the programs, because you can't hear the sound as you are setting the level. So determining the correct volume is somewhat of a hit-or-miss proposition.

The board operator can run the cues in a couple of different ways. There are standard *transport controls* at the bottom left of the cue list window, with very familiar arrow icons. On an older reel-to-reel tape deck, the tape was "transported" or moved through the machine using certain controls like play, pause, stop, fast forward, and fast reverse. The word *transport* is now used to describe the set of icons that have the same effects, only with digital rather than mechanical equipment.

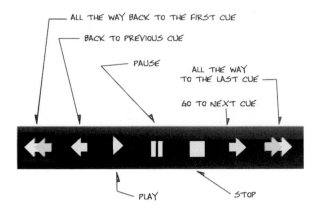

TRANSPORT ICONS

A large Go button on the screen will start a cue when you click on it with the mouse. This method is probably the best, because it is completely unambiguous, but the transport buttons allow more options. On QLab, the spacebar can be used in place of either the Go button or the transport buttons.

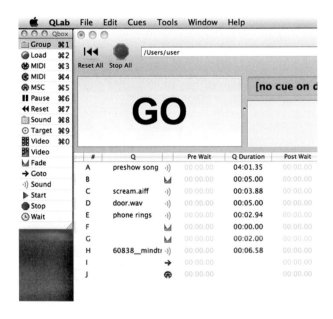

VECTORWORKS

Back in the day, all drafting was done by hand, using a T-square and triangles, but now computers reign completely. Drafting is different from freehand drawing in that the images are done to *scale*, meaning that all parts of the drawing are proportional to one another, and that they are a specific amount smaller than the actual objects they represent. One of the most common scale sizes for theatrical drawings is 1/2″ equals 1′-0″. That means that if you use a ruler to measure some part of the drawing, and the ruler says that part is half an inch long, the real object it represents is 1 foot long.

DRASTICALLY DIFFERENT SIZES!

THE SCALE OF A DRAWING IS VERY IMPORTANT

The scale drawings of that earlier time were done on special translucent paper so that *blueprint* copies could be made by passing light through them to a coated paper below. The coated paper was developed in an ammonia bath so the lines would show up. Making copies in that way was expensive and cumbersome, but printers had not yet been invented. When computers and large-format printers came along, one of their first uses was to create scale drawings digitally, and then print them out, eliminating the blueprinting process. (Blueprints had white lines on a dark blue background and were very hard to read.) One of the first *CAD* or *computer-aided design* programs was *AutoCAD*, which is still very widely used today. AutoCAD originated in the early 1980s, when personal computers were in their infancy.

Vectorworks (VW) is a competing CAD program that is used by many people in the entertainment industry because there is an entertainment-specific version called Spotlight. *Vectorworks Spotlight* has many tools for lighting designers, as well as the standard architectural drawing setup. VW was originally developed for Macs, but can now be used on either Macs or PCs.

The name "Vectorworks" has an interesting connotation that speaks to the difference between any CAD program and an image-editing program like Photoshop. Whatever the type of computer or computer program, lines, shapes, colors, on the screen must somehow be documented and recorded. Photoshop does that using the raster method, which records the look of each individual pixel on the screen. As a result, you can manipulate the image one pixel at a time. That makes it possible for the brushes in Photoshop to move in any direction the mouse moves, and for the eraser to remove only what you want it to. But the trade-off is that Photoshop files are huge, and would never have been possible on early computers and their very small memories.

Vector programs are different. The computer remembers line placement by creating a mathematical formula that says "this line starts here and stops there." You should think of the drawing as individual lines, rectangles, circles, and so forth that come together to form a drawing. In Photoshop, you can remove part of a line with an eraser. In Vectorworks, you must select the line first, and then push it back to the desired length. The computer writes a new equation that reflects that change. When you draw with Vectorworks, you should consider the philosophy of vector graphics in organizing your work. It is easiest to rough in lines first, waiting until later to worry about assigning attributes like line weight and color.

One of the best things about a vector program over a raster program like Photoshop is *scalability*. Scalability means that you can make an image larger or smaller without disfiguring it. If you enlarge a 72-dpi JPEG image to something like 500 percent, the pixels become very large on the screen, and the image becomes a grainy collection of squarish dots. That does not happen with a vector program. The lines become thicker as you zoom in, but they don't break down into dots.

Thinking globally, CAD programs are a huge advantage over what has become known as "hand drafting." That is especially true in theatre, where things change rapidly, and drawing an entirely new plan by hand at a moment's notice just isn't possible. VW is an especially great program for lighting designers, because it has so many tools aimed at creating light plots. Lighting design requires a lot of detail in record keeping, and computers are great at that.

The Vectorworks program is very complex, and this chapter is only the briefest outline of how to visualize its properties. There are some very fine online resources that can help you with the details of this program. You should think of this as a "cheat sheet" just to help you get started.

PHOTOSHOP ERASES INDIVIDUAL DOTS OR PIXELS. IMAGES OFTEN HAVE FUZZY EDGES FOR BETTER BLENDING.

ERASER ICON LOOKS LIKE A "PINK PEARL" ERASER

Pink Pearl

THE ERASER TOOL CAN HAVE A FUZZY EDGE LIKE THIS, OR A SHARP EDGE. SELECT THE TYPE YOU NEED FROM THE BRUSHES PALLET.

AN ERASER BRUSH CAN MOVE THROUGH THE MIDDLE OF A LINE. THERE ARE NO RESTRAINTS ON ITS MOVEMENTS.

VECTORWORKS IS DIFFERENT. IT WORKS BY RESHAPING OBJECTS LIKE LINES. THEY HAVE VERY SHARP EDGES.

2D SELECTION TOOL

CLICK ON THE LINE TO SELECT IT. ENDPOINT GRAB HANDLE WILL APPEAR.

DRAG THE ENDPOINT BACKWARD UNTIL THE LINE IS THE LENGTH YOU WANT.

The workspace

When you open VW, go to File > Workspace Preferences and choose Spotlight. That will set up the workspace so that all of the theatre-specific tools are available. If you choose any other workspace, the Spotlight tools won't be on your monitor. An unnamed file will open with the program, and if you are starting something from scratch, you can use that file to begin your work. Or you can open some other file that was already established.

The menu bar at the top of the workspace has many familiar names on it like File and Edit, along with the lesser known Page and Palettes. VW must be able to work with drawings of many different sizes and scales. Use the Page menu to set the scale of your drawing, which is often 1/2″ for something like a plan view or elevations. Traditional sizes for drawings have been either 24×36 or 36×42, and in VW that is selected by choosing *Print Area*. In the past few years, many designers have gotten away from this practice and tend to make elevations and detail drawings on much smaller pages that are easier to print out and can be made into a booklet.

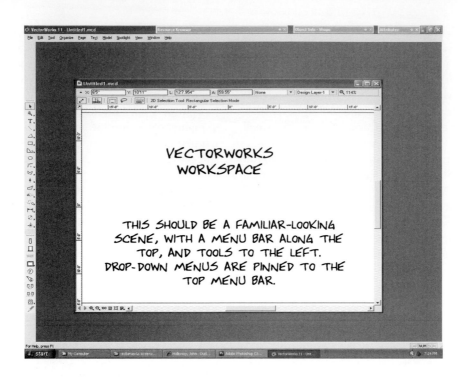

VECTORWORKS
WORKSPACE

THIS SHOULD BE A FAMILIAR-LOOKING
SCENE, WITH A MENU BAR ALONG THE
TOP, AND TOOLS TO THE LEFT.
DROP-DOWN MENUS ARE PINNED TO THE
TOP MENU BAR.

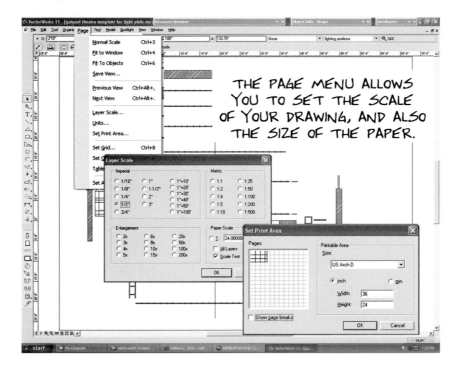

THE PAGE MENU ALLOWS
YOU TO SET THE SCALE
OF YOUR DRAWING, AND ALSO
THE SIZE OF THE PAPER.

The Page menu is also used to determine the *grid size*, which is the network of blue lines in the background. They are very helpful when lining up objects on the page. You can also set the *origin*, which is the point from which everything is measured. One of the great things about VW is that you don't have to worry if you've done this wrong, because you can change it all later and the drawing will just update itself, and you won't have lost anything. With hand drafting, once you started on a certain piece of paper, you were stuck with it.

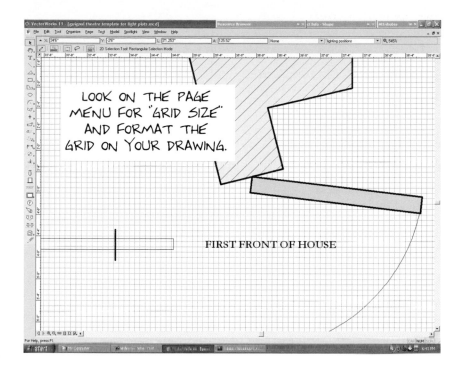

The *Palettes menu* is similar to what you would expect from one called "Windows," except of course that this was originally a Mac program. It allows you to open up all the various "toolboxes" used in creating and formatting a drawing. There are a lot of them, and unless you have a really huge monitor, it is best to open only the ones you need at the moment. You can open and close palettes at will at any time during the drawing process.

Vectorworks palettes

- *2D tools*—has drawing implements like the line tool, rectangle, the arrow selection tool, and the text tool. These tools are used constantly when drawing and should be kept close by.
- *Attributes*—is used to assign alternative qualities to an object on the drawing. An object is one definable thing, like a line, rectangle, or collection of text.

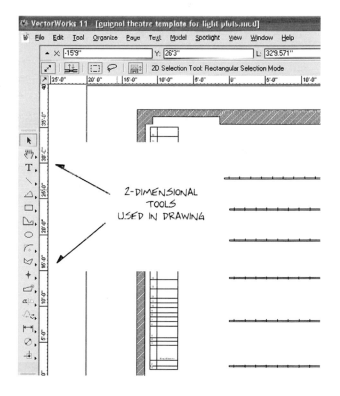

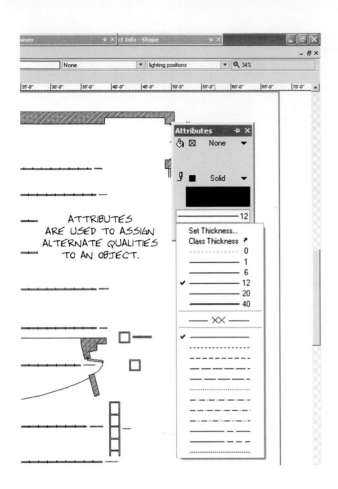

ATTRIBUTES ARE USED TO ASSIGN ALTERNATE QUALITIES TO AN OBJECT.

- *Resource browser*—a window that allows you to import already constructed objects from a catalog. They are as different as a section of truss or a Fresnel. Like all browsers, it has the ability to retain favorites.
- *Object info box*—is very similar to what one would expect after right-clicking and choosing "properties" on a PC. It is very helpful in assigning information like color and dimmer numbers to lighting instruments.
- *Spotlight*—has icons related to placing theatre-specific items on a plot, especially the instrument insertion tool used for placing lighting fixtures.

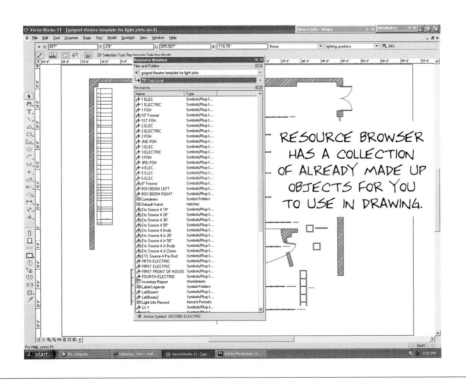

RESOURCE BROWSER HAS A COLLECTION OF ALREADY MADE UP OBJECTS FOR YOU TO USE IN DRAWING.

OBJECT INFO BOX

LISTS THE PROPERTIES OF OBJECTS, AND IS ESSENTIAL WHEN CREATING A LIGHT PLOT.

BE SURE TO LEAVE IT PINNED TO THE TOP MENU BAR

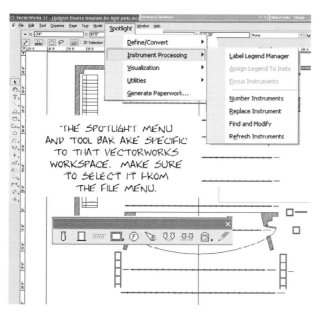

THE SPOTLIGHT MENU AND TOOL BAR ARE SPECIFIC TO THAT VECTORWORKS WORKSPACE. MAKE SURE TO SELECT IT FROM THE FILE MENU.

labeled X and Y that tell the distance of the cursor from the origin. The origin is set from the Page menu, and is a measuring point like most other graphs. You can change it as you go along so that its placement is convenient for the moment. The L box tells the length of a line.

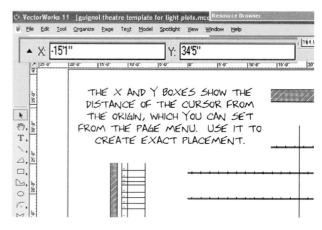

THE X AND Y BOXES SHOW THE DISTANCE OF THE CURSOR FROM THE ORIGIN, WHICH YOU CAN SET FROM THE PAGE MENU. USE IT TO CREATE EXACT PLACEMENT.

There are many other palettes and menus for other purposes. The tops of the palettes have small pushpins on them that allow you to pin them to the blue bar across the top of the screen. Clicking on the pin changes its orientation from up and down to sideways. When the pin is sideways, the palette will collapse upward out of the way when it is not in use.

Drawing

The rectangle, circle, and line tools are used to draw most objects. At the top of the workspace are boxes

Click on a line or rectangle to select it. You will see small handles or *end points* on objects that have been selected and are ready to be manipulated. Use the arrow to drag one of the handles, making a line longer or shorter. Manipulate rectangles and circles in the same way. Use the arrow tool to drag entire objects around on the page. You can nudge selected items on the screen using the four arrow keys on your keyboard, but only after pressing down the Shift key. Without the Shift key, the entire page moves, which can be quite disconcerting if you aren't expecting it. When you draw a line or a rectangle or an arc, holding down the Shift key at the same time will change the way that the object is formed, keeping it proportional to the original.

After you have created some portion of your drawing and are ready to format it, use the Attributes palette to assign different qualities. Use the arrow tool to select the object and the attributes menu to change its appearance. Draw a marquee box around a number of items to select them all at once. If you hold down the Shift key while using the arrow, you can select a number of items by clicking on them one after the other.

The *group* and *ungroup* commands are listed under the *Organize menu*. Select a number of lines that make up one object and group them together so that they can be manipulated all at once. Ungroup separates them again.

Layers

Vectorworks uses *layers* to help organize complicated drawings. All of the layer commands are located under the Organize menu. It is often helpful to separate drawings according to things like the theatre itself, Act I scenery, Act II scenery, light fixtures, lighting positions, or whatever separations make sense for your particular situation. There are a number of layer options that allow

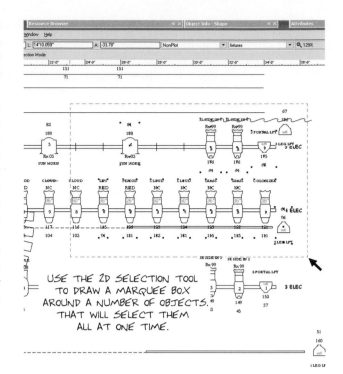

USE THE 2D SELECTION TOOL TO DRAW A MARQUEE BOX AROUND A NUMBER OF OBJECTS. THAT WILL SELECT THEM ALL AT ONE TIME.

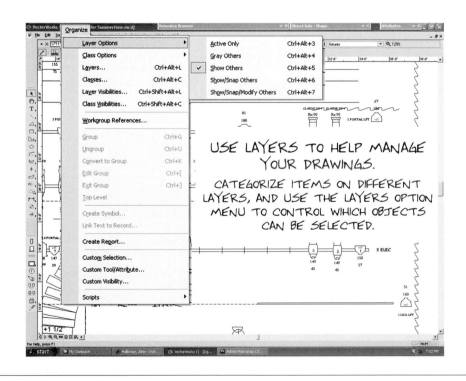

USE LAYERS TO HELP MANAGE YOUR DRAWINGS.

CATEGORIZE ITEMS ON DIFFERENT LAYERS, AND USE THE LAYERS OPTION MENU TO CONTROL WHICH OBJECTS CAN BE SELECTED.

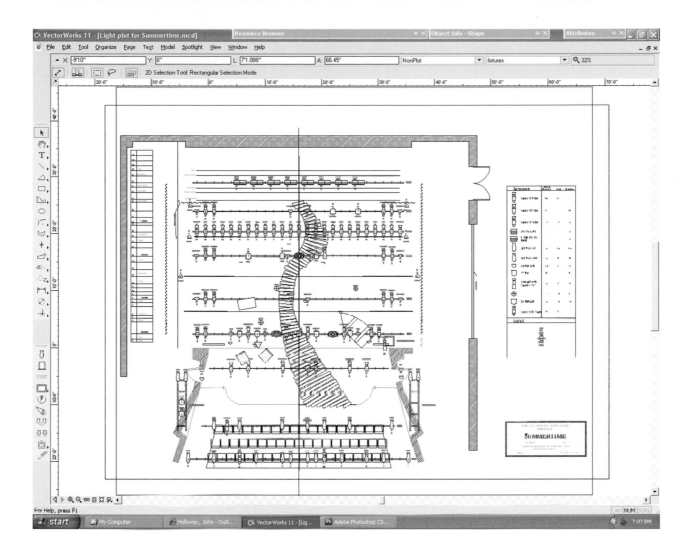

you to protect parts of the drawing while working with others. The layer you are working on is the *active layer*. You can change layers using the Layers dialog box at the top of the workspace.

Organize > Layer Options > Gray Others will keep the active layer black but make all other layers a gray color. That makes it easier to spot what is in the active layer. With that setting, you can select objects in the active layer and move them around the page without accidentally moving anything from another layer. Organize > Layer Options > *Show, Snap, Modify Others* will allow you to work with all layers at one time.

Spotlight

All of the previous instructions work with any VW workspace, but the real beauty of the program for entertainment work is its ability to create light plots. A light

plot shows the location of light fixtures on the stage, and also gives information about circuiting, color, and patterns.

The process works best if you set up your drawing by marking the *lighting positions* on the plan drawing first, and then adding the fixtures and other information later. Open a new layer and name it "lighting positions." Draw in pipes used for electrics and front of house positions. Click on the first one to select it. Navigate to Spotlight > Define/Convert > *Convert to light position* and assign the appropriate name. As a part of its record-keeping duties, VW keeps track of lights that are placed on a designated lighting position. That sort of thing is very tedious to do by hand, so you want to make sure that the computer does it instead. Later on, VW will reflect this information in a hookup sheet that is automatically (a relative term) generated from the plot information.

Use the Resource Browser to select lighting fixtures you would like to place on the plot. Navigate through the browser to find the appropriate company products, and the specific fixture, and click to select it. Click next on the *Fixture Insertion tool* from the Spotlight palette. Click the place on the drawing where the fixture goes and the icon for your light will show up there. You have the option of rotating it while it is still selected. If you want to place more of the same type of fixture, click the drawing in other places to do that—you do not need to go through the selection process again.

Use the Object Info box to include information about the light. Type in all necessary information about color, purpose, and templates in the dialog boxes. The placement and unit numbers will be automatically added by the program.

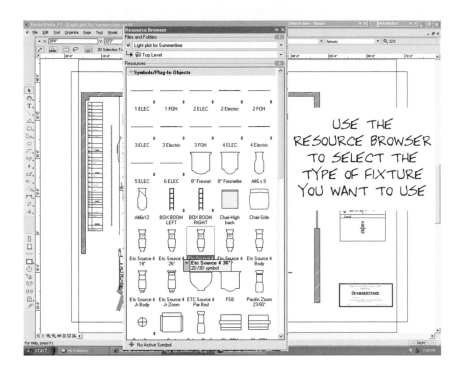

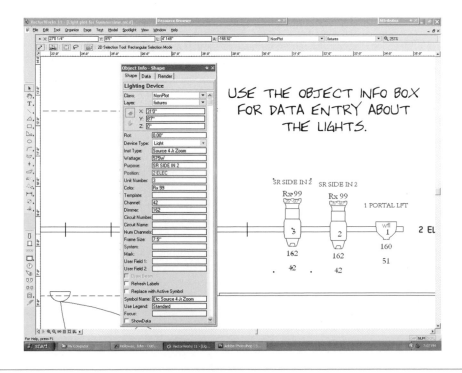

To add instrument numbers, select the group of instruments you would like to number sequentially and navigate to Spotlight > Instrument processing > Number instruments. A dialog box allows you to choose the numbering system you would like to use.

VW Spotlight allows you to configure the way information about a fixture is arranged around its icon on the plot. That process is handled by the *Label Legend Manager*, which is found via Spotlight > Instrument processing > Label legend manager. Use this tool to add the labels you would like to have, and to place them on the fixture. The setup is a bit complex, but Spotlight remembers your preferences for subsequent plots.

Select Spotlight > Utilities > Key to instrumentation to place a key on the drawing that references the choices you made with the Label Legend Manager.

Use Spotlight > Generate paperwork to create a hookup for your light plot. *Generate paperwork* opens a dialog box with lots of different possibilities. You can configure the Excel-like spreadsheet to display the

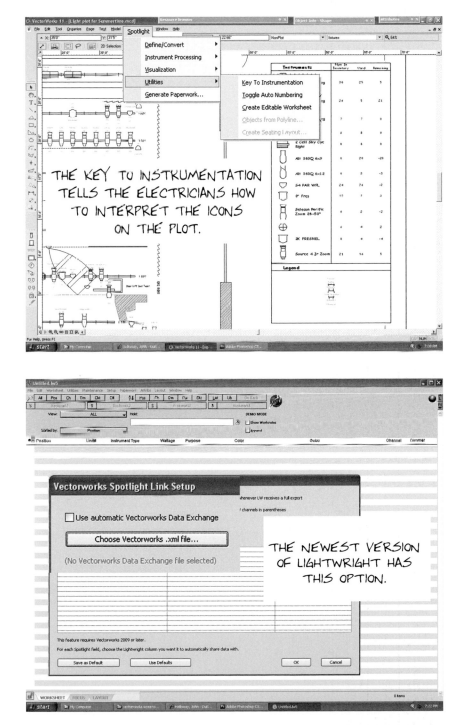

information in many different ways. These spreadsheets are a good way to find mistakes in the plot they are generated from. The process works much better on newer versions of the program. The program *Lightwright* has been around for many years and is an excellent resource for managing paperwork. Newer versions of Lightwright for Vectorworks are more compatible with one another and can be used in unison on either a Mac or a PC.

Vectorworks does *not* auto-save, so be sure to save your work frequently to avoid losing it. The program seems to have an almost unlimited ability to undo past actions (Ctrl-Z), but on occasion you may make a mistake that you cannot back out of. In such as case, you may prefer to close the program without saving your work. When you reopen it, the file will revert to

the last saved point, which might be back before the unfixable mistake occurred.

Drawing over a drawing

A lot of theatre work includes very loosely drawn, organic-looking shapes that are more at home in Photoshop than they are in Vectorworks. Fortunately, this technique allows you to convert that sort of drawing to a vector version of itself. If you draw something freehand, you can scan it into Photoshop and save a digital copy of it. Different tools can be used to manipulate and improve the drawing until it has the desired appearance. Use the Vectorworks Import option from the File menu to bring in your image to the workspace.

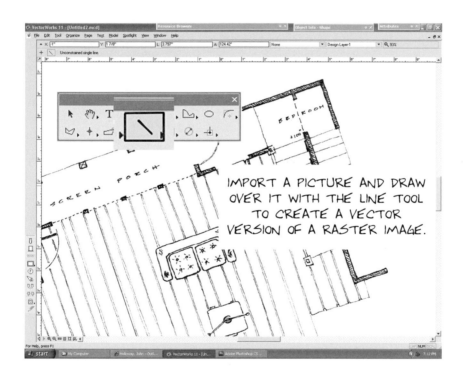

Use the magnifying tool to zoom in very closely on the drawing, and use the line tool to draw over the imported image, tracing a copy of it. Be sure to use different layers for the image and your tracing so that

they don't interfere with one another. Use a large number of small, straight lines to accomplish the drawing of curved lines.

CHAPTER 13

STAGE MANAGEMENT

Stage managers have many responsibilities related to rehearsing and performing theatre. They are typically the first to arrive and the last to leave. It is a tough job, but also very rewarding. Throughout the process of producing a play, a stage manager should be the center of communications in sharing ideas and information, whether they be artistic, administrative, or technical in nature. That may be a simple statement, but the true challenge of the job is keeping up with the many ways this information is presented, and making sure that it gets disseminated in an accurate and timely fashion. Professional stage managers are members of the *Actors' Equity Association* (AEA), the union for actors. It has been that way since the union was formed, when virtually all stage managers were people whose acting careers had gone awry. That is no longer axiomatic.

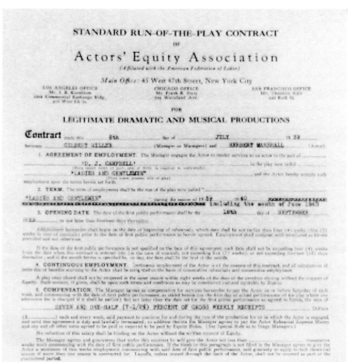

AN EXAMPLE OF AN EQUITY CONTRACT FROM THE 1950s

THE CONTRACT MENTIONS THAT THIS IS A "LEGITIMATE" SHOW, WHICH MEANS IT IS NOT A VAUDEVILLE TYPE PERFORMANCE, BUT RATHER A SHOW WITH A SET SCRIPT AND PLOT.

STAGE MANAGERS ARE UNION MEMBERS OF ACTORS' EQUITY ASSOCIATION RATHER THAN IATSE, THE UNION FOR STAGEHANDS. EVEN SO, STAGE MANAGERS HAVE A LOT OF INTERACTION WITH THE CREW OF A SHOW, AND OFTEN IDENTIFY MORE WITH STAGEHANDS THAN WITH ACTORS.

CALLING THE TECHNICAL CUES FOR A SHOW IS AN IMPORTANT JOB FOR A STAGE MANAGER, SO THAT ACTIVITY IS DETAILED IN THIS CHAPTER.

DIFFERENT ORGANIZATIONAL STRUCTURES

Some theatre organizations have a position known as the *production stage manager*, who may have larger administrative responsibilities than a traditional stage manager. In commercial theatre, a person hired as the *company manager* controls the business side of things, issuing paychecks, making travel arrangements, filing tax forms, and so forth.

doi: 10.1016/C2009-0-23409-X

In a school setting, where students serve as stage manager, the role of stage manager (SM) is generally more limited to organizing rehearsals and calling cues for a show. Each theatre organization is somewhat different, and has its own rules. Equity stage managers must follow the rules set down in the AEA contract with their group. Equity has contracts with many different organizations, but in each case the contract is published as a booklet that contains all the *work rules* for that venue. All unions have work rules, which are used to define responsibilities, duties, rights, and privileges.

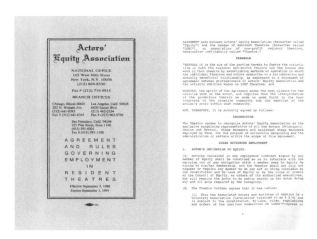

THE COVER AND FIRST PAGE OF THE EQUITY CONTRACT WITH LORT THEATRES BACK IN THE 1990S.

A UNION CONTRACT SPELLS OUT THE RULES AND OBLIGATIONS OF THE PARTIES, SO IN ESSENCE IT IS THE "RULE BOOK" FOR THE RELATIONSHIP. SCHOOL THEATRES DON'T USUALLY HAVE A RULEBOOK, BUT THEY DO HAVE AGREED UPON DUTIES AND RESPONSIBILITIES.

MATTERS SUCH AS THESE ARE NOW POSTED ON THE AEA WEBSITE RATHER THAN BEING PRINTED ON PAPER. YOU CAN GO TO THEIR WEBSITE AND CHECK THE ENTIRE DOCUMENT.

This chapter presents, in a roughly chronological order, the way things happen, beginning with design meetings, auditions, the rehearsal process, production meetings, tech rehearsals, dress rehearsals, and finally the running of the performances.

First Meeting with the Director

At some point, you should have a first meeting with the director. It is best to do this as early as possible so that the two of you can discuss how to work together in putting together the play. You should get some idea of the director's artistic view of the piece, and find out how the director would like the process to develop. Some directors like to shape the production organically, or in a loose manner. Others are much more structured. Be

sure to ask questions about this particular director's process. Be honest with the director. If you don't have any experience in a particular area, let him or her know so that he or she can help you learn.

Design Meetings

Sometime early on, weeks or maybe months before rehearsals begin, designers will start working with the director to solidify the way the show will look and sound. The role of the stage manager in these meetings is to take notes of the ideas that are put forward and to publish a record of the discussions. This will help keep the director and the designers on track with one another. A bit of efficiency on your part will greatly aid the process. Be sure to disseminate the notes as quickly as possible, as they are of little use days or weeks later. Social networking sites can be an excellent resource for that process, but be careful not to post sensitive information in a place where the public at large can find it.

Auditions

There is a wide diversity of style in how directors like to hold *auditions*, and the only way for you to find out how your director works is to ask him or her. Find out when and where the auditions are to be held. Most theatre organizations have a place to post information known as the *call board*. The director may want you to post a notice on the call board detailing how actors should prepare for the auditions. Some directors want actors to come with a prepared selection. Some choose to have the actors read from the script of the play that is being done. Sometimes it is both. There may be singing or dancing auditions. If actors must read from a script, make sure that copies are available. Often times, the scripts will have been ordered in advance, but if not, you will need to make copies of the pertinent pages for use at the auditions.

It is usually best to set up a table in the theatre to use in processing the auditionees. This will give you a place to lay the scripts and the *audition forms*. Consult with the director about what information should be required on the audition form, but the most obvious data should be name, phone number, email address, sex, height, weight, hair color, as well as any activities that may conflict with the rehearsal schedule. Quite often, the theatre or the director may have a standard form already made up. You should expect to make announcements to the auditionees about who the director wants to see, and to perform other crowd-control duties. Use *assistant stage managers* (ASM) to help do this. (*ASM* is a more frequently used term on its own, as stage managers are not usually called SMs.) If you are paying attention to the process, you will be able to anticipate what the director wants to do next, and will be much more helpful as a result.

The AEA requires two assistants for a musical, but only one for a straight play. This is because musicals are more complex and harder to run. Your theater probably has its own rules about assistants, or perhaps they will leave those details up to you. You will find that off-book rehearsals run much better with at least one assistant. Stage managing is a skill that is best learned by observing others, so assisting is a way to move into stage managing on your own.

After auditions are completed, the director will make decisions regarding the *cast list*. On occasion, the director may ask for help with this, but for the most part he or she won't need you, and especially not your opinion as to whom should be cast. Stage managing is a "people" job, and good managers have good *people skills*. Even if the director asks your opinion about an artistic matter, it is best to be conservative in your answer. The director may wish instead to confer with an *assistant director* (AD). Assistant director is a position that carries with it an expectation of artistic input; that is, the *AD* is often asked to do research, or to help rehearse scenes, take acting notes, and generally give opinions about how the work is progressing artistically. Some directors use the stage management staff to take notes, but they never really want your honest opinions on artistic matters.

A stage manager should be careful to avoid breaking any confidences that exist with the director. You may well have access to sensitive information that the director would not like the cast to know. If you gossip about such matters, the director will soon find out. You will not be an effective stage manager if the director must hesitate to tell you things. Acting in a consistently professional manner will build confidence in you as a person, and as a member of the production team.

THE FIRST READ-THROUGH

The *first read-through*, which often includes designers and other artistic/administrative staff, is an informal chance for the company to meet and hear the play for the first time as a group, especially if it is a new play. Optimally, the designers will be on hand to explain elements of their work to the acting company. The director will have comments to the group as a whole, and there may be introductions and other such "get to know each other" functions. Then the cast will read through the play.

You may be asked to read *stage directions*, or help in some other way. It is the director's rehearsal; you are there to make sure that things go smoothly. Quite often, it is best to have this meeting in a room with a large table where the participants can sit and face each other comfortably. You should ask about the director's preference in advance and make the necessary arrangements. Some people call this *table work*. It is a good idea to time this rehearsal so that there is some idea of how long the play will run. You should make it a practice to record the *run time* of any rehearsal that doesn't stop for a significant portion of the play. You probably don't need to time blocking rehearsals, because they stop and start so frequently.

PRODUCTION MEETINGS

Most theatre organizations have some sort of *production meetings*, which are sometimes very informal, perhaps after a rehearsal or on the spur of the moment. For other theatres, production meetings are very well defined, happening each week (or even every day) at a specific time set aside expressly for them. This is a time when the nuts and bolts of a production are discussed: things like schedules, how many crew people are needed, how to handle problems discovered in rehearsal, and so forth. All are given a chance to review their work for the past week and to comment on any problems they see on the horizon. Many times there is a discussion of how to integrate the work of different departments, such as when scenery will be ready for painting, how to paint the floor and focus lights on the same day, or where in a costume to hide a radio transmitter. Quite often it seems that an inordinate amount of time is spent discussing socks, or how many people it will take to pull a rope, but the meetings are really a very important tool in keeping the production process running smoothly.

During the rehearsal process, the director may mention that an extra lamp is required in a certain scene, or that a costume needs a pocket, or that perhaps a door could open the opposite direction, or that thunder and lightning are required at a certain point. Be sure to take notes about those revelations, and to mention them at the next production meeting.

It is very important that the stage manager or an assistant take precise notes about the decisions made at production meetings, or all of that sock discussion time will have gone for naught. You should type up a brief summary of each meeting and email this to all interested parties. Generally speaking, actors should not be included, because they are not part of that process.

Preparing for Rehearsals

You must do a number of things during the table work, before the standing rehearsal phase begins, in order to get ready for the process. The following section describes things that are always included, but there may be others that are specific to the production you are managing.

Tape out the set in the rehearsal area

The scenery designer will supply you with a *plan view* of the setting, and you must use tape to mark it out on the floor. This is to give the director and the actors an understanding of the spaces involved, and to aid in the blocking process. Use a *scale rule* to measure the drawing, and a regular tape measure to transfer the full-size dimensions to the stage or rehearsal studio floor. If you don't know how to do this, ask someone (perhaps an assistant) who does. It is important to do this work properly so that the actors get a true sense of how much space they have for certain scenes.

Use either vinyl *electrical tape,* or narrow strips of *gaff tape,* or *cloth spike tape* to mark the stage. The electrical tape comes in many colors, and you may wish to use that if your layout has multiple scenes and is very complicated. That will make it easier for the actors to orient themselves. If you use gaff tape instead, rip off narrow strips so that less tape is used. This not only saves on tape, but it is much kinder to the floor. Tape often pulls up the paint on the floor, and less tape equals less damage. White is good for a black stage floor. Electrical tape has some quirks. The vinyl tape stretches a lot when you pull it off the roll, so let it draw back up

some before sticking it to the floor or it will come back up later. Tape pulling up in the middle of the first rehearsal is a rookie mistake that you should avoid in order to save face.

Find rehearsal props/costumes

You probably won't have the real props until just before tech rehearsals, so you need to find some stand-ins to use until that time. Your *rehearsal props* should be about the same size and weight of the real thing, so that actors will have a chance to practice realistically. A block of wood with a rope on it can be a microphone, or a bundle of fabric can be a baby doll. A plastic soda bottle would not be a good substitute for a whiskey bottle, because the liquor bottle is much heavier. Find something closer to the actual size and weight.

You will often need things like a couch or chairs. Most of the time you can set up chairs in a row for a sofa, but other times you must improvise. You shouldn't necessarily expect the designer or the shop to help you with this, other than offering advice as to whether your choices are appropriate. They are busy with their own chores.

The wardrobe department may have a supply of *rehearsal skirts* and other items that can be used to simulate costume pieces. If you need something specific, you should ask about it in the production meeting. You cannot expect wardrobe to supply your rehearsal with too many specific items, because that is really your job. Actors should be expected to wear appropriate clothing from home to rehearsals. For men that might include a suit jacket or shoes with a leather sole. Women might be asked to wear low-heeled pumps, also known as *character shoes.*

The stage manager is often responsible for scheduling *costume fitting* appointments for the actors. Ask the wardrobe department for a list of who they would like to see, available times, and how long an appointment should last. You are responsible for scheduling, because you have contact with actors at rehearsal that others do not have. You can discuss this process at production meetings.

Make a production/prompt book

Your *production book* should contain copies of all your paperwork. Things like a *contact sheet,* rehearsal schedule, crew list, and other things that are needed for your particular show. The main component is your *prompt script.* This is used to mark blocking, and for cues during the run of the play.

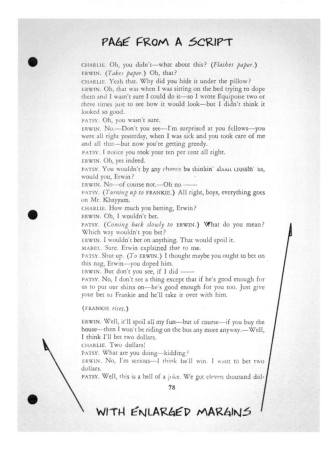

The method of making a prompt script is largely a matter of personal preference, but there are some givens. If you received a small *acting edition*–type script, make a photocopy of it to use in creating your book. Although technically a copyright infringement issue, everyone does this to make a stage manager script, and it is expected. Make each page of the script its own single copy so there will be lots of space to make notes. You may wish to enlarge the print so that it is easier to read and so that there will be more space between the lines. By the end of technical rehearsals, the need for extra white space will be well understood.

THE REHEARSAL PHASE

The first few rehearsals are typically *blocking rehearsals*, and you will need your prompt script from the get-go in order to write down the blocking notes. *Blocking* is a catch-all term for movement on the stage. If there is a very large cast, and the blocking is complex, you may wish to make a number of 8½×11-inch copies of the ground plan to go in your book so that you can mark the exact locations of actors on the stage. Writing down the blocking could be something you do yourself, or it could be an ASM chore. It is important to be accurate, because actors will definitely ask "Where do I enter?" many times before the show opens.

At some point the actors will be *off-book*, meaning that they are no longer allowed to use their scripts on stage. They will have, however, the option to *call for line* if they cannot remember one. An ASM should be located near the front of the stage to supply the lines as they are called for. This is often a delicate balance between saying too much and saying too little. Actors are taught not to break concentration when calling for a line. It is important for the person *on the book* to follow along very closely and to speak right up with the proper line the instant it is called for. Choose a person who is capable of focusing on that job without being distracted. *Feeding lines* means to offer them so that the actor can repeat them just after being prompted. If possible, you should rotate the duty of being on book to keep one person from getting too bored. Having an ASM follow the book for you will keep you free to observe the overall process and to jump in where necessary. If there are starts and stops, you may need to move furniture around, or call "lights up" or something else that will keep the rehearsal moving and make everyone's work more efficient.

Usually, directors have a run-through early on after the blocking is completed in order to see how the pieces fit together. Be sure to time this *stumble-through* so that an idea of the running time can be determined. It is important to let the design staff know when this is happening so that they have an opportunity to observe the rehearsal. This is especially important for lighting designers, who must know something about the blocking in order to complete their work.

Sometimes sound is an integral part of the performance, and you may need to provide music in order for certain scenes to be rehearsed effectively. Most of the time, this is done with a jam box you bring in yourself for this purpose. You or an assistant should cue up the sound and play it at the appropriate moment. This process is much easier in the modern age of CD burners and MP3 players.

You should familiarize yourself with the physical plant of the theater, including where lights can be turned on and off, and which doors lead where. Lights used for general illumination at rehearsals are called *work lights*. Remember to set out the *ghost light* at the end of the rehearsal.

Tech rehearsals

Many schools use the dry/wet tech system. A *dry tech* rehearsal is used to set cues with no actors present, and a *wet tech* tries them out at a rehearsal where actors are present. The dry tech is often referred to as a *cue set*, because lighting, sound, and scenery cues are determined at that rehearsal. A *cue-to-cue* rehearsal skips over the dialogue inside a scene, and jumps from one cue to the next.

Actors don't usually attend the dry tech, because they would spend a lot of time waiting and becoming frustrated. Much of the action centers on a collaboration between the lighting designer and the director, looking at different lighting schemes and deciding which ones they want to use for the play. Sometimes the designer will arrive with a number of cues already worked out, or the whole thing may occur at the dry tech. Either way, it is a time-consuming enterprise. The same thing happens with sound design, and with

moving scenery around the stage. Each change in the lighting is distilled into a *cue*. Your job as stage manager is to write down in your book the exact moment each cue should happen, and what number has been assigned to that cue. Cues are given numbers in order to organize them, so you can call for them efficiently during the run of the show. Sometimes sound cues have letters, so that there is less confusion. You may work on just light cues, then sound and set cues, or they may be all done at once. Lighting cues are generally marked as electrics, sound as sound, and scenery as either fly or deck.

In your book you might begin with a cue sequence something like this:

House to half GO

This cue asks for the house lights to dim 10 to 20 seconds before the play begins. The audience knows the show is about to start, and they turn their attention to the stage.

House out and Electrics 2 GO

This sequence asks for the house lights and preset lights to go out for the play to start. The theatre becomes dark.

Fly 1 GO

The curtain begins flying out in the dark.

Electrics 3 and Sound out GO

The preshow music fades down as the lights fade up on the first moment of the play.

Electrics 1 is generally the *preshow preset* that the audience sees as they enter the theatre. That could be lights on the curtain if one is used, or it could be an interesting look for the stage if it is not. At any rate, the first cue is called just before the *house opens*.

It is very important for you to be well organized when writing down the cues in your book during the dry tech. There may easily be a hundred or more cues in a single show, and you are the only person who is taking notes on their placement—everyone else is looking at other things. If you don't write the cues down properly in your book, a great deal of time setting them will have been wasted.

Your assistants will probably be asked to move around the stage as ersatz actors and/or to help move props around the stage. Because they have been in rehearsals, and know how the show works, they can instruct the *deckhands* and *prop guys* as to where things go. (Note that the word "guy" used in theatre just means "person," and doesn't necessarily indicate male gender.)

Quite often, it is necessary to mark where something should go when it is brought on stage. *Spike* two legs of a chair or two corners of a box. You can use colored tape to separate out spikes that overlap one another. *Glow tape* is sometimes used if the stage will be very dark when the prop is brought out.

At the end of every rehearsal, you should remind the crew of their next call time. It is common for call times to change during this period, because so many things are still being worked out. Tell the crew not to leave the theatre without checking in first.

After the cues have been set, but before the next rehearsal, you need to mark your prompt script so that you can *call the show*. Calling the show means listening to and watching the actors on stage, and alerting the crew when to take their cues. In order to call the show, you need to have the cue WARNs and GOs marked in your prompt script. The exact method of marking them is governed by personal preference, but some techniques are fairly standard.

Cues must often happen on a particular line or perhaps one particular word within that line so the marking must be done with some precision. Most stage managers mark the word placement in the text and draw a pencil line off to the margins of the script. Pencil is important, because cues are very frequently changed between tech rehearsal and opening night. Mark the cue type and number in the margin so that the pencil line connects the cue number and the correct word in the script. It should read something like ELEC 23 GO, or SOUND 7 GO, depending on the actual placement.

Notice that the GO word is placed last. When you actually make the call, the crewperson involved should take the cue *exactly* on the word "Go." This is one way in which a high degree of precision in cuing can be achieved. Stagehands are taught to be very meticulous about taking cues exactly on the word "Go" and not before or after. You should reinforce that standard.

Most stage managers give *warnings* for cues, and those should be written down in the book as well. Quite often a number of cues can all be warned at the same time when they are in close proximity to one another. Warns or *standbys* (either term is appropriate) should be announced in the opposite manner to a GO. The correct phrasing is "Standby electrics 23 and sound 7." Announcing the call as a standby *first* will avoid confusion as to the nature of the call. The warns should be marked in your script in the same manner as the GOs, with pencil lines and marginal notations.

Cue calling is typically done via *intercom headset*, which is especially true when speaking to assistant stage managers, the light board operator, and spot operators. If you assign one assistant to stage left and the other to stage right, they can be your eyes and ears as to what is going on backstage. You should position your desk to get the best view of the actors on stage, and/or use any video monitoring equipment available. If the sound operator is responsible for playback only, he or she may

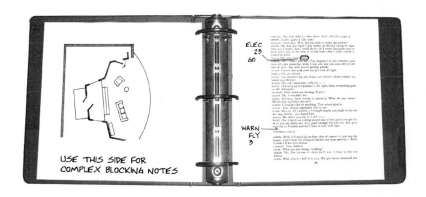

USE THIS SIDE FOR
COMPLEX BLOCKING NOTES

PROMPT BOOK

IT IS HELPFUL TO HAVE LOTS OF EXTRA WHITE SPACE AROUND
THE SCRIPT SO THAT YOU HAVE ROOM TO MARK THE CUES,
AND TO MAKE NOTES ABOUT OTHER THINGS THAT MUST
HAPPEN DURING THE SHOW.

be on headset as well. Sometimes when that person is mixing sound reinforcement, he or she needs both ears to listen to the show. In that case, a *handset* is used instead.

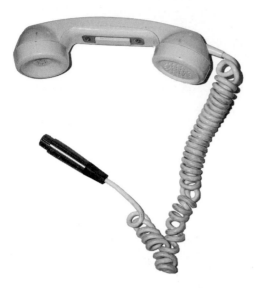

SOMETIMES A HANDSET
IS USED IN PLACE OF A HEADSET
WHEN THAT PERSON MUST HEAR
WITH BOTH EARS

The standard intercom headset has an earpiece and a microphone. The earpiece is called a *muff* (as in earmuff) and the headset can be either the single- or double-muff type. *Double-muff* headsets are frequently used when the show is very loud, like a concert, but in a much quieter stage show, a *single-muff* headset allows the user to hear both the stage manager and the show that is going on around them. The *headset mike* on most models will turn itself off when rotated to the up position, which places it on top of the head.

SINGLE MUFF HEADSET
WITH ATTACHED MICROPHONE

Intercom headsets are meant to be used in combination with a *beltpack*. The headset plugs into the beltpack, which has a couple of adjustment features. A switch turns the microphone on and off. A knob or thumbwheel adjusts the volume of the earpiece. Most types have an LED indicator *call light* to warn the user that someone is calling them to pick up the headset.

BELT PACK FUNCTIONS

PUSH THE SIGNAL BUTTON TO LIGHT THE LED, WHICH
LETS OTHERS KNOW TO PUT ON THEIR HEADSET.

THE THUMBWHEEL ADJUSTS THE VOLUME OF
YOUR EARPIECE (NOT YOUR MICROPHONE).

PUSH THE MIC BUTTON TO TURN YOUR MICROPHONE
ON AND OFF. DON'T LEAVE YOURS ON UNATTENDED!

Backstage protocol dictates that users be careful to turn the mike off when it is not in use, so as to keep down unwanted noise. This is especially true when laying your headset down. Make sure to turn it off so that (a) it doesn't make a loud bang when you lay it down, and (b) extraneous noise doesn't run through the system while you are away. Avoid standing too close to a stage light, because induction from the filament will create a 60-cycle hum in the entire system. Some intercom systems have more than one *channel* so that the stage manager can select who can hear what he or she is saying. Switches turn various channels on and off.

THIS PARTICULAR INTERCOM HAS TWO CHANNELS, A & B. YOU CAN ROUTE INFORMATION TO SPECIFIC PERSONNEL BY SELECTING WHICH CHANNEL THEY CAN RECEIVE. "LINK" CONNECTS THE TWO CHANNELS TOGETHER. VARIOUS KNOBS ARE USED TO ADJUST VOLUME LEVELS.

The wet tech is generally the most chaotic period of any show. Everyone is dashing about, preparing for their individual tasks. For this rehearsal, the actors are called, as well as the crew, and they will be excited about the new elements being added. Try your best not to be overwhelmed by the hubbub going on around you, but rather learn to enjoy it instead. Everyone will be happier that way.

Frequently, a *tech table* is set up in the auditorium of the theatre for you to use during the tech rehearsals. Lighting and sound control may be located nearby. This is because a large amount of cross-talk must occur between the designers, the director, and the stage manager. A close-knit grouping makes it easier to communicate. Position an assistant at the stage manager's desk backstage in order to operate the cue lights.

Another means of communication is via *cue lights,* which are controlled by switches on the stage manager's desk. When the switch is turned on, a cue light is lit. This is a warning for action to take place, so the switch should be turned on a reasonable amount of time before the cue is to occur. If the time span is too short there won't be enough time to get ready. If the time span is too long, the stagehands will get bored and look away just as the light goes off. Cue lights are a good way to communicate with the fly rail, or with deckhands, because many of them can see the light all at once, and because it doesn't unnecessarily burden them with equipment. When the cue light is switched off, it is the same as if the stage manager has said "Go." Use tape and a marker to indicate which switch controls which light. It might seem that you would just remember it, but often things become a bit hectic at the SM desk, and it is good to be able to react in a hurry.

You may be required to call followspot cues, or they may be taken on their own, or called by some other electrician. Spot cues often contain a *frame number*, which is the color of the spot, and some means of describing the person to be followed with the spot. Because there is generally more than one followspot in use, each one is given a number for identification. Thus the spot call goes like this: "Spot one in a frame two, pick up Mrs. Lovett upstage left on her entrance." That is a lot for a busy stage manager to say, and in a professional situation spot calls are frequently handled by an electrician who knows the show well. You may not have that luxury in a school show.

Tech week is the time between the dry tech and opening night. In commercial theatre, the term "production" is used instead, and it often lasts more than one week. It is a busy period full of last-minute changes and phrases like, "Oh, just one more thing …." The stage manager really begins to take the over show during

this period. Opportunities to stop and make changes become fewer and fewer. Most directors avoid stopping during a *dress rehearsal*, because it disrupts the artistic flow of the actors. The last dress rehearsal before opening is called the *final dress*.

The stage manager should have a list of things that must happen in order for the show to start. Making a list of them will ensure that they all get done, as it is very easy to forget one of a hundred things when there is no list. Be sure to delegate chores to assistants and crew, but keep an eye on things and insist that they have lists as well.

It is customary to have a *sign-in sheet* posted on the callboard near the *stage door* for actors to sign, showing that they are in the theatre. This is good practice to follow, because it will let you know right away if someone is missing. You must telephone someone immediately if he or she is missing. Stage managers alert the actors and stagehands when *half-hour* has been reached. In commercial theatre, IATSE work days are measured from the half-hour call, and it is very important to the stagehands. Most stage managers also make 15-minute and 5-minute calls. *Places* means that the show is about to start, and that cast and crew alike should make their way to their opening positions without delay.

THE STAGE DOOR TYPICALLY LEADS TO THE DRESSING ROOM AREA.

IT IS BAD MANNERS TO ADMIT PEOPLE WHO ARE NOT INVOLVED WITH THE SHOW.

CHAPTER 14

HARDWARE, FABRICS, ADHESIVES, AND OTHER THEATRICAL SUPPLIES

Hardware is such a commonly used word that we tend to overlook its original intended meaning. Try thinking of it as two separate words. When you look at it that way, hardware consists of wares, or products, that are generally made from a hard substance, metal. That could be a fairly good definition of hardware, especially back in the day. Plastics are used now for many hardware items that were once made of steel or brass, but the vast majority of hardware is still metallic in nature. I think that originally the word *hard* was used to differentiate these supplies in name and concept from the wooden structures they were used to connect. There are literally hundreds of thousands of pieces of different types of hardware available today, for use in dozens of different construction crafts. Most of the hardware in this section was developed for use in building things other than theatre scenery. Stage carpenters have found creative ways to use hardware that suits their particular craft, and I will point those out as they come along. Sometimes it is important to know what the original use of the piece was, so that gets mentioned from time to time.

A trip to a hardware store, though, can reveal many products that don't really fit that description at all. Glue certainly doesn't, and yet it is often the best way to assemble wooden structures. There are many different types of adhesives, for wood, plastics, and even metal. This chapter also includes things like wire, sandpaper, and fabrics that are used so frequently in a theatre scene shop that they are often kept "in stock" and ready to use at any moment. It isn't really practical to make a separate trip to the hardware store every time you need some hot-melt glue.

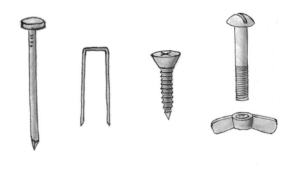

FASTENER TYPES

doi: 10.1016/C2009-0-23409-X

FASTENERS

Fasteners are used to connect building materials. It is the preferred modern term for the hardware group containing *nails*, *staples*, *screws*, and *bolts*. Each one of these fastener types has different qualities that separate it from the others. A nail is different from a staple, and a screw is not the same as a bolt. Sometimes the differences are a bit vague, but there are commonly understood definitions. It is important to know the names and definitions of things—not simply to be able to ask for them, but also because knowing how something works can help a technician to understand why it might be important to choose one piece of hardware over another.

Nails

Nails were some of the earliest fasteners in common use, at least in part because they require very little technology to produce. The Industrial Revolution brought about the ability to use machines to easily manufacture all sorts of things in mass quantities, including metallic hardware. Before that, all metalworking was done by hand, one piece at a time. Early nails were made by cutting across bars of flat stock at a slight angle, and this type of nail is known today as a cut nail. Cut nails are triangular in shape, and if laid head to toe and side by side, it is easy to visualize how they were made. These nails are still manufactured in small quantities for historical restorations.

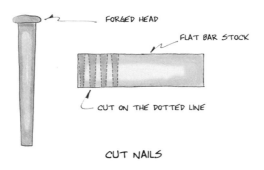

FORGED HEAD

FLAT BAR STOCK

CUT ON THE DOTTED LINE

CUT NAILS

The method of categorizing nail sizes was developed over a long period of time, and it is one of those fun, obscure things to know about. It is related to a method that was also used to price them when they were produced in England some centuries ago. As you can imagine from seeing how early nails were cut, the larger the nail, the harder it was to produce and hence more expensive. Making cut nails was a labor-intensive undertaking. The present system of sizing is related to the cost of making nails back at that time. The small letter d is used to represent the word *penny* in England. When this system originated, one hundred of the larger nails cost

16 cents, which was a great deal of money at that time. Of course, we've had quite a bit of inflation since then. The important thing to remember is that the larger the nail, the higher the penny number, and the smaller the nail, the lower the penny number.

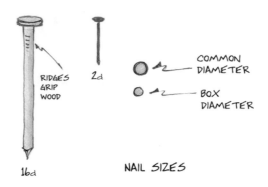

RIDGES GRIP WOOD

2d

COMMON DIAMETER

BOX DIAMETER

16d

NAIL SIZES

In modern times, a two-penny is the smallest size nail available. The 16d nail is the largest commonly used in woodworking. A 2d nail is about 1 inch long, while a 16d nail is about $3\frac{1}{2}$ inches long, which should give you some indication of the relative sizes. Smaller nails are usually called *brads*, and larger ones are called *spikes*.

Constructing a home requires a considerable number of fasteners. Modern nails are made from wire rather than bars of steel. They are quickly and easily manufactured by large machines that can turn out thousands in a minute. The prices of today's nails are mostly related to the cost of the steel wire and distribution of the finished product. Allowing for inflation, they are quite inexpensive by comparison to the earlier version. Wire nails are easily distinguishable from cut nails, because the modern type is round in cross section rather than squarish like the antique cut nails.

Modern machine-made nails are more precise than a cut nail, yet even so it is not really necessary to be terribly exacting in making them. If a 16d nail is said to be about $3\frac{1}{2}''$ long, it might well be $3\frac{1}{4}''$ or $3\frac{5}{8}''$. The work that they do does not require an exact tolerance. The diameter of the nails is related to the length and is an arbitrary but standard gauge. The longer a nail is, the larger its diameter is.

Even so, there are two classifications of diameter, box and common. *Box nails* are thinner than *common nails*. A 16d box nail is skinnier than a 16d common nail, but a 4d common nail is smaller in diameter than a 16d box nail, because the whole nail is smaller. Box nails are usually best for scenery, because they are thinner and tend to split lumber less easily. Most fastener outlets stock nails in even penny sizes from 2d to 16d. Above size 16d, nails tend to come in even multiples of 10, like 20d, 30d, 40d, and so forth. These larger sizes are not of much use to the scenic technician as a nail per se, but if you bend the head at a 90-degree angle, a nail can become a replacement hinge pin, and often the larger sizes fit better.

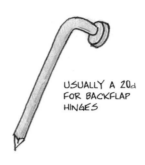

USUALLY A 20d FOR BACKFLAP HINGES

BENT NAIL FOR HINGE PIN

Any nail smaller than 2d is generally referred to as a brad, and the length is given in inches such as $\frac{7}{8}$ or $\frac{3}{4}$. Nails today are most usually sold by the pound, although some hardware stores have them in small boxes of arbitrary amounts. Traditionally, a standard full box of nails weighs 50 pounds. That is a very large number of 4d box nails, but not so many 16d common.

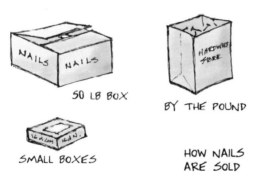

NAILS NAILS

50 LB BOX

HARDWARE STORE

BY THE POUND

SMALL BOXES

HOW NAILS ARE SOLD

There are several different types of nail heads. The most recognizable is the standard flat head. This kind of head is used for most nailing, especially when the heads will not show in the final product. The head of this type of nail is easy to grasp and remove with a claw hammer whenever that is necessary. However, the nail head serves another purpose that is not so obvious, but is the real reason it exists. The head prevents the nail from being pulled entirely through a piece of lumber. In most construction scenarios, a thin piece of wooden material is being nailed to a thicker piece, such as a sheet of $\frac{1}{2}''$ plywood being nailed to a 2×4. If the nail had no head, movement in the wood could easily work the

nail through the plywood, and the two pieces would come apart. The head keeps that from happening. It is important to drive nails all the way down so that the heads are snug to get the greatest holding power from them.

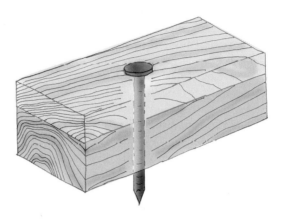

THE HEAD OF A NAIL KEEPS THIN PIECES OF WOOD FROM SLIDING OFF THE NAIL SHAFT.

The *finish nail* is another type. Many people mistakenly think that a finish nail has no head, but in reality it has a very small head that is intended to be driven completely beneath the surface of the wood it is holding down. The small head is large enough to get a grip on the wood, but tiny enough to leave only a minute entrance hole on the surface of the wood. A close inspection reveals that there is a small dimple on the finish nail head that may be used in conjunction with a *nail set* to "set" the head just below the surface of the work. The resulting hole may later be filled and sanded so that it does not show. This technique is how the finish nail got its name, because it is to be used in "finishing" work, such as applying trim to doors and windows.

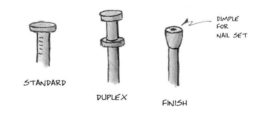

STANDARD

DUPLEX

FINISH

DIMPLE FOR NAIL SET

TYPES OF NAIL HEADS

A duplex or double-headed nail looks much the same as a standard nail, except that there are two heads on the shaft about half an inch apart. The double-head approach is meant to secure the wood with one head, and to leave the other head for pulling the nail out at some future date.

Another category of nails is meant to be used in a *nail gun*. Most nail guns are pneumatic, meaning that they run on air pressure. They are covered in the chapter on tools. Nails of this type must be manufactured to a much closer tolerance than ordinary nails, because they need to precisely fit through the gun without jamming. Most often these nails come in some sort of strip, which is glued or taped together as a means of organizing them. Each company has its own patented method of producing nails that is different from everyone else's, so that the nails are usually not interchangeable. In recent years, competing nail manufacturers have sprung up to make generic "brand x"–type nails for some of the guns. Some of these work fine, and some cause the nail gun to jam frequently.

Nail guns have traditionally been sold at a very low price in order to get people to buy them. That guarantees a long-term commitment to buying a particular type of nail, and that is where the money is made. The nails tend to be somewhat expensive. It is best to consider the economic ramifications of nail gun politics when buying a particular type. It is not a good idea to buy a gun that uses inordinately expensive or difficult-to-find nails. Exact brands differ from region to region.

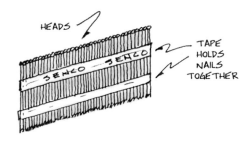

NAILS FOR A PNEUMATIC GUN

A good finish nailer is an indispensable tool in the modern scene shop. Nail guns speed up your work tremendously, and there are some techniques that are almost impossible without one. Most guns will hold a variety of nail lengths from 1 inch to 2 inches, and that should fit most of your needs.

The holding power of small finish nails is not very great. Sometimes that is okay, and other times it is not. Many of the construction methods depicted in this book require that wooden joints be glued together. Glue joints are very strong, but the parts must be closely held together until the glue has a chance to bond. In some types of construction, clamps are used for that purpose, but putting them on is a very slow and tedious process. Pneumatic finish nails are a great way of pinning the joinery together until the glue sets. Even though the tiny pneumatic nails don't have much holding power, they are easy to put in, and they hold well enough for the short time they are needed.

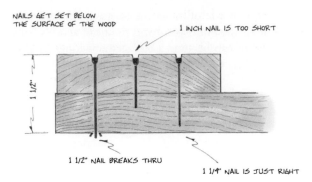

MAKING A NAIL SELECTION

One thing to remember about these nails is that—like all finish nails—they are meant to be set into the surface of the work about $\frac{1}{8}''$. If you are using them to join two pieces of 1-by stock (that are really $\frac{3}{4}''$ thick), care must be taken to select a nail that will not go through the far side of the work. The two pieces of wood are $1\frac{1}{2}''$ thick when placed together. If a $1\frac{1}{2}''$ nail is used, the setting of the nail will send it $\frac{1}{8}''$ through the wood. A nail $1\frac{1}{4}''$ long would be a better choice.

Some nail guns are meant to be used with much larger nails, and in general construction, they are meant to assemble the wooden skeleton or *framing* of a house. They are ideal for construction that involves 2×4 lumber, and can really speed things up if you are building scenery from that type of material. Large nail guns of this sort may be called framing guns, because of the type of work they are used for.

Staples

Staples are used in a very similar manner to nails, but there are some important differences. A nail is one metallic shaft, whereas a staple has two *legs* connected by a top section known as the *crown*. The physical manner in which staples connect materials together is different from a nail in a very important way.

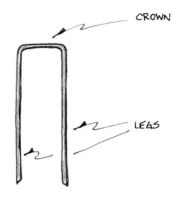

PARTS OF A STAPLE

Everyone is familiar with a desk stapler, which uses very small staples to batch together loose sheets of paper. This kind of stapler uses a small metal plate to bend the ends, or legs of the staple over after they have passed through the last sheet. Construction staples are different, in that they are a much heavier gauge and are not intended to be bent over. The legs simply go all the way into a piece of wood in the same manner as a nail. Even so, the staple is much better at connecting thin materials, and a sheet of paper is an extreme example of a thin material.

Staples are a better choice for certain applications than nails are. The most obvious example of this is when you must attach very thin pieces of plywood to a thicker substrate. A nail gun nail sets its nails in $\frac{1}{8}$". If the plywood you are using is $\frac{1}{4}$" thick, that leaves the nail only $\frac{1}{8}$" to grip the plywood. It is very easy for the plywood to work its way off of the nail under these circumstances. With a staple, the crown of the staple tends to catch a certain amount of the wood fiber under itself and uses it to hold the thin ply to the framing underneath.

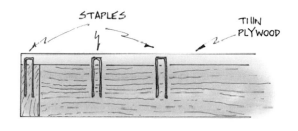

WHEN USING A THIN COVERING MATERIAL, STAPLES GRAB SOME OF THE WOOD AND HOLD IT DOWN RATHER THAN SHOOTING RIGHT THROUGH

Construction staples come glued together in a strip, just as desk staples do. They are generally classified by the length of the leg in inches—$\frac{3}{4}$", $1\frac{1}{2}$", and so on—and by the width of the crown. Most staples have a crown that is either $\frac{1}{4}$" or $\frac{1}{2}$" wide. Quarter-inch-wide staples will not fit into a gun intended for $\frac{1}{2}$" crowns. The manufacturing principles and the sales philosophy of this type of staple are much the same as for pneumatic nails.

Staples are also best suited to other thin materials, such as fabric or cardboard or paper, but a large construction stapler may be too powerful for them, and might shoot the staple right through. Hand-operated, manually powered staplers are useful for stapling smaller objects. A fabric stapler is a pneumatic gun that shoots very small-gauge staples that are often used in upholstery work.

Some staples are not intended to be used in a gun. There are fencing staples, which are essentially U-shaped bent nails with two sharp ends, and also insulated staples designed for electrical work. Modern insulated staples are made of two small 2d nails that are connected by a piece of plastic. Plastic is used in this application, because it does not conduct electricity. It is not a good idea to use a metal crown staple on electric wires because of the chance that the staple will be driven too far and cut through the wiring insulation. That would cause a short circuit. Only the insulated staples are approved by the National Electric Code.

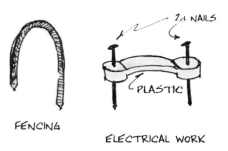

FENCING

ELECTRICAL WORK

Screws and bolts

Screws and bolts are fasteners that use *threads* to hold themselves in position. Threads are the ridges found on the side of the shaft of a screw or bolt. A close inspection will reveal that a thread is really one long ridge that curves around and around, spiraling from one end to the other.

Sometimes it is easy to become confused about the difference between screws and bolts. Generally speaking though, bolts are used with a *nut* that holds the bolt in place. The nut has female threads that match the male threads on the bolt. On occasion, female threads are tapped into a hole drilled into a metal structure or housing. Then a bolt can be screwed into that pre-threaded opening rather than using a nut. The threads on a bolt are sometimes called *machine threads*. Bolts have a blunt end.

Screws have a pointy end and make their own pathway into wood, plastic, or sheet metal. They compress the material on either side in order to form that hole. The male threads of the screw grip the walls of the hole with much more holding power than a nail does. Screws form their own female threads in the work material.

Even though these descriptions hold true most of the time, some smaller bolts are referred to as machine screws. This is a plot hatched by manufacturers, just to make the whole thing more confusing. But if you recall that bolt threads are called *machine* threads, it is a bit easier to understand.

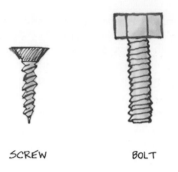

SCREW   BOLT

Screws and bolts come in a variety of different head shapes so that you can select a style that works well for the particular job at hand. Perhaps the most common type is the *flat head*. The flat head is used when it is necessary to maintain a flat surface, with none of the screw head protruding above the surface of the work. This kind of head is often used to attach certain types of hardware, such as hinges, picture hangers, hanging irons, and so forth. The cone-shaped flat head is manufactured to fit into countersunk holes in the hardware just mentioned.

Some screws and bolts have a *round head*. It is intended to be more decorative and to show above the surface. Round heads are often found on stove bolts, the ¼″-diameter bolts used to hold scenery together. Older-style sheet metal screws have a head similar to the round head, but with a flattened top. This kind is called a *pan head*, because it is the same basic shape as the interior of a cast-iron skillet. Sheet metal screws are not intended to sink in flush, because the material they are used on will not allow it. The pointy ends of these screws are used to connect pieces of thin sheet metal, and as a result the screws themselves are made from very hard steel. This theoretically allows them to work their way through the metal without dulling or breaking. Pan-head screws are difficult to install with a power tool, so other types are more popular now, especially the hex head.

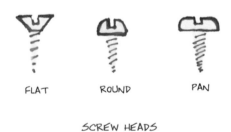

FLAT   ROUND   PAN

SCREW HEADS

Two very popular *drives* are used for screw heads: the *standard slot* and the *Phillips*. The drive is the part of the screw that is used to force or drive it into the work. When screws were made by hand, slotted heads were the only type feasible to manufacture, but in the machine age, the Phillips drive has all but totally replaced it. The Phillips drive is much easier to use with a power screwdriver, which is the only logical way to drive the thousands of screws it takes to put together a stage setting. In recent years, there has been a move toward even more functional shapes, with the most successful being the *square drive*.

SLOTTED   SQUARE

PHILLIPS

TYPES OF DRIVES

The major problem encountered in using a power screwdriver (such as a variable-speed drill) is that the driver bit tends to slip out of the screw head. This can lead to deforming the head in such a way as to make it impossible to get the screw in or out. The Phillips head handles this problem much better than the slotted head, and the square drive is better than the Phillips. The only problem with the square drive is that they are more difficult to find in all sizes. As a result, you might wind up with a mixture of half square and half Phillips drive screws in the shop. Obviously, production will be streamlined if only one kind of fastener is used, and there is no need to change bits back and forth. Perhaps in the future, the square drive will overwhelm the Phillips drive in much the same manner as Phillips replaced slotted.

The diameter of a screw is determined by a gauge number that is fairly arbitrary in nature. A common gauge of screw for attaching hinges is the #8. To give some basis for comparison, #2 screws are tiny, whereas a #12 screw is about the largest commonly found. The practically microscopic screws used on things like eyeglasses have numbers like 00 or 0000. The length of screws is described in inches or fractions thereof.

Not all screws are manufactured in the same way, or are of the same quality. Ordinary wood screws have a thread that does not extend all the way from the point to the head, but rather stops short of the top, leaving a portion of the shank smooth. Another type of screw known as a *tapping screw* has threads that are continuous. The tapping screw also seems to have sharper threads, and they are much easier to drive.

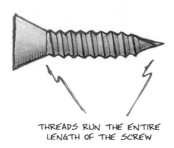

THREADS RUN THE ENTIRE
LENGTH OF THE SCREW

TAPPING SCREW

Drywall screws are extremely popular today. They were developed to hang wallboard in houses. These screws are very long and thin, and have a distinctive appearance. They have what is called a *bugle head*, which looks and works much the same as a Phillips flat head. Drywall screws are most often black in color. They come in two gauges, #6 and #8, with the #6 diameter being the most useful. The lengths are somewhat odd, generally being $\frac{7}{8}''$, $1\frac{1}{4}''$, and $1\frac{5}{8}''$ for the shorter screws, and then jumping up into the 2″, 3″, and even 4″ ranges.

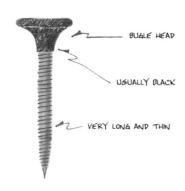

BUGLE HEAD

USUALLY BLACK

VERY LONG AND THIN

DRYWALL SCREW

Drywall screws are very hard and brittle, so the heads tend to break off if too much torque is used to drive them into the work. If a drywall screw is sticking through the back of a piece of scenery, it can be easily snapped off with a hammer, or even your foot. This would not be even remotely possible with any ordinary type of screw, and serves as a demonstration of how hardness and malleability are inversely proportional, an issue that often comes up in the steel made to construct tools. Drywall screws need to be made of especially hard steel because of their length and their thin nature. Some drywalls have a twin set of threads rather than just one long continuous thread. The bigger, single threads hold better in wood.

Tech screws are a specialty item and are mostly available from a dedicated fastener outlet, although you can find a limited selection of them in some hardware stores. (If you spell "tech" with a K, it becomes Tek, a well-known brand name.) They are intended to drill into thin steel, such as 16-gauge square tube, and then create their own machine threads that will secure the screw in place. They are at their best when you are attaching wood to metal. Tech screws are usually either #10ga or #8ga in diameter and are available in a variety of lengths. There are three types of heads: a large bugle head, a pan head, and a hex head. All of them are intended to be used in conjunction with a power driver, because tech screws cannot be driven by hand. The hex type is much easier to install, but it leaves a rather large and unsightly head above the surface of the wood. The flat-headed type is harder to spot once the scenery has been painted.

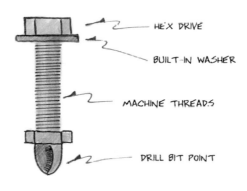

HEX DRIVE

BUILT-IN WASHER

MACHINE THREADS

DRILL BIT POINT

TECH SCREW

As mentioned earlier, the difference between screws and bolts lies in the type of thread that is used. Screw threads are pointy at the end that must start into the wood, and the threads flare outward so that they can gain more purchase on the surrounding material. Machine threads are exactly the same from beginning to end, so that they are in sync with the threads found on a matching nut. Tech screws have a drill bit on the end that creates the hole for it in the steel. The screw then taps its own treads in the metal. Normally, a bolt must have a hole drilled for it in advance, whereas a screw tends to make its own pathway. So tech screws are an interesting blend of the two.

Bolts are sized by their diameter and by their length in inches. The diameter is given first and the length second, as in "quarter-inch by three-inches." Metric bolts are not commonly used in scenery building in the United States. Very small bolts under $\frac{3}{16}''$ in diameter are sometimes referred to as machine screws and given a gauge number starting at #10 and going down.

Threads on a bolt are proportional to the size of the bolt itself, so that the threads of larger bolts are larger than the threads of smaller bolts. The number of threads is often listed with the size of the bolt, as in quarter-inch/20. Thread descriptions are given in *threads per inch*, or *tpi*. Each diameter of bolt has a normal number of tpi, but sometimes manufacturers will deviate from the norm for a specific purpose, and you may find that even though your replacement bolt is of the same diameter, it still will not work properly. Quarter-inch bolts have a standard 20tpi, and $\frac{3}{8}''$ have a standard 16tpi. Those sizes rarely have any other option. But very small machine screws like the #8 or #6 are often found with a variable number of threads.

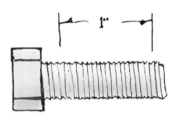

16 TPI
(THREADS PER INCH)

Almost all screws and bolts are threaded right-handed, which means that to tighten them you should turn to the right, or clockwise. To remove, apply force to the left, or counterclockwise direction. Someone long ago came up with the helpful phrase, "Righty tighty, lefty loosey."

The load capacity of heavy-duty bolts is rated with marks on the bolt head. These marks relate to a numbering system for toughness. Rated hardware is guaranteed to hold a certain amount of weight. Grade 8 bolts are the strongest, but grade 5 is a more common hardware-store variety. Many types of hardware have both rated and unrated versions.

Hex heads are a very popular drive for bolts, and as such they are intended to be used with a wrench. The amount of force used to tighten bolts is described as *torque*. A wrench applies much more leverage to a bolt than a screwdriver does. The higher torque of a wrench will get the bolt much tighter than a screwdriver can. Bolt head sizes naturally correspond to wrench sizes in inches. The size of the head and the size of the shank of a bolt are two separate issues. The size of a bolt as it is listed at the hardware store refers to the size of the shank, not of the head. So a $\frac{1}{4}''$ bolt has a $\frac{7}{16}''$ head.

The heads of *carriage bolts* are entirely different. They have a smooth, slightly rounded head with no gripping surface. The carriage bolt has a bit of square shank just below the head that is meant to be used in conjunction with a square hole in a metal surface, or with a *torque washer* into wood.

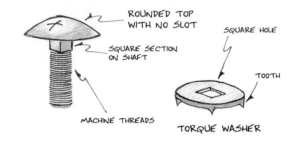

ROUNDED TOP WITH NO SLOT
SQUARE SECTION ON SHAFT
MACHINE THREADS
SQUARE HOLE
TOOTH
TORQUE WASHER

CARRIAGE BOLT

A torque washer has a square hole in the center and teeth on the outside edge. The teeth dig into a wooden surface and prevent the carriage bolt from turning while the nut is tightened. If a carriage bolt is used in wood without a torque washer, and the threads of the bolt are disrupted in some way, it may be impossible to remove the bolt without an angle grinder. Many people like the tight way the heads fit against the side of a platform.

Threaded rod can be purchased in lengths from 36" up. They come in all the popular diameters and can be useful when regular bolts are not long enough. Threaded rod does not have a head, but works quite well if you use nuts at both ends.

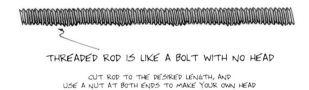

THREADED ROD IS LIKE A BOLT WITH NO HEAD

CUT ROD TO THE DESIRED LENGTH, AND USE A NUT AT BOTH ENDS TO MAKE YOUR OWN HEAD

Nuts are most often hex-shaped, but some older types are square. A really old bolt might also have a square head. *Wing nuts* are just about the only other type, and they are very helpful because they can be made finger-tight without the use of a tool.

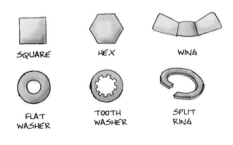

SQUARE
HEX
WING
FLAT WASHER
TOOTH WASHER
SPLIT RING

BOLT HEADS, NUTS, & WASHERS

It is generally best to use *washers* with bolts, because this spreads out the holding force of the bolt over a greater surface area for the pieces being bolted together. This makes it much less likely that the bolt will pull itself through the hole and cause the joint to fail. Also, washers keep the action of tightening the nut from marring the surface of the work and make it easier to get the nut tight. You should always turn the nut, not the bolt, especially if the bolt is holding together steel pieces. This helps protect the threads on the bolt from becoming damaged. Regular washers are generally known as *flat washers*. *Split-ring* washers and *tooth washers* may be used where vibration is a problem. These types of washers keep tension on the nut at all times and prevent it from working itself loose.

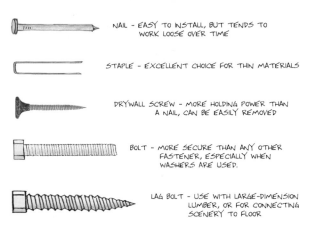

NAIL - EASY TO INSTALL, BUT TENDS TO WORK LOOSE OVER TIME

STAPLE - EXCELLENT CHOICE FOR THIN MATERIALS

DRYWALL SCREW - MORE HOLDING POWER THAN A NAIL, CAN BE EASILY REMOVED

BOLT - MORE SECURE THAN ANY OTHER FASTENER, ESPECIALLY WHEN WASHERS ARE USED.

LAG BOLT - USE WITH LARGE-DIMENSION LUMBER, OR FOR CONNECTING SCENERY TO FLOOR

FASTENER COMPARISON CHART

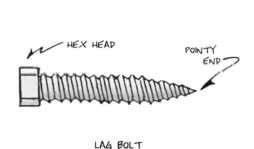

HEX HEAD

POINTY END

LAG BOLT

A *lag bolt* is a hybrid type of screw/bolt. They look like large screws that have a hex head on them. They are sized like a bolt, but go in like a screw. They are most often used to secure large items like lighting towers to the deck. Lag bolts often require a pilot hole for insertion.

Choosing the correct fastener

In general, staples have more holding power than nails, screws have more holding power than staples, and bolts are more secure than screws. If two wooden pieces are glued together as well as nailed or stapled, the strength of the joint will be much stronger. A properly applied adhesive creates a much stronger bond than you might think, but the words "properly applied" should be considered very carefully. It is virtually impossible to disassemble wooden pieces that have been glued together, so don't use glue if you need to take something apart later on.

Screws work really well for joining wooden structures when disassembly is planned in the future, and drywall screws are very popular for that sort of thing. Bolting is generally the most secure way of fastening

parts together. Anything that hangs overhead should be bolted for safety reasons, and if there is any question at all about the weight of the piece, be sure to use rated bolts and other hardware. This is especially true when the load is pulling on the fastener along its length. A sideways force creates a shearing stress, which is generally less likely to pull two wooden structures apart, because that would require the total failure of the wood surrounding the joint. But if the force is one that pulls along the length of the fastener, it is much easier for a nail, staple, or screw to fail. In that case, a bolt with appropriately sized washers has much more holding power.

HINGES

Hinges are crucially important to the rigging of stage scenery. Except for fasteners, they are used more than any other type of hardware. You are familiar with how hinges work when hanging a door, but in the theatre they are used in a much larger variety of applications. There are many different types of hinges, some of which have specialty uses and are manufactured with that single purpose in mind. Hinges are often used in scenery as a fastening or connecting device and not because they can be made to swivel back and forth.

The shaft that runs through the *barrel* of the hinge and holds the two *leaves* together is known as the *pin*. Some hinges have tight pins that are permanently attached to the hinge. A loose pin hinge can be separated into two halves when its pin is removed. If one leaf of the hinge is connected to one piece of scenery, and the second to another unit, you can disassemble the two units by just removing the pins.

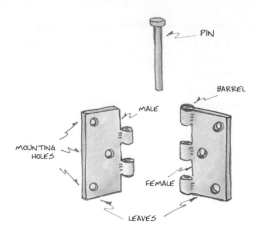

PARTS OF A HINGE

Butt hinges are used to hang doors. The name is derived from the fact that this type of hinge is intended to butt up against the edge of the door. In woodworking, boards that meet at their edges are said to be butting against one another, and when connected in this way the result is called a *butt joint*. An inspection of any butt hinge will show that the two leaves or sides are much taller than they are wide. If you compare the shape of the hinge to the edge of the door where it is used, the specific shape of the butt hinge makes sense. Butt hinges are meant to be used in pairs, as one alone would not provide much stability when the door swings open. Heavy or heavily used doors may have three or even four hinges on them.

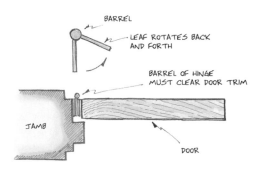

HOW A BUTT HINGE WORKS

Butt hinges are usually sized by the height of the leaf. Three-inch butts are fairly small; four-inch butts are quite large. The width of the leaves is proportional to the height, with the theory being that heavier doors will also be thicker doors. For theatrical use, the 3-inch size is large enough for most applications. Some modern-day butts have rounded corners. These corners are to complement the use of a router and jig

in creating the mortise that the hinge fits into. A straight corner hinge is generally more preferable when a jig is not used.

Strap hinges are shaped like two isosceles triangles joined at the base. This type of hinge is intended to be used on gates and other such flat structures. Strap hinges attach to the front of the gate, and the reasoning behind their shape is contingent upon that manner of attachment. Butt hinges are shaped to fit the edge of a door, but strap hinges are shaped to take advantage of the large flat surface of a gate front. Strap hinges are best when a large, very heavy-duty hinge is required. Its shape makes it a natural candidate to be bolted to a bulky scenic unit. A close relative of the strap hinge is the *T-hinge*, which is like a strap hinge on one side, and a butt hinge on the other. The unique shape of this hinge can be useful in certain situations.

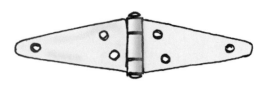

STRAP HINGE

Another type of hinge may be referred to as a "saloon-door" or "kitchen-door" hinge, but is technically known as a *double-action, spring-loaded hinge*. Swinging doors are frequently required to facilitate stage movement. Directors love to have doors swing back and forth to reveal characters in a comedy. Mounting a swinging-door hinge can be quite a challenge, as it is somewhat more complicated than a butt or strap hinge. The common type of swinging hinge operates by using two spring-loaded barrels that are located on either side of the door. Rather than having two leaves, as most hinges do, this type has three. The center one serves only to connect the two barrels. This leaf is not attached to either the door or the jamb.

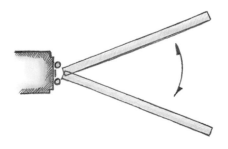

DOOR SWINGS BOTH WAYS

Around the top of each hinge barrel are a series of holes. A steel pin is used to turn the disk where the holes are located. (The manufacturer will most likely supply a special tool, but after you have lost it, a nail with the point ground off will do nicely.) Rotating the disk winds a spring that gives the hinge its ability to swing. A small pin is used to prevent the spring from unwinding. There are two barrels on each hinge, and all of the barrels on all of the hinges must be wound in order for the door to operate properly. It is possible to vary the speed of the closing of the door by adjusting the amount of tension on the springs.

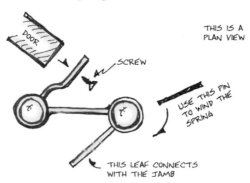

THIS IS A PLAN VIEW

SCREW

USE THIS PIN TO WIND THE SPRING

THIS LEAF CONNECTS WITH THE JAMB

SWINGING DOOR HINGE

This type of hinge comes in a variety of sizes, which mostly have to do with the thickness of the door slab. The hinge must be large enough to properly fit on the edge of the door. If the door is too thick for the capacity of the hinge, there will be no place for the barrels to fit. A close relative of the swinging door hinge is the *double-action hinge*, which swings in much the same way, but is not spring-loaded. These may be used on folding screens, but are not really sturdy enough to be used on very heavy scenery.

There are a number of different types of cabinet hinges. Some of them greatly resemble butt hinges and are used in more or less the same way, but on a smaller scale. Some are meant to be face mounted like a strap hinge.

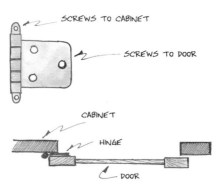

SCREWS TO CABINET

SCREWS TO DOOR

CABINET

HINGE

DOOR

CABINET DOOR HINGES

The most popular type of cabinet hinge is the *self-closing flush-mount*. These are used for American-style doors, which do not cover the entire front of the cabinet. On this type of cabinet, the face frame and one half of the hinge are visible when the door is closed. This type of hinge attaches to the back of the door, and to the front of the face frame. The modern self-closing type does not actually close the door, but will hold it shut without using any type of catch or latch. Self-closing cabinet hinges are very cheap, plentiful, and easy to install without any special tools. An offset, or inset type, is available for doors whose backs are not on the same plane as the front of the face frame, but rather are inset $\frac{3}{8}''$ into the opening.

The *continuous* or *piano hinge* is similar to the butt hinge, except that it has a very long leaf. Piano hinges run the length of a door of some type, like the lid of a piano. They provide a sturdier connection than a series of smaller hinges.

CONTINUOUS OR PIANO HINGE

The *backflap hinge* is a type of hinge made especially for theatrical use. It is generally not used in the traditional way—that is, to allow a piece to rotate. The backflap is more often used as a connector that holds scenery together. It allows stagehands to take scenic units apart, and then put them back together easily and quickly. Backflap hinges are indicative of the kind of methodology that gives scenery its knock-down, pull-apart, throw-on-a-truck, and reassemble-for-act-three-in-Peoria style. Early-twentieth-century wooden scenery revolved around this portability factor. Traditional scenery is constructed so that it is lightweight and movable, whether the intent is to tour or to allow for the production of a play with multiple scenes that must be reset. In commercial theatre, virtually all scenery is built elsewhere and must be trucked in to the theatre. The use of backflap hinges has traditionally been a critical link in this methodology. Hinging and bolting scenery together are covered in detail in the construction chapters.

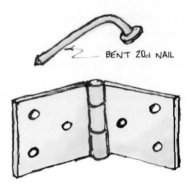

BENT 20d NAIL

LOOSE-PIN BACKFLAP

this is not possible for some reason, the pins can be pulled and the jack removed from the scenery. Sometimes several flats joined together will need to be stiffened so that they do not bend where they are hinged. A stiffener may be hinged to the back of the flats so that they remain rigid. Hinging the stiffener with loose-pin backflaps will make it possible to remove and reattach it easily. Even if scenery does not need to be moved during a show, being able to easily assemble/disassemble facilitates things like painting and moving the scenery around the shop.

You can examine the backflap hinge for clues on how to use it effectively. Notice that the leaf of the hinge is more or less square in nature. This would tend to indicate that it is not meant to be used on the edge of lumber as a butt hinge is, but rather on the face of some framing member. Most backflaps are *loose-pin*, and the pin supplied is a bent shaft, giving it a small handle to grasp, so that it is easy to remove and replace the pin.

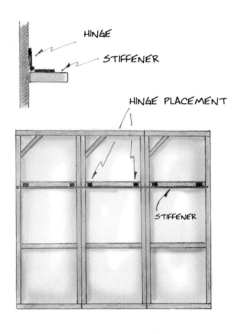

HINGE

STIFFENER

HINGE PLACEMENT

STIFFENER

BACKFLAP HINGES
ON A STIFFENER

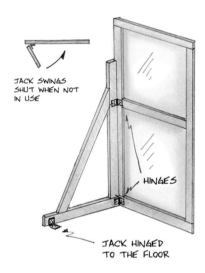

JACK SWINGS
SHUT WHEN NOT
IN USE

HINGES

JACK HINGED
TO THE FLOOR

BACKFLAP HINGES USED
ON AN L-JACK

Loose-pin backflaps are often used to join groups of flats or other scenery. Attach the hinges to the backside of the framing so that removing the pins allows you to separate the flats from one another. This hinge may also be used to attach L-jacks to the back of a flat in order to keep it upright. When not in use, jacks may be folded over against the back of the flat, or, if

Another use for this versatile hinge is to connect scenery to the floor. If it is not practical to use a stage weight to hold an L-jack to the deck, then a hinge may be used for the same purpose. You can also use this same technique to secure the bottoms of stairs, newel posts, columns, and any other scenic element the hinge will fit onto.

When using a backflap for some purpose in which the pin will never need to be removed, it is best to use a tight pin hinge, or to replace the original pin with *pin wire*. Pin wire can be bent over at the ends to ensure that it does not fall out unintentionally. Although you can buy pin wire by the pound from a supplier, I have found it less expensive to buy the kind of wire that is used to hang suspended ceilings and to cut my own. This wire is quite stiff and useful for other projects as well.

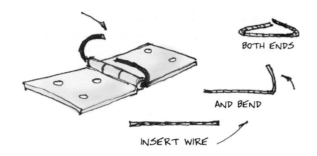

BOTH ENDS

AND BEND

INSERT WIRE

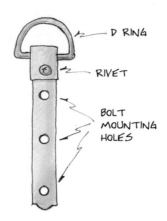

D RING

RIVET

BOLT MOUNTING HOLES

HANGING IRON

You might try using the tight-fitting original pin to put the scenery together, and then knock it out and replace it with a *bent nail*. This serves to give the joint just enough slack to fit together easily. Twenty-penny nails are a good fit for the 2″ backflap size.

If necessary, backflaps may be trimmed with a grinder to fit an odd shape. Sometimes you may need to bend them with a hammer and vise, and this can be done without too much effort. There is a certain brand of backflap hinge that has notches cut into it to make this a simpler process, but they are somewhat more expensive, and the notches that make them easier to bend also make them easier to break.

Backflap hinges come in several different sizes, running from 1″ to 2″. There is some merit to having a variety of sizes, but the 2-inch size is the most effective, so you may wish to stick with those. It is easy to recycle hinges, as there is little to go wrong unless they become bent in some way. The 2-inch variety is a heavier gauge and will last longer.

Hanging Hardware

Connecting scenery to a batten and flying it out overhead is one of the oldest methods of changing from one set to another. Soft goods like drops can be simply tied to a batten using their own tie lines, but built scenery is heavier and requires another approach. Specific pieces of hardware have been created for just this purpose. Safety is key when flying scenery, and it should be, because hanging heavy objects overhead is dangerous. The chance for disaster is high if an accident should occur. A further explanation of the use of theatrical flying equipment may be found in the chapter on rigging.

One of the oldest types of flying hardware is the *hanging iron*. It is basically a length of bar stock that has been doubled over to accommodate a *D-ring* at one end. The D-ring connects with a hanging cable. Holes along the length of the hanging iron are used to bolt it to a scenic unit. A hanging iron is actually made from steel, but it is quite common in the theatre to call anything metallic an "iron." It is important to bolt the hardware on, so that it is very securely fastened.

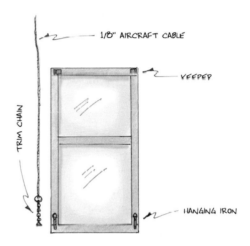

1/8″ AIRCRAFT CABLE

KEEPER

TRIM CHAIN

HANGING IRON

PUT THE HANGING IRON AND TRIM CHAIN ON THE BOTTOM FOR EASIER ADJUSTMENTS

Notice that the hanging iron is placed at the bottom of the flat rather than the top. Suspended scenery rarely hangs exactly straight the first time, and generally needs to be adjusted after it is up in the air. It is much easier to make adjustments while you are standing on the floor rather than from the top of a lift or ladder.

Trim chains are used to adjust the length of a hanging rig. They typically consist of a welded ring, a 2-foot length of $\frac{3}{16}$″ chain, and a snap hook. The chain is used to adjust the length of the cable, and this in turn adjusts the trim of the scenery. It is a fairly easy thing to lift the low side of the piece and adjust a trim chain up or down a link or two. Because the chain passes through the D-ring, moving up a 1-inch link will raise the side only half an inch.

Chains are often also used at the top to attach the cable to the batten. They should be wrapped around the batten at least once, and then use a shackle to connect the chain back to itself.

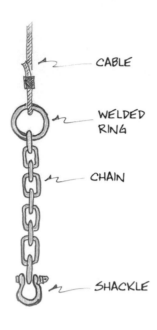

CABLE

WELDED RING

CHAIN

SHACKLE

TRIM CHAIN

On occasion it is necessary to make smaller adjustments to a trim than are possible by using chain. A *turnbuckle* can shorten a hanging cable by a tiny amount. The turnbuckle is essentially a very long nut with an eyebolt sticking out of it at either end. One of the eyebolts has a left-handed thread, and when the center section is rotated, the two eyebolts come closer together, or farther apart, depending upon the direction the center portion is turned. Turnbuckles are available in a large variety of sizes, from only a few inches to several feet in length. Most of the time they are not necessary on a simple piece with only two lines, but can really help out on a complicated hanging job in which many lift lines are needed.

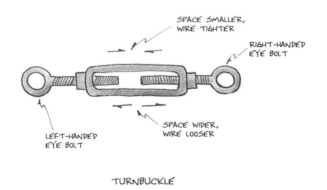

SPACE SMALLER, WIRE TIGHTER

RIGHT-HANDED EYE BOLT

LEFT-HANDED EYE BOLT

SPACE WIDER, WIRE LOOSER

TURNBUCKLE

There are several different ways to keep the cable firmly attached to the top of the flat. Half of a backflap hinge works on a lightweight piece. A D-ring plate with no ring is a more heavy-duty alternative. One problem with either of those approaches is that the scenery tends to tip forward some, because all of the weight is hanging on the downstage side of the hanging cable. You can get around that problem by drilling a hole in the top of the scenery, and feeding the wire rope through it. If the framing of the scenery is beefy enough, the hole might be enough, but often times it is prudent to install a steel plate on the back of the unit to keep the cable from pulling through the side of the hole. Be sure to use bolts rather than screws on any hanging hardware.

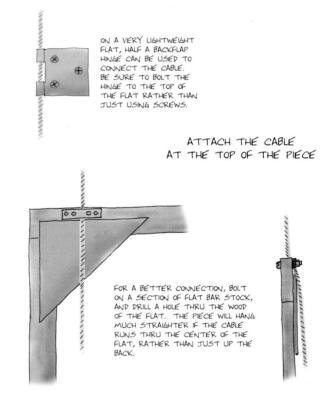

ON A VERY LIGHTWEIGHT FLAT, HALF A BACKFLAP HINGE CAN BE USED TO CONNECT THE CABLE. BE SURE TO BOLT THE HINGE TO THE TOP OF THE FLAT RATHER THAN JUST USING SCREWS.

ATTACH THE CABLE AT THE TOP OF THE PIECE

FOR A BETTER CONNECTION, BOLT ON A SECTION OF FLAT BAR STOCK, AND DRILL A HOLE THRU THE WOOD OF THE FLAT. THE PIECE WILL HANG MUCH STRAIGHTER IF THE CABLE RUNS THRU THE CENTER OF THE FLAT, RATHER THAN JUST UP THE BACK.

A *D-ring plate* is used in a quite similar manner as the hanging iron. However, this hanging hardware is shaped differently and may be used in places where a hanging iron might not fit. Most of the time, the hanging iron is used with the D-ring at the top and the iron vertical; the D-ring plate is used lying flat, which makes bolting it securely even more important.

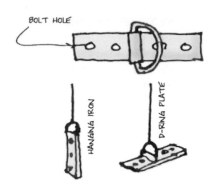

BOLT HOLE

HANGING IRON

D-RING PLATE

D-RING PLATE

Aircraft cable is used in hanging scenery, because it has a very high load rating. Essentially, this is a twisted rope that is made from steel strands. A large ⅜″ or ½″ variety is used in arena rigging. In the theatre, ¼″ aircraft cable is used in rigging the counterweight arbors. Most scenery involves less weight, and the size of the cables used is correspondingly lighter. Most scenery is hung using ⅛″ cable, which is rated from 1,000–2,000 pounds to its breaking strength. The actual amount varies from one manufacturer to the next and is stamped on the side of the reel that the cable comes on. The ⅟₁₆″ diameter cable is rated at about 400 pounds; the ¼″ goes up to 7,000 pounds. These are the breaking strengths, of course, and it is prudent to maintain a safety factor of at least 4, so the safe load should be derated by that amount.

SPOOL OF 1/8″ AIRCRAFT CABLE

Quite frequently, the cables are painted black so that they don't show so much in the lights. It is also possible to purchase cable that has already been painted or powder-coated by the manufacturer.

A *rope thimble* is used to protect the line from being bent over and kinked. It is very important to avoid a sharp bend when using wire rope. It is less forgiving than a line made from more pliable fibers like polypro-

pylene or nylon. Kinking the cable will make it more difficult to use and will also greatly reduce its breaking strength. There are different sizes of thimbles for different diameter ropes and cables.

WIRE ROPE   THIMBLE

Often called by its trade name *Crosby*, a *wire rope clamp* can be used to fasten the aircraft cable around the thimble. Wire rope clamps are quite commonly used to secure lift lines to a stage batten. It is the accepted practice to use two of these clamps when attaching cable to a thimble or a batten, as this better ensures that the connection will hold if one them has been improperly installed or vibrates loose.

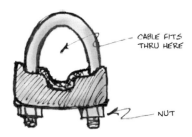

CABLE FITS THRU HERE

NUT

WIRE ROPE CLAMP

The bottom saddle part of the clamp should be attached to the tail side of the cable. This is often referred to as the "live" end.

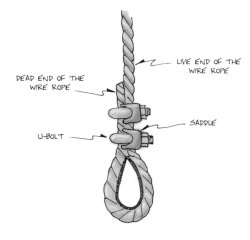

DEAD END OF THE WIRE ROPE

LIVE END OF THE WIRE ROPE

SADDLE

U-BOLT

WIRE ROPE CLAMPS ARE MEANT TO FIT THIS WAY

Swage fittings are used in the same manner as wire rope clamps, but the main difference is that the Crosby is removable, and the swage fitting is not. Once a swage fitting is secured to the cable, it is impossible to get it back off, unless you simply cut off the few inches of cable that are involved. Swage fittings are cheaper than wire rope clamps and are much neater on the cable. They are also easier to put on but do require a special *crimping tool.* A different size crimper is needed for each size of cable. Some tools are made with several different apertures that will fit more than one diameter of wire rope. Special cutters must be used on the wire rope, so that the end is not overly deformed so much that it will not fit through the hole in the swage fitting. A common trade name for a swage is *Nicropress Sleeve.*

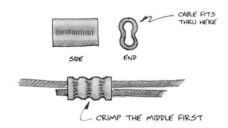

SWAGE FITTING

Screw eyes and *eyebolts* are very useful in rigging many different things backstage, but avoid using them for hanging anything from a batten unless the weight of the item being hung is very, very low. It is generally unsafe to use this hardware to hang heavy items over the stage. Sometimes, a large diameter–rated eyebolt can be used through metal framing, but screw eyes should only be used for small prop items, and never to hang anything weighing more than a few ounces. When using an eyebolt in metal framing, be sure to use a flat washer to avoid having the nut pull through.

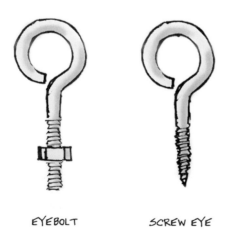

EYEBOLT   SCREW EYE

Eyebolts have a machine thread and are used with a nut, like a regular bolt. Screw eyes have a pointed screw thread and are intended to be used in wood only, like a screw. Screw eyes come in a wide variety of sizes that are somewhat arbitrary. Eyebolts are described by the diameter of the rod they are bent from, such as $\frac{1}{4}''$ or $\frac{1}{2}''$. Take the direction of force of the cable pull into consideration when using an eyebolt. Cable pulling at an oblique angle is more likely to cause the eyebolt to fail. Rated hardware has a known load rating and is much safer to use.

Quick links resemble an oval chain link, but one side has a nut that may be used to create an opening for the passage of chain links, rope thimbles, and other hardware. When properly closed, the quick link is very secure and will not come open accidentally. Quick links are sized according to the diameter of the link material. It is problematic that the opening in the link is often not large enough to fit over what you would like to attach it to. Some quick links are rated for a specific load, but most are not, and thus are not appropriate for rigging purposes.

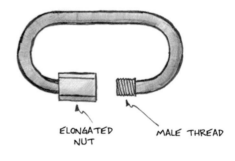

ELONGATED   MALE THREAD
NUT

QUICK LINK

Shackles are used in much the same way as a quick links, but they are manufactured in much larger sizes, and for much heavier loads. The shackle has a bell and is designed to connect two lines to one, but may also be used for a one-to-one connection. The removable bolt is called the *pin,* and it is accepted practice to use the shackle with the pin facing down, as most of the time a bridle is hung in that way. Never rig two cables to the bell of a shackle, because it places stress on the pin. Shackles are almost always rated hardware and are the best choice for overhead rigging.

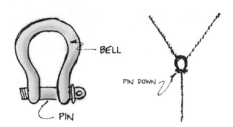

SHACKLE

Snap hooks are used to quickly connect cables or chains. They have a somewhat oval shape, with one end of the oval being larger than the other one. They are very commonly used on lighting safety cables where the load rating is not such a concern. *Carabineers* are a type of climbing hardware that work in much the same way. Because they are used for climbing, they almost always have a load rating, but they are somewhat clumsy to use for most rigging applications where steel cable is used.

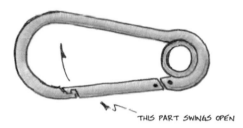

THIS PART SWINGS OPEN

SNAP HOOK

An *S-hook* is a piece of heavy wire that has been bent into the shape of an S. A pair of pliers is used to close the ends around something you are hanging. This piece of hardware is not easily removed, except with a pair of bolt cutters. They should not be used for overhead hanging because the hook may open up and fail if too great a load is applied. Also, it is not uncommon to see someone forget to bend the ends of the hook closed, and if used in this way, the hooks are almost certain to come loose at the worst possible moment. S-hooks are more appropriate to a variety of prop uses.

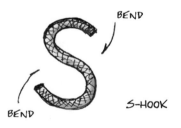

BEND

BEND

S-HOOK

Some large-sized, shop-built S-hooks were being used for the national tour of *Grand Hotel* when disaster struck, as related by this story in the *Denver Post* on April 14, 1991:

*PLAY HAS BRUSH WITH DISASTER
And the show went on. The old theater adage was put to the test yesterday at the Auditorium Theatre. During the matinee finale of *Grand Hotel*, with the entire cast on stage, a lighting and electrical harness weighing several hundred pounds fell from the rafters and crashed onto the stage. It missed the cast members, none of whom missed a beat; many members of the audience thought it was all part of the show. After the performance, a few cast members were overheard backstage saying that they had been frightened to death, but the evening performance was scheduled to go right on time.

April 14 has always been a bad day for theatres. The author witnessed the event from stage left, and found it an impressive lesson on the importance of safety in rigging.

Rota-Locks are used to join two pipes together at a right angle. They come in two parts. One is a rod that has been bent into a double U–shape and then welded together at the end. The other piece is a spacer that fits in between the two pipes that have been slipped into the U-shapes. The spacer part has a bolt on it that may be turned to tighten the joint. Rota-Locks are manufactured for all sizes of schedule-40 black steel pipe from 1″ to 2″ ID. The only real problem with the use of these clamps is that the pipe must be slipped into the clamp from the very end, and this is sometimes difficult to do.

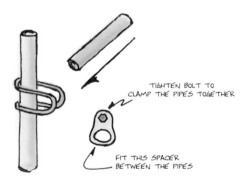

TIGHTEN BOLT TO CLAMP THE PIPES TOGETHER

FIT THIS SPACER BETWEEN THE PIPES

PIPE CLAMPS

A similar piece of hardware, the *Cheeseborough clamp*, locks itself around the pipe by means of a bolt and wing nut and has the added advantage of working with the pipe at any angle, not just 90 degrees.

HARDWARE, FABRICS, ADHESIVES, AND OTHER THEATRICAL SUPPLIES

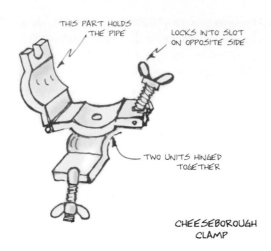

THIS PART HOLDS THE PIPE

LOCKS INTO SLOT ON OPPOSITE SIDE

TWO UNITS HINGED TOGETHER

CHEESEBOROUGH CLAMP

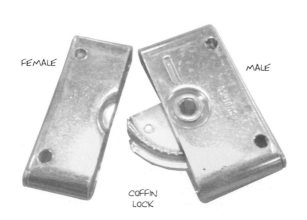

CLAMP USED TO CREATE A PIPE GRID

Casket locks consist of a male and a female side, with the male side having the moving parts. The two halves are connected to two different pieces of scenery, and then a $\frac{5}{16}''$ hex key is used to lock them together. There is a cam-shaped hook inside the male half that rotates around and grabs two projections inside the female half. Because the hook in the male is a cam, it draws the female side toward it as it rotates.

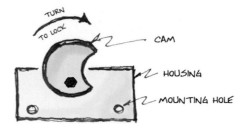

TURN TO LOCK

CAM

HOUSING

MOUNTING HOLE

COFFIN LOCK

Screen door handles come in many sizes and weights. They are quite useful as a "gripping" point when attached to a unit of scenery. They are relatively inexpensive and reusable.

SCREEN DOOR HANDLE

A *cane bolt* is used to secure rolling scenery to the floor. It is very similar to a *barrel bolt* used on a door, with the exception that the cane bolt sinks into a hole drilled in the floor or deck. When the bolt is pulled upward and turned to the side, it will stay up and out of the way. When the handle is rotated to the center position, the bolt slides downward and into the hole in the floor, which holds the unit in place.

Casket or *coffin locks* are a great way to connect heavy pieces of scenery. Casket locks are most often used to lock two or more platforms together, and a full discussion of this process may be found in the chapter on decking. These locks can also be used in a wide variety of applications to join scenic units in much the same manner as loose pin hinges, although the method of attaching the lock is much different.

CANE BOLTS SECURE ROLLING UNITS TO THE STAGE FLOOR

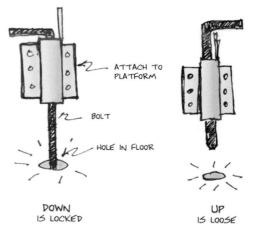

ATTACH TO PLATFORM

BOLT

HOLE IN FLOOR

DOWN IS LOCKED

UP IS LOOSE

FEMALE

MALE

COFFIN LOCK

There are several types of flat pieces of steel that may be used to connect wooden framing members. *Corner braces* form a flat right angle and are especially useful on the bottom corners of stock 4×8 platforms to keep the 2×4 s from pulling apart. *Angle irons* are similar in concept but are made by bending a straight piece of bar stock. Angle irons may often be used in the same connective manner as a backflap hinge, whenever the pieces need not be disassembled. Both come in a wide variety of sizes. You can easily bend an angle iron to an obtuse angle by laying it on a section of steel pipe and tapping it with a hammer.

The best type of caster for theatre use has a plate on the top of it and can be bolted to the bottom of a piece of scenery. Casters that fit into a socket, like furniture casters, are not generally strong enough to fit theatrical needs. Casters are said to be of either the *swivel* type, or the *rigid* type. Swivel or "smart" casters rotate and allow the scenery to be moved in different directions. Rigid, or "dumb" casters are fixed, and will run scenery back and forth along the same pathway. Some situations call for swivel, and others demand rigid casters.

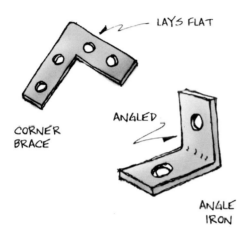

CORNER BRACE

LAYS FLAT

ANGLED

ANGLE IRON

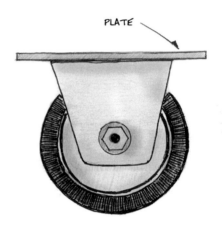

PLATE

RIGID CASTER

Casters

Casters are wheels used to roll something. There are many different sizes, types, and styles to choose from, but only a few are really useful for moving scenery. Lots of casters are intended for use on furniture, and they are not nearly strong enough to move heavy scenery.

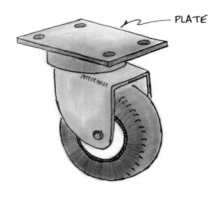

PLATE

SWIVEL CASTER

Casters are most often described by the size of the wheel and their load capacity. It is best to use casters that are rated significantly higher than the actual load. This makes for a much smoother ride. It is axiomatic that the larger in diameter the wheel, the easier it will be to move the wagon. Larger wheels are less prone to becoming stuck on or in irregularities in the stage floor. The other side of the coin is that large swivel casters require more clearance room to swivel, which makes it more difficult to stop and reverse direction.

One interesting type of caster is the *universal* type, which has three small wheels on a revolving base. This allows the caster to carry more weight on small wheels that can be fitted into a low space under a scenic unit. Quite often it is nice to be able to make a piece that is very low to the ground. Universal casters are also able to swivel in a smaller space. More information about using casters can be found on the Web site.

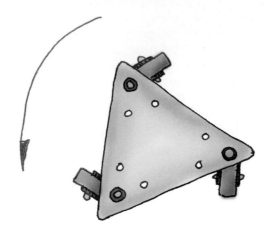

THIS TYPE IS USUALLY RATED FOR A HIGH LOAD
AND IS VERY LOW TO THE GROUND

bond. When used on wood or some other porous material, the holding power of either of these two glues will generally exceed the strength of the material itself. Hence the wood will pull apart before the glue joint does. It is important to spread the glue evenly over the entire joint surface to achieve maximum holding power.

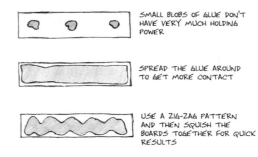

SMALL BLOBS OF GLUE DON'T HAVE VERY MUCH HOLDING POWER

SPREAD THE GLUE AROUND TO GET MORE CONTACT

USE A ZIG-ZAG PATTERN AND THEN SQUISH THE BOARDS TOGETHER FOR QUICK RESULTS

APPLYING WOOD GLUE

Manufacturers use a variety of substances to manufacture the wheels used on casters. The best ones most often have a steel center hub and a tire made of neoprene or hard rubber. Plastic wheels or wheels that are made entirely of steel are not generally acceptable, because of the amount of noise they create when the unit is being rolled. Plastic casters also cannot carry very much weight.

ADHESIVES

Aliphatic resin glue, which is often called *carpenter's glue*, is probably the most commonly used adhesive in building scenery. It has a yellow color that makes it easy to differentiate from white glue like Elmer's. Regular white glue is in the family of *polyvinyl glues.* Either one will do the same job, but yellow glue bonds more quickly and with greater strength than white glue. Carpenter's glue is the best choice for most woodworking, but not especially for adhering muslin to a flat. The white glue gives you a bit more time to work before it is too stiff to move the fabric around. White glue also dries clear, which can be an advantage in certain situations. As a rule of thumb, yellow glue bonds to two-thirds of its holding power in about 20 minutes; the white glue requires about an hour. Getting the maximum hold from either takes 24 hours.

Neither of these glues is a good gap filler, which means that the parts being joined should be smooth, well fitting, and tightly held together in some way while the bond is formed. Jostling the joint while the glue is setting up will greatly reduce the holding power of the

It is difficult to tell much difference in quality between the various brands of these two glues. Years ago, yellow glue was somewhat more expensive than the white, but this is no longer true. You get a much better value if you buy these glues in gallon bottles. But the smaller applicator-type bottles are a must when actually using the glue. Of course you can also fill up other kinds of squeeze bottles and use those as well.

GALLON   PINT

WOODWORKING GLUE

After a year or so of storage, the yellow glue tends to form stringy clots in the jug that jam up the flow of the liquid. If that starts to happen, the glue is past the point where it is usable. A few years ago, manufacturers developed Type II yellow glue, which is said to be waterproof. This may be a good choice of adhesive if the scenery is to be used outdoors, but it is not normally necessary for a show in the theatre.

Sobo is a brand of flexible white glue that can be used on materials that must bend after the adhesive has dried. It is often used on fabrics.

Contact cement is an adhesive that works by first bonding to the two separate material surfaces, and then to itself. It is very commonly used to adhere laminates like Formica to a table or countertop. There are two basic types, the original that is quite flammable and really high in VOCs (volatile organic compounds—not a good thing; see the text box for more information), and a newer type that is water-based. Clearly, the water-based type is a wise choice for use in the theatre, although it does not have all the holding power of the original.

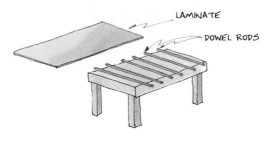

POSITION THE LAMINATE WITH THE RODS IN PLACE TO KEEP THE TWO SURFACES APART, THEN PULL THE RODS OUT ONE BY ONE

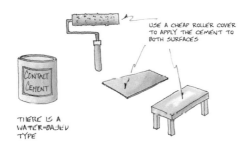

THERE IS A WATER-BASED TYPE

AS SOON AS THE CEMENT IS NO LONGER WET YOU CAN JOIN THE TWO SURFACES TOGETHER, BUT REMEMBER THEY WILL BOND RIGHT AWAY

The cement is rolled or brushed onto both of the two pieces to be joined. Use the cheapest possible short-nap rollers and foam brushes for this purpose, because the applicators will be ruined by the end of the project. It is important to let the adhesive dry for at least a half an hour or so, or until it is clear and dry to the touch. Often it will go on green or tan and dry clear. The contact cement will not bond properly unless it has dried prior to the two surfaces coming together. Exact times and conditions can be found on the label.

This type of glue bonds immediately on contact. Sometimes if only the least bit of touching has occurred, the parts can be yanked quickly apart, but there are no guarantees. It is best to have a means of closely positioning the parts without having them touch each other. When laying countertops, rods are placed on the surface of the counter so that the laminate can be positioned. When all is ready, the rods are pulled out one at a time as the laminate is pressed against the wooden underlayment. It is important to press the two materials together firmly, perhaps using a roller or rubber mallet, but clamping is not required. Laminate is generally cut a bit large and trimmed off later with a router so that exact positioning is not required.

Contact cement is a good adhesive for building up blocks of polystyrene foam for carving. Unlike construction adhesives, it leaves no residue on the inside of the block that is difficult to carve through. The water-based cement will not "eat" the foam, and it makes a very good bond, as it connects entire surfaces.

🌼 GREEN IDEAS TIP BOX

Volatile Organic Compounds

We have become accustomed to thinking of anything *organic* as being somehow better than the normal, or at least more natural and good for the environment. This is not true with VOCs, and the reason lies in the meaning of the word *organic* as used in chemistry. Organic chemistry is the study of compounds having a hydrogen/carbon base, which generally includes things like coal tar dyes, diesel fuel, and oil-based paint. So a paint or solvent that has a high *volatile organic compound* content releases a lot of hydrocarbons into the air as it dries. Fumes like that are toxic, and you should take care to avoid inhaling them in mass quantities. If there is a suitably efficacious substitute for a high VOC compound, then it only makes sense to use it instead. The Environmental Protection Agency (EPA) has been calling on manufacturers to reduce these compounds for many years, which has led to the near disappearance of oil-based paints.

Barge cement is a flammable contact cement of the older type that is often useful for small prop jobs. It comes in a can with a brush applicator in the cap, much like rubber cement. It is an excellent product for emergency repairs.

Construction adhesive is a very thick liquid or mastic. It is often used to glue together foam pieces. It will also stick foam to wood, steel, aluminum, acrylic sheet, or just about anything else. A longer explanation of its use may be found in the section on working with foam. One of the advantages of this type of adhesive is that it is an excellent gap filler and can be used to connect parts that do not fit well. Normally, this product comes in a caulking tube, but you can also find it in gallon cans. *Liquid Nails* is a brand of construction adhesive that has been around for many years. Make sure to use the original formula. It will melt a bit of the foam, but it holds much better than any other type. Construction adhesive is also great to use in connecting wood to metal square tubing, when tech screws alone are not enough.

but there are many, many, prop uses. It is also great for foam rubber.

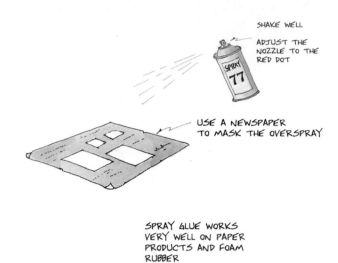

SHAKE WELL

ADJUST THE NOZZLE TO THE RED DOT

SPRAY 77

USE A NEWSPAPER TO MASK THE OVERSPRAY

SPRAY GLUE WORKS VERY WELL ON PAPER PRODUCTS AND FOAM RUBBER

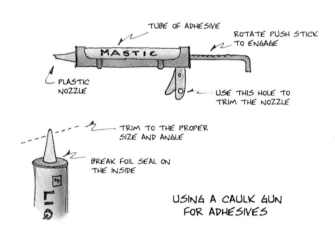

TUBE OF ADHESIVE

ROTATE PUSH STICK TO ENGAGE

MASTIC

PLASTIC NOZZLE

USE THIS HOLE TO TRIM THE NOZZLE

TRIM TO THE PROPER SIZE AND ANGLE

BREAK FOIL SEAL ON THE INSIDE

USING A CAULK GUN FOR ADHESIVES

Spray 77 is an industrial adhesive from 3M that has become available in retail outlets in recent years. It is an excellent glue to use in adhering either paper or a paper-thin material to a smooth flat surface. Shake well, line the nozzle up with the red dot, and spray an even coat over the entire surface of the paper. Use newspapers to prevent the overspray from ruining the tabletop or floor. Carefully position the paper and press it flat. Allow the glue 60 seconds or so to get tacky on the paper for before placement. That allows the paper to stretch out a bit and reduces the number of bubbles that may appear on large sheets. Small sections are not affected as much because the stretching of the paper is proportionally smaller. Wallpaper stretches in much the same way. Spray 77 gets used quite often for mounting thin paper on heavier stock,

The 3M company has several spray adhesives that are identified by a number and can be used in much the manner as the 77 is.

Zap is a brand of *cyanoacrylate* or super-glue that is sold at woodworking stores, but there are other brands as well. There are several different formulas for specific purposes, as well as a kicker that speeds up the bonding time. This product is not recommended for general woodworking, but it is handy to have around for the occasional odd problem. You can use it to glue small parts together when speed is of the essence. It is important to not use too much or the setup time will take too long. It really does take just a drop. The kicker causes the glue to set up almost immediately. Be sure to follow the instructions exactly. Generic types of this glue are available just about anywhere, but you will most likely find the kicker only at a specialty woodworking store.

Tape

Gaffer's tape is a cloth tape with adhesive on the back that gets its name from its original use by movie electricians. It is available in many different colors, but black and white are generally the most useful. The standard size is a 2-inch-wide, 60-yard roll. There are several different brands, and many stagehands have a particular brand that they insist is the best. Some are thicker and stiffer than others and might be better suited to your particular situation. Some leave less sticky residue behind when you pull them off of something.

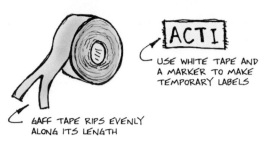

USE WHITE TAPE AND
A MARKER TO MAKE
TEMPORARY LABELS

GAFF TAPE RIPS EVENLY
ALONG ITS LENGTH

GAFFER'S TAPE

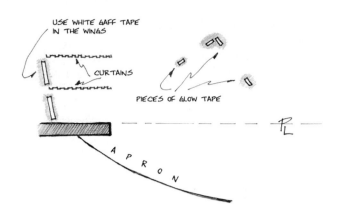

USE WHITE GAFF TAPE
IN THE WINGS

CURTAINS

PIECES OF GLOW TAPE

APRON

GLOW TAPE CAN'T CHARGE UP IN THE WINGS
WHERE THERE IS NO LIGHT. IF YOU USE TOO
MUCH OUT ON THE STAGE, IT WILL BE
DISTRACTING IN A BLACKOUT.

One of the great things about this tape is that it can be ripped along its length into very narrow strips when odd sizes are required. The white can be used for putting labels on boxes and hampers, rail linesets, or dressing room doors. It can be ripped into strips to mark sightlines or to be used as spike marks. The black is useful when you need it to disappear into the darkness of the backstage void. It is often used on electrical cables (hence the gaffer connection). The main advantage of gaff tape over ordinary duct tape is that the fabric nature of gaff tape makes it stronger and more malleable.

Glow tape is a plastic tape that is impregnated with a fluorescent powder that glows in the dark. The powder soaks up light energy and then releases it when darkness comes. It is often used for *spiking* the stage floor and for marking dangerous dropoffs like stairs or the front of the stage. "Spiking" means to put marks on the stage floor that indicate the placement of scenery or props. The advantage is that, theoretically at least, the tape will glow in the darkness of a scene-change blackout. The pieces out on the stage floor that are exposed to direct stage lights glow very brightly in the darkness. On the other hand, if this tape is used in the wings where there is no light to charge it up, the chemical will hardly be visible at all. Strips of white gaffer's tape work better when the marks are in a place that is perpetually dark.

Vinyl electrician's tape (e-tape) is used to provide extra coverage for wiring insulation. It is stretchy and easy to bend around uneven joints. It is a good insulator. The most common color is black, but there are many other colors available. Electrician's tape is often used to color-code wires or even scenic units. It can be used when there are a great many spike marks on the stage floor, and there is a need to be able to differentiate between them. The most useful colors for electrical purposes are green for the ground, white for the neutral, and black, red, and blue for the hots. You can use the same tape to color code the different lengths of jumpers used for lighting purposes.

Some theatrical supply companies sell a narrow-width variety of gaff tape that comes in many different day-glow colors. It is meant for use as spike tape and is really better than vinyl electrical tape for that purpose, because it doesn't stretch so much. E-tape is designed to stretch to several times its own size so that it conforms to the odd shape of wires twisted together. That can be problematic when spiking the floor, because the tape stretches when you pull it off the roll, and if you don't wait for it to shrink back up before sticking it down, it will tend to curl up off the floor later. The gaffer/spike tape won't do that.

Masking tape is a paper adhesive tape that was designed to be used as a temporary mask while painting cars. It works great when you are using a sprayer. The original type is a tan color, but a blue variety is currently marketed as *painter's tape*. Masking tape is cheap in comparison to other types of tape and is often used when some other type would really be better. Remember that masking tape is not designed to be left on any surface for more than 24 hours. After that length of time the paper and glue begin to dry out, and the tape will either let go entirely, or it will become so permanently stuck that it must be scraped off. It should not be used to mark the floor of a rehearsal space, or for any other semipermanent application.

Teflon tape is a nonsticky type of tape that may be used in the place of pipe dope to secure the threads of a pipe connection from leaking. It is wrapped around the male end two or three times in a clockwise direction.

Floral tape is a paper tape that uses wax as an adhesive. As the name implies, it is often used in making floral arrangements, especially with silk flowers. It is slightly stretchy and works well for wrapping the stems together. Its green matte finish is more or less invisible when viewed from the audience.

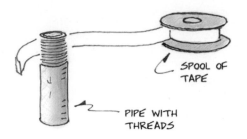

TEFLON TAPE ON PIPE THREADS

SPOOL OF TAPE

PIPE WITH THREADS

80 GRIT SANDPAPER IS FAIRLY ROUGH

220 GRIT SANDPAPER IS MUCH FINER

STEEL WOOL

SANDING SUPPLIES

Everyone is familiar with Scotch-brand Magic Mending tape, as it is used to hold papers together, but this type of tape is also useful on glass or mirrors. On paper, the slightly frosted appearance goes away when the tape is pressed down. On glass, the frosted look stays and can be used to create an etched or beveled look to the surface.

SANDPAPER

As the name implies, *sandpaper* is a sheet of paper or cloth that has a granular substance (which is usually not really sand) stuck to one side. This abrasive side is used to wear away the surface of some other material, most often wood but also plastics and even metal. Sheets of sandpaper are a standard 9×11-inch size. Many power sanders use either one-half or one-quarter of a standard size sheet. Belt sanders use a round *belt* of sandpaper rotating between two drums. These belts are manufactured to fit a particular size of sander. Random orbit sanders use a round sanding pad with either an adhesive back or Velcro to attach the disk to the sander.

Most sheets of sandpaper are made in either an A or a C weight. The C weight is thicker and heavier than the A. The C weight is typically used for coarser grit sandpaper. The *grit number* is a measure of the size of the granules on the paper; 80-grit is a coarse paper that may be used to roughly shape wood or plastic. It is very aggressive and will remove a large amount of wood in a short while. It leaves a somewhat rough surface, but one that most people would find suitable for painting with theatre techniques.

Many other grits are available. A grit of 150 is a reasonably fine number for sanding wood; sanding coats of finish on furniture might require a grit in the 300 or 400 range. In the author's opinion, most wooden scenery is smooth enough for painting after a quick workout with the 80-grit paper.

If an extraordinarily smooth surface is required, *steel wool* may be used. Steel wool is made from very fine steel shavings and is like an SOS pad without the soap. Steel wool comes in several grades from #2 to #0000. The #2 is fairly coarse; the #0000 is extremely fine. Steel wool is very handy for polishing metal surfaces, like the top of the table saw.

FABRICS

Fabrics are very important in building scenery. Theatres have a lot of curtains and drops, as well as fabric-covered flats and other scenery. Fabrics are often used as a means of creating painted scenery that is portable and lightweight.

Scenic *muslin* is the most common theatrical fabric. Muslin is a lightweight, all-cotton fabric that creates an excellent paint surface. It is often used for painted backdrops or for cycloramas. It is also used to cover the surface of soft covered flats, although when very high strength is required, some shops may use canvas for this purpose. *Canvas* and muslin are both made from unbleached cotton threads, but the threads used for the canvas are larger in diameter, and as a result the fabric is heavier and coarser. It is important that theatrical canvas/muslin be manufactured from 100-percent cotton in order for the painting and sizing techniques of the theatre to be effective. Canvas tends to come in narrower widths, usually 72 inches or less. The ounce weight of canvas refers to how much the fabric weighs per square yard, so naturally the heavier the weight the thicker and more durable the fabric will be.

Muslin is easily available in widths up to 120 inches, and much greater widths are possible—up to 35 feet in size. The largest sizes are most often used for cycloramas or for translucent drops where a seam would be unsightly. You should select the width of the fabric in the same way that you would choose the length of lumber being used for a specific project. The width chosen is a function of the width of flats being covered, or of drops being sewn together. The weight of the fabric may be light, medium, or heavy, but the heavy weight is recommended for most scenic uses. Canvas is often found in a variety of colors, but muslin is most often the natural off white. Sky cyc muslin is sometimes sold as a light-blue color, as this enhances the ability to color the cyclorama a light-blue sky hue.

Most theatrical fabrics are available as either flame-proofed (FP) or non-flame-proofed (NFP). Fabrics are very flammable, and if the fabric is not flame-proofed by the manufacturer, it should be treated in the shop. Often flame-proofing in the shop is more efficient, but some fire marshals won't allow it.

A number of theatrical specialty fabrics are available only from a theatrical supplier. One of these is *scrim*, which is a net-like material with rectangular openings. It is often used to create transparent curtains. White and black are the popular colors. Scrim is generally available in widths around the 16- to 18-foot range or in the 30-foot range. Thus you could construct a scrim that is either 18 feet tall by any width, or a scrim that is 30 feet tall by any width, or a scrim that is 30 feet wide by any height. It is not practical to sew two pieces of scrim together, as the seam would show when the translucent quality of the scrim is put to use.

Bobbinette is a similar material with hexagonal openings that are somewhat larger than those found in a scrim. It, too, can be found in white or black colors. This material may be used for cut drops, and is available only in very large widths. An even larger opening is found on *scenery netting* that has square openings 1 inch in either direction. Netting is also used to create cut drops. *Textilene* is a new material that looks very much like scrim, but is actually a nonwoven plastic material. It is incredibly strong and resilient, but is not available in really wide widths.

Velour is a heavyweight, plush fabric that is used to make curtains. It is most often found as a 54-inch-wide fabric in a wide variety of colors. Velour has a nap like carpet does, which means that the pile will look different when it runs in different directions. Care must be taken to make sure that the nap on two adjoining panels is running the same way. You can do this by brushing the pile with your hand and seeing how the light reflects off the fabric. Black velour has incredible light- and sound-absorbing qualities, and is an excellent choice for making a basic set of borders and legs. It is often used to cover masking flats, and other parts of scenery that the designer would like to disappear backstage. Like canvas, the thickness of velour is given in the number of ounces per square yard.

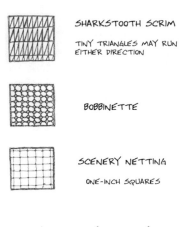

SHARKSTOOTH SCRIM
TINY TRIANGLES MAY RUN EITHER DIRECTION

BOBBINETTE

SCENERY NETTING
ONE-INCH SQUARES

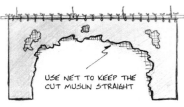

USE NET TO KEEP THE CUT MUSLIN STRAIGHT

NET-LIKE FABRICS

A less expensive alternative to velour is *duvetyn/commando* cloth. Sometimes this fabric is called duvetyn when it is lighter in weight and commando cloth when it is heavier. Sometimes it depends on which part of the entertainment business you work in. Most people in theatre call it duvetyn. This fabric has no true nap like velour, but it does have a brushed, textural surface giving it a matte appearance. Like velour, duvetyn is most popular in black but comes in a variety of colors. The black is very handy for masking flats and can be stapled onto scenery to cover small gaps that were not foreseen in the design process. Duvetyn scraps can also be used to drape things backstage that you do not want the audience to see.

Burlap is a fabric made from jute. Jute is a rough fiber that has an oily resin in it. As a result, it is quite flammable and must be heavily treated with a flame retardant. It has a rough texture, much like the bags used to hold potatoes or coffee, which are made from the same material. Its natural color is, of course, that of jute, but burlap is also available in a wide range of colors. Colored burlap tends to be of a somewhat more regular weave than the natural. The texture of burlap makes it a favorite with designers, as is *erosion cloth*, a very loose type of jute netting.

Cheesecloth is a very lightweight, loosely woven fabric closely resembling gauze. It is generally not used as a fabric per se, but rather as a coating for other materials. This material is available from a theatrical supplier, but you may prefer the type sold in fabric stores that comes in a box. It is easier to use for projects like coating foam-built scenery. The theatrical gauze or cheesecloth is much more difficult to apply. More information about that is available in Chapter 23.

CHEESECLOTH COMES FOLDED INTO FOUR LAYERS

100 YDS CHEESECLOTH

IN A BOX

Webbing is a narrow strip of heavy, stiff material that is used to beef up the edges of a drop or curtain. It is typically used only on the top edge, where the grommets are placed. It can sometimes be used in the construction of furniture, or to make straps of one sort or another. The original type of jute webbing is $3\frac{1}{2}''$ wide and comes in a roll. There are two red (or sometimes blue) stripes down the length of the webbing, which are useful in lining up the placement of grommets. A newer type is made from polyester and is much more durable when used on a drop.

Grommets are brass rings used to reinforce the holes made in the top of a drop. They allow ties to be used in fastening the drop to a batten. The standard size of grommets used in that way is #2. Grommets must be installed with a grommeting hole cutter and setter. They are placed on 1-foot centers. More about webbing and grommets and how they are used can be found in Chapter 5.

FLAME-PROOFING

It is important to *flame-proof* scenery, as mentioned earlier. Flame-proofing means that a treated wooden or fabric material may char but will not support an open flame. "Fireproofing" is another thing entirely. It is generally not possible to accomplish that condition unless your scenery is built entirely from steel (or perhaps concrete and rocks for an outdoor drama). Many communities have a requirement that scenery should resist burning for a certain amount of time when heated with a match. The fire marshal in your community has the legal authority to make all decisions as to how much flame protection is required, as well as other safety concerns like fire exits and such.

TWO TYPES OF FLAME RETARDANT

ONE CAN BE ADDED TO PAINT, AND THE OTHER SPRAYED ON AS A FINAL COATING

There are many different flame-retarding compounds on the market. Some are liquids that get sprayed on after the scenery is painted, and some are additives that you can put in the paint itself. Some are intended specifically for nonporous plastics. Follow the instructions that come with the compound. Retardants are available from most theatrical suppliers.

CORDAGE

Ropes and other lines used for tying are very important when working on stage. The most basic old-style type of rope is the hemp line, so-called but actually made from manila, a similar fiber that is derived from a relative of the banana tree. The rope itself is formed by twisting the fibers into several loose strands, known as yarns, and then twisting the yarns into a rope. This type of line has a definite right-hand twist, known as its *lay*. The lay becomes a factor when coiling a rope. Ropes of this type come in various diameters that are given in inches. The working strength of a rope is derived from its breaking strength, usually with a safety factor of 4. For example, if the breaking strength of a certain line is 400 pounds, then the safe working load limit would be 100 pounds. Knots, abrasions, and dirt will all greatly reduce the actual breaking strength, which is why the safety factor is used.

Many modern ropes are made from synthetic fibers such as nylon, polyester, or polypropylene. These ropes are generally more expensive than a hemp rope, but they are stronger and will last longer. Nylon is perhaps the fiber of choice, as it is fantastically strong, flexible, and lightweight.

Sash cord is a very popular theatrical line. It was originally intended for use on the type of older window that used a counterweight hidden in the wall to balance out the weight of the sash. It is a woven rope, which means that there is an interior core of fibers that are surrounded by a woven casing. Because the fibers are not twisted together, the rope is less likely to become twisted up and tangled. Sash cord is excellent for tying knots, and for lashing together scenery backstage, but it is not especially strong. Nylon ropes are often made by the same technique and are among the strongest lines available. Sash cord has a matte white sizing added to it; nylon has a shinier appearance. The natural color of nylon is milky white, but it can be dyed any color. Modern-day sash cord has a cotton exterior with synthetic fibers on the inside, and is the line of choice for rigging a traveler track.

Tie line is used in many different situations backstage, and is technically known as #4 black trick line. It is about ⅛″ in diameter and seems very sturdy, but it is important to remember that according to the manufacturer, the safe working load is only 16 pounds. This kind of black tie line is most often available on a 3,000-foot reel and can be found either glazed or unglazed. The glazed version tends to last longer, but it is harder to tie. Ties for electrics should be about 30 inches long in order make two wraps around the pipe. Double wrapping makes it easier to keep the tie line tight when making a bow knot. Ties that are all the same length are easier to use.

Wire used to make suspended or drop ceilings is an excellent source of pin wire for loose-pin backflap hinges. It is about the diameter of a thick wire clothes hanger, and comes in lengths 10 or 12 feet long. This wire can be used for all sorts of properties construction projects, because it is quite sturdy but can be easily bent with pliers.

Floral wire is a much thinner wire that can be used for much more than flower arrangements. It is a steel wire that has been painted green on the outside.

Cable ties are typically used to secure flexible cable or line to a rigid structure. They can be used in lots of different ways, especially when you would like to make a more permanent connection than tie line or tape would allow. Cable ties are often made from nylon for strength, and have many ridges along their length. When the free end of the tie is pushed through a slotted head at the other end, the ridges catch on the head in a ratcheting fashion, so that the strip feeds in but cannot

be pulled back out. This allows you to get the tie on very tight. But as the strip cannot be removed from the head, cable ties are essentially one-use items, and wire cutters are generally required to get them off. They are at their best in a semipermanent situation.

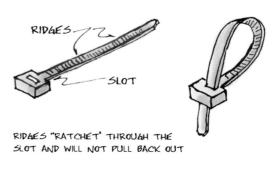

RIDGES "RATCHET" THROUGH THE SLOT AND WILL NOT PULL BACK OUT

CABLE TIE

PAINT AND OTHER COATINGS

The artistic painting of scenery is outside the scope of this book, but it seems appropriate to have a technical discussion of paint and what it is made of. This short discussion of paint attributes will help you understand the types of coatings found in a scene shop. There are several fine books about the actual techniques of painting scenery.

Paint in general, no matter what type it is, is composed of three basic parts: the *pigment*, which gives the paint its color; the *vehicle*, which makes it a fluid; and the *binder*, which causes it to stick to the surface you are painting.

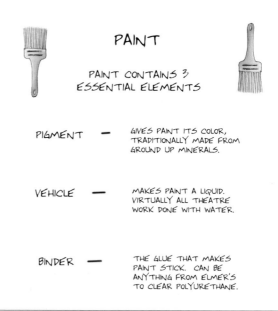

PAINT

PAINT CONTAINS 3 ESSENTIAL ELEMENTS

PIGMENT — GIVES PAINT ITS COLOR, TRADITIONALLY MADE FROM GROUND UP MINERALS.

VEHICLE — MAKES PAINT A LIQUID. VIRTUALLY ALL THEATRE WORK DONE WITH WATER.

BINDER — THE GLUE THAT MAKES PAINT STICK. CAN BE ANYTHING FROM ELMER'S TO CLEAR POLYURETHANE.

For many centuries, the pigment in paint was made from ground-up minerals. Much of it still is. Raw sienna was made from soils found in Sienna, Italy. Cadmium yellow was made from a ground-up version of that element. Renaissance painting masters employed apprentices who were charged with grinding up the pigments to a fine powder and then mixing them with linseed oil to make paint. They used the minerals as pigment; linseed oil was both the vehicle and the binder. Until fairly modern times, scenic artists used similar *dry pigment* to mix their paint with hide (animal) glue and water to make the paint used in theatre.

Some years ago, *casein* paints were developed, which had their pigments already mixed together into a liquid paste that could be purchased in gallon containers. This alleviated a lot of work in preparing the paints from scratch. Nowadays, most paint of this sort is made with a synthetic binder rather than the original casein milk-based type, but they work in very much the same way. There are a couple of dozen standard colors, and all others are mixed from those, much like an artist uses tubes of watercolor paints to mix the exact colors she needs for her painting.

IDDINGS (NOW ROSCO) CASEIN-BASED PAINT
HAS BEEN AROUND FOR MANY YEARS.
IT HAS NO THICKENER LIKE LATEX PAINTS
AND IS EASIER TO MAKE INTO WASHES AND GLAZES

On the other hand, ordinary house paint generally starts with a base made of *titanium oxide*, a whitish mineral that thickens the paint substantially. Water is the vehicle, and a latex or acrylic compound is used as the binder. Thick paint is less likely to drip off a brush and is easier for a homeowner to use, but the titanium oxide has the effect of "whiting out" the pigment color. Thus it is often difficult to get pure colors with house paint. The thickness is also problematic when painting a drop, because the flexible nature of the fabric demands a very thin, flexible coating that has more in common with a dye than with house paint. Synthetic casein paints come in gallon cans as a very thick paste, but can be reduced with water to make an extremely thin paint, which is excellent for fabrics like muslin. House paint cannot be thinned down in that way without losing a lot of its brilliance.

SOME STORES SELL A CLEAR BASE
THAT YOU CAN MIX WITH PIGMENTS
TO MAKE YOUR OWN COLORS.

Another type of paint gaining appeal with scenic artists is made from *Universal Tinting Colors*. Paint stores use these colorants to add pigment to their products. There are about 11 standard colors. Most paint manufacturers have several different *bases*, made up in advance, that have varying amounts of binder in them. Deeper colors have more pigment added, and thus need more binder in the base. Binder and pigment are the expensive components in paint, so deeper colors are always more expensive. The tinting colors themselves do not contain the titanium oxide thickening agent, which is already in the base. It is important to remember that Universal Colorants are pigment only, and that a binder must be used with them in order to make the paint stick to the surface of anything you apply it to. Many different glue or glue-like products can be used for the binder, including white glue, clear paint base, and water-based polyurethane. Mixing paint in this way allows the artist to create very specific colors from the tints, and to create a coating that is free of titanium oxide.

UNIVERSAL COLORANTS

THESE PIGMENTS ARE USED BY PAINT STORES TO COLOR THEIR PAINT.
YOU CAN USE THEM IN THE SAME WAY, WITH WATER AND GLUE.

Water-based polyurethane is a much better choice for stage work than the original, which was made from some incredibly messy, high-VOC chemicals. It can be tinted with pigment to form glazes or used to protect a surface that has already been painted. Water-based polyurethane comes in gloss and satin varieties, but either one will impart a shiny depth to underlying paint. This substance is a favorite of faux finish painters.

Bronzing powders are ground up metallics like bronze, brass, copper, and aluminum. They are mixed together with glue and water to make a type of paint that creates a faux metallic surface. You should be very careful not to breathe in the unmixed, dry powder, because it is bad for your lungs.

One scenic unit might be constructed of a combination of metal, wood, and plastic. Each of those materials reacts with paint in a different way. Treating them all with the same type of undercoat creates a smoother, more finished appearance. Several products can be used to create a solid base for faux finish painting on scenic units that are made from a mix of different materials. Products such as *Jaxsan* 600, *elastomeric*, and *Sculpt or Coat* work equally well to even out the appearance of the various parts of the scenery and create a more homogeneous texture. They are liberally applied to the scenery before painting.

THIS PLASTIC BOTTLE
CONTAINS SMALL
ALUMINUM PARTICLES
THAT CAN BE MIXED
WITH VEHICLE AND
BINDER TO MAKE A
SILVERY COATING

THIS TYPE OF ELASTOMERIC COATING
IS WIDELY AVAILABLE AT HOME CENTERS

Drywall *joint compound* is used in construction to finish off wallboard used to cover interior walls. It is more or less the same thing that people mean when they use the word "spackle." It is often used to create smoother surfaces on wooden scenery as well. Joint compound is very easy to work with, and is not generally considered to be toxic, so there is no problem getting it on your hands. It is very easy to sand off with ordinary sandpaper. The one drawback to this material lies in its somewhat rigid nature: it tends to crack and fall off if the scenery is bent in some way. Scenic artists have several uses for a compound called *dope*, which is made from joint compound and white glue.

BUCKETS OF JOINT COMPOUND ARE USED
TO FINISH DRYWALL IN A HOUSE. THEY ARE
INEXPENSIVE, AND JOINT COMPOUND IS OFTEN
USED TO FILL SMALL HOLES IN WOODEN SCENERY

Bondo can be used when joint compound is not strong enough. This material is used for automotive body work, and is more or less indestructible. It can be sanded, sawn, and drilled into; much like plastic or wood. Bondo has two parts: the base material and a cream hardener. The two should be mixed with some precision, so that a proper setup time is achieved. This material must be used quickly, because Bondo hardens in a matter of minutes. It is an exothermic chemical reaction, so hot temperatures speed up the setup period. Joint compound must dry through evaporation, and a thick application can take several days, but a thick application of Bondo actually sets up faster than a thin one, because the heat retained in the center causes a faster chemical reaction. Bondo will stick to just about everything, so some care must be taken when applying it. It is much harder to sand than joint compound, but can be molded with a Surform when it is not quite hardened.

CHAPTER 15

WOOD, LUMBER, AND OTHER BUILDING MATERIALS

Wood and *lumber* are not interchangeable terms, although there is a direct relationship between the two of them. Wood refers to the species of tree that lumber comes from. Lumber is a product that is manufactured from wood. Lumber has a uniform size and fits into certain categories, so theoretically all 2×4s that are 10 feet long are exactly the same size. All lumber is made of wood, but not all wood is made into lumber. Plywood panels are made from logs, just like lumber is, but they are a manufactured product that often uses parts of many different trees sliced up and glued back together.

Trees and the wood that comes from them can be divided into two different types: *hardwoods* and *softwoods*. You would naturally assume that the wood from a hardwood is higher in density than that from a softwood, and for the most part this is true, although the two divisions are really defined in a way other than just how dense they are. Hardwoods are designated as coming from broad-leafed trees. These are generally deciduous trees that lose their leaves in the winter and then grow a new set in the spring. Hardwoods as a group are usually denser than softwoods—hence the obvious names—but this is not always the case. Well-seasoned (dried) yellow pine varieties can be much denser than some varieties of mahogany.

A BUNDLE OF ONE BUILDING MATERIAL, IN THIS CASE 2×4S,
IS KNOWN AS A UNIT. THE BOARDS LYING OFF TO THE SIDE
OF THE MAIN STACK ARE "CULLS." THE BOARDS NOBODY WANTED
BECAUSE OF A DEFECT- IN THIS CASE SEVERAL ARE QUITE BOWED.

TREES AND WOOD

Softwoods are coniferous trees that have a needle-like leaf structure. The most common varieties in North America are pine, spruce, redwood, cedar, and fir. *Fir, pine,* and *spruce* are the three types of wood most often used to produce lumber. There are many different varieties of pine trees, but they can be separated into two main types, *yellow* and *white.* Stage scenery has traditionally been constructed of white pine. White pine is an extremely workable wood for building scenery, as it is soft and easy to cut, it has a straight grain pattern, and it is widely available at a reasonable price. Yellow pine is much heavier and is more susceptible to splitting. Fir is quite often used to make interior trims and moldings.

At least a cursory understanding of the mechanics of how trees grow can help you understand how wood will react when it is used for building stage scenery. Because trees grow naturally, they are prone to quirks that cannot be entirely eliminated by the lumber milling process.

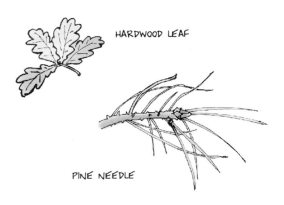

HARDWOOD LEAF

PINE NEEDLE

Many people seem to think that trees grow upward out of the ground, but this is not the case. In reality, they grow from the top up and from the outside out, and not from the center or bottom. Tree bark protects an interior layer of fibers known as the *cambium* or sapwood. The cambium layer of a tree is the area where growth rings originate. Everyone has seen growth rings, which are evident when looking at a cross section of a tree trunk. These rings are added to from the outside, which is to say that each year's growth ring, provided by the cambium layer, is added to the outside of the tree trunk, just under the bark. Bark is very much like skin for a tree and protects the cambium layer from weather and disease. Bark is rough because it must constantly expand as the tree grows.

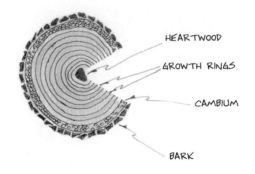

CROSS SECTION THRU
A TREE TRUNK

The cambium is responsible for transporting water and nutrients from the ground to the leaves. It is really a mass of tiny tubes much like blood vessels. These fibers are very strong and pliable along their length, but they are not bound together all that well. It is possible to strip the fibers from some trees into long strings. This works with other plants as well. Hemp fibers are stripped from the stalk of that plant and then twisted into rope. You may think of a stalk of celery as being indicative of the mechanics of the structure of a tree. The stalk will bend along its length, but will easily snap across its width. After it does, the stringy fibers that make up the stalk are plainly visible.

THE CAMBIUM LAYER IS MADE UP
OF MANY SMALL TUBES THAT
RUN FROM THE ROOTS UPWARD

Celery grows to its full size in one season, so there is no division of growth rings. A tree can grow over hundreds of seasons, and the *heartwood,* or interior of the trunk, is the remaining evidence of many years' cambium layers. The heartwood is the rigid material that gives the tree its strength and ability to remain erect.

The way a tree grows means that objects on the outside of the tree trunk will eventually be enveloped by it. If a sign is nailed to the exterior of a tree trunk, some years later the tree will have grown around it, causing the sign to eventually disappear. The same thing can happen to wire fences and other manmade objects in the forest.

THIS OAK
HAS GROWN AROUND A SIGN

As you have seen, trees grow from the outside out, but they also grow from the top up. Because the bulk of a tree is added to by the growth of the cambium layer outward, there is no way for the trunk to elongate itself. A tree gets taller when new limbs sprout on top of it.

Trees grow taller and straighter if other trees surround them, like you would expect in a forest. This forces the tree to grow upward to get to the sun, and causes the lower limbs to fall off. As a result the trunk of the tree, which is the source of lumber, is longer and taller and has smaller knots. The grain is straighter in a forest tree, and lumber from it is less likely to warp out of shape. Most lumber today comes from farm-grown trees that are planted just the right distance apart to get maximum production, and the highest-quality grain structure.

If a limb should die, rot, and fall from the tree, leaving a small protuberance or stump, this stump will in time be covered over by the natural growth of the trunk. If this tree is eventually cut down and sawn into boards, the dead limb will show up as a *knot* or knothole.

TREE ALL ALONE   TREE IN A FOREST

HOW THE CAMBIUM
GROWS AROUND A
DEAD LIMB

LUMBER

Lumber refers to wood from a tree that has been cut to a specific dimensional size for use in construction. Lumber is called by its *nominal* size, which is its name size, and not the actual size of the board. That is a curious idea, and bears some explanation. When logs are harvested to be used as lumber, they are sawn into planks using a very large circular blade saw. The logs themselves are quite large in cross section and require a blade several feet in diameter in order to get through the entire log. The teeth on such a blade are very big. The resulting cut is rough, and because of the difficulty in making precise cuts in so large and heavy an object, the size of the planks is not very exacting.

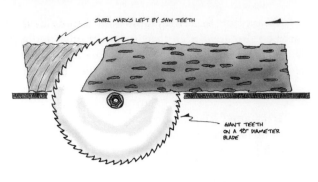

SWIRL MARKS LEFT BY SAW TEETH

GIANT TEETH
ON A 48" DIAMETER
BLADE

THE SAWMILL PRODUCES VERY ROUGH PLANKS
THAT MUST BE MILLED SMOOTH

= 2″), and that twice the milled or actual size of a one-by is equal to the milled size of a two-by (3/4″ + 3/4″ = 1½″). Thus if two pieces of one-by material are placed on top of one another, they will have the same nominal and/or milled thickness as a piece of two-by material all on its own. Inch symbols (″) are used to represent the word *inches*. The symbol for feet is given as (′). The nominal widths of construction lumber are in even numbers of inches, beginning with 4. The chart shows the thickness and width of common lumber sizes in both the nominal and milled categories.

LUMBER SIZES CHART
NOMINAL TO MILLED

	4	6	8	12
1X	3/4 X 3 1/2	3/4 X 5 1/2	3/4 X 7 1/4	3/4 X 11 1/4
2X	1 1/2 X 3 1/2	1 1/2 X 5 1/2	1 1/2 X 7 1/4	1 1/2 X 11 1/4

* SOME MILLS MAKE THAT 5 1/4 - THERE ARE SOME REGIONAL DIFFERENCES

In the late nineteenth and early twentieth centuries, buildings were constructed in a rougher way than they now are. Lath-and-plaster construction was much more forgiving of uneven walls and rooms that were not exceptionally square, and rough-cut lumber straight from the saw was fine. Today, modern home builders require a more accurate dimension size. Most lumber is really cut for the home construction industry, which is a very large market, and not for the scenery construction business, which is very small by comparison. To accommodate the need for more accurate lumber, rough-sawn planks are sent through a planer to smooth and shape them to an exact size. This milling process reduces the size of the lumber by a certain amount and is what causes the *milled size* to be somewhat smaller than the nominal or name size. The milled size is the actual size of a piece of lumber, but the nominal size is what we call it.

There are some similarities in the milled sizes, making it quite easy to remember all of them. As mentioned earlier, all of the 1× thicknesses are actually ¾″ thick, and the 2× thicknesses are really 1½″ thick. All of the milled widths are ½″ narrower than the nominal size, except for the 8″, 10″, and 12″ boards, which are ¾″ smaller. These four rules enable you to memorize the entire chart. Lumber sizes have not always followed this pattern. Milled sizes have gotten smaller several times over the years, and perhaps will again. Wood has a tendency to shrink up as it dries, but only across the width. Wide boards tend to shrink more proportionally, so sometimes they are slightly smaller than expected.

Larger sizes of lumber such as 4×4 and 4×6 are available, but they are not commonly used in the construction of lightweight stage scenery.

Dimension lumber is cut to evenly numbered lengths starting at 8 feet long and running through 16 feet (8′, 10′, 12′, 14′, 16′). The written description of specific lumber sizes is given using the formula thickness × width × length, and the feet and inch marks are left off. Thus a 1×4 that is 10 feet long would be expressed as a 1×4×10. If this standard form is used, then anyone familiar with the industry should understand what you mean. The inch and feet symbols are not shown in an effort to simplify the notation.

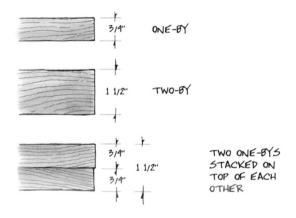

3/4″ ONE-BY

1 1/2″ TWO-BY

3/4″
1 1/2″
3/4″

TWO ONE-BYS
STACKED ON
TOP OF EACH
OTHER

Light construction lumber comes in two main thicknesses. These are most often called by the names *one-by* (1×) and *two-by* (2×), referring to 1 inch thick by some variable width, or 2 inches thick by some width. This is a nominal size. The milled or actual sizes are ¾″ for a one-by and 1½″ thick for a two-by. It is interesting to note that twice the nominal size of a one-by is equal to the nominal size of a two-by (1″ + 1″

Quite often, and especially when building traditional soft covered flats, a need arises for a one-by material that is slightly narrower than a 1×4. As you can see from the chart, no such size is commercially available. It is common practice to rip down 1×12 lumber in order to get a theatrical size called the 1×3. These 1×3s are not available at the lumberyard. The width of 1×3 boards is determined by the largest practical width that can be gotten when dividing a 1×12 into four equal sections. Allowing for the width of the saw blade, this ripped down size is 2⅝", so the actual milled size of a 1×3 is ¾" × 2⅝". It is an important size to remember when figuring lumber cut lists for flats.

Because lumber is formed from a natural source rather than being manufactured, the quality of individual pieces varies, and lumber is divided into grades based on how good it is. The major factors used in lumber grading are grain structure, dryness, and the types and quantity of knots. Lumber with a straight grain structure is the best for construction. Grain that curves and swirls, or that varies greatly in size and consistency, indicates a tree that grew under stress. These boards are more prone to splitting, breaking, and warping.

Lumber is generally dried in a *kiln* to remove excess *sap*, which naturally occurs in the wood. Sap is the nutrient-rich fluid that flows up the fibers of the cambium layer, and allows the tree to grow. But after it is cut, an overabundant amount of moisture left in the wood can cause boards to warp and shrink. Lumber that is not thoroughly dried before construction begins will tend to shrink after the structure has been completed and make the joints pull apart.

Even thoroughly dried wood expands and contracts in accordance with the amount of moisture in the air. In humid conditions, wood grain absorbs water from the air and swells across its width, but the length of a board is not affected in the same way. The absorption of moisture by the growth layers causes them to swell like a sponge, but they grow only fatter, not longer. As a result, only the width of wood is affected—not the length. This factor is very important in furniture making, but doesn't seem to cause so much trouble with scenery.

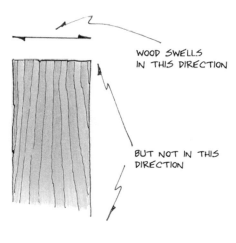

WOOD SWELLS
IN THIS DIRECTION

BUT NOT IN THIS
DIRECTION

WOOD SWELLS
ACROSS THE GRAIN

Knots are formed by limbs that dropped off the trunk as the tree grew. If the knots are small and solid, they have little effect on the structural soundness of the piece of lumber, but if they are large and loose, quality is greatly reduced. *Loose knots* are just that; the wood in the center of the knot is easily moved with the fingers or is missing entirely.

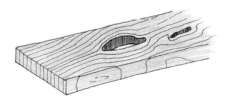

A LOOSE KNOT

A grading system has been established in order to differentiate between various grades of lumber. Obviously, higher grades are more expensive because they are more desirable. In *construction-grade* lumber, the grades are #1, #2, and #3. Number-three grade is sometimes known as *utility*. Number-one grade lumber is of a very high quality, having a straight grain pattern and a minimal number of small knots. Number-two has more knots that tend to be larger and more pronounced. Number-three lumber contains loose knots that fall out and leave a hole. Number-one grade is quite expensive and rarely available; number-three is often limited in construction work to braces or other members that will not be retained in the finished product. This leaves the number-two grade as the predominant choice for most construction. This designation has become so prominent that often the grade of the lumber is not listed, but even so, it is #2.

Another grading system is used for *finish-grade lumber*. Finish lumber is usually meant to be used in the construction of moldings, cabinets, windows, doors, and other such very exacting work. Finish lumber is much more expensive and is of a much higher quality. Finish lumber is often sold in its rough-cut state, with the customer being expected to plane the boards to a smooth finish. The grades of finish lumber are A, B, C, and D. Sometimes A and B are lumped together as a grade known as firsts and seconds. Professional scenery building shops often use finish lumber, because very high labor costs make the proportional share of money spent on excellent materials less of a concern. Expectations of the client are also higher.

Finish lumber that is sold without the benefit of having been planed is generally known as *rough-cut lumber*. Rough-cut lumber of this type has no standard dimensional size like regular construction lumber. In order to make the most efficient use of the tree, the lumber is left as wide and as long as is possible, and there are no sizes given other than thickness. The thickness of rough-cut lumber is given in quarters. A rough-cut board that is 2 inches thick is called an *8-quarter board*. A 1-inch-thick board would be a 4-quarter board.

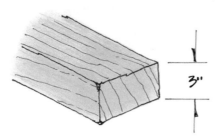

USING THE QUARTER SYSTEM, A THREE-INCH-THICK BOARD IS EQUAL TO 12 QUARTERS

Finish lumber is priced by a volume measurement known as the *board foot*. One board foot is equal to a volume that is 1 inch thick by 12 inches square. Another term is the *running foot*, which refers to the total length of all boards involved without regard to their width or thickness. If you have ten 1×4s and each one is 12 feet long, then you have 120 running feet of 1×4.

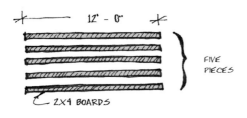

THERE ARE 5 PIECES OF 2×4 LUMBER.

EACH ONE IS 12'-0" LONG.

5×12=60

THAT IS A TOTAL OF 60 RUNNING FEET.

HOW MANY RUNNING FEET?

Back in the day, it was quite common for lumberyards to list their prices by the board foot, but *stick pricing* is much more common today. A "stick" is one piece of lumber. A price is given for each length of each type of board. Rough-sawn lumber is still sold by the board foot, because the pieces are not uniform, and contain different volumes of wood. Most do-it-yourself, chain-store lumberyards have only #2 lumber priced by the stick.

Because lumber is derived from natural sources, it has a tendency to bend into odd shapes after it has been cut into pieces and milled to an exact size. Each one of these defects can be overcome during the construction process, but the approaches to doing that are different. There are three main ways for this to happen. It is helpful to be able to tell them apart.

The first of these defects is *cup*. Cupping is most pronounced when a board is harvested just to one side of the center of the trunk. Unfortunately, this is the most common location for cutting 1×12s used in building scenery. As a result, the growth rings appear with a preponderance of the softer, lighter-colored wood on one side of the board. That side will shrink a bit more in the drying process, and the board will curl some to that side as a result.

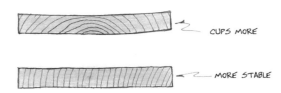

END GRAIN DIFFERENCES

The effect of cupping is reduced when lumber is cut into narrow strips. When the amount of the curve is divided between the boards, it becomes proportionally smaller and may virtually disappear.

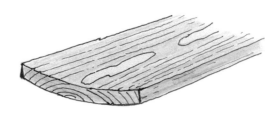

THIS BOARD IS CUPPED

The second defect is known as *bow*, which occurs along the length of the grain. It is seen as either a turn to one of the flat sides, or to one of the edges. If the bow is a gentle curve along the entire length of the piece, then it can often be worked out as a consequence of internal bracing, as in a soft cover flat with toggles. If the bow is the result of a large knot, causing the board to take a sudden turn, it is usually better to try to cut around the knot, and use the board for two shorter pieces.

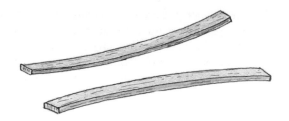

THESE BOARDS ARE BOWED

THIS BOARD IS REALLY WARPED

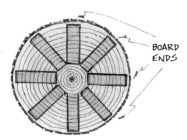

QUARTER-SAWN BOARDS HAVE THE MOST STABLE GRAIN PATTERN

MOST LUMBER IS CUT THIS WAY BECAUSE IT IS MORE ECONOMICAL

Warp is used to describe the twisting of a board from one end to the other like a piece of licorice. It is very difficult to remove this defect by using internal bracing. It is best to use this sort of board for very short pieces of stock in which the proportional amount of warp is reduced.

Lumber mills can maximize production by slicing a log down the center, and then cutting slabs from the resulting halves. Although that produces more lumber, it means that some boards pass near or through the heartwood of the tree, leading to a less desirable board. Some boards are said to be *quarter-sawn*, meaning that an extra effort is made to saw up the log so that the grain of the wood stands on end as it passes through each plank.

PLYWOOD

Plywood differs from dimension lumber in that it is a product *manufactured* from wood rather than being wood simply cut into strips. The main advantages of plywood are that it comes in large sheets, it is very strong, and it is less prone to splitting. Remember that the wood of a tree was originally the slender tubes forming the cambium layer. They run up and down the length of the trunk. The fibers themselves are very strong from end to end, but the bonds that hold them together are much weaker, and as a result wood tends to tear or split along its length. So although you can bend a *long* piece of lumber quite a bit, a *wide* one will snap if you cut a short piece of it and apply pressure.

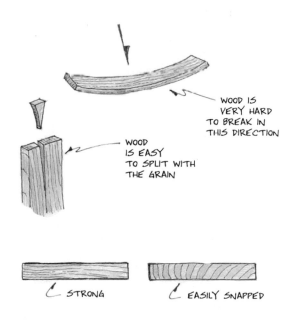

WOOD IS VERY HARD TO BREAK IN THIS DIRECTION

WOOD IS EASY TO SPLIT WITH THE GRAIN

STRONG

EASILY SNAPPED

GRAIN DIRECTION INFLUENCES WOOD STRENGTH

The standard size of a sheet of plywood, and most other sheet goods, is 4'-0" by 8'-0". By comparison, the widest commonly available lumber is only 12 inches wide. However, lumber comes in much longer lengths than plywood. So the choice between plywood or lumber can often be made on the basis of what size pieces you need for a particular project.

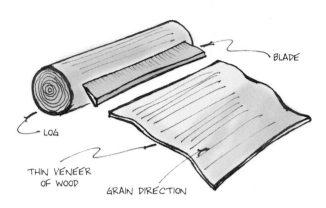

PEELING VENEER FROM A LOG BY
THE ROTARY METHOD

Plywood is made by peeling layers of wood off of a large log in much the same way that a handheld pencil sharpener shaves tiny layers of wood off the end of a pencil. This method of forming plies is known as *rotary cutting*. Sometimes the plies are called *veneers*. The layers of wood are glued together to form large sheets.

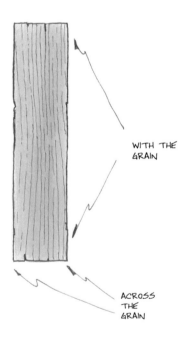

WITH THE
GRAIN

ACROSS
THE
GRAIN

DEFINITION OF TERMS
WITH AND ACROSS THE GRAIN

Plywood develops its great strength from the way that the grain of various layers is oriented. You have seen that the strength of wood lies along the length of the fibers. The fibers are much stronger and more pliable along their length than are the bonds that hold them together. It is fairly easy to split the fibers apart from one another, but it is much more difficult to break them lengthwise. If the grains of the various sheets of veneer that make up the plywood are oriented at right angles to one another, the resulting structure will have extraordinary strength in both directions.

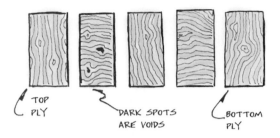

ALTERNATING WOOD GRAIN IN PLYWOOD

That is how plywood is formed—by gluing together the layers of shaved wood with the grain of adjoining plies running in alternating directions. Both of the exterior top and bottom plies on any one sheet are oriented so that the grain of the wood is running along the 8-foot length of the sheet. This means that there are normally an odd number of plies, no matter what the exact number is. The grain pattern of rotary-cut veneers is always rather extreme, because the cutters are constantly weaving in and out of the various growth rings. On occasion, this is called a "flame" pattern. Sometimes this makes it difficult to determine exactly which way the grain runs, but if you look at the entire sheet, you will be able to see it.

The plies are stacked up, with a layer of glue sprayed between each one. The adhesive sets up quickly in the presence of heat and great pressure. A press is used to squeeze the assembly together until the glue bonds. After the plies are securely joined together, the sheet is cut to its 4×8 size, and if the grade of plywood calls for it, the surface is sanded smooth to an exact thickness.

Plywood is made from many different types of trees, both hardwood and softwood. Most common construction-grade plywood is manufactured from either yellow pine or fir. The type and quality of wood used to make plywood are reflected in its grade.

Plywood is graded with the letters A, B, C, and D. Because there are two distinct sides to a sheet of plywood, two letters separated by a slash mark are used to describe the sheet: for example, A/C or C/D, where A represents the good side, and C the bad side. Statistically, you would think that there are 16 grades of plywood, (4×4=16), but in reality there are far fewer. Not all of the possible combinations of letters exist as grades of plywood. The most common grade of yellow pine plywood is C/D, which is frequently used as an underlayment in home building. It is minimally sanded on the outside and is therefore very rough. Knotholes are abundant on both sides. B/C yellow-pine ply has been plugged and sanded on one side and is rough on the other. The type of plywood to use depends on your budget and the kind of work being done. There are a number of factors to determine when making a selection, but it is almost impossible to fill all the defects in C/D ply.

THE B SIDE OF A
SHEET OF B/C PLY

ANY KNOTHOLES
ARE FILLED AND
SANDED SMOOTH

YELLOW PINE
PLYWOOD SIDES

THE D SIDE OF A
SHEET OF C/D PLY

KNOTS ARE LEFT
OPEN, AND THE
TEXTURE OF THE
ENTIRE SIDE IS
MUCH ROUGHER

Fir plywood is much lighter than yellow pine and tends to warp less. Back in the day, A/C fir plywood was a fraction of the cost it is now, and was used extensively. At the time, mills were not able to effectively peel yellow pine logs into suitable veneers. Plantation-grown hybrid trees are different, and yellow pine plywood is now the norm. A/C fir has one excellent side that is very smooth, but the good side of B/C yellow pine is almost as smooth. However, fir plywood warps much less and is not nearly so heavy.

When a very good grade of plywood is needed, A2 cabinet-grade ply may be the answer. This type of plywood has two sides graded A. It is usually made from birch or some other similar wood. Sometimes, A2 plywood has an inner core of birch veneers and an outer skin of a more exotic wood. This material is quite dense and is very heavy as a result.

A2 is often touted as being very solid and having no voids. A *void* is an empty space on one of the interior plies of a sheet of plywood. They are quite common in construction-grade plywood and usually show up as a slot on the edge of a sheet after it has been cut. They are most often caused by a knothole or some other defect in one of the plies. A2 is generally sanded very smooth on both sides.

Fir and yellow pine plywood sheets come in a variety of thicknesses from $\frac{1}{4}''$ to $\frac{3}{4}''$ in $\frac{1}{8}''$ increments ($\frac{1}{4}$, $\frac{3}{8}$, $\frac{1}{2}$, $\frac{5}{8}$, $\frac{3}{4}$). The actual thickness of a sheet of yellow pine plywood is a bit smaller than the nominal size. Generally, $\frac{3}{4}''$ is actually $\frac{23}{32}''$, and other thicknesses are also $\frac{1}{32}''$ smaller. This slight difference will most likely not matter in what you are building. The true size of A/C fir ply is exactly the nominal size. Plywood can generally be depended on to be exactly 4 feet by 8 feet and exactly square. It is often useful as a squaring-up device in constructing scenery.

Lauan is a mahogany plywood variety that is imported from the Pacific Rim. The major advantages of lauan are that it is often less expensive than American plywood and has a much smoother finish that takes paint well. It is, however, not nearly as dense as domestic plywood, and that makes lauan less structurally sound.

 GREEN IDEAS TIP BOX

According to the American Panel Association—the governing body for plywood manufacturers—the forest products industry plants about a billion trees every year, and there is more forest cover in the United States now than there was in 1920. Tree farms dot the southern states, and are often used to manufacture B/C and C/D plywood used to construct scenery as described in this book. You may notice that there are many tips on how to use plywood to create laminated structures that were at one time more likely to be constructed from dimension lumber. Yellow pine plywood is cheaper by comparison, and very abundant. On the other hand, lauan products are generally *not* made from sustainable forests, so you may wish to consider that when selecting materials, as well as the fact that lauan is neither as strong nor flame resistant as yellow pine.

This material is most commonly available in a ¼″ thickness, but may also be found in ½″ and ¾″ varieties. The ½″ variety is especially good for small-profile pieces that must be cut out with a jigsaw. Because this material is made in countries where the metric system is used, the sizing can be a bit off, but the sheets are generally just as square as any other type of plywood. The actual thicknesses of the various sizes are 6, 12, and 16 millimeters, which are a bit smaller than ¼″, ½″, and ¾″.

There are several other "engineered" wood products that come in sheets, but are not technically considered to be plywood. Most of the time that has to do with the way that the grain structure of the wood is treated.

OTHER MATERIALS SOLD IN LARGE SHEETS

A number of other building materials are sold in sheet form. These include hardboard, particleboard, MDO, OSB, foam insulation, and acrylic sheet.

Hardboard is often called by its trade name, *Masonite*. It is made from finely ground wood particles that are glued together into a very dense cardboard-like material. The tempered version is semiwaterproof. Hardboard comes in ⅛″ and ¼″ thicknesses. Sometimes there are two slick sides, and sometimes one side has a burlap-like texture. The lack of a grain structure greatly reduces the strength of this material and is a serious drawback. It is also very heavy, but it is quite often used as floor covering where those shortcomings are not as important. Hardboard can stand up to the punishment of casters, and the weight is not so much of a problem once it is on the floor. Hardboard is also used to make pegboards of the sort used in retail stores and closets.

TOOLS ON PEGBOARD

Oriented-strand board (OSB) is made from wood chips arranged so that they overlap one another. The overlapping nature of the wood fibers gives OSB a structural integrity not found in particleboard (described next). It develops a great deal of tearout when cut, but has the advantage of maintaining a flat stability that is not usually found in B/C yellow pine plywood. Plywood tends to keep a great deal of its strength when cut into narrower 8-foot strips, but OSB does not.

ORIENTED STRANDBOARD

Particleboard is similar to hardboard, in that it is made from sawdust that has been glued together into sheets. The particles are larger, and the sheets are much thicker. It is often used for countertops or speaker enclosures where a very dense material is actually a plus. Particleboard is usually not suitable for scenic use, because it is extremely heavy, and because it is completely lacking in strength, due to the absence of any sort of grain structure.

MDO, or *Medium-density overlay*, is a yellow pine plywood product that has been surfaced with a layer of thick, dense paper, giving it a very smooth surface. It is quite water-repellent and is often used for outdoor signs. It can have a number of scenic uses. It is very strong, and the surface of the paper is as slick as tempered Masonite.

The nongrain plywood substitutes are fine for many projects, especially when full or nearly full sheets are used. They are not as successful when cut into strips and used as a substitute for dimension lumber. Care must be taken to consider the limitations of particleboard and OSB when selecting materials for certain projects. Finding quality lumber has become more difficult, and as a result ¾″ plywood has become a replacement for one-by lumber in many applications. As a result, it is often cut into long, thin strips resembling 1×3 s or even narrower slats. Plywood works fairly well in that application, but particleboard is generally a very poor choice because it breaks so easily.

PLASTICS

Foam insulation can be found in two main types. *Expanded polystyrene* is made from tiny plastic beads that are expanded and fused together to form large hunks of foam, which are then sliced into sheets. It is white in color, and when carved with a Surform or wood rasp, will come apart into small beads. It comes in a variety of thicknesses and widths.

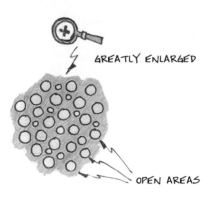

GREATLY ENLARGED

OPEN AREAS

EXTRUDED POLYSTYRENE HAS A VERY FINE SPONGE-LIKE TEXTURE

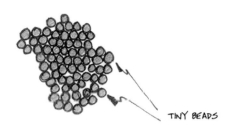

TINY BEADS

EXPANDED POLYSTYRENE IS MADE UP OF MANY TINY BEADS

Extruded polystyrene was originally manufactured only by the Dow Chemical Company under the name Styrofoam. It does not flake off in beads, but it has a more homogeneous texture that is something like a sponge. It is more difficult to carve, but it is better at maintaining sharp edges. Real Styrofoam is always blue or gray. A competitor's very similar product is pink. More information about foam products can be found in Chapter 23.

Acrylic sheet is often referred to by the trade name Plexiglas. It comes in clear, mirrored, white, black, and a variety of colors. It is rather expensive, but is also much safer than using glass onstage. Acrylic sheet will break, but does not shatter like glass, and the resulting pieces are not nearly as sharp or dangerous as real glass. Acrylic sheet can be found in a wide range of thicknesses from $\frac{1}{16}''$ to several inches, but the $\frac{1}{16}''$, $\frac{1}{8}''$, and $\frac{1}{4}''$ sizes are by far the most common and usable.

This acrylic sheeting bends quite easily and automatically returns to its original state when released. If acrylic sheet is heated to near its melting point with a heat gun, it can be bent at a sharp angle, and that angle will be retained when the plastic cools. It can be cut and drilled with ordinary woodworking tools, but care must be taken, as the material is very brittle. The main drawback to acrylic sheet is that it scratches so easily.

CHAPTER 16

HAND TOOLS

Once upon a time, when speaking to my class about tools, I would begin my remarks with the statement that tools are really just an extension of our own bodies. And then I'd continue with how our fingers can grasp things but a wrench or a pair of pliers can do it with more force, which is a normal humanistic approach to the subject. One year, as I was standing before the class prepared to say just that, a student remarked, "You're not going to tell us that tools are an extension of our own bodies, are you?" and of course I said no. At least until now. I guess I wasn't the first person to think of that. Even so, it is good to approach a technical subject like tools by seeing how they relate to human beings.

CABINET FOR HAND TOOLS
IN A UNIVERSITY SCENE SHOP

MEASURING AND MARKING TOOLS

Undoubtedly, the most commonly used measuring tool is the measuring tape. It is a tool that seems obvious and self-explanatory at first glance, but it is actually much more complex than you might think. Physically, the standard type consists of a thin metal strip that is rolled up inside a plastic or metal housing. This strip is called the *blade*, and it is connected to a wind-up spring that retracts it into the housing. The blade is curved from side to side so that it has a certain rigidity when extended. That is to say that it stiffens and can be played out to a distant point. The width of the blade (the best are 1 inch wide) governs the effectiveness of its ability to be extended in this manner, and narrow blades will not go as far. Generally, there is a button or catch of some sort that locks the blade in an extended position.

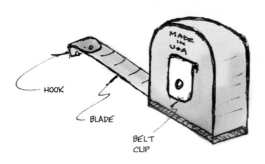

TAPE MEASURE

A small metal piece is attached to the end of the blade and is used to catch the end of a board that you are measuring. On close inspection, this *hook* appears to be quite loose, and the casual observer might attribute this looseness to shoddy workmanship on the part of the manufacturer.

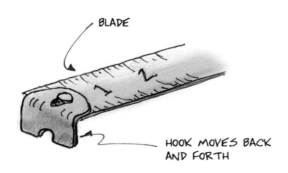

BLADE

HOOK MOVES BACK AND FORTH

There is, however, a reason for the hook's looseness. It is intended to shift position in order to accommodate both inside and outside measurements. The hook does that by moving back and forth to account for its own thickness. When used for a measurement to the inside of a space (such as the inside of a cabinet), the hook slides toward the user, making its outside the point of absolute zero. When hooked over the end of a board it will extend outward, making its inside the point of absolute zero.

You can adjust the accuracy of a tape measure by bending its hook. Using a pair of pliers, bend the hook until the tape reads accurately when tested against an object of known size. If the hook has been flattened out by stepping on it or some other misadventure, it should be readjusted before further use.

The blade is marked with a series of numbers and lines that are used to reference measurements. Most tapes can measure an object down to the closest sixteenth of an inch. That is the distance between the smallest marks on the blade.

The fractional sizes used in woodworking may seem quite odd at first when compared to the metric system, but they are actually derived in a very logical way that comes from dividing distances in half. The largest mark between any two of the inch designations is used to indicate one half of an inch. The two next-longest marks indicate one-half of that distance, or one-quarter of an inch. Next is one-eighth of an inch, and finally the smallest lines are used to measure one-sixteenth of an inch. One-sixteenth is equal to half of a half of a half of a half of an inch. If you are unsure which lines represent which fraction, simply look in the middle of the inch to find the half, the middle of the half to find the quarter, the middle of the quarter to find the eighth, and the middle of the eighth to find the sixteenth. Or count how many of a particular size space are between two inch marks. If there are eight of them, then those are the $\frac{1}{8}''$ spaces and/or marks.

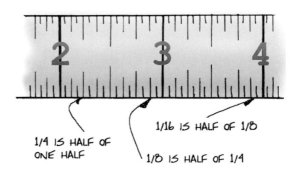

1/4 IS HALF OF ONE HALF

1/16 IS HALF OF 1/8

1/8 IS HALF OF 1/4

Notice that the numbering system on a tape measure has two different sets of numbers, one along each edge of the blade. The first consists of numbers that are all inches. Twenty-five feet, a common tape-measure length, is equal to 300 inches. On the other side, both feet and inches are shown, so that you have measurements such as 10 feet 2 inches. That equals 122 inches. Look from side to side on the blade to convert systems. Dimensions listed on a plan sometimes use one method and sometimes the other, so the tape is manufactured to accommodate either one. If you are ever looking at a plan, and would like to convert feet and inches to just inches, you can look up the answer by cross-referencing it on the tape rather than by multiplying.

Another series of numbers is marked in red ink. They start at 16 and continue onward to include 32, 48, 64, 80, 96, and so forth. These numbers are, of course, multiples of 16. They are printed in red to make them easier to locate. Sixteen inches is the normal center spacing for framing members, like studs in the wall of a house. Most tools are designed for the home construction market rather than for scenery building. This can sometimes leave us with extraneous information, but in this case you may find occasions to also frame scenery on 16-inch centers.

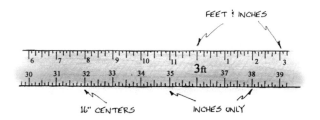

TAPE MEASURE MARKINGS

STEEL TAPES ARE DIFFERENT, BECAUSE THEY ARE MEANT TO MEASURE LARGER DISTANCES. THE BLADE DOESN'T RETRACT ON ITS OWN.

Another type of tape measure is more often used in the theatre itself rather than in the shop. A 50- or 100-foot cloth or *steel tape* that can be reeled in like a fishing rod is helpful for laying out the locations of large units of scenery. This kind of tape is also used for measuring the trim heights of battens by lightly attaching the end of the measuring tape to the batten with adhesive gaffer's tape and then flying the batten out. Hold the correct distance marking to the floor with your foot, and when the tape becomes taut, the proper height has been reached. It is fine to step on this kind of a tape measure, because it is already flat. Repeatedly stepping on a tape with a rigid curved blade will eventually ruin it.

A *framing square* can be used for both measuring and marking. There are many different types of squares, but this one gets its name because it is often used in laying out the framing (or structure—studs, joists, and rafters) of a house. The best framing squares are made of aluminum, because that makes them lightweight and rustproof. There are inch markings along all the sides.

Because this tool is often used to compute roof pitches, some of the markings may be in twelfths of an inch rather than in sixteenths of an inch. Roof pitches are expressed by stating a rise and a run in twelfths of an inch, such as $9/12$ or $12/12$. Twelfths of an inch will not work if you are measuring sixteenths or eighths. Be aware of that when using this square as a measuring tool. The framing square is most often used to check or create 90-degree angle corners and to mark stair carriages.

A relative of the framing square is the *Speed Square*, which is used in much the same manner. Speed Squares are smaller and sturdier than their larger cousins and also have a lip along one edge to make it easier to line them up with a board. They are very commonly used to mark the alignment of framing members. There are knock-off brands with names like "Fast Square."

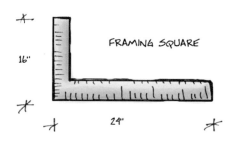

FRAMING SQUARE

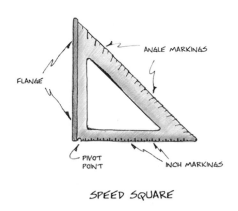

SPEED SQUARE

Drywall squares look like a large metal version of the T-square that was once used for drafting. They are not terribly accurate, but they make excellent straight edges and are also useful for jobs such as laying out where nails should go in order to run into hidden framing when you are building hardcover flats or platforming.

BLUE CHALK

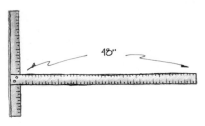

DRYWALL SQUARE

The *chalk line* is excellent for marking long straight lines. This tool consists of a fishing-type reel housed in a box filled with chalk dust. String on the reel becomes coated with the chalk. If the string is stretched between two points it will form a straight line, and snapping (pulling the string up slightly and letting it go) the string will leave chalk dust on the surface of whatever you are marking. Be sure to stretch the string tautly to ensure that the line is really straight.

A large wooden *compass* is essential for marking circles. You can easily make this tool from scrap lumber and a bolt.

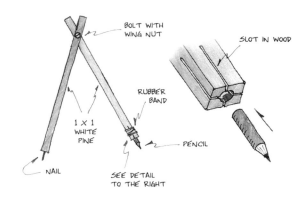

LARGE SHOP-BUILT COMPASS

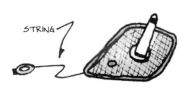

CHALK LINE

It is often easier to run the string past the two marks so that the line is longer than you really need. If the points are extremely far apart, have a third person hold the center of the string, and snap the line twice, once from either side of the middle third person.

Shake the box and hold it with the pointy end down to get extra chalk on the string as it comes out of the tool. Chalk is usually blue, but other colors are available. The red is meant to make semipermanent lines in concrete, so you may have trouble getting that color off if you use it for woodworking. Painters like to use powdered charcoal instead of chalk.

For even larger circles, *trammel points* are used. These are essentially small clamps that can be attached to a wooden slat. One of the clamps forms a pivot point and the other holds a pencil. Two slats can be joined together if necessary. This type of rig is much more accurate than the old "string and a pencil" method. If trammel points are not available, a very satisfactory shop-built compass can be put together with slats of wood, a nail, and a hole drilled for the pencil. This alternative method is not quite as easy to use, but it can give excellent results.

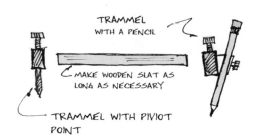

TRAMMEL
WITH A PENCIL

MAKE WOODEN SLAT AS
LONG AS NECESSARY

TRAMMEL WITH PIVIOT
POINT

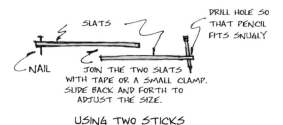

SLATS

DRILL HOLE SO
THAT PENCIL
FITS SNUGLY

NAIL

JOIN THE TWO SLATS
WITH TAPE OR A SMALL CLAMP.
SLIDE BACK AND FORTH TO
ADJUST THE SIZE.

USING TWO STICKS

TWO METHODS OF MARKING
LARGE CIRCLES

Levels are used to check whether objects are level to the horizon, or *plumb* with a line that is perpendicular to the horizon. Those are the proper terms: "level," being flat, and "plumb," being upright. Most levels have several small vials with air bubbles inside of them. The vials are placed so that they are either in line with the length of the tool or perpendicular to it. That facilitates using the level either horizontally or vertically. A level with a longer body is generally more accurate. Short levels with magnets on them are very nice when working with steel tubing. Each vial has two marks toward its center. The middle of the vial bulges slightly to help steady the bubble inside. When the bubble is directly between the two marks, the level is in proper alignment.

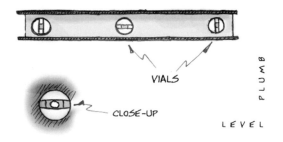

VIALS

CLOSE-UP

PLUMB

LEVEL

WHEN THE BUBBLE IS CENTERED
THE OBJECT IS LEVEL OR PLUMB

WRENCHES, PLIERS, AND THE LIKE

These tools are used for gripping and turning and come in a multitude of varieties for special purposes. A choice should be made as to which tool is the most appropriate for a particular task. Using the wrong tool can be very frustrating; using the right one will make any job easier.

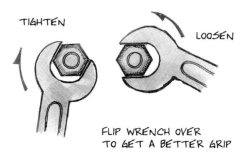

TIGHTEN

LOOSEN

FLIP WRENCH OVER
TO GET A BETTER GRIP

The most commonly used wrench in most theatres is the *Crescent* or *adjustable wrench*. The Crescent Tool Company invented this type of wrench, and in modern usage, any brand of adjustable wrench is often referred to as a Crescent or "C" wrench. A Crescent by any name is identifiable by its peculiar half-moon shape. The jaws of the wrench can be adjusted to different sizes by turning a screw-threaded device with your thumb. A C wrench is essential when hanging or focusing lights, as lighting equipment uses so many different sizes and types of bolts.

ADJUSTABLE

CRESCENT WRENCH

An *open-end wrench* is similar in appearance to a Crescent wrench, except that it is not adjustable. A set of these wrenches is required so that you'll have the correct size. Quite often, there are actually two different sizes incorporated into the same wrench, one at either end. Notice that the ends are fixed at an angle to the body of the tool. This allows you to get a wider range of motion when using the wrench in a tight space. You can get a better angle to start from if you flip the wrench over each time you reposition it.

CHROME   STEEL

OPEN END WRENCH

A *box-end wrench* wraps entirely around a hex-headed bolt and makes for the surest possible grip. When a C wrench slips off while you are turning a bolt, the corners of the head are damaged. Sometimes they become so rounded off that a wrench will no longer work. Box-end wrenches are less prone to slipping and damaging the bolt. They generally come in sets that are double ended, just like the open-ended wrenches.

BOX END WRENCH

Socket wrenches are very similar to box-end wrenches in the way that they grip a bolt head. The difference lies in the method of attaching a handle.

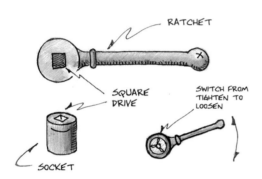

SOCKET WRENCH

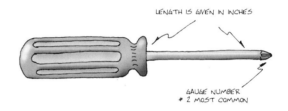

PHILLIPS HEAD SCREWDRIVER

Sockets typically use a ratcheting handle that can be set to turn freely one way and grip in the other. This negates the need to remove the wrench from the bolt head in order to gain fresh purchase, and makes for especially speedy tightening and loosening. Deep sockets are useful when the end of the bolt protrudes a good distance through the nut and might cause the wrench to bottom out with a normal shallow socket.

The *drive* of the ratchet refers to the size of the square nub that fits into the top of the socket. The most common drive size is $3/8$″.

Screwdrivers are relatively self-explanatory, other than that the tips must correspond to the drive of the screw, and naturally the most popular types are slotted and Phillips. Square-drive and TORX are also available. Screwdrivers come in different sizes, both in length and diameter. The diameter is a gauge size, and the #2 is appropriate for a #8 wood screw of the sort that is used to attach hinges to a flat.

Pliers are the most quintessential gripping tool, and the most likely to be considered an "extension of the human body." Most pliers are *not* designed to be used on bolt heads, and indeed will often scar a bolt or nut and make it difficult to deal with later on. So don't use them in that way. Some types of pliers are really meant to be used as cutting tools and not with any type of fastener at all.

Slip-joint pliers are the most common type. They can be used for gripping and holding different-sized objects when fingers are not strong enough. The slip-joint part comes from the fact that the rivet holding the two halves together can be adjusted, allowing the jaws to accommodate either very small pieces or very large pieces, depending on the placement of the rivet. This tool has a wide range of uses, such as gripping small wires or crimping together an S-hook.

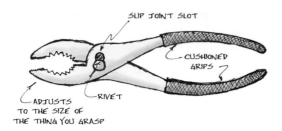

SLIP JOINT SLOT

CUSHIONED GRIPS

RIVET

ADJUSTS TO THE SIZE OF THE THING YOU GRASP

SLIP-JOINT PLIERS

Needle-nose pliers are very similar, but have a long, pointy snout for small objects.

NEEDLE-NOSE PLIERS

Vise Grips (another brand name) are specialized pliers that can clamp and lock into place with great force. They are adjustable for a wide range of sizes. Vise Grips have an amazingly large variety of uses when you need a tool that can be clamped in place. They are particularly handy for removing stripped-out screws when there is enough of the head or body sticking out to get a grip on it.

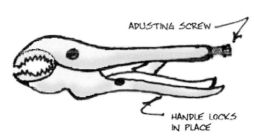

ADUSTING SCREW

HANDLE LOCKS IN PLACE

VISE GRIPS

Diagonal pliers or "dikes" are actually intended to cut pieces of wire or small metal hardware like pins or nails. You may also find them to be an excellent tool for misapplied pneumatic nails or staples. Use them to grip, rather than cut through the nail, and then twist the dikes and pull the nail out. The twisting motion is meant to gain leverage, just like a claw hammer. Of course, this won't work on larger sizes of hand-driven nails, because the amount of force you would need is too large.

DIAGONAL PLIERS

Bolt cutters really aren't pliers at all, but they are kind of similar in appearance. As the name implies, this tool can be used to cut off bolts, but also chain, metal rods, and the occasional padlock.

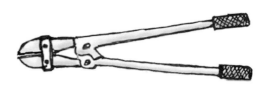

BOLT CUTTERS

You can get much more leverage on the cut if you place the bolt as far as possible into the jaws of the cutters, close to the pivot point. Padlocks are made with hardened steel and will ruin your bolt cutters after a few cuts.

Pipe or "monkey" wrenches are intended to grip a round object, most often a pipe. They are adjustable to fit different pipe sizes. *Pipe wrenches* grip in only one direction at a time and thus must be flipped over in order to go from tightening to loosening. (So any monkey wrench can be left-handed if you just turn it over.) If you are connecting two pipes with a coupling, use two wrenches facing in opposite directions.

PIPE WRENCH

The Felco company invented this type of *cable-cutting pliers*, which tend to be rather pricey. They are more delicate than you would think, and shouldn't be used to cut other ordinary objects. The jaws are angled so that the front part comes together first, which forces the cable inward and greatly reduces the amount of fraying that occurs when making the cut. An ordinary pair of dikes won't do that. The 7″ cutters are big enough for the ⅛″ aircraft cable used to hang most theatre scenery. You will need something larger for ¼″ cable used to rig battens.

CABLE CUTTER JAWS

TIPS COME TOGETHER FIRST AND TRAP THE CABLE FOR A CLEAN CUT

HAMMERS AND MALLETS

There are two basic categories for hammers: those used for driving nails and all others. Nail-driving hammers are of course the most common in a woodworking shop. Other types include rubber mallets, sledgehammers, wooden mallets, and ball peen hammers. This second grouping is used for various tasks like demolition and metalworking.

The standard nail-driving hammer has a 16-ounce head, although they are also manufactured in lighter and heavier weights. There is a *curved claw* version and a *straight claw* type. The claw is the opposite side from the portion used to pound in nails. The curved claw is best for removing nails, as it allows the user to rock the hammer along the claw to gain leverage and more easily pry out the nail. A straight claw is easier to slip in between boards and pry them apart. Either one is about the same when it comes to driving nails.

There is a definite difference in the quality of various hammers. The steel used in the head of the hammer should be hard enough not to wear away or be deformed by nails. You may have seen cheap hammers made from very soft steel whose claws have been bent and twisted from the force of removing nails. On the other end of the spectrum, if a hammer is made from steel that is too hard, it may be brittle as a result. Chips of the hammer head itself can shatter and fly away and are very dangerous. Some years ago, OSHA came up with guidelines for manufacturers about grinding some steel from the striking area of hammers to make them less likely to chip. You can see that the edges of a hammer are chamfered at a 45-degree angle.

The handle of a hammer is also important. It should be sturdy and unlikely to break. Steel handles are sturdiest, but they transmit a high degree of shock and vibration to the elbow. Prolonged use may result in tendonitis. Wooden or fiberglass handles are really the best. When using a hammer, try to keep in mind that it is intended for driving nails and not for pounding concrete or steel beams or other such items.

Using a hammer to drive nails takes a moderate amount of skill gained through practice. Holding the handle near its end increases the amount of leverage and hence force that is transmitted to the driving of the nail. However, the same statement can be applied to the striking of your thumb if your aim is not very good. Your thumbs will no doubt appreciate choking up a bit on the handle until your hand-eye coordination catches up with your enthusiasm. In this modern age of pneumatic nail guns and staplers, hammers have become somewhat outmoded, but skill with this basic tool is still important.

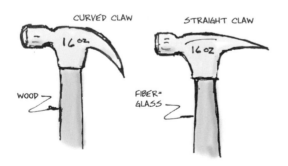

CURVED CLAW   STRAIGHT CLAW
16 oz   16 oz
WOOD   FIBER-GLASS

WOODWORKING HAMMERS

START OUT HOLDING THE HAMMER LIKE THIS

AND WORK YOUR WAY UP TO THIS
AS YOUR SKILLS IMPROVE

Rubber mallets are used when a soft, cushioned blow is required. The same is true of plastic or wooden types. Forcing together mortise and tenon joints and putting the lid on a can of paint are both examples of this concept. *Sledgehammers* are used primarily for demolition, although a large, rubber-coated Deadblow is excellent for forcing decking pieces into place. *Ball peen hammers* are intended exclusively for the shaping of sheets of metal. You probably won't have much need for them unless you are crafting props or some other specialty item.

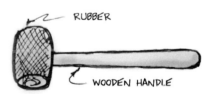

RUBBER MALLET

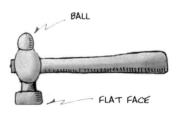

BALL PEEN HAMMER

CLAMPS

Clamps are used to hold things together. There are many various types, because there are many different kinds and shapes of things to hold together. The most common type is the *C-clamp*. The origin of the name should be obvious from its appearance. These clamps come in many sizes, but the 4-inch variety seems to be the most useful in a theatre shop, because the jaw opens wide enough for two 2×4s and/or anything smaller. This type of clamp has very great holding power, but it may leave indentations on soft materials such as white pine lumber. If this is likely to be a problem, use some small blocks of scrap lumber as pads.

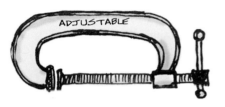

C-CLAMP

Wooden clamps are useful, because they have very deep jaws and can clamp the interior of an item far from the edge of the piece. They are also the most adjustable for clamping at odd angles, but learning to operate the jaws can take a bit of practice. This clamp is less likely to leave depression marks on your work.

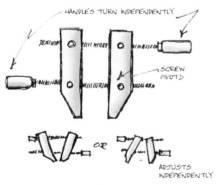

WOODEN CLAMP

Pipe and *bar clamps* are useful for clamping items that are very wide or long. They can be used for squeezing in or adjusting the framing of platforms or flats. A bit of room is required in order to turn the handle and tighten the clamp. Pipe clamps are made from a length of ¾″ steel pipe and some commercially manufactured ends. You can make up virtually any length of clamp, as this type uses pipe ordinarily found lying around the shop. It is often handy to have a clamp longer than an

8-foot sheet of plywood, and a pipe clamp of that size is easily made up. When a less cumbersome size is required, you can exchange the long pipe for a shorter one. Bar clamps work the same way, but you are stuck with the length of flat bar that came with the clamp.

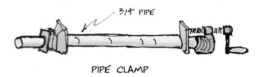

PIPE CLAMP

Vise Grip clamps (not to be confused with the pliers of the same brand name) are very easy to put on and have a great amount of holding power. The somewhat pointy ends of the clamp can be useful when the item being clamped is small. Once the size of the opening has been properly set, it is very easy to apply and/or remove this clamp. They are great for welding tabs and/or hinges onto square tubing. The mechanics of the handles are just like the pliers, but the jaws have been replaced with a clamp shape.

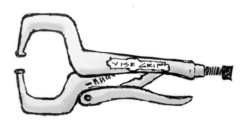

VISE GRIP CLAMP

Spring clamps are somewhat like giant clothespins. They do not have a terrific amount of holding power but are very easy to attach. They are quite popular for pinning backstage draperies and other lightweight chores.

SPRING CLAMP

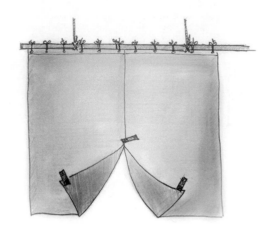

USE SPRING CLAMPS TO HOLD THE CURTAINS OPEN

HAND-HELD POWER TOOLS

There are two basic types of small power tools. They are separated by the kind of power used to operate them. The most common and well-known power source is electricity, from either a wall outlet or a battery. Tools powered by compressed air are known as *pneumatic tools*, which are less well known to the public but very important in a shop. There are pneumatic versions of virtually all tools. Some of them are not nearly as efficient as their electric counterparts, but pneumatic nailers and staplers are much more efficient than electric ones. You need an *air compressor* to use them. A compressor and its delivery system of pipes and hoses represent a sizable monetary investment, but one that is well worth the investment for a shop when compared to the resulting savings in time and labor.

A LARGE CAPACITY AIR COMPRESSOR

AN ELECTRIC MOTOR DRIVES A PISTON THAT COMPRESSES AIR INTO THE TANK

GREEN IDEAS TIP BOX

Nickel-cadmium or *Ni-Cad batteries* are what make the new cordless world spin. They can be recharged hundreds of times, but eventually they will wear out and no longer hold a charge. When that happens, it is important to recycle them, because the nickel/cadmium mixture inside is highly toxic. So putting them in the landfill is harmful to the environment. If the batteries are recycled, the toxic substances inside can be made into new products. Some Ni-Cad batteries have this phone number printed on them: 800-8-BATTERY. This is a help line to find a recycler in your area, and is good for all makes and models.

ELECTRICAL TOOLS

Recent years have brought major breakthroughs in battery technology, especially the sort that are used in a variety of power tools. Battery-powered drills and/or screw guns are the most popular, with the obvious advantage being a greater freedom of movement when the tool is free from a power cord that must be dragged about. Modern battery-powered drills are almost as powerful as their corded cousins, and the batteries last for hours, even under heavy use. For someone who suffered through the development of less-efficient batteries, it truly is incredible. Battery-powered drills possess an amazing amount of torque (driving power) for their size. You may still need an older, corded drill for heavy jobs like using a paint mixer or drilling large holes in steel, but battery power is the best choice for day-to-day work.

The voltage rating of a battery drill makes a big difference in how well it cuts through difficult materials. The higher the voltage is, the greater the *torque*. All of the new types have a ratcheting chuck that works really well without a key— you just tighten them with your bare hands. Battery-powered drills often have a torque setting on the chuck that allows the user to select the exact amount of force that is applied. This will allow you to stop screws from damaging soft materials like sound-deadening insulation.

BATTERY - POWERED DRILL

THIS TOOL IS TYPICAL OF THE TYPE OF CORDLESS DRILL OFTEN USED AS A "SCREW GUN." IT HAS A PHILLIPS DRIVER TIP IN IT. THE POWER OF THE DRILL IS A FUNCTION OF THE VOLTAGE, AND AT 18 VOLTS THIS ONE HAS LOTS OF POWER. THE BATTERY CAN BE RECHARGED MANY TIMES AT THE CHARGING STATION.

CHUCK REQUIRES NO KEY

TORQUE SETTING

SET THIS FEATURE TO PROVIDE THE PROPER TORQUE FOR THE JOB YOU ARE DOING. WHEN THE DRILL REACHES THAT AMOUNT OF FORCE, THE CHUCK BEGINS TO RATCHET, AND DOESN'T TURN ANYMORE. USE A LOW SETTING FOR SCREWS GOING INTO SOFT MATERIALS. USE THE MAXIMUM SETTING (DRILL BIT) FOR TIMES WHEN YOU NEED THE MOST TURNING FORCE.

At its most basic level, an electric hand drill consists of a motor, a trigger or switch that turns the motor on, and a *chuck* that is used to clamp a drill bit to the motor. The chuck rotates to move three jaws placed inside of it. They come together or apart, depending on the direction you rotate the chuck. When a drill bit is placed inside, the chuck is rotated until the jaws are firmly seated against it. Hand-tightening is fine for most drills, but some older types and/or heavy-duty ones use a *chuck key* to lock the bit in place. Gear teeth on the chuck correspond to teeth on the chuck key. These teeth make it possible to lock the chuck very tightly. A *drill press* is a large, stationary type of drill. They always use a chuck key.

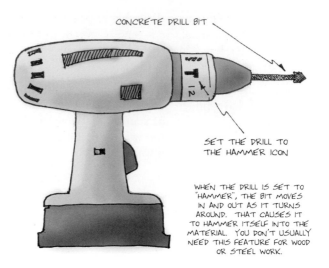

CONCRETE DRILL BIT

SET THE DRILL TO THE HAMMER ICON

WHEN THE DRILL IS SET TO "HAMMER", THE BIT MOVES IN AND OUT AS IT TURNS AROUND. THAT CAUSES IT TO HAMMER ITSELF INTO THE MATERIAL. YOU DON'T USUALLY NEED THIS FEATURE FOR WOOD OR STEEL WORK.

A HAMMER DRILL WORKS DIFFERENTLY

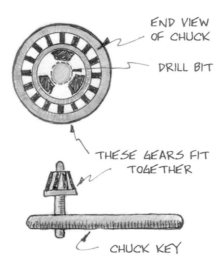

END VIEW OF CHUCK

DRILL BIT

THESE GEARS FIT TOGETHER

CHUCK KEY

Not all chucks are the same size. Some really small ones may accommodate only a ¼″ drill bit, but most modern cordless drills go up to ½″. A ½″ chuck will accommodate a bit shaft of up to that size.

Some more powerful drills are designed to bore large-diameter holes into wood or steel, and have only one slow speed. They usually have a cord, and are physically much larger. Others are of a type called *hammer drills*, meaning that not only do they spin, but the bit also oscillates forward and backward as well. This feature is especially helpful when drilling into concrete.

But most drills are of a type known as *variable-speed reversible*. When you pull on the trigger, the amount of pressure dictates how fast the drill rotates. So a light pressure makes the drill spin very slowly, and pulling the trigger all the way back runs it at maximum speed. This feature is very important when using a drill as a *screw gun*. Slower speeds are essential when driving screws. Years ago, special types of drills were manufactured especially for driving drywall screws, but now just about any cordless drill will do that.

Driving Phillips-head screws is a common task, and of course it is much easier with a power tool. When using a drill to install screws, remember to "push hard, pull softly." If you pull the trigger switch in hard all the way, the drill will turn far too fast for you to control it. Use a soft touch on the trigger. But push hard against the screw with the drill so that the driver bit stays firmly seated in the screw head. It is also best to use a slower speed when drilling through steel or other metals in order to avoid overheating and damaging the bit.

It is important that the drill be reversible, because screws frequently need to be taken out as well as put in. Most drills have a switch near the trigger that selects forward or reverse.

A COLLECTION OF DRIVER BITS

THERE ARE MANY DIFFERENT TYPES AND SIZES. GENERALLY SPEAKING, PHILLIPS BITS WORK MUCH BETTER THAN STANDARD.

Not all Phillips screwdriver bits are the same. Some have a very long shank, and some are meant to fit into special bit holders. There are different diameter sizes as well, much like a regular hand-held screwdriver. The #2 diameter is best for most jobs, unless you are using very small screws. Some of the #2 bits have a special, narrower shape that makes them work especially well with drywall screws.

There are a number of different types of drill bits. The most common are the twist drill, the spade bit, and the hole saw. It is important to know something about how the different types work so that you can choose the right bit for a particular job.

A *twist drill* has a spiral shape, as the name implies, and is intended for use in wood, metal, or plastic. (Only a special masonry bit should be used in concrete.) Twist drill bits are usually half an inch or smaller in diameter, because sizes larger than that tend to be quite expensive. The spiral flute is meant to carry the waste product away from the tip of the bit. These bits are somewhat difficult to sharpen once dull. With a bit of practice, you can sharpen the tips with a bench grinder, but great care must be taken to maintain the original bevel. Twist drills come in a tremendous number of diameters, usually separated by a $\frac{1}{64}''$ difference, but the sizes corresponding to bolt sizes are the most useful.

SHANK REDUCED

TWIST DRILL BIT

A *spade bit* is a flat piece of metal with a round spindle that fits into the chuck of a drill. It is meant to be used in wood or other soft materials only, and will not work in steel. They somewhat resemble a garden shovel—hence the name. Spade bits are much easier to manufacture than twist drills are and as a result are much less expensive. Because the size of the cutting part of the bit is not in any way bounded by the size of the shank that fits into the drill chuck, it is easy to find quite large spade bits, all with $\frac{1}{4}''$ shanks. It is common to find this type of bit up to $1\frac{1}{2}''$ diameter. For anything larger than that, a hole saw (described next) should be used. Spade bits are also known as *paddle bits*.

SPADE BIT

As the name implies, the *hole saw* is actually a round saw blade that is rotated by the drill. Hole saws vary greatly in quality and price, and can be found in sizes up to 6″ in diameter. The larger sizes should be used in a more powerful $\frac{1}{2}''$ corded drill.

HOLE SAW

DRILL DIRECTION

Remember that drill bits are intended to cut only when the drill rotates in a forward, clockwise direction. If you notice that the drill bit you are using does not seem to be working at all well, check whether the motor reversing switch is set properly. It is difficult to see which way the chuck is spinning when the drill is operating at full speed, and it is easy to reset the switch without knowing it.

Belt sanders are the most aggressive type of power sander and do the most work in the least amount of time. An endless belt of sandpaper moves along on two revolving drums. A mechanism allows you to shift the two drums closer together to allow for belt changing. An adjustment knob makes very small changes in the alignment of the front drum in order to make the belt "track" properly. This alignment prevents the belt from running to the edge of the drums and coming off, and/ or from getting jammed against the other side. The sander must be running when the adjustment is made, and it is best to hold the tool upside down in order to see what affect the adjustments are having.

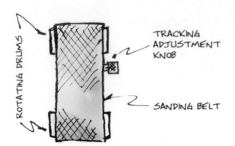

ROTATING DRUMS

TRACKING ADJUSTMENT KNOB

SANDING BELT

BOTTOM VIEW OF BELT SANDER

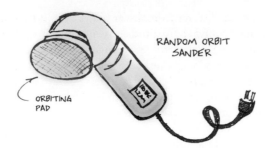

RANDOM ORBIT SANDER

ORBITING PAD

Sandpaper grits are an indication of how rough the paper is and how aggressively it will wear away any material you are sanding. A 40-grit belt is extremely rough and effective; 100-grit is more suitable for sanding smooth to a paintable surface. When using a belt sander, it is important to remember this rule of thumb: if you want to sand something so that it becomes flat, be sure to use the flat, bottom part of the sander. Move the tool around a lot while you are sanding, much like you might move a steam iron around while removing the wrinkles from fabric. The front end is rounded where the belt curves around the roller, and sanding with that part makes the work go really fast, but it is difficult to get a smooth surface. Sometimes you may wish to have an uneven surface, such as when distressing wood to make it look older and more worn. The rounded front part of the sander is perfect for that type of work.

ROUNDED END

THE FLAT SIDE IS BEST FOR SMOOTHING

BELT SANDER

At first glance a *random orbit sander* looks like it just spins in a circle, but in fact this sander has a system of gears that moves the sanding pad along a random path. They work amazingly well, especially on curved surfaces. They are very aggressive, but because the sanding pad moves in a random orbit rather than just spinning, it leaves no swirl marks behind. An ordinary orbital sander often leaves sanding marks that look a lot like the curved scrapes left behind by a circular saw blade. The random orbit sander is much easier to manipulate than a belt sander and can be used in tight situations. It is great for smoothing rounded corners.

A good *jigsaw* is an essential tool in any theatre shop, because of the preponderance of odd-shaped items that scenery work demands. Jigsaws use a "bayonet" type of blade. This is a flat piece of metal with sawteeth that is connected to the saw at one end. The jigsaw moves the blade up and down, thus creating the cutting action.

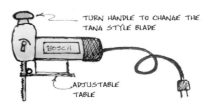

TURN HANDLE TO CHANGE THE TANG STYLE BLADE

BOSCH

ADJUSTABLE TABLE

JIGSAW

The best jigsaws have several features to look for that make them much easier to use than cheaper varieties. One of these is the *tang-style blade* that can be inserted into its holder and held in place by a set-screw from the very top. Some brands use a set-screw that is placed through a hole in the blade itself. This hole in the blade is of course a weak spot that can cause premature blade breakage. The tang-style blades are much easier to change.

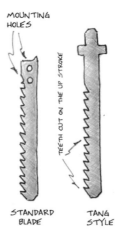

MOUNTING HOLES

TEETH CUT ON THE UP STROKE

STANDARD BLADE

TANG STYLE

JIGSAW BLADES

Another feature to look for is the ability to adjust the blade to kick outward as it travels up and down, leading to a much more aggressive cutting stroke. As with any saw blade, the more aggressive your cutting becomes, the more splintering—or tearout—will result. It is good to be able to adjust blade kick to a particular material and work situation.

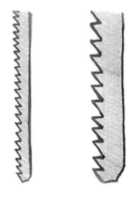

THE NARROW BLADE HAS A SMALLER TURNING RADIUS BUT IS MORE PRONE TO BREAKING THAN THE WIDER BLADE

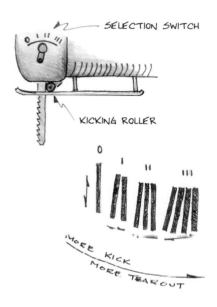

SELECTION SWITCH

KICKING ROLLER

MORE KICK
MORE TEAROUT

SELECT THE PROPER AMOUNT OF KICKING ACTION FOR YOUR JOB

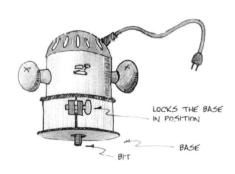

LOCKS THE BASE IN POSITION

BASE

BIT

PARTS OF A ROUTER

Jigsaws can be used to cut out curved and otherwise odd-shaped pieces. Because the blade is free at one end, it can be inserted into a hole drilled in the interior of a piece and then used to cut out a shape in the middle of it. There are many kinds of blades for different types of materials, such as wood, plastic, and metal. The size of the blade from front to back makes a great difference in the turning radius of the blade. Some jigsaw blades are very small from front to back, and this allows them to cut very tight curves. Of course, the smaller the blade, the more likely it is to break.

Routers are used to create a decorative edge along a piece of wood, and also to trim the outer edge of wood or plastic sheets, and especially (in theatre) the thin plywood covering a hard-cover flat. The basic moving parts are a very high-speed motor, a base that can be adjusted up and down, and a *collet*. The collet is similar to a drill chuck and is used to clamp router bits in position. Unlike drill bits, router bits are intended to cut from the side of the bit rather than from the end, as when drilling a hole. There are many different types of router bits that may be used to cut profiles along the edge of a piece of wood.

Routers have either a ¼″ or a ½″ collet. Some have two different interchangeable collets. Those sizes are meant to match up with the diameter of the shank portion of the router bit, which is the part that is fitted into the collet. Half-inch bits are generally more stable and give a better cut. The horsepower rating of a router is relative to the strength of the motor.

The *router base* is adjustable up and down, allowing the operator to extend a variable amount of the bit below the surface of the base. Only the portion of the bit that has been extended below the base will actually cut anything. Varying the amount of bit will alter the profile that can be cut.

A *flush-trim bit* is used to trim the edges of hard-cover flats or other scenic elements. A roller on the bottom of the bit means that it will trim the cover to the exact size of the underlying framing, negating the need to make hyper-accurate cuts for the cover.

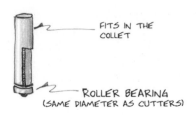

FITS IN THE
COLLET

ROLLER BEARING
(SAME DIAMETER AS CUTTERS)

FLUSH TRIM BIT

You can buy many different types of router bits to form decorative edges on wood trim. One of the simplest is the *round-over bit*, which is very popular in a scene shop. It is used to give wooden structures a finished appearance and to remove unwanted sharp and splinter-prone edges. The very similar *chamfer bit* does the same thing, but at a 45-degree angle instead. Remember that the bit represents the negative shape of the profile that will actually be created.

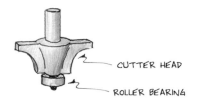

CUTTER HEAD

ROLLER BEARING

ROUND-OVER BIT

A hand-held *circular saw* is commonly called a Skil saw because the Skil Tool Company was an early manufacturer. (That seems to happen an awful lot.) Many other companies now manufacture what is generically called a *circular saw*, which does, in fact, use a circular blade very similar to that used on other, larger, shop saws. This blade is usually smaller, as the tool is intended to be guided by hand. There is much more information about circular blades in the next chapter.

THIS CIRCULAR SAW HAS A TABLE ON
THE BOTTOM. THE GUARD RAISES UP
AS YOU ENTER THE WORK

Most of the cutting in home building is done with a circular saw. In a theatre shop that is equipped with stationary cutting tools, this saw is not used as much, but it can still be very handy for cuts that are difficult to make on the larger tools. That most commonly occurs when making straight cuts in plywood that are not at a right angle to the edges, and/or when the sheet cannot be fed into the table saw for some other reason. Often, it is much easier to maneuver the saw through a large piece of work than to maneuver the work through a saw. You can find instructions for making a circular saw guide on the Web site. The guide is very useful for making more accurate long cuts in plywood.

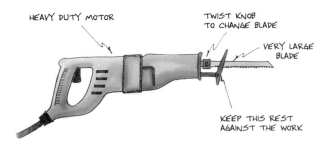

HEAVY DUTY MOTOR

TWIST KNOB
TO CHANGE BLADE

VERY LARGE
BLADE

KEEP THIS REST
AGAINST THE WORK

RECIPROCATING SAW

The Sawzall tool was named by the Milwaukee Electric Tool Company. It is generically known as a *reciprocating saw*. It is often more of an "anti-tool," because it is frequently used to tear scenery apart after the show is over with. The blade on a reciprocating saw is very much like a larger version of the jigsaw. A reciprocating saw is in its element when there are large, oddly shaped pieces to be dismembered in a hurry without much regard for accuracy. You can buy different types of blades to use on either metal or wood. The metal blades are especially nice for tearing apart scenery made from steel square tube.

PNEUMATICS

Some tools are work more efficiently when they are powered by compressed gas, and nailers/staplers definitely fit into this category. The pistons inside them are driven by the sudden release of air pressure from an outside source. They are connected to that source with a flexible hose. *Pneumatic* (meaning powered by air) tools require an air compressor. It is dangerous to use bottles of other compressed gases, especially the oxygen type used in some types of welding, but really any kind of compressed gas bottle.

There are several manufacturers of pneumatic guns, and each one produces equipment in its own style.

Although the guns are somewhat different in their specific mechanics, the basic concept of how they propel a fastener is the same.

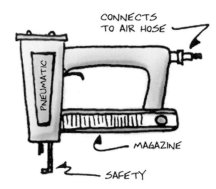

CONNECTS
TO AIR HOSE

PNEUMATIC

MAGAZINE

SAFETY

TYPICAL STAPLER

A piston inside the gun drives a shaft, which in turn forces a nail or staple down into the wood. Most guns are not intended to be used in metal or concrete, although one special type does in fact penetrate thin sheet metal. The nails are connected together either with glue, tape, or plastic retainers. There is generally some sort of *magazine* to fit the nails into, and that feeds them up to the driving piston.

The nails are fed through the magazine toward the drive shaft by means of a spring mechanism that creates a semiautomatic type of firing sequence. Both staplers and nail guns are equipped with a *safety* at the point where the nail or staple fires out of the gun. The safety must be pressed against a solid object in order to fire, preventing the user from accidentally shooting a nail into the air and possibly hitting another person. The safety is not entirely foolproof, and if it becomes bent or coated with glue it may stick in the fire position. So be careful not to leave your finger on the trigger when moving the gun around the shop. Of course, you should never stick anything into the linkage to purposely circumvent the safety.

A major cause of nail gun accidents occurs when a nail comes out the side of a board and strikes a finger.

This can be a common problem if you are holding two boards together and fail to shoot the nail in straight. Sometimes a nail will curve out the side when it strikes a dense area inside the board, and there is really no way to predict when that will happen. It is a good practice to avoid putting your fingers anywhere a nail could conceivably shoot out the side of your work. Because it is also common for carpenters to use their fingers to judge when joints are lined up properly, you should make it a habit to line up the joint, and then move your finger before firing.

Staplers and finish nailers typically set nails below the surface of the board, with the theory being that filler will later be used to make the point of entry invisible. When selecting a length of fastener to be used, it is important to take this fact into account. Pick a slightly shorter size to ensure that the nail does not come out the far side when you are holding the work. If your hand or leg or some other body part is in contact with the backside of the wood, a too-long nail will come through into your flesh. So it is a good idea to avoid putting any part of your body under the board.

NAILS CAN COME OUT THE
SIDE OF THE LUMBER

OUCH! BE CAREFUL!

Numerous other tips for the use of nail guns can be found in the chapters on construction.

CHAPTER 17

SAWS AND WOODWORKING

Constructing wooden scenery requires some excellent carpentry skills. Woodworking in the theatre has more in common with cabinet building than it does with most home construction like framing. Cabinet work is very exacting, and it results in freestanding units that are transported to the work site for installation. The cabinets are assembled inside an already existing structure, and have many moving parts. The framing structure of a house is stationary, and for the most part it really doesn't matter how heavy it is, or whether it can be moved. Scenery must be lightweight enough to at least move from the shop to the theatre, and quite often, from one theatre to another.

Scenery is built in parts, or units, that are later assembled in the theatre. Many times scenery must also be moved during a show—either hand-carried, rolled, or flown out on a rigging system. Moving the scenery around puts extra stress on its structure, which must be taken into account when the units are designed.

In truth, building scenery is not like any other type of construction work. Stage carpenters are called upon to build very complicated units within a very short time span. There are often requirements for "magic" tricks, like an actor who gets sucked into the floor, walls that fly out on cue, or a bed that folds up into a table. If you were to ask a house carpenter for a bridge that flies out of the way for Act II, you would most likely receive a blank stare in return. A theatre carpenter will ask how fast and how high.

STUDENTS RIPPING 1X
ON A TABLE SAW WITH A GUARD AND A DUST COLLECTION SYSTEM

doi: 10.1016/C2009-0-23409-X

TYPES OF JOINTS

You need to master many small techniques in order to become a proficient carpenter. You may wish to keep this book handy in the shop so that you can refer back to it as you go along. It would be difficult just to read through this material and jump right into carpentry work. An apprentice period of working in the shop is required in order for you to work safely and efficiently. There are dozens of different woodworking tools in most theatre shops. Some of them were mentioned in the previous chapter. The tools in this chapter are so commonly used and so complex that they deserve some special attention. Of special interest are the table saw, the radial arm saw, the power miter saw, and the band saw. This chapter also covers some general woodworking terms and practices.

Marking lumber and cutting it to size is an essential skill in any woodworking shop. Three main types of basic joinery cuts comprise the lion's share of woodworking. *Ripping* wood means cutting it along or with the grain. Because the grain in a piece of lumber generally runs along the length of the board, rip cuts tend to be very long. You might rip down some pieces of 1×12 lumber so that they become 1×3s instead. *Cross-cutting* is done across the grain, at a 90-degree angle. It is often associated with trimming boards to length. You might cut some random lengths of 1×3 down to a specific length like 9'-10½". *Miter cuts* are used to trim the ends of boards or molding to some angle other than 90 degrees. The most common of these would be a 45-degree angle cut, such as might be used to make a picture frame. There are many, many combinations and permutations of these types of cuts, but it seems helpful to begin with some way of organizing these different concepts to make them easier to remember. Curved cuts, such as can be done on a band saw, or using a jigsaw are also important.

There are some special names for the way that wooden parts fit together. When the end of one cross-cut board hits directly upon another one at a 90-degree angle they are said to be butting into one another, and if you nail them together like that, a *butt joint* is created.

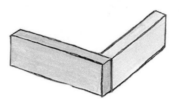

BUTT JOINT

If you connect two boards together so that their faces are overlapping one another, this creates a *lap joint*. If you cut away half of the material from either board so that the overlap then keeps the faces of the two boards on the same plane, you will have a *half lap*.

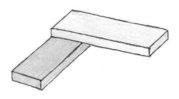

LAP JOINT

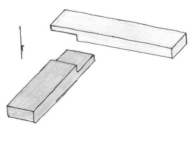

HALF LAP

Connecting two boards using a thin piece of plywood creates a *covered joint*.

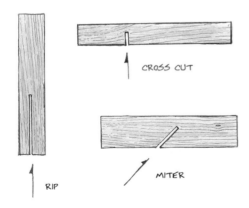

THREE TYPES OF CUTS

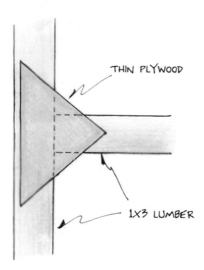

COVERED JOINT

often with painted scenery. *Joiner* is an archaic term for a carpenter. One of the mechanicals in Shakespeare's *Midsummer Night's Dream* is Snug the Joiner.

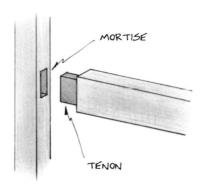

MORTISE AND TENON

If you lengthen a board by using another piece of the same material, and then join the two sections with a third piece, the covering piece is called a *scab*.

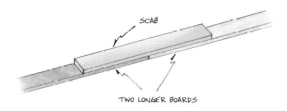

SCAB JOINT

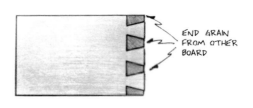

DOVETAIL

A *dado* is a slot cut into a piece of wood large enough so that another piece of wood can fit into it.

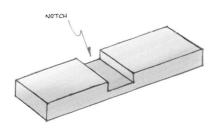

DADO CUT

There are lots of other joining techniques, such as mortise and tenon, dovetail, dowels, and finger joining. These joints are much more difficult to produce, and are typically reserved for furniture where the beauty of the joinery is meant to show. That doesn't happen too

CIRCULAR SAW BLADES

Just to be clear, it is the blade that is circular and not the saw. As the name indicates, a *circular saw blade* has a round shape with teeth located around the outside edge. This type of blade cuts when it is rotated at a high speed and the teeth are pressed against the wood you are cutting. They are used in many different types of saws. Circular saw blades are sized according to their diameter in inches, so a 10-inch blade is therefore 10 inches in diameter. The hole in the center is used to connect the blade to the saw. The post on the saw that it fits onto is called an *arbor*. Most blades have either a ⅝″ or a 1″ arbor hole that corresponds to a specific saw, which has an arbor one of those sizes.

Small teeth on a circular saw blade result in a finer cut with less *tearout*. Tearout is the splintering that occurs in wood as the blade passes through it. Blades with large teeth are commonly referred to as *ripping blades*, and those with smaller teeth as *cross-cutting blades*. Larger teeth are fine when ripping lumber, because the wood is less likely to splinter when it is cut with the grain. Larger teeth are more aggressive and better suited to making the long cuts that are associated with rip sawing.

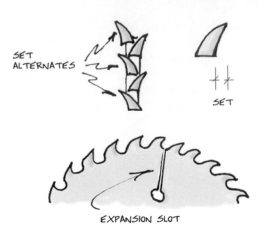

SET ALTERNATES

SET

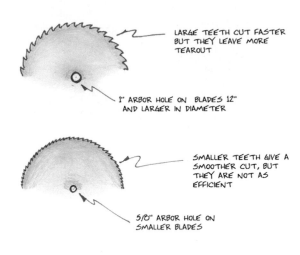

LARGE TEETH CUT FASTER BUT THEY LEAVE MORE TEAROUT

1" ARBOR HOLE ON BLADES 12" AND LARGER IN DIAMETER

SMALLER TEETH GIVE A SMOOTHER CUT, BUT THEY ARE NOT AS EFFICIENT

5/8" ARBOR HOLE ON SMALLER BLADES

CIRCULAR SAW BLADES

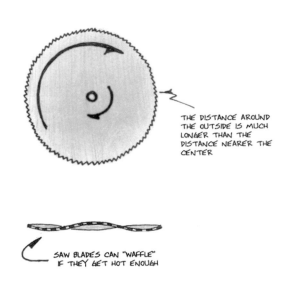

EXPANSION SLOT

SET IN A SAWTOOTH

THE DISTANCE AROUND THE OUTSIDE IS MUCH LONGER THAN THE DISTANCE NEARER THE CENTER

Sawteeth are either the traditional type that are an integral part of the blade, or are built with tips made from carbide steel. Traditional blades require that the sawteeth be slightly bent over at the tip. This is known as *set* in the blade and is a very important part of how the blade works. We are all aware that friction causes heat, and if there is any doubt, rubbing your hands together rapidly will prove the point. When a circular saw blade is spinning at high speed (which it must do in order to cut), a great deal of heat is generated by the blade rubbing against the piece of wood that it is cutting. Set in the blade teeth is used to minimize this friction by separating the wood from the body of the blade by a slight amount. Sawteeth are bent to the side in an alternating pattern, first to one side and then to the other. Because it is really the tips of the teeth that do all of the cutting, setting the teeth will ensure that the pathway that they cut through the board is a small amount larger than the body of the blade. This reduces friction and heat.

If the body of the blade gets too hot, it tends to warp out of shape. This happens because the circumference of the outside part of the blade is much larger than the circumference of any interior part of the blade. As the blade expands and warps, more friction is created and the heat buildup gets worse. Some blades have slots cut into them in several places around the outside circumference so that the blade can heat up and expand a bit without deforming.

SAW BLADES CAN "WAFFLE" IF THEY GET HOT ENOUGH

HEAT CAUSES EXPANSION OF THE BLADE

The pathway cut through the wood by the blade is called the *kerf*, and that part of the wood is reduced to sawdust in the cutting process. If you were to cut halfway through a plank and then stop, the kerf is the leftover slot in the wood. The kerf disappears when you have finished cutting, just like your lap disappears when you stand up.

KERF

In recent years, circular saw blades have become increasingly high-tech as advances in technology have made it possible to manufacture them with ever increasing precision. Computer-controlled lasers and water jets can cut very complex shapes in tool steel that were not possible with older stamping methods. Also, you may have noticed that some blades have teeth that are not bent at the tips, but rather seem to have an entirely different piece of metal attached at that point. These blades are known as *carbide blades*, because tungsten carbide is used to make the blade tips. Tungsten carbide is an extremely hard and durable metal alloy.

THIS TOOL MEASURES HARDNESS BY PRESSING A POINT INTO THE STEEL AT A CERTAIN PRESSURE, AND THEN MEASURING THE SIZE OF THE INDENTATION

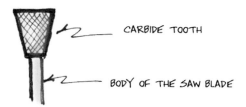

CARBIDE TOOTH

BODY OF THE SAW BLADE

The Rockwell Scale lists the density or hardness of a variety of different types of steel alloys. They are not all the same, but rather have been created specifically because they have different properties. It is axiomatic that the harder something is, the more brittle it is. Tungsten carbide, being very dense and hard, can be honed to an incredible sharpness and can retain that edge for a very long time. Those are excellent qualities for a sawtooth. Conversely, this material is brittle and quite easy to shatter, which is not a quality you would ask for in a large chunk of metal spinning at high speed. As a result, manufacturers design blades with the carbide alloy used only in small amounts that are welded onto the tips of the teeth, like caps.

The body of the blade is composed of regular *tool steel* that is much more malleable. In this way, each part of the blade is made from the ideal material for that part. Carbide teeth are often ground into very advanced shapes at the factory, and these enhance their cutting abilities. They do not have set in the traditional sense, but rather each of the carbide tips projects to both the left and right sides.

One drawback to carbide blades is that they are often impossible to sharpen effectively, because of the intricate nature of the shape of the teeth. The greatly increased efficiency of these blades more than offsets the added expense. They stay sharp much longer than an ordinary blade.

Although circular saw blades have been mentioned specifically, the concept of set in the teeth and the way a kerf is formed is true of all types of blades.

THE RELATIVE HARDNESS OF TUNGSTEN CARBIDE IS A ROCKWELL C SCALE NUMBER OF ABOUT 72, WHICH IS NOT MUCH LOWER THAN A DIAMOND. THE HARDNESS OF TOOL STEEL LIKE YOU WOULD FIND IN THE BODY OF A SAW BLADE IS IN THE 50s, AND MILD STEEL LIKE THAT FOUND IN SQUARE TUBE FOR SCENERY BUILDING IS IN THE 10 TO 20 RANGE.

THE TABLE SAW

The *table saw* gets its name from its basic shape, which does indeed resemble a small table. The horizontal metal surface is referred to as the "table," and is the most easily recognized feature. Another important part is the *rip fence* or guide. This is the metal and/or wooden structure that runs from the front of the saw to the back and is adjustable as to its distance from the saw blade.

The table saw uses a circular saw blade that is engineered to run parallel to the rip fence. As you may have already realized because of the rip fence, the table saw is most commonly used to rip lumber or plywood to a specific width. Basically, this involves taking long boards or sheets of plywood and feeding them through the saw to create long, thin strips of material, such as a 1×3.

There are several adjustable features on any table saw. These are the rip fence, the angle of the blade as it intersects the table, and the height of the blade above the top of the table. There are wheels or knobs of some sort on the front and/or side of the saw that operate the blade-moving mechanisms. The specific workings of a table saw differ from one manufacturer to another, but these features are a standard requirement of any table saw.

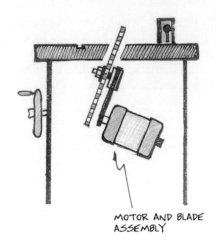

MOTOR AND BLADE ASSEMBLY

TILTING THE BLADE FOR AN ANGLED CUT

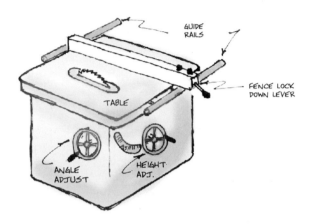

PARTS OF A TABLE SAW

It is important to be able to raise and lower the blade so that materials of varying thicknesses may be cut. It would be quite dangerous to leave the blade extended to its full height at all times. The normal rule of thumb is to set the blade to rise above the work about half an inch or so, enough to cut efficiently, but not so much as to be an undue hazard.

The rip fence is the most commonly adjusted feature of the table saw. The fence determines the size or width of the material being ripped. The distance is set by measuring between the face of the fence and the saw blade. Many shops add a better surface to the rip fence than was supplied by the manufacturer. Generally this involves some sort of plastic material that is slick, but will not wear away too soon. A low-friction material makes it easier to feed the wood through the saw.

ONLY LEAVE ABOUT 1/2" OF BLADE EXPOSED ABOVE THE WORK

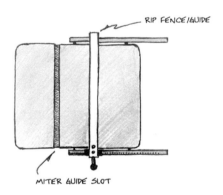

RIP FENCE/GUIDE

MITER GUIDE SLOT

SLOT AND FENCE SHOULD BE PARALLEL

Some types of cuts will work only if the saw blade does *not* cut all the way through the work, and you must carefully measure how much is sticking up from the table.

The blade can be angled to produce a beveled edge along the side of a ripped board.

The standard fence has an adjustment feature that allows you to realign it so that it remains perfectly parallel with the blade. If the blade and fence are not true, it is very difficult to feed work through the saw. A stable and secure rip fence is really important on a table saw. Aftermarket products are available to enhance the performance of most saws.

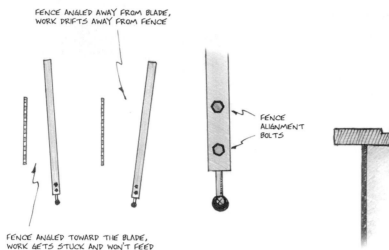

FENCE ANGLED AWAY FROM BLADE,
WORK DRIFTS AWAY FROM FENCE

FENCE ALIGNMENT BOLTS

FENCE ANGLED TOWARD THE BLADE,
WORK GETS STUCK AND WON'T FEED

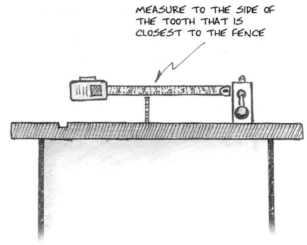

MEASURE TO THE SIDE OF
THE TOOTH THAT IS
CLOSEST TO THE FENCE

RIP FENCE ADJUSTMENTS

It is important to use a guard on your table saw. On newer equipment, the saw has been engineered so that the guard is attached to the motor rotation shaft, and a thin metal plate extends upward to the table. When wood is ripped on this type of saw, the metal plate holding the guard is aligned with the kerf coming out of the saw. Wood passes on either side of the plate. On older models, a guard extends from the back and fits on both sides of the blade. One problem with this type of guard is that it tends to obstruct the passage of large sheets of plywood when they are being ripped on the saw. Sometimes there is an arm that extends from the ceiling or wall, and the guard rests on that and the guard is not so much in the way. No matter what type of guard is used, remember that it makes the saw only *safer*, not completely *safe*, and that you need to be very alert at all times when using power tools.

With most types of woodworking equipment, the material being cut is marked in some way, and then the cutting tool is aligned with that mark in order to make the cut. The table saw is different.

With the table saw, the fence is adjusted to a specific point. When the cut is made, the gap between the fence and the blade determines the size of the finished product. In order to be precise, you measure between the fence and the part of the blade that is closest to the fence. You can use an ordinary tape measure for this.

Put the hook up against the fence and move both the fence and tape until the correct distance reads against the blade tooth. If you check the discussion of blade tooth set, you will realize that the closest point will be either the extreme edge of one of the carbide teeth or one of the teeth that has its set bent in the direction of the rip fence. If you measure to the middle of the blade instead, the resulting rip will be too narrow

by half the width of the saw kerf. If you measure to the far side of the blade, the rip will be too narrow by the width of the entire kerf, most likely about $\frac{1}{8}''$. In woodworking, $\frac{1}{8}''$ is quite a bit, and anything you build so sloppily will be rather poorly done.

Most saws have some sort of built-in measuring device. If yours is properly calibrated, it will work just fine, but if you are unsure about that, the measuring technique just mentioned can be used to double-check. Measure the distance with a tape and then compare your findings to the distance listed on the saw. If you change the blade, you may need to recalibrate the built-in device if the replacement blade has a significantly different set to its teeth.

When ripping material on the table saw, you should begin by standing in front of the saw with your feet a comfortable distance apart. Most saws are set up for a right-handed person, and the fence is to the right of the blade. Stand to the left side of the board you are ripping. It is very important to keep the work firmly planted against the fence as you pass it through the saw. If it drifts a way, the result will be too narrow. Also, drifting away from the fence increases the chance of a kickback. When the board is fed through far enough to reach the far side of the saw table, your partner can pull it on through the saw. It is best to work with a partner until you have had enough experience and guidance to be safe and confident in your use of the saw.

USING A PUSH STICK

STAND ON THE LEFT, SO THAT YOU CAN
SEE THE WORK AGAINST THE FENCE

It is a good practice to use a push stick to help feed the work through the saw, and this is always true when the piece you are cutting is small and brings you too close to the blade. Be sure to use any guards and/or hold downs that are required for your particular tool.

Using the table saw should not require a great deal of strength, but rather is more of a balancing act, especially when the work is deftly fed through a well-maintained saw. If there is a great deal of resistance to the work passing through the saw, you should check to see whether the fence is in proper alignment to the blade, whether the blade is in good condition, and whether you have properly held the board against the rip fence.

Most table saws have a slot milled into the top of the table that allows for the passage of a *miter guide*. This is sometimes referred to as a T-square. The miter guide slides back and forth in the slot and can be used to cross cut and/or make miter cuts. This is a somewhat cumbersome undertaking, and it will work only for relatively short boards. Longer pieces are much more easily cut on the radial arm saw.

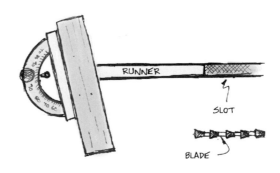

MITER GUIDE

Tool manufacturers like to make their products do as many different jobs as possible so that they are more attractive to buyers. Just because it is possible does not mean that it is particularly safe or efficient.

The saw blade arbor should be aligned with the table at the factory or when you initially set up the tool, and it will rarely need adjustment. The rip fence is a different matter. You can use the miter guide slot to check the alignment of the fence to the blade by sliding the fence next to the slot and seeing whether the two are parallel. If they are not, then adjust the fence so that it matches the slot. In reality, you may find that the saw is easier to use if there is just a tad more room at the side of the blade away from the front. This allows the work to pass through more easily. If the blade is not parallel to the table, consult the manufacturer's instructions about truing up the blade.

Some shops install an auxiliary table around the saw's own table so that it is easier to cut large pieces of plywood. In this way, you can cut through a section of plywood without worrying about the scrap part sagging and hitting the floor. This auxiliary table will use up a great deal of floor space and may not be appropriate for all shops.

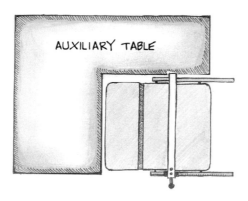

AUXILIARY TABLE

RADIAL ARM SAW

The *radial arm saw* is sometimes known as a bench saw or overhead arm saw. The three different names taken together are actually a good description of how this saw works. The radial arm saw is best suited to cross-cutting long pieces of lumber such as 2×4s or 1×3s. Usually, the saw itself is fitted with a long table or bench that

extends to either side of the saw. It is used to support the length of the boards being cut. The actual motor and saw blade are mounted on an overhead arm, which allows that assembly to roll back and forth when pulled over the bench holding the piece you are cutting. The overhead arm can be pivoted radially from a point in the back of the saw in order to make miter cuts.

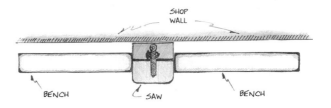

PLAN VIEW OF A RADIAL ARM SAW

The surface of the cutting table that comes with the saw is made from plywood or particle board, because it is necessary for the blade to cut slightly into this surface in order to cut all the way through your work. Toward the rear of the table is a fence that is used to align the *work* (material being cut). The track of the saw blade is at a right angle to the fence. The wooden fence will most likely need to be changed once a week or even more frequently if the saw gets heavy use. Changing the fence is an easy thing to do, and it will increase the accuracy of your cuts. A badly cut-up fence can also be a safety hazard.

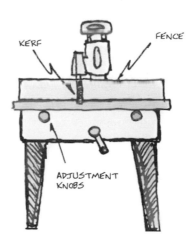

RADIAL ARM SAW

A pair of clamps on the bottom of a radial arm saw is used to easily remove and replace the rear fence. Make a new fence from a section of 1×3 or 1×4, whose length is cut to the width of the saw table. It is an easy matter to remove the old fence and put in the new using the clamps.

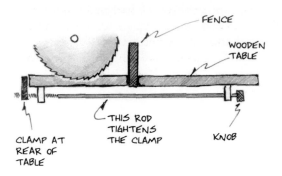

SIDE VIEW OF CLAMPING MECHANISM

A crank in front of the saw is used to raise and lower the blade. The blade should be lowered far enough into the table so that it cuts all the way through the wood, but not so far as to cut too deeply into the table. You must raise and lower the saw motor/blade assembly when changing blades, and also if you need to change the angle of the blade for a miter cut.

The "radial" part of the saw name refers to the way this saw can be adjusted to rotate to an angle other than 90 degrees. On most saws, a locking mechanism disengages to allow the operator to turn the arm to any point up to 45 degrees. This would by definition be a miter cut rather than a cross cut. The mechanism is different on various machines, but the basic principle is the same. There should be some kind of marking dial that will let you know the precise number of degrees the arm has been pivoted to.

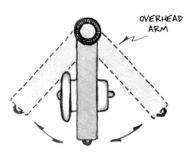

SAW ARM PIVOTS

Some saws allow the user to also turn the motor and blade assembly to an angle other than vertical. When both of the pivoting features are used in conjunction with one another, the resulting cut is known as a *double miter*. Naturally, these types of cuts take a toll

on the wooden fence and table. Each new angle will leave a new cut mark in the fence and on the wooden surface of the table, and will require frequent replacement if you do it often.

The most common size radial arm saw is the 10-inch, meaning that the blade is 10 inches in diameter, but it is possible to buy an industrial model that is 12, 14, or even 18 inches in diameter. Up to a point, the larger and heavier a saw is, the more stable it is. That is a good thing when you leave the arm set at 90 degrees to the fence, but readjusting a 14-inch saw to various angles can be a real bear—not to mention that the large table is somewhat difficult to replace. Rather than use this saw for making miter cuts, you may consider a comparatively inexpensive power miter saw to cut small trim pieces. A power miter saw is designed specifically for the purpose of cutting angles and is much more efficient at it. If the pieces you have to cut are really wide, you may have to use the radial arm saw.

The radial arm saw is at its best when there is a table or bench on both sides of the saw. The tables support the length of lumber that you are cutting. In the ideal situation, it is best to have an entire 16 feet on both sides of the saw. The longest commonly found lumber is 16 feet long, and a table that size on both sides will give you complete flexibility in cutting. If that is not possible, most right-handed carpenters like to have a longer bench on the left-hand side.

Some carpenters use a jig along the bench that has been marked with measurements back to the blade. That allows them to line the end of the board up with preset marks and avoid having to measure with a tape each time. If you are working in a shop with many other people with varying skill levels, it may be difficult to keep a jig like that properly calibrated. Your shop probably has its own policy set, and you can just follow those guidelines.

MEASURING JIG ON A RADIAL ARM SAW

Before cutting a piece of dimension lumber to length, you should trim one of the ends of the board so that it is perfectly square and even at that end. Most sawmill lumber is cut to only an approximate length, and the mill workers are not known for using the utmost care in trimming the ends.

Typically, boards are about half an inch longer than the stated amount and cut at a small angle. There are often cracks at one the end of a piece of lumber that are caused by the board drying out more at the end while banded together in a unit. This very common defect is known as *checking*. Trimming the end will get rid of this also.

TRIM THE END OF A BOARD
TO STRAIGHTEN IT AND
REMOVE CHECKING

After trimming one end, you may need to flip the board around to get to the opposite one. If there is enough room on the bench, slide the board to the other side of the saw blade. Use a tape measure to mark the length of the cut. Take care to measure the board along one side rather than diagonally. This is all the more important on wider boards, for which the diagonal will cause your measurement to be much shorter than it should be.

DON'T MEASURE AT AN ANGLE, OR THE BOARD
WILL BE SHORTER THAN YOU THOUGHT

Mark the cutting spot as close to the edge of the board as possible so that the mark will be easy to align with the blade. For the utmost in accuracy, make a tiny

pencil dot on the very corner of the board, and then enlarge the mark by making a "V" with the dot being the apex. This V mark is sometimes called a *crow's foot*, and it is used by all types of carpenters to mark the exact placement of a cut. The dot by itself would be difficult to find. A line on the board can be misleading if it is not exactly straight, and you are unsure which part is the true length. The point of a V mark is unambiguous.

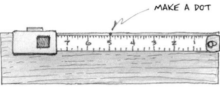

THE SMALLER THE DOT, THE MORE EXACT
THE MEASUREMENT WILL BE

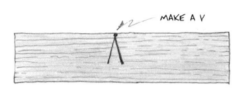

MEASURING A BOARD

A new fence on the saw will make easy to line your cut mark up with the blade, because the kerf in the fence will be exactly the same size as the blade. Therefore you need only to line the V mark up with the proper side of the kerf. Once you have had occasion to cut several hundred flat framing parts from a giant cut list, you will appreciate how easy it is to line the mark up to the fence when there is a clean setup. Over time, vibration from the saw motor, and just general wear and tear will cause the kerf in the fence to become larger and less accurate.

One of the most commonly made errors in using the radial arm saw is lining the board up with the wrong part of the kerf. Let us say that you have marked a board to be cut to 1'-0". You have made your tiny dot close to the edge, and then made the dot into a V. You have marked the board from the right-hand side, so as a result, the portion of the board you want to keep is to your right. To which part of the fence kerf should you align the cut mark, the left side, the center, or the right side?

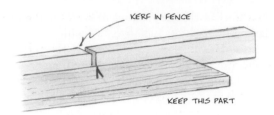

LINE THE V UP WITH THE
PROPER SIDE OF THE KERF

The answer is found by considering what happens when the blade cuts through the wood. The blade is not like a knife, which would merely part the two sections without a reduction in the overall amount of material. The blade cutting through the wood creates a kerf, and reduces a portion of it to sawdust. For all practical purposes, it simply ceases to exist. You must not allow any part of the kerf line space to occupy any part of the board you want to keep. After all, you have gone to great lengths to ensure that the measurement you made was very exacting. If the measurement is exact and you later shorten the piece with the saw blade, then by definition it cannot be the right size.

Align the cut mark with the kerf so that none of the "keeper" is lost. If your keeper board is to the right side of the fence kerf, then you should line the V mark up with the right side of that kerf. If, on the other hand, the keeper piece were on the left-hand side, then you would need to line the V mark up with the left side of the fence kerf. The center of the kerf is never an option.

It is often necessary to cut a number of short pieces from the same board. It would be tempting to simply measure all of the pieces at one time down the length of the board, and cut them all at once. This method does *not* work, because it does not allow for the passage of the saw blade and the creation of the kerf. Measuring that way will cause each succeeding section to be just a little bit smaller than it should be, about the same width as the blade.

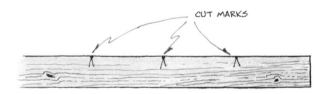

IF YOU MAKE A SERIES OF CUT MARKS
ALL AT THE SAME TIME
EACH PIECE WILL BE TOO SMALL

A good method of cutting a large number of same size multiples is to use a *stop block*. This is a small block

of wood clamped to the fence of the radial arm saw. First mark a board in the usual manner, and place your mark up against the fence as you normally would, but do not cut it yet. Take a scrap piece of lumber and clamp it to the fence in the appropriate place so that it is just at the end of the keeper piece. You can cut your first piece and a virtually unlimited number of others without measuring again. Gently slide the raw stock over against the stop block and cut each piece in turn. If the board that you are cutting the parts from is large, and you bang it into the stop block very hard, the block will move from its intended position. A Vise Grip clamp is excellent for holding the stop block, because it is so easy to operate. It is a good idea to spot check the size of the completed parts with a tape measure. The only thing worse than cutting a board to the wrong length is cutting a hundred of them to the wrong length.

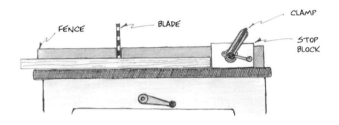

USING A STOP BLOCK

Care must be taken when using a stop block that parts do not get trapped between the blade and the block and get kicked back. This can happen when the already cut piece gets loose and turns at an angle. Of course, when the piece is at an angle, the length is increased on the diagonal, and it will tend to become jammed at first and then thrown clear by the spinning blade. This tends to be more of a problem with small pieces. You can lessen the problem by cutting the stop block at an angle to the work, so that only the point is touching.

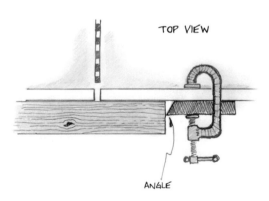

LEAVE AN ANGLE ON THE STOP BLOCK
TO MAKE IT WORK BETTER

However you have measured your cut, the method of actually sawing the board is the same. Make sure that none of your fingers is in the path of the blade as it crosses the table, firmly press the board against the fence, and steadily draw the saw across the board until it is completely cut through. The speed at which material is fed into a tool is known as the *feed rate*. It will take a bit of practice to learn the exact feed rate for any particular saw, but here is a rule of thumb. If the motor becomes bogged down and slows, you are cutting too fast. If there is excessive smoking from the blade, you are most likely going too slowly, and the rubbing of the blade in the same location is resulting in excessive heat buildup. (Of course, the latter might also be an indication that the blade is dull and should be changed and/or sharpened.) Do not pull the blade much farther toward you than is necessary to cut the board, as doing so will greatly increase the possibility of a kickback. Most saws have an automatic return spring that pulls the blade and motor rearward to its resting position. It is much kinder to the equipment to gently return the saw to its starting position than to allow the spring to slam it back there.

There are several different types of anti-kickback devices manufactured for radial arm saws. Be sure to read the manufacturer's safety instructions for the particular saw you are using.

THE POWER MITER SAW

Sometimes this tool is known as a *power miter box*. That is because it was developed from an earlier, nonpowered tool. Like many names, this one came about over a period of time and has been expanded to reflect changes in technology. *Miter boxes* have been around for thousands of years and were originally intended to be used with a handsaw. They consist of a wooden box with saw kerfs at common miter angles.

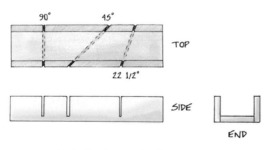

OLD WOODEN MITER BOX

A section of wood trim is placed inside the box, and a saw is used to cut the trim along the same lines as the

preexisting kerf. The saw blade is held true to the desired angle by the wood surrounding the kerf.

Although this type of low-tech solution is inexpensive and straightforward, it is also not terribly effective. It is difficult to secure the trim inside the box. Using a handsaw is, of course, slow and difficult when compared to a modern power saw. The miter box is limited to a small number of predetermined angles, and as such is not very flexible. Theatre work requires the use of many odd angles, much more so than ordinary home construction, in which right angles are generally interrupted only by the occasional 45-degree angle. Theatre settings abound with odd shapes, raked stages, and other such interesting-looking but difficult to build structures.

The power *miter saw* is easily and quickly adjustable to any angle up to 45+ degrees. It has a fence in the back that may be used in the same way as the fence on a radial arm saw. Naturally, the electric motor makes the actual cutting quite easy to do. Most saws are capable of adjusting not only to miter to one side or the other, but also on the opposing axis, making it possible to double miter. Nominally, the maximum number of degrees is 45. But most saws actually go to 46 or 47 so that you can cut angles to fit corners that aren't exactly square.

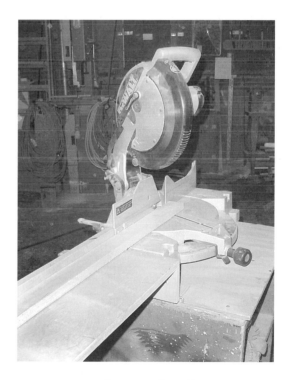

POWER MITER SAW

A power miter saw usually operates by pivoting from the rear. The blade goes through a slot in the surface when cutting, and the entire table, motor, and blade assembly rotates when changing the angle, making a consumable wooden top unnecessary. Most have a degree marker in front to use in adjusting the saw. The rotation mechanism itself has automatic stops at 90, 45, and 22½ degrees, because these are the most commonly used angles. When aligning a cut mark, you must bring the blade down so that it is almost touching the wood, as there is no kerf in the fence to use as a reference point. Because there is no kerf in the fence to line up the cut, and because the blade comes down in the middle of the work, it is really better to mark the wood in the middle rather than on the edge, but that only works for a cross cut at 90 degrees. Some newer saws have a laser light that comes on to illuminate a line along which the blade will cut. This light may therefore be used to line up the cut.

Rather than having a hinge point, some miter saws slide along two bars when you are making a cut. The method for aligning one of these saws is more like you would expect on a radial arm saw.

Be very careful when using a power miter saw. There is a great temptation to hold on to pieces that are too small. Don't do that. Instead, use a large section of trim, cut the desired angle on the end, and then cut the other angle while holding onto the large leftover section. This way, your hand will not come so near the blade.

HELPFUL HINTS FOR CUTTING ANGLES

When joining two angled pieces together so that the mitered ends match, the two ends must be cut to the same number of degrees in order for them to fit together properly. If the overall angle is 90 degrees, the angle of each member should be 45 degrees. If the overall angle is 60 degrees, each individual piece should have an angle of 30 degrees. If the angles of the two boards are not the same, the beveled ends will be different sizes and the mismatch will be noticeable.

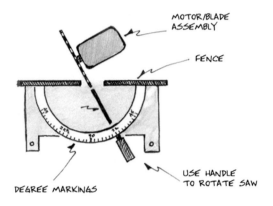

CHANGING THE ANGLE ON A
MITER SAW

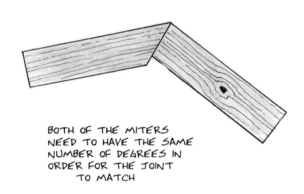

BOTH OF THE MITERS
NEED TO HAVE THE SAME
NUMBER OF DEGREES IN
ORDER FOR THE JOINT
TO MATCH

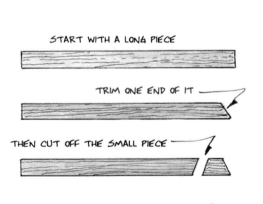

START WITH A LONG PIECE

TRIM ONE END OF IT

THEN CUT OFF THE SMALL PIECE

SAFELY CUTTING SMALL PIECES
ON A POWER MITER SAW

Cutting angles confuses many people. You may find it difficult to decide how to measure an angle, and from which point. In reality, there are a few simple rules to follow that will make the entire process clear, or at least translucent. But first, a bit of geometry review.

A rudimentary knowledge of geometry can save time when working with odd shapes. An understanding of how *complementary* and *supplementary* angles interact will make it clear how many angles in a construction problem are actually the same. Look at the trapezoidal structure. Assume that the shape is regular, and that the left side is the mirror image of the right side. The top and bottom lines are parallel to one another. If you are given the span of just one angle, you can determine all the others by using simple geometry.

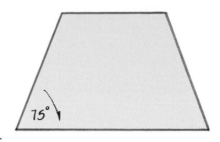

TRAPEZOID WITH EQUAL SIDES
AND A PARALLEL TOP AND BOTTOM

All of the angles in the trapezoid have been described from a starting point of just one.

Angles such as those shown here are often greater than 45 degrees, and it has already been stated that most power miter saws will not cut an angle greater than 45 degrees. Neither will most radial arm saws or table saw miter guides. The secret is that you are usually not really cutting the larger number of degrees, but rather the smaller complement of the angle.

The next drawing shows how supplementary angles are derived from the one angle that was originally given.

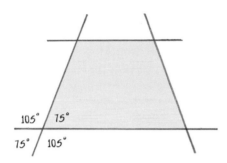

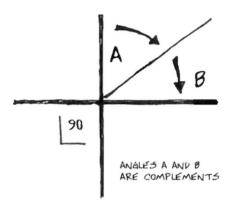

ANGLES A AND B
ARE COMPLEMENTS

Develop the concept further until the angles of the bottom are extended to the top left. Remember that the top and bottom sides of the trapezoid are parallel to one another.

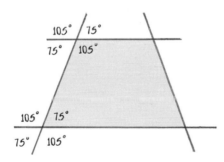

Note that the complement of an angle is the angle that when added to the original angle, adds up to 90 degrees. In the present case, an angle of 75 degrees on the drawing is actually the complement of the true angle of 15 degrees. The complementary angle is used because the trapezoid drawing shows an angle measured from one *side*, whereas the degree markings on your miter saw are measured from the *end* of the board. The saw is set up so that it is operating from a starting point that is already at a right angle to the length of the section of lumber you are about to cut.

If the left and right sides are mirror images of one another, angles for both sides are inferred to be the same.

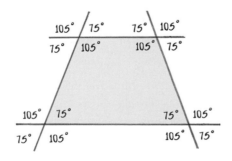

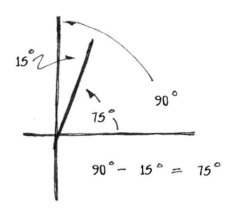

Mistakes occur. If you have determined an angle and it does not fit, the simplest thing to try next is to subtract the angle you have from 90 degrees and try again. This trick quite often works when you become confused; at least, it works for me when I do. Subtracting from 90 degrees will give you the number of degrees in the complementary angle.

It is not unusual to receive drawings that have no degree markings at all, but rather size dimensions only. There is an easy method of marking angles without knowing what the angle degrees actually are.

First, lay out a pattern of the perimeter of the shape. This may well occur as a natural consequence of laying out the platform top or some other construction. If not, you can draw the shape on a large piece of paper, or on the floor. There is a lengthy discussion of this technique in Chapter 22.

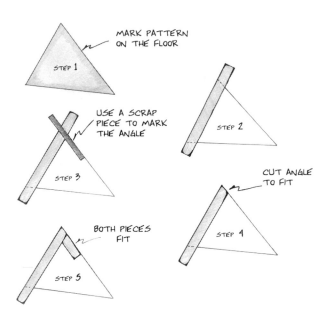

HOW TO MARK AN ANGLE
WITHOUT KNOWING THE DEGREES

Lay a length of lumber along the edge of one of the lines of the full-scale pattern you have drawn. Mark the end of it with a pencil by holding a section of scrap along the intersecting line. Take this marked piece to the power miter saw and align the saw blade with the pencil mark you've made. If you cut the board and save both parts, you can lay them in place on your pattern and see if they fit. This is a very expedient method of working with angles, and much faster than using a protractor or bevel gauge. You may never need to know the number of degrees for any of the angles, but if you do, you can read them off the gauge on the saw itself. This method is very accurate, because it uses a proportionally large scale to figure the angles. A full-scale

pattern is 24 times larger than a half-inch scale drawing.

CUTTING CROWN MOLDING

One of the most common jobs done on a miter saw is cutting moldings. The most challenging of these is *crown molding*, because of the way that type fits in the corner of the ceiling at an angle.

IN A HOUSE, CROWN MOLDING GOES IN THE CORNER BETWEEN THE WALLS AND CEILING. ON A STAGE SET THERE GENERALLY ISN'T A CEILING, SO THE MOLDING IS ATTACHED ONLY TO THE WALL. IN THIS PICTURE, THE CROWN MOLDING HAS BEEN INSTALLED AND FILLED WITH LATEX CAULK - READY FOR PAINTING. A SEPARATE TRIM PIECE LIES BELOW THE CROWN.

If crown molding were solid, it would be much easier to visualize how to make it fit on the wall. But to save material, the molding is milled so that there is an open space in the corner where no one can see it. On the back of the crown are two small flat surfaces: one that touches the wall, and one that touches the ceiling. Between them is a larger flat surface that connects them. The larger flat surface is the edge of the part that is open.

Most stage settings don't have a ceiling, and the crown molding is only attached to a wall, which is not a very stable arrangement. You can improve the stability by adding a nailing strip across the top of the wall.

Crown moldings don't fit the wall at a 45-degree angle like you might think they would. Instead, the lower part extends farther down onto the wall than the top part does onto the ceiling. The bottom of the molding has the outward sticking part of the ogee curve, and often has an extra detail as well and needs to be

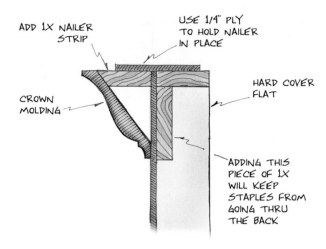

ADD 1X NAILER STRIP

USE 1/4" PLY TO HOLD NAILER IN PLACE

HARD COVER FLAT

CROWN MOLDING

ADDING THIS PIECE OF 1X WILL KEEP STAPLES FROM GOING THRU THE BACK

IT'S POSSIBLE TO SIMPLY STAPLE THE TRIM TO THE TOP OF A GROUP OF FLATS, BUT THE CONNECTION ISN'T VERY STRONG. THIS METHOD SUPPORTS THE CROWN MOLDING BETTER.

longer for aesthetic reasons. It is important to know which way the molding should hang.

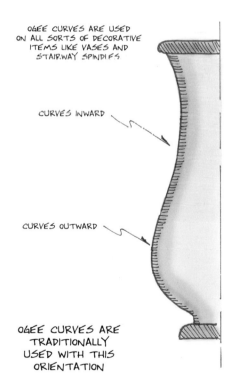

OGEE CURVES ARE USED ON ALL SORTS OF DECORATIVE ITEMS LIKE VASES AND STAIRWAY SPINDLES

CURVES INWARD

CURVES OUTWARD

OGEE CURVES ARE TRADITIONALLY USED WITH THIS ORIENTATION

The molding fits together at one of two basic angles—an inside corner or an outside corner. On an inside corner, the bottom of the trim meets the corner, but on the outside the top will actually extend farther

than the corner itself to a point where it meets another piece of trim on the continuing wall.

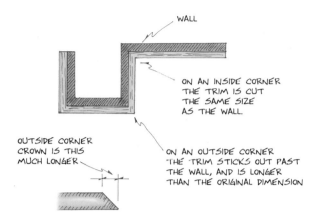

INSIDE AND OUTSIDE CORNERS FIT DIFFERENTLY

WALL

ON AN INSIDE CORNER THE TRIM IS CUT THE SAME SIZE AS THE WALL.

OUTSIDE CORNER CROWN IS THIS MUCH LONGER

ON AN OUTSIDE CORNER THE TRIM STICKS OUT PAST THE WALL, AND IS LONGER THAN THE ORIGINAL DIMENSION

IT IS MUCH EASIER TO MARK THE SECTIONS OF MOLDING BY HOLDING THEM UP TO THE WALL AND MARKING THEM, THAN BY MEASURING THE WALL AND THEN MARKING THE TRIM.

CUT AN INSIDE CORNER FIRST SO THAT THE TRIM WILL FIT AGAINST THE WALL, AND THEN MARK YOUR CUT FOR THE OUTSIDE CORNER.

It is best to cut the inside corner angle first and then measure the length of the trim by holding it up to the wall. Carefully place the molding on the miter saw so that it is at the same angle it will later take on the wall. Pretend that the saw fence is the wall, and that the table is the ceiling. *The trim is upside down from where it will go on the wall.* Set the saw for a 45-degree angle and make your cut. You may wish to mark the location of the top and bottom of the crown with a pencil on the saw table and fence, so that it is easier to line things up the next time. Or, if you are using a nailing strip, lay a section of it on the saw to hold the crown in place at the correct angle.

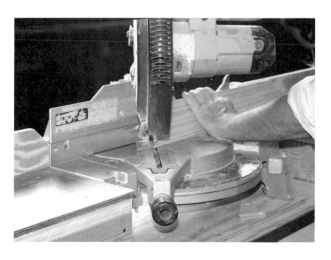

Hold the molding up to the wall and mark where the corner meets up with the bottom side of it. The cut you make will angle away from your mark, making the piece longer than the point where the pencil mark is.

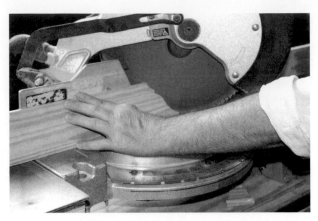

SWING THE SAW 90 DEGREES AROUND
TO CUT THE OPPOSITE ANGLE

IT LOOKS LIKE THE BLADE IS ABOUT TO CUT OFF THIS
FELLOW'S ARM, BUT IN REALITY THE BLADE IS SEVERAL
INCHES AWAY FROM IT. IT IS IMPORTANT TO KEEP A
VERY STEADY GRIP ON THE TRIM, AND TO NOT GET
YOUR FINGERS TOO CLOSE TO THE SAW BLADE.

USE A PENCIL TO MARK THE SIZE ON THE MOLDING
DIRECTLY FROM THE WALL, RATHER THAN USING A
TAPE MEASURE. THIS METHOD IS MUCH LESS
PRONE TO MISTAKES. THE WALL IN THE PHOTO IS
ON ITS BACK, AND A NAILING STRIP ATTACHED.

A COMPLETED OUTSIDE CORNER

Put the molding back on the saw in just the same way you had it before, and line the mark up with the blade. Notice that the two cut lines, the first one you made and this second one, are actually parallel with one another on the piece of crown molding. This is much more noticeable on a small section. Hold the piece you've just cut back up on the wall to make sure that it fits, and then nail it on with a finish nailer.

It is easiest to start at the next inside corner and then work your way back to the outside corner of the piece you just finished, rather than to cut an opposite outside corner and try to then fit the inside one last. That won't allow you to mark the piece on the wall. It is certainly possible to measure and cut to length, but it is much harder to visualize how the parts fit together. When you cut the next section, you will need to rotate the miter saw table 90 degrees in order to get the correct angle.

You can twist the trim a little bit this way or that to get a better fit when you attach it to the wall. If one of the sides runs past the other a small amount, sand that off to improve the fit. Use a bit of painter's caulk if there is a small gap that needs filling.

Homebuilders often use a method called *coping* to install crown moldings, because it maintains a better fit when the wood dries and shrinks a bit over a long period of time. It is done by cutting the trim off at a 45-degree angle, and then using a coping saw to remove all of the wood up to the face. That method is somewhat more complex, and seems unnecessary for something so temporary as a theatre show.

THE BAND SAW

Band saws are at their best cutting curves and other odd shapes, although they often have rip fences and miter guides as well. However, unlike the table saw and the radial arm saw, the band saw can be used *freehand*. This means that the piece you are cutting does not need to be guided by a fence or other such implement, but rather may be manipulated by hand. It is possible to rotate the work through the saw in ways that would be extremely dangerous with a circular saw blade.

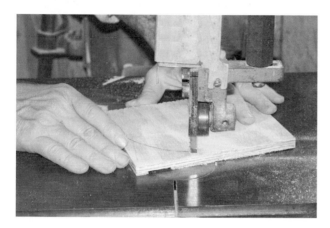

The name *band saw* is derived from the type of blade used. Band saw blades are exactly what the name implies—a thin metal strip that has been welded together to form an endless metal band with teeth on it. There are many different styles of blades for various cutting situations. The two main variables in band saw blade manufacture are the number of teeth per inch and the width of the blade from front to back. As with any saw, the larger the teeth (and the fewer per inch) the more aggressively the blade will cut, and also the rougher that cut will be. Six teeth per inch (tpi) is a blade with very large teeth, while 32 tpi is very fine. You may find that 10 or 12 tpi is the best for general-purpose work. Large teeth create a higher degree of tear out (splintering), and the sides of the wood that have been cut by the blade will have a rougher texture to them. Smaller teeth will of course result in a much finer cut, but the cutting will be slower and more difficult.

Band saw teeth need to have a fair amount of set to them in order to make cutting curves easier. The extra set allows the blade to cut to the side better. Another factor in cutting curves is the width of the blade from front to back. The smallest size is usually ⅛″, and the largest can be 1½″ or so on a very large industrial machine. The thinner the blade, the tighter the possible cutting radius will be.

The best size of blade for general work is probably either ⅜″ or ½″. These sizes allow the cutting of rea-

sonably small radii, but they are large enough to stand up to some fairly hard use without breaking prematurely. Band saw blades are made by cutting a strip of blade material to a specific length and welding the two ends together to form the band. The weakest point in this structure is the weld, and if it is not executed properly, the blade will break at that point prematurely.

The length of the strip is determined by the size of the saw itself and must be known when new blades are ordered. The easiest way to measure the blade length is from a broken blade, but you can also measure the inside of the saw itself.

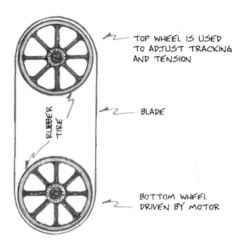

BAND SAW WHEELS

A band saw operates by spinning the blade over two (sometimes three) wheels inside the housing of the saw. The wheels have rubber tires on them to cushion the blade as it rotates. The tires have a slight crown in the middle, which causes the blade to center itself there. Outwardly focused inertia, sometimes called centrifugal force, causes the blade to seek the largest possible diameter of orbit around the wheel, and the blade will therefore center itself in the middle of the tire.

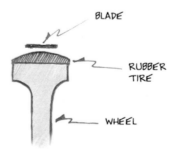

The bottom wheel is usually the drive wheel and is connected to the motor via a belt. The top wheel has a pair of adjustment knobs to keep the blade tracking properly. One knob tightens the blade by increasing the distance between the two wheels. The other is used to tilt the top wheel so that it is in proper alignment with the bottom one. This process is similar to the one used to adjust the belt on a belt sander. These adjustments are amazingly forgiving, but a saw too far out of whack will result in excessive vibration and blade wear, in much the same way that improper front end alignment will affect a car.

TOP OF A BAND SAW

The band saw has a table that is used to support the work. This table is generally similar to that on a table saw, but smaller. There may be a means of attaching a rip fence, and you will most likely find a slot for a miter guide. The rip fence comes in handy when cutting foam. Most band saw tables will rotate to an angle, making it possible to cut bevels on the machine. On a band saw the table rotates rather than the blade as on a table saw. It is not practical to angle the two large wheels.

Just below the surface of the table is a *blade guide*. There is a similar guide on the guard that slides up and down to cover the blade. These guides are very important to the proper operation of the saw, and without them it is not possible to use the saw with much accuracy. The function of the guides is to prevent the

blade from flaring to the side when a piece of work is fed through the saw. They are especially important for cutting curves. The pressure of cutting curves will bend the blade way out of alignment and make precise work impossible if the guides are not in good working order.

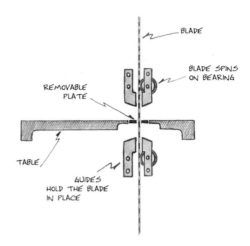

BAND SAW BLADE GUIDES

The guides should fit close to the blade to hold it steady, but they should not touch enough to deflect the blade at rest, as this would create a high degree of friction and heat. There are most likely some type of removable leaves that make it possible to alter the thickness of the guides from front to back in order to accommodate the thickness of the blade. Obviously, the guide will need to be thicker for a ¾″ blade than for a ⅛″ blade. There should be some kind of roller bearing to the rear of the guide that the back of the blade can press against when resistance is met in cutting wood. A roller bearing is used, so that it spins rather than allowing the rear of the blade to cut into its surface.

Installing a band saw blade is a matter of threading the blade through the machine and into its proper position. You should of course disconnect the saw from power before opening it up. Use the top wheel adjustment knob to move the two wheels closer together. After the blade has been put into position around the wheels, use the same knob to increase the distance and tighten the blade. Most likely there will be some sort of gauge to tell you when there is sufficient tension on the blade. If not, tighten the blade and pluck one side like a string on an upright bass. It should be taut enough to make a musical note. Trial and error will teach you the tone to listen for as an indication that the proper tension has been reached. If the blade is too tight, the saw will often make a squealing noise when you start it. If it is too loose, it may slip on the tire and slow down when cutting thick material.

It is possible to install the blade inside out, so that the teeth are pointed up rather than down. It makes sense that the saw cuts downward, because that presses the work against the table. If the teeth are pointing up, flip the blade inside out to reverse their orientation.

The band saw is one of my favorite saws to use, because it is so much quieter than any other and because most of the sawdust comes out at the bottom of the saw rather than hitting you in the face. There is hardly any danger of kickback, which is a constant concern with a circular saw. It is often fun and relaxing to cut odd shapes on the saw. Do not be lulled into some false sense of security, as the band saw can be just as dangerous as any other saw. Remember to wear safety glasses and to observe all the safety tips for your particular saw. One of the most important rules is appropriate use of the guard that covers the upper portion of the blade. It is adjustable up and down. Never leave more than an inch of blade exposed above the material you are cutting. Actually, this is a matter of craftsmanship as well, because the closer the blade guide is to your work, the more accurate it will be.

The band saw is an excellent choice for cutting lightweight materials such as polystyrene foam. Foam is so light that it tends to vibrate too much in a table saw, and on occasion the vibration will create a kickback. This will not happen on a band saw.

There are a few techniques for cutting curves that will make your work more accurate. One of these is to start a curved cut with the "soft" side of the cut. If you have a curve that must gently begin at one straight side, this is the soft side. Begin with the side of the work parallel to the blade and gently turn the wood into the blade. If you do not cut enough material off the first time, go back and try again. It is much better to cut too little than too much.

It is very common to cut circles on the band saw. Most of the time you can simply mark out the curve with a compass, and freehand the circle on the saw. But sometimes more precision is required, and a *jig* can be used to align all the parts perfectly. A jig is a shop-built tool that helps a carpenter in doing a specific job. This particular jig will allow you to make really exacting curves. It takes a bit of time to get the saw set up for the first circle, but from then on they go really quickly.

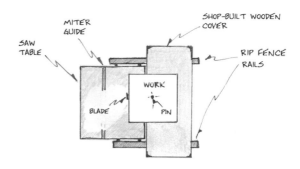

MAKE A WOODEN INSERT THAT YOU CAN NAIL INTO. PUT A PIN THROUGH THE CENTER OF THE WORK, AND ROTATE THE WOOD THROUGH THE SAW.

MAKING MANY PERFECT CIRCLES

A wooden top on the band saw table is required to make this jig work. If your band saw has rails for a rip fence, you can easily make something that slides on and off of the table. If not, you may need something that covers the entire saw table.

Cut some squares to the same size as the diameter of the circles you want to cut. Find the centers by marking across the corners diagonally. Put a pin through the center where the two marks cross each other. This can be as simple as driving a nail through the wood, if having a small hole in the middle is not problematic. Place the work on the saw table and press the pin down into the surface of the added-on wooden cover. Make sure that the pin is directly across from the blade, and that the edge of the plywood square is touching the edge of the band saw blade. Start the saw, and rotate the work 360 degrees to make a circle. To cut multiples, place the squares on the table one at a time and cut.

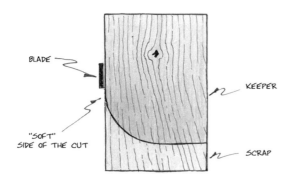

START YOUR CUT FROM THE SOFT SIDE

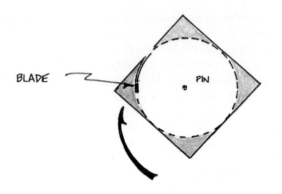

ROTATE THE WORK THROUGH THE SAW
ALL THE WAY AROUND

Another common task is to cut a slot or notch in a piece of wood. To do that, cut one side, pull the work out, and then cut the other side. Use the blade straight in to *nibble* away at the bottom of the notch.

MAKE THE FIRST CUT STRAIGHT IN, THEN PULL THE WORK OUT

MAKE THE SECOND CUT IN

PULL BACK JUST A BIT, AND THEN CUT OVER TO THE FIRST CUT

CUT STRAIGHT INTO THE SLOT AS MANY TIMES AS NECESSARY TO CLEAR THE NOTCH

CUTTING A NOTCH WHEN THE BLADE IS TOO LARGE TO TURN

Sometimes you need to cut a curve that is very close to the turning limits of the blade. It may be that the saw comes close to cutting a particular curve but binds just a little too much to be workable. In this case, you can cut a curve near the one you need, but leaving about ⅛″ or so along the outside. If you then come back and cut the original curve, the blade will bind less, because the small strip of wood is more easily deflected than the solid piece that was there. Leaving the small ⅛″ strip makes the finish cutting more stable. If the curve is way too tight for the blade, you can try cutting many small lines that are tangent to the curve. These methods work only on outside curves—not on inside curves.

CUTTING SHARP CURVES

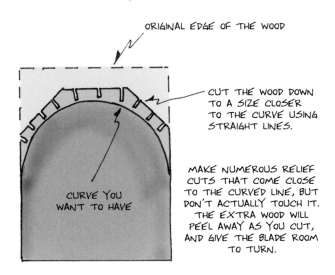

ORIGINAL EDGE OF THE WOOD

CUT THE WOOD DOWN TO A SIZE CLOSER TO THE CURVE USING STRAIGHT LINES.

CURVE YOU WANT TO HAVE

MAKE NUMEROUS RELIEF CUTS THAT COME CLOSE TO THE CURVED LINE, BUT DON'T ACTUALLY TOUCH IT. THE EXTRA WOOD WILL PEEL AWAY AS YOU CUT, AND GIVE THE BLADE ROOM TO TURN.

If you are cutting a small or lightweight piece, put your thumbs and forefingers on the work, and your other fingers on the saw table. This will help keep the piece steady and decrease vibration as you rotate it through the saw. It also keeps your fingers farther from the blade. There are limits to this. If the piece is too small, the danger of cutting your finger is too great to risk it. If you are not sure if the piece is too small, it probably is.

CUTTING DADO AND HALF LAP JOINTS ON A RADIAL ARM SAW AND BAND SAW

All of the techniques thus far have been accomplished with one cut, but the dado and half lap joints require more than that. Either one can be accomplished with a standard saw blade, but a special *dado blade* can make the job go faster. Most blades are of the stacked dado type, in which two blades are used on the same saw. Naturally, the two blades together create a wider kerf than one alone would. In addition, special chippers are used between the two outside blades, so that they are spaced apart even wider. The chippers come in a variety of thicknesses, so that different size dado slots are possible by stacking them together in various combinations.

by nibbling away sections of wood from repeated passes of the saw.

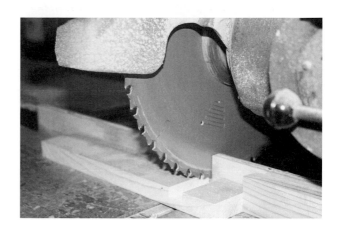

Cut all of your pieces to length before setting up the saw for the dado cuts. Remember to make them full length from one side of the frame to the other, with no allowance for overlapping, as would be necessary for a butt joint.

REGULAR TYPE BLADE

CHIPPER

CHIPPERS HAVE TEETH ONLY ON THE ENDS

USE SEVERAL CHIPPERS IN THE STACK TO CREATE A BLADE AS THICK AS YOU NEED TO CUT THE PROPER SIZED DADO

THIS BLADE GOES ON THE OPPOSITE SIDE OF THE STACK

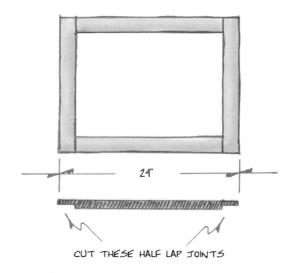

24"

CUT THESE HALF LAP JOINTS

EVEN THOUGH IT APPEARS THAT THE RAIL IN QUESTION SHOULD BE CUT TO A LENGTH SHORTER THAN 24" BY TWICE THE WIDTH OF THE MATERIAL, IT IS ACTUALLY THE FULL 24" BECAUSE IT EXTENDS THE WHOLE DISTANCE IN MAKING THE HALF LAP.

The dado blade increases the width of the kerf, but a regular blade will work just as well, albeit more slowly,

How to make a half lap at the ends of two pieces of 1×3? Normally, the radial arm saw cuts all the way through a piece of wood because the blade extends into the table a short distance. But the blade can be raised and lowered by using the crank in the front. Raise the blade up to a level that is ⅜″, or half the thickness of the ¾″-thick stock. Use a ⅜″-thick board to judge the distance, but check that by making several passes through two different pieces of one-by stock. Hold the two together to see if the resulting kerf is just the right depth. Adjust as required.

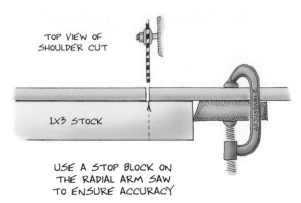

TOP VIEW OF SHOULDER CUT

1X3 STOCK

ADJUSTABLE

USE A STOP BLOCK ON THE RADIAL ARM SAW TO ENSURE ACCURACY

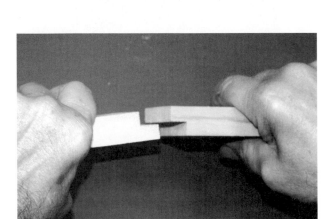

Remember that a 1×3 is nominally 1″ thick and 3″ wide, but that the actual milled size is ¾″ × 2⅝″. The half lap needs to be cut into the ends of the board far enough so that the entire width of the 1×3 will fit onto it.

Place the 1×3 on the radial arm saw, and align your mark with the left side of the kerf. Pull the saw across the work to make the cut, and then push it back to its rear position. Move the work over a slight bit to the left and repeat the process, so that another section of wood is removed. Nibble away in that fashion unto all of the excess wood has been removed. If you've installed a dado blade, it may take only a couple of passes of the saw, but a regular blade takes quite a few.

You need to cut at least two pieces like this in order to create one lap joint, but most of the time a large number of pieces must be cut for multiple joints. In that case, use a stop block on the saw to make the job go faster, and to increase accuracy. All of the pieces will be exactly the same when a stop block is in place.

If you have a well-calibrated band saw, the process of creating half lap joints can be speeded up by making the shoulder cut with the radial arm saw, and then moving to the band saw to finish the joint. This technique requires a sturdy band saw with a blade that is at exactly a 90-degree angle to the table. Set the rip fence ⅜″ away from the blade, and/or clamp a wooden block onto the table at that distance. Raise the guard up above the 3″ required by the 1×3 stock. Feed the wood into the saw gently so that the blade cuts the face of the lap joint. Your feed rate should be fairly slow, because the 3″ thickness places a strain on the saw. Because you are cutting into the board only a short distance, you will need to pull the work back out after the cut is finished.

Dado cuts can also be made in the center of a board, so that another one fits across it, creating an X.

Create a dado cut down the length of a board using the table saw.

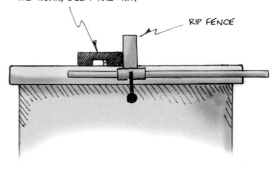

DADO IS CUT UPSIDE DOWN.
THE BLADE DOES NOT GO
ALL THE WAY THROUGH
THE WORK, JUST HALF-WAY

RIP FENCE

CUT A DADO THE LENGTH OF A
BOARD ON THE TABLE SAW

CHAPTER 18

CONSTRUCTING FLATS

The basic rationale behind building flats is to provide a lightweight structure with a surface that represents a large flat area such as a wall. In earlier times, flats were essentially a large artist's canvas onto which all decoration such as windows, doors, wallpaper, and sometimes even furniture were painted. Lashing the flats together to form a room was a method of constructing stage sets that was inexpensive and made the sets easily transportable. In this modern era, audiences expect to see a more realistic and three-dimensional setting.

There are two main types of *flats*: the traditional type covered with a soft material such as muslin or canvas, and an alternate type that has a hard plywood covering. The two different approaches are called soft-covered and hard-covered flats respectively. Hard-covered flats are often called TV or Hollywood flats because they are used in those industries. In either case, any kind of flat is constructed around a framework that delineates the outside profile and that provides enough internal support to maintain the structural integrity of the flat. This structure, usually unseen by the audience, is called the *framing*.

The skills you learn in building flats are easily transposed into building more complex units. Flat-like structures are used in building all sorts of things. The basic techniques of measuring, cutting, and joining are essential no matter what you are making. Cut lists are used in all construction projects, whether you are using wood, plastic, or metal. It is important to learn to visualize how units fit together, and how that interaction dictates the sizes of their individual parts.

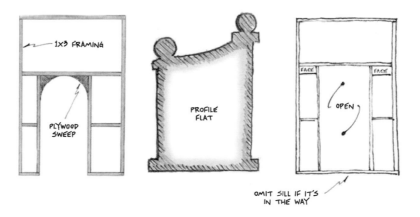

FLATS DON'T HAVE TO BE JUST RECTANGLES

SOFT-COVERED FLATS

The most common *soft-covered flat* is a rectangular structure covered with fabric. The covering is usually muslin, an all-cotton fabric that can be purchased in quite large sizes from theatrical suppliers. (See Chapter 14.) Do not use muslin from a retail fabric store that may have synthetic fibers in it. This type will not shrink properly during the sizing process. Soft-covered flats may be covered with scenic canvas instead when extreme durability is required. Sometimes duvetyn, velour, or some other type of specialty fabric may be used. Black duvetyn or velour can be used to make excellent masking flats. Even so, heavyweight muslin is the standard type of covering for a painted flat. Scenic muslin is usually made on special looms in Asia and can be purchased from one of many different supply houses.

The framing for a soft-covered flat of this sort is joined together in a traditional way, using framing parts with names derived from general woodworking practice.

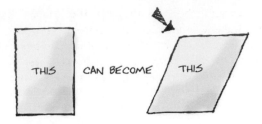

WHEN FORCE IS APPLIED AT AN ANGLE

ONE TRIANGLE WILL STRENGTHEN ALL THE CORNERS

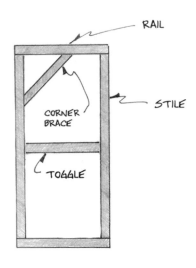

PARTS OF A FLAT FRAME

Any horizontal member is known as a *rail*. Any vertical member is a *stile*. Internal framing members that help to brace the rails or stiles are called *toggles*, whether they run vertically or horizontally. Quite often these are referred to with both names, such as in "toggle rail." A brace that runs diagonally across one corner of a flat is called a *corner brace*. This brace is used to reinforce the squareness of the flat and to keep it from deforming into a parallelogram.

The corner brace creates a triangular form at the corner of the flat. Triangles are a very strong structural form, because there is no easy way to deform the shape. In order to do so, you must change the size of a leg, or bend it in some way, which requires a lot of force. The corner brace triangle is used to stiffen and reinforce the larger rectangle. If one corner of the rectangle is held rigid at 90 degrees, the other three corners must follow suit. Corner braces are needed only if the flat is very large.

The rails, stiles, and toggles of this type of flat are joined together using thin pieces of plywood that are fastened to the rear faces of the boards. It is easy to see why when a flat is viewed from the edge.

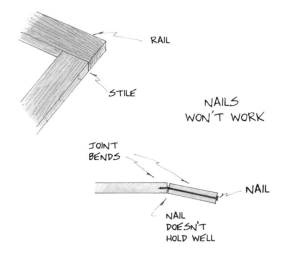

RAIL

STILE

NAILS WON'T WORK

JOINT BENDS

NAIL

NAIL DOESN'T HOLD WELL

There are two obvious problems in nailing through the rail into the stile. There is a high probability that the wood will split because of the nail and/or that the nail will bend. This joint would be weak and prone to failure in either case. You could turn the wood on its side and form the butt joint that way. But the muslin covering of the flat would tend to bow the sides inward when it shrinks in during the sizing process.

Thin plywood blocks attached to the rear of the framing are an excellent way of avoiding all these problems. The ¼″ plywood pieces are known as *corner blocks* and *keystones*. They form a covered joint. It is easy to understand the derivation of the name "corner block," but the origination of "keystone" is a bit more obscure. It comes from the shape of a stone block that forms the top of a Romanesque archway. These blocks were cut into the shape of a trapezoid and were used as a decorative and functional flourish.

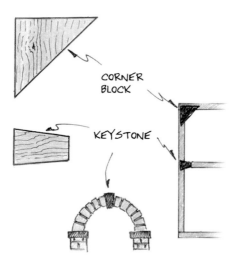

Traditional keystones for flat building were made into this shape so that the wide portion of the keystone is attached to the stile, and the narrow portion (which is the same width as the toggle) attached to the toggle rail. That meant more surface area would be glued to the stile and less where the toggle is smaller anyway. However, the trapezoid shape is difficult to cut, because the sides are not parallel, and the angle of the saw must be changed repeatedly. Many shops forgo the traditional keystone shape and use a plain rectangle for the keystone.

On a flat, the top and bottom rails always extend to the very edge of the flat, covering the ends of the two stiles. This is done to protect the stiles when moving the flat. It keeps the wooden framing from splitting if the flat is dropped on its corner. Having the top and bottom rails extend all the way from side to side is such a hard-and-fast rule that the orientation of a flat can be determined just by observing the manner in which the framing pieces are overlapped. This is helpful when there is a mix of different flats and some of them are wider than they are tall.

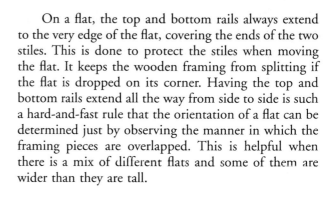

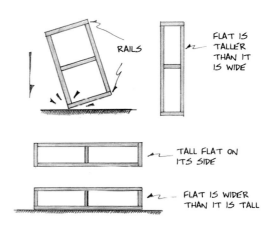

TOP AND BOTTOM RAILS
RUN ALL THE WAY SIDE TO SIDE

A center support or toggle is used to maintain the shape of a flat. Sometimes, especially on larger units, the side stiles tend to curve inward when the flat's covering is attached and stretched. One or more toggles will prevent the stiles from bowing toward the center. The rule of thumb is to place a toggle every 4 feet or so

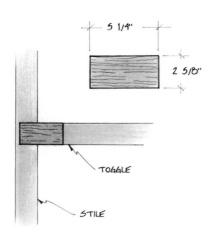

KEYSTONE PLACEMENT

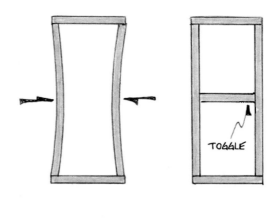

TOGGLES ARE USED TO PREVENT
THE SIDES OF THE FLAT FROM
BOWING INWARD

All of the framing members of a flat are cut from one-by material, traditionally white pine. In many shops, soft-covered flats are constructed from 1×3s, unless they are quite large, and then 1×4s are used. This is somewhat a matter of personal preference.

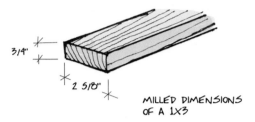

MILLED DIMENSIONS
OF A 1X3

The 1×3 has odd dimensions. As you may recall from Chapter 15, all nominally 1-inch-thick boards are actually ¾″ thick after they have been through the milling process. So that dimension seems correct, but the width is odd. If you go to the lumber-yard, the widths of one-by material are all even measurements like 4, 6, 8, 10, or 12 inches. So a 1×4 is the smallest commercially available size. That turns out to be somewhat heavier than is required for most flats. The added weight actually makes the flat structure weaker when the flats are moved around. The weight of the flat makes it more likely that it will get twisted out of shape enough for the joints to come loose. A theatre 1×3 is made by ripping down a 12-inch-wide board into four equal pieces that are 2⅝″ wide. Four times 2⅝″ is actually only 10½″, but remember that the saw kerf takes away some of the material.

Rectangles that are taller than they are wide are undoubtedly the most common type of soft-covered flat. They are often used as wall sections. But that is not the only type. On the contrary, the variety of flats is virtually limitless. Door and window flats are also very popular.

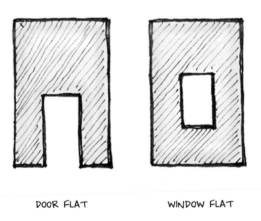

DOOR FLAT   WINDOW FLAT

The next step in learning about flat construction is to develop an understanding of how framing is used to form a specific profile or outline. There are several basic concepts used to determine how a flat will be framed. Begin by determining which parts will form the outside profile of the flat.

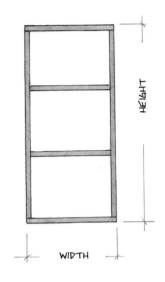

HEIGHT

WIDTH

THUMBNAIL SKETCH

It is good to make small thumbnail sketches of scenic units on sheets of paper as you go along. The sketches are used to make up cut lists of the individual parts that you'll need and also serve as a construction guide during the assembly process. Some shops do a whole series of technical drawings that are really just CAD versions of these same sketches. Sometimes that approach is very helpful when a scale drawing is needed.

Visualizing each flat or platform or stair unit as a separate entity makes it easier to focus on the construction of each one as a single unit. It is important to think of and to construct scenery as individual parts, because that feeds into the requirement that stage scenery be portable. If you build an entire wall as one huge unit, you won't be able to move it anywhere later on.

Sketch a simple flat by starting with a rectangle delineating the outside profile, and then put in the interior parts. Support the stiles with a toggle at least every 4 feet. Because this unit is 10 feet tall, two evenly spaced toggles have been sketched in. One toggle would have left two spaces 5 feet tall. Two toggles will leave three spaces, each about 3′4″ tall. Neither one nor two works out to exactly 4 feet, but the best answer for the number of toggles in this example would be two.

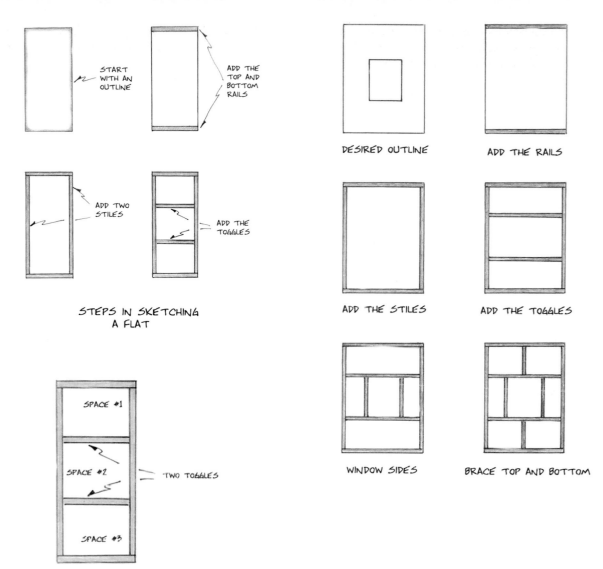

START WITH AN OUTLINE

ADD THE TOP AND BOTTOM RAILS

ADD TWO STILES

ADD THE TOGGLES

STEPS IN SKETCHING A FLAT

DESIRED OUTLINE

ADD THE RAILS

ADD THE STILES

ADD THE TOGGLES

WINDOW SIDES

BRACE TOP AND BOTTOM

SPACE #1

SPACE #2

TWO TOGGLES

SPACE #3

TWO TOGGLES MAKE THREE SPACES

As another example, imagine that you have been requested to build a window flat 6 feet wide and 10 feet tall. The window inside the flat should be 3 feet wide and 4 feet tall. The window is centered side to side in the space, and the bottom of it is 3 feet from the floor. It is easy to sketch out the flat using just this information. Begin with the outside profile, and then continue with the inside profile of the window opening.

Keep in mind that your sketch should be of the *back* side of the framing, meaning that you are viewing it from the rear. If the flat is symmetrical from left to right, there is no difference, but if not, you must be sure to show the correct view. It will not be possible to install the keystones and corner blocks later on if the flat is laid out face up.

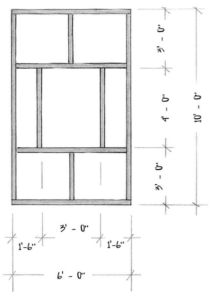

3' - 0"

4' - 0"

10' - 0"

3' - 0"

3' - 0"

1'-6"   1'-6"

6' - 0"

A DIMENSIONED SKETCH

In the window flat example, there is a nonstructural reason to place the toggles in a specific location. Rather than simply divide the available space into thirds, the two toggle rails are positioned so that they become the top and bottom of the window opening. Because the flat is more than 4 feet wide, two additional toggle stiles are used to brace between the toggle rails and the top and bottom rails.

Door flats are framed in a similar fashion, except that the opening extends all the way to the floor, and the bottom rail is split into two parts. Toggle placement is used to delineate the top of the door opening.

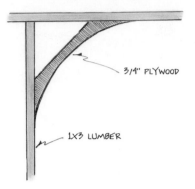

3/4" PLYWOOD IS THE SAME THICKNESS AS THE 1X3 SO IT WORKS WELL FOR A SWEEP

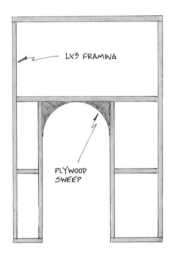

ARCHED DOORWAY

There is no reason why flats must be composed of straight lines and 90-degree angles, other than the fact that these are the easiest flats to build. The framing members can be cut at any angle and joined together with blocks and keystones cut to match.

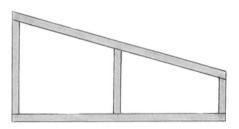

EXAMPLE OF A FLAT THAT IS NOT A RECTANGLE

All of the flats presented thus far have been rectilinear, but flats are not limited to that shape. One easy variation is to use a framing piece known as a *sweep*. Sweeps are used to create a curved profile, most commonly at the top of a window or doorway. Sweeps are cut from $\frac{3}{4}''$ plywood so that the thickness of the sweep matches the thickness of the one-by used to frame the flat. Sometimes the plywood is left whole when the sweep is very small, but more often the material around the curve is trimmed away to reduce the weight of the unit. Use a large wooden compass or a set of trammel points to mark the curve. Connect the sweep to the main structure using keystones or specially cut shapes of $\frac{1}{4}''$ plywood as required.

Sometimes designs require flats that mirror an object with a completely irregular shape. To construct this type of flat, begin with an interior composed of straight lines that fill most of the space. Then add to the profile with $\frac{3}{4}''$ plywood, much like when installing sweeps. The principle is the same; the shapes are simply more complex. The profile edges can be attached with $\frac{1}{4}''$ ply that has been cut to the specific size and shape of the profile.

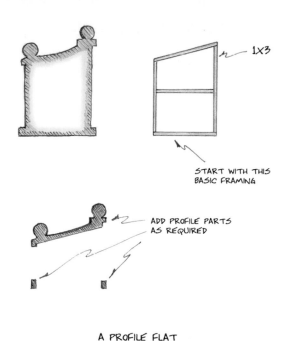

1X3

START WITH THIS
BASIC FRAMING

ADD PROFILE PARTS
AS REQUIRED

A PROFILE FLAT

among them. Woodworking is always done using fractions. It is important not to mix the two up in construction work, because it makes the lists harder to do. Fractions are often actually easier to work with than decimal points, and you can do the math in your head rather than needing a calculator. At any rate, any answers you come up with must be measured with a tape that is marked in fractions, not decimal equivalents. Calculators are available that operate in feet and inches rather than decimals. You may wish to try one but will probably find out that you don't really need it after a short while, because the problems are so easy once you get the hang of them.

$$1/2 = 1 \div 2 = 0.5$$

THE SLASH MARK
MEANS "DIVIDED BY"

CUT LISTS

A *cut list* is essential when building just about anything. You make a cut list the same way for any project, although the sizes of lumber and other materials change from job to job. Making a cut list involves using feet and inches, as well as fractional parts of inches. Fractions of an inch were covered earlier when talking about tape measures in the chapter on hand tools. The divisions of the tape relate to repeatedly dividing one inch in half. One-quarter is equal to half of a half, one-eighth is half of that, and so on. Before beginning an in-depth study of how to figure cut lists, here is a short review of adding and subtracting fractions.

FRACTIONS AND ENGLISH-STYLE MEASUREMENTS

Fractions are an indication of an amount that is divided by another amount. The slash symbol (/) actually means "divided by," so the fraction $\frac{1}{2}$ really indicates 1 divided by 2, that is, a whole that is split into two equal parts. The fraction $\frac{1}{4}$ represents a whole that has been divided into four equal parts. One-quarter could also be expressed as the decimal equivalent of 0.25, which is the number you will get when you divide 1 by 4 on your calculator. Many math problems are much easier to work when using decimal equivalents of fractions. The math problems used in determining cut lists are not

The top number in a fraction is the *numerator*, and the bottom is the *denominator*. In order to add fractions together, you need to make sure that they have a common denominator. Before $\frac{1}{4}$ and $\frac{1}{2}$ can be added together, you must change the denominator 2 into a 4 so that a commonality is achieved. You can do that by multiplying the fraction $\frac{1}{2}$ by the fraction $\frac{2}{2}$. Two halves equal 1 and will not change the value of $\frac{1}{2}$. Multiplying any number by 1 will not change its value. To multiply fractions, multiply the two numerators and then the two denominators.

$$\frac{1}{2} \quad \text{NUMERATOR}$$
$$\quad \text{DENOMINATOR}$$

$$1/2 \times 2/2 = 2/4$$

$$1/4 + 2/4 = 3/4$$

Subtracting fractions is essentially the same process of finding a common denominator and then subtracting the numerator. If you want to subtract $\frac{1}{4}$ from $\frac{1}{2}$, then 4 will again be the common denominator, creating the equation $\frac{2}{4} - \frac{1}{4} = \frac{1}{4}$.

Another example is shown in the following figure.

$$3/4 - 5/8 = ?$$

$$3/4 \times 2/2 = 6/8$$

$$6/8 - 5/8 = 1/8$$

Working with Feet and Inches

The *dimensions* used in a construction project have the added complexity of being large enough to require adding and subtracting whole feet and inches as well as just fractions. Although fractions are used to subdivide inches, you should never express foot measurements in fractional portions such as "two and one-half feet." Rather, you should say, "two feet, six inches."

There is a shorthand method of expressing feet with a mark similar to an apostrophe ('), and inches with marks similar to quotation marks ". (Of course, you don't call them that in measuring—they are feet marks and inch marks.) Two feet, six inches is written as 2'-6". Two feet, six and one-half inches is written 2'-6½". Always insert a dash between the feet and the inches, but not between the inches and the fraction.

NOTATION EXAMPLES

2'-0" .... NOT 2'

2'-0 1/2" .... NOT 2'-1/2"

0'-2 1/2" .... UNLESS ALL DIMENSIONS IN ALL INCHES

2'-6" .... NOT 2 1/2'

If the measurement is an even two feet, the notation should be 2'-0", with the zero inches included to make the reader certain that there are actually no inches included rather than think that the writer has neglected to write the number of inches down. On occasion, you will need to express a measurement that includes a fractional portion of one inch, but no whole inches, such

as 2'-0½", and you are seeing the proper notation method written here.

Sometimes measurements are given in all inches rather than in feet and inches. A tape measure is equipped to deal with that because one side of the blade is in feet and inches and the other side is in all inches. Traditionally, if no part of what you are building is larger than 8 feet, then all dimensions are given in inches, but this rule is not always followed. Flats are almost always at least that size, and as a result flat cut lists are usually done in feet and inches. If you are building step units, or some other smallish scenery, it may be easier just to use all inches. There may be a specific reason to choose one method over the other, but once you have done so, stick with it. Never mix all inch dimensions with feet-and-inches dimensions, because it is very easy to get confused about the numbers. Twenty inches (20") and two feet (2'-0") tend to look very much alike, and they are very close in actual length. You cannot tell just from looking at the size on a scale drawing which one you have. It is often difficult to read feet and inches marks when they are written in pencil on a scrap board. If you make it a habit to use one system for an entire project, you will have fewer mistakes.

In the following figure are a few practice examples of adding and subtracting feet and inches.

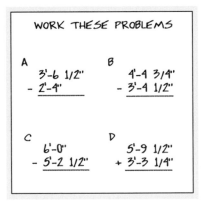

WORK THESE PROBLEMS

A
3'-6 1/2"
- 2'-4"

B
4'-4 3/4"
- 3'-4 1/2"

C
6'-0"
- 5'-2 1/2"

D
5'-9 1/2"
+ 3'-3 1/4"

The first problem, A, is fairly easy, as it is possible to subtract the 4 inches from the 6½ inches cleanly and arrive at an answer of 2½ inches. Three feet minus two feet leaves one foot, and therefore the answer to the first problem is 1'-2½".

The second problem, B, is a bit more of a challenge, as you must first convert the fractions so that there is a common denominator. Multiplying ½ by ²⁄₂ results in the fraction ²⁄₄. Two fourths subtracted from three fourths is one fourth. The rest of the second problem is straightforward and the answer should be 1'-0¼". Note that a 0 is used to denote the absence of any whole inches.

The third problem, C, involves shifting feet to inches in order to work the problem. The figure 6'-0" is a whole number of feet, and therefore no inches are present to use in subtracting the 2½". Before the problem can be solved, you must convert one of the feet into inches. You can do this by borrowing one foot from the feet column and increasing the number of inches by 12. Because there are 12 inches in a foot, you have neither lost nor gained anything by re-expressing the amount as 5'-12". Go a step further and convert one of the inches into a fractional amount so that you have something to subtract the half-inch from. Now the number is written as 5'-11½". From here you can do the normal math and arrive at a length of 0'-9½" for the third problem. Again, you can see that a 0 has been used to indicate that the number of feet is nil rather than simply missing.

The final problem, D, is one of addition rather than subtraction and is distinguished by the fact that in adding the 2-inch amounts together, a sum greater than 12 is reached. It is then proper to reduce the number of inches by shifting them over to the foot column, adding 1 to that total. The answer to problem four is 9'-0¾".

they are the topic of this chapter, that is what will be discussed. If the size and shape of the flat are given, a carpenter should be able to work out a cut list for constructing a standard flat without too much more information. In order to form a cut list, it is necessary to make a drawing of the structural framing of the sort that was talked about in the first part of the chapter. It is not generally essential that this type of drawing be to scale, though they often are. Small sketches of technical ideas for individual units are helpful in visualizing what they look like, and you can use them to generate a cut list.

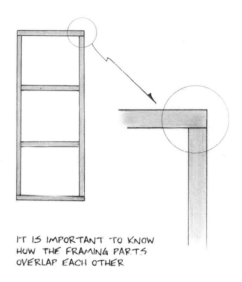

IT IS IMPORTANT TO KNOW HOW THE FRAMING PARTS OVERLAP EACH OTHER

It's important to indicate on the sketch exactly how the framing pieces intersect. Basically that means which pieces overlap which others. Dimensions are given to the outside of the structure. If covered butt joints are used to join the 1×3 lumber, only one of the pieces will extend all the way to the outside edge. Any other piece intersecting it will have its length shortened by the width of the 1×3. The math part of making a cut list is mostly about deciding which boards are the boards that get shortened, and then subtracting some amount from their length.

The next drawing shows that the top rail and the bottom rail run continuously from side to side, and the two stiles stop short of the top and bottom. Also, the center toggles do not run all the way to the outside, but are shortened by the width of the two stiles. This drawing has been dimensioned, and you can see the lines and numbers used to give the overall size of the flat. The dimensions in this drawing are to the outside of the object. Extension lines are used to indicate the exact point where the dimensions apply.

HOW TO CONVERT FEET TO INCHES
AND INCHES TO
FRACTIONAL NUMBERS

CONSIDER THE PROBLEM

    6'-0"
 - 5'-2 1/2"
 _____

    6'-0" = 5'-12"

    5'-12" = 5'-11 2/2"

THEREFORE:

    5'-11 2/2"
 - 5'-2 1/2"
 _____
    0'-9 1/2"   ANSWER

Cut lists are made from dimensioned drawings of scenery. Someone—most of the time, the scenic designer—has drawn out elevations of what the scenery looks like. These are scale drawings that show the shape and size of flats that must be constructed. Of course, flats are just one type of unit used in scenery, but as

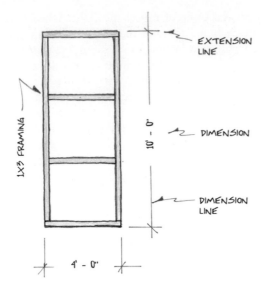

EXTENSION LINE

1×3 FRAMING

10' - 0"

DIMENSION

DIMENSION LINE

4' - 0"

To get the length of the styles, subtract $2\frac{5}{8}'' + 2\frac{5}{8}''$ from the overall 10'-0" measurement. $2\frac{5}{8}'' + 2\frac{5}{8}'' = 5\frac{1}{4}''$. When that amount is subtracted from 10'-0", the answer is $9'\text{-}6\frac{3}{4}''$. On the list, you should make a notation of 2 @ $9'\text{-}6\frac{3}{4}''$. This, of course, indicates that two pieces at this length are required to build the flat.

$$\begin{array}{r} 10'\text{-}0'' \\ -\ 0'\text{-}5\ 1/4'' \\ \hline \end{array}$$

$$\begin{array}{rl} 9'\text{-}12'' & \text{DIFFERENT WAYS} \\ -\ 0'\text{-}5\ 1/4'' & \text{OF EXPRESSING} \\ \hline & \text{THE SAME} \\ & \text{NUMBERS} \end{array}$$

$$\begin{array}{rl} 9'\text{-}11\ 4/4'' & \\ -\ 0'\text{-}\ 5\ 1/4'' & \\ \hline 9'\text{-}6\ 3/4'' & \text{ANSWER} \end{array}$$

Years ago, it was necessary to explain that the @ symbol means "at," but thanks to the miracle of texting, that explanation is no longer needed!

The previous drawing shows a flat that is 4'-0" wide and 10'-0" tall. There are two toggles. The framing is to be cut from 1×3 #2 white pine. When forming a cut list, begin by listing the longest required pieces first and work your way down in order to the shortest. The parts are ranked that way to ensure that they will get cut out in that same order. The reason for that will be explained later in the chapter. Looking at the drawing, it is apparent that the longest pieces are the two stiles. The stiles are often the longest pieces if you are making wall flats for a box set. Most of the time, flats are taller than they are wide.

The stiles are both the same size. It is normal to assume that the top and bottom of the flat are parallel with one another unless there is information to the contrary. It is apparent that as the two stiles do not reach either the top or bottom, their overall length should be decreased by twice the width of the framing material, which in this case is 1×3 lumber that has an actual milled size of $2\frac{5}{8}''$ wide. The number to subtract from the overall height is twice $2\frac{5}{8}''$, or $5\frac{1}{4}''$.

The exact size of the framing lumber in this example is not as important as realizing that calculations are made on the basis of whatever that size is. Sometimes 1×4 framing is used on flats, and of course in that case, the milled size of the framing lumber would be $3\frac{1}{2}''$. Whatever size you are using, you need to subtract the width of the two pieces of lumber from the overall height in order to arrive at the proper length.

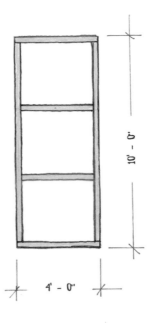

10' - 0"

4' - 0"

The next longest pieces are the top and bottom rails. You can see from the drawing that these two parts are continuous from side to side, and are dimensioned at 4'-0". Therefore, the next item on our list is 2 @ 4'-0". No math is required, because the dimensioned size on the drawing and length of the actual part are the same.

The final items for your cut list are the two center toggles. Again you can note that these do not run all the way from side to side, but rather dead end at the *inside* of the stiles. Again you need to add 2⅝" and 2⅝", and again the sum will be 5¼". I have added these two numbers together many, many times over the years and somehow the answer is always the same. I'm sure that after you have worked a few of these problems, you will simply remember some of the most common math answers. After subtracting the 5¼" from 4'-0", the answer is 2 @ 3'-6¾".

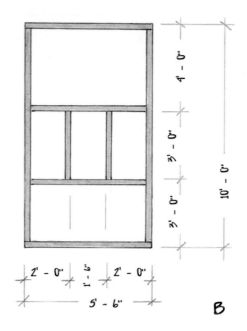

PRACTICE PROBLEM   **B**

CUT LIST

2 @ 9'-6 3/4"

2 @ 4'-0"

2 @ 3'-6 3/4"

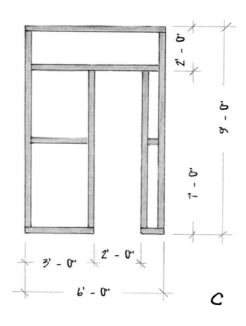

PRACTICE PROBLEM   **C**

The answers to the practice problems can be found after the Helpful Hints box.

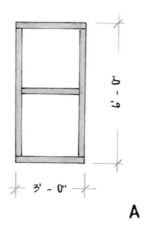

PRACTICE PROBLEM   **A**

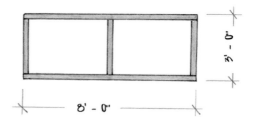

PRACTICE PROBLEM   **D**

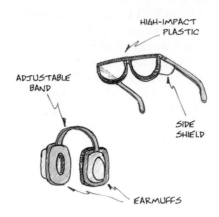

SAFETY GLASSES AND HEARING PROTECTOR

common sense. If you think that something is dangerous, then it probably is, and you should take precautions. Sometimes there are dangers that are not so obvious.

That is why it is important to read and understand all the safety procedures outlined in the instructions that come with any tool. Although many tools are similar, individual examples have eccentricities that you may not know about unless you read the instruction book or receive specific instruction in the use of that tool from a qualified person. The most important safety consideration is to pay attention to what you are doing. Most accidents seem to occur when a worker has a lapse of concentration in using a tool.

The first requirement for building anything is a cut list. For this project, suppose that you have a drawing for a flat that is 3 feet wide and 12 feet tall. The cut list has been worked out to the side. If you are actually building this project, you may wish to use some other dimensions; just work up a sketch with sizes that meet your needs.

ANSWERS

A
2 @ 5'-6 3/4"
2 @ 3'-0"
1 @ 2'-6 3/4"

B
2 @ 9'-6 3/4"
2 @ 5'-6"
2 @ 5'-0 3/4"
2 @ 3'-0"

C
2 @ 8'-6 3/4"
2 @ 6'-9 3/8"
1 @ 6'-0"
1 @ 5'-6 3/4"
1 @ 3'-0"
1 @ 2'-6 3/4"
1 @ 1'-0"
1 @ 0'-6 3/4"

D
2 @ 8'-0"
3 @ 2'-6 3/4"

FLAT CONSTRUCTION

Now that you are armed with the ability to create a cut list from a drawing or sketch, it is time to bring together the skills learned in several different sections and try a construction project. Before using power tools in the shop, it is important to review some safety issues.

Safety in a theatre shop should be stressed at all times. People of all different skill levels work there. It is important to wear safety glasses with any type of cutting tool, and hearing protectors with any tool that is loud enough to be annoying. Is it necessary to wear safety glasses and a hearing protector when using a hand screwdriver? Probably not, but if someone else is using an angle grinder right next to you, the answer would be a definite yes. The most important aspect of safety is

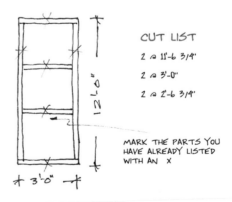

CUT LIST

2 @ 11'-6 3/4"

2 @ 3'-0"

2 @ 2'-6 3/4"

MARK THE PARTS YOU HAVE ALREADY LISTED WITH AN X

TYPICAL ROUGH SKETCH AND CUT LIST

Rip down a 1×12 to get enough stock to build this flat. Of course, the 1×12 you start with will need to be at least 12 feet long, or the 1×3s that you rip down will be too short to cut to the proper length.

By definition, #2 white pine has certain defects that prevented it from being sold as a higher grade of lumber, so the 1×3 lying on your shop floor has some imperfections in it. The process of sorting lumber according to quality is known as *culling*. The culls are the pieces deemed unusable for a particular purpose; however, remember that a length of 1×3 that is totally unsuitable for a long stile might be just fine for a shorter rail, which is why it was important to list the parts of your flat in order from longest to shortest.

Some pieces are obviously too bowed or warped to use. (Cupping is not usually a problem with such narrow strips.) To get a good view of how distorted a certain board is, hold one end up to your eye and look down to the end of it as though you were looking down a pool cue. This makes it easy to determine how much bow or warp there is over the length of the board. If the defect involved is a gentle bow, it can easily be removed by correctly positioning the flat's toggles. If there is a sharp bend where a knot is located, that piece is probably not going to be usable. Cull all of the pieces, and set aside the ones that are best suited to cutting the long stiles.

Use the radial arm saw to cut the two stiles to their proper length. Remember to trim off the end of the 1×3 first so that you have a nice square starting point. Trimming will also remove the small drying out cracks, or checks, that often appear at the very end of a board. There should be plenty of length to do this even if you are using 12'-0" stock, because the boards from the lumberyard are just a bit longer than that. Also, the stiles are shorter than 12'-0" because of the way they are interrupted by the top and bottom rails.

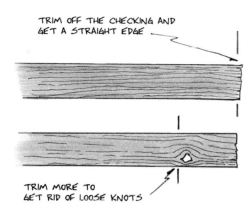

TRIM OFF THE CHECKING AND GET A STRAIGHT EDGE

TRIM MORE TO GET RID OF LOOSE KNOTS

TRIM THE END OF THE BOARD BEFORE CUTTING A PIECE TO LENGTH

Next, cut the 3'-0" rails, and then the two toggles. Cut around large knots wherever it is possible. Refer back to the chapter on woodworking and saws for more information on measuring and marking for the radial arm saw (RAS). If a RAS is not available, a power miter saw is the second best choice. You can set up a miter saw with benches on either side so that it works almost the same.

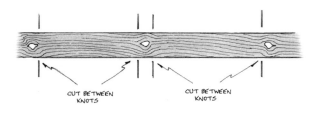

CUT BETWEEN KNOTS   CUT BETWEEN KNOTS

CUT SHORTER LENGTHS FROM LESS DESIRABLE MATERIAL

The corner blocks and keystones are next. The best material to use is ¼" A/C fir plywood, but B/C ply is almost as good. It's not a good idea to substitute lauan or Masonite for your corner block material. The lauan is far too spongy and will quite easily break under stress. Masonite is stiffer, but its lack of grain structure is a major fault. There seems to have been a general shift toward using B/C pine plywood, and even though this material is somewhat heavier than the fir, it is a reasonable substitute if ¼"-thick A/C fir is not available. The small size of the blocks makes the weight somewhat of a nonissue, and even the high degree of warp found in yellow pine plywood is not such a problem, because the blocks are so small. B/C yellow pine plywood is very strong, much stronger than either lauan or hardboard.

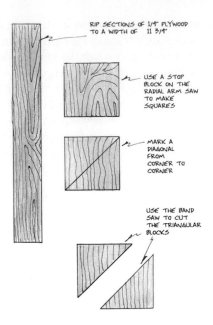

RIP SECTIONS OF 1/4" PLYWOOD TO A WIDTH OF 11 3/4"

USE A STOP BLOCK ON THE RADIAL ARM SAW TO MAKE SQUARES

MARK A DIAGONAL FROM CORNER TO CORNER

USE THE BAND SAW TO CUT THE TRIANGULAR BLOCKS

CUTTING CORNER BLOCKS

 GREEN IDEAS TIP BOX

Trees are one of America's most abundant and renewable resources. Virtually all yellow pine trees used in making plywood are grown on plantations, that is, farms in which the trees are planted in rows like any other crop. They are planted at just the right distance apart to grow straight and tall for maximum lumber production. When one crop is harvested, another is planted in its place. Most agricultural crops mature in a matter of months, but trees take several decades. The cost of yellow pine plywood is more stable than for other varieties, because the industry that grows them has been planned and is predictable.

Wood has much more strength along the length of its grain than it does across the grain. That is why plywood is manufactured with the grain of the various plies running in opposition to one another. As a result plywood is very strong in all directions. But when using ¼" plywood, this theory must be modified a bit to accommodate the fact that this thin material has only three plies. Obviously, there are two plies running one way and only one in the opposite direction. Therefore ¼" plywood has much more strength in one direction than it does in the other. When using it for a corner block, make sure that the two grains that are visible on the top and bottom run *across* the crack resulting from the joining of the stile and rail. The tendency of the two boards is to flex at the joint so that they bend with the crack as the corner of the bend.

The size of corner blocks is somewhat flexible, but should be somewhere in the neighborhood of 12 inches. Something slightly smaller than 1 foot, such as 11¾", is an excellent size when you consider the 4×8-foot size of a sheet of plywood. You can rip four strips of 11¾" wide plywood on the table saw, and then cut those strips into squares with the radial arm saw. If you were to make the blocks exactly 12" square, only three strips could be made from a 4'-0" wide sheet because of the loss incurred when the saw kerf is taken into consideration. Use a stop block on the radial arm saw to ensure that all of the blocks are perfectly square. The band saw is used to slice the squares from corner to corner, creating the triangular shape required for a corner block.

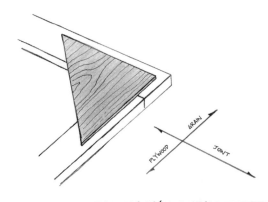

PLYWOOD GRAIN
JOINT

RUN THE PLYWOOD GRAIN AT A 90-DEGREE ANGLE TO THE DIRECTION OF THE JOINT

If the grain of the block runs in the same direction as the crack, the joint will not be nearly as strong. You can see from the drawing that the two blocks shown cannot be cut from the same square unless one of them is flipped over after cutting. That would put the bad side up. It is better craftsmanship to show the good side of the plywood (A or B) as the exposed side—the one you can see from the back. If you flip the triangle over, one of the sides will have to be the rough side.

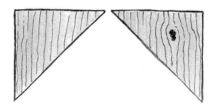

IT TAKES CUTTINGS FROM TWO DIFFERENT SQUARES TO MAKE A PAIR OF LEFT- AND RIGHT-HANDED CORNER BLOCKS

You can avoid this by making a set of left- and right-handed blocks when you cut them on the band saw. Do this by scribing your diagonal cut lines in opposite directions. When making a large number of corner blocks, it is more efficient to cut a number of them at one time by stacking the blocks together and cutting through all the layers at once. When using this method, it is possible to organize the left- and right-handed blocks by stacking the squares so that the grain on them is alternately vertical and horizontal. When a stack such as this is cut, there will automatically be an even number of left- and right-handed blocks.

TO MAKE LOTS OF CORNER BLOCKS STACK THE BLANKS UP WITH THE GRAIN ALTERNATING AND CUT THEM ALL AT ONE TIME

One final step must be taken before the corner blocks are ready for use. It is common practice to chamfer the edges of the plywood blocks in order to keep them from splintering later on, and that is easily done on a stationary belt sander. A stationary belt sander is the same as a handheld one, except that it is larger and you are meant to move the work in relation to the tool rather than the tool in relation to the work. If the stationary version is not available, you can do almost the same thing by turning the handheld belt sander upside down and depressing the constant run button next to the trigger. Just be sure that your particular sander can do this safely, and be aware that it may move around a bit due to vibration. It is easier to bring the work to the tool when the part you are sanding is so lightweight that you would have to hold it in place anyway. Sanding the corners should be a rapid process requiring no more than a few seconds for each block. Only the good side of the plywood needs to be chamfered, as the rough side will be pressed against the framing of the flat, and doing that side would just create an unsightly crack between the two pieces. Sanding will help to give your work a finely crafted appearance.

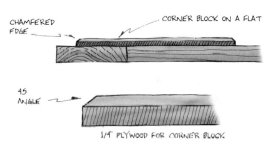

CHAMFERED EDGE / CORNER BLOCK ON A FLAT

45 ANGLE

1/4" PLYWOOD FOR CORNER BLOCK

CHAMFERING THE EDGE REDUCES SNAGS AND SPLINTERING. IT GIVES YOUR WORK A MORE PROFESSIONAL APPEARANCE.

Keystones are manufactured in a similar process, except of course that they are a rectangular shape rather than a triangle. Making the traditional trapezoidal shape is usually too time-consuming for the amount of extra strength it allows. Some people call the rectangular version a "strap." Rip down some of the 1/4" plywood into strips that are 2 5/8" wide. Cross cut these strips into pieces 5 1/4" long, and then chamfer the edges of the good sides.

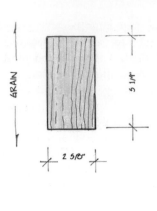

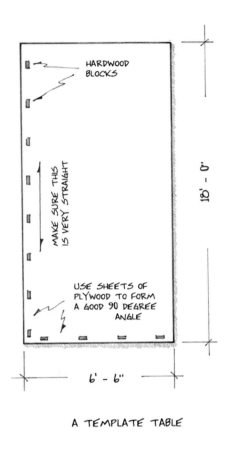

A table 6'-6" wide and 18'-0" long is a good size. This is somewhat larger than the 6'×16' size that is generally the largest practical limit for a flat. Blocks of wood along two adjacent sides form a guide. This guide is used to capture the framing and hold it in place. The resulting corner should be as square as possible, because it will be used to square up your flats.

KEYSTONE

Remember to keep the grain of the plywood running the length of the keystone. That keeps the strength of the grain running across the joint as it did on the corner blocks. If for some reason you are building a structure that requires extra strength, use a corner block in place of a keystone.

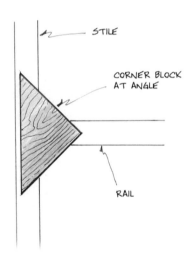

SUBSTITUTE A CORNER BLOCK FOR A KEYSTONE WHEN MAXIMUM STRENGTH IS NEEDED

A *template table* makes it much easier to assemble the parts of a flat. A template is a set of guidelines used to shape something else. Templates are used in such diverse pursuits as drafting and setting up word processing documents. In flat building (and other types of construction), they are used to square up the framing as it is put together. Many shops have constructed a large wooden table to use as a template, but a wooden floor works just as well. It is imperative to be able to nail into the surface of the template in order to hold your parts in alignment while working on the flat. You can also use a number of platforms laid edge to edge for this purpose.

A TEMPLATE TABLE

The first step in laying out the parts for assembly is to place the bottom rail against the bottom of the template. If there is any bow (*crown*) in the board, it should point toward the inside of the flat so that the structure will not rock when it is in its upright position. There should not be very much bow in such a short piece of 1×3. Next, place one of the stiles along the side of the table where the positioning blocks are. Make sure that the crown of this piece is pointed toward the inside of the flat as well. (Crown is another word for bow.) Using 6d finishing nails, secure these two pieces to the table, taking care to straighten them out along the blocks as you go. Try not to put any nails in the places where the corner blocks and keystones will need to be connected. Do not drive the nails in all the way; instead, leave the heads up a bit, so that it will be easier to remove them later on. Use the fewest nails possible to accomplish your purpose.

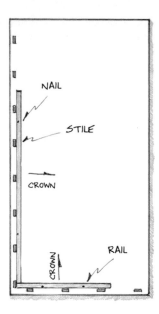

SECURE THE STILE AND RAIL
BUT DON'T PUT NAILS WHERE
THE CORNER BLOCKS WILL GO

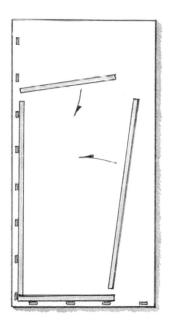

LINE UP THE CORNERS OF THE
REMAINING RAIL AND STILE

Set the remaining stile and rail in position, making sure to again point the stile's crown toward the interior of the flat. Adjust all corners so that they are flush with one another and nail down these last two pieces. When

tacking down the second stile, it is important to use nails only at the very ends of the piece, and close to the edge, where they will be out of the way of the corner blocks. That allows the stile to move as you remove the bow. If the nails are too far from the end, the joints will be dislocated when the stile is straightened. Very thin 6d finishing nails will make it less likely that the 1×3 will split when you nail so close to the end. Place the toggles in position and use them to press the second stile outward. If all of the pieces have been cut to the right sizes, the bow or crown should be removed and the flat should now be straight, square, and true.

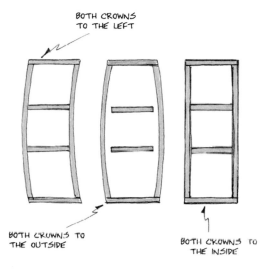

FOR BEST RESULTS, POINT ALL THE
CROWNS OR BOW TO THE INSIDE OF THE FLAT

If the amount of bow in the two stiles is relatively the same, it will have almost no effect on the finished product, because the force of one side pushing in is an equal but opposite reaction to the force of the other side. If you are making just one flat, you will have very little choice in the matter. But if you are making flats for an entire show at one time, there will most likely be a number of same-length stile pieces to choose from, and you can pick matching pairs for the various flats. It is much easier to make many flats all at once than to cut and assemble them one at a time. In industry that is often referred to as *economy of scale*, meaning that if you spread the cost of preparing to build a product over many multiples, the cost per unit is reduced. That philosophy works for building all sorts of things. It is very efficient, but of course, not nearly as much fun as making things one at a time.

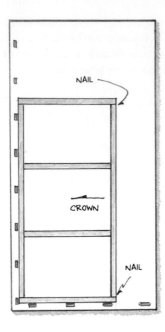

FOR A 1×3, MAKE A MARK 1 5/16" TO
EITHER SIDE OF THE TARGET AMOUNT

are close enough together that a partner may not notice the difference until it is too late.

TOGGLES SHOULD BE EVENLY SPACED

The up/down position of the toggles has never been written down on any of the construction sketches. It is common practice not to dimension the exact location of internal bracing. It is a given that the toggles will be evenly spaced inside the opening. In this case, there are two toggles, but they create three spaces inside the flat. If you had three toggles, there would be four spaces, and with four toggles five spaces, and so forth.

The number of spaces is used to calculate the placement of the bracing rather than the number of toggles. Divide the total distance by the number of spaces to determine the size of each one. In this case you divide 12′-0″ by three and arrive at 4′-0″. Sometimes, the toggles are used to brace something that will be added to the flat later on, such as a chair rail or some other piece of trim. In that case, dimensions may show the toggles are to be installed at a particular height from the bottom of the flat.

Imagine another case where the overall distance is 16′-0″ and the number of toggles is five, resulting in six spaces. Dividing 6 into 16 gives $2\frac{4}{6}$ feet, which is not an easy number to work with. Sometimes the numbers work better if you convert to all inches and try that way. Doing that, 16 × 12 = 192, a number that is easily divisible by 6. You can convert the resulting 32 inches back to 2′-8″, or simply continue to work with the inches if that is easier. If you write it down anywhere, be sure to use 2′-8″, because all of the other dimensions have been in feet and inches. If you write 32 instead, it may be misinterpreted as 3′-2″. Those two dimensions

In the example that goes with our project, the two toggles lie at 4′-0″ centers from the end. But that measurement is actually to the center of the toggles, and there is nothing on a 1×3 that marks the center of the board. You could measure $1\frac{5}{16}″$ to the center of the toggle and place a mark there, but the more accepted method is to measure the stiles at 4′-0″ and 8′-0″ and then to make a mark $1\frac{5}{16}″$ on either side of that point. That marks the two corners of the end of toggle itself and is a more accurate way than merely using the center of the toggle. $1\frac{5}{16}″$ is half of $2\frac{5}{8}″$.

An easy way to find half of any fraction is by doubling the denominator. In essence, you are multiplying the fraction by $\frac{1}{2}$. $\frac{1}{2}$ times a/b = a/2b. $\frac{1}{2}$ times $\frac{5}{8}$ is $\frac{5}{16}$.

When toggles are placed every 4′-0″, you can hook the tape measure over the bottom of the flat and make a mark $1\frac{5}{16}″$ to each side of each multiple of 4′-0″, or (in inches) 48″ and 96″. Mark both stiles since there are two ends to every toggle. Mark them all at once and avoid moving the tape for each measurement, because that allows placement error to creep in.

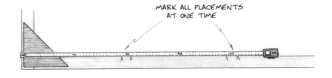

MARK ALL PLACEMENTS
AT ONE TIME

MARKING WHERE TOGGLES GO

After all of the framing for the entire flat has been tacked in place, attach the corner blocks and keystones. The traditional practice is to inset the blocks $\frac{3}{4}″$ from the outer edge of the flat. This is done in order to allow another flat made from $\frac{3}{4}″$-thick stock to fit evenly against it when making a 90-degree corner. This is done even if there is no immediate need for that to happen, as flats are often considered to be "stock" scenery, intended to be reused at a later date.

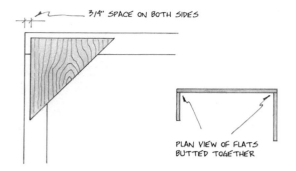

CORNER BLOCKS TRADITIONALLY HAVE A 3/4" INSET TO ALLOW THEM TO FORM A CORNER WITH ANOTHER FLAT

I have always gone along with this principle out of a sense of tradition unless there is a reason to deviate from it, and besides, it is easier to tack the framing to the table if there is a space around the edge where the nails can go. It is a fairly simple matter to mark all the corners and toggle locations by using a scrap length of 1×3 held on edge. Putting the blocks closer to the edge will result in a stronger structure, so if there is a concern about strength, you should definitely place the blocks closer to the edge. But if you inset at least a quarter of an inch, you will have a much better-looking result.

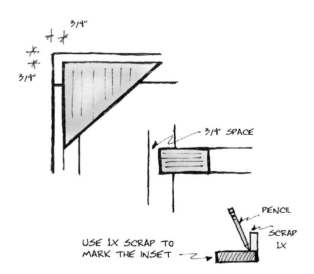

USE 1X SCRAP TO MARK THE INSET

Use a construction stapler with ¾"-long staples in it to attach the ¼" plywood blocks to their proper positions. Staples are the fastener of choice, because the crowns of the staples won't pull all the way through the thin blocks of plywood like finish nails from a nail gun

are likely to do. Naturally, any sort of power tool will be much faster than doing the job by hand. Sometimes a shop will use screws for this operation, but that seems like a bit of overkill when glue is used.

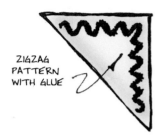

ZIGZAG PATTERN WITH GLUE

The strongest bond is formed by using a healthy application of aliphatic resin (yellow carpenter's) glue when attaching these blocks. Apply the glue using a kind of zigzag pattern. Put the block in place and then squish it back and forth a couple of times to spread the glue. You can pull one of the blocks back off every once in a while to confirm your gluing technique. The larger the surface area of the glue joint, the stronger the bond will be. Several small dots of glue on the back of the plywood block just won't do. You have only four or five minutes to get things arranged after putting the glue on, as carpenter's glue will start to set after that time. So don't put the glue on until you are ready to staple. Remember that the glue will hold much better than any fastener you could possibly use. For the most part, fasteners really only hold the wooden pieces together while the glue sets up.

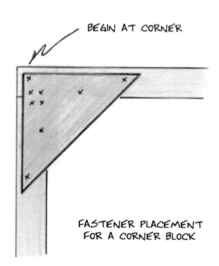

FASTENER PLACEMENT FOR A CORNER BLOCK

A traditional pattern is used to nail, staple, or screw the blocks in place. It is a good lesson in nailing technique, so you should use it for tradition's sake, even though using glue lessens the need for such exactitude. The pattern is as follows: one in each corner, two on either side of the joint, and one in the inside center on each leg. If you start with the staple that goes in the corner of the flat, it will make it much easier to line up the other two corners. From an engineering standpoint, it makes sense to secure the ends of the block and also the joint break. The center fasteners are added for good measure.

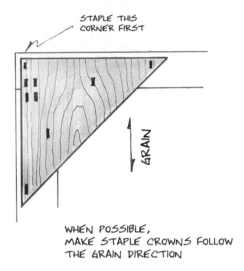

STAPLE THIS
CORNER FIRST

GRAIN

WHEN POSSIBLE,
MAKE STAPLE CROWNS FOLLOW
THE GRAIN DIRECTION

Keystones are fastened in the same way, but their rectangular shape creates a "double five" of dominoes appearance. Again, there is a staple in each corner, but this time four instead of three. If you are neat and tidy with the nail pattern, your work will have a more professional appearance. *There will be less flaking of the top veneer of the plywood if the crown of the staple follows the same direction as the grain of the plywood.* The crown is the top part of the staple, the section that holds the two legs together. If you are using lauan for your corner blocks instead of plywood (which the author cautions against) the thin and porous nature of the lauan may allow the staple to shoot all the way through when the crown is going the same direction as the grain.

When all of the corner blocks and keystones have been put in place, it is a good idea to wait just a few minutes for the glue to set up somewhat before removing the nails that are holding it in place on the template table. After the flat has been separated from the table, check it over for defects and remove any puckers from the front that were caused by the 6d nails. This will prepare the flat for covering and sizing. When building a show, it is common to generate a large stack of flat frames before going on to the covering stage. Some flats are constructed for use as structural members and may never be covered at all.

COVERING THE FLATS

Most painted flats are covered with either muslin or canvas. Both fabrics are made from unbleached cotton, with the difference being that the canvas is made from heavier threads and is therefore thicker and more durable. Heavyweight muslin is generally acceptable as a covering, because university shows tend to be of fairly short duration and extra strength is not required. Being constantly loaded in and out of theatres takes a heavy toll on scenery.

Some flats are covered with thin plywood rather than fabric. Most of the time that is because the designer wants to attach something to the surface of the flat that would not work well with a fabric cover. There may be a need to hang lots of artwork on the walls. There may be trim pieces that cannot be accommodated in any other way. Traditionally, flats with a hard cover are made in the "Hollywood" style as described later on, but on occasion traditional flats are used. The main problem encountered in using a hard cover on a traditional-style flat is that when plywood is placed on the thin edge of the 1×3, the framing tends to curl up, and it is difficult to get the flat to straighten out when it is assembled.

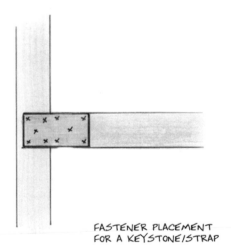

FASTENER PLACEMENT
FOR A KEYSTONE/STRAP

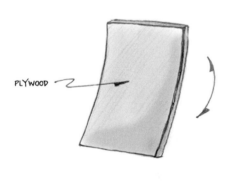

PLYWOOD

PUTTING PLYWOOD ON SOFT-COVERED
STYLE FRAMING CAN MAKE IT BOW

There are many different ways to affix muslin to a flat. The old-style method was to use tacks around the center of the flat, and animal glue (which is something akin to hot glue with a brush) to glue the muslin in place. Tacks are required due to the "instant stick" nature of this adhesive. The use of animal or hide glue has diminished in recent years both for political reasons (like where it comes from) and also because it is very messy to use. Hide glue must be heated in a special pot, and must be kept warm for hours on end. It is not the best thing you have ever smelled (because of where it comes from). Obviously, there is a risk of being burned by the glue. Today this sort of adhesive is mostly reserved for making expensive wooden musical instruments. For centuries, luthiers have appreciated the tone that hide glue gives to stringed instruments. It is also used in antique furniture repair.

THIS FLAT IS USED BY A PAINTING CLASS, SO THE COVER IS JUST STAPLED ON

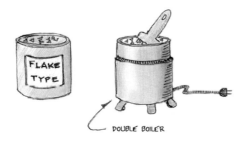

DOUBLE BOILER

HIDE OR ANIMAL GLUE IS BOUGHT BY THE POUND AND IS HEATED IN A GLUE POT

Some people stretch the muslin around the edges of the flat and staple it in the back as with an artist's canvas. This method does a good job of finishing off the raw edge of the flat. It is a good approach when the edges are likely to show to the audience. The downside is that the rear side of the flat is somewhat messy, and it may be difficult to attach hardware as a result.

Another method is to glue the muslin onto the face of the framing using the technique shown from here on. Begin by laying the flat face up on top of some saw-horses. Pull enough muslin off of the roll or bale to cover the flat. Leave 3 or 4 inches of extra fabric around the outside edges, and rip the muslin to the desired size. Ripping is actually much better than using scissors for this purpose because the muslin will rip much straighter than you can possibly cut it. Scissors are helpful in making a small notch to start the rip. Pull off the excess strings and drape the muslin over the toggles on the inside of the flat.

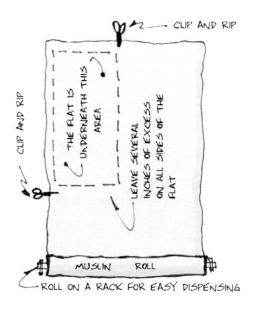

CLIP AND RIP

CLIP AND RIP

THE FLAT IS UNDERNEATH THIS AREA

LEAVE SEVERAL INCHES OF EXCESS ON ALL SIDES OF THE FLAT

MUSLIN ROLL

ROLL ON A RACK FOR EASY DISPENSING

Brush a generous helping of white glue onto the outer perimeter of the flat, spreading the glue over the entire surface of the 1×3. Do not put glue on any of the inside toggles or other framing. The muslin should be attached only on the outside, leaving the inside free. The only exception to this would be for a window flat, or some similar structure where the muslin is to be trimmed on the inside.

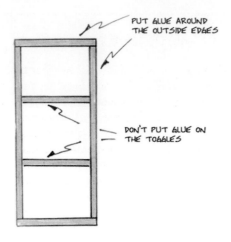

PUT GLUE AROUND THE OUTSIDE EDGES

DON'T PUT GLUE ON THE TOGGLES

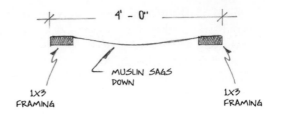

4' - 0"

MUSLIN SAGS DOWN

1X3 FRAMING

1X3 FRAMING

MUSLIN SHOULD SAG ABOUT 1" OVER 4 FEET

Pick up the muslin and place it gently on the surface of the flat and into the glue. This will take at least two people, and on a large flat, four. Walk around 90 degrees to the middle of the long sides of the flat and pull opposite one another to lightly stretch the muslin and press it very gently into the glue. Work together toward one end of the flat, straightening and pressing until that one end is finished, and then back to the middle, working toward the opposite end.

When the flat has been checked for puckers and bad glue spots, set it aside for at least 8 hours to let the glue dry. This gluing technique requires a high degree of finesse during the laying down and straightening out process, but once you have mastered it, it is much faster and easier than any other I have used. See the helpful hints section for some additional advice.

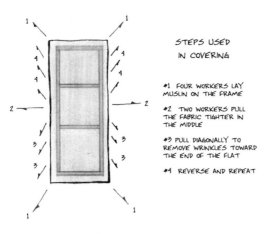

STEPS USED IN COVERING

#1 FOUR WORKERS LAY MUSLIN ON THE FRAME

#2 TWO WORKERS PULL THE FABRIC TIGHTER IN THE MIDDLE

#3 PULL DIAGONALLY TO REMOVE WRINKLES TOWARD THE END OF THE FLAT

#4 REVERSE AND REPEAT

MUSLIN LAYING ON TOP OF FRAMING

DRILL A 1/4" HOLE IN THE CAP AND USE THE ENTIRE GALLON JUG AS A GIANT SQUEEZE BOTTLE

GLUE

USE A 2" POLY BRUSH, OR SOME OTHER CHEAP TYPE TO SPREAD THE GLUE. DO NOT USE EXPENSIVE LINING BRUSH

Try not smear the glue around too much when positioning the muslin, because if you wipe it all off, there will be nothing left to adhere the fabric to the wood. It is not necessary to stretch the muslin tightly. It is actually better to leave some sag in the material, but no more than an inch on a 4-foot-wide flat. You have used enough glue if you can feel a slight dampness through the fabric, but it is not good to have wet, sticky glue on the surface of the fabric. When it is dry, glue prevents scenic paint from soaking into the cotton fibers. Casein paint will have a noticeably lighter hue in the glue-coated areas.

Trimming is best accomplished with a utility knife, or perhaps just the blade from one. Stretch the excess fabric off to the side and down just a bit in order to find the corner of the wooden framing. Puncture this spot and hold the blade up against the side of the 1×3. Trim the muslin by running the blade along the edge of the flat. Try to make the edge of the muslin exactly flush with the framing. Use one long motion to slice the muslin so that the cut is as smooth as possible.

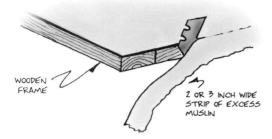

WOODEN FRAME

2 OR 3 INCH WIDE STRIP OF EXCESS MUSLIN

Sizing simply means to shrink the muslin fabric down to its proper size and tension by using a solution of very watery glue and/or paint. The normal ratio is in the neighborhood of 15 parts water to 1 part glue, but the exact amount is not all that crucial. A bit of paint in the mixture will make it easy to tell which part has been treated. Sometimes, when speed is of the essence, you might use a base color selected by the paint department. You can actually see the cover shrinking and tightening right away. It may be necessary at some point to check the edges of the flat for small sections of loose muslin, and to reglue these with a small bottle of Elmer's.

HARD-COVERED FLATS

Hard-covered flats are more appropriate when durability is a prime factor. The name comes from the thin sheets of plywood that form the covering. Hard-covers are at their best when smaller flats are required, such as in a TV studio and sometimes a movie set. The weight of the plywood becomes a major problem on larger flats. Most television scenery tends to be in the 9- to 10-foot-tall range. The nice thing about the hard-covers is that it is possible to cut holes in them to run cables or fog hoses or the like without destroying the structural integrity of the flat. Pictures can be hung just about anywhere without the need to install additional toggles, as is necessary with a traditional muslin-covered flat. These factors are especially helpful in television, where many decisions are not made until the very last moment and are difficult to predict. TV flats are often cut up to allow a new camera angle, or entire walls are moved around. The philosophy is that if the camera doesn't see it, it doesn't matter. In live theatre, the audience is free to look wherever they wish, and you must pay a bit more attention to the overall appearance of the setting. Being as neat as possible backstage is especially important in live theatre, because the stage manager cannot call out "cut" if something falls over backstage. The show must go on.

Hard-cover flats are definitely the more modern type, especially considering the high degree of realism required nowadays. Hard-cover flats are generally easier to build, more durable, and easier to connect together. But a stage carpenter should know how to build either type, as well as how to extend the techniques used to build them into the construction of other units.

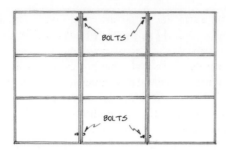

HARDCOVER FLATS CAN BE BOLTED
TOGETHER THROUGH THE FRAMING
ON THE BACKSIDE

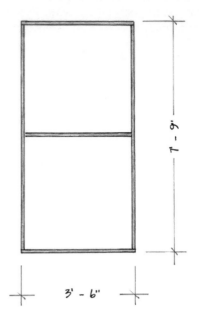

7' - 9"

3' - 6"

NOTE THE THINNER APPEARANCE
OF THE FRAMING WHEN IT IS
TURNED ON EDGE FOR A
HARDCOVER FLAT

MATH PROCESS

3/4" + 3/4" = 1 1/2"

7 - 8 2/2"
- 0' - 1 1/2"
7 - 7 1/2"

TV flats are built with the framing on edge, so that the wall is quite thick by comparison to the standard type. Flats are often bolted or screwed together edge to edge through the framing.

Soft-covered flats must be hinged together in back. As mentioned, it is possible to build a traditional soft-covered frame and then cover that with plywood. There are occasions where that is the best way to go. This section was written with the "on edge" type of framing in mind.

Because the entire face of the framing is covered with plywood, there is typically no need for corner blocks or keystones, or even corner braces. Hardcover flats are somewhat easier to construct than their traditional counterparts. Making a cut list is similar to the earlier process, but the sizes are different because of the way the framing is placed on edge. In the first example, the flat is no larger than 4 feet by 8 feet. The reason for this should be clear—the plywood covering is available in sheets no larger than that. It is possible to build a hardcover flat larger than 4×8, but special framing techniques must be used.

The overall dimensions are 3'-6" × 7'-9". As you would expect, the stiles are the longest framing pieces, and should appear first on the cut list. Remember that the milled thickness of a one-by is actually ¾″. Just as with the muslin flat cut lists, you must subtract the thickness of the two rails from the overall height of the flat to determine the length of the two stiles.

The length of the two rails is the overall width of the flat, 3'-6". The center toggle is found by again subtracting 1½″ from the overall width. Hence our cut list is expressed as shown here:

CUT LIST

2@ 7' - 7 1/2"

2@ 3' - 6"

1@ 3' - 4 1/2"

A window flat can be designed in the same way that a soft-cover version is, with internal framing forming the window area. Here is an example of that process:

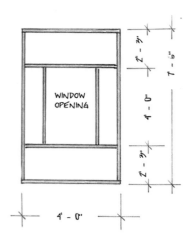

DIMENSIONS OF A HARDCOVER
WINDOW FLAT

The examples so far are flats smaller in size than 4 feet by 8 feet. To go larger than that requires a way to join the sheets of covering plywood together. The normal structural framing can be used to help with that, but you need some extra parts to make it all work.

The ¾″ width of a one-by is not wide enough to accommodate the joining process. Each plywood edge would have only ⅜″ resting on the framing, and that is not really enough for a reliable connection. A good method of enlarging that surface area is to turn a framing member on its side so that the widest surface is flush with the front of the regular framing. This type of framing member is called a *facing piece*. The facing pieces do not add much to the structural stability of the flat, but they work well for their intended purpose of attaching the cover. Here is an example of a flat that uses this technique. Notice that the facing piece is used in addition to the normal toggles.

The large surface area provided by the facing piece is excellent for gluing the plywood covering to the frame. You can see in the next drawing how the concept of facing pieces is used to frame a window flat that is larger than 4 feet by 8 feet.

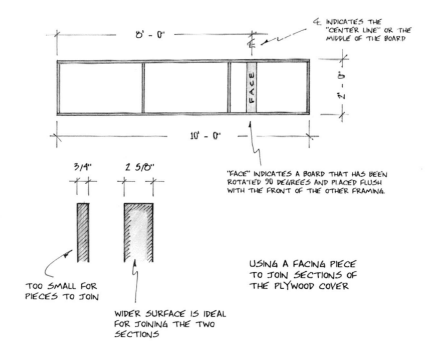

USING A FACING PIECE
TO JOIN SECTIONS OF
THE PLYWOOD COVER

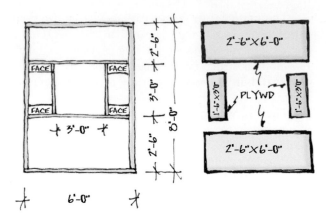

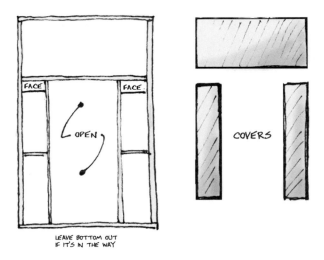

The final example is that of a door flat. The bottom rail passes all the way across the bottom of the flat, including the space that is left open for the doorway. This will leave a threshold that an actor must step over in passing through the door, but it greatly enhances the strength of the flat.

COVERING A HARDCOVERED FLAT

Notice how the facing members are situated so that the plywood covering pieces will be easy to cut and easy to install. The plywood covers are all simple rectangles. This method is much easier than trying to cut the lauan into a more complex shape, and also ensures that all edges of the covering are connected to the framing.

Sometimes a flat must have a solid covering wider than 4 feet. In that case, the facing pieces are arranged so that the plywood is applied horizontally. In reality, this would be a very heavy flat, and the excessive weight should be considered when deciding whether or not to use this method. Perhaps a series of smaller flats could be used instead. You can see there is a framing piece running up the middle of the flat that intersects the facing pieces. This internal stile must be notched to allow for passage of the facing pieces.

It is possible to build the unit without this framing member, but great care will need to be exercised in moving the flat, or the two sides of the doorway may easily be torqued to the breaking point. The action of the play may not allow for this member to be used. Sometimes a flat piece of metal, or bar stock may be used in place of the lumber. If so, the *sill iron* should be made from $\frac{1}{8}'' \times 1''$ stock, and be made to run all the way from side to side, underneath the regular framing. Sill irons are a traditional part of soft-cover flats used in touring.

CONSTRUCTION

Joining the framing of a hard-covered flat is pretty straightforward, although it is necessary to bear in mind that the flat should be put together face up, rather than face down as with a muslin flat. It is not necessary to use the template method, because the plywood covering will square up the flat. Be sure to use plenty of glue on the joints, although glue alone will not hold the framing together because of the small surface area involved. The glue does help, however.

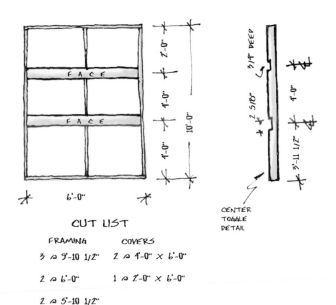

CUT LIST

FRAMING	COVERS
3 @ 9'-10 1/2"	2 @ 4'-0" × 6'-0"
2 @ 6'-0"	1 @ 2'-0" × 6'-0"
2 @ 5'-10 1/2"	

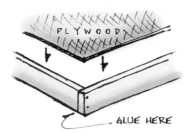

GLUE HERE

likely go unnoticed, but a crack that size in the covering would most certainly show.

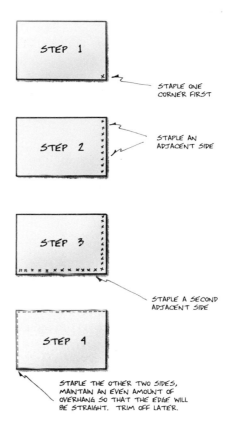

STEP 1 — STAPLE ONE CORNER FIRST

STEP 2 — STAPLE AN ADJACENT SIDE

STEP 3 — STAPLE A SECOND ADJACENT SIDE

STEP 4 — STAPLE THE OTHER TWO SIDES, MAINTAIN AN EVEN AMOUNT OF OVERHANG SO THAT THE EDGE WILL BE STRAIGHT. TRIM OFF LATER.

ATTACH THE PLYWOOD COVER

When measuring the placement of internal framing pieces, remember to use the measurement $\frac{3}{4}''$ rather than $2\frac{5}{8}$. A Speed Square is helpful for making sure that the toggles are square to the rest of the framing. After marking a location with two small Vs, use the square to mark a line through one of them and across the board. You can use this mark to line up the toggle when nailing. Often there is a slight discrepancy in the widths of the various framing pieces caused by mistakes in the ripping process. Be sure to flush the tops of the boards with the top of the framing, because that is the front of the flat.

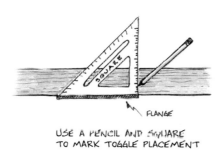

FLANGE

USE A PENCIL AND SQUARE TO MARK TOGGLE PLACEMENT

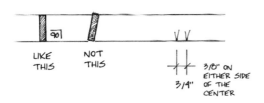

LIKE THIS   NOT THIS   V V

3/4"   3/8" ON EITHER SIDE OF THE CENTER

MARKING THE TOGGLE PLACEMENT

You must cut the plywood pieces that cover the front of the flat in advance of beginning the construction process, or there will be a problem with the glue setting up prematurely. It is often best to cut the covering parts a bit large, say $\frac{1}{16}''$ or even $\frac{1}{8}''$. That will allow enough extra so that they can hang over the edge a small amount after the cover is stapled on. You can trim this edge flush later. It is difficult to cut out all the framing parts and the covering parts and get them to all fit together closely without cheating a bit in this way. If the overall size of the flat were off by $\frac{1}{8}''$, it would most

Begin attaching the cover by putting glue on the tops of all framing parts that will be touched by the first section of plywood. Carefully lay the covering in place and adjust it so that one of the outside corners is aligned and flush. The other parts of the cover need not be exactly in place, but just close. Don't worry about them now. Staple the one corner, and then flush up and staple one of the adjacent sides starting from the corner where you began. Use a staple every 8 inches or so, aligning and stapling each point in turn. The most common mistake is to try and line up the whole thing at once. It is not really practical to do that, and it is completely unnecessary.

After the first side is done, return to the corner where you began and staple the adjacent side in the same manner as the first one. This process is used to square up the framing, and making one of the corners square should have the same effect on the rest. If the flat is 4×8 or smaller, it's an easy matter to finish up by stapling the remaining two sides. If you have oversized your plywood (sometimes even if you have not), there will be a small overhang on one or both of the two remaining sides. Do not pull the framing outward and flush the two surfaces in the middle unless it already fits that way at the corner. If you do, you will create a curve on that side of the flat. Try instead to leave the same amount of overhang along the entire length of the side. This is fairly easy to do if you feel the amount of overhang at the corner with your finger and then use the same finger to judge the amount of overhang as you work your way around the flat.

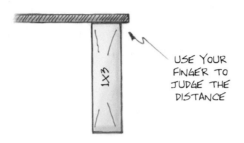

Be sure to run a line of staples into the internal framing parts as well as the outside edges. Use a straightedge to mark the location of the framing by looking at nail holes on the side. Longer lines can easily be marked using a chalk line. A drywall square can also be helpful.

After the covering has been completed, it is time to trim and fill the flat. Use a router with a *laminate trimming bit* to shave off the excess covering material. This type of *flush trim bit* has a large roller bearing on the bottom that makes for a smooth passage along the side. Because the cutters are exactly the same diameter as the bearing that rides on the framing, the cover will be trimmed to exactly the same size as the framing. Before starting, be sure to check for any nails or staples that might be sticking out, as these will permanently damage the bit.

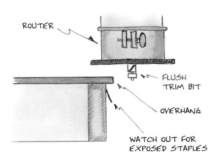

USE A ROUTER TO TRIM THE COVER

You can use joint compound to fill the joints and cracks that are a natural result of the construction process. If there will be a great deal of movement associated with the piece, it might be best to use auto body filler, but the joint compound is much easier to use and is incredibly cheap. A 5-gallon bucket costs only a few dollars and will last a very long time. Use the thicker variety.

Lots of different types of scenery are made using the same techniques as described for the construction of hardcover flats. You can extend these methods to many other projects.

It is very common to use plywood strips for the framing parts when the size of the unit is small, less than 8 feet in any direction. You can make the width of the plywood anything required by the plan, wider than would be possible with dimension lumber. Wider framing is used to make things like squared columns. If the unit needs extra strength, thicker stock can be used for the covering. If you need to make a profile piece that has a decorative edge, try using $\frac{1}{2}''$ plywood for the cover, because this will hold up better if the profile is complicated. The profile edge can overhang the framing by several inches with no problem.

Fitting together a large number of flats so that the cracks between them don't show is an ongoing struggle. There is really no elegant solution unless the problem has already been solved in the design process. If the design calls for a huge, flat, featureless wall, there is very little the carpenter can do to help the situation. Most designers incorporate breaks into the design that allow the set to be constructed of reasonably sized parts. Quite often there is a column or corner, or some other vertical diversion that will allow two flats to be joined without the edges showing. It is not a good practice to expect to use filler on joints of this sort after the scenery has been erected.

A few words of advice about the size of flats or other scenic units: if you need more than two stagehands to carry a piece, it is big. If four stagehands can't carry it, it is too big and you should either cut it in half or put wheels on it. And last, if it won't fit through the shop door, it won't make it to the stage.

HELPFUL HINTS

- A nail gun will make the process of nailing the framing together much easier to do. The Senco SFN1 gun with the 1½″ DA 17 nails or something equivalent is an excellent choice. This is a lightweight gun and is well balanced. The 1½″ nails are a good length to use for the framing. You may find that ¼″ crown staples are also excellent. You need that sort of stapler for the cover, so one tool can do both jobs.
- Be careful about where your fingers rest when the nail is fired into the wood. It is fairly easy for the nail to come out the side and into your finger if you leave that digit in the way. The flip side of this is that it is much easier to tell if parts are in line using your finger than by looking at them. Just be careful to move your finger before each shot.
- Use good quality yellow glue on the joints, and remember that this type of adhesive begins to set in just a few minutes. Plan ahead and have all your parts ready in advance.
- Lightly sanding the corners of the flat with 100-grit sandpaper will reduce splintering and give the flat a more finished look. Do not round the corners over very much if there are flats that need to fit flush against one another, as this will only make the crack appear larger.
- Remember when applying the joint compound that the idea is to fill the holes and not to create a build-up on the surface of the flat. Any amount extra that dries on the surface of the flat will have to be sanded off later, a time-consuming and thankless job.
- Staples must be used to attach the plywood covers, as nails will zip right through.
- The covering material of choice is often ¼″ lauan, a type of plywood from the Pacific Rim. This material has a very tight grain structure, and this grain does not "telegraph" through a paint job. Good-quality lauan is sometimes difficult to find. You might have better luck at a lumberyard servicing the cabinet-making industry than at a home center. Lauan is also discussed in the chapter on lumber and sheet goods. Just be aware that lauan is not terribly sturdy; ¼″ domestic plywood is much stronger, but has a grain pattern that is very easy to spot even after it is painted. Some shops glue muslin or even canvas on the outside of the plywood and framing to achieve a more paintable surface that is extremely durable.

CHAPTER 19

BUILDING STAIR UNITS

Actors can't get from one stage level to another without stairs. It is a rare stage setting that does not include them in some way, whether just one step up to a low platform or as a long set of backstage *escape stairs*. Stairs come in many different types that may be constructed to fit a particular need, but there are some properties held in common by all the various types.

There are three main parts to any set of stairs. The *treads* are what you step on when going up or down. *Risers* are the part of the unit that "rise" from one tread to another, and the *carriages* are the side pieces used to "carry" the weight of the entire unit. Steps vary greatly depending upon the types of materials used, steepness, whether they are left open or boxed in, and stylistic differences.

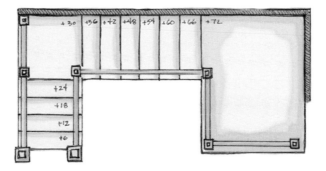

MANY DIFFERENT PARTS WORK TOGETHER
TO CREATE A SET OF STAIRS

STEP BASICS

There are a few general concepts to understand about how the human body relates to moving up and down to different levels. Everyone has tripped over a section of sidewalk that is suddenly higher than the surrounding area. You have also sat down in a chair that is lower than you think and had a sudden sensation of falling. This happens because the body accustoms itself to certain distances and rhythms and comes to expect them. The same principle makes it possible for me to type these words or for a musician to play the piano without either of us looking at the keys.

When climbing a set of stairs, your body develops a rhythm to its movement, and if one of the steps is of a different height, that unexpected difference may cause you to trip. For this reason, it's important that all risers be of the same height, and likewise, for all treads to be of the same depth. Without that, a set of stairs can be very dangerous.

doi: 10.1016/C2009-0-23409-X

You can determine the rise of steps by dividing the total number of rises into the total height. Stage stairs are usually easy to plan because stage platforming tends to be in even amounts. If a platform is exactly 2 feet tall you can determine riser height in even numbers. If you want to have a rise of 6 or 8 inches (commonly used increments), then you can divide that riser height evenly into a platform height of 24 inches. A 9-inch riser wouldn't work, because that height will not divide cleanly into 24 inches. Nine-inch risers will fit neatly, however, with a platform height of 36 inches. Divide the height of the platform by the individual riser height to get the number of rises required. The number of risers is one more than the total number of treads, if the platform itself is used as the top step.

their feet. That works well on the way upstairs, even if the tread is quite shallow. But if the front part of your foot is hanging off the tread on the way downstairs, that movement will seem very unnatural and difficult. Normally, it is best not to exceed a slope of 45 degrees with any stair unit. Bearing these limits in mind, a stair with a 9-inch tread (run) and a 9-inch rise is the steepest acceptable unit. But those proportions are very steep and will require a sturdy handrail and good clip light. An 11-inch tread depth is much more actor-friendly. Most building codes call for measurements no steeper than a 7-inch rise and 11-inch run.

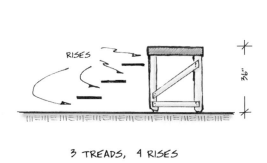

3 TREADS, 4 RISES

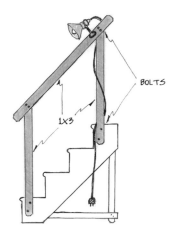

AN EASILY CHANGED HANDRAIL
FOR ESCAPE STAIRS

The height of the rise is usually a design consideration and is determined on the basis of artistic concerns that are beyond the scope of this book, although there are some practical points that should be taken into account. It is best for a technician to understand how choices are made to better interpret the design safely.

It is hard for the average person to ascend a stair that has a rise of over 9 inches. It is just too far to raise your foot every time you take a step. Strangely, it is also difficult to negotiate a stair with a very shallow rise, say less than 6 inches. Perhaps this is because we are just not used to them.

Treads should never be less than 9 inches deep if an actor is to come down the stair with any sense of grace. As a general rule, it is much easier to climb a difficult set of steps than to descend. Most people walk with their weight resting on their toes and the balls of

Quite often, a set of drawings for a particular show may indicate that escape stairs should be "pulled from stock" or are otherwise left to the discretion of the carpenter. As a result, you may have occasion to determine a common riser height on your own, apart from any plans supplied by the designer.

In order to figure out the common height of each riser, you need to know the overall height that the stairs must ascend, and also the number of steps that will be used. It should be easy to find the overall height, as this is the distance from the floor to the level the stair reaches. The number of steps is a bit trickier, as you will need to choose a number that will result in a rise of between 6 and 9 inches. Of course, if you guess

STAIR TERMINOLOGY

Rise and run: The measurements of height and depth for a stair unit.

Riser: The vertical connection of two levels or steps.

Tread: The part you step on.

Carriage: The side framing that keeps the treads and risers together.

Newel post: A large post that anchors the end of, or a bend in, a section of railing. The newel post at the bottom of a stairway is usually the most ornate.

Baluster or spindle: An upright piece used to support the handrail. Spindles are rounded and usually turned on a lathe.

Landing: An area used for a change in a stairway's direction. This is most common when a number of different sections or flights of steps are used.

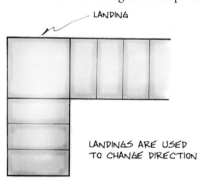

LANDING

LANDINGS ARE USED TO CHANGE DIRECTION

---

the wrong number, you can always try again with no harm done.

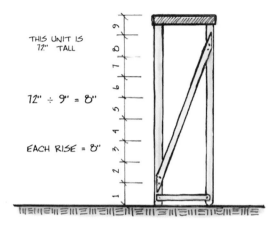

THIS UNIT IS 72" TALL

72" ÷ 9" = 8"

EACH RISE = 8"

This illustration shows a 6'-0" platform. It is easier to work this sort of problem using all inches, which would be 72". Nine inches would be the tallest possible rise, and 72" divided by 9 results in eight rises to get from the floor to the top of the platform. One of the 9" rises is actually the space that occurs between the top step and the platform. As a result, this stair would have eight rises but only seven treads. You could just as well use a riser height of 8", which would mean nine rises and eight treads. A 7" rise would result in 10.3 risers, which of course wouldn't work.

The preceding problem was made quite a bit simpler by virtue of the fact that the first two sets of numbers divided evenly. Unfortunately, this does not always happen, and quite often the process goes a bit more like this: imagine that the platform height is 8'-6", which converts to 102". Guessing that 11 rises might work, 11 into 102 gives you 9.3 inches per rise. A rise of 9.3" is in excess of the 9" maximum we have set for ourselves. If you substitute 12 for the number of rises and do the math, you will discover that with 12 rises, each individual rise would be 8.5 inches. This is lucky, because the decimal number 0.5" is easy to convert to a fractional equivalent of $\frac{1}{2}$". If you need an easier climb, then 13 rises would give you an average of 7.8 inches each. Again, 7.8 is a decimal number, slightly more than $\frac{3}{4}$".

A decimal expression such as 7.8 may be converted to a woodworking fraction by using a ratio to determine the number of sixteenths that a base-ten number equals. Use the equation $z/10 = x/16$. In this equation, z represents the number of tenths and x is the number of sixteenths—a fraction that you can find on a tape measure. The conversion of 7.8 to a woodworking fraction goes like this:

```
TO CONVERT BASE 10
DECIMALS TO SIXTEENTHS
USE THIS EQUATION FOR A RATIO:

    2/10 = X/16

    EXAMPLE:

    8/10 = X/16
    X = (8·16)/10
    X = 128/10
    X = 12.8
WHICH ROUNDS OFF TO ~ 13/16
```

The rounding off will leave a margin of error that is really too small to be of importance. As you can see, it is far easier to start out with a more user-friendly decking height, or to choose the $8\frac{1}{2}''$ riser height. But that may not always be an option.

A STEP-BUILDING METHOD

Here is a method of building stairs that uses nothing other than $\frac{3}{4}$-inch plywood. It is presented first because it is an easy and straightforward way to build a small step unit based on very clear engineering principles. Using only one material streamlines the process, and it produces a neat and clean piece of work, which should be a major objective of any craftsman.

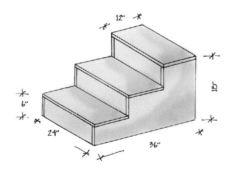

This step unit has a 6″ tall rise and a 12″ deep tread. There are three treads in total, and the width of the steps is 24″. Remember that the steps are constructed exclusively of $\frac{3}{4}$″-thick plywood. In order to construct this unit, you will need to develop a cut list of the parts.

Most people find it easier to make the list of parts in order from the most easily understood to the most difficult to figure out. The easy answers give clues to the difficult ones, which works well in many different situations. Remember that determining the overlapping members is critical to forming a cut list.

A close examination of the drawing reveals that the $\frac{3}{4}''$ plywood pieces used for the three treads stretch all the way from the left side to the right side of the unit. They also extend from the very front to the very back of the 12-inch dimension. There are no other structural members overlapping them that would make the tread pieces smaller than the listed dimensions, so you can determine that there are three treads @ 12″ × 24″. It makes sense that the treads rest on top of the other parts, because they are weight-bearing. If the treads were nailed on the inside of the other parts, only the nails would be supporting them. The shear strength of a nailed joint like that is not very high.

```
CUT LIST


TREADS ...    3 @ 12″ X 24″
```

The next part to consider is the bottom riser. Notice in the drawing that this riser piece fits inside, between the two carriages. The overall dimension of the width is 24″, so to get the width of just the riser piece, you must add $\frac{3}{4}'' + \frac{3}{4}''$ and subtract that from the overall width of the unit.

```
SUBTRACT THE
THICKNESSES OF THE
TWO CARRIAGES


24″ - (3/4″ + 3/4″) = 22 1/2″


ALL THE RISERS AND
NAILERS FIT BETWEEN
THE TWO CARRIAGES
```

Similarly, you can see that the overall height of the tread from the floor is given as 6″, but that this measurement is to the top of the tread while the riser only reaches up to the bottom of it. The tread is ¾″ thick.

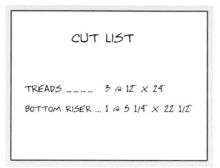

The remaining two risers require a bit of explanation, because they have parts that join in a way that cannot be seen in the original drawing of just the outside of the unit. A section view through the center shows the hidden internal parts

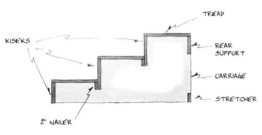

SECTION VIEW OF INTERNAL PARTS

You can see from the exterior drawing that the second and third risers have the same width as the first one did. The height of the next riser is not decreased by ¾″ as the first one was. It starts ¾″ *below* the *top* of the first tread, and winds up ¾″ *below* the *top* of the next one. So nothing is gained or lost. Even though ¾″ is lost by subtracting the thickness of the tread on top, it is regained by adding back the thickness of the tread on the bottom. In addition, the section view shows that these two risers extend below the underlying tread by a distance of 2 inches. This allows for a second piece of ¾″ ply to be scabbed onto the front of the riser.

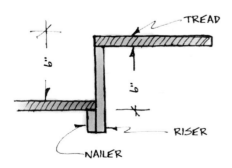

When the 2″ is added, the total height of the riser is 8″. These risers should be listed as 2 @ 8″ × 22½″. The 2-inch piece of plywood is added in order to give the tread a framing member to rest upon. If this were not done, then the rear of the tread would be supported only by nails driven horizontally through the bottom of the riser next to it. Many steps are made in that way, but it proves to be an inherently weak structure. The nails easily bend, and the glue bond breaks. Adding the 2-inch nailer prevents that from happening.

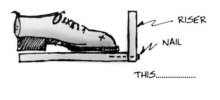

THIS.............

CAN EASILY BECOME

GLUE BOND BREAKS
NAIL PULLS OUT
UNIT FAILS

There are some rules with this construction method that make it quite easy to figure a cut list. The first riser piece is always ¾″ shorter than the overall height of the rise. All other risers, regardless of how many there are, will be 2″ taller than the given riser height. The 2″-wide nailers we have been discussing are of course only 22½″ wide, because they fit to the inside of the carriages. The horizontal member at the back of the step unit and which supports the top tread will also be 22½″ wide, with the other dimension varying depending on the width of the step unit. Very wide steps require a beefier member, but a 3½″-wide strip should prove sufficient for this small unit. The 3½″ width was selected because it is the same as the milled width of a 1×4. If there is a supply of 1×4 white pine on hand, you can substitute it for a plywood version of this part.

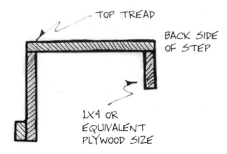

The two carriages are the only remaining items for your cut list. These pieces are not rectangles, but rather a more complex shape. Because of that, it isn't possible to describe them merely by saying they are "so wide by so long." Instead, you must make a small sketch and dimension the parts.

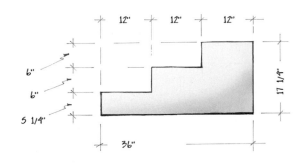

CARRIAGE DIMENSIONS FOR CUT LIST

The section of the carriage that corresponds to the bottom riser is dimensioned at 5¼″ just as the riser was and for the same reason, because it fits under the tread rather than to the side of it. The next two rises are an even 6″ each, as they both lose and gain ¾″ from their respective treads. The depth of the tread is given at 12 inches. Note that the overall height is 17¼″, ¾″ smaller than the height of the finished unit.

CONSTRUCTING THE STEPS

Use the table saw to rip the ¾″ plywood into strips of the proper width and the radial arm saw to cut the

strips to length. The project will be more aesthetically pleasing if the grain of the exterior veneer on the plywood runs the length of the pieces. B/C yellow pine plywood is probably the best choice of material, because it is readily available and will create a nice finished appearance. C/D is not normally recommended, because it is usually too warped and full of voids to fit together well enough to be structurally sound when cut into small pieces. Use all of the measuring and marking skills you learned from the chapters on woodworking and flats. This method of construction depends upon a high degree of accuracy from the cutting process, and parts that are not the right size will not fit together well.

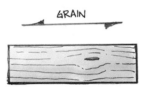

FOR BEST RESULTS, RUN GRAIN THE LENGTH OF YOUR PARTS

Because the carriages are not a simple rectangular shape, they require a bit more work to cut out. If the unit is small with only a couple of steps, then it might be best to cut out a rectangle that is the proper overall size, and then to cut notches to form the required shape. If the step unit is larger, with a number of steps, that might be too wasteful a process. If you are making many units at one time, there will probably be some intuitive manner of laying out the parts that will save on materials. At any rate, mark lines for the parts using the sketch you made as a guide, transferring the measurements and connecting the marks with a straightedge. Use either the band saw (if the part will fit) or a jigsaw to cut along the lines. Remember to make the kerf fall on the side of the line that will become scrap.

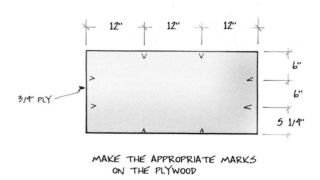

MAKE THE APPROPRIATE MARKS
ON THE PLYWOOD

3/4" PLY

12" 12" 12"

6"
6"
5 1/4"

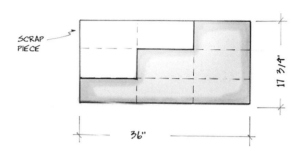

SCRAP PIECE

17 3/4"

36"

CONNECT THE DOTS WITH LINES,
AND DRAW IN THE PROFILE OF THE
CARRIAGE

the two pieces apart to see if that was enough. Pressing the two pieces together and then squishing slightly from side to side will help to spread the glue. Yellow aliphatic resin (carpenter's) glue is the best. It has very fast bonding properties, so be aware that once this glue is applied, you have only a few minutes before the glue begins to set. If you disturb the glue bond after it has begun to gel, but before the bond is completed, the strength of the connection will be greatly reduced.

Finishing nails or staples from a gun do not have a great deal of holding power, so the glue really is essential. It is good to make a habit of gluing together more or less every joint on all projects, unless you know from the outset that they will need to be taken apart at some point in the future. When that is the case, screws or bolts are the preferred fasteners.

Many nailers set the nail (or staple) an eighth of an inch or so into the surface of the plywood. Be sure to bear this in mind when selecting the length of fastener to use. For a double layer of $\frac{3}{4}$"-thick plywood, a $1\frac{1}{2}$" fastener is really too long. The *set* of the fastener by the nail gun would cause this length to protrude from the back of the underlying piece of plywood. That can lead to some nasty cuts on anyone handling the scenery and looks just awful. Use a slightly shorter $1\frac{1}{4}$" nail or staple instead.

The second phase of assembling the steps is to connect the risers and the carriages together. Remember that the carriages have a good and a bad side, and of course the good side should face outward. It is easiest to stand one of the center risers on end, put glue on the end that is up, then lay the carriage on top of the riser. If you nail the center riser first, you can balance the carriage while you go about the business of nailing it. Once a second riser is attached, the pieces will stand up on their own and make it much easier to finish the job. Standing the risers on end will also keep the glue from running off the edge as quickly. Be sure to flush what will become the top of the riser to the top of the carriage, and the face of the riser with the front of the carriage.

Assembly is made easier by following a certain order of work. Connect the 2"-wide nailers to the 8"-wide risers first. Keep track of the good and bad sides of the plywood, because of course you want to put the good side facing outward. For the two riser parts, this means attaching the 2"-wide strip to the good side of the 8"-wide riser, taking care to align it with the bottom and the two sides.

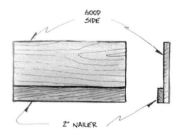

GOOD SIDE

2" NAILER

ATTACH THE 2" NAILER TO THE
GOOD SIDE OF THE RISER

A nail gun or a construction stapler will greatly speed up assembly. Use glue to help adhere the two surfaces. Apply enough so that the surfaces are completely coated. You can learn to gauge this amount by putting on the glue in a zigzag pattern and then pulling

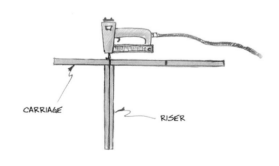

CARRIAGE

RISER

TURN THE RISER ON END TO
ATTACH THE CARRIAGE TO IT

Once you've completed the task of joining the three risers and the support that goes at the back of the top tread, flip the unit over and attach the second carriage in the same way. Gluing helps hold the wood together. Use enough fasteners to hold the parts together well, but not so many that they split the plywood apart.

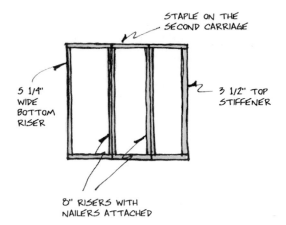

STAPLE ON THE SECOND CARRIAGE

5 1/4" WIDE BOTTOM RISER

3 1/2" TOP STIFFENER

8" RISERS WITH NAILERS ATTACHED

After attaching the second carriage, turn the step unit upright and nail on the treads. The assembly of carriages and risers may not be especially square when you look at them. That's because we've done nothing so far to make them so. Use the treads to square things up. Each one should, unless something has gone horribly awry in the cutting process, have four 90-degree angled corners, and two sets of equal sides. This is the ideal shape to use in squaring up a structure.

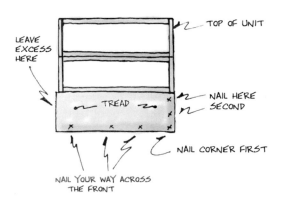

LEAVE EXCESS HERE

TOP OF UNIT

NAIL HERE SECOND

TREAD

NAIL CORNER FIRST

NAIL YOUR WAY ACROSS THE FRONT

START IN THE CORNER FLUSH UP TWO ADJACENT SIDES TO SQUARE THE STEP UNIT

Put glue on the surfaces that lie underneath the bottom tread, and set the tread into position. Adjust the tread until one of the front corners is perfectly aligned with the corner of the riser and carriage, and put one

nail in this corner. Twist the entire step unit until the side of the tread is flush with the carriage, and secure that back corner with a nail. The short side of the tread is connected to the assembly. Now nail the front of the

HELPFUL HINTS

- Don't try to align all the parts completely before you begin to nail. Line up only the section you are nailing at the time.
- B/C plywood is $\frac{1}{32}$″ thinner than the nominal size. There are two sides to the unit, so the stairs will be $\frac{1}{16}$″ narrower than planned. You can cut the treads that much smaller to make them fit better, or make the length of the risers that much longer.
- If the tread is slightly too small from front to back, leave a space in the back where it isn't so noticeable.
- A *stretcher* at the bottom of the step unit in the only remaining free corner will help to prevent the plywood carriages from warping inward.

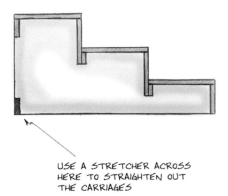

USE A STRETCHER ACROSS HERE TO STRAIGHTEN OUT THE CARRIAGES

- The width of the nailer that holds up the back edge of the treads does not have to be 2 inches. That is simply a number I chose because it is easy to add with other numbers. If you are planning to construct a very wide unit of more than 60 inches or so, increase the size of this member to accommodate the longer span. You can build steps up to 96 inches in width using this method and a $3\frac{1}{2}$″-wide nailer. The steps require no center carriage and are completely rigid, with no detectable deflection in the center. Methods that require the use of one or more center carriages are much more difficult to assemble.

tread, beginning at the first corner you attached and then working your way across to the other side. Aligning two adjacent sides and securing them will automatically square up the entire unit. It is the same process that was used to square hard-cover flats in an earlier chapter. It is essential to remember to square up the unit as you go along. A nail every 8 inches or so is generally sufficient. Use each one to resquare the unit as you go along.

ALTERNATIVE BUILDING TECHNIQUES

Sometimes the design of a stair makes it necessary to use an alternative method of step building. This is often true for stairs with many steps, or when an open-riser look is mandated. Some stairs are curved, or at an angle. Some must be made from metal.

Long or tall stairs are most commonly made using the *stringer* technique. Any step unit that rises more than 3 feet or so in height will be very heavy when constructed with a solid carriage. In this case, the stringer style is much lighter and is generally preferred.

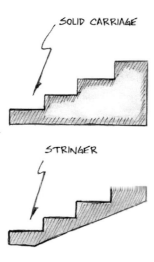

The drawing illustrates the difference between the two types, which seems quite significant. In reality, the stringer style is constructed in more or less the same manner as the previous demonstration, except for the diagonal nature of the carriage, and the method of marking the notches. This style of carriage is actually somewhat easier to lay out and cut than the closed style. The process is begun by ripping a strip of ¾″ plywood for the stringer. If an 8-foot-long section of plywood will not be long enough, it is possible to *laminate* together thinner stock to make up the stringers. Be sure to offset the joints in the laminating process to produce a stronger member.

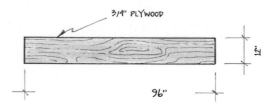

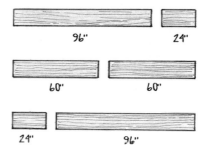

IF YOUR STRINGER PIECE MUST BE LONGER THAN 8'-0', YOU WILL NEED TO LAMINATE IT TOGETHER FROM 1/4" THICK PLYWOOD

WHEN LAMINATING PARTS TOGETHER, OFFSET THE JOINTS AS MUCH AS POSSIBLE. PUT GLUE OVER THE ENTIRE SURFACE OF THE JOINT WITH A PAINTBRUSH OR ROLLER.

For most applications, a 12-inch-wide strip of plywood is wide enough for the stringer, although if the stair is to have unusually high rises, deep treads, or a great many steps, it may be necessary to increase the width of the strip to 15 or perhaps 16 inches. It is important that the stringer be large enough to maintain its strength even after the notches have been cut into it.

After the stock for your stringers has been ripped to the proper width, you can mark the location and angle of the notches for the steps. Use a *framing square* for this job. It is best to use a regular square that is 16 inches on one side and 24 inches on the other. A Speed Square will not work. An aluminum square is by far the easiest to use because it is much lighter, and the numbers are easier to read. Remember that with most framing squares, the markings on one side are in twelfths of an inch and in sixteenths of an inch on the other side. The twelfths are used to work on roof pitches and are of little use in scenery building, so you should use the side marked in sixteenths. If you are not sure which is which, count the number of small spaces between the inch marks.

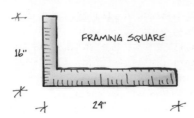

FRAMING SQUARE

16"

24"

Another helpful tool that is an adjunct to the framing square is the *stair gauge*. Gauges are essentially small clamps that may be fastened to the edge of the framing square. They make it easy to repeatedly find the same spot on your framing square and function as a jig to increase the accuracy of your layout.

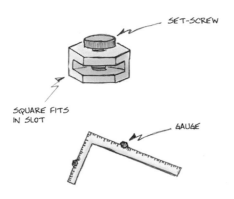

SET-SCREW

SQUARE FITS
IN SLOT

GAUGE

STAIR GAUGES CLAMP ONTO THE SQUARE
SO THAT YOU CAN EASILY RETURN TO
THE SAME SETTING

Assume that you wish to lay out a set of stairs with a rise of 6 inches and a tread depth of 10 inches. Take the framing square and lay the corner of it across the plywood so that the 6-inch mark on the short side of the square is even with the near edge of the plywood. Rotate the framing square until the 10-inch mark on the long side of the square lines up with the same edge of the plywood strip. If you have a set of stair gauges, attach them to the square so that it is easy to return to the alignment you set up.

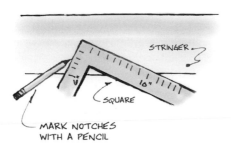

STRINGER

SQUARE

MARK NOTCHES
WITH A PENCIL

Use a pencil to trace around the outside edge of the square and mark one tread depth and one rise. It is best to start at the bottom of the stringer when marking the layout. There is one really tricky part to the process. The bottom rise, as laid out on the stringer, must be shorter in height than the remaining rises by the thickness of the tread, which in our case is ¾". Use the framing square and measure down from your tread line 5¼" in two widely divergent places, making sure that you are measuring at a right angle to the tread line.

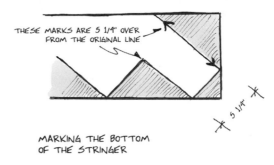

THESE MARKS ARE 5 1/4" OVER
FROM THE ORIGINAL LINE

5 1/4"

MARKING THE BOTTOM
OF THE STRINGER

Use the square as a straightedge to draw a line parallel to the original tread line, and that runs through the 5¼" marks. You have established the very bottom of the stringer, the part that makes contact with the stage floor.

From this point, it is a fairly simple matter of drawing in as many repetitions of the first riser/tread layout as are required to reach the desired height for the stringer. When the top tread line is marked, don't mark the corresponding rise line upward, but instead mark a line downward from the tread line to finish off the step.

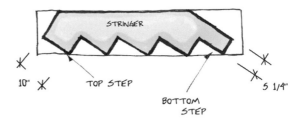

STRINGER

10"   TOP STEP   5 1/4"

BOTTOM
STEP

Construction of this type of step unit is basically the same as our first unit, save for the fact that that the carriage is shaped differently. The riser section subassemblies are built first, and then attached to one of the stringers. Then the opposite stringer is connected, and finally the treads are used to square the unit. You will need help with these stringers, because they are so much bigger and heavier than the carriages in the smaller unit discussed earlier.

At this point you may well wonder how this type of stair remains upright, as the carriage does not reach all the way to the floor in the back. One way is to leg the stair so that vertical framing members keep the unit erect. You will need two legs in the back and enough bracing to keep the whole thing together.

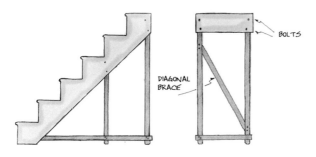

LEGS ON A STRINGER-TYPE STAIR

Notice the triangles formed by the bracing in the drawing of the freestanding stair on the last page. You can see one large triangle in the side view created by the horizontal rail, the upright member, and the stair itself. In the rear view, you can see two triangles that share a hypotenuse. Triangles are a very strong structural form and are often seen in various types of bracing.

If the stair connects with a sturdy enough platform, it is easy to use that platform to support the stair. If more than one set of stairs is connected to the platform (a front set and escape, for example), the stairs may actually enhance the stability of the platform by acting as diagonal bracing.

Sometimes the design calls for stairs that have open risers; that is, the piece that physically makes up the riser itself is left off. These stairs have a more open appearance to them. In this case, the type of all-plywood construction we have been discussing will not work. A ¾-inch plywood tread is not nearly strong enough to support the weight of a person, even when the steps are very narrow, without being joined with a riser. Therefore a thicker and stronger tread material must be used. Most commonly, two-by lumber of some sort is used, probably a 2×12 or a 2×10, as any narrower dimension would be too small for the tread. This type of stair usually has carriages made from a 2×12 also, and they must be cut out with the stringer method if the overall height of the stair is more than 12 inches.

When 2×12s are used, the thickness of the treads will be 1½″ rather than ¾″. As a result, the bottom rise will need to be marked 1½″ smaller on the bottom of the stringer rather than ¾″ as noted in the earlier exercise. This type of stair unit may appear to be airier and lighter to the eye, but it is in reality much, much heavier. It lacks the "portability factor" required by most stage scenery. It will also tend to be less precise, and to warp out of shape more easily, so it is not such a good choice from an engineering standpoint.

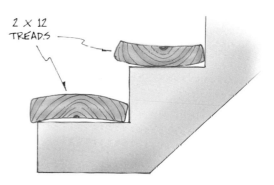

2 X 12 TREADS

2 X 12 LUMBER TENDS TO CUP, AND MAY NOT LAY FLAT ON THE CARRIAGE. IT'S ALSO VERY HEAVY

It is possible to make this unit entirely from laminated plywood by using three layers of ½″ ply on the stringers. You can use a double lamination of ¾″ ply for the treads instead of dimension lumber, with the advantage being that the resulting material is more stable. If you glue the plywood together so that only the good side is out, its appearance is enhanced, and any natural bow in the plywood will tend to cancel itself out.

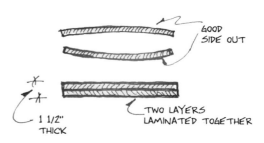

GOOD SIDE OUT

1 1/2" THICK

TWO LAYERS LAMINATED TOGETHER

In recent years, stair units constructed from steel tubing have become very popular. *Square tube* is a popular choice for metal construction, because it is much easier to cut and fit together than any other shape. Tube cutting and joining techniques are shown in Chapter 21. Steel square tube framing presents a very light, open quality to the audience, which belies the fact that it is often rather heavy instead. However, the unique look of the material has made it a popular choice for designers, especially when the design calls for an industrial look. Although the steel itself is very heavy, it can be joined in ways that use less material, and some structures are not as heavy as you might think.

For steel square tube construction, use thin plywood or lauan to make a pattern in the shape of a carriage, as discussed earlier. Cut square tube parts to fit the jig and weld them together. Chapter 21 goes into detail about how to use wooden blocks to make a temporary jig that will hold the parts in position while they are being welded. After the carriages have been constructed, use straight pieces of tubing to connect the two carriages and form the support for plywood treads.

An alternative method is to create rectangular metal frames for the treads, and join them together with runners on the sides of the step unit. Angle the bottom ends of the runners so that they mate with the floor at the proper angle.

MAKE A PATTERN FROM SCRAP PLYWOOD AND USE IT TO BUILD A JIG FOR THE SQUARE TUBE STRUCTURE

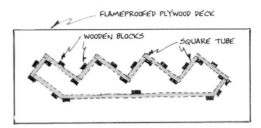

FLAMEPROOFED PLYWOOD DECK

WOODEN BLOCKS   SQUARE TUBE

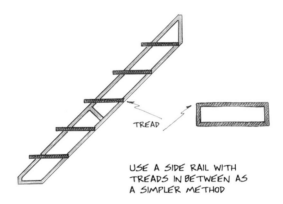

TREAD

USE A SIDE RAIL WITH TREADS IN BETWEEN AS A SIMPLER METHOD

CHAPTER 20

DECKING METHODS

Generally speaking, platforming is the most difficult and expensive scenery to build. Platforms are more heavily constructed than most other stage scenery, because of the weight they must carry—not only the weight of the setting that is placed upon it, but the combined pounds of all the actors as well. Moving objects like actors create what is known as a *live load*, which requires a sturdier structure than a *static load*. Actors who are dancing, or running, or jumping up and down create a load that is really several times their combined weight, because their mass is multiplied by their acceleration to arrive at the force or load acting on the platforming. A group of dancers running to one side of the stage and suddenly stopping causes a great deal of sideways or *lateral stress* on the structure that elevates the platforming. Care must be taken to assure that any decking system is safe for the type of load that will be placed on it.

The words *platform* and *deck* are often used interchangeably. In a subtle way, "decking" tends to indicate platforms that are part of a system, and saying "deck" or "platform" often means a single piece.

You may notice in this chapter how many of the techniques and processes mentioned earlier in the book are also useful in constructing platforms. Flip back to some of the earlier chapters for more information about tools, woodworking, and wood products like plywood and lumber.

COMMERCIALLY MANUFACTURED DECKING

THIS PLATFORMING SYSTEM WAS DESIGNED AS PORTABLE STAGING FOR CONCERTS IN LARGE ARENAS. IT IS VERY EASY TO SET UP, BUT IS NOT SUITABLE FOR THEATRE WORK BECAUSE IT IS TOO HEAVY, AND ISN'T VERY ADAPTABLE.

doi: 10.1016/C2009-0-23409-X

STOCK DECKING

Most permanent theatre companies use stock decking units to decrease the cost of using platforms. The most common size for a stock platform is the 4×8, because that is the size of a sheet of plywood. It is often cost effective to have some other stock sizes too, such as 2×8 and/or 4×4. These dimensions are a good fit with a 4×8, and in combination they create a large variety of platform shapes. You may find that your particular theatre benefits from some other types as well. A prudent designer considers the use of standard units in designing a show, so as to reduce the cost of construction. Directors like platforms, because they create different levels between actors, and you will have many encounters with decking over a lifetime in show business.

Professional scenery-building shops often use either aluminum rectangular tubing or $\frac{5}{4}$ clear lumber to frame a platform. That makes for an excellent product, but can be a bit pricey for smaller theatres and/or universities. Nonetheless, when building stock platforms that will be kept for a very long time, it is generally good to splurge on the best materials you can afford. Stock platforms are in constant use for years before they are no longer viable. In view of how long they last, the expense seems worthwhile. Try to have a global approach to designing the decking, so that all the parts are interchangeable. When constructing oddly shaped platforms for one specific show, a less extravagant approach may be sufficient.

The projects discussed so far have mostly used one-by lumber or plywood for the framing. Platforms typically need something stronger and more rigid, so 2×4 dimension lumber is often used. It will stand up to years of difficult and/or indifferent use. Sometimes 1×4 framing is enough for a throw-away that doesn't carry much of a load, especially if it sits on the floor. The best covering material is $\frac{3}{4}''$ plywood. It is thick enough to make a secure cover with minimal spring to it. A 4×8 platform built with a $\frac{3}{4}''$ plywood top requires a support framing member every 24″ in order to keep deflection and vibration to a minimum. A sketch of the framing for a stock platform built with 2×4 lumber and a $\frac{3}{4}''$ thick plywood top is shown, with a cut list.

You can see that the end rails of this stock 4×8 platform are 4′-0″ long and run all the way from side to side, while the toggle rails fit to the inside of the stiles, and as a result are only 3′-9″ in length. Staggering the joints in this way locks the framing together securely. If all of the rails were 3′-9″, it would be remarkably easy to pull the stiles off of the sides of the platform. You can connect the framing together with 16d box nails or 3″ drywall screws, but before doing that, be sure to cut notches for the coffin locks.

STILE IS TOO EASY TO PULL OFF.
OVERLAP END RAILS THE OPPOSITE WAY

Coffin locks are cam-operated fasteners that are attached to the sides of decking and used to join the platforms together. They negate the use of bolts or C-clamps for that purpose. Coffin locks allow you to lock platforms together quickly and easily, using a $\frac{5}{16}''$ hex key. During setup, the decking can be laid out face up and in the position it will eventually occupy. Bolting platforms together can be quite problematic when the height of the decking is too short for a person to crawl under. Bolting together a large number of heavy platforms upside down and then trying to flip them over can be quite a challenge, and it places a lot of stress on the decking.

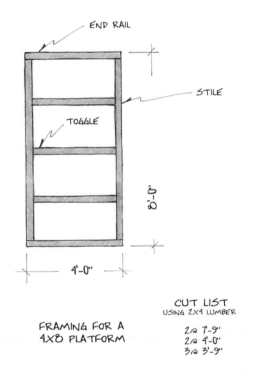

FRAMING FOR A
4×8 PLATFORM

CUT LIST
USING 2X4 LUMBER

2@ 7-9'
2@ 4'-0'
3@ 3'-9'

DRILL KEY HOLE
FOR MALE HALF ONLY

If you install the male and female locks in carefully considered locations, they will always match up, even when the platforms are laid out in many different ways. Most often, individual platforms are laid side by side, or end to end when they are used together. Sometimes you need to place one platform across the ends of two others or to create an L-shape.

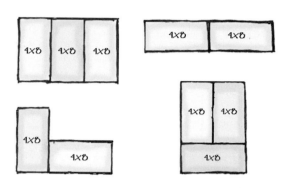

DIFFERENT WAYS OF JOINING
4×8 PLATFORMS

Coffin lock placement for the method in this book is centered exactly 1'-0" from each corner of the 4×8 stock platform. In this way, no matter how the platforms are turned, the male/female sides will match up properly. You can see that from side to side and from end to end, the platforms always have two locks touching, which makes for a very strong joint. When the platforms meet from side to end, this is not always the case, but if one platform connects the ends of two, the connection is again optimum.

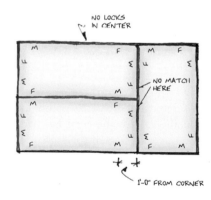

POSITIONING
THE COFFIN LOCKS

A careful measurement of a casket lock reveals that it is just a bit smaller than 3⅜" wide and ⅝" thick. Cut that size notch into the 2×4 framing to allow for installation. The notches should be 1'-0" from each

corner, because that measurement works well when some of the stock platforms are 2×8s. In that case, the lock will fall dead center on the 2-foot end. Because the 2×4 framing members overlap one another, the notch will fall exactly 1'-0" from the end on the rails, but on the stiles which fit to the inside of the rails, the distance is only 0'-10½". To avoid some tedious repetition in measuring and marking, make a jig that handles the chore for you. In order to easily register the jig on a 2×4, it is designed from a piece of ¾" stock that has been ripped to 3½" wide. You can make your jig for marking the notch locations to these specifications:

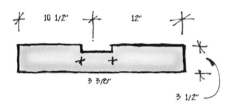

NOTCH MARKING JIG

To use this jig, simply lay it on top of the board, line up the top and bottom with the edges of the 2×4, the end of the jig with the end of the board, and trace around the inside of the notch. Use the 1'-0" end for marking the rails that run from side to side, and the 0'-10½" end for the 7'-9" stiles. Use a jigsaw to cut out the notches, or if a large number of platforms are being built, use the radial arm saw with a dado head cutter installed.

CUT NOTCHES BEFORE
YOU ASSEMBLE THE
FRAMING

Nail the framing together with 16d nails. Begin by connecting the perimeter box. Be sure to accurately measure the placement of the interior framing. It is important for all of the internal parts to be consistent. These are stock platforms, and having exactly interchangeable parts will pay dividends later on in ways that are not apparent now. There really is no way to overstate the importance of having your work be neat and tidy. It is the mark of a craftsperson who takes pride in their work.

Measuring the internal parts calls for finding the center of the 2×4s, and then the edges, in the same way as on a flat. Using a standard tape measure, follow along the side of the previously connected rectangle until you reach 2'-0". Count backward ¾", which is half of the thickness of the 2×4. Make a V mark. Count forward ¾" to 2'-0¾" and make another V mark. Move forward to the 4'-0" placement and repeat the procedure, and again at the 6'-0" toggle. Do this on both stiles, taking care to start the measurement *from the same end.* Now you have marked both sides of both ends of all three toggles. Marking the two corners is a much more accurate method of working, and once it becomes habit, it takes no longer than marking just the center. Marking the center of the two-by creates a problem of determining the center of the end of the 2×4 when putting it in place.

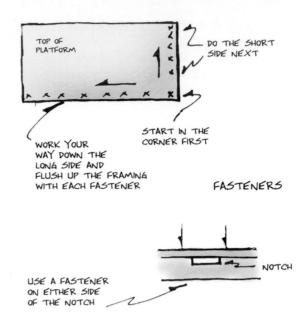

TOP OF PLATFORM

DO THE SHORT SIDE NEXT

START IN THE CORNER FIRST

WORK YOUR WAY DOWN THE LONG SIDE AND FLUSH UP THE FRAMING WITH EACH FASTENER

FASTENERS

USE A FASTENER ON EITHER SIDE OF THE NOTCH

NOTCH

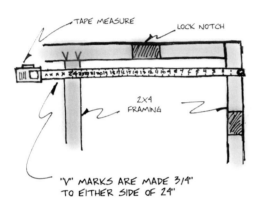

TAPE MEASURE

LOCK NOTCH

2×4 FRAMING

"V" MARKS ARE MADE 3/4" TO EITHER SIDE OF 24"

Lay the plywood decking in place and attach it. On a permanent unit like this, it is best to glue the plywood down, as this is the most secure way to join the parts and will help to prevent squeaking later on. You can use either yellow carpenter's glue, or if the 2×4 stock is a little rough, a construction adhesive like Liquid Nails may work better. The thicker mastic is an excellent gap filler, while the aliphatic resin carpenter's glue is not. Following the common practice that you have seen before, begin by aligning one corner of the unit, while leaving the others merely close. Use 1⅝" #6 drywall screws to secure the plywood tops. This may seem like overkill when used with the glue, but remember that these platforms will be around for a very long time. Work your way along the abutting 4'-0" side, squaring up and fastening as you go, one step at a time. Go back to the original corner and work your way along the contiguous 8'-0" length in the same fashion. Because the framing of a platform is very rigid, you many need to use one or more pipe clamps to square the 2×4s to the plywood.

Use the same procedure as before to ensure that the finished platform is square. Attempting to line up all parts of the platform at one time is not productive and is really just a waste of time. It is far better to begin in one corner and square things up as you add new fasteners. A sheet of ¾" A/C or B/C plywood is extremely square, as it comes from the factory. You can place great faith in the ability of plywood to square up your work and will rarely be disappointed.

Mark the holes for attaching the casket locks. It is imperative that you use a jig for this step in order to maintain accuracy. It also speeds up the work by at least an order of magnitude. You can easily make up a set of jigs used to mark coffin lock placement in about an hour or so, and over a period of time, the effort will be well rewarded.

The ½" by 3⁷⁄₁₆" block is intended to fit inside the notches you cut into the framing earlier. The perforations on top are used to mark the exact placement of the holes to drill for inserting the ⁵⁄₁₆" hex key, and for the two screws that hold the coffin lock in place. The notch in the 2×4 to the right has been arbitrarily selected to be the male part of the lock. (See the earlier drawing of positioning the coffin locks.) Using that system, any platform side has two notches for locks. The one on the left will be female, and the one on the right will be male. That selection was arbitrary, and the right could be a female instead. The original selection is inconsequential, but it is crucial to maintain continuity once a selection has been made.

As you can tell from looking at the jig, different mounting holes are required for each sex. Use the jig to mark placement of the holes, and drill the holes with the appropriate size bit. The keyway requires a ½" hole

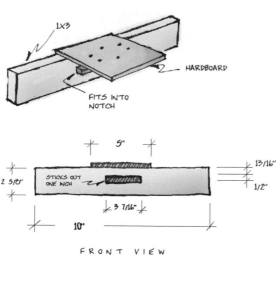

1X3

HARDBOARD

FITS INTO
NOTCH

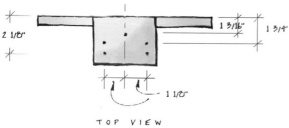

5"

2 5/8"

13/16"

STICKS OUT
ONE INCH

1/2"

3 7/16"

10"

FRONT VIEW

2 1/8"

1 3/16"   1 3/4"

1 1/8"

TOP VIEW

HOLE PLACEMENT JIG
FOR COFFIN LOCKS

in order to have enough room to easily accommodate the $\frac{5}{16}''$ hex key. If you use $2\frac{1}{2}''$ #12 flathead Phillips wood screws to secure the locks, an $\frac{1}{8}''$ pilot hole with the appropriate countersink should do the job nicely for those two screws. Install the male half of the lock with the label up, as this will ensure that the key will turn to the right to lock the device and to the left to unlock.

LABEL UP

MALE HALF

The screws holding the female side of the coffin lock in place will match up well with the 2×4 framing along the edge of the platform, but the screws on the male will not. Instead those screws will fit just to the inside of the 2×4 framing, and not really penetrate the wood properly. Even so, they will hold the lock in place adequately. If you would like a neater appearance, glue a small block of one-by material under the notch and the screws will rest between the block and the 2×4 frame. If the platform is framed with one-by material rather than 2×4 stock, you can drill $\frac{1}{4}''$ holes for flat-head bolts rather than using screws. In either case, drill a *countersink* hole for the head to fit into. You don't want anything to stick up above the surface of the plywood.

Using casket locks greatly lengthens the service life of stock platforms. Drilling bolt holes in platforms to lock them together degrades the framing, and over a period of time, it will render the decking unfit for use. The coffin lock system really comes into its own when you are loading the show into the theatre. That process is much, much, easier, and you can connect platforms that are lying directly on the stage floor or have very short legs that you would not normally be able to reach under. As the decking is laid out right side up, there is no need to turn anything over.

Another procedure that will increase the life span of a stock platform is to use *corner irons* to hold together the outside perimeter of the framing. Use the flat irons on the bottom of the platform rather than on the inside of the corner, because they are the easiest to install, and because they do not interfere with the installation of legs. Legs may need to be attached to the inside corner of the framing.

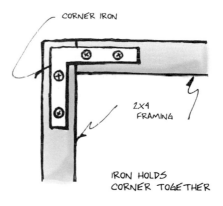

CORNER IRON

2×4
FRAMING

IRON HOLDS
CORNER TOGETHER

Select a corner iron that is at least 4 inches long on each side so that there will be enough screw holes for the iron to gain good purchase. The iron will keep the end rail from pulling away from the stile, which it is prone to do. Gluing this joint together is not a viable solution, as there is too much stress, and the bond will not hold.

Oddly Shaped Decking

You can't platform every show with just rectangles. Quite often, stock sizes are used for the majority, and then odd-shaped decks are built to fill in. The best method for constructing them is to cut out the plywood top first and then use this shape as a *full-scale pattern* used in marking the 2×4 framing. This method reduces the amount of information that must be predetermined, and hopefully also reduces the errors that may come from that process. As an example, assume that you need to construct a platform that is half of a 4×8 sheet of plywood, and that is a triangle formed by drawing a line diagonally from corner to corner. Here is a dimensioned drawing of the unit in question:

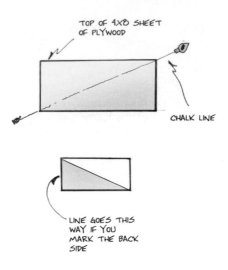

TOP OF 4×8 SHEET OF PLYWOOD

CHALK LINE

LINE GOES THIS WAY IF YOU MARK THE BACK SIDE

THE SHEET OF PLYWOOD DOES ALL THE MEASURING FOR YOU

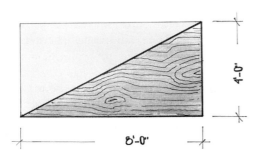

MAKE A PLATFORM FROM HALF A SHEET

The sketch provides all of the information required to construct this platform, even though you have not been given any information about the number of degrees in any of the angles other than the one factory corner, which can be assumed to be a right angle. Using the full-scale pattern method, it is not necessary to know these angles, which in any case are rarely given on the designer's plans.

In order to cut out the plywood for the top of the unit, mark a straight line from corner to corner on a sheet of ¾″ ply. A chalk line is very handy for this purpose. Make sure that the plywood is good side up when you do the marking, or you may wind up with a piece that is cut out upside down. If you want to mark on the back to reduce the amount of saw tearout on the good side, just be sure to mark everything mirror image. You can use either a jigsaw or a circular saw to make this cut. If you choose the circular saw, try using the guide shown on the companion Web site, so that the cut is exactly straight.

After the top of the platform has been cut out, lay it across a pair of sawhorses so that the corners are unobstructed. Trim the end of a piece of 2×4 to make it square and line it up with the 4'-0″ side of the triangle. (You may wish to cut the 2×4 to a length only slightly longer than that side so that it is less cumbersome.) Square up one end with the 90-degree-angle corner, and use a pencil to scribe the length and angle of the plywood onto the 2×4 from underneath. Use the band saw or power miter box to cut the board to length. If you use the power miter box, make a note of the degrees involved, as you will need to know the angle later on for another part. For the moment, you need only to adjust the saw by eye so that it matches to your marked line, and then cut the 2×4.

When using this method, it is best to attach each framing member as you go along, because it will simplify the marking process. Otherwise, the piece you just cut will tend to move while the next piece is being marked. For an irregular deck that will not go into stock at the end of the show, you probably won't want to glue the pieces in place. That makes it almost impossible to get anything back apart, and there may be some salvageable pieces. It is enough to screw the top to the framing with 1⅝″ drywall screws. After this first section has been attached, hold another length of 2×4 under the 8-foot-long side and scribe the resulting angle from the plywood pattern. You will not be able to cut this angle on most power miter saws, because it is too steep. The saw will not swing around that far. The best way is to use a large band saw if you have one that will accommodate the piece. If not, a circular saw may be used. Cut halfway through on one side, and then turn the 2×4 over to do the same on the second side.

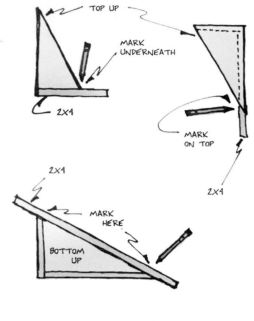

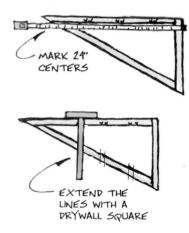

USE THE PLYWOOD
TO MARK THE FRAMING

must first do some layout on the bottom of the platform to determine the toggle locations. Measure along the 8-foot side of the platform, marking both sides of a 2×4 toggle as was described earlier in this chapter in the section about stock platforms. It is not practical to do both sides, as the hypotenuse of the triangle is at an angle. You need a different way of marking that side. Use a drywall square or some other large square to extend your existing marks to the angle side. Square the straightedge up with the known side, and extend the marks outward at a 90-degree angle. It is only necessary to mark the 2×4 framing, not the entire expanse of plywood. Set a length of stock in place flush with the straight side, and scribe the required length and angle from the opposite side. These three toggles can be cut on the power miter box.

Use 16d box nails or long drywall screws to join the framing where it intersects. A pneumatic framing nailer will greatly speed up the process. The plywood decking should be secured to the toggles with drywall screws. It is probably not necessary to secure the framing of a short-lived platform with corner irons, unless there is some special reason to do so. Sometimes, especially if a show is to be set up a number of times, it is best to put coffin locks on the sides of the platform that will abut a stock platform, or if it is easy to reach under the decking, you can just C-clamp the units together.

After the piece has been cut, screw it into place and turn the entire platform upside down. The final perimeter framing member may be marked by laying a length of 2×4 stock over the space it will occupy and scribing the two ends. The end of the board with the most obtuse angle can be cut on the power miter box using the same degree setting as before. The opposite angle will be the same as the one previously cut on the band saw. After this last perimeter framing is connected, it is time to mark the interior toggles.

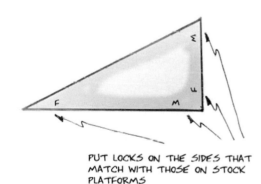

PUT LOCKS ON THE SIDES THAT
MATCH WITH THOSE ON STOCK
PLATFORMS

MARK 24'
CENTERS

EXTEND THE
LINES WITH A
DRYWALL SQUARE

Each toggle will be a different length, but each one will have one end that is a 90-degree angle, and another that is the same angle as was earlier cut on the power miter box. Before you can cut the toggles to length, you

Curved Platforms

You may find it necessary to build decking with curved edges, and there is generally no way to make 2×4 framing fit exactly on the curved edge of the plywood top. If the top of the platform can be left as an overhanging lip, the framing can be ordinary 2×4 construction. A ¾″ ply top can have an overhang of 2 or 3 inches without suffering any ill effects. If the curve requires more than this, you may try doubling the thickness of the plywood along the edge.

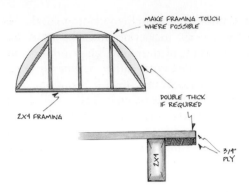

MAKE FRAMING TOUCH
WHERE POSSIBLE

2X4 FRAMING

DOUBLE THICK
IF REQUIRED

2X4

3/4"
PLY

PLATFORM WITH A ROUND EDGE

NAIL

PENCIL

SPRING
CLAMPS

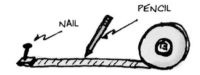

NAIL

PENCIL

CIRCLE MARKING IMPLEMENTS

To mark the curve, use a set of *trammel points* if it is part of a circle, or use the grid method shown in the section on full-scale patterns if it is irregular. Trammel points are essentially small clamps attached to a strip of wood to form a very large beam compass. One of the clamps has a steel pin that serves as the stationary point, and the other clamp has a holder for a pencil. You can use strips of white pine left over from ripping down 1×3s as the "beam" part of the compass. It is best to use a lightweight connection because it gives more control over the marking process. A substitute for the trammel points is to use two small strips of wood that are held together with small spring clamps. Put a 4d nail through the end of one of the strips to use as the stationary point, and drill a pencil-size-diameter hole through the end of the other. (Make it just a shade small.) Squeeze the pencil into place, and you are ready to go. The size can be adjusted by removing the clamps and sliding the strips of wood back and forth. Do not use a string with a pencil tied to the end of it, because the string will either stretch, break, or get caught on something. Sometimes, for a very large arc, you may consider driving a nail into the stationary point and using a steel measuring tape to strike the arc.

After the curve has been established, you can draw in some lines to represent placement of the framing members. It is best to do this in some logical way, but the actual placement is somewhat arbitrary, especially if the curve is irregular.

Bending plywood is usually made from either lauan or birch that has been laminated together like regular plywood, except that there are two thick plies and one very thin ply. The barrel version has the grain of the thick plies running the 4-foot direction on the sheet. If you rip a 4-inch-wide strip from a sheet of that type bending ply, the 8-foot-long section will be exceedingly bendable, and can easily be wrapped around the edge of a curved surface such as a platform.

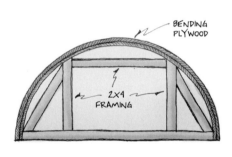

BENDING
PLYWOOD

2X4
FRAMING

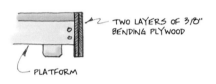

TWO LAYERS OF 3/8"
BENDING PLYWOOD

PLATFORM

USE BENDING PLYWOOD AROUND THE
OUTSIDE EDGE OF THE PLYWOOD TOP
* THIS WILL INCREASE THE SIZE OF THE PLATFORM

Make your framing touch the edge of the curve in as many places as possible in order to give the plywood more support. You can also add small braces that go between the platform top and the facing. Remember when you lay out the curve that anything you add to the outside will make it larger.

LEGGING METHODS

There are many different ways to give height to the kind of platforms we have been discussing, but all of the methods fall into one of two categories. The first is to put individual legs on each of the platforms, and the second is to build a structure that will support a number of platforms all at once. Choose the type that works best for your situation. Individual legs are the best solution when the platforms are either very low to the ground, and/or when the platform area is very small. On the other hand, a large expanse of decking several feet off the stage floor definitely calls for some kind of support structure.

Perhaps the most popular way of legging in small theatre companies is to bolt 2×4 legs into the corners of the platforms. This approach doesn't require too much instruction, as it is very straightforward and intuitive. Most theatres use $\frac{3}{8}''$ carriage bolts to connect the legs. Carriage bolts are a good choice because the small, rounded heads allow two platforms to be locked together side by side without the bolt heads getting in the way. A problem associated with this practice, however, is that drilling the bolt holes tends to degrade the stock platforms. You can mitigate that somewhat by using the same holes through the platform framing each time you add a new set of legs. The 2×4s themselves are much beefier than what is really necessary to hold up the load. The compression strength of a 2×4 leg is tremendous, and it will hold up a great deal more weight than you are ever likely to place on it. Smaller framing members will support just as well if they are properly constructed.

The major engineering problem associated with legging is to provide *lateral* strength to keep the structure from twisting out of shape to the side, and/or from "corkscrewing." Care must be taken to keep the legging structure rigid. If all of the parts stay in position, the structure will be safe. If any of the parts bends or twists the structure will fail.

The upright parts have a *compression* load that pushes straight down the length of the board. Even smallish boards work well in that situation, because wood has excellent compression strength when used this way. *Stiffeners* and *braces* are used to keep the upright parts in position. Lateral forces from things like actor movement tend to disturb the equilibrium of the system and work against the bracing, which must be designed to counteract lateral forces. *Tensile strength* is the ability of a material to withstand a load that may cause it to bend or break. When individual legs are used, the platform framing itself is responsible for imparting tensile strength, and it is not an issue with the legs. It is important to securely fasten legs of any type to the platform framing.

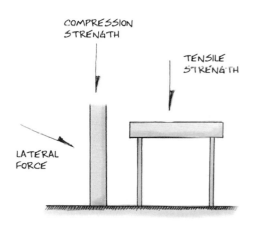

Platform legs are generally much longer than they are wide, and the narrowness of the surface attached to the platform framing gives them a tendency to pull away from it. Bolting on 2×4s is a good way to avoid pulling away, but bolting is generally harmful to the platform. Another solution to the problem is to use a *V-leg*. They are called this because of the shape of their cross section. It is essentially two pieces of 1×4 that have been glued and stapled together. This is a cost-effective method of manufacture, because there are often scraps of this material left over from the construction of other scenery. If this material is not available, you can rip down strips of $\frac{3}{4}''$ plywood. V-legs have two sides forming a corner, and that shape has more ability to withstand twisting in relation to the platform framing. Also, because there are two boards joined at a right angle, the leg is strengthened against bowing out of shape. One single 1×4 would be very dangerous in that regard. It is important to glue the two halves of the leg together so that they remain firmly attached to one another.

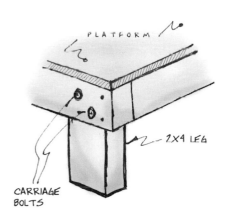

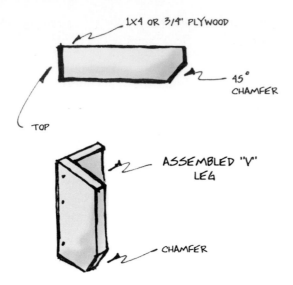

1X4 OR 3/4" PLYWOOD

45° CHAMFER

TOP

ASSEMBLED "V" LEG

CHAMFER

side, and two on the wide side. Try not to get too close to the edges, or the white pine will split, but the farther apart the fasteners are, the more secure the leg will be. If you are using $\frac{3}{4}$″ ply for the legs, the danger of splitting is greatly reduced, but the screws are harder to install and may require pilot holes. If six legs are used on a 4×8 platform, there will be no unsupported span of more than 4'-0″. That is compatible with the strength of a platform constructed with 2×4 lumber and a $\frac{3}{4}$″ plywood top.

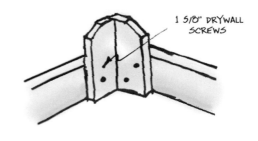

1 5/8" DRYWALL SCREWS

PLYWOOD TOP UPSIDE DOWN

The method of manufacture goes as follows. Determine the length of the leg from the height of the platform less the amount of the thickness of the material covering that platform. If the lid of a platform is $\frac{3}{4}$″ ply and the height of the decking overall is 12″, then the length of the leg stock should be $11\frac{1}{4}$″. Plan on using six legs on each 4×8 stock platform.

LEG PLACEMENT ON A 4X8 PLATFORM

Cut all of the legs at one time using the radial arm saw and a stop block. Use the power miter box to put a small bevel, or chamfer, on the outside edges of the leg. This increases the chance that the leg will sit flat on a slightly uneven surface, and besides, it is a very handsome look. It is much easier to do the beveling before the two halves of the leg have been joined.

Connecting the two sides is a simple matter of gluing and then stapling them with a pneumatic gun. Notice that due to the overlap, one of the sides of the completed leg is wider than the other. Sometimes it is helpful to assemble the legs so that half are formatted one way and half the other so that they match on the platform. But structurally, it really doesn't matter.

Attach the V-legs to the platform from the inside with $1\frac{5}{8}$″ drywall screws. Put one screw on the skinny

As a rule of thumb, you can consider that a platform with V-legs or 2×4 legs needs no lateral support if it is 12″ or less in height. The width of the leg is large enough, and the distance of the platform from the floor low enough that the structure has little danger of breaking loose under normal conditions. Only $7\frac{3}{4}$″ of each leg is exposed below the bottom of the framing. It is imperative, though, that the platforms and legs be properly constructed and assembled.

For heights over 12″, bracing is required. Sometimes it is enough to simply band the bottom of the legs with a 2″-wide strip of $\frac{3}{4}$″-thick material that will keep the legs from being twisted outward. If the height warrants it, diagonal bracing should be used. Note how the bracing runs in different directions for added strength. You should use similar bracing even when bolted-on 2×4 legs are used. They are prone to failure from the same kinds of lateral forces.

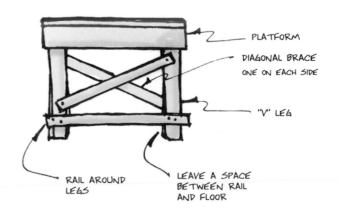

PLATFORM

DIAGONAL BRACE ONE ON EACH SIDE

"V" LEG

RAIL AROUND LEGS

LEAVE A SPACE BETWEEN RAIL AND FLOOR

- There is some concern that the screws may not have enough holding power to make a safe connection. It is important to use screws that are long enough, and to make sure that they are tightly installed. There should be no gap of any kind between the leg and the framing.
- Make sure to use the proper number of legs in your system. Six legs per 4×8 platform is slightly redundant and will provide extra protection. Do not use fewer.
- If the plywood top of the platform has been "glued and screwed," it will provide some measure of protection from the leg pressing upward and creating a structural failure when the lid detaches from the framing.
- If the load on your platforming is high, you can add a safety feature by gluing blocks on the outside of the leg structure so that the load from the platform frame is transferred to the leg by more than just the screws holding the leg to the frame.

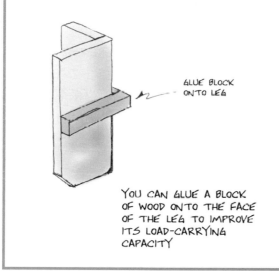

GLUE BLOCK ONTO LEG

YOU CAN GLUE A BLOCK OF WOOD ONTO THE FACE OF THE LEG TO IMPROVE ITS LOAD-CARRYING CAPACITY

Putting individual legs on a large number of platforms can become quite expensive in both labor and materials, because of the unnecessary duplication of the upright members and also the problem of how cumbersome the units can become. It is quite easy for one or more of the decking units to become out of square, especially if they are very tall. The more of them there are, the less likely they will all fit together properly. Individual legs are fine when the decking area is very

small and/or low to the stage floor, but larger and taller decks require a different approach.

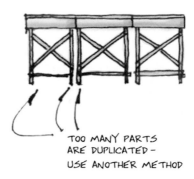

TOO MANY PARTS ARE DUPLICATED – USE ANOTHER METHOD

CARRIERS

Carriers get their name from the way they carry the weight of the decking. They are intended to hold several platforms at once, and the effectiveness of this method increases with the number of platforms involved. It does not work particularly well with just one or two. Sometimes it's best to make taller carriers from welded steel frames, and there is a discussion of that process in the section on steel frame construction, Chapter 21. Here I will concentrate on wooden carriers, but the principles of one type carry over to the other.

Carriers are essentially short stud walls, like those in a house but made from different materials. You can use either 1×4 or 2×4 lumber, but the thinner one-by type requires more precision in construction and use, and more attention to lateral bracing. If that is problematic in your particular situation, consider 2×4 construction. The 1×4 type is definitely a more elegant product. Adjust the cut list numbers to reflect the types of materials you are using.

The size and shape of the decking area are of great importance in designing the carrier system. For the purposes of this discussion assume that the deck being constructed is 20 feet by 24 feet in size, and that it should be 18″ tall. Here are two possible ways to get this size using standard 4×8 platforms connected together with coffin locks.

Support the deck so that there is no span greater than 4′-0″. You can accomplish this by running the carriers on four-foot centers. If the carriers are made from either 1×4 or 2×4 stock, the 3½″ wide lumber is spacious enough to support the 2×4 framing of two platforms at once. It is crucial that platform framing rest firmly on the carrier.

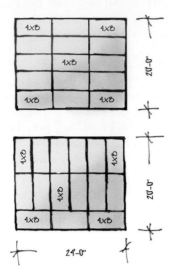

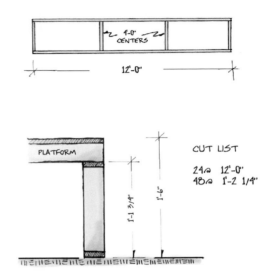

hand, a cut list can be determined for carriers. Notice that there are quite a few pieces involved, but considerable time is saved by using interchangeable parts that can be cut out all at once. Remember to rank the cut list from the longest pieces to the shortest, because this is the order in which they should be cut. It will be easy to find the material suitable for the short sections after the long ones are finished.

In laying out the placement of the carriers, it is important to make choices that will make the job of setting up the decking easier. Sections of carrier that are too large or too small will make the job harder to accomplish. The following figure shows one possible solution to the carrier layout problem. Note that all of the units are the same size. That will make it easier to manufacture them.

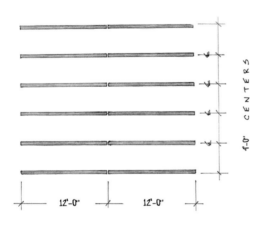

PLAN VIEW OF CARRIER LAYOUT

The next step in developing a plan for this project is to determine the overall height of the carriers. For the V-legs, you subtracted only the thickness of the platform covering material, but for this type of support it is necessary to account for the thickness of the entire platform, framing and all, because all of the platform will be resting on the carrier. In this demonstration, the thickness of the platform is $4\frac{1}{4}''$. Hence the overall height of the carrier is $13\frac{3}{4}''$. With that information at

One really advantageous aspect of using the carrier method is that resting the framing of the platform on the carrier increases the stability of the platform. The load on top of the platform is assumed by the entire structure and the full width of the chord of the framing members rather than just the portion connected by the legging screws.

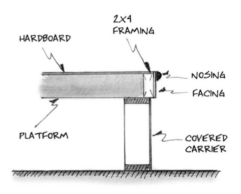

MAKE SURE THAT THE PLATFORM FRAMING STAYS ON THE CARRIER

The carriers are glued and nailed together in the normal way, but they also need some kind of lateral bracing. Without it, they will tend to rack out of shape into a parallelogram, and the entire deck might fall. The importance of keeping the upright members vertical is paramount. The 1×4 uprights have enough compression strength to hold up a reasonable load, but compression assumes only a downward force. If the uprights are allowed to tilt, failure is imminent. You can avoid this by bracing the uprights diagonally.

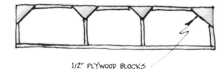

1/2" PLYWOOD BLOCKS

THESE BLOCKS ARE ESSENTIAL

SOLID COVER

The rack bracing is applied using ½" plywood corner blocks similar to those used to put together standard soft-cover flats, only thicker. Glue and staple them into place. If your load is very heavy, consider using thicker materials or metal framing. Sometimes it works out well to cover the entire surface of the carrier so that it is really a hard-cover flat. This type may be used to form its own facing material, and is great for the downstage side, especially if the platform is allowed to hang over a bit.

If the carriers are reasonably short, and the size of the decked area is large, then the carriers may be screwed to the floor and to the undersides of the platform framing. Do the layout by measuring the placement of the decking area, and then setting the carriers on 4-foot centers. The carriers on the outside edge should be flush with the edges of the platforms. Make sure that the interior carriers are placed where the platforms join, and that both decks are supported. If the decking is higher and more support is required, use triangular rack braces.

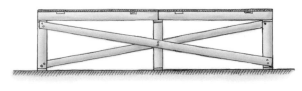

USE TRIANGLE FORMING RACK BRACES
AS REQUIRED

SOUND DEADENING

Hard shoes pounding against the ¾" plywood top of a platform can make a most distracting noise. The clomping and thudding of feet in a blackout remove much of the magic of the moment. The easiest way to deaden this type of unwanted sound is to carpet the platforming. Unfortunately, the carpet approach is not always feasible because of design factors. Here is a method of deadening sound with insulation and hardboard that works quite well and has the added bonus of also improving the appearance of the deck. It works well for in-house shows, but would be far too difficult to load in for a tour show.

Use one of several different types of thin insulating materials. Homasote works well, or perhaps extruded foam insulation with a foil cover. Either of these loosely compacted materials is intended to insulate a house from cold, but it will insulate sound vibrations just as well. Foam insulation is a bit less likely to fall apart, and it is not as flammable or possibly toxic as the asphalt-impregnated type of Homasote. The material chosen should be relatively thin (about ½"), and should come in 4×8 sheets. It is crucial that all of the sound-deadening *substrate* be the same thickness. This method is at its best on large areas, and it can become problematic on small sections of oddly shaped decking.

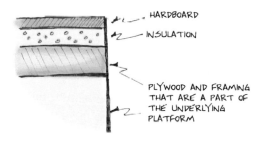

HARDBOARD

INSULATION

PLYWOOD AND FRAMING
THAT ARE A PART OF
THE UNDERLYING
PLATFORM

Refer to the sketch of a decking layout composed of stock 4×8 platforms. The deck measures 20'-0" × 20'-0". The most straightforward method of joining the decks together is shown. The second layout describes a way of putting down the insulation so that the joining cracks of the insulation do not fall in line with the joints of the 4×8 platforms. This will prevent the *telegraphing* of uneven joints upward toward the finished surface.

The final step in the process is to lay down sheets of ¼" hardboard to use as a paintable surface. The finished product will appear much flatter and more solid than just using the tops of the platforms themselves. The foam is too flimsy to be the top layer. You can use a layer of just hardboard with no foam at all, but of course that provides only minimal insulating results, although it does greatly improve the physical

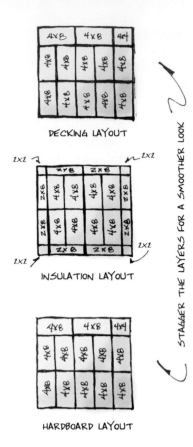

DECKING LAYOUT

INSULATION LAYOUT

HARDBOARD LAYOUT

STAGGER THE LAYERS FOR A SMOOTHER LOOK

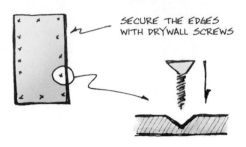

SECURE THE EDGES
WITH DRYWALL SCREWS

MAKE COUNTERSINKS SO THAT
SCREW HEADS DO NOT STICK UP
PAST THE SURFACE

appearance of the deck. A layer of hardboard is very frequently used on decking, even if sound deadening is not required. Be sure to stagger the hardboard away from the underlying joints.

It is not necessary to attach the insulating material to the platforms. It will lie there just fine on its own, and in the end will be securely bound by the hardboard. Anything over half an inch thickness of insulation is troublesome to manipulate when putting down the deck. It is important to use a material that will hold together well if you intend to reuse the panels consistently.

Tempered $\frac{1}{4}''$ hardboard makes the best cover. The hardboard is installed with the same orientation as the original platforms. It is not necessary that you follow the exact same plan, but that is often the most expedient thing to do.

Make small *countersink* holes in the surface of the hardboard about every foot around the outside perimeter of the sheet. Use $1\frac{1}{4}''$ drywall screws to fasten the hardboard to the deck. Add more screws to the center of the sheet as required to securely fasten it.

The surface of hardboard is very slick. You should plan on painting new sheets before any scheduled rehearsals.

STRESSED-SKIN PLATFORMS

Sometimes a special type of platform is required, for which the standard construction methods are simply inappropriate. This could be because a platform must cover an unusually large span, and/or must have a clean and streamlined appearance. Sometimes the bottom of the platform will be seen. *Stressed-skin platforms* have both a top and a bottom cover, so the bottom looks just as good as the top. The way in which they are constructed makes them much more rigid, and more supportive than the traditional platforming method, even though they might actually be thinner than a traditional platform constructed with 2×4s and a $\frac{3}{4}''$ plywood top.

The secret to stressed-skin manufacture lies in the way the bottom cover or "skin" keeps the platform from bending under stress. In order for any structure to bend, two things must occur. The top must compress, and the bottom must stretch. Bending of this sort will eventually cause the structure to break when the force applied is enough to stretch the material past the breaking strength of the fibers that hold it together.

The bottom skin in a stressed-skin platform prevents the bottom of the structure from stretching because it spreads the stress of the load over the entire platform rather than letting it concentrate on one framing member. All of the materials used in a stressed-skin structure are intended to work in concert, and they must be securely joined together into a monolithic unit, or the structure will fail. All of the joints in a wooden platform of this type must be properly glued together in order for the system to work. This concept cannot be overemphasized.

You can build this type of platform using $\frac{1}{2}''$ plywood for the tops and $\frac{1}{4}''$ ply for the bottoms. Make sure to use a good grade of plywood that is very strong, lightweight, and has a paintable surface. It is possible to

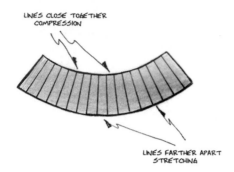

LINES CLOSE TOGETHER
COMPRESSION

LINES FARTHER APART
STRETCHING

THIS DRAWING MIMICS THE
EFFECTS OF BENDING. NOTICE
HOW THE LINES ON THE CURVE
ARE FARTHER APART ON THE
BOTTOM AND CLOSER TOGETHER
ON THE TOP. THE BOTTOM
STRETCHES, WHILE THE TOP
COMPRESSES.

After the framing has been glued and nailed together, the top of the platform may be attached. The plywood should be used to square up the framing in the usual way, by starting at one corner and working the two adjacent sides. The framing used in this platform will be prone to bowing because of its length, but because it is more limber, it will be easier to work into place than framing on a 2×4 deck. If there is a problem keeping the internal framing in place during this process, cut a number of spacers to keep the framing from wandering. Remove them before sealing the bottom.

Be sure to use sufficient yellow aliphatic resin glue to ensure that the plywood is completely adhered to all of the lumber framing over the entire surface of the one-by. It is very important to glue every inch of every joint on a stressed-skin platform. Staple the top plywood to all of the framing, not just the perimeter, so that it will be held together firmly while the glue sets up. A pneumatic gun really makes this job easier.

use ½″ ply for the top surface rather than the normal ¾″ because the framing members of the platform are much closer together and will reduce the amount of flex created by footfalls. The load rating can be improved by increasing the top to bottom thickness of the framing members. In general, it is a good policy to keep the weight of this type of platform down. Stressed-skin platforms tend to be rather large, and any reduction in weight is greatly appreciated by the stagehands. This type of decking is not intended to be covered with the sound-deadening materials described previously.

Use ¾″ thick dimension lumber for the framing of stressed-skin platforms. Care should be taken to avoid knots that seriously impair the structural integrity of the lumber. Framing members should be designed to run across the open span, even if this is the entire length of the platform. Space the members at no more than 12″ apart, on center. This will provide sufficient support for the ½″ plywood top.

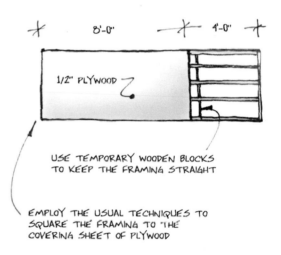

8'-0"   4'-0"

1/2" PLYWOOD

USE TEMPORARY WOODEN BLOCKS
TO KEEP THE FRAMING STRAIGHT

EMPLOY THE USUAL TECHNIQUES TO
SQUARE THE FRAMING TO THE
COVERING SHEET OF PLYWOOD

If the size of the top requires more than one sheet of plywood, the two adjoining sheets should be scabbed together securely. This is very important, and the structure will fail if it is not done properly. Glue and nail a 4″-wide slat of ½″ plywood to the underside of one of the plywood sheets, half on and half off. The protruding half will be used to connect the second sheet. Do not cut notches in the framing to let in the connecting slat, but rather use several small pieces. Notches may well remove too much of the white pine framing for it to support properly in the weakened condition. Do extend the connecting slat so that it covers as much space as possible between framing members. Again, it is very important that all wooden surfaces that touch each other have a proper glue bond. Nails alone will not hold.

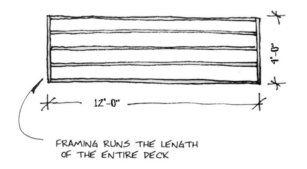

4'-0"

12'-0"

FRAMING RUNS THE LENGTH
OF THE ENTIRE DECK

WIDTH OF THE FRAMING MEMBER
DEPENDS ON THE LENGTH OF THE
SPAN, WEIGHT, AND TYPE OF LOAD.

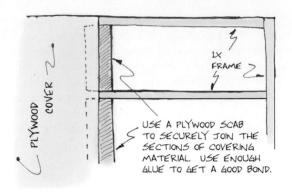

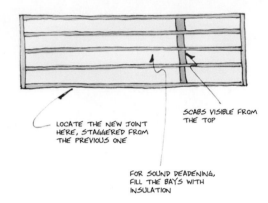

USE A PLYWOOD SCAB TO SECURELY JOIN THE SECTIONS OF COVERING MATERIAL. USE ENOUGH GLUE TO GET A GOOD BOND.

LOCATE THE NEW JOINT HERE, STAGGERED FROM THE PREVIOUS ONE

SCABS VISIBLE FROM THE TOP

FOR SOUND DEADENING, FILL THE BAYS WITH INSULATION

BOTTOM OF THE UNIT

After you have let the glue set up, turn the platform upside down so that the framing is visible. If the platform needs sound deadening, add that to the inside before enclosing the bottom. The least expensive method is to use fiberglass roll insulation. It is cut and inserted into the "bays" just like in the walls of a house. Care must be taken that insulation on the framing is not allowed to interfere with the glue joint on the bottom skin.

The $\frac{1}{4}''$ bottom ply should be attached in the same manner as the top was, including the use of the connecting scabs. Proper installation of the joining scabs is even more important on the bottom skin, which is subjected to stresses that want to pull it apart. The bottom plywood is what gives this technique its name, because the $\frac{1}{4}''$ plywood is the "skin" that is "stressed." If the bottom skin comes loose from the structure, or two connected pieces come apart from one another, a catastrophic failure of the structure will occur. Make sure that the plywood joint on the bottom falls in a different place than the top did.

After the glue has cured overnight, use a flush trim router to clean up the edges. Stressed-skin platforms must use some kind of carrier-type structure to elevate them, because there is no place to attach any sort of individual leg. If steel frame legging is used, the decking can usually be held in place by virtue of its own weight when wooden blocks are attached to the underside of the platform to keep it from sliding. You can also use hinges or other angular fasteners.

BLOCKS GLUED TO THE BOTTOM OF THE PLATFORM

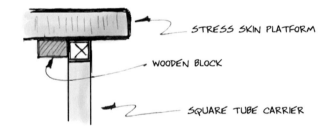

STRESS SKIN PLATFORM

WOODEN BLOCK

SQUARE TUBE CARRIER

CHAPTER 21

METAL FRAME CONSTRUCTION

In recent years, metal framing has become increasingly popular as a medium for scenic construction. The use of welded steel or aluminum tubing allows scenery to be constructed from materials that are smaller in cross section, more securely joined, and in some cases lighter than traditional wood framing. This method has the added advantage of being very quick to assemble using easily constructed jigs. Furthermore, there is actually more salvageable material left from steel framing than from the wooden type. Metal framing from tubing is the only logical approach to constructing some scenic units with open structures and odd angles.

YOU CAN MAKE ALL SORTS OF INTERESTING SHAPES WITH STEEL THAT JUST AREN'T POSSIBLE WITH WOOD.

MATERIALS

The phrase *metal framing* could mean either aluminum or steel. There are advantages and disadvantages to either product. Aluminum is much lighter than steel, but steel is considerably stronger than aluminum, which has a tendency to crack and shatter. Welded steel square tube is much less expensive than its extruded aluminum counterpart. Aluminum is more difficult to weld than steel is, and requires special inert gas techniques that are more difficult to produce. Aluminum framing is very popular with companies who build scenery for tours of rock-and-roll shows because of its light weight, but they have almost unlimited financial resources. Steel framing is much more popular with schools and smaller theatre companies.

doi: 10.1016/C2009-0-23409-X

Square tube gets its name from the shape of the cross section, which is, of course, square. It is quite often the most useful shape, although tubing is also manufactured in round or rectangular cross sections. Steel tube is *bent* into shape from flat bars of metal, and as a result, one side of it has a seam where the edges of the bar have been welded together. This seam generally appears as a slightly darker, sometimes bluish stripe.

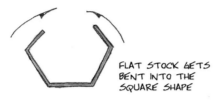

FLAT STOCK GETS BENT INTO THE SQUARE SHAPE

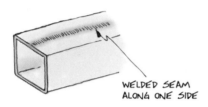

WELDED SEAM ALONG ONE SIDE

Aluminum is extruded through a die in order to get whatever particular shape is required. Cutting and grinding steel framing requires the use of special metalworking equipment, whereas the much softer aluminum can usually be cut and shaped with ordinary woodworking tools. Welding aluminum requires a TIG or MIG welder, whereas steel may be worked with an ordinary arc welder, or even *oxyacetylene*.

This chapter is written with steel tubing in mind, because it is more widely used, but there isn't that much difference in the types of structures you can build with either one.

Building the structural parts of a set from steel square tube can actually be less expensive than using wooden parts. The difference in price is due to the way steel joints are welded together. The resulting connections are much stronger than any kind of wooden joinery, and you can easily make angular shapes that are much more difficult with wooden scenery. Less bracing is required, so fewer running feet of material are needed for steel structures than for traditional wooden methods.

Steel tubing is available in many sizes and cross sections. A reasonably well-stocked supplier should have square tube in a variety of sizes from half-inch to 4-inch. *Rectangular* tubing is available in sizes like 1×2 inches, 1×3 inches, 2×3 inches, and so forth. Other useful shapes are *angle iron*, which has two sides and is shaped like an L, *channel*, which is U-shaped, *flat bar*, which is one flat piece and *round bar*, which is a solid round

OXYACETYLENE RIG

shape. *Round tubing* is hollow on the inside, which makes it different from round bar. Round tubing and steel pipe are not the same thing. *Black steel pipe* used in plumbing is generally much thicker than the tubing meant for welding structures. Even so, black steel pipe is frequently used in constructing scenery.

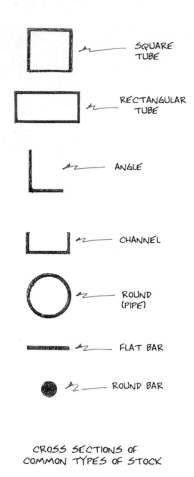

CROSS SECTIONS OF
COMMON TYPES OF STOCK

thickness of the wall. For lightweight structures, it is generally best to use the thinnest wall available. The 20-ga tubing is an excellent lightweight material, but it can be somewhat difficult to find, because it is not very popular for general construction. The 16-ga is much more common. Unless you are building something that must withstand extreme forces (in which case you should perhaps consult a professional engineer), it is best to steer clear of really thick tubing like 10 ga. It is just too heavy for most theatrical use. You can spot thick wall tubing by looking at the corners. Thicker wall tubing has rounder corners. This makes sense when you think about how square tubing is made by bending a flat piece of steel into a square shape and welding the sides together.

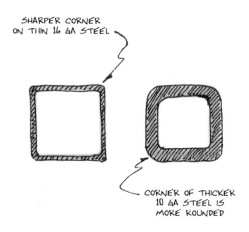

THICKER STEEL HAS
MORE ROUNDED CORNERS

Pipe is sized by its *inside diameter* or ID. The wall thickness varies in proportion to the diameter according to the *nominal pipe size*, or NPS, but is generally between ⅛″ and ³⁄₁₆″, so 1-inch pipe is actually almost 1⁵⁄₁₆″ on the outside. Other types of structural steel such as square or round tubing are sized by their *outside diameter* or OD. Of course, it is much easier to make up a cut list if you are given the exterior dimensions of the materials.

The two most common wall thicknesses of black steel pipe are known as Schedule 40 and Schedule 80. Schedule 40 is the most available; Schedule 80 is much thicker and heavier. Pipes are really meant to hold pressurized water on the inside; square tube is not.

The wall thickness of tubing is described with a *gauge system*. The smaller the gauge number, the thicker the tubing wall. The same gauge numbers are used to describe the thickness of all steel pieces. As in the case of wire gauges, the method of doing so is the exact opposite of what would seem logical. As a point of reference, 10-ga tubing is approximately ⅛″ thick; 16-ga tubing is about ¹⁄₁₆″ thick (16 ga, ¹⁄₁₆″ is easy to remember). From a structural standpoint, the outside dimension of the tubing has the most impact on the rigidity of something you make from it, rather than the

Most square tubing comes in 24-foot lengths, which is an excellent thing if you need long pieces. Many construction projects that include plywood parts are centered around 8- or 12-foot lengths, so the 24-foot size is appealing in that regard, as those numbers divide into 24 evenly. Some smaller size tubing comes in 20-foot lengths; black steel pipe is a standard 21-foot size.

The 1½″ size square tube is very popular for several reasons. First of all, 1½″ is the same thickness as any wooden two-by. It is often handy to work with materials that are the same thickness, because the parts line up better. Second, it is difficult to obtain thinner gauges in larger tubing that is really intended for heavy construction purposes, and in theatre we are always concerned about the weight of portable scenery. Last of all, and perhaps the most important, the cross section of 1½″ square tube is large enough to have a fair amount of rigidity all on its own, without being doubled, or made into a truss. For most projects, you can estimate that it has approximately the same strength and rigidity as a 2×4. Some small units are better constructed from 1″ or even ¾″ stock when that rigidity is not required. *Structural Design for the Stage*, by Holden and Sammler (Focal, 1999), is an excellent resource for anyone interested in studying the structural properties of specific materials.

Structural steel tubing of the sort used to construct scenery is composed of *mild steel*, a name given to steel with a low carbon content that has excellent malleability and a Rockwell C scale hardness number in the 20s. It is easily drilled with ordinary tools.

WELDING EQUIPMENT

Two very common types of welders are used to join steel. One is the generic *arc welder* and the other is the *metal inert gas* type, which is abbreviated as *MIG*. A MIG welder is by far the easiest kind of welder to use for welding mild steel and is far and away the most popular choice. A MIG welder is somewhat more expensive to purchase than a standard arc welder, because its mechanism is much more complicated.

An arc welder is essentially a very large rectifier unit that changes AC power into DC power. Electronically, some machines are constant current while others are constant voltage. Two long cables are attached to the output of the machine. The *ground* has a clamp on the end that gets connected to the steel you are welding. The other cable has a smaller clamp to hold an *electrode*, which is a consumable wire stick coated with *flux*. The flux is a catalyst that aids in the welding process by

producing CO_2 gas when heated by the welding process. The CO_2 gas prevents the steel from oxidizing at high temperatures. When the electrode is brought into close contact with the steel, a circuit is completed between the (usually) positive output of the welder, the electrode, the steel being welded, the ground clamp, and the negative terminal of the welder.

VOLTAGE PRESSURE CREATES A HOT SPARK

ARC WELDING MELTS THE STEEL ELECTICALLY

Because the electrode is only tangentially in contact with the steel, the electricity must jump across that small gap in order to complete the circuit. When that happens, a small spark or *arc* is created. The arc is very hot and melts the steel. The electrode gets hot also, and the tip of it melts as well. Protected by the flux, molten steel from the electrode mixes with the molten steel on the edges of the joint being welded. Three pieces of steel are being melted and joined: the two pieces being connected and the electrode from the welder itself. When the molten steel cools and hardens, all three should be joined at the molecular level, so that theoretically they are all one homogeneous crystalline structure. (In reality, the heating and cooling make a slight difference in the composition of the welded area.)

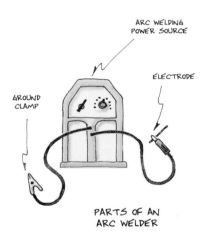

ARC WELDING POWER SOURCE

ELECTRODE

GROUND CLAMP

PARTS OF AN ARC WELDER

There are several fairly problematic consequences of arc welding. Of course the light produced is extremely bright and will cause serious injury to your eyes if you look at it from a close distance. (The distance from the arc while you are welding is very, very close.) Special equipment must be worn to protect your eyes while welding, and the glass is so dark that you cannot see anything other than the light from welding through it when it is in place. The electrode will complete the circuit the instant it is in close proximity to the steel (close enough for the voltage pressure to force electrons across the gap, as discussed in Chapter 6). So it is difficult to coordinate your movements to get the electrode in position, get the helmet in place, and then strike the arc.

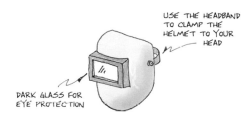

USE THE HEADBAND TO CLAMP THE HELMET TO YOUR HEAD

DARK GLASS FOR EYE PROTECTION

PROTECTIVE HELMET FOR MIG OR ARC WELDING

The helmet is strapped securely to your head. It is hinged on the side so that a quick neck motion will cause it to fall down into place. Newer types have a lens that senses the light from the welding process and electronically darkens in an instant, making it much easier to coordinate your movements.

The electrode is consumed by the welding process and must be frequently changed. The flux, the very hot steel, and oxygen from the air combine to form *slag* on the surface of the steel while you are welding. The slag is messy and can get in the way of future welding. It must be removed by hand after the welding process is completed.

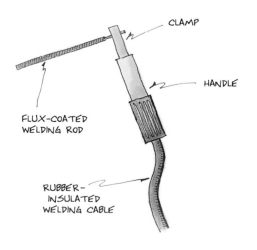

CLAMP

HANDLE

FLUX-COATED WELDING ROD

RUBBER-INSULATED WELDING CABLE

The MIG welder addresses some of the difficulties of using an electric arc when welding. An MIG welder

also uses a large rectifier to change AC power into DC power. It also has two cables that carry electric current and complete a circuit. One of them has a grounding clamp, but the other has a *nozzle* in place of the electrode found on a regular arc welder. The nozzle emits an *inert gas* that surrounds the joint while welding is taking place. The inert gas, most often an *argon/CO_2 mix*, protects the molten steel from oxygen in the air. There is no flux on the wire, and as a result no slag is formed on the weld. (Some wire welders do not use the inert gas method, and *do* in fact have flux-coated wire. They are not technically considered to be MIG welders.)

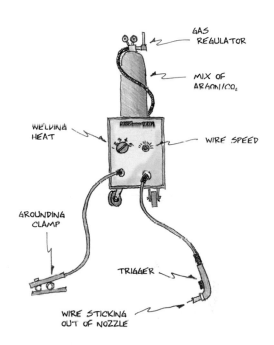

GAS REGULATOR

MIX OF ARGON/CO_2

WELDING HEAT

WIRE SPEED

GROUNDING CLAMP

TRIGGER

WIRE STICKING OUT OF NOZZLE

BASIC PARTS OF A MIG WELDER

A MIG welder is sometimes called a *wire welder*, because it uses a spool of wire in place of the electrode that is found on a standard arc welder. The wire is fed through the nozzle from a spool that contains enough of the wire to last for a very long time in even a very busy shop, so it does not need changing very often. This means that you do not have to stop welding to insert a new rod. The arc on a MIG welder is not struck until you pull a trigger on the nozzle. This makes coordinating the welding process much easier to do. You can rest the wire in the nozzle on the joint to be welded, cover your eyes with the hood, and then pull the trigger to start the welding process.

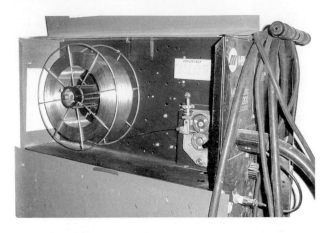

SPOOL OF WIRE IN A MIG WELDER

LOTS OF BLOBS AND SKIPS

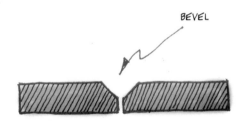

GRIND DOWN THE CORNERS OF
THICK STEEL PIECES FOR
BETTER WELDING PENETRATION

Remember that welding requires you to melt both of the parts forming the joint, and to allow the resulting metals to flow together so that they become indistinguishable from one another. A good weld should have a "puddled" appearance, because the steel is highly viscous when in the liquid state.

NOTE THE EVEN PUDDLING ALONG
THE LENGTH OF THE WELD

You should be able to see that both parts melted and that the resulting joint line shows evidence of it. If the weld looks like many globs of steel stuck on the surface, the metal did not really flow together. There has been no *penetration* of the heat into the underlying metal.

If the metal you are welding is really thick, it may be necessary to prepare the joint by grinding so that the heat from the arc can melt the steel all the way through its thickness. If you are welding 16-ga tubing, that will not be necessary, because the tubing wall is so thin.

Make the weld itself by slowly moving the electrode or wire back and forth across the joint line. Make sure that heat from the arc is applied to both surfaces. If you move too quickly, there will not be enough heat to properly melt the two parts. If you move too slowly, there will be too much heat and the steel will completely melt and drop out, creating a hole. Some people describe the movement across the joint as a zigzag pattern, and others as making small circles with the nozzle. On a MIG welder, pulling the nozzle back from the joint will reduce the amount of heat present at the weld. Moving closer will make the weld hotter. If you pull back too far, the gas will not be able to completely encase the welding area, and also the wire may melt before it gets close enough to the steel to complete the circuit. This can cause a popping sound while you are welding. It will also happen if the wire speed is too high. Different diameters of wire are available, and of course the heavier gauges are meant for thicker welds. About 0.035 is a good size for 16-ga tubing.

The MIG welder has a *heat control knob* with numbers like 1 through 5 that can be used to regulate the voltage pressure of electrons through the welder, and hence the temperature of the arc. (Some machines control current instead.) The higher the voltage, the more heat concentrated on the weld. Use a higher setting for thick materials and a lower setting for thin materials. If the steel surrounding the weld tends to melt and fall through the tubing, the temperature is too hot. Coordinate the temperature with the wire speed for a good weld.

WIRE SPEED KNOB

One other variable is the pressure of the *gas flow*. This is set by a regulator on the tank of gas, and generally doesn't need to be adjusted after setting up the tank when you first get the welder. A glass vial has a small bead inside it that should float about halfway up when the argon/CO_2 mix is running through the welder. It sits on the bottom of the vial when the welder is idle.

HEAT SELECTION KNOB

Another variable is the speed of the wire coming out of the nozzle. Generally speaking, the *wire speed* should be higher if you are welding at a higher temperature, but this is somewhat variable, so you will need to experiment to discover the best setting. If the wire pushes the electrode away from the weld, the wire speed is too fast. If the end of the wire melts into a ball before getting to the weld, the speed is too slow. Again, you need to adjust the wire speed and temperature in tandem, so that a good balance is struck. It is different for thicker/thinner materials, but after a while you will have an intuitive understand of the appropriate settings for the type of welding you most frequently do.

The newest types of welders have a different scheme, in that you must set the thickness of the material and wire gauge. The welder automatically sets the voltage and wire speed parameters.

Reading this chapter will not qualify you as an expert at using either an arc or MIG welder. It takes more time than that, and you need to have personal instruction. The few preceding paragraphs were meant as an overview of the process. The rest of this chapter is concerned with how to prepare, cut, and assemble parts for welded steel scenery. That is actually the most difficult and time-consuming part of the job.

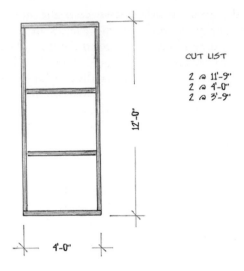

CUT LIST

2 @ 11'-9"
2 @ 4'-0"
2 @ 3'-9"

MAKE FROM 1 1/2"
STEEL SQUARE TUBE

SOME SAFETY CONCERNS

The light produced by any type of welding will cause extensive retina damage if you stare at it, especially if you are very close at hand, that is, when you are the person welding. But the light can be problematic from a distance as well, so it is good to use *protective screens* if others are in close proximity. The lenses found in sunglasses, or even cutting torch goggles, are not enough protection from the bright light.

The welds are very hot for some time after you make them, and will cause a severe burn if you touch the steel shortly after welding it. You can get a nasty sunburn on exposed skin if you weld for a long period and don't cover up your arms or neck. Use all the protective gear required for your particular equipment. This includes, at the very least, safety glasses, a helmet, special gloves, and screens to mask other workers from your welding. Be sure to read, understand, and follow all of the safety instructions that come with your welder.

---

a result, the length of the upright stiles will be 3 inches shorter than the overall dimension, while the rails run the full length of the nominal size.

Now that you have a cut list, you must cut the steel. Aluminum can be cut with woodworking equipment, but steel requires special techniques.

The most practical tool for cutting small sections of steel in a small shop is the *chop saw*, sometimes known as a *cut-off saw*. This is really sort of a misnomer, as a chop saw is really a type of grinder and not a saw at all. Rather than using the teeth of a blade to cut, this tool *grinds* the metal away with an abrasive blade. The blades must be changed frequently, as the abrasive material is also worn away during the cutting process. Small chop saws are relatively inexpensive, around $300, and are a very expedient and forgiving way to cut steel.

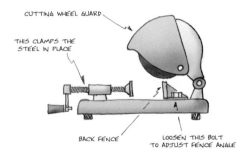

CUTTING WHEEL GUARD

THIS CLAMPS THE
STEEL IN PLACE

BACK FENCE

LOOSEN THIS BOLT
TO ADJUST FENCE ANGLE

PARTS OF A CHOP SAW

CUTTING AND FITTING THE PARTS

The most difficult part of metal construction is cutting the pieces and making them stay put while you are welding them. After the parts are joined, grinding the welds flat can be another lengthy chore. Of course, any cutting job necessitates the development of a cut list.

The process of making a cut list for this welding project is exactly the same as the process of making a cut list for a flat, or a step unit, or a platform. Overall dimensions are given on the drawing, and your task is to determine which framing members overlap the other members. This drawing indicates that the top and bottom rails overlap the upright members in the same way they would on a hard-cover flat. The directions say to construct the unit from 1½" 16-ga square tube. As

They function in much the same way as a power miter box, with a hinge in the back that lets the user press the grinding blade down onto the work. This allows gravity to work for you when cutting. There should be a metal plate or fence on the table of the saw that allows the user to cut angles. This is done by loosening a pair of bolts and rotating the plate to the desired angle. There are marks on the plate to indicate angles, but they are often not very accurate. Perhaps the manufacturer of your particular chop saw will have improved on the design, but if not, you might try using a Speed Square to set the saw to either 90 or 45 degrees. For other angles, use the power miter box to cut a 3- or 4-inch-wide board to the desired angle, and then use this pattern to set the angle on the chop saw. Hold the length of the board against the fence, and then lower the blade. Adjust the fence so that the angle of the pattern board matches the blade, and tighten the fence into place.

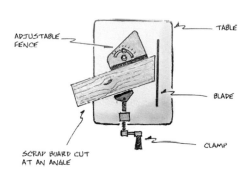

ADJUSTABLE FENCE

TABLE

BLADE

CLAMP

SCRAP BOARD CUT AT AN ANGLE

CUT A BOARD ON THE MITER SAW AND USE IT TO SET THE ANGLE

The saw should have a clamp of some sort in the front so that the steel can be securely held in the saw while cutting. A chop saw sprays out a shower of sparks while it cuts the steel, and you should take care to protect yourself and others. Be sure to follow all the safety rules listed on the tool. Be especially mindful of the fire danger from the sparks. If you've never used a chop saw before, you will most likely be surprised by the abundance of sparks that the tool creates. They can get into sawdust and smolder for a very long time before a fire is noticed.

BE CAREFUL!

THE CHOP SAW MAKES LOTS O' SPARKS

A *metal-cutting band saw* is another common steel-cutting tool. This type of band saw is very different from the kind used in woodworking, but the blades are very similar in either case. The metal cutting band saw blade greatly resembles one used in a hacksaw, with small teeth that weave back and forth to create the necessary set for cutting. The band saw itself warps the blade outward so that it can cut through material that would otherwise be too large for the throat of the tool. There are both portable and stationary versions of this tool. Either one is much quieter than a chop saw, and does not produce sparks, but they are much, much slower at cutting through the material.

METAL CUTTING BAND SAW

If you have the room, and will be cutting a lot of steel, it might be worth your while to set up a radial-arm-saw-type bench for your saw. The steel pieces are quite long and supporting them with a bench is very convenient. If you place a fence all down the length of the table, you can easily attach stop blocks for making multiple cuts. Create a holder for a chop saw by installing wooden blocks to hold the feet in place. A stationary metal cutting band saw has feet on it that you can attach to the floor.

If no wall space is available, you can work on a non-flammable concrete floor instead. Make up a number of wooden blocks that are the same height as the top of the saw table from the floor. They can be used to hold the tubing up off the floor and level with the saw. This creates a flexible method of supporting the tubing while cutting, because you can move the blocks around as required.

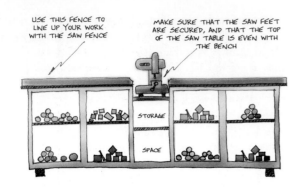

USE THIS FENCE TO
LINE UP YOUR WORK
WITH THE SAW FENCE

MAKE SURE THAT THE SAW FEET
ARE SECURED, AND THAT THE TOP
OF THE SAW TABLE IS EVEN WITH
THE BENCH

STORAGE

SPACE

THIS BENCH FOR A CHOP SAW
IS SIMILAR TO ONE FOR A RADIAL ARM SAW

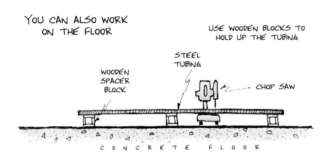

YOU CAN ALSO WORK
ON THE FLOOR

USE WOODEN BLOCKS TO
HOLD UP THE TUBING

WOODEN
SPACER
BLOCK

STEEL
TUBING

CHOP SAW

CONCRETE FLOOR

Each piece must be marked and cut in turn, in much the same manner as working on a radial arm saw. Don't try to rush the cut; let the chop saw work at its own pace. The speed used to cut any material is called the *feed rate*. If the motor on the chop saw, or any other cutting equipment, begins to slow down and bind excessively, you are moving too fast. It is also possible to move too slowly, causing the work to heat up unnecessarily from excess friction.

After the steel is cut you will need to dress the ends a bit to remove *burrs* left by the chop saw. It is pretty easy to do this with a few strokes of a large, rough *file*. A grinder can also be used, and it is really a matter of personal preference. Some of the pieces will have an open end exposed in the finished product, and may need to have the interior burr removed as well. A file will fit inside easily. It is not necessary to spend a great deal of time in treating the ends of pieces that will be welded together. However, it is sometimes difficult to jig up the parts if there is a large burr on the end of the tubing. If the defect is small, it will most likely melt away during the welding process. Most burrs on the inside will not show.

Steel tubing is often coated with a layer of oil. The steel mill does this to keep the product from rusting while it is at the supplier. It is generally a nasty, grimy sort of oil, and for years I have suspected that it is one way of recycling used motor oil. Sometimes there's a little, and sometimes there's a lot. It is best to take care of the oil problem shortly after the stock arrives by wiping it down with a spray cleaner like 409 or Simple Green and rags or paper towels. It's a dirty job, but someone has to do it! It is important to get at least the major portion of the oil off the tubing, so that it is not there when you are welding. The suspect oil could otherwise be vaporized into an inhalable gas by the welding process. Besides, it is very messy.

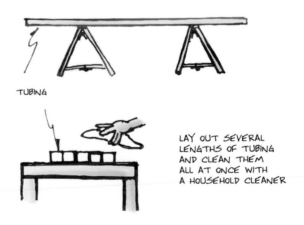

TUBING

LAY OUT SEVERAL
LENGTHS OF TUBING
AND CLEAN THEM
ALL AT ONCE WITH
A HOUSEHOLD CLEANER

ASSEMBLY

Unless you are making something really small like a cane bolt holder, you may find that creating the *welding jig* takes more time than any other part of the fabrication process. It is really important to hold the tubing steady while you are welding, because heat from the arc causes the steel to expand and warp out of shape, a process generally referred to as *heat distortion*. Heat distortion can move the parts you are welding a significant amount, and cause your project to be very much less than square. There are many different ways of creating a welding jig. The easiest is to make marks on the floor and hold the steel members in place with stage weights. This method is best when the parts are very large, and the number of units is very small.

Tape out a sizable right-angle pattern on the concrete floor of the shop, and use it in much the same way as a template table is used to square up flats. Lay down several sheets of plywood and use them to mark the right angle. Using several sheets of plywood will ensure that the angle is proportionally large enough to enhance accuracy in the layout.

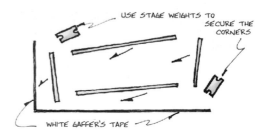

USE STAGE WEIGHTS TO SECURE THE CORNERS

WHITE GAFFER'S TAPE

SQUARING THE FRAME

Concrete floors are often uneven. It is a good idea to make up a supply of small wooden wedges to use in leveling the joints. You can make these from short sections of 1×12 that are cut diagonally on the band saw. That will keep the grain going the length of the wedge. It is important to use wedges or some other type of *shim* to arrange the faces of the square tube so that they are on the same plane with one another before welding.

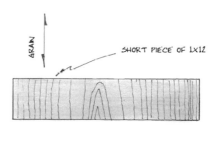

GRAIN

SHORT PIECE OF 1×12

USE THE MITER SAW TO CUT A FEW WEDGES FROM EACH END OF A LONG PIECE

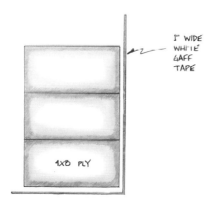

1" WIDE WHITE GAFF TAPE

1×8 PLY

USE SHEETS OF PLYWOOD AND WHITE TAPE TO MARK OUT A REALLY LARGE RIGHT ANGLE

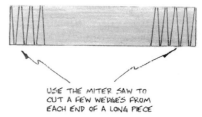

WEDGE

WEDGE

MAKE SURE THAT THE TOPS OF BOTH PIECES OF TUBING ARE ON THE SAME PLANE

Start with the bottom rail, and then add a stile. Stage counterweights may be used to hold the ends of the square tube in place. They are quite heavy and, of course, will not burn. If your theatre uses old-style lead weights it would probably not be a good idea to use them for this purpose, as they might easily melt and/or become toxic.

USE WEDGES TO LEVEL OUT THE DIFFERENT PIECES OF SQUARE TUBE

If you will be tech screwing some other material to the square tube, avoid having the welded seam side up when laying out the unit. Because the heating and cooling of the welding process tempers the metal, the seam is oftentimes much harder steel than the regular mild steel of the body of the tube, and it will be more difficult to get the tech screws to start there.

Using stage weights to pin down the corners of a unit lying on a concrete floor is a good way to stabilize the parts of a large frame, but if the parts are smaller and more complex another method is called for. It is at its best when you need to reproduce a number of the same units. A welding shop uses a template table with a sheet of steel on its top. Individual parts are tack-welded to its surface to hold them in place while welding the joints, and that is a good method, but if your shop is mostly a woodworking facility, you probably don't have space for that kind of table. Instead, use the same wooden-topped template table used to build flats. Use small wooden blocks to hold the parts in place. Cut a number of them from half-inch plywood, somewhere in the neighborhood of 1 inch by 2 inches. The exact size doesn't matter as much as that they are all the same.

USE 1/2" PLYWOOD TO CUT A LARGE NUMBER OF UNIFORM BLOCKS, ALL ABOUT 1" BY 2".
IF THESE BLOCKS ARE ALL THE SAME IT WILL BE EASIER TO MAKE UP A WELDING JIG.

Plywood is best, because it won't split apart the way dimension lumber can. Half-inch is a good thickness because it doesn't interfere with welding the sides of the steel as much as a thicker block would. They are very easy to attach to the table using a nail gun. If you use nails about 1" long, it will be easy to remove the blocks when you are finished.

The first step in laying out the jig is to establish a right angle of wooden blocks on the table, which you can do with the same trick as before, using sheets of plywood. Lay down the first couple of parts that go in that corner, and hold them in place with more blocks, especially toward the ends. Add more sections of precut tubing and lock them in place with more blocks. Use only as many as necessary, but enough to positively hold the steel tubing in place. After you've welded this first unit together and removed it, you can fit more precut sections into the jig and weld another almost instantly. It takes a bit of time to put the jig together, but once you have it, you can make a large number of identical units in a very short time.

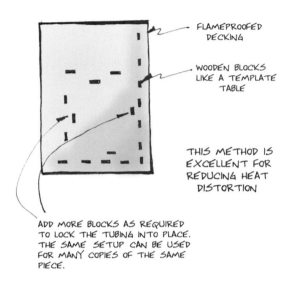

FLAMEPROOFED DECKING

WOODEN BLOCKS LIKE A TEMPLATE TABLE

THIS METHOD IS EXCELLENT FOR REDUCING HEAT DISTORTION

ADD MORE BLOCKS AS REQUIRED TO LOCK THE TUBING INTO PLACE. THE SAME SETUP CAN BE USED FOR MANY COPIES OF THE SAME PIECE.

If a table is not available, or is not large enough, try locking together a number of 4×8 platforms to make a larger surface. A wooden top is important so that you can nail down the blocks. Be careful when welding, though, because the steel gets very hot, about 2600 degrees, and wood ignites at around 500 degrees Fahrenheit. It's a good idea to keep a spray bottle of water around to douse small flames that pop up from the plywood. Always make sure that the area is clear of sawdust and other flammable materials.

The process of creating jigs from wooden blocks will arise several more times, when special situations are discussed. Making up a welding jig is an important part of the metal frame construction concept.

If you examine the butt joint between two pieces of square tubing, you will see that there are four seams between the two pieces. The most obvious are the face seams, which occur between the end of one piece and the side of another. They result in a *face weld*. The inside corner between the two can be joined with a *fillet weld*. Opposite to the fillet is a seam that shows the thin edge of the end of the tubing. It is generally not practical or advisable to weld that seam.

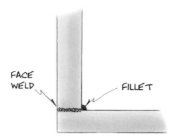

FACE WELD

FILLET

All welds leave at least a small bump out on the surface of the seam, so another piece of steel will not lie perfectly flat against it. In order to smooth out the bump, you must grind off the part of the welded seam that is sticking out from the face of the tubing. An *angle grinder* is used to do that. The grinder blade is actually a gritty material very similar to what you would find on a chop saw used to cut the metal to length. As you grind away metal, the blade is also consumed, eventually becoming too small to be useful.

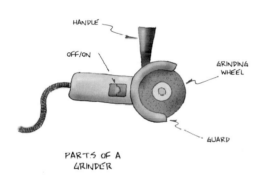

HANDLE

OFF/ON

GRINDING WHEEL

GUARD

PARTS OF A GRINDER

Much like a belt sander, the way you hold a grinder has a lot to do with how aggressively it removes unwanted material. If you hold it at a steep angle to the work, it will remove the metal very rapidly, but also tends to create an uneven surface. Holding it at a flatter angle will create a smoother surface.

You do not need to grind all of the welds, but rather only the ones that create a problem in fitting other parts together. It is only necessary to make the area flat, or nearly so. Most novices tend to go too far and create a depression at the site of the weld, which requires more work than necessary and also tends to weaken the joint. Grinding is a noisy, smelly, and somewhat unpleasant chore, and it is best to keep it to a minimum whenever possible. Remember to consider where the sparks are going. Always wear eye and hearing protection when using any type of grinder.

Fillet welds don't need to be ground down, because they don't fit up against anything. Because of that,

GRINDING AT A STEEP ANGLE TENDS TO DIG INTO THE WORK

GRINDING AT A SHALLOW ANGLE CREATES A FLATTER SURFACE

many people tend to connect units with fillets rather than face welds, which means that no grinding is necessary. That technique works really well when a third member will be welded at a right angle to the first two, as would happen when making a box-like structure. The process of welding the third member actually makes the face weld for you.

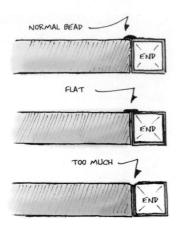

NORMAL BEAD

END

FLAT

END

TOO MUCH

END

DON'T GRIND OFF SO MUCH
AS TO WEAKEN THE WELD!

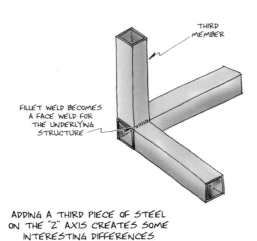

THIRD
MEMBER

FILLET WELD BECOMES
A FACE WELD FOR
THE UNDERLYING
STRUCTURE

ADDING A THIRD PIECE OF STEEL
ON THE "Z" AXIS CREATES SOME
INTERESTING DIFFERENCES

A Practical Example

The following concept of how to arrange steel square tube supports for decking is based on using three standard 4×8 platforms that are joined together with casket locks. The finished deck will be 2 feet tall. When designing decking systems involving square tubing, it is best to think of the platforms as a group, rather than as separate pieces. The system is put together from five main subassemblies that bolted together to form an overall structure. Here is a drawing to use as an example:

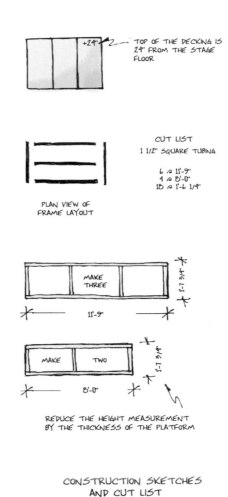

+24" TOP OF THE DECKING IS
24" FROM THE STAGE
FLOOR

CUT LIST
1 1/2" SQUARE TUBING

6 @ 11'-9"
4 @ 8'-0"
18 @ 1'-6 1/4"

PLAN VIEW OF
FRAME LAYOUT

MAKE
THREE

1'-7 3/4"

11'-9"

MAKE   TWO

1'-7 3/4"

8'-0"

REDUCE THE HEIGHT MEASUREMENT
BY THE THICKNESS OF THE PLATFORM

CONSTRUCTION SKETCHES
AND CUT LIST

But welding the fillets alone does not connect the steel parts as securely as the face welds do. If you are concerned about the structural integrity of what you are building, it is best to weld all the seams together. If your welding skills are good, you won't really need to grind that many of them, especially not those that don't show and don't affect the assembly of the parts.

If you are making a large number of multiples, weld all the frames on one side first, and then stack them with the unwelded side up. That makes it easy to weld all of the reverse sides at one time. You can attach the ground to the bottom frame, and it will not need to be moved until the entire stack of frames has been completed. Contact will be preserved through the entire group.

The decking frames require an upright member about every 4 feet when using $1\frac{1}{2}''$ 16-ga steel square tube. That spacing is enough to hold the weight of the decking and a reasonable amount of live load as well (live load indicating movement, as with people). *It is critical to keep the upright members vertical.* The compression strength of a 1½″ section of steel square tube is tremendous, but if the support structure is allowed to warp out of shape, disaster is imminent. Generally speaking, the greater surface area a decking unit has, the more stable the structure will be. No matter what type of legging system you use, ten 4×8 platforms linked together will have much, much more stability than one alone.

Rather than legging three separate 4×8 platforms, one system is used for all of them. The 11′-9″ frames stretch all the way from one side of the deck to the other, and therefore tie the three platforms together for more stability. Notice that these longer sections are designed to fit inside the shorter 8′-0″ frames. This is done in order to reduce the number of different-sized units to be constructed, and feeds into the wooden block jig philosophy of construction. Although five frames need to be built, there are only two different jig setups.

The word *frame* is used to indicate a flat, welded together section. One of the advantages of using flat sections is that they stack and store in a small amount of space. Another is that the overall unit can be dismantled easily, and just as easily reassembled using bolts. The trade-off is that some parts are duplicated. When it is assembled, this carrier system duplicates a few of the uprights used to hold up the weight of the load. That is especially true in the corners where two frames come together. In this example, six extra uprights must be cut: one for each corner and two at the ends of the center frame. That amounts to approximately 9 feet of square tube material out of 115 feet total, which is less than 10 percent extra.

Notice that the interior toggles are placed on approximately 4′-0″ centers, meaning that the centers of the uprights are 4 feet apart. On the 8′-0″ frames, it is essential to locate the uprights at precisely the center in order to facilitate the connection of the middle frame. But placement of uprights on the longer frames is not as critical, as they don't connect with anything else. Even so, you should make them all the same since they will be done on a jig anyway, and you might wind up using them differently later on.

Connect the metal frames together using ¼″ bolts and wing nuts. Bolting is a very secure method of joining them. ¼″ bolts are heavy-duty enough, considering that the connecting bolts have no load on them; they are just used to keep the parts from separating. Washers are a good idea, especially if you oversize the holes at ⅜″. Oversizing the holes makes it much easier to get the bolts through the frames. Especially if you consider that each bolt must pass through four walls, two on each piece of square tubing. A ¼″ hole is barely large enough for a bolt to fit through one hole. A larger ⅜″ opening allows for easy alignment and bolting of what are often awkwardly large frames.

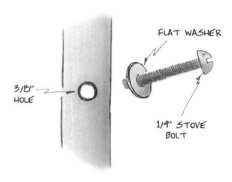

ACCOMMODATING ODD SHAPES

Sometimes nonrectangular platform shapes are required. These frames do not fit together in the tidy manner of our earlier example. Care must be taken to keep the frames located under the decking in such a way that the wooden framing of the platform and the steel frame of the legging system will work in concert. It is imperative that these two members come into contact with one another at least every 4 feet, although the steel framing of the leg frames and the wooden framing of the platforms do not need to be exactly the same shape. Here is an example of the relationship between the decking and the carrier frames:

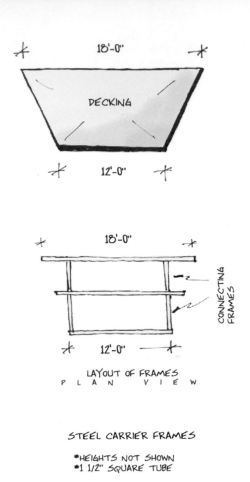

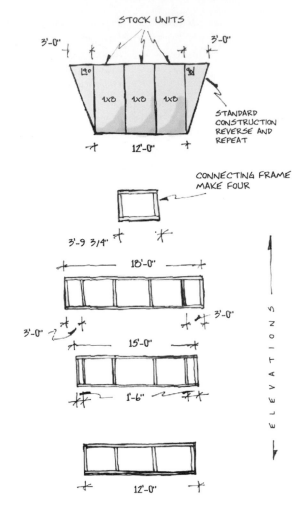

As seen in this example, the steel support frames are still used in a rectilinear way, and the normal bolting method may be used. The joining of the steel undercarriage and the wooden decking are not necessarily continuous with one another, but the rule of maintaining contact at least every 4 feet is preserved. This type of setup is easily constructed, because the parts are easy to measure and they fit into the jig well, but the process is best suited to a situation where the platform will not need to be faced. It will work well with a fabric skirt that is attached to the wooden frame. This type of underpinning is functional, but not really something you would like for the audience to see. Here are some sketches for the individual parts:

It would be better if the metal carriers holding up the decking could match the shape of the wooden parts. The framing of the wooden decking would lie directly atop the horizontal members of the carriers. The large diagram shows how that can be accomplished using hinges. Unlike in the earlier example, you can cover these frames with plywood or some other material so that they mask the underside of the platforms. In order to determine the exact sizes of the metal frames, lay out a full-scale replica of the unit to use as a pattern. Because you are copying a decking piece, it is best to build the platform first, and use it as the pattern.

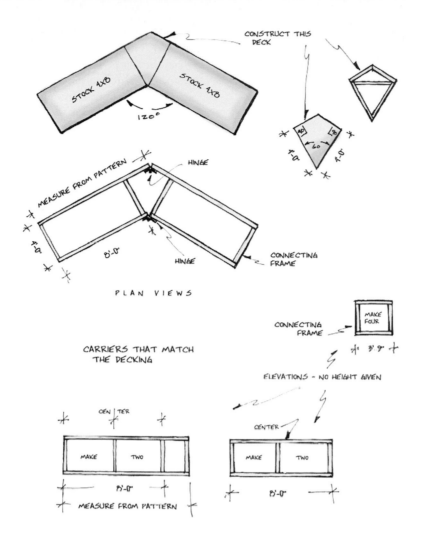

CONSTRUCT THIS DECK

STOCK 1×8   STOCK 1×8

120°

HINGE

MEASURE FROM PATTERN

4'-0"   8'-0"   HINGE

CONNECTING FRAME

PLAN VIEWS

CARRIERS THAT MATCH THE DECKING

CONNECTING FRAME   MAKE FOUR

3' 9"

ELEVATIONS - NO HEIGHT GIVEN

CEN TER

MAKE   TWO

8'-0"

MEASURE FROM PATTERN

CENTER

MAKE   TWO

8'-0"

Only one angled piece of decking must be built from scratch, as the other two sections are managed by using standard 4×8 platforms. After constructing it, lay out the entire footprint of the decking so that it can be used as a pattern.

The steel framing sections must meet at an angle, but cutting miters on all of the frames is too difficult a process, and even if you did manage it, the angles on the horizontal parts would not fit the sides of the uprights well. It isn't possible to change the geometry of the square tube into a triangular shape, as you might with a wooden part.

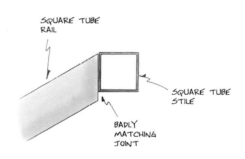

SQUARE TUBE RAIL

SQUARE TUBE STILE

BADLY MATCHING JOINT

IF YOU CUT THE END OF THE RAIL AT AN ANGLE, IT WILL NOT MATCH WELL WITH THE UPRIGHT

It is better to hinge the frames so that they touch *corner to corner*. This means that the frames will need to be shorter that the overall dimensions of the platform faces.

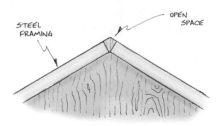

STEEL FRAMING

OPEN SPACE

STEEL FRAMING STOPS
SHORT OF THE CORNER

A method of computing the actual size must be developed. Using a 1½″-wide strip of plywood, mark a line along the edge of the decking to simulate the placement of the square tube framing. Make a line at a 90-degree angle from this line wherever the lines cross in the corners. This reveals the true sizes of the frames.

Hinges can be used to connect the uprights at odd angles. It is difficult to bolt or screw hinges in place on a metal frame, but it is easy to simply weld them on. Three-inch butt hinges fit rather well on 1½″ square tubing. It is best to use the square-cornered type, and make sure that they are steel, not brass. Most hinges are brass plated, which will not affect the process. Loose-pin backflap hinges are not well suited to this project because they are too flimsy, and the same could be said about any other hinge smaller than the 3″ butt.

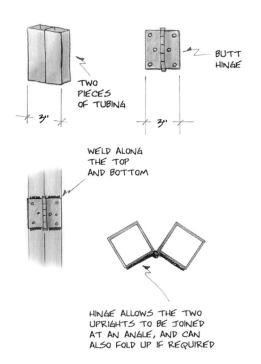

TWO
PIECES
OF TUBING

← 3″ →

BUTT
HINGE

← 3″ →

WELD ALONG
THE TOP
AND BOTTOM

HINGE ALLOWS THE TWO
UPRIGHTS TO BE JOINED
AT AN ANGLE, AND CAN
ALSO FOLD UP IF REQUIRED

Weld the hinges on after the frames have been constructed and trial fitted on top of the pattern. Setting

up on the pattern ensures that the angles are properly adjusted. Vise Grip clamps are an excellent way to hold hinges in place while they are being welded. If the hinges are located to the inside of the unit, they will not be in the way of any covering that might be attached to the frame. Loose pins made from bent 30- or 40-penny nails will make it easy to connect the hinges together.

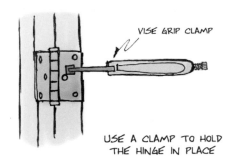

VISE GRIP CLAMP

USE A CLAMP TO HOLD
THE HINGE IN PLACE

CONNECTING THE PLATFORMS

Here are a couple of different ways to connect the wooden platform sections to the steel frame undercarriage. The method you choose is dependent upon how many platforms there are, the way they will be used, and/or the materials that are on hand and easily available. Stressed-skin platforms can be held in place by small wooden blocks similar to what were used to create a welding jig. When placed in the right spots, they keep the decking from sliding off, while gravity holds it down.

Perhaps the easiest method is to drill ³⁄₁₆″ holes through the top member of the steel frames and use 2½″ drywall screws to connect the wooden framing of the decking to the square tube. These holes are easier to drill from above, before the platforms are set down on the frames. The weight of the platform will keep it pressed against the metal frame; the screws are just to prevent the platform from slipping off the side.

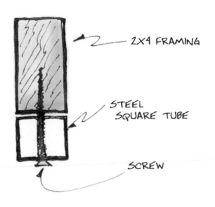

2X4 FRAMING

STEEL
SQUARE TUBE

SCREW

If the decking system must be struck and reassembled repeatedly, it might be best to weld *flanges* onto the tubing instead. If the flanges are placed to the inside of the 2×4 platform framing, they will be out of sight, but will still prevent the platforms from sliding off the undercarriage. The setup can occur by simply laying the decking into place after the steel framing has been erected. Similarly, your load-out will not be held up by waiting for screws to be removed. It is often helpful to bend the flanges in slightly in order to make the parts fit together more easily. Be sure to put enough flanges in the proper locations, not only to keep the platform on the frames, but also to keep the frames from racking out of shape.

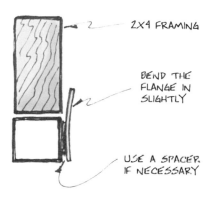

2×4 FRAMING

BEND THE FLANGE IN SLIGHTLY

USE A SPACER IF NECESSARY

A similar result can be achieved by attaching wooden blocks to the inside of a platform's 2×4s. If the wooden blocks stick out past the bottom of the framing for an inch or so, the platform can be held in place with no fasteners. Uniform blocks of ¾″ plywood may be used for this purpose, and if properly installed, will still allow the platforms to be stacked up squarely.

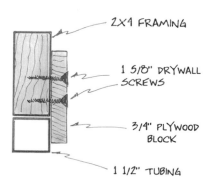

2×4 FRAMING

1 5/8″ DRYWALL SCREWS

3/4″ PLYWOOD BLOCK

1 1/2″ TUBING

You've seen three different ways to connect stock wooden decking to metal framing, but what about connecting the framing to the stage floor? Sometimes the decking system is so large, heavy, and solid that there is no need to attach it to the floor. This is especially true

of wide and low decks that have no tendency to tip over. When the footprint of the platforming is small, and the height is substantial, it is best to lag bolt the bottoms of the frames to the floor. A ⅜″ × 4″ lag bolt is a good size. Drill ½″ holes in the steel frames while they are still in the shop.

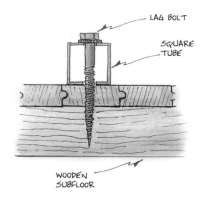

LAG BOLT

SQUARE TUBE

WOODEN SUBFLOOR

MAKE SURE THAT THE BOLTS GO FAR ENOUGH INTO THE FLOOR

A ¼″ pilot hole into the wooden floor will make it easier to screw in the bolt. This method may be used to secure spot towers, lighting towers, and other such metal frames. Use lag bolts of a proper size, and be sure that the flooring is solid enough to hold the threads of the lag bolts. Traditional wooden stage floors were made of several layers of wooden parts, so that they provide an excellent substrate for lag bolts, but you should make sure that is true when working in an unfamiliar space.

IMPACT DRIVER FOR LAG BOLTS

The kind of steel framing discussed so far can be dismantled and stacked against the wall when not in use. It is very easy to move about (except for the weight) and can be fitted into a truck without using up too much space. The flat nature of all of the pieces makes them easy to assemble with the types of jigs already discussed. Sometimes though, it is preferable to put the frames together into cubes. This method will avoid the doubling of vertical support elements in the corner of an assembled frame and hence will require less material. It also creates an airier, more open look if the framing is to be visible to the audience. This approach is at its best when the size of the decking piece involved is quite small and it won't need to be disassembled.

The concept is simple, but the execution is somewhat more complicated. The problem lies in arranging all the parts so that they are square to one another in a three-dimensional rather than two-dimensional setting. Arranging two dimensions on the jig is easy, but squaring in two directions requires some new techniques.

Make a new squaring up jig that works when the unit is on its side, 90 degrees from the original placement. The height will be the same as before, but you will need to move the end blocks over to accommodate the new width.

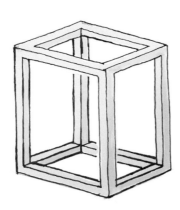

MAKING ONE SOLID PIECE
HAS A NEATER APPEARANCE,
BUT IT IS MUCH MORE
DIFFICULT TO CONSTRUCT

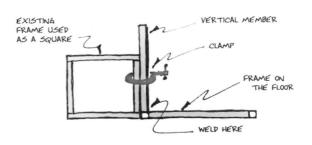

EXISTING FRAME USED AS A SQUARE

VERTICAL MEMBER

CLAMP

FRAME ON THE FLOOR

WELD HERE

TACK WELD EVERYTHING FIRST.
THIS ALLOWS FOR SOME ADJUSTING
AND REDUCES THE EFFECTS OF
HEAT DISTORTION.

Begin by constructing two side frames in the normal manner. These frames will be connected directly by horizontals rather than by using additional frames. You don't need a 2×4 framed platform to finish off the top. Tech-screw ¾″ plywood to the top instead.

Something must hold the original frames plumb while welding the new parts on. Use an unattached frame to do that. As shown in the previous diagram, the frames are easy to clamp to one another, and if all has gone well they should be a perfect right angle.

YOU CAN MAKE THE TOP WITH
JUST A LAYER OF 3/4" PLYWOOD.
IT DOESN'T NEED TO BE FRAMED
WITH 2X4S, BECAUSE THE UNIT
NEVER COMES APART.

TACK WELDS ARE SMALL
CONNECTIONS THAT
HOLD THE STEEL
TOGETHER TEMPORARILY.
THE STEEL DOESN'T HEAT
UP ENOUGH TO EXPAND AND
CAUSE HEAT DISTORTION.
TACK THE PARTS TOGETHER
FIRST SO THAT THE
STRUCTURE IS HELD IN PLACE.
COME BACK AND COMPLETE
THE WELDS LATER.

It is best to *tack-weld* this sort of work and get all of the parts in position before completing the welding. Double-check the squareness before finishing the welds. Heat distortion can be a real problem and will warp the entire structure out of alignment. When a piece of tubing is welded on one side, it will tend to draw up toward that side as it cools. Tack-welding parts, and making sure that they are firmly braced during welding, will reduce that effect.

Welding supply shops carry *magnetic squares* that work in the same way as the larger squaring up frames. They are much easier to put on, but their small size can be a drawback. Use whichever method seems the best at the time.

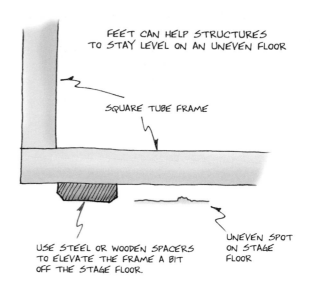

FEET CAN HELP STRUCTURES TO STAY LEVEL ON AN UNEVEN FLOOR

SQUARE TUBE FRAME

USE STEEL OR WOODEN SPACERS TO ELEVATE THE FRAME A BIT OFF THE STAGE FLOOR.

UNEVEN SPOT ON STAGE FLOOR

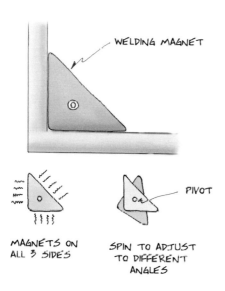

WELDING MAGNET

MAGNETS ON ALL 3 SIDES

PIVOT

SPIN TO ADJUST TO DIFFERENT ANGLES

Sometimes you may need to ensure that a structure can be exactly leveled out over a slightly uneven surface and the best way to do that is to use *leveling feet*. There are several different kinds, but be sure to use heavy-duty ones with at least a ⅜″ bolt on them. In a pinch, you can also use a carriage bolt, but they are not as easy to adjust.

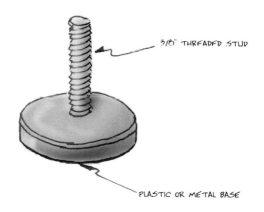

3/8″ THREADED STUD

PLASTIC OR METAL BASE

LEVELING HARDWARE WITH THREADED STUD

You may feel from time to time that a *rack brace* is needed to keep a welded frame from deforming into a parallelogram. This is unusual, especially if you weld the faces of the tubing together. Rack braces are a good idea when there is a high lateral stress on the structure.

Height Adjustments

Not all stage floors are exactly level. Sometimes bumps are left over from old paint, tape, or uneven boards. Consider adding small plastic feet to the bottoms of the carriers at regular intervals.

There are several ways of tapping threads for the bolt, and the simplest is to drill an appropriately sized hole and then ream out threads with a tap.

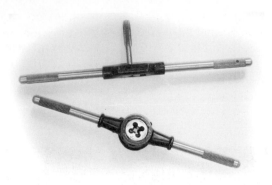

TAP IS ON THE TOP, DIE ON THE BOTTOM

Taps and *dies* are designed to thread all sorts of things. Dies are used to put male threads on a shaft, while taps are used to install female threads inside a hole. The problem with tapping this tubing is that the 16-gauge metal isn't thick enough to produce more than one thread, and the leveler will soon work itself loose. Try welding on a thicker metal plate for more grip.

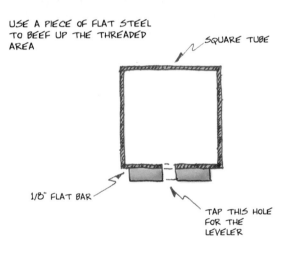

Another approach is to weld a nut to the bottom of the frame. This variation isn't as craftsman-like, but it gets the job done and is actually stronger because the nut is so much thicker than the metal plates.

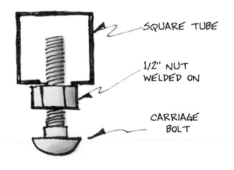

CUTTING STEEP ANGLES

A chop saw won't cut an angle steeper than 45 degrees. You may occasionally find the need to do so, especially if constructing a metal L-jack brace.

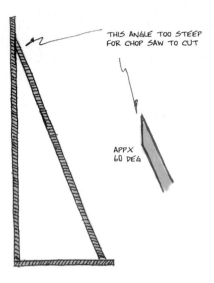

FIND ANOTHER WAY TO CUT ACUTE ANGLES

The stile and rail end in right-angle cuts, but the rack brace is different. The bottom angle where it intersects the rail is less than a 45-degree angle, but the top angle is probably close to a 60-degree angle. The exact amount isn't important, because you can mark the angle directly on the steel with a straightedge using the full-scale pattern method. Use a grinder with a cut-off wheel to do the actual cutting.

The *cut-off wheel* is essentially a very thin grinding wheel that is meant to cut through the steel rather than to smooth it out. Its thinness produces less of a kerf, and allows the wheel to move through the metal more easily. Hold it at a right angle to the work when you are cutting. After a bit of experience, you will notice that there is a tendency for the wheel to get caught in the steel while you are cutting, and that sometimes it may shatter because it is so thin. Be sure to wear protective gear. You can avoid this problem to some extent by marking the steel all the way around and not penetrating the tubing by more than a small amount.

different from the normal type that has a metal plate with mounting holes. You can drill a hole through the steel itself, insert the stem of the caster through it, and then use a locking nut or a regular nut with a lock washer to hold it in place. This method is very easy, but the stemmed casters are less available than the plated kind. They are available only in the swivel type.

Another method of attaching casters is to weld on a *mounting plate* that matches the mounting plate on the caster itself. Drill holes in the shop-built plate that match the ones in the caster.

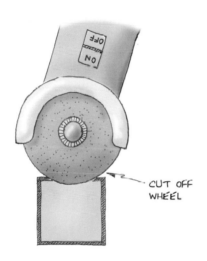

DON'T GO TOO DEEP WITH THE CUTTING WHEEL, OR IT WILL BIND IN THE STEEL

CUT OFF WHEEL

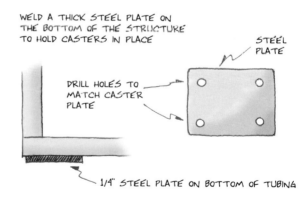

WELD A THICK STEEL PLATE ON THE BOTTOM OF THE STRUCTURE TO HOLD CASTERS IN PLACE

STEEL PLATE

DRILL HOLES TO MATCH CASTER PLATE

1/4" STEEL PLATE ON BOTTOM OF TUBING

Either of these two methods results in a very solid attachment.

CASTERS ON STEEL FRAMING

Casters can be attached to steel framing in one of two different ways. The first is to use a *stemmed caster* that has a bolt sticking out the top. Stemmed casters are

BENDING METAL TUBING

A *tube bending machine* consists of three wheels, two of them stationary, and a third drive wheel that can be moved toward them in small increments. The drive wheel can be put into motion with a crank. It is used to force the tubing through the machine.

together so that multiple copies can be made using the same formula. If you need several arcs all with the same radius, try making a longer piece of the curve and then cutting it into sections.

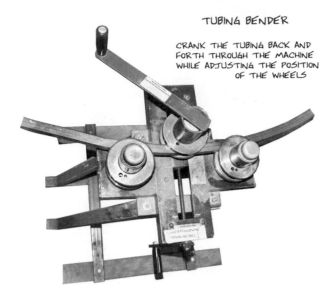

TUBING BENDER

CRANK THE TUBING BACK AND FORTH THROUGH THE MACHINE WHILE ADJUSTING THE POSITION OF THE WHEELS

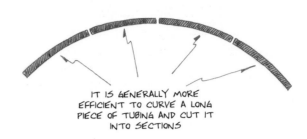

IT IS GENERALLY MORE EFFICIENT TO CURVE A LONG PIECE OF TUBING AND CUT IT INTO SECTIONS

The drive wheel is cranked toward the two stationary wheels in very small amounts via a screw thread. Turning the bolt forces the wheels toward each other. Each time that happens, the tubing is forced to curve just a bit more in order to fit between the wheels. You can adjust the amount of curvature in the tubing in proportion to the distance between the wheels. It is best to do this slowly, and to make many passes back and forth rather than to hurry, because that places too much strain on the equipment and the tubing alike.

EXTENSION LEGS

Extension legs are used to adjust the height of decking or some other unit, when the amount of difference between one leg and another is very great. They are excellent for outdoor setups, where the terrain is apt to be extremely variable. They are created by using two different-sized pieces of square tubing that nest inside one another. They can be adjusted by extending or collapsing the interior section in proportion to the exterior one. Holes along the side make it possible to insert a pin to lock the members into position. An outer leg of $1\frac{1}{2}''$ tubing is approximately $1\frac{3}{8}''$ on the inside, so that a $1\frac{1}{4}''$ tubing leg can easily slide in and out.

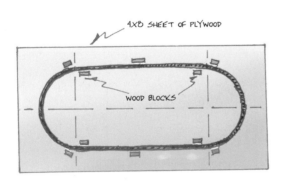

4X8 SHEET OF PLYWOOD

WOOD BLOCKS

DRAW OUT A FULL-SCALE PATTERN ON A SHEET OF PLYWOOD AND CURVE THE PIECES TO MATCH IT. LATER ON YOU CAN USE THE SAME PATTERN AS A JIG TO HOLD THE PARTS TOGETHER

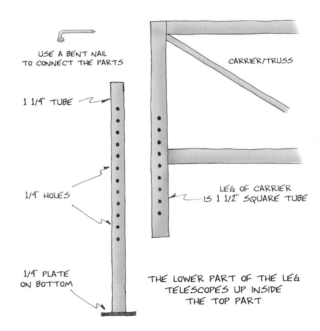

USE A BENT NAIL TO CONNECT THE PARTS

CARRIER/TRUSS

1 1/4" TUBE

1/4" HOLES

LEG OF CARRIER IS 1 1/2" SQUARE TUBE

1/4" PLATE ON BOTTOM

THE LOWER PART OF THE LEG TELESCOPES UP INSIDE THE TOP PART

A full-scale pattern can be used to judge when the curve is correct. You should keep track of how many turns you've made on the bolt that brings the wheels

Because the legs are meant to be used as a group, it is important to standardize construction so that all pieces are identical and interchangeable. The parts are easily cut to the same length, but the holes must also be identical. To do this, a jig is required.

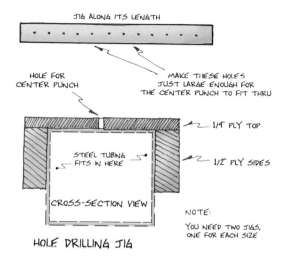

JIG ALONG ITS LENGTH

HOLE FOR CENTER PUNCH

MAKE THESE HOLES JUST LARGE ENOUGH FOR THE CENTER PUNCH TO FIT THRU

1/4" PLY TOP

STEEL TUBING FITS IN HERE

1/2" PLY SIDES

CROSS-SECTION VIEW

NOTE:
YOU NEED TWO JIGS, ONE FOR EACH SIZE

HOLE DRILLING JIG

The holes are placed on 1-inch centers, which is close enough to allow for small adjustments, but not so close as to require excessive drilling to create them. Notice that one of the jigs is meant to fit snuggly on the 1½" and the other on the 1¼" tubing. The holes in the jig are just large enough for a *center punch* to fit through. A center punch is used to make a small dent in metal so that a drill bit naturally goes to the center of it. Punch both sides of the leg rather than drilling all the way through it. This will increase precision and all burrs will be to the inside of the tubing.

A JIG LIKE THIS MAKES CUTTING ON THE DRILL PRESS MUCH EASIER

Make a square plate from approximately ³⁄₁₆" steel and weld it to the bottom of the smaller extension leg.

That will prevent it from sinking into the dirt. When setting up the decking, a collection of ½" and ¾" plywood blocks can be used as shims to spread the load even more, and adjust the height of individual legs to plus or minus ¼".

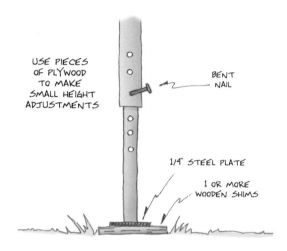

USE PIECES OF PLYWOOD TO MAKE SMALL HEIGHT ADJUSTMENTS

BENT NAIL

1/4" STEEL PLATE

1 OR MORE WOODEN SHIMS

How Trusses Work

A *truss* is a structural member that is specially designed to be both strong and lightweight at the same time. It is strong because it is made up of many small triangles, and it is lightweight because the interior is composed mostly of open space. Thin steel or wooden members are used to create the triangles. The connection points are called *nodes*. A typical truss looks something like this:

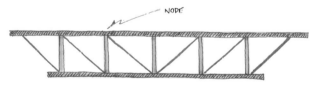

NODE

THIS TYPE OF TRUSS MADE OF WELDED STEEL IS COMMONLY USED TO SUPPORT ROOFS

THE DIAGONALS MAKE TWO TRIANGLES OUT OF ONE SQUARE

Triangles are very strong geometric shapes, because it isn't possible to deform them without bending one of the members, or destroying a node that connects them. This is not true of any other polygon, all of which can be distorted by altering the connection angle of a node.

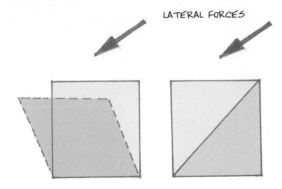

LATERAL FORCES

A SQUARE CAN BE DEFORMED INTO A PARALLELOGRAM
WHEN LATERAL FORCES ACT ON IT. THE SIDES OF
THE SQUARE ROTATE AROUND THE NODES. THAT
ISN'T POSSIBLE FOR A TRIANGLE UNLESS ONE OF THE
SIDES IS BENT.

Trusses are very *rigid structures*, and are not intended to bend. If a truss deflects over a certain amount, catastrophic failure is imminent. Bending is a sign that either the nodes or the connecting members have been loaded past capacity. On the other hand, a single piece of steel tubing can flex to a curved shape and then return to its original linear shape. As that happens, the top of the tube compresses, and the bottom stretches.

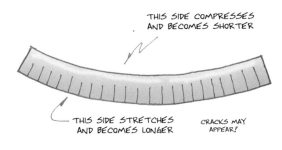

THIS SIDE COMPRESSES
AND BECOMES SHORTER

THIS SIDE STRETCHES
AND BECOMES LONGER

CRACKS MAY
APPEAR!

HOW MATERIALS BEND
THINNER MEMBERS BEND MORE UNDER THE SAME AMOUNT OF FORCE

The closer the top and bottom are to one another, the easier it is for a member to bend, because the top and bottom don't need to compress and stretch as much to create the radius of the arc. Thinner members bend more easily than thicker ones, which is a fairly intuitive concept.

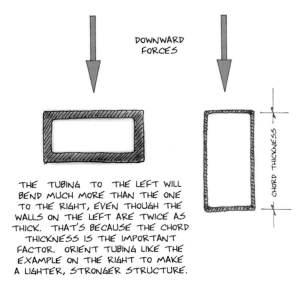

DOWNWARD
FORCES

CHORD THICKNESS

THE TUBING TO THE LEFT WILL
BEND MUCH MORE THAN THE ONE
TO THE RIGHT, EVEN THOUGH THE
WALLS ON THE LEFT ARE TWICE AS
THICK. THAT'S BECAUSE THE CHORD
THICKNESS IS THE IMPORTANT
FACTOR. ORIENT TUBING LIKE THE
EXAMPLE ON THE RIGHT TO MAKE
A LIGHTER, STRONGER STRUCTURE.

A truss creates a rigid structure that is lightweight, yet able to support large loads by separating the top and bottom beams. Greater separation means that the top and bottom must stretch/compress more than they are able to do. The most common type of truss is created by top and bottom beams connected with verticals, where diagonals are used to stiffen the structure by dividing it into triangles.

A practical example of how trusses can be used to create weight-bearing decking units can be found on the Web site.

CHAPTER 22

FULL-SCALE PATTERNS

Full-scale patterns are used to produce work that does not lend itself to an ordinary cut list. Some units of scenery are so oddly shaped that the normal methods are simply impossible. This frequently occurs when lots of angles are used, or if the shapes are curved. The full-scale pattern technique allows you to mark framing parts directly from the patterns, or in some cases the pattern is marked on plywood that becomes a part of the unit. Most of these techniques have been touched on in other chapters, but it seems best to organize them all in one place. Theatre scenery tends to have very fanciful shapes and profiles that require the builder to be more inventive than carpenters engaged in general construction.

Throughout history, painters have used a *grid technique* to reproduce scale drawings into full size. If a drawing has been rendered in $\frac{1}{2}''$ scale, each $\frac{1}{2}''$ on the drawing is equal to $1'\text{-}0''$ in full size. You can use this method by dividing the drawing into $\frac{1}{2}''$ squares, and the surface you would like to transfer the design to in $1'\text{-}0''$ squares. You can transfer the drawing to the larger scale one square at a time with a high degree of accuracy. Scenic artists use this method daily in their work. If a *profile piece* of scenery is to be constructed, the same technique will serve the stage carpenter well.

SOME UNITS CAN'T SIMPLY BE MEASURED WITH A TAPE
AND MARKED FOR CUTTING WITH A CROW'S FOOT.
THEY REQUIRE A MORE COMPLEX APPROACH.

USING A GRID

Gridding a profile quite often requires the input of a scenic artist. Most often the carpenters will lay out plywood, grid it off into 1-foot squares, and then request that the scenic artist or

doi: 10.1016/C2009-0-23409-X

designer mark the profile. Depending on the personalities involved, you might wind up marking the outlines inside the squares and then just getting them checked by a more artistic member of the team. (Unless, of course, *you* are that person.)

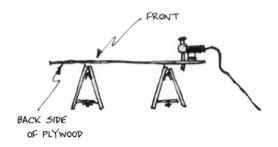

FRONT

BACK SIDE
OF PLYWOOD

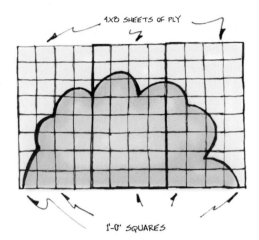

4X8 SHEETS OF PLY

1'-0" SQUARES

GRIDDED OFF
1/2" SCALE
DRAWING

JIGSAW TEETH CUT
ON THE UPSTROKE

MARK THE DRAWING
ON THE BACK
WHENEVER POSSIBLE

You can also reduce tearout by cutting with the grain. As you may recall, ripping creates less tearout than cross-cutting, because ripping cuts with the grain. You may be able to line the plywood up in such a way as to keep as many lines as possible running with the grain of the wood. Obviously, this is problematic when cutting curves. But tearout is also reduced if you cut at an angle that pulls on the wood fibers rather than pushing them. If you are cutting at an angle to the grain, one side of the kerf will be pushing, and the other side will be pulling. Make sure that the keeper piece is on the pulling side of the kerf. If you have a large curve, it is possible to reverse the angle of your cut where the grain direction changes and make the entire curve smoother.

Charcoal is a great medium to do the marking, because it leaves dark, bold lines and is easily erased. Once the outline of the piece has been marked in charcoal, it is a good practice to retrace it with a Sharpie marker so that the line is clearer. Charcoal tends to vibrate off the plywood during the cutting process, and having a clear and indelible mark makes the job of cutting much easier. The more complicated the work is, the more important it is to retrace. One word of caution: lacquer-based pens can be difficult to paint over. This is especially true if the paint is a light color.

After the design has been laid out, cut the profile edges with a jigsaw. The teeth on a jigsaw blade cut on the upstroke so that the saw is pulled against the work. That keeps the saw from bouncing around so much. Unfortunately, that also means that most of the tearout tends to occur on the top of the plywood. You can mark the pieces on the backside so that the front will have a cleaner edge. If the design is really complicated, this can be more trouble than it is worth, and it may not be necessary.

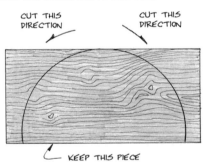

CUT THIS
DIRECTION

CUT THIS
DIRECTION

KEEP THIS PIECE

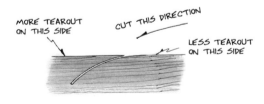

MORE TEAROUT
ON THIS SIDE

CUT THIS DIRECTION

LESS TEAROUT
ON THIS SIDE

CUT SO THAT THE BLADE
PULLS THE GRAIN ON
THE SIDE YOU WANT TO KEEP

Very often, the profile you are working with will be on several sheets of plywood that must be joined together later. It is difficult to get the cut on one sheet to line up exactly with the cut on the next one. This is especially true of marks that were made with charcoal and markers. It is often better to leave extra material at the joints and to trim that excess off after the panels have been joined together.

LAYOUT PATTERNS

A related method uses a full-scale pattern to mark angled pieces where dimensions are known, but angles are not. This often occurs when building scenery. It is generally more accurate to use this method, which does not include determining the angles from a scale drawing. "Scaling" from the drawing can lead to some fairly large errors, as the drawing is so small in relation to the true size of the scenery that a pencil dot can be as much as an inch. If you make a large pattern from dimensions on the plan, you are using the best information to build the piece.

The drawing shows a hard-framed portal that must be constructed from steel square tube. The offstage edge is square, with lengths of steel meeting at 90-degree angles. The inside profile is full of odd angles, and we don't know what they are. You are given the dimensions of the scenery and the locations of the angled intersections. That is all the information you need to do a layout of the portal.

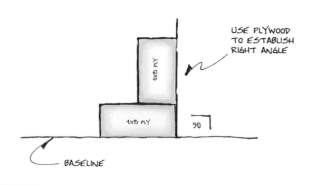

CONSTRUCT THIS HARD PORTAL FROM 1 1/2" SQUARE TUBING AND 1/4" PLYWOOD

The first step is to mark the outside and inside profiles of the shape on the floor. The floor is a good place for this procedure, because it requires no preparation other than sweeping. The floor is always there and doesn't cost anything. Sometimes it makes more sense to do the layout on plywood, and other times you may want to use paper.

You will be marking the framing pieces by laying them on top of the drawing, and there is no need to move the drawing around. This particular unit is made from welded steel, so a concrete floor is an obvious choice for fire safety reasons. It is fairly large, and it would be difficult to lay out enough platforms to do a wooden block jig. The jig seems less necessary, as only one copy will be built. Heat distortion is less of a problem on a large flat piece that has relatively few parts for its size. These are all factors to consider when deciding how to go about your work. Start the layout procedure by snapping a chalk line on the floor in a convenient location.

SNAP A BASELINE ON A CLEAN FLOOR

Form a line at a 90-degree angle perpendicular to the original by using one of the following methods. Use a sheet (or several sheets) of plywood to form the angle. Lay one edge of the sheet on the line, and draw along the adjacent side to form the 90-degree angle. This is much more accurate than using a framing square, because the plywood is so much larger, and the proportional amount of error that can creep in is much smaller.

USE PLYWOOD TO ESTABLISH RIGHT ANGLE

4X8 PLY

4X8 PLY

90

BASELINE

As an alternative you can use the *"3–4–5" method* of creating a right angle. For any triangle with sides that are 3, 4, and 5 units long, the corner formed by the intersection of the 3-unit and 4-unit sides will be a right triangle. This holds true for triangles that are multiples of these numbers such as 6–8–10 or 9–12–15.

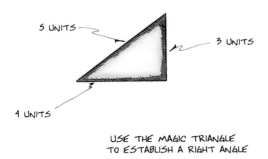

USE THE MAGIC TRIANGLE
TO ESTABLISH A RIGHT ANGLE

Measure along your base line 12'-0", and mark the beginning and ending points. Then use two tape measures, one to measure up 9'-0", and the other to triangulate the 15'-0" between the 9'-0" mark on the tape, and the 12'-0" mark on the floor. That will establish a right angle. This technique is easiest to do with three people—one to hold the end of each tape measure on its respective mark, and the third to move the tapes back and forth until the 12'-0" and the 15'-0" marks are aligned with one another. Make sure that you are consistent about which side of the tape measure you are using. Drawing a line through this point and the original corner mark will establish a line perpendicular to the base line.

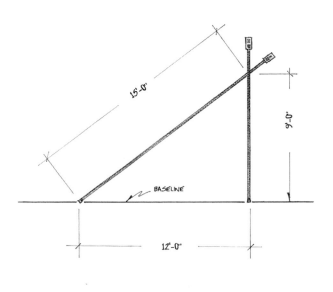

USE LARGER MULTIPLES OF 3, 4, 5
FOR GREATER ACCURACY

Once the base line and the 90-degree tangent have been established, you can plot the remaining points. Measure along the x axis to determine the width of the unit. It is possible to establish another 90-degree angle for this line, but it is much easier to simply measure twice, once toward the top and once at the bottom, and connect the dots.

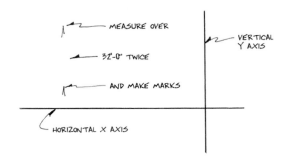

MEASURE OVER TWICE AND SNAP
A NEW LINE TO MARK THE OTHER SIDE

The same method may be used to establish the top line of the unit. The remaining points are plotted according to their measurements from a known position by following the dimensions shown on the sketch. Often it is helpful to think of the layout as a graph with an x and a y axis, and the layout of the remaining points is a process of measuring from these axes. The widths of the two leg bottoms can be measured directly from either side of the portal. The remainder of the points that establish the diagonal lines can be plotted up from the bottom and over from one of the sides. The lines between the points can be drawn in with a straightedge, or if the distance is too great, use a chalk line. Whatever the method, it is best to finish by darkening in the line with a Sharpie so that it will be easy to see and less likely to be accidentally swept away.

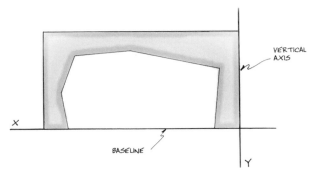

PLOT POINTS IN RELATION TO THE
X AND Y AXES. THEN CONNECT
THE POINTS WITH STRAIGHT LINES

The next drawing shows how the portal is divided into several different parts, or units, and how the framing is to be placed. The decisions about where the break lines fall are made in accordance with the realities of what size materials are available, and what it is reasonable to expect humans to carry and assemble. Generally speaking, fewer parts means less expense, but they can be much more difficult to assemble and transport. Try to make units that can be carried by no more than four stagehands. If it takes more than that, the piece is probably too large.

Also look for natural break lines in the design of the scenery itself. Quite often there is already a difference in paint color, or a piece of trim running along the scenery. It is clear that your break lines will show much less if you follow the same path.

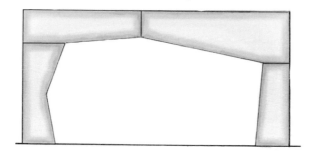

DIVIDE THE PORTAL INTO BUILDABLE PORTIONS
ALONG REASONABLE BREAK LINES

The steel square tube that was specified to frame this portal is 1½″ wide. Rip a scrap piece of plywood to that same width and use it to mark the placement of the framing members. Lay the jig along the outside edges of the pattern and use it to make a mark 1½″ to the inside. Take care to properly mark the overlapping of the framing, accurately mapping out which sections extend all the way to the side and which ones stop short. Measure the proper placement of all the required toggles using the method described in earlier construction chapters.

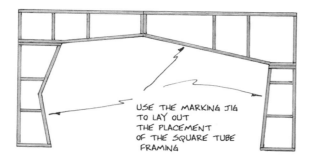

USE THE MARKING JIG
TO LAY OUT
THE PLACEMENT
OF THE SQUARE TUBE
FRAMING

This portal will be covered with sheets of plywood, so take that into consideration when deciding where the toggles should go. The 1½″ square tube is wide enough to join the seams of adjacent plywood panels using tech screws. Your 1½″-wide marking tool should make it easy to mark the actual sides of the toggles. When all of these steps are complete, and you have established your pattern, it is time to begin marking the actual pieces to be cut. Notice that you have not formed a cut list, and that we do not yet know any of the angles involved.

Marking the pieces is a matter of laying a section of the square tube on the pattern, and then using a straightedge to transfer the angle and the length to the tube. Make certain that the piece of tube is flush with all the edges of the pattern except the one you are about to mark. Close one eye as you adjust the straightedge so that it is lined up with the mark on the floor. The tricky part is to hold the marker so that it is directly above the line on the floor. There is a tendency to mark the piece with the correct angle, but too long or too short. It takes a bit of practice to get this technique down pat.

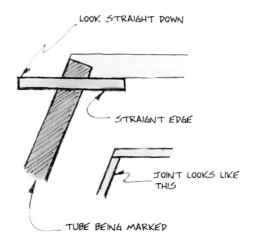

LOOK STRAIGHT DOWN

STRAIGHT EDGE

JOINT LOOKS LIKE THIS

TUBE BEING MARKED

Lay the square tube in the *chop saw*, and adjust the saw until it is set at the proper angle. Lower the blade and sight down the side of it to check for proper alignment. This is rather like looking down the length of a board to see whether it is bowed or warped. If you are using this technique on a wooden structure, substitute "power miter box" for "chop saw." After the angle has been cut, lay the resulting piece back down on the pattern to check it for the proper size. You may want to refer to the discussion of angles in Chapter 17 where I talk about the relationship that angles have to one another in the same shape. Many of the angles in this project are the same. It is, of course, easiest to cut all of one angle and then all of another. If you are ever uncertain which other angles are the same as one you have just cut, put that first piece down on the pattern in various places to look and see. After all of the pieces of square tube have been cut and laid in place, the full-scale pattern they are lying on makes a wonderful layout jig for welding.

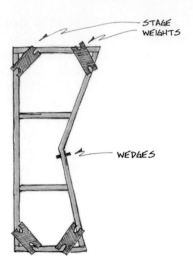

USE THE STANDARD
METAL FRAME TECHNIQUES

CHAPTER 23

WORKING WITH FOAM

The trade name *Styrofoam* is used in the vernacular to indicate a number of different plastic products. These foam products are useful in building scenery, because they are so lightweight and easy to shape. One of the drawbacks of foam construction is that the foam is also easily torn up by even moderate use. There are ways of coating the foam to give it a tougher exterior, hence making it more useful to use. Foam is at its best when used to construct large, oddly shaped structures like rocks, geometric forms, or perhaps more finely crafted large trims like cornice pieces. It is easy to create very textural surfaces with foam. The foam adds a lot of bulk, cheaply, and without making a unit too heavy.

CORNICE MADE FROM EXTRUDED POLYSTYRENE

FOAM PRODUCTS

Styrofoam is a *polystyrene* product made by the Dow Chemical Company. Like Kleenex, or Masonite, or Plexiglas, there is a tendency to call any similar foam product by the same name. Actual Styrofoam is an extruded polystyrene product that is bluish in color. *Extruded* means that the polystyrene material is forced through a die, and the shape of the die determines the shape of the sheet of foam. A cutter slices off the sheet after 8 feet of it has been extruded through the die. Styrofoam is an open-cell foam, and it has a spongy texture on the inside. Usually it is sold in 4 × 8 sheets of varying thickness, most often ¾", 1", and 2". In construction, it is used for insulation purposes.

Most Styrofoam is manufactured with score marks at certain intervals that make it possible to break the foam into 16"- or 24"-wide strips without using a saw. Sometimes this scoring is problematic when cutting the foam to other sizes. This type of polystyrene has a smooth texture when cut, and tends to retain sharp corners. It is easy to cut with a saw, but not as easy to carve as other types of foam. It is at its best when a smooth texture is required.

© 2010 Elsevier Inc. All rights reserved.
doi: 10.1016/C2009-0-23409-X

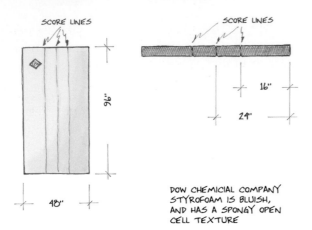

SCORE LINES

SCORE LINES

96"

48"

16"

24"

DOW CHEMICAL COMPANY
STYROFOAM IS BLUISH,
AND HAS A SPONGY OPEN
CELL TEXTURE

Expanded polystyrene is easily recognized by its white color and pebble-like texture. As the explanation of its manufacture indicates, it is composed of small, $\frac{1}{8}''$ diameter beads of foam that are stuck together. When carving this type of foam, the beads separate from one another, making expanded foam quite easy to carve, especially for large, rounded shapes. The residue from the carving process looks like the stuffing used for beanbag chairs.

Expanded polystyrene is a similar yet different product. Expanded foam is manufactured by putting tiny polystyrene pellets into a cooker. The pellets are exposed to steam heat, swell in size, and stick together. The size of the vat determines the size of the foam blank that is produced. Many different local companies produce expanded polystyrene through this process. The ones in my area make an original blank of foam that is 2 feet thick, 4 feet wide, and 16 feet long, much larger than the extruded product. The blanks are then cut into smaller sections. If you go directly to a factory (which may well be a more approachable operation than you think), it is possible to purchase these large chunks and/or smaller sections that have already been cut up. Sometimes this type of foam is sold in fairly large pieces for use as flotation units for docks or houseboats. Large blocks can be easier to use for sculptural projects, but most often, thinner sheets are more practical.

At the factory, the large sections of foam are sliced into a more usable size with a *hot wire machine*. A hot wire is just that—a special type of wire with enough direct current passing through it to make it hot enough to slice the foam by melting its way through it. Quite often it is possible to see the slightly curved striations from the cutting process on the face of a sheet of foam.

BEADBOARD IS EASIER TO CARVE
INTO LARGE ROUNDED SHAPES

WHEN WORKED, IT
FLAKES OFF IN
TINY WHITE BEADS

Carved polystyrene is a great way to simulate stone work for arches, columns, and cornices. These structures normally have a somewhat rough texture in the real world, so the naturally knobby texture of the foam is not a distraction. It is generally better to build a framing support structure and to cover that with a thin layer of polystyrene than to make the entire unit from solid foam. But it is certainly possible to use foam in a structural way, especially if a coating material is used to reinforce the structure. Sometimes foam can be used to make very nice stucco when a really rough textural quality is required. Foam is easily cut with a variety of woodworking saws and can be shaped with conventional carving and smoothing tools.

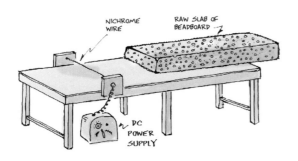

NICHROME
WIRE

RAW SLAB OF
BEADBOARD

DC
POWER
SUPPLY

HOT WIRE FOAM CUTTER

Use a respirator when cutting the foam on a table saw, because the heat of the blade rubbing against the foam tends to make it melt just a bit. You should always wear at least a dust mask to screen out the ever-present bits of foam that are in the air, even when carving by hand. The particles are very large, so an ordinary dust mask will work for them.

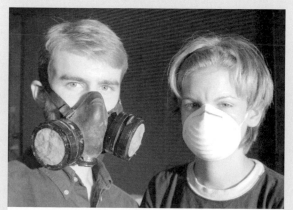

RESPIRATOR OR DUST MASK

CHOOSE THE RIGHT PROTECTION

Most safety in the shop is really just a matter of common sense. Although there is no obvious danger in working with foam, it only makes sense to take at least minimal precautions. If you must break down the foam chemically, be sure to wear an approved respirator, not just a dust mask. Do it outside, or in an area with good exhaust fans.

PORTAL PROJECT EXAMPLE

It will be easier to discuss the properties of foam, and how to work with it, by visualizing a theoretical project. Let us say that you will be building a large portal that must frame the entire stage. The design calls for an arched opening bordered with a stone trim. The portal should be constructed in small segments that can be bolted together and hung from a batten. Of course, the stone work should be very light, as the entire portal is meant to fly up on a batten. Because the bottom of the arch is well within reach of actors and stagehands, it is best to give the stone a protective coating that is strong enough to withstand the occasional bump and scratch.

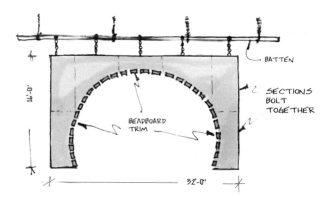

BATTEN

SECTIONS BOLT TOGETHER

BEADBOARD TRIM

16'-0"

32'-0"

The portal must be designed around transportable panels. You should construct the stone work so that the transitions between panels do not show any more than absolutely necessary. Proportion the stones in the arch so that a mortar joint line appears wherever there are two panels joined together. This is fairly easy to do since the stones are of somewhat random size anyway.

In this example, the wooden parts of the portal are made as hard-covered flats, and are easiest to build in 4×8 chunks. Soft-covered flats would work just as well, or even something framed with metal tubing. This particular design was for a rather small proscenium opening, so the hard-covered flat approach was the most appealing.

Once the framing structure is completed, rip expanded polystyrene strips to the proper size. You need some to cover the thickness of the arch, and also the part that faces the audience. Making the stonework in two parts means that they can be more easily glued to the wooden structure. The part that makes the portal look thicker is often called a *reveal*.

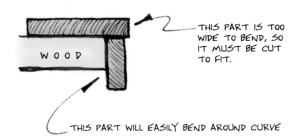

THIS PART IS TOO WIDE TO BEND, SO IT MUST BE CUT TO FIT.

THIS PART WILL EASILY BEND AROUND CURVE

Keep in mind that the larger the pieces, the harder they are to bend. The piece of foam used to create the reveal easily bends enough to match the curve, because the bend happens along its thinner side. If the facing piece is narrow, you can just bend it on as well. If not, you might be able to kerf it, making relief cuts that help it bend, or you can try using two smaller strips glued together. If the facing piece is really wide, you may need to cut it along curved lines, but this greatly increases the time required to build the unit. If you must make take the curved cut approach, mark one side of the foam from the wooden structure of the portal, and then use a spacing block to mark the width.

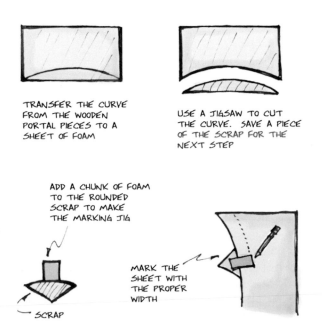

TRANSFER THE CURVE FROM THE WOODEN PORTAL PIECES TO A SHEET OF FOAM

USE A JIGSAW TO CUT THE CURVE. SAVE A PIECE OF THE SCRAP FOR THE NEXT STEP

ADD A CHUNK OF FOAM TO THE ROUNDED SCRAP TO MAKE THE MARKING JIG

SCRAP

MARK THE SHEET WITH THE PROPER WIDTH

If you need to kerf the foam, lay several of the sections together side by side and cut notches about halfway through the foam at regular intervals. The notches will make the foam bend much more easily. It is important that the spaces between cuts be even, or the foam will not bend evenly and will tend to break at the irregular spot. The spacing of the cuts, and their depth, are both a function of how flexible the foam slat will need to be when completed. It is best not to go overboard in cutting the notches, or they may be visible in the finished product.

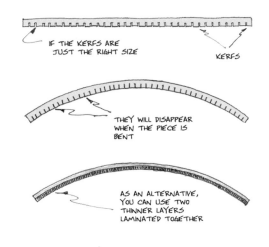

IF THE KERFS ARE JUST THE RIGHT SIZE

KERFS

THEY WILL DISAPPEAR WHEN THE PIECE IS BENT

AS AN ALTERNATIVE, YOU CAN USE TWO THINNER LAYERS LAMINATED TOGETHER

KERFING WORKS WELL ON FOAM BECAUSE IT IS SO EASILY STRETCHED AND COMPRESSED

Not all expanded polystyrene is of the same quality. Some manufacturers grind up old trimmings and mix them back into the mixture for new foam. This is fine up to a point, but if too much is used, the foam becomes brittle and will not bend very far without breaking.

This project requires a large number of relatively narrow strips of foam material. The foam is very light in comparison to plywood, so it is easy to handle when you carry it around the shop. You might be lulled into thinking that it will be easy to rip on the table saw because it is so lightweight. Just the opposite is true. You should exercise extreme caution when using the table saw with foam products. They tend to jump around in the saw, and get kicked back unexpectedly. It is much easier to rip the foam on a band saw that has a rip fence. If your band saw does not have a fence, it may be possible to clamp a board on the table so that it produces the same effect.

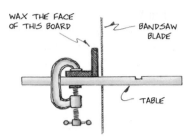

WAX THE FACE OF THIS BOARD — BANDSAW BLADE

TABLE

CONNECT TWO BOARDS
AT A 90-DEGREE ANGLE.
CLAMP TO TABLE TO
MAKE A RIP FENCE.

Attach the foam using Liquid Nails and pins. The pins (usually largish nails or pin wire) will be removed after the adhesive has had time to set up. Liquid Nails is a *mastic*, or highly viscous liquid adhesive, that has been around for decades. It is commonly used as a construction adhesive for gluing panels to floor joists and walls. It comes in a tube and is applied using a standard *caulk gun*. It works well for foam construction, because its thick, gooey texture tends to make the foam stick together from the moment the pieces touch. Yellow carpenter's glue and/or white polyvinyl glue will stick foam to wood, but the drying time is greatly extended because the foam prevents ventilation of the joint. Woodworking glues don't work well when joining foam with foam. Water-based contact cement or "green glue" is also a possibility, but the drying time required and the "instant stick" nature of that adhesive are definitely negative qualities for this project.

usually the melting effect is not enough to prevent the foam from bonding. The company that manufactures Liquid Nails has recently come out with a new line of special formulas, and one of them purports to be designed especially for use on foam. It takes much longer to set up and does not stick nearly as well as the original formula, although it is less detrimental to the foam, and one must consider what fumes are created as the foam melts. Even so, the original Liquid Nails is extremely effective. There are other, newer formulations from other companies such as *Power Grab*, but I've not found that they work as well, although they are less destructive to the foam. Mastics are also available in bucket containers, so that you can apply them with a knife. It is generally easier just to stick with the caulking tube approach. Use this product in a well-ventilated area.

You need not be too particular when applying the foam to the wooden structure. Most of the time it is better for the foam to over run the joint a bit. Any tiny amount of extra foam is easily removed with a carving tool later on. Do not try to trim the ends of the slats until after they are attached to the wood and the adhesive has had time to set up. They can be quite easily trimmed with an ordinary handsaw after the unit is stable. The pins may be pushed through two different layers of foam or may be driven through a slat of foam and then slightly into the wooden structure. Do not drive the nail in any farther than is absolutely required, or it will be difficult to remove later on.

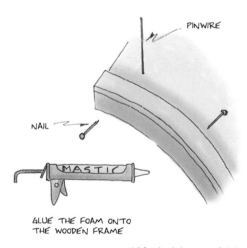

PINWIRE

NAIL

GLUE THE FOAM ONTO THE WOODEN FRAME

USE NAILS AND WIRE AS PINS TO HOLD IT IN PLACE

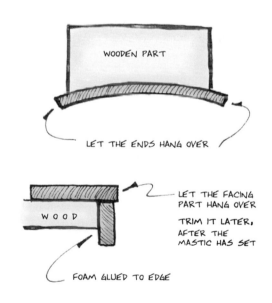

WOODEN PART

LET THE ENDS HANG OVER

WOOD

LET THE FACING PART HANG OVER

TRIM IT LATER, AFTER THE MASTIC HAS SET

FOAM GLUED TO EDGE

The major problem involved in using any petroleum-based adhesive on foam is that the adhesive tends to melt the foam. Liquid Nails is no exception, but

As indicated earlier, the ends of the foam pieces can be cut off with a handsaw. There are few occasions in the modern world when a hand tool is actually better than a power tool, but working with expanded polystyrene is one of them.

Expanded polystyrene is often called *bead board* because of the way the particles flake off when you cut it with a saw or carve it with other tools.

Use the handsaw to rough out sections of a carving. You will get much better control with a handsaw, because it cuts more slowly than a power tool. A loose hacksaw blade with gaffer's tape on one end is also good, especially for smaller cuts. Use the fastest cutting tool that you can without endangering yourself or the foam. It is hard to make really small cuts with a full-sized handsaw.

The very best tool for carving bead board is the *Surform*. It greatly resembles a cheese grater. Surforms are made by the Stanley Tool Company in a variety of types. Some are long and flat, some are long and curved, and some are short and either flat or curved.

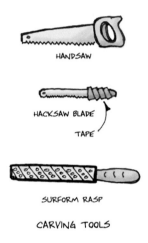

HANDSAW

HACKSAW BLADE

TAPE

SURFORM RASP

CARVING TOOLS

The Surform you select for a particular job is largely a matter of personal taste, but the longer ones seem to work the best for rounding things over, like the foam in this project. Like its relatives the file and the wood rasp, there is a handle part and a cutter part. This tool was originally intended to shape wood by peeling it away just like a cheese grater grates cheese. It is highly effective at pulling apart the small beads that make up the foam, and with a little practice you will be able to round over the edges of the foam with ease.

Sandpaper is another useful tool for carving foam. In this case rougher is better, and 80-grit is about the smallest grit aggressive enough to work efficiently. You can use it to finish off the project after the rough carving is complete. If you can locate some 30- or 40-grit paper, you can actually use it for carving, because it is rough enough to do that. A sanding block is good for the rough carving paper. Sanding blocks can be made in a variety of shapes, and the foam will assume the negative shape of the block.

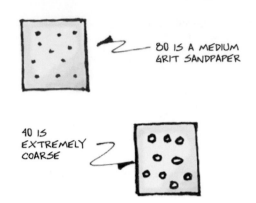

80 IS A MEDIUM GRIT SANDPAPER

40 IS EXTREMELY COARSE

Begin carving the stone archway by laying out the joint lines. A regular Sharpie marker is the best tool for writing on foam. Mark the joints an appropriate distance apart, making sure that one falls at each junction between two panels. Use the Surform or a rounded-over sheet of sandpaper to carve away the indentation.

When using sandpaper by hand, avoid tearing the sheet. Fold it into fourths and use it that way. This will give you a semistiff pad to work with. When one-quarter of the paper is exhausted, turn or refold the pad so that a new surface is exposed. This makes the sandpaper much easier to hold and to use. Sometimes folding the already quartered paper one more time can make the perfect tool for carving the joint lines.

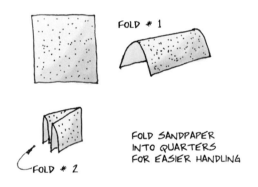

FOLD # 1

FOLD # 2

FOLD SANDPAPER INTO QUARTERS FOR EASIER HANDLING

Rounding the edges of the foam is best done with the Surform. Work on the project with the unit lying face up. Begin by trimming off any excess foam where a facing piece overlaps a side piece. Hold the tool so that the grater is cutting on the downstroke. This will prevent the facing foam from accidentally being pulled away from the face of the flat. Keep the Surform at a slight angle and lightly work the entire surface. Hold it flat against the edge. Move the tool around to different areas in an even pattern—a little here, a little there. Don't try to take too much off in any one pass of the Surform. It is much better to use a light touch, because the carving will go really fast anyway. If you go too fast, you will not be able to tell when you are getting a nicely smoothed profile.

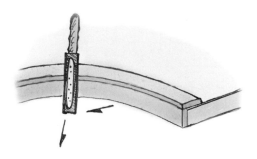

MOVE THE TOOL DOWN AND TO THE SIDE. HOLDING THE SURFORM TIGHT TO THE BOTTOM PIECE OF FOAM WILL TRIM THE OVERHANGING PIECE TO THE SAME SIZE

To shape the outside corner of the foam, hold the Surform so that the length of it is running the same direction as the corner to be rounded over. Lightly run it up and down the length of the corner. Begin by chamfering off a 45-degree bevel and then slowly alternate the angle of the Surform between 90 and 0 degrees. Do not press too hard with the tool, but rather just skim the surface, rotating back and forth until the desired curvature is obtained. The inside corner is shaped in a similar manner, but the Surform must be held at a slight angle in order for it to fit into the curve. Use some 80-grit to finish smoothing the curve and any touching up that must be done. Sometimes it is helpful to lay the various pieces of the portal together so that there is a means of judging that the same amount of curvature is maintained throughout. Once you have the hang of it, this is really an easy and fun process.

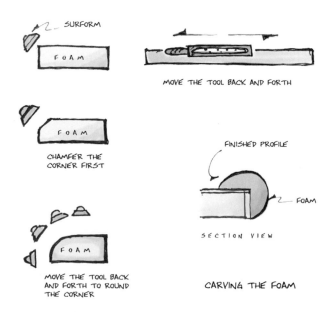

SURFORM
FOAM

MOVE THE TOOL BACK AND FORTH

CHAMFER THE CORNER FIRST
FOAM

FINISHED PROFILE
FOAM
SECTION VIEW

MOVE THE TOOL BACK AND FORTH TO ROUND THE CORNER
FOAM

CARVING THE FOAM

Because this foam is well within reach of the stage, the surface should be coated with something to toughen it up and prevent damage. The most effective method is to coat the foam with a layer of *cheesecloth*. When sealed in place with paint, the cheesecloth forms a tough "skin" that is both flexible and resistant to abrasion. It will not offer much protection from sharp punctures or being repeatedly stepped on.

The flexible nature of the cheesecloth coating makes it work well with the compressible and resilient polystyrene. On occasion, when a smoother texture is required, it is possible to substitute lightweight muslin for the cheesecloth, but the muslin is much harder to apply. Cheesecloth is a gauze-like material that was at one time used in draining cheese. (And it still is, as far as I know, which isn't far at all.) It has a very loosely woven appearance, much like a very fine net. The variety required for this technique is 100 percent cotton. Synthetic fibers will not work, as the sealer will not adhere properly to them.

Cotton cheesecloth is commonly available from large fabric stores in boxes of 100 yards. Buying the cheesecloth by the box is a good idea, because it is cheaper that way, and it often takes more of the fabric for any given project than you would think. Theatrical fabric suppliers sell a gauze material that they often refer to as "cheesecloth." It comes in wider widths and has a finer weave. It is much more difficult to work with than the fabric-store variety and is not recommended unless you need a fine texture.

The sealer used in sticking the cheesecloth to the foam is usually leftover paint, but just about any water-based liquid with glue in it will work. You can gather all the remaining paint that is still usable from recent projects and mix it together in one 5-gallon bucket. It is imperative to use water-based paints. A gallon of flat black latex and the proper ratio of flame-retardant additive will produce an excellent all-around gray basecoat, back paint, and cheesecloth sealer all in one. The mixture should be left slightly thick for use with the cheesecloth—several steps more viscous than is normal for back paint. If you don't have any paint that you would like to get rid of, or would like to use a specific color, you can use straight latex out of the can. It takes quite a bit of paint to get the cheesecloth to stick properly.

Begin with the foam unit on sawhorses at a comfortable height. When pulled from the box, cheesecloth is about 9" wide and is folded over so that it is four layers thick. Sometimes it is appropriate to use the cloth with that many layers, but it is usually easier to work with one or two. One layer is fine for most projects.

The key to making the application job run smoothly is to start by properly draping the cheesecloth. It is helpful to put down a coat of paint first and then to lay the cheesecloth down onto the paint while it is still wet. This will keep the cloth in place while you are draping it. Lay the cloth so that it extends onto the surface of the plywood at least an inch or so, and leave enough hanging down to wrap around to the wood on the back of the flat. This will ensure that the foam becomes securely anchored to the flat.

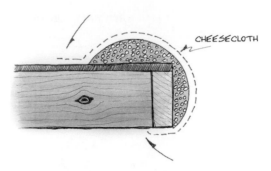

EXTEND THE CLOTH AROUND TO THE BACK FAR ENOUGH TO MAKE A GOOD CONNECTION TO THE WOODEN STRUCTURE SO THAT THE FOAM WILL NOT PULL OFF EASILY

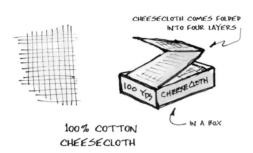

CHEESECLOTH COMES FOLDED INTO FOUR LAYERS

100 YDS CHEESECLOTH

IN A BOX

100% COTTON CHEESECLOTH

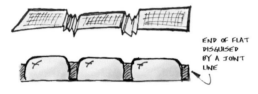

END OF FLAT DISGUISED BY A JOINT LINE

DRAPE THE CHEESECLOTH SO THAT THERE IS PLENTY OF SLACK TO PROJECT DOWN INTO THE JOINTS. IT IS BETTER TO HAVE TOO MUCH THAN TOO LITTLE.

Leave a fold of the cheesecloth at each joint depression so that there will be enough slack in the material for it to be forced down into the crack with a wet paintbrush. You needn't be too picky about this procedure. By the end of it, paint will be all over your hands and arms up to the elbow. If the cheesecloth is not positioned exactly, pick it up and move it around. It is far better to leave a bit of extra slack in the cloth than to have it wind up stretched tight over a joint line. That would effectively wipe out the carved detail. For a project like this, it matters little if the cloth is overlapped or folded over itself in places; indeed, this can sometimes create a desired amount of extra texture.

Don't be too stingy with the paint. The gauze should be completely saturated in order to adhere properly to the foam. When dry, the foam/cheesecloth combination is incredibly tough, much like a hide, and the extension of the cloth onto the surrounding wood makes it very difficult for the foam to become dislodged from the wooden structure.

MAKING A CORNICE

Another common use for foam is to make a large, built-up *cornice*. A cornice is used at the top of a wall and is theoretically less likely to be damaged. It is better not to use cheesecloth, because of the rough texture the cloth creates. A cornice is usually a smoother piece of work, and should have the appearance of wood or plaster. It is problematic to use foam for trims that are within reach of the stage floor because it is just too fragile. If you are planning on moving the set around to different theatres, I wouldn't recommend this technique, because the foam is too easily destroyed. But it works really well for a short-run show. The blue Dow Styrofoam or some other extruded polystyrene type is the best material for this job, because it is so much smoother than bead board.

The structural design for a cornice of this type must take into consideration the materials that are used to construct it. It works best to build up the cornice from strips of foam that have been ripped down on the band saw or table saw. It is fairly easy to glue together a number of 8-foot or longer sections and then cut these to the proper length and angle. That makes cutting the angles less problematic than trying to miter each piece individually, which would be an awful lot of mitering. Instead, put together stock parts that are long enough to cut the needed pieces. Avoid having a butt joint between two pieces on the same wall by laminating together sections long enough to reach from corner to corner.

Here is an example of a cornice that is designed for polystyrene construction:

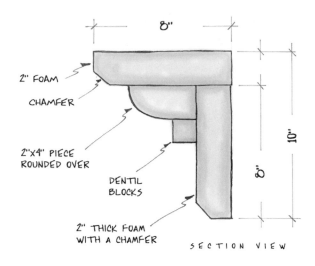

2" FOAM

CHAMFER

2"x4" PIECE
ROUNDED OVER

DENTIL
BLOCKS

2" THICK FOAM
WITH A CHAMFER

8"

10"

8"

SECTION VIEW

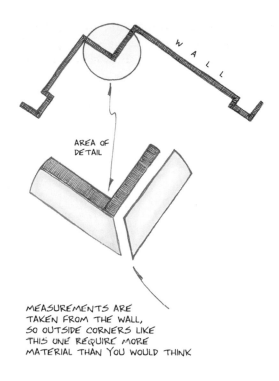

WALL

AREA OF
DETAIL

MEASUREMENTS ARE
TAKEN FROM THE WALL,
SO OUTSIDE CORNERS LIKE
THIS ONE REQUIRE MORE
MATERIAL THAN YOU WOULD THINK

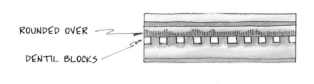

ROUNDED OVER

DENTIL BLOCKS

FRONT ELEVATION

The section view reveals the size and shape of each trim member. You also need to know the total length of trim required for all of the wall sections together. Estimate the lengths from your ground plan. Some of the walls may be longer than 8 feet in length and thus will require the construction of an extra-long section of trim. It is possible to connect the foam pieces with offsetting joints so that the finished product extends to virtually any length, but at some point the length of the cornice will make it simply too cumbersome to deal with effectively. Remember that outside corners require an extra amount of material, and that cutting miters in general tends to use up the trim faster than expected. It is much easier to make a few extra lengths of cornice from the outset than to be forced to replicate a section of complex trim at the last moment. This particular molding includes a *dentil* type of detail, which is essentially a series of blocks glued on with a space between each one.

The first task is to determine the widths of all the parts and the number of strips required of each size; forming them into a cut list. It is best to rip down all of the foam parts on the band saw. You can use a table saw, but the foam is so light it tends to jump around in the saw and get kicked back. Be cautious if you do decide to use a table saw.

Sometimes there are 45-degree-angle chamfers that must be ripped along one or more of the pieces. It is best to cut the strips to size first, reset the saw, and then cut all of the chamfers at the same time. If you need to do that on the table saw, use a hold-down or *finger board* to keep the foam in place. Start the foam through the saw by pushing, and then have an assistant pull the strip through the rest of the way. Use a scrap board to hold the trailing end in place. This will greatly reduce the tendency of the foam to kick back. The same techniques work well on the band saw, even though there isn't much danger of a kickback on that saw.

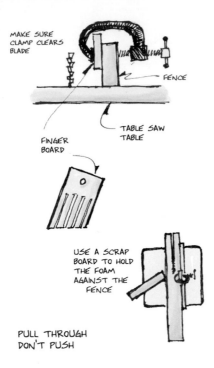

MAKE SURE CLAMP CLEARS BLADE

FENCE

FINGER BOARD

TABLE SAW TABLE

USE A SCRAP BOARD TO HOLD THE FOAM AGAINST THE FENCE

PULL THROUGH DON'T PUSH

Bring the parts together and squish them back and forth a few times to further spread the glue. This will also have the advantage of using suction power to hold the parts together while they bond. Use nails, pin wire, stage weights, or whatever is necessary to hold the parts together as they dry. When all of the trims are together, go back and check the connections several times, as they tend to pull apart.

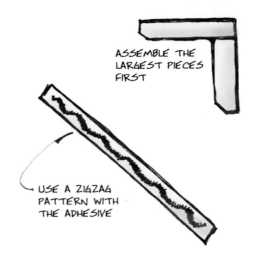

ASSEMBLE THE LARGEST PIECES FIRST

USE A ZIGZAG PATTERN WITH THE ADHESIVE

Once the foam has been ripped into strips, cut the sections to length. If you are making nothing but 8-foot-long units, the job is already done. A 10-foot section requires 8-foot and 2-foot lengths. You may need to also use lengths of 4 and 6 or 5 and 5 feet if the molding needs extra stiffening. When making longer sections, remember to stagger the location of the joints.

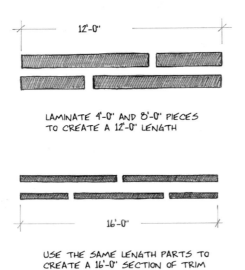

12'-0"

LAMINATE 4'-0" AND 8'-0" PIECES TO CREATE A 12'-0" LENGTH

16'-0"

USE THE SAME LENGTH PARTS TO CREATE A 16'-0" SECTION OF TRIM

Connect the strips of foam together to form the cornice. Apply a zigzag pattern of Liquid Nails to the edge of the back section and attach this piece to the top section. Use the adhesive on any surfaces that are to be glued together.

A zigzag pattern spreads the adhesive out over a larger area, increasing the holding power of the glue.

Do not hurry the curing period. It is best to assemble these parts in the late afternoon and come back to them the next morning.

Save the dentil molding until last. Use the radial arm saw to cut a strip of foam into the necessary cubes. It would be really time consuming to measure the placement of each cube. Use the cubes themselves to do the spacing instead. It is common for the space between the blocks to be the same distance as the size of the blocks themselves. You can use unattached blocks to set the spaces between the cubes you are gluing on.

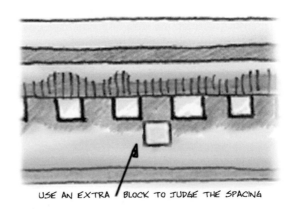

USE AN EXTRA BLOCK TO JUDGE THE SPACING

DON'T WORRY ABOUT BEING EXACTLY RIGHT WHEN YOU PLACE THE DENTIL BLOCKS. YOU JUST NEED TO BE CLOSE ENOUGH THAT NO ONE WILL NOTICE THE DIFFERENCE.

MAKE SMALL ADJUSTMENTS TOWARD THE END OF THE CORNICE SECTION SO THAT THE BLOCKS END EVENLY.

The dentil mold does not have to fit with any other parts, so it is necessary to make sure only that the measurements are close enough to look good. It is common to have to pull some of them off and respace them to accommodate the miter joints. Because the blocks are very small, air can get around the edges, and it is much easier to use regular carpenter's glue to attach the dentil mold than to use mastic.

The cornice parts must be cut to length and mitered on the ends to fit around the wall angles. You can compute the sizes on paper with measurements taken from the actual walls. If the walls are straight, plumb, and the angles involved are true, then it is a fairly straightforward process. Measure along each of the walls to verify the length of each one, because sometimes there is a discrepancy between the plans and the actual construction. Because you are cutting the cornice to fit on the wall and not on the printed plan, it is best to go right to the source for your measurements.

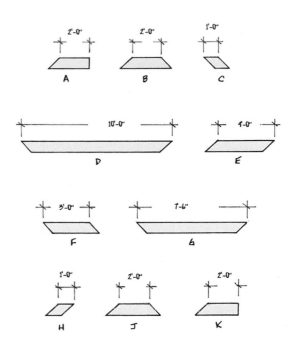

MAKE A CUT LIST WITH SKETCHES OF THE PARTS SO THAT IT WILL BE EASIER TO TELL WHICH WAY TO CUT THE MITERS

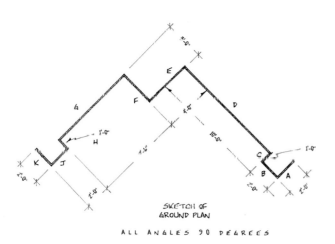

SKETCH OF GROUND PLAN

ALL ANGLES 90 DEGREES

Make a small sketch of each piece of trim as you include it on your cut list. Show the angle that must be cut and the direction that it runs. Dimension the sketch with the size you measure from the wall. Indicate which part of the angle the dimension relates to. This will reduce confusion when you begin cutting.

If there is an unknown angle, use a scrap board and the power miter saw to determine the angle by trial and error. Cut the board and hold both halves in the corner. If the joint is open, reduce the number of degrees. If the points do not meet, make the angle more acute.

There are two ways of cutting the mitered angles. One method is to use a very large band saw. It must have a guard that you can raise high enough to accommodate the 8″ height of the trim. That can be a problem. The other is to construct an old-style wooden miter box large enough to house the 8″ depth of the cornice.

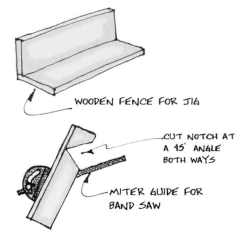

WOODEN FENCE FOR JIG

CUT NOTCH AT A 45° ANGLE BOTH WAYS

MITER GUIDE FOR BAND SAW

the wall surface, and so must be marked to the backside of the cornice. It takes a bit of practice to learn to visualize the placement of the pieces and the direction that the angles run. Making the cut list with diagrams of this sort will help.

If it is not possible to cut the trim on a band saw, a large miter box will work just as well, perhaps better. The miter box is definitely more accurate, and the only downside is the time required to put it together. The box will be easier to use if it is the same size as the trim you are cutting. A tight fit will prevent the piece from moving around while you are cutting it. The cornice in the example is 8″ across the top, and 10″ tall, so these are the dimensions of the inside of the jig.

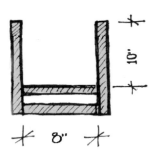

10″

8″

SECTION THROUGH A MITER BOX

A band saw large enough to accommodate an 8″-tall item probably has a *miter guide*. The stock miter guide is probably a bit small to handle such a large piece. Enlarge it by adding a wooden jig to the guide. The jig is merely two pieces of plywood glued and nailed together and then bolted to the miter guide. Make it as large as will comfortably fit on your band saw. The wooden section will be easier to use if there is an equal amount of wood, and hence weight, on either side of the miter guide. If you put the jig together and use the band saw itself to cut the 45-degree angle notch out of the base, the resulting V will be usable as a reference point in lining up the cornice on the jig. Most of your cuts will be either 45 or 90 degrees. This jig will not cut angles greater than 45 degrees.

You could make a box from just three boards, but the structure would be really weak to cut such large and cumbersome trim. It is better to have more strength in the bottom of the jig, which you can easily get by using two pieces across the bottom span rather than just one. Leave a small space in between them. Make the side boards wide enough so that they will stick up 10″ even after the bottom part is taken into consideration.

The length doesn't matter so much, but it is nice if the box is at least 3 feet long so that it is stable enough to work well. Glue and staple the boards together. Slots cut into the sides of the box are used to guide the handsaw used to cut the actual cornice. The slots must be cut so that they accurately represent the angles you need. The table saw can be used to begin the cuts by using its miter guide and running the box through the saw upside down. The table saw is very accurate, but will not be able to cut all of the way through the sides of the box, so use a circular saw or a jigsaw to complete the cut.

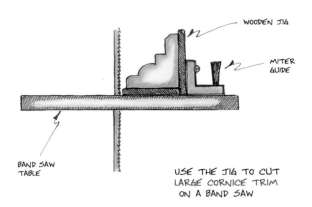

WOODEN JIG

MITER GUIDE

BAND SAW TABLE

USE THE JIG TO CUT LARGE CORNICE TRIM ON A BAND SAW

Cutting the foam is somewhat of a balancing act, but the cornice is very light and, of course, there is almost no resistance to the blade cutting through the piece. A second person may be required to aid in holding up the far end. Make sure there are no pins left in the foam that can damage the saw. It is advisable to begin by cutting the longest pieces first. The cut list was made so that there is a diagram of each section to better define the angle directions. All of the measurements are from

BOTTOM OF MITER BOX

YOU CAN USE THE TABLE SAW TO ACCURATELY START THE SLOTS

For this project, you need a 90-degree cut and two 45-degree cuts, one going in each direction. The directions for marking the individual pieces of cornice are the same as for the method that used the band saw. Making the miter box is time-consuming, but it is much easier to cut a cornice in a miter box than it is on the band saw.

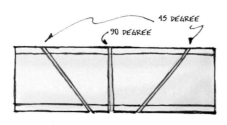

PLAN VIEW OF A MITER BOX

Cut all of the sections of cornice in turn and check each against the wall flats to verify that all is well. Use some 80-grit sandpaper to finish off any rough spots on the foam. It may be necessary to remove a few of the dentil blocks and fudge the spacing a bit to make them look right. Sometimes it is easier to wait until the end to put the dentil blocks on the trim. Use latex caulk on the rough spots. It is pliable enough to work well with the bendable foam.

An easy way to attach the cornice to the wall is to use some ¼" plywood strips adhered to the top of the cornice with Liquid Nails. The strips need to extend off the rear of the cornice molding far enough so that they can be screwed to the tops of the flats. The only thing holding the cornice is the glue, so make sure the bond is good.

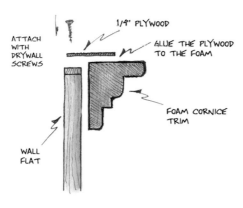

ATTACHING THE CORNICE
TO THE WALL FLATS

It is nice to give the surface a coating of some kind of heavy sealer for protection as well as to give it a slicker looking finish. Products like *elastomeric* are excellent for this purpose. It is imperative that you determine that

any sealer used is compatible with the chemical nature of the foam.

TOMBSTONE PROJECT

TOMBSTONE PROJECT

Creating a tombstone is a really fun student project. Perhaps I've built too many versions of *Tom Sawyer* and *A Christmas Carol*, but it seems that the theatrical demand for tombstones is quite high. At any rate, this graveyard monument uses all of the skills you've learned so far. Here are some construction sketches for the piece:

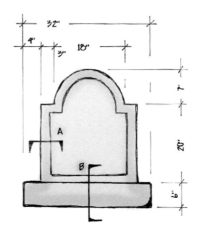

DIMENSIONS FOR THE PROJECT

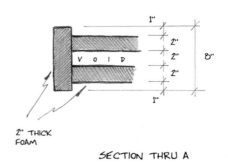

SECTION THRU A

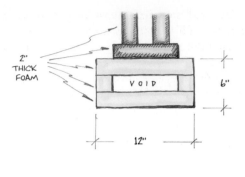

2"
THICK
FOAM

VOID

6"

12"

SECTION THRU B

It would be possible to carve this piece from one solid chunk of foam, but that is harder to find, and it makes more sense to use readily available sheet goods instead. The exterior of this unit will give the appearance of being massive and sturdy, but actually the tombstone is hollow inside. This reduces the amount of product used, and hence the cost.

Start by cutting out the front and back pieces of the vertical slab. The layout consists of a rectangle and half a circle, which are easily laid out using a drywall square, a compass, and a Sharpie marker. Cut the pieces out with a jigsaw, and use the first one as a pattern for the second.

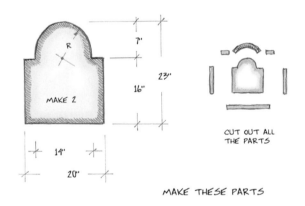

R

7"

23"

16"

MAKE 2

14"

20"

CUT OUT ALL
THE PARTS

MAKE THESE PARTS

The edging around the vertical portion of the tombstone is made of the same 2"-thick foam. Rip an 8-foot-long section of it to use as stock. The straight sections are easily cut to length, and it matters little which way the joints overlap. The edging for the rounded top will need to be kerfed in order for it to bend enough to fit the diameter of this curve. The radius is small, so the kerfing must be quite severe and will require an extra technique.

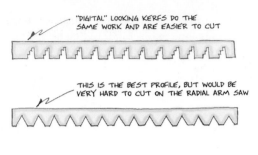

"DIGITAL" LOOKING KERFS DO THE
SAME WORK AND ARE EASIER TO CUT

THIS IS THE BEST PROFILE, BUT WOULD BE
VERY HARD TO CUT ON THE RADIAL ARM SAW

USE THE RADIAL ARM SAW TO KERF THE FOAM

Set the radial arm saw so that the blade is ¾" above the table. Make a mark on the wooden guide that is 1" to the right of the kerf where the blade passes through the fence. Each time the blade passes through the foam, move the stock 1" to the right as indicated by the mark on the fence. When you have prepared a long enough section to cover the distance around the semicircle, reset the blade ½" higher than it was. Repeat the kerfing operation, but this time cut away foam just to the side of the previous pass. Repeat again with a shallower cut if necessary. This will form a kind of "digital"-looking dart or V shape in the foam that will close up as the foam is bent around its circle.

CONNECT THE
FRONT AND BACK
SIDES

THEN ATTACH
THE KERFED
PART OF THE
EDGING

USE SCRAP PIECES
AS SPACERS

Assemble the top section using two or three pieces of scrap foam as spacers, and join the vertical slab sections using Liquid Nails. The spacers are used to keep the sections 2" apart, and to give the total thickness of 6". Glue on the 8"-wide top strip you kerfed earlier, leaving about an inch of overhang on either side. It will be difficult to gauge the exact length of this piece, because it fits on a circle. Just remember that it is easier to trim a bit more off the kerfed section than it will be to make a new one. Glue on the two flanking pieces to help keep the curve in place while the Liquid Nails sets up. Attach the remaining trim pieces and set the entire assembly aside until the mastic has bonded sufficiently to hold while you work on rounding over the corners.

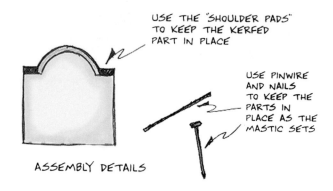

USE THE "SHOULDER PADS" TO KEEP THE KERFED PART IN PLACE

USE PINWIRE AND NAILS TO KEEP THE PARTS IN PLACE AS THE MASTIC SETS

ASSEMBLY DETAILS

Cut out pieces for the top and bottom of the base. Rip enough of the 2″ × 2″ stock to fit around the perimeter of the hollow structure. Cut the 2″ × 2″ strips to length, and glue all of the parts together. Set this section aside to dry.

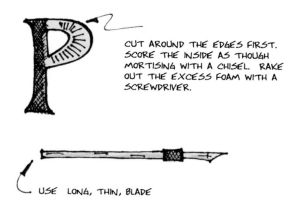

BASE

It is easiest to work on carving and finishing these two subassemblies while they are apart, and then to join them before the cheesecloth is put on. Use the Surform to even any parts that are sticking out, and round over all the corners. Most builders agree that the more you round over, the older and more weathered the finished product will appear. You may wish to add a few cracks and some lettering. Use a Sharpie to mark the lettering and a pointy *X-Acto knife* to cut them out. Normally, a large-handled utility knife is better for any type of cutting, but in this instance, a long and thin blade is the best. Cut straight in around the outside edges and rake out the center like a chiseled mortise. Smooth all surfaces with a piece of 80-grit sandpaper.

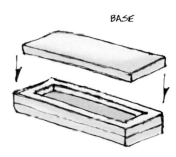

CUT AROUND THE EDGES FIRST. SCORE THE INSIDE AS THOUGH MORTISING WITH A CHISEL. RAKE OUT THE EXCESS FOAM WITH A SCREWDRIVER.

USE LONG, THIN, BLADE

The final step before painting is to cover with cheesecloth. This project is a bit more challenging to cover than the stonework was. It is best to cut the cloth into 12″ or 18″ squares of single thickness before beginning, because large sections are too hard to control. Bunch up the cloth where it must fit down into crevices like the letter carving. If the cheesecloth does not go down into the cracks properly, your hard work creating texture will tend to disappear.

POWER CARVING METHODS

A very quick, but messy way to carve any kind of polystyrene foam is to use a drill and a *wire wheel*. Some wire wheels are intended to be used to remove rust and old paint from wrought iron railings and the like. These wheels are perfect for carving, because they are mounted on a shaft and can easily be inserted into a drill.

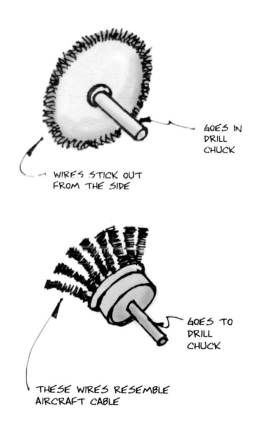

GOES IN DRILL CHUCK

WIRES STICK OUT FROM THE SIDE

GOES TO DRILL CHUCK

THESE WIRES RESEMBLE AIRCRAFT CABLE

There are two main types. One of these is 2 or 3 inches in diameter with a brush of wire around its outside edge. The other has what looks like short lengths of wire rope sticking straight ahead out of a central hub. Both of these types of wire wheels are used to carve by inserting them in a variable-speed drill and simply gouging and shredding the foam from the surface of the block. This technique can be used to create a number of really rough textures, like stucco, bark, or rock. The hub with the wire rope sticking straight out is the easiest to control; the other wheel is more aggressive about removing the foam. They both spew out an unbelievable amount of foam chips. Safety glasses and a respirator are a must, and you can expect to be completely covered from head to toe with small bits of foam. A good shop vac is essential for cleanup. I have found that any time foam is involved in a project it is best to sweep and vacuum up the leavings right away so that they are not tracked all over the theatre.

INDEX